ILLUSTRATED STORY OF WORLD WAR II

READER'S DIGEST

ILLUSTRATED STORY OF WORLD WAR II

THE READER'S DIGEST ASSOCIATION, INC., PLEASANTVILLE, NEW YORK

CONTENTS

Introduction

On September 2, 1945, the Japanese surrendered aboard the battleship *Missouri,* of the U.S. Pacific Fleet, in Tokyo Bay, bringing to an end the bloodiest war man has ever known. It was six years and one day since Adolf Hitler, the German dictator, sent his armies into Poland, igniting a conflict that would spread warfare from the skies of London to the sands of North Africa, from Scandinavian mountains to Italian farmlands, from Atlantic shipping lanes to the waters and islands of the Pacific, from the jungles of Southeast Asia to the hedgerows of Normandy.

World War II was fought by more men over more of the globe, with greater loss of life and destruction of property, than any other war. Seventy million soldiers took part; 16 million of them were killed—nearly 1 out of 4. Another 18 million civilians died because of the war. The total of wounded and missing, soldiers and civilians, will never be known. Neither the United States nor the rest of the world would ever be the same again. The advent of the Nuclear Age, under the pressures of war, in itself forever changed the military and political patterns of life on this earth.

Though not drawn into the war until late in 1941, twenty-seven months after its start, the United States lost more men than were killed in the Civil War on both the Union and Confederate sides. Nearly 300,000 Americans—out of an armed force of 16 million—gave their lives in the struggle. Winston Churchill expressed what free men were fighting for when Britain early in the war stood virtually alone against the German blitzkrieg:

> Upon this battle depends the survival of Christian civilization. . . . Hitler knows that he will have to break us in this island or lose the war. If we can stand up to him, all Europe may be free and the life of the world may move forward into broad, sunlit uplands. But if we fail, then the whole world, including the United States, including all that we have known and cared for, will sink into the abyss of a new Dark Age.

Britain did stand firm. But the foes of freedom moved on relentlessly elsewhere. In the next two years, Nazi forces conquered nearly all of Europe, penetrated deep into

Russia and threatened to seize Moscow itself, drove across North Africa and seemed on the verge of invading the Middle East. America provided material for Britain and Russia, and took economic action against the Japanese, who had been at war with China since 1931. Otherwise, our nation was divided by debate and controversy over what we should do. Germany, Italy and Japan were aggressors against nations that had sought only peace. But we had not been attacked. Then, out of the skies over Hawaii on December 7, 1941, came Japanese planes to bomb Pearl Harbor, sending many great ships of America's Navy to the bottom. On that "day of infamy," a nation that had tried to avoid this international conflict was suddenly at war with the most savage enemies. Through nearly four years of work and sacrifice, America would cast off the burden of the longest economic depression in its history to become the most productive and most powerful nation in the world.

"The days of business as usual were past," writes historian Louis L. Snyder. Within a year after Pearl Harbor the United States was equaling the entire Axis war production, though the enemy had a head start of ten years. By the end of the war the United States had produced 300,000 planes, 87,000 tanks, 2,400,000 trucks, 17,900,000 firearms, 61,000 pieces of heavy artillery and many millions of tons of shells, bombs and other explosives. "From tens of thousands of factories," according to Mr. Snyder, "came finished tools of war, more war matériel than produced by the rest of the world combined. It was an awesome example of audacious planning, mass activity, prodigious energy."

In his account in this book of the Battle of the Philippine Sea, Peter Maas dramatizes how well the American miracle of production made itself felt in the war. He describes the arrival of Vice Adm. Marc A. Mitscher on the flag bridge of the carrier *Lexington* in June 1944, and he adds that she had replaced the first *Lexington,* sunk in the Battle of the Coral Sea on May 7, 1942. Mr. Maas tells of the launching of planes from the *Yorktown,* a ship named for the *Yorktown* sunk off Midway, June 7, 1942. In that same Battle of the Philippine Sea we find the aircraft carriers *Princeton, Cowpens, Bunker Hill, Essex, Monterey* and *Belleau Wood.* We find also the battleships *Indiana* and *South Dakota. None of these ships existed in December 1941.* All told, after most of the American Fleet was left twisted and shattered at Pearl Harbor, American shipyards produced 10 battleships, 25 cruisers, and enough submarines, destroyers and other combat vessels to bring the entire total to 1265 brand-new men-of-war.

By contrast, Mr. Maas also touches upon the sinking of the Japanese carrier *Taiho* during those June days in 1944. Torpedoed by the American submarine *Albacore,* the *Taiho* sank several hours later. It was a sad loss for the enemy, for the ship was the pride of the Imperial Navy, the newest and most modern carrier the Japanese had produced. The *Taiho* was also the *only* Japanese carrier completed after the war began.

In addition to providing combat vessels, American shipyards produced 5200 other ships. On June 6, 1944, the very day the largest invasion fleet in the history of the world was moving across the Channel to the shores of France, America was able to send a fleet of 110 troop and cargo vessels escorted by the most powerful naval force in history to Saipan, halfway across the world. In Europe and the Pacific these invasion fleets were covered by enough aircraft to provide absolute superiority over the once-vaunted enemy air forces.

While making the tools of war, the American people at home fed and clothed themselves, bought $157 billion worth of war bonds and paid the heaviest income taxes in their history. Every family was, in one way or another, participating in the war effort. But their attention was constantly centered on the man engaged in actual combat. Whether rifleman or general, pilot or admiral, he was the focus of his countrymen's deep concern. And the battles themselves, on the ground, in the air and at sea, held our people in prayerful suspense. Even before the smoke lifted from the battlefield, we sought to know, *What really happened?*

Today, the passage of time and the accumulation and sifting through of documents have placed World War II in clearer perspective. The great moments, the great turning points, can be explored in depth. Much is known now that was once obscured in the chaos of battle. At last we can survey "the way it was."

Such a comprehensive survey is what the editors of the Reader's Digest present in the *Illustrated Story of World War II*. In words and pictures this book moves over the panorama of the war as it unfolded, focusing on the march of events, the very atmosphere of the conflict itself—not on what might have been, but on the moment when leaders weighed the situation and acted.

From an enormous stockpile of memoirs and eyewitness accounts, histories and biographies, news dispatches and official publications, from thousands of photographs, the editors of the Reader's Digest have selected and illustrated fifty-seven outstanding stories. To make it easy for the reader to follow events, the Reader's Digest *Illustrated Story of World War II* also provides thirty-five maps, each telling its own story about a crucial phase or battle.

The editors have been aided in their task by Brig. Gen. S. L. A. Marshall, one of the ablest historians of World War II. He is credited with originating the "after-battle critique," now the standard method for collecting the details of military operations in the field—a technique similar to the debriefing system used to record from their own fresh recollections our astronauts' voyages into space. General Marshall was the first military historian in the Pacific in the years 1943—44. Then, appointed Chief Military Historian of the European Theater of Operations, he took part in the action and reconstructed the key battles, from the first landing on the Normandy beaches to Berlin. His help was invaluable to the editors in selecting and, in some cases, writing the stories in this book that best describe the great moments of the war.

The Reader's Digest *Illustrated Story of World War II* recounts not only the military but the human drama. It tells what it was like to be caught up in that gargantuan struggle, from the moment when the first bombs fell on Pearl Harbor to the atomic blows that brought about the ultimate surrender. It brings to life again the unforgettable episodes of nobility and agony, of despair and triumph.

To all Americans who took part in the war, to our allies and to a new generation inheriting a world shaped by that war, this book is dedicated.

ILLUSTRATED STORY OF WORLD WAR II

The first smoke of war stains the skies
of Pearl Harbor as the battleship *Oklahoma* (right), hit
repeatedly by Japanese torpedoes, capsizes and settles, while the
battleship *Maryland*, berthed alongside, suffers little damage.

PEARL HARBOR

THE TRAGEDY, THE CALL TO ARMS

THE JAPANESE PLAN FOR EMPIRE

At five minutes before eight o'clock, Hawaiian time, on the morning of December 7, 1941, a Japanese airman dropped a bomb on Pearl Harbor. It was the first of many to fall upon the great American Naval base where the bulk of the U.S. Pacific Fleet was moored on that never-to-be-forgotten day when a sneak attack drew the United States into the Second World War and Japan herself on to ultimate disaster.

Ironically, the United States, more than any other nation, was responsible for awakening Japan from her ancient isolation and sending her on her reckless quest for power and dominion. Unwelcome though Commodore Matthew C. Perry was when his four warships dropped anchor in Yedo (now Tokyo) Bay in July 1853, his visit served to stir the dreams of empire that were soon to arouse the island people of Japan. Thus began, after more than 200 years of strict seclusion, a sudden exposure to Western ideas, production techniques and military systems. In the short space of eighty-eight years, Japan turned herself from a feudal state into a nation with an army and a navy trained and equipped to rival those of the great European powers.

Prodded by her militaristic leaders, Japan launched an attack on China. The Sino-Japanese War (1894–95) gave victorious Nippon possession of Formosa (Taiwan) and the Pescadores (see map on opposite page). A few years later the Russo-Japanese War (1904–05) broke out over rival claims in Korea and Manchuria. Russia was brought down in defeat, with Japan acquiring the southern half of Sakhalin Island and Port Arthur. (Russia's lease of Kwantung Peninsula, in the southern part of Liaotung Peninsula, Manchuria, was taken over by Japan in 1905 and renewed in 1915.) The Japanese continued their expansion by annexing Korea in 1910.

Japan entered World War I on the side of the Allies in 1914. She occupied numerous German colonies in the Far East and later, as a member of the League of Nations, was given a mandate over the Caroline, Marshall and Marianas islands, with the exception of Guam (ceded to the United States by Spain in 1898).

Anti-Western feelings within Japan became intensified when, at the Washington Naval Conference in 1921–22, the Japanese Government agreed to keep her Navy smaller than those of Great Britain and the United States in a 5-5-3 ratio. Two years later the United States passed an immigration act barring Japanese and certain other nationalities.

For some time a master plan had been evolving to give Japan domination of Southeast Asia and the islands of the western half of the Pacific. This meant the removal of all Western influence. The Greater East Asia Co-Prosperity Sphere, as the territory was called, extended from the Kurile Islands southeast to the Marshall Islands, west to Netherlands East Indies (now Republic of Indonesia), and in a great curve to India.

In 1931 the Japanese overran Manchuria, later turning it into the puppet state of Manchukuo. Condemned by the League of Nations for her act, Japan resigned her membership. Clashes with the Chinese blazed into warfare in 1937, in which Peiping (now Peking), Shanghai, Nanking, Hankow, Canton and the important rail center of Tungshan (now Suchow) were captured.

In February 1939 Japan seized Hainan Island, and after the fall of France in 1940, her troops moved into northern Indochina with the permission of Vichy France. She occupied the entire country in midsummer of 1941. The ultimate objective was the seizure of the rich Southern Resources Area.

A critical stage in international relations was reached when the United States clamped down a total embargo, freezing all Japanese assets in America. Negotiators were sent to Washington to try to settle the disagreement between the two countries. But the talks were only a blind. The plans of the Japanese war party were set; war was to begin with the attack on Pearl Harbor.

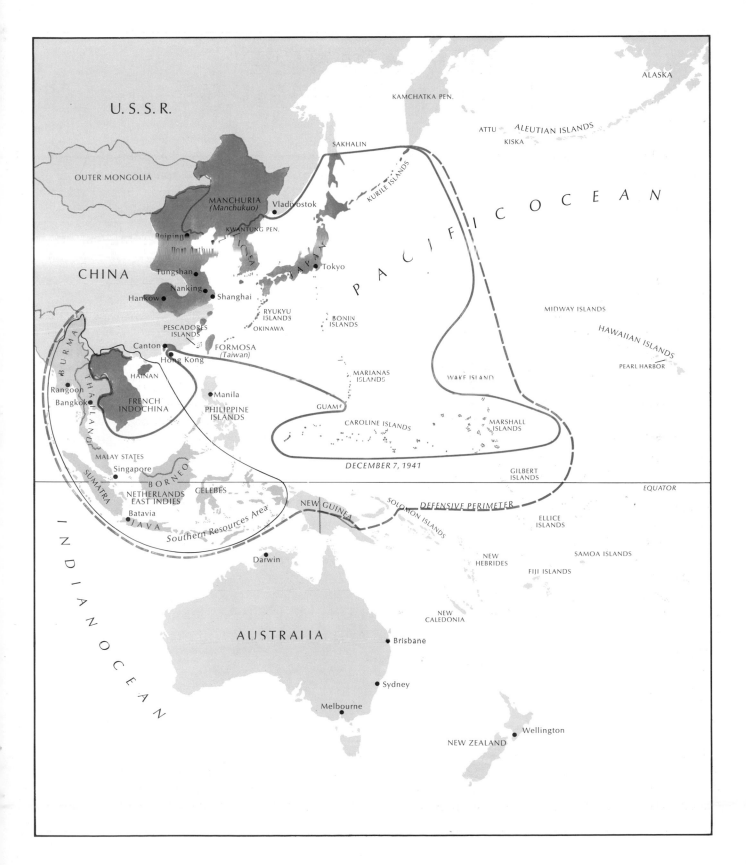

A Japanese "Kate" torpedo bomber speeds away from Hickam Field after dropping its cargo of death. Only a few American planes were able to get into the air and give battle.

I LED
THE ATTACK ON
PEARL HARBOR

BY CAPT. MITSUO FUCHIDA

The assault on the U.S. Naval base at Pearl Harbor as seen from the cockpit by the commander of the first wave of Japanese planes.

"We want you to lead our Air Force in the event that we attack Pearl Harbor."

It was all I could do to catch my breath. It was now late September 1941, and if the international situation continued to intensify, the attack plan called for execution in December. There was no time to lose in training for this all-important mission.

In mid-November, after the most rigorous training, planes were taken on board their respective carriers, which then headed for the Kurile Islands, traveling singly and on different courses to avoid attention. Then, at six on the cloudy morning of November 26 [November 25 east of the international date line, in Hawaii and the United States] our twenty-eight-ship task force, including six carriers, left the Kuriles.

Vice Admiral Chuichi Nagumo was in command of the Pearl Harbor Attack Force. "In case negotiations with the United States reach a successful conclusion," he had been instructed, "the task force will return immediately to the homeland."

Our course was to be between the Aleutian and Midway islands, so as to keep out of range of American air patrols, some of which were supposed to extend 600 miles. We sent three submarines ahead to report any merchant ships sighted, and maintained a constant alert against U.S. submarines.

Strict radio silence was observed throughout, but we listened for broadcasts from Tokyo or Honolulu to catch any word about the outbreak of war. In Tokyo a liaison conference between the Government and the High Command was held every day from November 27 to 30 to discuss the U.S. proposal of the 26th. [This was the sharp rejection by Washington, on November 25, of "minimal conditions" for peace submitted by Tokyo on November 17.] It was concluded that the proposal was an ultimatum tending to subjugate Japan and making war inevitable, but that peace efforts should be continued "to the last moment."

The decision for war was made at an Imperial Conference on December 1. Next day the General Staff issued the order: "X day will be December 8" [December 7, Hawaiian and U.S. time]. Now the die was cast. We drove headlong toward Pearl Harbor.

Why was that Sunday chosen as X day? Because our information indicated that the American Fleet returned to Pearl Harbor on weekends after training periods at sea. Also because the attack was to be coordinated with our operations in Malaya, where air raids and landings were scheduled for dawn of that day.

Intelligence reports on U.S. Fleet activities were relayed to us from Tokyo: DECEMBER 7 [December 6, Hawaiian and U.S. time]: NO BALLOONS, NO TORPEDO-DEFENSE NETS DEPLOYED AROUND BATTLESHIPS IN PEARL HARBOR. ALL BATTLESHIPS ARE IN. NO INDICATIONS FROM ENEMY RADIO ACTIVITY THAT OCEAN-PATROL FLIGHTS BEING MADE IN HAWAIIAN AREA. LEXINGTON LEFT HARBOR YESTERDAY. ENTERPRISE ALSO THOUGHT TO BE OPERATING AT SEA.

We were 230 miles due north of Oahu shortly before dawn on December 7 when the carriers turned and headed into the northerly wind. The battle flag was now flying at each masthead. There was a heavy pitch and roll that had caused some hesitation about taking off in the dark. I decided it was feasible. Flight decks vibrated with the roar of aircraft engines warming up.

Now a green lamp was waved in a circle. "Take off!" The engine of our foremost fighter plane built up to a crescendo—and then the plane was off, safely. There were loud cheers as each plane rose into the air.

Within fifteen minutes 183 fighters, bombers and torpedo planes had taken off from the six carriers and were forming up in the still-dark sky, guided only by signal lights of the lead planes. After circling over the fleet formation, we set course due south for Pearl Harbor. The time was 6:15 a.m.

Under my direct command were 49 level bombers. To my right and slightly below me were 40 torpedo planes; to my left, about 200 meters [218 yards] above me, were 51 dive bombers; flying cover for the formation were 43 fighters. [Captain Fuchida's totals of aircraft under his command vary slightly from official U.S. figures. See page 25.]

At seven I figured that we should reach Oahu in less than an hour. But, flying over thick clouds, we could not see the surface of the water and had no check on our drift. I switched on the radio direction finder to tune in the Honolulu radio station and soon picked up some music. By turning the antenna I found the exact direction from which the broadcast was coming and corrected our course. We had been 5° off.

Now I heard a Honolulu weather report: "Partly cloudy, with clouds mostly over the mountains. Visibility good. Wind north, ten knots."

A more favorable situation could not have been imagined. About 7:30 the clouds broke, and a long white line of coast appeared. We were over the northern tip of Oahu. It was time for our deployment.

A report came in from one of two reconnaissance planes that had gone ahead, giving the locations of 10 battleships, 1 heavy cruiser and 10 light cruisers. The sky cleared as we moved in, and I began to study our objectives through binoculars. The ships were there, all right. "Notify all planes to launch attacks," I ordered my radioman. The time was 7:49.

Bombs fell on Ford Island, on Hickam Field, where heavy bombers were lined up, and on Wheeler Field. In a short time huge billows of black smoke were rising from these bases.

My level bomber group kept west of Oahu past the southern tip of the island. None but Japanese planes were in the air. Ships in the harbor still appeared to be asleep. The Honolulu radio broadcast continued normally. We had achieved surprise!

Knowing the General Staff would be anxious, I ordered the following message sent to the fleet: WE HAVE SUCCEEDED IN MAKING SURPRISE ATTACK. REQUEST YOU RELAY THIS REPORT TO TOKYO.

Now I saw waterspouts rising alongside the battleships. Our torpedo bombers were at work. It was time to launch our level-bombing attacks, so I gave the attack signal. All ten of my squadrons formed into a single column with intervals of 200 meters.

As my group made its bomb run, American antiaircraft from shipboard and shore batteries suddenly came to life. Dark-gray bursts blossomed here and there until the sky was clouded with shattering near-

misses that made our plane tremble. The counterattack came less than five minutes after the first bomb had fallen.

My squadron was headed for the *Nevada,* which was moored at the northern end of Battleship Row on the east side of Ford Island. When it was nearly time for bomb release we ran into clouds and circled over Honolulu to await another opportunity. Meanwhile, other groups made their runs.

Suddenly a colossal explosion occurred in Battleship Row. A huge column of dark-red smoke rose to 1000 feet, and a stiff shock wave reached our plane. A powder magazine must have exploded. The attack was in full swing; smoke from fires and explosions filled most of the sky over Pearl Harbor.

Studying Battleship Row through binoculars, I saw the big explosion had been on the *Arizona.* She was still flaming fiercely, and since her smoke covered the *Nevada,* the target of my group, I looked for some other ship to attack. The *Tennessee* was already on fire, but next to her was the *Maryland.* I gave an order changing our target to this ship.

As the lead bombardier dropped his bomb, the pilots, observers and radiomen in the other planes shouted, "Release!"—and down went all our bombs. I lay flat on the floor to watch through a peephole. Four bombs in perfect pattern plummeted like devils of doom. They grew smaller and smaller until they looked like poppy seeds and finally disappeared just as tiny white flashes appeared on and near the ship.

From a great altitude near-misses are much more obvious than direct hits because they create wave rings in the water which are plain to see. Observing two such rings plus two tiny flashes, I shouted, "Two hits!" I felt sure considerable damage had been done. I ordered the bombers that had completed their runs to return to our carriers, but my plane remained to observe and conduct operations still in progress.

Pearl Harbor and vicinity had been turned into complete chaos. The *Utah* had capsized. The *West Virginia* and *Oklahoma,* their sides almost blasted off by torpedoes, listed sharply in a flood of heavy oil. The *Arizona* was listing badly and burning furiously. The *Maryland* and *Tennessee* were on fire.

During the attack many of our pilots noted the

(Right) *Destination: Pearl Harbor. Within the space of fifteen minutes, all 189 planes of the first Japanese assault wave were airborne. One here is given a rousing "Banzai" send-off by the carrier's crew.*

(Left) *Japanese flyers on the carrier Sho-kaku get final briefing before setting out on their "divine mission" to bomb Pearl Harbor.*

(Below) *Capt. Mitsuo Fuchida commanded first assault wave of the Pearl Harbor raid.*

brave efforts of American fliers to get planes off the ground. Though greatly outnumbered, they flew straight in to engage our craft. Their effect was negligible, but their courage commanded admiration.

It took the planes of our first attack wave about one hour to complete their mission. By the time they were headed back to our carriers, having lost 3 fighters, 1 dive bomber and 5 torpedo planes, our second wave of 171 planes swept in.

The second attack achieved a nice spread, hitting the least damaged cruisers and destroyers. This attack also lasted about one hour, but owing to the increased return fire it suffered higher casualties—6 fighters and 14 dive bombers.

After the second wave headed back to the carriers, I circled Pearl Harbor once more to observe and photograph the results. I counted 4 battleships definitely sunk, 3 severely damaged. Still another battleship appeared to be slightly damaged, and extensive damage had been inflicted on other types of ships. The seaplane base at Ford Island was in flames, as were the airfields, especially Wheeler.

My plane was about the last to get back to the fleet, and I was summoned to the bridge immediately. Admiral Nagumo's staff had been engaged in heated discussion about the advisability of launching another attack.

"Four battleships definitely sunk," I reported. "We have achieved a great amount of destruction at airfields and air bases. But there are still many targets which should be hit."

I urged another attack. Admiral Nagumo, however—in a decision which has since been the target of much criticism by naval experts—chose to retire. Immediately flag signals were hoisted, and our ships headed northwest at high speed.

The white wakes of Japanese torpedoes reach out toward easy targets, the Oklahoma *and* West Virginia, *moored along Battleship Row on the southeast shore of Ford Island.*

One of the attacking Japanese airplanes is hit by American fire and goes down in flames during the Pearl Harbor assault. Out of a total of 360 enemy planes comprising the two waves, only twenty-nine were lost. U.S. air power was practically destroyed.

A Navy tug is sent to assist the battleship Nevada, seen in the background. Torpedoed by Japanese aircraft as well as hit repeatedly by bombs, the Nevada managed to get moving under her own steam in an effort to escape the holocaust. Her gallant sortie ended when she was beached at Waipio Point.

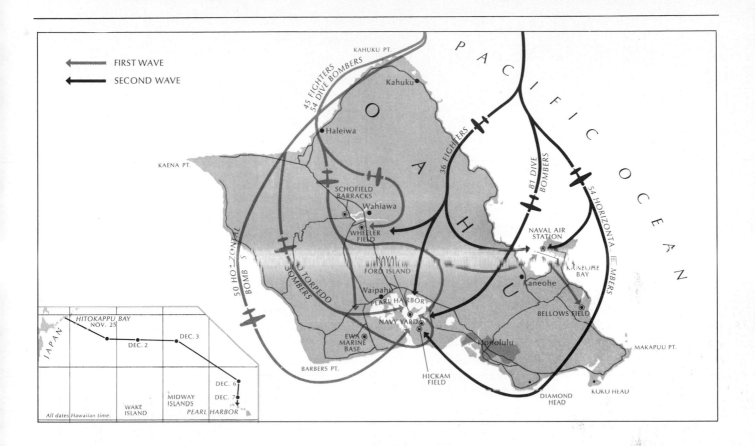

FIRST WAVE
SECOND WAVE

TWO HOURS OF DEATH AND DESTRUCTION

The attack on Pearl Harbor had been planned by the Japanese as early as January 1941. The enemy fleet consisted of 6 aircraft carriers bearing 414 airplanes, 2 battleships, 3 cruisers, 9 destroyers, 3 submarines and numerous auxiliary craft. It sailed from the Kurile Islands on November 25, 1941 (U.S. time), under strict radio silence and complete blackout. The northern route to the objective with its prevailing bad weather and high seas was deliberately taken to lessen the chance of detection by U.S. aircraft or merchant ships. Well ahead of the main Japanese force was a group of submarines, 25 to 28 in number. Five of these carried midget two-man submarines fastened to their decks.

At 6 a.m. on December 7 the signal was given for the attack. The assault was made in two waves: the first by 50 horizontal (level) bombers, 40 torpedo bombers, 54 dive bombers and 45 fighters; the second by 54 horizontal bombers, 81 dive bombers and 36 fighters.

There were 94 ships of the U.S. Navy in Pearl Harbor on that Sunday morning of December 7, 1941. Of these, 70 were combat vessels, including 8 battleships.

The Japanese planes met no opposition. While their fighters and dive bombers attacked the airfields at Wheeler, Hickam, Kaneohe, Bellows and Ewa, torpedo and horizontal bombers concentrated on Pearl Harbor. Surprise was complete. The

double file of great U.S. battleships was struck again and again. When the first wave of planes had spent its fury, the second wave tore in on the ripped and blazing targets.

In less than two hours the winged raiders were gone and the ships of the Japanese striking force were withdrawing into the northwest. The savage assault had taken a serious toll—7 of the 8 U.S. battleships had been either sunk or badly crippled; 3 cruisers had suffered severe damage, as had 3 destroyers. Of a total of 394 U.S. planes, 188 were demolished and 159 damaged; 2403 Americans were killed and 1178 wounded. The Japanese lost 29 aircraft, 5 midget submarines and 1 full-sized submarine.

The moored battleship California *is engulfed by flames and smoke from burning oil following torpedo hits by Japanese planes. The struggle to keep the ship afloat was lost, and she settled to the bottom of the harbor.*

REMEMBER PEARL HARBOR!

BY BLAKE CLARK

An American journalist tells what it was like that Sunday morning when the bombs began falling on the Hawaiian island of Oahu.

I have been close to the horrors and glories of one of the most crucial battles in America's history. Its beginning, on a calm, sunny Sunday morning in one of the most peaceful spots in the world, was a rumbling noise of what I thought was coast artillery practice, then this radio announcement: "Keep calm, everybody. Oahu is under attack. This is no joke. The emblem of the Rising Sun has been seen on the wings of the attacking planes."

Typical of the surprise attack was the experience of the commanding officer at the Kaneohe Navy Seaplane Base. He was having his breakfast coffee. Hearing planes, he looked out the window and saw three flights of three planes each, flying low and making a right turn into the entrance of the bay.

"Those fools know there is a strict rule against making a right turn!" the Commander exclaimed, leaping to his feet. The first alarm was the screeching of his automobile tires coming downhill to the administration building. The mustard-yellow planes now flew low, one behind the other, no more than fifty feet above seaplanes that lay anchored in the bay. A hundred yards away were two boats of young seamen passing each other, the shifting crews of the anchored planes. The Japanese opened up. Machine-gun bullets made a wide lane of geysers that led straight to the boats and the anchored planes. The planes went up in flames. A few of the boys escaped.

On the seaplane ramp, gun crews rushed out to salvage machine guns from burning planes and set them up. Streams of fire converged upon the attackers. For fifteen or twenty minutes this strafing attack kept up, the line of planes going continuously up and down, crossing each time directly over the planes on the ramp.

During the lull that followed, men commandeered all available cars and drove them to staggered positions on the airfield, so that if enemy planes tried to land they would crash into the cars. Civilian employes helped put out fires and manned bulldozers to push burning planes away from the hangars.

Lieutenants George Welch and Ken Taylor, sitting in the officers' club at Wheeler Field, saw dive bombers swoop low over the ammunition hangar and drop their bombs. The lieutenants rushed out to their car. They hit 100 miles an hour on the way to their planes. They did not stop to hear the size or number of planes attacking, but rose to battle and headed straight for a squadron of a dozen or more of the Japanese planes flying over Barbers Point. They accounted for three of the enemy before they had to return for refueling.

One of Welch's three machine guns jammed, and Taylor was wounded in the arm and leg. Before Welch's gun could be unlocked or Taylor's wound receive first aid, a second wave of fifteen Japanese planes swept in. Taylor had been advised not to return to the air because of his wounds, but he and Welch took off immediately.

The Japanese were soon on Taylor's tail. Welch, behind them, dived on the one most dangerous to his partner, letting fly with all his guns. The enemy plane burst into flames and crashed; Taylor escaped. Welch followed another plane seaward, caught it five miles offshore and gave its two-man team an ocean grave.

These fighters were not alone. An old-timer, Lieutenant Sanders, led a unit of four planes up through an overcast of 6000 feet. He saw a group of six Japanese planes bombing an airfield and signaled his men to attack. The Japanese saw them and fled. The unit came in fast; Sanders opened up on the leader. The Japanese plane smoked up, faltered and fell into the sea.

Lieutenant James Sterling was hot after one of the enemy. A Japanese plane was on his tail. Sanders closed in, but the attacker was already pouring bullets into Sterling's plane, and it burst into flames. The

---

(Above right) *The sneak attack made a shambles of the U.S. Naval Air Station on Ford Island, destroying aircraft and installations.* (Below) *The figure of a U.S. soldier is outlined against the flames of a civilian home that was set afire when it was struck by the wreckage of a downed Japanese airplane.*

American continued to fight the Japanese plane ahead, and they all went into a dive—the Japanese in front, Sterling still firing at him, the second Japanese after Sterling, and Sanders following through. Down they plunged, motors roaring at full speed. Only Sanders pulled out.

At Hickam Field the Japanese first attacked planes drawn up in front of the hangars. In the second and most destructive raid, two rows of high-flying bombers dropped heavy demolition bombs directly on the most populous section of the field. For what seemed a full minute after the bombs landed, nothing happened. Then the mess hall (large enough to house six basketball courts), the guardhouse, the fire station, the huge barracks and an immense hangar all seemed to rise intact from the ground, poise in midair and drop back to the earth in fragments.

Ground defenses were now going full blast and accounted for several raiders. Green men acted like veterans, time and again dashing out under fire and taking over machine guns whose operators had just been killed.

Twenty men were caught in a turret on the *Arizona,* the battleship most devastatingly bombed. A hot blast enveloped them. They felt a pressure on their eardrums. Nauseating gas and smoke smothered them. There was confusion and danger of panic, but at one command—"Quiet"—not a word was spoken. A seaman produced a flashlight, and they found their way through the thick smoke to the ladder. The man sent to open the hatch took a long time, but the men waited quietly in the heavy smoke.

When the hatch was opened they burst out upon an amazing sight. The forward part of the ship was a mass of flames and shattered, twisted metal. Bodies lay thick on the deck. Men were running out of the fire, falling on the deck, jumping over the side. Japanese planes were flying low over the ship, strafing the fleeing seamen. Out of the chaos the men heard a voice of calm reassurance.

"Take it easy. Don't get excited. Leave the ship for Ford Island." It was the surviving ranking officer. He went into the flames. Many who came out with him were so badly burned that they were barely able to stand. They stumbled along, feeling their way, helpless; yet not a man gave way to panic.

The officer worked swiftly, surely, and took no shelter from the Japanese, who continued their strafing. Many of the wounded and some of those unhurt would have failed to get off the burning ship had it not been for this officer's courage. Men took heart from his calmness, forgot about themselves and turned to help others escape. Not until the last boat pulled away with the final load of wounded did the officer leap overboard and swim ashore.

On one ship a chaplain in ecclesiastical gown was setting up his reader's stand for the morning service. At the attack he dashed to where some men were dealing out arms and grabbed a machine gun. Using his stand for a prop, he set up the gun and fired away.

We learned in Honolulu that Sunday how narrow the dividing line is between the soldier and the civilian in wartime. Soon after the bombing started, a call came into the headquarters of the Hawaii Medical Association. The voice just said: "Pearl Harbor! Ambulances! For God's sake, hurry!"

Within twenty minutes doctors and volunteer workers had stripped the insides of more than 100 delivery trucks of every description, equipped them neatly with previously prepared stretcher frames and were speeding to the scene of action.

Women of the Motor Corps, in every available car, were carrying men to Pearl Harbor. The three-lane highway was an inferno. Army trucks, official and unofficial emergency wagons, ambulances, Red Cross cars and hundreds of taxis rushing officers and men to their battle stations screamed up and down the six-mile road. The Motor Corps women were equal to the task.

The Army wounded were taken to Tripler Army Hospital. Surgeon King put in an emergency call for surgical teams to the doctors of Honolulu. Then occurred one of life's breathtaking coincidences. At that very moment, about fifty Honolulu doctors were listening to a lecture on war surgery delivered by Dr. John J. Moorhead of New York. The audience departed in a group for Tripler.

By another coincidence Dr. Moorhead had recently demonstrated a new survival instrument that locates metal in the body. The instrument proved its worth that morning, saving precious hours that would have been spent waiting for X rays to be developed.

At eleven o'clock, when plasma from the local blood bank was running low, Dr. Forrest Pinkerton made a short appeal over the radio for blood. In half an hour 500 people were waiting at the doors of Tripler Hospital. The staff of trained technicians worked at twelve tables, but could not take the blood as fast as it was offered. Some donors stood in line for seven hours.

Convalescents in the Navy Hospital were hastily evacuated to temporary quarters outside to make room for the injured, streaming in on stretchers. Numbers of young seamen had lost arms or legs, hundreds were burned. The spirit of these boys was unbelievable. The most impressive fact about the hospital, filled with wounded, many suffering unto death, was the silence —no confusion, no crying out.

Each afternoon for days, numbers of Pearl Harbor's 2403 heroic dead were buried, simply and with dignity, without crowds of onlookers. On each grave was a bouquet of flowers. A row of tight-lipped, khaki-clad marines stepped forward, raised their rifles and fired three volleys. A bugler sounded taps.

On New Year's Day, Honolulu paid its respects to the dead in a memorial service. Hundreds of persons attended, each wearing a flower lei in honor of the dead. They gathered around the long wide trenches in which rows of men who had fought side by side now lay side by side, each in his own coffin. Six Hawaiian girls sang the slow sweet strains of "Aloha Oe."

Fleet Chaplain William A. Macguire spoke in a firm voice: "Don't say we buried our dead with sorrow. They died manfully. They were buried manfully. And we will avenge their deaths, come what may!"

America's first requiem for its war dead takes place at a mass burial at Kaneohe, Oahu. In less than two hours on the morning of December 7, 1941, a total of 2403 Americans were killed in the succession of Japanese air attacks that marked U.S. entry into World War II.

WHY THE SNEAK ATTACK SUCCEEDED

BY LOUIS L. SNYDER

A leading historian probes the chicanery the Japanese employed to gain the element of surprise at Pearl Harbor, and the strange twists and turns of fate that aided them.

Early on Sunday morning, December 7, 1941, a young boy was scooting along on his bike from Honolulu to Pearl Harbor, the chief U.S. Naval base in the North Pacific. He was carrying an urgent communication from Washington. General George C. Marshall, U.S. Chief of Staff, recognizing that negotiations with Japan had broken down, had sent an alert to Pearl Harbor. An attempt to send the message by Army radio having failed because of bad static, it was forwarded through commercial channels to Honolulu. The Honolulu office gave it to the boy with instructions to get it to Pearl Harbor as quickly as possible. He was on his way when the first bombs fell. He dived for a roadside ditch and stayed there for two hours while bombs hurtled from the skies.

Not long before, there had been indications that something was radically wrong. But by a combination of unfortunate circumstances the attacking Japanese were able to achieve complete surprise.

At 6:45 a.m. the American destroyer *Ward,* on routine patrol duty off the naval base, identified and sank a Japanese midget submarine. No one on the destroyer dreamed that it might have been a part of a large task force.

During the first two weeks of September 1941, Japan's senior Naval officers met in conclave at the Naval War College in Tokyo to discuss the strategy of an attack on Hawaii. A month later, on October 5, a selected group of pilots was briefed on the plan. On November 5 came Combined Fleet Top Secret Operational Order No. 1, to be followed within two days by Order No. 2 calling specifically for an attack on Pearl Harbor.

The task force sailed from Tankan (Hitokappu) Bay in the Kurile Islands on November 25, 1941 (U.S. time), under radio silence and with instructions to sink any vessels encountered.

On November 30 came the code message, EAST WINDS, RAINING, the signal for all Japanese diplomatic and consular agents in the United States to destroy their papers. The next day came the radio message, CLIMB MOUNT NIITAKA, to the Japanese task force. It was the irrevocable, fateful order to attack Pearl Harbor.

The warships refueled at sea on December 2 and set their course toward Pearl Harbor (see map inset on page 25). The rendezvous point, 1460 miles northwest of Pearl Harbor, was reached on December 3.

Shortly after 7 a.m. on December 7, two U.S. soldiers were watching their mobile radar set on the northern slope of Oahu. An oscilloscope signal began to blip wildly. The screen showed what seemed to be a swarm of aircraft approaching at a distance of 137 miles. One of the soldiers immediately informed an officer by phone. The officer's answer was disastrous for many men at Pearl Harbor. He told them to ignore the signals, assuming they indicated friendly B-17's expected from the mainland. It was a human mistake, but a costly one.

Less than a half hour later, through the fleecy clouds over Kahuku Point, came the roar of the first wave of Japanese planes.

The man who engineered the attack on Pearl Harbor was Adm. Isoroku Yamamoto, Commander in Chief of the Imperial Japanese Navy. In the belief that "the fiercest serpent can be overcome by a swarm of rats," the Admiral carefully amassed an armada of aircraft carriers long before December 7, 1941, and supervised the training of a force designed to obliterate American power in the Pacific.

In mid-October 1941 Prince Fumimaro Konoye, who had struggled for moderation, resigned as premier. He was succeeded by Gen. Hideki Tojo, the "Razor Brain," whose new Cabinet of Army and Navy officers "smelled of gunpowder." The anti-American campaign went into high gear.

"The rise or fall of our Empire depends upon this battle," Adm. Isoroku Yamamoto told his officers before Pearl Harbor.

sible for the conduct of their Government if an answer was delayed.

The response came on November 26, 1941, in a strongly worded note presenting these counter-demands by Washington: Withdrawal of Japanese forces from China and Indochina; a joint guarantee of the territorial integrity of China; Japanese recognition of the Chinese Nationalist Government of Chiang Kai-shek; a nonaggression pact among the Pacific powers; future adherence of Japan to the rules of law and order in her relations with other countries; and Japanese withdrawal from her association with the Axis powers. In effect, the Japanese were being asked to make a complete about-face.

Meanwhile, "Magic," the U.S. Army and Navy cryptanalytic division, which had broken the Japanese radio code, was intercepting messages which made it clear that Tokyo had little confidence in the Washington peace negotiations. One important communication was missed by the Americans: On November 5, 1941, the Combined Fleet Top Secret Operational Order No. 1 was issued.

On November 25 the Japanese task force under Vice Admiral Nagumo sailed toward Hawaii. Simultaneously, the Japanese Foreign Minister, Shigenori Togo, instructed Nomura in Washington to avoid giving the impression that Japan wished to break off negotiations.

In Tokyo on November 30, 1941 (U.S. time), an Imperial Conference made a formal decision to strike. A fleet of warships and transports was sent to the Gulf of Siam in a successful effort to confuse U.S. Army and Naval Intelligence, which believed that Japan would strike at the East Indies or possibly Singapore. Washington sent an inquiry to Tokyo regarding Japanese intentions.

On December 6, 1941, Japanese forces poured from troop ships and planes into Indochina. Simultaneously, "Magic" intercepted Tokyo's answer to Secretary Hull's counter-demands of November 26. It was a flat rejection.

That same day President Roosevelt dispatched a personal appeal to Emperor Hirohito:

There came about an elaborate piece of playacting by the Japanese militarists, planned so that Japanese Naval units could have time to reach Pearl Harbor for the surprise attack. On November 14, 1941, Tojo's special envoy, Saburo Kurusu, arrived in San Francisco on his way to Washington to assist the Japanese Ambassador, Adm. Kichisaburo Nomura, in a last-ditch effort to "maintain the peace." Kurusu announced to the press that he had come "to make a touchdown." It is highly probable that neither he nor Admiral Nomura was aware that they were being used as decoys in a fixed game.

At the negotiations on November 17, 1941, with Secretary of State Cordell Hull, the Japanese representatives presented a list of "minimum demands": An end to the American financial and economic embargo; cessation of military and economic aid to China; a hands-off policy in China; recognition of Manchukuo; full access to the Netherlands East Indies for Japan; and acknowledgment of Japan's "Greater East Asia Co-Prosperity Sphere." The envoys requested Hull to bring the demands to the attention of President Franklin D. Roosevelt, since they could not be held respon-

I address myself to Your Majesty at this moment in the fervent hope that Your Majesty may, as I am doing, give thought in this definite emergency to ways of dispelling the dark clouds. I am confi-

31

dent that both of us, not only for the sake of the peoples of our great countries but for the sake of humanity in neighboring territories, have a sacred duty to restore traditional amity and prevent further death and destruction in the world.

On the next day, December 7, 1941, there was no reply from Tokyo. The Japanese emissaries, Kurusu and Nomura, had asked for an audience with Secretary of State Hull at one o'clock that afternoon, Washington time. He agreed to meet them at 1:45 p.m. They arrived at 2:05, just twenty minutes late. Hull kept them waiting another fifteen minutes in an outer room of his office.

Richard L. Turner, an Associated Press newsman, reported:

Gone was the blithe breezy aplomb that had characterized their numerous previous visits to the Department. There was a tight-lipped, almost embarrassed smile for newsmen, and an absolute refusal to answer questions. Kurusu paced the diplomatic reception room. Nomura sat stolidly upon a leather divan; only a frequently tapping foot betrayed his perturbation.

At this moment Hull received the flash that the Japanese had attacked Pearl Harbor. The envoys were admitted to his office. Nomura handed him the final Japanese reply to the American formula for peace in the Pacific. Hull gravely read the mixture of insults and misstatements, charging among other things that the United States was guilty of scheming for an extension of the war. Then the Secretary of State turned to the Japanese Ambassador and responded with a verbal blasting without precedent in the history of American diplomacy.

In a voice choking with anger, Hull said, "I must say that in all my conversations with you during the last nine months I have never uttered one word of untruth. This is borne out absolutely by the record. In all my fifty years of public service I have never seen a document that was more crowded with infamous falsehoods and distortions—infamous falsehoods and distortions on a scale so huge that I never imagined that any government on this planet was capable of uttering them."

Wordlessly, the Japanese left.

At Pearl Harbor the United States was suffering greater naval losses than in the whole of World War I. Half the U.S. Navy was crippled and American striking power in the Pacific was for the time almost completely paralyzed.

The reaction in Japan was ecstatic. In blazing headlines the *Japan Times and Advertiser,* mouthpiece of the Foreign Office, claimed: U.S. PACIFIC FLEET IS WIPED OUT! The paper asserted that Japan had reduced the United States to a third-class power overnight, as witness direct accounts and photographs from forces which carried out the attacks.

Only a few hours after Pearl Harbor, Emperor Hirohito issued a formal declaration of war, couched in terms of medieval grandiloquence:

We, by grace of Heaven, Emperor of Japan, seated on the throne of a line unbroken for ages eternal, enjoin upon you, our loyal and brave subjects: We hereby declare war on the United States of America and the British Empire.

Adolf Hitler underwent a rare moment of euphoria when he heard the news from Pearl Harbor. This was language he understood and approved. Once again the Japanese had proved to his satisfaction that they deserved the title of "honorary Aryans" which he had bestowed on them.

Congress agreed that "a state of war has been thrust upon the United States" and declared that a state of war existed with Germany and Italy. Within a week some thirty-five nations, representing one half the world's population, were at war, and most peoples of the world were either directly or indirectly involved.

The Japanese attack awakened all Latin America to its grave danger. Within five days nine Caribbean countries (Costa Rica, the Dominican Republic, Haiti, Honduras, Nicaragua, El Salvador, Cuba, Guatemala and Panama) declared war on Japan, Germany and Italy. Most other American nations broke off diplomatic relations with the Axis within a few weeks, but Chile and Argentina held back until 1943. Brazil's declaration of war against Germany and Italy on August 22, 1942, had a profound effect all over South America and the Caribbean. Argentina finally declared war in March 1945.

Four days after the attack on Pearl Harbor, Italy and Germany declared war on the United States.

Japanese Ambassador Kichisaburo Nomura (left) and Special Emissary Saburo Kurusu smilingly flank Secretary of State Cordell Hull on the way to the White House. At that very moment the Japanese attack force under Vice Admiral Nagumo was steaming toward Pearl Harbor.

"A date that will live in infamy," President Roosevelt calls December 7, 1941, as he faces a joint session of Congress the next day to seek a declaration of war against Japan. Seated behind the President are Vice President Henry A. Wallace (left) and Speaker of the House of Representatives Sam Rayburn of Texas.

AMERICA
ON THE BRINK
OF WAR

BY EUGENE LYONS

The United States in the 1930's was passing through one of the noisiest, wildest, most colorful periods in its history. Here is a lively reminiscence of the nation in those turbulent times before the bombs fell on Pearl Harbor.

The outbreak of World War II in the fall of 1939 culminated a decade that had begun with a different type of worldwide disaster—the Great Depression. These two tragedies encompassed a period of death, destruction and suffering for all mankind. The moods of the American people, the issues that excited them, were related to international events.

Yet the United States remained overwhelmingly isolationist, with the Congress determined to steer clear of entanglements abroad. Fears for the nation's own security, of course, were aroused by Nazi threats and aggressions in Europe, and even more so by the fanatic expansionist drive of Japan's military caste in Asia. American sympathies were increasingly engaged by the fate of victimized nations and peoples. But the image of Fortress America, safe behind its ocean ramparts, was strong in the public mind.

Sharp disagreements on the proper role of the United States in foreign affairs gained momentum as the world situation deteriorated. Pressures for action to curb fascist ambitions were at times heavy. The climate of noninvolvement, however, was too pervasive to permit what the majority denounced as meddling.

The gloom of the Depression years began to be dissipated after Franklin D. Roosevelt became President in 1933. People who used to sing "Brother, Can You Spare a Dime?" now joined in singing "Happy Days Are Here Again." Roosevelt's "Fireside Chats," however grim the subject matter, were suffused with gaiety and confidence.

As in other times of general suffering and confusion, hucksters of "cure-alls" set up their soapboxes. There was Huey Long, Governor of Louisiana and later U.S. Senator, promising to make "every man a king" with himself as the "Kingfish." An assassin's bullet cut him down in mid-career. There was the "radio priest," Father Charles E. Coughlin, in Royal Oak, Michigan. Through his Sunday afternoon broadcasts—with an audience estimated at its peak at 30 million—and his magazine *Social Justice,* he lambasted both Roosevelt's New Deal and the "money changers" as servants of capitalism.

A more sober crusader was Dr. Francis E. Townsend, whose program called for $200 a month to all unemployed persons over sixty, on condition that the money be spent within a month. To millions of aging Americans this perpetual-motion economics seemed to make sense. On the fringes, in the last prewar years, came organizations such as the Christian Fronters and Christian Mobilizers, and sideshows like William Dudley Pelley's Silver Shirts of America and Fritz Kuhn's goose-stepping German-American Bund—uniforms, swastikas and all.

Perhaps to escape from the tedium of joblessness or welfare work, people engaged frantically in song and dance and other diversions. Hordes of jitterbugs writhed to the beat of ever-new varieties of swing. It was a time of incandescent name-bands—Artie Shaw, Gene Krupa, Glenn Miller, Tommy Dorsey and others. The exciting sounds of Benny Goodman's clarinet and Harry James's trumpet were loud in the land. The aristocracy of jazz was headed by Duke Ellington and Count Basie, composers and bandleaders both, while homemade titles were worn by a hot-lipped trumpet player named Louis ("Satchmo") Armstrong and a wild tap dancer called Bill ("Bojangles") Robinson.

The curtain was beginning to come down on vaudeville even while its eventual successor, television, was still in the laboratory. Professional sports were big. Joe Louis socked his way to the world heavyweight title in 1937 and when he kayoed Max Schmeling the following year it was hailed as scientific proof that Hitler's "master race" wasn't so masterly after all. A similar test had been won two years before at the Berlin Olympics when another black American, Jesse Owens, outran his Nordic competitors and all others. In baseball a rash of heavy hitters such as Jimmy Foxx, Lou Gehrig, Hank Greenberg, Joe DiMaggio and the newcomer Ted Williams packed them into the major-league parks.

Drinking was legal again, as of the end of 1933, after fourteen not-so-parched years. Shorn of its drama of speakeasies, pocket flasks, rumrunners and gang wars, the indulgence seemed a bit tame. But what was lost in the quality of defiance was made up in sheer quantity. Besides, the Prohibition Era was kept going, fresh and bloody, in gangland stories on the nation's screens, where Edward G. Robinson, Humphrey Bogart, George Raft and other gun toters did their stuff.

Movies reached new heights of fiscal glory. The great Charlie Chaplin shared honors with a moppet "Little Colonel" named Shirley Temple. And Karl Marx didn't have a chance against the Marx Brothers, then in the prime of their zaniness.

Another hallmark of the time was a spate of games for the millions, some newly invented, others newly popularized: bingo, pinball, miniature golf, a something-for-nothing chain-letter craze. The arrival and survival of the French-Canadian Dionne quintuplets stirred up more popular interest than the death of 100,000 Chinese under Japanese fire in far-off Nanking. The 1937 sinking of the American gunboat *Panay* on the Yangtze River made headlines, but not as big as those made three years earlier by the FBI hunt and slaughter of Public Enemy No. 1, John Dillinger.

Radio came of age, luxuriantly, both as entertainment and as a channel for information. Millions tuned in on Amos 'n' Andy, Kate Smith, Fred Allen and Jack Benny. "Information Please," "The Quiz Kids" and "Take It or Leave It" drew vast audiences.

On the more serious side, political commentators flourished as never before or since. Opinion-makers such as Elmer Davis, Raymond Gram Swing, Dorothy Thompson—to mention only a few—rated tremendous public attention. Sunday nights, "Mr. and Mrs. America and all the ships at sea" tuned in eagerly for the gossip and guesses of Walter Winchell, delivered at machine-gun speed. The whole population, so it seemed, was glued to its radio receivers as H. V. Kaltenborn reported from Europe, blow by blow, on the Czechoslovak crisis and other way stations on the road to Armageddon.

The theater would remember the 1930's as a time of unforgettable hits like *The Man Who Came to Dinner, Arsenic and Old Lace, Life with Father* and the musi-

cal *Of Thee I Sing*. The merely entertaining was balanced by plays of social significance, including *Pins and Needles,* a musical developed by the International Ladies Garment Workers Union. The ordeal of sharecroppers was on view year after year in *Tobacco Road.* The intrusive war theme was reflected, among many others, by Robert Sherwood's *Idiot's Delight* and *There Shall Be No Night.* The latter switched its locale from Finland to Norway, its Soviet invaders transformed into Nazi Germans, after the German invasion of Russia. On the screen Chaplin took on the German Fuehrer single-handedly in *The Great Dictator.*

That there were real jitters under the jitterbugging was demonstrated by a bizarre episode one evening in October 1938. That was when Orson Welles put the H. G. Wells fantasy *The War of the Worlds* on the airwaves. Presented realistically in present-tense news bulletins with blood-chilling sound effects, it convinced thousands of panic-stricken listeners that an actual invasion by people from Mars was taking place.

As the clouds over Europe and Asia grew more ominous, Americans were absorbed in reading and then seeing *Gone with the Wind* and *The Grapes of Wrath,* and in digesting *Life Begins at Forty.* Against the background of the Munich crisis, the agony of conquered Hungarians and Czechoslovaks and the Japanese atrocities in China, they were singing and dancing to "Flat Foot Floogie with the Floy Floy," "A-Tisket A-Tasket" and other edifying songs.

After the European war broke out in September 1939, the overwhelming nationwide support drawn by Bundles for Britain pointed up American sympathy for Great Britain in its dark hour: some 1.5 million people volunteered their services through more than 2000 local branches.

In the United States the isolationist-interventionist dispute, simmering for many years, burst into the full fury of a "Great Debate." It would stir and divide the nation for twenty-seven months like no other debate since that on slavery prior to the Civil War. Recrimination and accusation touched heights of frenzy.

Immediately after the Nazi assault on Poland, opinion polls showed that over 80 percent of Americans still opposed any intervention carrying a risk of war. Only after the fall of France in June 1940 did a meager majority favor meaningful aid to the Allies.

The line between isolation and intervention was not as sharp as the terms suggest. There were gradations

"Joltin' Joe" DiMaggio shows the form that carried him to a 56-consecutive-game hitting streak in the summer of 1941.

Radio listeners of the 1930's relished the low-key wit of comedian Fred Allen, seen here with his wife, Portland Hoffa.

36

Republican presidential nominee Wendell Willkie campaigns in 1940 at his birthplace, Elwood, Indiana. Defeated by FDR, he cooperated actively in the President's war effort.

(Left) *Symbols of a peaceful "World of Tomorrow" are a 728-foot trylon and 180-foot-wide perisphere at the 1939–40 New York World's Fair. Before the fair ended, World War II had erupted.*

(Below) *On October 29, 1940, Secretary of War Henry L. Stimson picks number for Selective Service as President Roosevelt watches.*

The fanatic appeal of Hitler reached into America during the prewar years. A group of ardent Nazi supporters wear the swastika and give the "Heil Hitler!" salute at Yaphank, Long Island.

37

of opinion, with large numbers of Americans holding in-between views. Few even among the leading interventionists were for entering the war, but they were willing to face the risks of extending maximum help to the democracies, short of war. The Committee to Defend America by Aiding the Allies, headed by the Kansas editor William Allen White, summed up the central interventionist concept in its very title.

Among the isolationists, only a handful of extremists—such as the Christian Fronters, the Silver Shirts and the German-American Bund—were pulling for a Nazi victory. The majority did not deny that Hitler was an evil force and Japanese brigandage detestable. But they argued that the United States was not directly threatened and that the Allies would win in the long run anyhow.

The die-hard isolationist forces were formidable. They included influential Senators and Congressmen; top-shelf progressives; Norman Thomas for the Socialist Party; and two powerful publishers: William Randolph Hearst, owner of a newspaper chain, and Robert R. McCormick, of the Chicago *Tribune*. They also had new associates in the Communists and fellow travelers, now zealous in denouncing the Allies following the Soviet-German nonaggression agreement.

The organized spearhead of isolationism was the America First Committee. It was strong, well financed and relentless in denunciation of the Government's interventionist moves. The outstanding isolationist was Charles A. Lindbergh, a national hero.

The most potent interventionist pressures were exerted less by words than by events. The relentless march of satanic evil from triumph to triumph offended the Puritan conscience of America. The strength of isolationism was being slowly eroded. In January 1939 Roosevelt's plea for repeal of the embargo on arms and munitions was brushed aside. Toward the end of the year, the rape of Poland having been completed, Congress repealed these provisions in the Neutrality Act of 1939, and authorized the sale of every type of armament on a "cash-and-carry" basis.

The Administration's priority goal was to rearm the United States as quickly and massively as possible—and in the process to generate productive capacity for the Allies. By the end of 1939 opposition toward this on Capitol Hill had collapsed. The President's requests for huge defense budgets, in January 1940 and repeatedly thereafter, were met with alacrity. In May he ob-

tained consent for the production of 50,000 planes a year, and a little later for a two-ocean Navy involving construction of 200 additional warships. Aggregate defense appropriations came to an impressive peacetime high of $28 billion; by the end of 1941 the total would reach $78 billion—in a time when dollars were worth about twice what they are today.

The "arsenal of democracy," geared to miracles of productivity, was thus operating at full blast before the Japanese struck at Hawaii. A major miracle was an abundance of employment that at last ended the ten-year Depression. A comprehensive Selective Service Act, the first peacetime draft in American history, was voted in September 1940. In that same month a unique horse trade was consummated: in payment for fifty World War I destroyers, the United States accepted sites for naval and air bases on British soil, from Newfoundland to British Guiana.

There was no "war" party when Roosevelt ran for his third term against Wendell Willkie in 1940. Both candidates were formally for keeping America out of the conflict. In accepting the Republican nomination, Willkie advocated the fullest aid to the Allies and approved the military draft then under discussion.

Clearly Great Britain could not have conducted its defense without American economic collaboration. In the first eleven months of the war, the British Commonwealth absorbed 95 percent of all American aviation exports, 90 percent of its armaments and munitions exports. To ease Britain's desperate condition after its losses of matériel at Dunkirk, mountains of obsolescent American equipment were released to it. In due time, however, the British ran out of cash, and to meet this crisis Roosevelt created the Lend-Lease program. It gave full access to American resources and industrial power for the conduct of the war on credit or, at the President's discretion, as gifts.

The Lend-Lease proposal was debated for two months. Made law in March 1941, the act gave the President unlimited authority to supply arms, planes, ships and everything else the Allies needed. Winston Churchill would say, in an address to a joint session of Congress: "Give us the tools and we will finish the job." He got the tools in overflowing quantities.

It was an open secret, moreover, that to protect the colossal shipments of war sustenance, the U.S. Navy was patrolling the western approaches of the Atlantic, under orders to destroy German or Italian men-of-war intruding into the patrolled area. Greenland and Iceland, occupied by the British after the fall of Denmark, were put under U.S. military control by the Danish Government-in-Exile. An unlimited state of national emergency was declared by President Roosevelt in a "Fireside Chat" on May 28, 1941. All Axis funds in the country were frozen the following month.

When Germany invaded Soviet Russia on June 22, 1941, Churchill and Roosevelt at once hailed Russia as a welcome ally. Quantities of Lend-Lease production were immediately diverted to the Soviets.

The climactic episode in the informal Anglo-American alliance was staged off Newfoundland, beginning on August 9, 1941. There President Roosevelt and Prime Minister Churchill, on their respective warships, met for a series of supersecret conferences at sea. The principal public product was the Atlantic Charter, an agreement (not as yet binding) on long-range war ob-

jectives—"the final destruction of the Nazi tyranny"—and details of the better world to follow. In addition, the two statesmen and their military staffs made strategic decisions on military collaboration, if circumstances made the United States a full-fledged belligerent.

The Newfoundland meeting, taken together with Lend-Lease, edged America closer and closer to war. Yet, almost on the eve of Pearl Harbor, a solid one third of Americans were still against entering the conflict. The debate, in truth, was never resolved by the people or the Congress. It was resolved by the hail of Japanese bombs on Pearl Harbor and the Hawaiian airfields. The promised "rendezvous with destiny" took place on the "day of infamy," December 7, 1941.

On September 2, 1940, America swapped fifty of its World War I destroyers with Britain for the right to build U.S. bases on British soil. The fifty ships beefed up a Royal Navy sorely pressed by the Nazis' vigorous U-boat campaign.

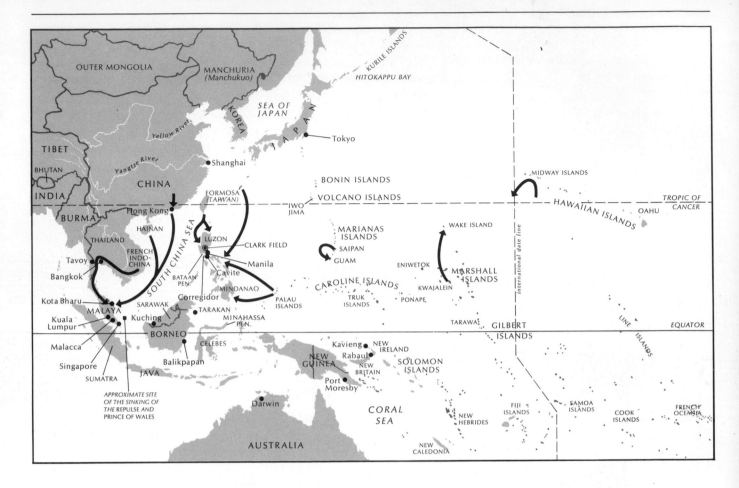

SURPRISE ATTACKS ACROSS THE PACIFIC

Triggered by the Pearl Harbor attack, Japanese forces invaded Thailand and Malaya. The island of Guam and Wake Island were overrun.

Air attacks were made on Manila, Shanghai, Singapore and Hong Kong. On December 9, 1941, resistance to the invaders ceased in Thailand, and a treaty of alliance was signed with Japan. The following day Japanese troops went ashore on Luzon, the northern island of the Philippines, and overcame an outnumbered American force. At Corregidor, an island fortress in Manila Bay, and on nearby Bataan Peninsula, the last defenders of the Philippines made their stand, fighting until May 6, 1942 (see pages 148–157).

The men of Nippon won victory after victory. Kota Bharu airfield in northeastern Malaya was taken after a bitter struggle. Hong Kong, the symbol of British power in the Far East, was forced into submission on Christmas Day 1941. Kuching, the capital city of Sarawak, fell on the same date.

A major offensive was mounted against the Philippines, the attackers using from 80,000 to 100,000 troops. Manila was bombed and bombed again, even after being declared an open city. On New Year's Day 1942, Japanese soldiers entered Manila and also captured the naval base at Cavite.

Invasion thrusts were made in the Netherlands East Indies, at Tarakan off Dutch Borneo and the Minahassa Peninsula in the Celebes. Kuala Lumpur in Malaya was overrun early in January, while Japanese forces crossed the Muar River, south of Malacca, after bitter fighting. The port and air base at Tavoy in Burma were captured January 18. Landings were made at Rabaul in New Britain, at Kavieng in New Ireland and at Balikpapan in Borneo.

By the end of January, the Japanese offensive was running ahead of schedule, thereby seeming to forecast the successful establishment of the "Greater East Asia Co-Prosperity Sphere" and the early realization of the Japanese goal.

(Above) *In a column of tanks and horses, the Japanese invaders move—apparently at a leisurely pace—over a road to Manila.*

(Left) *Planting sticks of dynamite on a bridge, Filipino soldiers prepare an explosive reception for the enemy.*

THE FALL OF SINGAPORE

BY NOEL BARBER

The events that led up to what Winston Churchill has called "the worst disaster and largest capitulation in British history" are described in this account of the downfall of the mighty fortress and naval base of Singapore.

While Singapore slept, at 1:15 a.m. on December 8, 1941 (December 7, U.S. time), the phone rang in Government House. Governor Sir Shenton Thomas lifted the receiver and heard the agitated voice of Gen. Arthur E. Percival, General Officer Commanding, Malaya. Percival reported that the Japanese had begun landing operation at Kota Bharu, a town 400 miles up the east coast of Malaya.

"Well," replied the Governor, "I suppose you'll shove the little men off!"

At that moment the war still seemed far away, but precisely three hours later, at 4:15 a.m., the first Japanese bombs came crashing down on the city. The raid by seventeen planes was not big, and possibly because the streetlights remained on, thousands of people never realized that it *was* a raid.

Long before dawn the attack was over. Sixty-one people had been killed and 133 injured. Most of the bombs had fallen in Chinatown, but one had shaken police headquarters in New Bridge Road. There Insp. Gen. "Dickie" Dickinson had already issued an order to round up every Japanese on the island.

By breakfast time the radio announced the Japanese attack on Pearl Harbor, and within moments the Singapore raid was forgotten. A number of Americans were on the island, and by midmorning there was visible evidence of a new partnership in arms—American flags seemed to appear out of nowhere.

The elation over America's entry into the war was reinforced by the first war communiqué issued from General Headquarters. Briefly, this announced that the Japanese attempt to land at Kota Bharu had been repelled. "All surface craft are retiring at high speed," the report stated, "and the few troops left on the beach are being heavily machine-gunned."

These reassuring words confirmed the belief that no significant attack could come from Malaya. The 400-mile peninsula was largely covered with dense tropical jungle, and a backbone of granite mountains zigzagged down its center. The Japanese had landed on the east coast where the roads were poor, and with the first monsoon rains drenching the countryside, no troops could hope to advance over the impassable terrain.

So the communiqué was accepted as good news in Singapore, and almost no one suspected how tragically misleading it was. The Japanese landing craft, having completed their mission, had retired at high speed. Kota Bharu was already in enemy hands.

"We have had plenty of warning and our preparations are made," announced the Order of the Day issued in Singapore on December 8. "We are confident. Our defenses are strong and our weapons efficient."

"I can't believe it!" cried George Hammonds, assistant editor of the Malaya *Tribune,* when he read the statement in the newsroom. "I can't believe anyone would deliberately tell so many lies!"

Hammonds had toured the island and Malaya many times, and he knew the boast was empty. Few of the 88,000 soldiers in the area—British, Australians, Indians and locally trained Asians—were jungle-trained, and some 15,000 were noncombatants. Many soldiers had landed only recently; they knew nothing of jungle warfare and little of discipline.

The island's vaunted 15-inch guns, Hammonds knew, would be totally ineffective against a land operation. Facing the sea, they had a limited traverse and their ammunition consisted solely of armor-piercing shells. Even worse, the supporting 9.2-inch guns had only thirty rounds of ammunition each. The British reckoned that if Singapore were surrounded, it would take six months before naval relief could arrive. Thus in the event of a siege the gunners would be able to fire one shell every six days.

Hammonds had his doubts, too, about the planes on the island, which included twenty-seven ancient torpedo bombers with old-fashioned open cockpits. If he had known the full truth, he would have been even

THE FALL OF SINGAPORE

more alarmed. Instead of the 336 first-line aircraft which had been promised to Malaya by the end of 1941, the R.A.F. had only 158 operational aircraft, most of them obsolete. Of the twenty-two airfields on the peninsula, fifteen had grass runways.

These airfields were a prime example of the bitter interservice rivalry which had plagued Singapore since 1925. For years there had been virtually no cooperation between the services. From the start the Navy had staked its reputation on the belief that any attack must come from the sea. The R.A.F. disagreed and had constructed the airfields without properly consulting the Army, which would have to defend them. In the uproar that followed Hammonds remembered one furious brigadier shouting, "Some of the bloody airfields can't *ever* be defended. The damn fools have built them in the wrong places!"

The quarrels between the services had never been resolved. They were complicated further when Prime Minister Churchill turned for help to his close friend, Alfred Duff Cooper, who had recently been sent to Singapore after leaving his job as Minister of Information. On December 10 Churchill sent Duff Cooper a telegram elevating him to a Cabinet position as Resident Minister for Far Eastern Affairs, and instructing him to settle emergency matters on the spot. But that afternoon, when a war council met in his home, he discovered that the commanders of the three services intuitively distrusted such an arrangement. Early in the meeting Air Chief Marshal Sir Robert Brooke-Popham calmly announced that he took orders from the Chiefs of Staff in London and not from Duff Cooper.

That evening George Hammonds was comfortably settled in a chair on the veranda of the Cricket Club. Ever since the raid he had been helping Jimmy Glover organize an emergency printing plant at Glover's home outside the city. (The original plant was located near the docks, a prime bombing target.) Now the job was done. A flatbed press, a new linotype and twenty tons of newsprint had been transferred to Glover's house, and 100 coolies had worked in relays for thirty-six hours, laying an underground cable to the machines.

As Hammonds relaxed, music blared from a radio in the Cricket Club bar, and freshly showered tennis players emerged from the locker room, boisterously demanding long cool drinks. Then suddenly the music stopped and the room became utterly still. The only sound was a voice from the radio which announced that H.M.S. *Prince of Wales* and *Repulse* had been sunk.

The silence continued for perhaps thirty seconds—until one old member dropped his glass. Like a starting pistol the sudden noise began a pandemonium of bewildered conversation.

Everyone in Singapore that evening remembers feeling the same stunning shock. The two great ships, pride of the British Navy, were a symbol of the Empire's power and prestige. Churchill had ordered them to Singapore because of the tremendous political effect of really modern ships in the Far East, even though no carrier support was available and the Admiralty had advised against the move. On December 8 the two warships had secretly slipped out from the harbor and up the east coast. Japanese reconnaissance planes had spotted them, and eighty-five bombers had been called to the attack. Both ships went down, with a loss of 840 officers and men.

By now the tactical advantage had been lost forever. In Malaya the Japanese moved swiftly inland, completely bypassing the "impenetrable" jungle. They commandeered bicycles and rode pell-mell through the rubber plantations and the roads that linked them together. Many wore nothing but shorts and undershirts, and they resembled the Malays so closely that it was often impossible to tell whether they were friend or foe.

It was a war for which even the few seasoned British troops were unprepared. To the Japanese the jungles and plantations presented few fears. To the British they were unknown worlds of tigers, snakes, bats and elephants—of unearthly noises and dripping vegetation, now hissing with torrential monsoon rains. In there the enemy could be anywhere or everywhere.

Then suddenly, having traversed jungle country where the British had insisted that tanks could never operate, the first Japanese tanks appeared, now maneuvering easily between the spacious squares of rubber trees. As they rolled south there was not a single British tank in Malaya to oppose them.

The R.A.F. was falling back, too. There were now only fifty planes fit for operation, and most of these were being withdrawn to Singapore. The Japanese had 530 aircraft, all of better quality. When twenty-seven Japanese bombers attacked Penang Island, off the northwest coast of Malaya, the British had no fighters in the sky. After devastating raids the island was quickly abandoned. When the Japanese arrived, they discovered a fleet of boats, junks and barges that the Army had failed to destroy. They used them to ship their men down the west coast so they could land behind the British lines.

In Singapore the reports were scattered and confusing, but by now the civilians were beginning to realize that the war in Malaya was not going well. The wounded were arriving on the island, and soon every room of the General Hospital was crowded.

By Christmas half of Malaya's tin mines and a sixth of the rubber plantations were in enemy hands. The Japanese were heading straight for Johore, at the tip of the peninsula, which pointed toward the northern beaches of Singapore.

Late on the night of December 26, Brig. Ivan Simson hurried to Flagstaff House, General Percival's residence in Singapore. Simson, perhaps above all other men, knew the danger Singapore now faced. He had been sent to Malaya four months earlier as Chief Engineer with instructions to improve the defenses of the area. Since then, he had traveled 6000 miles by car, plane and horseback, and he had learned more about the country's defense weaknesses than any other officer. But he had been able to do little about them.

Everywhere he went, it seemed, he met with indifference. During his tours, for example, he discovered that the troops had been given almost no instruction about antitank measures, although he knew that War Office pamphlets on the subject had been sent from London many months before. Simson found the pamphlets stacked by the hundreds in the cupboards of the military headquarters in Singapore.

But the greatest shock he received came when he inspected the northern beaches of the island. They were completely undefended. No gun or pillbox or even a strand of barbed wire marked the shore. In fact, on Sundays bathers still flocked to the beaches where across narrow Johore Strait, less than a mile wide, they could see the tip of the Malay Peninsula.

Time and again Simson had pleaded for fortifications on these shores, but General Percival had always refused categorically, without any explanation. Now, grimy and dead tired, Simson arrived at Percival's house. He had just returned from the front with a message for the General, and he hoped once again to get permission to fortify the northern beaches.

Percival was about to go to bed, but he asked Simson in and offered him a whisky. Gratefully Simson accepted. He took off his Sam Browne belt and revolver and delivered his message. Then, instead of leaving, he drew a deep breath and announced that he would like to discuss the subject of defenses.

Percival looked startled, but he sat down with a tired expression and prepared to listen. Tall and thin, with two protruding teeth, he was a difficult man to "warm up." Simson spoke quietly and with eloquence.

It now seemed inevitable that the Japanese would soon reach Johore and attack Singapore across the strait, he said. He had the staff to fortify the northern shores with pillboxes, gun positions, antitank defenses, underwater obstacles, fire traps, mines and barbed wire. He could even illuminate the water at night. He had all the materials; they had been available long before the Japanese attack. The job was now a matter of extreme urgency, but it could still be done.

It was a powerful plea, but Percival was not moved. Simson put down his whisky glass and leaned forward. "I must emphasize the urgency of doing everything to help our troops," he said. "They are tired and dispirited. They've been retreating for hundreds of miles. And please remember, sir, the Japanese are better trained and better equipped."

At first Simson had tried to speak dispassionately, but as the clock moved toward two in the morning and he seemed to be making no impression, he found it increasingly hard to control his anger. "It has to be done *now*, sir," he pleaded, "before the area comes under enemy fire."

Incredibly, Percival still refused to change his mind.

At last, in desperation, Simson cried, "General, I've raised this question time after time. You've always refused, and you've always failed to give me any reasons. At least tell me one thing—*why* are you taking this stand?"

Percival finally gave his answer. "I believe that defenses of the sort you want to throw up are bad for the morale of troops and civilians," he said.

Simson got to his feet, suddenly feeling quite cold and realizing that except for a miracle Singapore was as good as lost. He put on his Sam Browne belt and started for the door. "Sir," he said as he left, "it's going to be much worse for morale if the Japanese start running all over the island."

And within two months Singapore had surrendered.

The victor and the vanquished: A gloating Japanese officer announces to a group of Allied prisoners that Singapore, the British Empire's "Gibraltar of the East," has fallen and that 70,000 of their comrades have been captured by the Japanese.

In Singapore, a Malayan mother wails over the body of her child, one of thousands killed by Japanese bombing. The British Naval base was battered from the air and ground for a month. Finally, on February 15, 1942, the "impregnable" fortress-island, its supplies of food, water and ammunition exhausted, was forced to surrender. The British families who remained were herded into concentration camps.

"Today we rule Germany, tomorrow the world!"
This pledge was fervently intoned by millions of Germans, day after day,
year after year. In an attempt to make it come true, Hitler harnessed the
country's scientific and industrial genius and forged
the most powerful military machine Europe had ever seen.

TYRANNY ON THE MARCH
DECADE OF AXIS VICTORIES, 1931-40

THE NAZI RISE TO POWER
Early German Conquests, 1936-39

Humiliated and disillusioned by its defeat in World War I, and racked by inflation and political unrest, Germany offered a perfect breeding ground for the totalitarian ideology of Adolf Hitler. On January 30, 1933, with his Nazi (National Socialist) party gaining strength, Hitler became Chancellor of Germany. He immediately began planning to restore the Fatherland to its former greatness by recovering all lost territory and adding more *Lebensraum* ("living space").

After the close of World War I, the Continent of Europe had been turned into a patchwork of new countries and shrunken old ones by the terms of the Treaty of Versailles. From the wreckage of the Austro-Hungarian Empire came the republics of Czechoslovakia, Austria and Hungary. Serbia and Montenegro vanished, to reappear as part of the new nation of Yugoslavia. Poland was reborn from land that had once belonged to Austria-Hungary, Russia and Germany. By absorbing Transylvania, Bessarabia and other territory, Rumania swelled to twice its former size. Finland, Estonia, Latvia and Lithuania broke away from revolution-torn Russia to gain their independence.

In addition to its loss of territory, which put large numbers of its people under foreign rule, Germany was allowed neither a navy nor an air force, only a skeleton of an army and a limited merchant fleet. Conscription was forbidden, as was the manufacture of heavy armament.

Renouncing the League of Nations, Hitler withdrew Germany's membership in October 1933. He restored conscription and began to build an air force and a fleet of submarines. In March 1935 he scrapped the hated Treaty of Versailles. On March 7, 1936, the Fuehrer ("Leader") sent his troops boldly into the demilitarized Rhineland, winning his gamble that France, who was strong enough to repulse the invasion, would fail to act.

Ignoring censure by the League of Nations, Hitler continued on his way toward total war. He began the construction of the Westwall fortifications—the so-called Siegfried Line—in opposition to the French Maginot Line. In March 1938 Nazi forces swarmed into Austria, Hitler's homeland, in a swift move of annexation. This was followed by a demand that Czechoslovakia give up the Sudetenland with its predominantly German population. With the Czechs mobilizing their army, war was temporarily averted by the notorious Munich Conference, where the prime ministers of England and France bowed to Hitler's wishes and persuaded the Czechs to surrender the Sudetenland for "peace in our time."

The year 1938 saw the further fragmentation of Czechoslovakia when a slice of the southern region was absorbed by Hungary, and Poland occupied Teschen. The next year Hungary annexed Ruthenia, while Hitler, despite his declaration that he would make no more territorial demands, seized Bohemia and Moravia. Scarcely pausing, he took Memel from Lithuania and demanded that Poland surrender a section of the Corridor so that East Prussia could be linked with Germany proper. In addition he ordered that the Free City of Danzig be given to Germany. In a weak effort to emulate the territory grabbing of his Axis partner, Benito Mussolini dispatched his Italian Army to conquer Albania in March 1939.

At last convinced that Hitler could never be trusted, England and France prepared for war, assuring Poland of their support if that country should resist attack. The final act came when Germany and the Soviet Union signed a nonaggression pact, in August 1939, in which the Soviets agreed to remain neutral in a German-Polish conflict.

Now secure from the menace of Russian attack, Hitler gave orders for his High Command to bring into readiness the long-prepared plans for the assault on Poland; on August 31, 1939, the order was given to attack the following morning.

FINLAND

NORWAY

SWEDEN

GULF OF FINLAND

ESTONIA

N O R T H   S E A

B A L T I C   S E A

LATVIA

U. S. S. R.

DENMARK

Copenhagen

Memel
MARCH 1939

LITHUANIA

ENGLAND

Hamburg

Danzig

EAST PRUSSIA

POLISH CORRIDOR

NETHERLANDS

Elbe River

Berlin

Oder River

Vistula River

Warsaw

BELGIUM

G E R M A N Y

P O L A N D

WESTWALL (SIEGFRIED LINE)

Rhine River

SUDETENLAND
SEPT. 1938

LUXEMBOURG

RHINELAND
MARCH 1936

MORAVIA
MARCH 1939

TESCHEN
OCT. 1938

Paris

MAGINOT LINE

C Z E

Prague

OCT. 1938

RUTHENIA
MARCH 1939

F R A N C E

BOHEMIA
MARCH 1939

C H O S L O V A K I A

Munich

Vienna

NOV. 1938

SWITZERLAND

AUSTRIA
MARCH 1938

Budapest

SLOVAKIA
OCT. 1938

HUNGARY

R U M A N I A

I T A L Y

Y U G O S L A V I A

B U L G A R I A

A D R I A T I C   S E A

CORSICA

MEDITERRANEAN SEA

ALBANIA
APRIL 1939

SARDINIA

49

HITLER'S SEIZURE OF EUROPE

BY WILLIAM L. SHIRER

This remarkable narrative, written by a famous correspondent, reveals in chilling detail the terror and savage fanaticism that marked the early years of Hitler's Third Reich.

When Hitler became Chancellor of the Third Reich in 1933, Germany's position could hardly have been worse. Virtually disarmed and nearly bankrupt, it was plagued by unemployment and torn by political dissension. It was by far the weakest big power in the West, and its neighbors, particularly Poland, France and the Soviet Union, were hostile, suspicious and well armed.

Yet in little more than seven years this vagabond from the gutters of Vienna transformed Germany into the mightiest state in Europe and, by a storm of conquests unprecedented in swiftness and scope, made it absolute master of half the Continent.

How did he do it? Acting with the speed, brutality and consummate trickery which were always the hallmark of his tactics, he first consolidated his authority inside Germany. On March 23, 1933, he maneuvered the Reichstag into turning over its constitutional powers to him, supposedly on a temporary basis. By passing a so-called Enabling Act, which made it possible for Hitler to rule by decree with a show of legality, the legislature committed suicide and signaled the end of parliamentary democracy in the Third Reich. For, armed with such sweeping powers, which he had no intention of giving up, he soon banned all opposition political parties and enforced the ruling by means of concentration camps and systematic terror.

He then proceeded to regiment all Germany, taking over and nazifying its institutions one by one. He destroyed the power of labor by seizing the trade unions' funds and imprisoning their leaders, and thereafter forbade all strikes. He bound farmers to the land as in the days of serfdom, suppressed small businesses and forced the businessmen into the ranks of wage earners. Similarly he seized control of the churches, took over the schools, prostituted the courts, muzzled the press and made it a Nazi propaganda arm.

In sum, he smashed all individual freedom and replaced it with a regimentation which was unparalleled even for the Germans. Yet he was rewarded with increasingly frenzied public adulation. Why?

The foremost reason was that whereas 6 million wage earners had recently been out of work, the average man now had a job and the assurance that he would keep it. Beyond that, whatever his crimes against humanity, Hitler had unleashed a dynamic force of incalculable proportions which had long been pent up in the German people.

To what purpose he would direct this resurgence of energy Hitler had already touched on in *Mein Kampf* (see pages 89–90) and in a hundred speeches. He would fulfill the two great passions of his life, which were the creation of a mighty military machine and the shaping of Germany's foreign policy toward conquest.

To talk peace, to prepare secretly for war and to proceed with enough caution to avoid preventive action by the Versailles powers — such were Hitler's tactics during his first two years in power. He built up the armed services with unflagging energy. The Army was ordered to treble its numerical strength, from 100,000 to 300,000, by October 1, 1934. Joseph Goebbels, Minister for Propaganda and Enlightenment, was admonished never to allow the words "General Staff" to appear in the press, since Versailles forbade the very existence of this organization. The official rank list of the German Army ceased to be published lest its swollen roster of officers give the game away to foreign intelligence.

Submarines, which Versailles prohibited, were under secret construction in Finland, the Netherlands

---

Hitler leaves a mammoth mass meeting with his top chieftains as row after row of brown-shirted troopers pay homage to the leader who promised that the "master race" would dominate the world. The celebrated Nuremberg rallies, first held in 1933, lasted a week and were filled with music, parades and rabble-rousing speeches.

and Spain. As Minister of Aviation—supposedly *civil* aviation—Hermann Goering put manufacturers to work designing warplanes, and training of military pilots began immediately under the camouflage of the League for Air Sports. By the end of 1934 rearmament, in all phases, had become so massive that it could no longer be concealed.

Then, on Saturday, March 16, 1935, the Chancellor decreed a law establishing universal military service and providing for a peacetime army of thirty-six divisions, roughly half a million men. That was the end of the military restrictions of the Treaty of Versailles—unless France and Great Britain took action. As Hitler had expected, they protested but did not act.

Hitler was now determined to occupy the demilitarized zone of the Rhineland. All through the winter of 1935–36 he bided his time. France and Great Britain, he could not help but note, were preoccupied with stopping Italy's aggression in Ethiopia, but Mussolini seemed to be getting by with it. Despite its much-publicized sanctions, the League of Nations was proving itself impotent to halt a determined aggressor.

On March 1 Hitler reached his decision, somewhat to the consternation of his generals. Most of them were convinced that the French would make mincemeat of the small German forces gathered for the move into the Rhineland. Nevertheless, on March 2, 1936, in obedience to his master's instructions, Gen. Werner von Blomberg, Minister of War and Commander in Chief of the Armed Forces, issued orders for the occupation of the Rhineland. It was, he told the senior commanders, to be a "surprise move." Blomberg expected it to be a "peaceful operation." If it turned out that it was not—that the French would fight—Blomberg had already planned his countermeasure, which was to beat a hasty retreat back over the Rhine.

But the French, paralyzed by internal strife and sinking into defeatism, did not know this when a token force of three German battalions paraded across the Rhine bridges at dawn on March 7. Just a few hours later the Fuehrer was standing in the Reichstag before a delirious audience, expounding on his desire for peace and his latest ideas of how to maintain it. That evening I noted in my diary the scene that followed:

" 'Men of the German Reichstag!' Hitler said in a deep, resonant voice. 'In this historic hour, when, in the Reich's western provinces, German troops are, at this very moment, marching into their future peace-time garrisons, we all unite in two sacred vows. . . .'

"He could go no further. It was news to this parliamentary mob that German soldiers were already on the move into the Rhineland. All the militarism in their German blood surged to their heads. They sprang, yelling and crying, to their feet, their hands raised in slavish salute. The new messiah played his new role superbly. His head lowered, as if in all humbleness, he waited patiently for silence. Then, his voice choking with emotion, he uttered the two vows:

" 'First, swear to yield to no force whatever in restoration of the honor of our people. Secondly, we pledge that we have no territorial demands to make in Europe! Germany will never break the peace!'

"It was a long time before the cheering stopped. A few generals made their way out. Behind their smiles, however, I could not help detecting a nervousness. I ran into General von Blomberg. His face was white, his cheeks twitching."

And with reason. The Minister of War, who five days before had issued in his own handwriting the order to march, was losing his nerve. But the French never made the slightest move to oppose the Germans. The most Gen. Maurice Gustave Gamelin, Chief of the French General Staff, would do was to concentrate thirteen divisions near the German frontier to reinforce the Maginot Line.

Even this was enough to throw a scare into the German High Command. Blomberg, backed by most of the officers at the top, wanted to pull back the battalions that had crossed the Rhine. As one of them testified at Nuremberg, "Considering the situation we were in, the French Army could have blown us to pieces."

It could have—and had it, that almost certainly would have been the end of Hitler, after which history might have taken quite a different turn, for the dictator could never have survived such a fiasco.

It was Hitler's iron nerve alone which now, as during many crises that lay ahead, saved the situation and, confounding the reluctant generals, brought success. Confident that the French would not march, he bluntly turned down all suggestions by the wavering High Command for pulling back.

"What would have happened," he exclaimed on March 27, 1942, in recalling the Rhineland coup, "if anybody other than myself had been at the head of the Reich? Anyone you care to mention would have lost his nerve. I was obliged to lie, and what saved us was my unshakable obstinacy and my amazing aplomb."

Hitler's successful gamble in the Rhineland brought him a victory more staggering and more fatal in its consequences than could be comprehended at the time. At home it fortified his popularity and his power, raising them to heights which no German ruler of the past had ever enjoyed. It assured his ascendancy over his generals, who had weakened at a moment of crisis when he held firm. It taught them that in foreign policy and even in military affairs his judgment was superior to theirs. Finally, and above all, the Rhineland occupation, small as it was, opened the way to vast new opportunities in a Europe whose strategic situation was irrevocably changed.

For France, it was the beginning of the end. Her allies in the East—the Soviet Union, Poland, Czechoslovakia, Rumania and Yugoslavia—began to realize that France would soon not be able to lend them much assistance because of Germany's construction of a Westwall behind the Franco-German border. The erection of this fortress line, they saw, would quickly change the strategic map of Europe, to their detriment. They could scarcely expect a France which did not dare, with her 100 divisions, to repel three German battalions, to bleed her young manhood against impregnable German fortifications while the *Wehrmacht* ("Armed Forces") attacked in the East.

The German Foreign Minister openly explained to the American Ambassador in the spring of 1936, "As soon as our fortifications are constructed and the countries of Central Europe realize that France cannot enter German territory at will, all those countries will begin to feel very differently about their foreign policies and a new constellation will develop."

This development now began.

Dr. Kurt von Schuschnigg, Chancellor of Austria, related in his memoirs, "I knew that in order to save Austrian independence I had to embark on a course of appeasement. Everything had to be avoided which could give Germany a pretext for intervention, and everything had to be done to secure in some way Hitler's toleration of the status quo."

"Everything," as it turned out, was not enough. But there was to be a breathing space. In his address to the Reichstag on January 30, 1937, Hitler proclaimed, "The time of so-called surprises has ended."

And, in truth, there were no spectacular surprises during 1937. The year for Germany was one of con-

solidation and further preparation for the objectives which, that November, the Fuehrer would lay down to a handful of his highest officers. It was a year devoted to forging armaments, training troops, trying out the new Air Force in the Spanish Civil War, developing ersatz gasoline and rubber, cementing the Rome-Berlin Axis and watching for weak spots in Paris, London and Vienna.

But even in this "peaceful" year, Austrian Nazis, financed and egged on by Berlin, maintained a campaign of terror in that country. Bombings took place nearly every day in some part of the nation, and in the mountain provinces there were massive and often violent Nazi demonstrations. Plans were uncovered disclosing that Nazi thugs were preparing to bump off Chancellor Schuschnigg.

Finally, in February 1938, Schuschnigg was summoned for a "conference" to Hitler's mountain retreat on the Obersalzberg, high above his residence at Berchtesgaden. A man of impeccable Old World Austrian manners, Schuschnigg began the conversation with a graceful tidbit about the magnificent view and the fine weather that day. Hitler cut him short: "We did not gather here to speak of the fine view or of the weather." Then the storm broke. "You have done everything to avoid a friendly policy," Hitler fumed. "The whole history of Austria is just one uninterrupted act of high treason."

Shocked at Hitler's outburst, the quiet-mannered Austrian Chancellor tried to remain conciliatory and yet stand his ground. After an hour of argument, he asked his antagonist to enumerate his complaints, but the Fuehrer simply launched into another tirade against Austria. He then gave Schuschnigg until the afternoon to "come to terms"—without specifying what the terms were.

That afternoon, after cooling his heels for two hours in an anteroom, Schuschnigg was ushered into the presence of Joachim von Ribbentrop, the new German Foreign Minister. Ribbentrop presented a two-page "agreement" which, he announced, must be signed forthwith. The Fuehrer would permit no discussion.

Schuschnigg felt relieved to have at least something definite from Hitler. But as he perused the document his relief evaporated. For here was a German ultimatum calling on him to turn the Austrian Government over to the Nazis within one week.

But what could he do? He was summoned again to

Hitler's subservient bow is deceptive as he greets eighty-six-year-old Marshal Paul von Hindenburg, President of Germany, at a ceremony in Berlin in 1934. Chancellor of the Reich for more than a year, ex-Corporal Hitler had seized near-dictatorial power and reduced the nation's World War I hero to a figurehead. Before the year was out, the President was dead, and the Fuehrer was master of Germany.

Heinrich Himmler, shown here standing at protective attention next to his master, Adolf Hitler, was chief of the S.S. (Black Shirts) and head of the Gestapo. As organizer of the Nazi concentration and extermination camps, he was responsible for the murder of millions of Jews and others opposed to Hitler's tyranny. After his capture in May 1945, Himmler avoided trial as a war criminal by committing suicide.

Master of the lie and the half-truth Dr. Joseph Goebbels, Reich Minister for Propaganda and Enlightenment, was handpicked by Hitler as one of his chief lieutenants. Here Goebbels vehemently proclaims in March 1934 that the Saar Territory, administered by France under a League of Nations mandate, must be returned to the Fatherland.

Hitler and some of his closest lieutenants—Rudolf Hess is at his right, Hermann Goering at his left—return to the famous Munich beer hall to commemorate the Nazi putsch of 1923. It was a fiasco: Hitler and others were arrested, the Nazi Party outlawed. But the publicity and subsequent jail sentence made Hitler a national figure.

Hitler. He found the Fuehrer pacing excitedly up and down in his study.

Hitler: "Herr Schuschnigg, here is the draft of the document. There is nothing to be discussed. I will not change one single iota. You will either sign it as it is and fulfill my demands within three days, or I will order the march into Austria."

Schuschnigg capitulated. He told Hitler he was willing to sign. But he reminded him that under the Austrian constitution only the president of the republic had the legal power to accept such an agreement. At this answer, Schuschnigg later recounted, Hitler seemed to lose his self-control. He ran to the doors, opened them and shouted, "General Keitel!" Then, turning back to Schuschnigg, he said, "I shall have you called later!"

This was pure bluff, but the harassed Austrian Chancellor, who had been made aware of the presence of high-ranking German generals all day, perhaps did not know it. General Wilhelm Keitel later told how Hitler greeted him with a broad grin when he rushed in and asked for orders. "There are no orders," Hitler chuckled. "I just wanted to have you here." Thirty minutes later Schuschnigg signed Hitler's document.

It was Austria's death warrant. Within four weeks, by a combination of ruthless military pressure, propaganda and subversion, the Nazis succeeded in taking complete control of Austria. In order to "legalize" this act of naked aggression, Hitler announced that a plebiscite on the so-called *Anschluss* ("political union") would be held on April 10.

In a fair and honest election the plebiscite might have been close. As it was, it took a very brave Austrian to vote No. In the polling station I visited in Vienna that Sunday afternoon, wide slits in the polling booths gave the Nazi election committee a good view of how one voted. In the country districts few bothered —or dared—to cast their ballots in the secrecy of the booth; they voted openly for all to see. I happened to broadcast at 7:30 that evening, a half hour after the polls had closed, when few votes had yet been counted. A Nazi official assured me before the broadcast that the Austrians were voting 99 percent *Ja.* That was the figure officially given later—99.08 percent in Greater Germany, 99.75 in Austria. And so, for the moment, Austria passed out of history.

Without firing a shot and without interference from Great Britain, France and the Soviet Union, whose military forces could have overwhelmed him, Hitler had added 7 million subjects to the Reich and gained a strategic position of immense value to his future plans. He now possessed in Vienna the nerve center of Central Europe and the gateway to Southeast Europe. Moreover, with his armies flanking Czechoslovakia on three sides, that country was militarily indefensible. There was no time to lose in taking advantage of it.

"Case Green" was the code name of Hitler's plan for a surprise attack on Czechoslovakia, first drawn up in June 1937. Now the easy conquest of Austria made "Case Green" a matter of some urgency; the plan must be brought up to date and prepared for.

The Republic of Czechoslovakia, which Hitler was determined to destroy, was the creation of the peace treaties, so hateful to the Germans, after World War I. It was the most democratic, enlightened and prosperous state in Central Europe. But it was gripped by a domestic problem which in over twenty years it had not been able entirely to solve: the question of its minorities, including the 3¼ million Sudeten Germans who lived within its borders.

The Sudeten Germans fared tolerably well in the Czechoslovak state—certainly better than any other minority in the country. But their plight was for Hitler a pretext (as Danzig was to be a year later in regard to Poland) for cooking up a stew in a land he coveted, confusing and misleading its friends and concealing his real purpose. Now he issued instructions to the Nazi-dominated Sudeten German Party that "demands should be made which are unacceptable to the Czech Government."

The stew began to simmer, and by the weekend which began on Friday, May 20, 1938, it was believed in Prague and London that Hitler was about to launch aggression against Czechoslovakia. The Czechs began to mobilize. Now Great Britain, France and the Soviet Union displayed a firmness and unity in the face of the German threat which they were not to show again until a new world war had almost destroyed them.

The Czech mobilization sent Hitler into a fit of fury, and his feelings were not assuaged by dispatches telling of continual calls by the British and French ambassadors warning Germany that aggression against Czechoslovakia meant a European war—even though the furthest the British would go was to warn that "in the event of a European conflict it was impossible to foresee whether Britain would not be drawn into it."

The Fuehrer, brooding in his mountain retreat, felt deeply humiliated by the Czechs and by the support given them in London and Paris. Nothing could have put him in a blacker, uglier mood. His fury was all the more intense because he was accused prematurely of being on the point of committing an aggression which he indeed intended to commit. That very weekend, in fact, he had gone over a new plan for "Green." But now it could not be carried out. Swallowing his pride, he ordered the Foreign Office to inform the Czech envoy on Monday, May 23, that Germany had no aggressive intentions toward Czechoslovakia.

In Prague, London, Paris and Moscow, government leaders breathed a sigh of relief. The crisis had been mastered. Hitler had been given a lesson. He must now know he could not get away with aggression as easily as he had in Austria.

Little did these statesmen know the Nazi dictator. After sulking at his Obersalzberg retreat a few more days, during which there grew within him a burning rage to get even with Czechoslovakia, he convoked the ranking officers of the *Wehrmacht* to hear a momentous decision: "Czechoslovakia shall be wiped off the map!" he thundered. "Case Green" was again brought out and revised. The first sentence of the new directive read: *"It is my unalterable decision to smash Czechoslovakia by military action in the near future."*

What "the near future" meant was explained in a covering letter. "The execution of 'Green' must be assured by October 1, 1938, at the latest." It was a date which Hitler would adhere to through thick and thin, through crisis after crisis and at the brink of war, without flinching.

About this time the first crisis arose within the German ranks—a rift between Hitler and some of the highest-ranking generals of the Army. The opposition to the Fuehrer's grandiose plans for aggression was led by Gen. Ludwig Beck, Chief of the Army General Staff, who henceforth would assume the leadership of such resistance as there was to Hitler in the Third Reich. Beck began to perceive that Hitler's policy of deliberately risking war with Great Britain, France and the Soviet Union—against the advice of the top generals—would, if carried out, be the ruin of Germany. On May 5 he wrote the first of a series of memorandums strenuously opposing any such action. They are brilliant papers, blunt as to unpleasant facts and full of solid reasoning and logic. Although Beck over-estimated the strength of will of Great Britain and France and the power of the French Army, his long-range predictions turned out, so far as Germany was concerned, to be deadly accurate.

Beck was convinced, he wrote in his May 5 memorandum, that a German attack would provoke a European war in which Great Britain, France and the Soviet Union would oppose Germany and in which the United States would be the arsenal of the Western democracies. Germany simply could not win such a war. Its lack of raw materials alone made victory impossible.

Hitler, however, pressed forward with his plans for aggression, and Beck now maintained that the generals had reached the limits of their allegiance. If Hitler insisted on war, they should resign in a body. In that case, he argued, war was impossible, since there would be nobody to lead the armies.

Beck was aroused as he had never been before in his lifetime. The whole folly of the Third Reich, its tyranny, its terror, its corruption, suddenly dawned on him. The German people must be freed from the Nazi thrall. A state ruled by law must be restored.

To further this purpose, Beck arranged a secret meeting of the commanding generals. His arguments left a deep impression on most of them, but no decisive action was taken. The meeting of the top brass of the German Army broke up without their having the courage to call Hitler to account, and Beck saw that he had been defeated by the spinelessness of his brother officers. On August 18 he resigned as Chief of the Army General Staff.

Here again Hitler showed his craftiness. Though he accepted Beck's resignation at once and with great relief, he forbade any mention of it in the press or in the official military gazettes. It would not do to let the British and French governments get wind of dissension at the top of the German Army at this critical juncture. Had they heard, one could speculate, history might have taken a different turning; the appeasement of the Fuehrer might not have been carried so far.

Less than a month later, on September 12, Hitler delivered a brutal and bombastic speech, dripping with venom against the Czech state, to a delirious mass of Nazi fanatics gathered in the huge stadium at Nuremberg. The repercussions were immediate. The outburst inspired a revolt in the Sudetenland, which, after two days of savage fighting, the Czech Government put down by rushing in troops and declaring martial law.

These women of Düsseldorf offer flowers to smiling Nazi invaders in March 1936, as Hitler's troops occupy the Rhineland in defiance of the Versailles Treaty. A French show of force could have ended the Nazi bluff. Similar bold tactics were to win for the Fuehrer still more sensational victories until, finally, appeasement could no longer satisfy him.

Next day the French Cabinet sat all day, remaining hopelessly divided on whether it should honor its treaty obligations to defend Czechoslovakia in case of a German attack, which it believed imminent. That evening the British Ambassador in Paris was summoned for an urgent conference with French Premier Édouard Daladier. The latter appealed to Neville Chamberlain to try at once to make the best bargain he could with the German dictator. At eleven o'clock that same night the British Prime Minister got off an urgent message to Hitler:

IN VIEW OF THE INCREASINGLY CRITICAL SITUATION, I PROPOSE TO COME OVER AT ONCE TO SEE YOU WITH A VIEW TO TRYING TO FIND A PEACEFUL SOLUTION. I PROPOSE TO COME ACROSS BY AIR AND AM READY TO START TOMORROW.

Ich bin vom Himmel gefallen!" ("Good heavens!") Hitler exclaimed when he read Chamberlain's message. He was astounded but highly pleased that the man who presided over the destinies of the mighty British Empire should come pleading to him, and flattered that Chamberlain who was sixty-nine years old and had never traveled in an airplane before—should make the long seven-hour flight to Berchtesgaden at the farthest extremity of Germany. Hitler had not even the grace to suggest a meeting place on the Rhine, which would have shortened the trip by half.

Hitler began his conversation with Chamberlain, as he did his speeches, with a long harangue about all that he had done for the German people, for peace and for an Anglo-German *rapprochement*. There was now one problem he was determined to solve. The 3 million Germans in Czechoslovakia must "return" to the Reich. Then he sprang his proposal: Would Britain agree to a cession of the Sudeten region to Germany, or would she not?

Chamberlain expressed satisfaction that they had now arrived at the crux of the matter. He replied that he could not commit himself until he had consulted his Cabinet and the French, but added that he could state personally that he recognized the principle of the detachment of the Sudeten areas. He wished to return to England to report to the Government and secure its approval of his personal attitude.

While the British leader was consulting with his Cabinet and the French authorities, Hitler went ahead with his military and political plans for the invasion of Czechoslovakia. But as the negotiations progressed, a

series of events occurred which made Hitler hesitate. In order to stir up war fever among the populace, the Fuehrer ordered a parade of a motorized division through the German capital at dusk on September 27, an hour when hundreds of thousands of Berliners would be pouring out of their offices onto the streets. It turned out to be a terrible fiasco—at least for the Supreme Commander. The people of Berlin simply did not want to be reminded of war. In my diary that night I noted down the scene:

"There weren't 200 people at the Wilhelmsplatz, where Hitler stood on a balcony reviewing the troops. He looked grim, then angry, and soon went inside, leaving his soldiers to parade by unreviewed."

Within the Chancellery there was further bad news. A dispatch from Budapest said that Yugoslavia and Rumania had informed the Hungarian Government that they would move against Hungary militarily if she attacked Czechoslovakia. That would spread the war to the Balkans, something Hitler did not want.

The news from Paris was still graver. A telegram from the German military attaché warned that France's partial mobilization was so much like a total one "that I reckon with the completion of the deployment of the first sixty-five divisions on the German frontier by the sixth day of mobilization." Against such a force the Germans had, as Hitler knew, barely a dozen divisions.

Whether Hitler was aware that the order was going out that evening for the mobilization of the British Fleet cannot be established. He knew that Prague was defiant, Paris rapidly mobilizing, London stiffening, his own people apathetic, his leading generals dead against him, and that his latest ultimatum on the Czech question expired at 2 p.m. the next day.

At 10:30 that night Hitler telegraphed an urgent letter to Chamberlain in London. His letter was moderate in tone, beautifully calculated to appeal to Chamberlain. It was a straw which the Prime Minister eagerly grasped. To the Fuehrer he replied: "After reading your letter, I feel certain that you can get all essentials without war and without delay."

The next day, a few minutes before 2 p.m. on September 28, just as his ultimatum was to expire, Hitler made up his mind. Invitations were hastily issued to the heads of government of Great Britain, France and Italy to meet the Fuehrer at Munich at noon on the following day to settle the Czech question. No invitation was sent to Prague. The Czechs were not even asked to be present at their own death sentence.

When Chamberlain interrupted a speech in the House of Commons to report Hitler's eleventh-hour invitation, the ancient chamber reacted with a mass hysteria unprecedented in its history. There was wild shouting and throwing of papers into the air; many were in tears and one voice was heard above the tumult which seemed to express the deep sentiments of all: "Thank God for the Prime Minister!"

Jan Masaryk, the Czech Minister, son of the founding father of the Czechoslovak Republic, looked on from the diplomatic gallery, unable to believe his eyes. Later he called on the Prime Minister and the Foreign Secretary in Downing Street to find out whether his country, which would have to make all the sacrifices, would be invited to Munich. They answered that it would not, that Hitler would not stand for it. Masaryk struggled to keep control of himself.

"If you have sacrificed my nation to preserve the peace of the world," he finally said, "I will be the first to applaud you. But if not, gentlemen, God help your souls!"

The talks at the Munich Conference, which began at 12:45 on September 29, were anticlimactic; they constituted little more than a mere formality of rendering to Hitler exactly what he wanted when he wanted it. For, despite their outward show of firmness, Hitler had by now sensed that both England and France would go to almost any lengths to avoid war. ("Our enemies are little worms," he told his generals later. "I saw them at Munich.") At every step, the more Chamberlain had conceded, the more Hitler had demanded—and got.

Shortly after 1 a.m. on September 30, Hitler, Chamberlain, Mussolini and Daladier affixed their signatures to the Munich Agreement, providing for the German Army to march into Czechoslovakia on October 1, 1938, as the Fuehrer had always said it would, and to complete the occupation of the Sudetenland by October 10. Hitler had got what he wanted.

Chamberlain returned to London in triumph. "My good friends," he announced to a cheering crowd, "this is the second time in our history that there has come back from Germany to Downing Street peace with honor. I believe it is peace in our time."

Under the terms of the agreement, Czechoslovakia was forced to cede to Germany 11,000 square miles of territory, in which dwelt 2,800,000 Sudeten Ger-

mans and 800,000 Czechs. Within this area lay all the vast Czech fortifications which had formed the most formidable defensive line in Europe, with the possible exception of the Maginot Line.

But that was not all. According to German figures, the dismembered country lost 66 percent of its coal, 86 percent of its chemicals, 70 percent of its iron and steel, 70 percent of its electric power. A prosperous industrial nation was split up and bankrupted overnight. And for what?

It has been argued that Munich gave the two Western democracies nearly a year to catch up with the Germans in rearmament. The facts belie such an argument. As Churchill, backed up by every serious Allied military historian, has written, "The year's breathing space said to be 'gained' by Munich left Britain and France in a much worse position compared to Hitler's Germany than they had been at the Munich crisis."

Germany was in no position to go to war against Czechoslovakia *and* France and Great Britain, not to mention the Soviet Union. Had it done so, it would have been quickly and easily defeated, and that would have been the end of the Third Reich.

For France, Munich was a disaster. Her military position in Europe was destroyed. After Munich, how could her remaining allies in Eastern Europe have any confidence in France's written word? What value now were alliances with France? The answer in Warsaw, Bucharest and Belgrade was, "Not much"; and there was a scramble in these capitals to make the best deal possible, while there was still time, with the Nazi conqueror.

And yet, despite his staggering victory, Hitler was disappointed with the results of Munich. "That fellow," he exclaimed on his return to Berlin, "has spoiled my entry into Prague!" Chamberlain had forced the Czechs to submit to all his demands and thereby had deprived him of a *military* conquest of Czechoslovakia, which was what he had really wanted all along.

"It was clear to me from the first moment," he later confided to his generals, "that I could not be satisfied with the Sudeten German territory. That was only a partial solution."

A few days after Munich, the German dictator set in motion plans to achieve a "total" solution. Utterly disregarding his pledge to guarantee the frontiers of the rump Czech state, he instituted a campaign of

(Above) *Arriving in Munich for the signing of the pact, British Prime Minister Neville Chamberlain reviews a guard of honor.*

(Left) *Hitler, gaining an undreamed-of victory, is ecstatic. Chamberlain, too, is pleased in his delusion that war has been averted. But another Briton, Churchill, was growling, "A total defeat."*

(Below) *Returning to England, Chamberlain waves the treaty and tells the welcoming crowd, "I believe it is peace in our time."*

propaganda and internal subversion designed to force the nation to break up, which would afford him a pretext to march in and "restore order."

On March 14, 1939, with the German armies poised along his country's frontiers, Dr. Emil Hácha, President of Czechoslovakia, a tired old man who was suffering from a heart ailment, came to Berlin to plead with Hitler for his nation's life. The Fuehrer received him courteously enough, but when it became clear that he would accept nothing less than total surrender of the Czechs, Hácha and his Foreign Minister balked.

"The German ministers were pitiless," one diplomat reported. "They literally hounded Dr. Hácha and his Foreign Minister around the table on which the documents were lying, thrusting the papers continually before them, pushing pens into their hands, incessantly repeating that if they continued in their refusal half of Prague would lie in ruins from bombing within two hours."

At last, after having collapsed in a faint and been restored to consciousness by injections given him by a German doctor, Hácha was forced to sign.

At 6 a.m. on March 15, German troops poured into Bohemia and Moravia. They met no resistance, and by evening Hitler was able to make his triumphant entry into Prague. A long night of German savagery settled over the Czech lands.

But now, suddenly and unexpectedly, Neville Chamberlain experienced a great awakening. On March 17 he jettisoned a prepared speech on domestic policy and quickly jotted down notes for one of quite a different kind.

"We are told," he said, "that this seizure of territory has been necessitated by disturbances in Czechoslovakia. If there were disorders, were they not fomented from without? Is this the last attack upon a small state or is it to be followed by others? Is this, in effect, a step toward an attempt to dominate the world by force? No greater mistake could be made than to suppose that this nation has so lost its fiber that it will not take part in resisting such a challenge if it ever were made."

It was obvious to anyone who had read *Mein Kampf,* or who glanced at a map and saw the new positions of the German Army in Slovakia, just which of the "small states" would be next on the Fuehrer's list. Chamberlain, like almost everyone else, knew perfectly well.

On March 31, sixteen days after Hitler entered Prague, Chamberlain told the House of Commons:

"In the event of any action which clearly threatens Polish independence and which the Polish Government considers it vital to resist with its national forces, His Majesty's Government would feel itself bound to lend the Polish Government all support in its power. I may add that the French Government has authorized me to make it plain that it takes the same position."

The news of Chamberlain's guarantee of Poland threw the German dictator into one of his characteristic rages. According to an eyewitness he stormed about the room, pounding his fists on a marble tabletop, his face contorted with fury, shouting against the British, "I'll cook them a stew they'll choke on!"

The next day, April 1, he was in such a belligerent mood that apparently he did not quite trust himself, for at the last moment he ordered that the direct radio broadcast of a speech he was to make be canceled, and that it be broadcast later from recordings, which could be edited. Even the broadcast version was spotted with warnings to Great Britain and Poland. But, as so often before, Hitler ended on a note of "peace": "Germany has no intention of attacking other people."

That was for public consumption. In the greatest secrecy Hitler gave his real answer to Chamberlain two days later, on April 3. In a top-secret directive to the Armed Forces, of which only five copies were made, he inaugurated "Case White"—the attack on Poland. "Preparations," it stipulated, "must be made so that the operation can be carried out any time from September 1, 1939."

The question now was whether Hitler could wear down the Poles to the point of accepting his demands, as he had done with the Austrians and the Czechs, or whether Poland would resist Nazi aggression—and if so, with what.

This writer spent the first week of April in Poland in search of answers. They were, as far as he could see, that the Poles would not give in to Hitler's threats, but that militarily and politically they were in a disastrous position. Their Air Force was obsolete, their Army cumbersome, their strategic position—surrounded by the Germans on three sides—almost hopeless.

Events now moved quickly. On April 7 Mussolini sent his troops into Albania. In the tense atmosphere of Europe this served to make the small countries which dared to defy the Axis more jittery. On April 13 France and Great Britain countered with a guarantee to Greece and Rumania. The two sides were beginning to line up.

Although the top brass of the *Wehrmacht* had a low opinion of Italian military power, Hitler now pressed for a military alliance with Italy, which Mussolini had been in no hurry to conclude. But on May 6, on a sudden impulse, Mussolini committed himself irrevocably to Hitler's fortunes by agreeing to sign an alliance. The consequences for Mussolini would prove disastrous; this was, indeed, one of the first signs that the Italian dictator—like the German—was beginning to lose that iron self-control which until this year had enabled them both to pursue their own national interests with ice-cold clarity.

The Pact of Steel, as it came to be known, was signed with considerable pomp at the Reich Chancellery in Berlin on May 22. The core of the treaty was Article III:

"If one of the High Contracting Parties should become involved in warlike complications with another power, the other High Contracting Party would immediately come to its assistance with all its military forces."

Article V provided that in the event of war neither nation would conclude a separate armistice or peace. In the beginning, as it would turn out, Mussolini did not honor the one article; nor, at the end, did Italy abide by the other.

The day after the signing of the Pact of Steel, May 23, Hitler summoned his military chiefs to the Chancellery in Berlin and told them bluntly that further triumphs could not be won without bloodshed, and that war, therefore, was inevitable. The Fuehrer's adjutant took notes. His minutes of the meeting are among the most revealing and important of the secret papers which depict Hitler's road to war. Here, before the handful of men who would have to direct the military in armed conflict, Hitler cut through his own propaganda and uttered the truth about why he must attack Poland and, if necessary, take on Great Britain and France. And yet, for all its bluntness, his discourse disclosed more uncertainty and confusion than he had shown up to this point. Above all, Britain and the British continued to baffle him, as they did to the end of his life.

Germany's economic problems, he began, could be solved only by obtaining more *Lebensraum* in Europe, and "this is impossible without invading other coun-

tries or attacking other people's possessions. Further successes can no longer be attained without the shedding of blood. It is a question of expanding our living space in the East, of securing our food supplies and also of solving the problem of the Baltic States. There is no other possibility in Europe. If fate forces us into a showdown with the West, it is invaluable to possess a large area in the East."

Besides, Hitler added, the population of non-German territories in the East would be available as a source of labor—an early hint of the slave-labor program he was later to put into effect.

The choice of the first victim was obvious.

"There is no question of sparing Poland, and we are left with the decision. *To attack Poland at the first suitable opportunity*. We cannot expect a repetition of the Czech affair. There will be war."

So there would be war. With an "isolated" Poland alone? Here the Fuehrer was not so clear. In fact, he became confused and contradictory. He must reserve to himself, he said, the final order to strike.

"It must not come to a simultaneous showdown with the West—France and England. If it is not certain that a German-Polish conflict will not lead to war with the West, then the fight must be primarily against England and France.

"Fundamentally, therefore: Conflict with Poland—beginning with an attack on Poland—will be successful only if the West keeps out of it. If that is not possible it is better to fall upon the West and to finish off Poland at the same time."

In the face of such rapid-fire contradictions the generals must have winced, perhaps prying their monocles loose, though there is no evidence in the minutes that anyone in the audience even dared to ask a question to straighten matters out.

But then Hitler came down to earth again and outlined a strategic plan which later would be carried out with amazing success.

"The aim must be to deal the enemy a smashing blow right at the start. Considerations of right or wrong, or of treaties, do not enter into the matter.

"The Army must occupy the positions important for the Fleet and the *Luftwaffe* ("Air Force"). If we succeed in occupying and securing Holland and Belgium, as well as defeating France, the basis for a successful war against England has been created.

"The *Luftwaffe* can then closely blockade England

from France and the Fleet undertake the wider blockade with submarines."

As May 1939 came to an end, German preparations for war were well along. The great armament works were humming, turning out guns, tanks, planes and warships. The able staffs of the Army, Navy and Air Force had reached the final stage of planning. The ranks were being swelled by new men called up for "summer training."

But formidable as German military power was at the beginning of the summer of 1939, Germany was still not strong enough—and probably never would be —to take on France, Great Britain *and* the Soviet Union in addition to Poland. As the fateful summer advanced, all depended upon the Fuehrer's ability to limit the war—above all, to keep Russia from forming a military alliance with the West.

There was reason for Hitler's concern in this respect. On July 23 France and Great Britain agreed to the Soviet Union's proposal that military-staff talks be held at once to draw up a convention which would spell out specifically how Hitler's armies were to be met by the three nations. The Western powers did not think highly of the Soviet Union's military prowess.

They finally sent a mission to negotiate with the Russians, but it did not arrive in Moscow until August 11. By that time it was too late. Hitler had already begun the diplomatic approaches that were to lead to the Nazi-Soviet nonaggression pact.

From the German point of view, there was no time to lose. August 19 was the decisive day. German warships—submarines and pocket battleships—would have to get off at once for British waters, if they were to reach their appointed stations by Hitler's target date for the beginning of the war, September 1—only thirteen days away. The two great army groups designated for the onslaught on Poland would have to be deployed immediately.

The tension in Berlin and especially on the Obersalzberg, where Hitler and Ribbentrop waited nervously for word of Moscow's intentions, was becoming almost unbearable. And then, at 7:10 p.m. on August 19, came the anxiously awaited telegram from the German Ambassador in Moscow:

SECRET. MOST URGENT. THE SOVIET GOVERNMENT AGREES TO THE REICH FOREIGN MINISTER'S COMING TO MOSCOW ON AUGUST 26 OR 27. MOLOTOV HANDED ME A DRAFT OF A NONAGGRESSION PACT.

But for the Germans the date set for the meeting was not soon enough. If Ribbentrop was not received in Moscow before August 26 and then if the Russians stalled a bit, as the Germans feared, the target date of September 1 could not be kept. The whole timetable for the invasion of Poland, indeed the question of whether the attack could take place at all in the brief interval before the autumn rains, depended upon it.

At this crucial stage, Hitler himself intervened with Stalin. Swallowing his pride, he personally begged the Soviet dictator, whom he had for so long maligned, to receive his Foreign Minister in Moscow at once. During the next twenty-four hours, from the evening of Sunday, August 20, when Hitler's appeal to Stalin went out over the wires to Moscow, until the following evening, the Fuehrer was in a state bordering on collapse. He could not sleep. In the middle of the night he telephoned Goering to tell of his worries about Stalin's reaction to his message and to fret over the delays in Moscow.

Next day Stalin's reply came: THE SOVIET GOVERNMENT HAS INSTRUCTED ME TO INFORM YOU THAT IT AGREES TO HERR VON RIBBENTROP'S ARRIVING IN MOSCOW ON AUGUST 23. J. STALIN.

On August 22 Hitler, having received this indication from Stalin himself that the Soviet Union would be a friendly neutral, once more convoked his top military commanders and apprised them that he probably would order the attack on Poland to begin four days hence, on Saturday, August 26—six days ahead of schedule.

Stalin, the Fuehrer's mortal enemy, had made this possible. For sheer cynicism the Nazi dictator had met his match in the Soviet despot. The way was now open to them to get together to dot the *i*'s and cross the *t*'s on one of the crudest deals of this shabby epoch.

The published treaty carried an undertaking that neither power would attack the other. Should one of them become "the object of belligerent action" by a third power, the other party would "in no manner lend its support to this third power." In a secret additional protocol Germany and the Soviet Union agreed to the partitioning of Poland.

War gets the green light: As Stalin looks on benignly, his Foreign Minister, Vyacheslav M. Molotov, signs the fateful Nazi-Soviet nonaggression pact—paving the way for the attack on Poland—on August 23, 1939. Next to Stalin stands Joachim von Ribbentrop, Nazi Foreign Minister. World War II began nine days later.

On August 25 Marshal Kliment E. Voroshilov met with the French and British military missions in Moscow for the last time. "In view of the changed political situation," he said, "no useful purpose can be served in continuing our conversations."

Buoyed up by the good news from Moscow and confident that Great Britain and France would have second thoughts about honoring their obligations to Poland after the defection of the Soviet Union, the Fuehrer on the evening of August 23 set the date for the onslaught on Poland: Saturday, August 26, at 4:30 a.m.

"There will be no more orders regarding Y day and X hour," Gen. Franz Halder, Chief of the Army General Staff, noted in his diary. *"Everything is to roll automatically."*

But he was wrong. On August 25 two events occurred which made Hitler shrink back, less than twenty-four hours before his troops were scheduled to break across the Polish frontier. On the afternoon of that day the Fuehrer had received the British Ambassador and told him that he "accepted" the British Empire, and was ready "to pledge himself personally to its continued existence and to commit the power of the German Reich for this."

He desired, Hitler explained, "to make a move toward England which should be as decisive as the move toward Russia. The Fuehrer is ready to conclude agreements with England which not only would guarantee the existence of the British Empire in all circumstances so far as Germany is concerned, but would also assure the British Empire of German assistance regardless of where such assistance should be necessary."

His "large comprehensive offer" to Great Britain, as he described it, was subject to one condition: that it would take effect only *after* the solution of the German-Polish problem." This ridiculous offer was obviously a brainstorm of the moment, for how could the British Government, as he requested, take it "very seriously" when Chamberlain would scarcely have time to read it before the Nazi armies hurtled into Poland at dawn on the morrow—the Y day which still held?

But behind the "offer," no doubt, was a serious purpose. Hitler apparently believed that Chamberlain, like Stalin, wanted an out by which he could avoid going to war. Could he not buy Great Britain's nonintervention by assuring the Prime Minister that the Third Reich would never become a threat to the British Empire?

He got his answer at about 6 p.m.—the news of the signing in London of a formal Anglo-Polish treaty which transformed Britain's unilateral guarantee of Poland into a pact of mutual assistance. This meant that Hitler had failed in his bid to buy off the British as he had bought off the Russians. His interpreter, who was in Hitler's office when the report arrived, remembered later that the Fuehrer after reading it sat brooding at his desk.

Very shortly his disconsolate brooding was interrupted by equally bad news from Rome. It struck the Fuehrer, according to the interpreter, like a bombshell. Mussolini, after expressing his "complete approval" of the Nazi-Soviet pact and his "understanding concerning Poland," came to the main point:

"If Germany attacks Poland and the latter's allies counterattack, I inform you that it will be opportune for me not to take the initiative in military operations in view of the present state of Italian war preparations. At our meetings the war was envisaged for 1942, and by that time I would have been ready."

Hitler read the Duce's letter and icily dismissed the Italian envoy. That evening the Chancellery echoed with unkind words about the "disloyal Axis partner." But words were not enough. The German Army was scheduled to hop off against Poland in nine hours. The Nazi dictator had to decide at once whether, in view of the news from London and Rome, to go ahead with the invasion or postpone or cancel it.

Pushed into a corner, Hitler swiftly made his decision: all troop movements would be stopped, the attack called off.

It took some doing to halt the German Army, for many units were already on the move. One motorized column was halted on the border by a staff officer who made a quick landing in a small scouting plane. In a few sectors the orders did not arrive until after the shooting had begun, but since the Germans had been provoking incidents all along the border for several days the Polish General Staff apparently did not suspect what had really happened.

"Fuehrer considerably shaken," General Halder noted in his diary on August 25, after the news from Rome and London induced Hitler to draw back from the precipice of war.

But it was rarely easy, even for his confidants, to penetrate the strange and fantastic workings of Hitler's fevered mind, affected as it was by now with acute megalomania. By the very next afternoon the Chief of the Army General Staff noticed an abrupt change in the Leader. "Fuehrer very calm and clear," he jotted in his diary.

There was a reason for this, and the General's journal gives it. "Get everything ready for morning of seventh Mobilization Day. Attack starts September 1."

And what of the Fuehrer's frame of mind that very night, the night of his irrevocable decision to plunge his nation, for the first time under his leadership, into all-out war? Here is an eyewitness description:

"Hitler suddenly got up and, becoming very excited and nervous, walked up and down saying, as though to himself, that Germany was irresistible. Suddenly he stopped in the middle of the room and stood staring. His voice was blurred and his behavior that of a completely abnormal person. He spoke in staccato phrases: 'If there should be war, then I shall build U-boats, build U-boats, U-boats, U-boats, U-boats.'"

Such was the atmosphere in which World War II was launched.

During these last days of peace, the overwrought and exhausted diplomats of all the nations concerned made innumerable scrambling eleventh-hour attempts at mediation. They were but a flailing of the air, completely futile, and, in the case of the Germans, entirely and purposely deceptive.

For at half after noon on August 31, Adolf Hitler had taken his final decision and issued the order that was to throw the planet into its bloodiest war.

Hitler was still not quite sure what Great Britain and France would do. He would refrain from attacking them first. If they took hostile action, he was prepared to meet it. As darkness settled over Europe on the evening of August 31, 1939, and some 1.5 million German troops began moving forward for the jump-off at dawn, all that remained for Hitler to do was to perpetrate some propaganda trickery to prepare the German people for the shock of aggressive war.

They were in need of the propaganda treatment which Hitler, abetted by Goebbels and Heinrich Himmler, had become so expert in applying. I had been about in the streets of Berlin, talking with the ordinary people, and that morning noted in my diary: "Everybody against the war. People talking openly.

How can a country go into a major war with a population so dead against it?"

Despite all my experience in the Third Reich I asked such a naïve question! Hitler knew the answer very well. The week before, on his Bavarian mountaintop, he had promised the generals that he would "give a propagandist reason for starting the war" and admonished them not to "mind whether it is plausible or not." "The victor," he told them, "will not be asked afterward whether he told the truth. In starting and waging a war it is not right that matters, but victory."

Now there remained only the concocting of a deed which would "prove" that not Germany but Poland had attacked first. For this shady business, careful German preparations had been made at Hitler's direction. For six days Alfred Naujocks, an S.S. (*Schutzstaffel,* or "Black Shirt") ruffian, had been waiting at Gleiwitz (now Gliwice), on the Polish border, to carry out a simulated Polish attack on the German radio station there. S.S. men in Polish Army uniforms were to do the shooting, and previously drugged concentration-camp inmates were to be left dying as "casualties"—this last delectable part of the operation had the expressive code name, "Canned Goods." There were to be several such faked Polish attacks, but the principal one was to be on the radio station at Gleiwitz.

"At noon on August 31," Naujocks related in his Nuremberg affidavit, "I received the code word for the attack which was to take place at eight o'clock that evening. I had a man laid down at the entrance to the station. He was alive but unconscious. I could recognize that he was alive only by his breathing. I did not see the gun wounds, but a lot of blood was smeared across his face. We seized the radio station, as ordered, broadcast a speech, fired some shots and left."

At daybreak next morning, the very date which Hitler had set on April 3, the German armies poured across the Polish frontier and converged on Warsaw from the north, south and west.

In Berlin the people in the streets were apathetic, despite the immensity of the news which greeted them in the morning newspapers. Perhaps they were simply dazed at waking up to find themselves in a war which they had been sure the Fuehrer would somehow avoid. Even the robot members of the Reichstag, hacks whom Hitler had appointed, failed to respond with much enthusiasm as the dictator launched into his explanation of why Germany found itself at war. There was

far less cheering than on previous and less important occasions when the Leader had declaimed from this tribune. He seemed strangely on the defensive, and throughout the speech, I thought as I listened, ran a curious strain, as though he himself were dazed at the fix he had got himself into and felt a little desperate about it.

But now there was no way out. On September 3 Great Britain and France declared war on Germany. That same night, at 9 p.m., the German submarine U-30 torpedoed and sank the British liner *Athenia* some 200 miles west of the Hebrides; 112 passengers, including 28 Americans, lost their lives. World War II had begun.

Brave and valiant and foolhardy though they were—at one point they actually counterattacked Nazi tanks with horse cavalry—the Poles were simply overwhelmed by the German onslaught. This was their, and the world's, first experience of the blitzkrieg: the sudden surprise attack; the fighter planes and bombers roaring overhead, spreading flame and terror; the Stukas screaming as they dived; the tanks, whole divisions of them, breaking through and thrusting forward thirty or forty miles in a day; the incredible speed of even the infantry, of the whole vast army of 1.5 million men carried on motorized wheels, coordinated through a maze of electronic communications. This was a mechanized juggernaut such as the earth had never seen.

Within forty-eight hours the Polish Air Force was destroyed, and in one week the Polish Army was vanquished, most of its thirty-five divisions either shattered or caught in a pincer movement that closed around Warsaw. By September 17 all Polish forces, except a handful on the Russian border, were surrounded. All was over except the dying in the ranks of Polish units which still, with incredible fortitude, held out.

It was now time for the Soviet Union to move in on the stricken country to grab a share of the spoils. The Kremlin, like every other seat of government, had been taken by surprise at the rapidity with which the German armies hurtled through Poland. Their success was most embarrassing to the Russians. On what pretext could they now intervene against the fallen state? On September 17 there was disagreement between the two unnatural partners over the text of a joint communiqué which would "justify" the Russo-German destruction of Poland. Stalin objected to the German version because "it presents the facts all too frankly." Whereupon he wrote out his own version, a masterpiece of subterfuge, and forced the Germans to accept it. It stated that the joint aim of Germany and the Soviet Union was "to restore peace and order in Poland, which has been destroyed by the disintegration of the Polish state, and to help the Polish people to establish new conditions for its political life." On that shabby pretext, beginning on the morning of September 17, the Soviet Union trampled over a prostrate Poland. The next day Soviet troops met the Germans at Brest.

So Poland, like Austria and Czechoslovakia before it, disappeared from the map of Europe. But this time Hitler was aided and abetted in his obliteration of a country by the Soviet Union, which had posed for so long as the champion of oppressed peoples. Hitler fought and won the war in Poland, but the greater winner was Stalin, whose troops scarcely fired a shot. The Soviet Union got nearly half of Poland and a stranglehold on the Baltic States. It blocked Germany from two main long-term objectives: Ukrainian wheat and Rumanian oil, both badly needed if Germany was to survive the British blockade. Even Poland's oil region, which Hitler desired, was claimed successfully by Stalin.

Why did Hitler pay such a high price to the Russians? It is true that he had agreed to it in August, in order to keep the Soviet Union out of the Allied camp and out of the war. But he had never been a stickler for keeping agreements and now, with Poland conquered by an incomparable feat of German arms, he might have been expected to welsh, as his Army urged, on the August 23 pact. If Stalin objected, the Fuehrer could threaten him with attack by the most powerful army in the world, as the Polish campaign had just proved it to be.

Or could he? Not while the British and French stood at arms in the West. To deal with Britain and France he must keep his eastern front free. This, as subsequent utterances of his would make clear, was the reason why he allowed Stalin to strike such a hard bargain. But he did not forget the Soviet dictator's harsh dealings as he now turned his attention to the western front.

Nothing much had happened there. Hardly a shot had been fired. It was beginning to be called the *Sitzkrieg* ("sit-down war") or the phony war. Here was the French Army, "the strongest in the world," as British Gen. J. F. C. Fuller has put it, "facing no more than

(Top right) Hitler's soldiers advance through a wreckage-strewn Warsaw street. Poland's Air Force was destroyed within two days and its Cavalry butchered by Nazi tanks. But despite German superiority in planes, tanks and men, Poland's capital held out for a month before surrendering on September 27, 1939.

twenty-six German divisions, sitting still and sheltering behind steel and concrete, while a quixotically valiant ally was being exterminated!"

For the West the inaction was costly. As General Halder said at Nuremberg, "The success against Poland was only possible by almost completely baring our western border. The French would have been able to cross the Rhine without our being able to prevent it." Why then did not the French Army, which had overwhelming superiority over the German forces in the west, attack, as General Gamelin and the French Government had promised the Poles in writing it would?

There were many reasons: Defeatism in the French High Command, the Government and the people; the memories of how France had been bled white in World War I and a determination not to suffer such slaughter again if it could be avoided; the realization by mid-September that the Polish armies were so badly defeated that the Germans would soon be able to move superior forces to the west and thus probably wipe out any initial French advances; the fear of German superiority in arms and in the air.

But now the opportunity for any effective offense had been lost. With the Polish armies destroyed, Hitler could turn his full attention, and the bulk of his forces, to the west.

Against the advice of his generals, who wanted time to refit the tanks used in Poland, the Fuehrer issued a directive on preparations for an attack through Luxembourg, Belgium and the Netherlands at as early a date as possible.

A secret memorandum which Hitler read to his military chiefs before presenting them the directive showed not only a remarkable grasp of military strategy and tactics but a prophetic sense of how the war in the west would develop. The chief thing, he said, was to avoid the positional warfare of 1914–18. The armored

(Bottom right) Jewish women and children freeze in a tableau of terror as they are herded into boxcars by Storm Troopers during the Nazi destruction of Warsaw. Their destinations were, in most cases, the gas chambers of the death camps. This photograph was used at the Nuremberg trials as evidence of Nazi brutality.

A German soldier, hurling a grenade during the invasion of Poland, exemplifies by his attitude the fierce Nazi aggression that overwhelmed Central Europe. "Close your hearts to pity," Hitler had said. "Act brutally. Eighty million Germans must obtain what is their right."

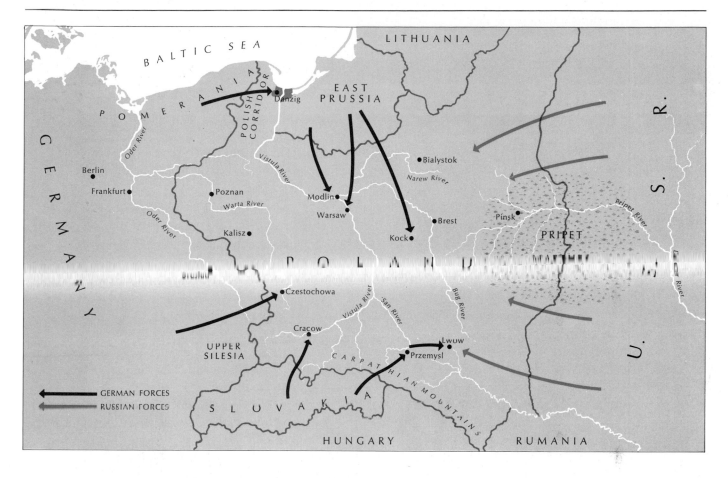

THE FALL OF POLAND: World War Begins

The Nazis unleashed a new type of mechanized warfare on Poland—the blitzkrieg, or lightning war. Panzer divisions of thousands of tanks, troop carriers and supply vehicles were sent speeding into Poland, while overhead screamed squadrons of dive bombers and fighters.

On September 1, 1939, fifty-nine Nazi divisions attacked from East Prussia, Pomerania, Upper Silesia and Slovakia. The Poles hastily mobilized their Army but they had little chance against the mechanized fury that was upon them. The *Luftwaffe,* in well-synchronized conjunction, knocked out railways, airfields, cities and vital communication centers.

The attack caught the Polish Air Force on the ground. Most of its planes were destroyed. German forces cut across the Polish Corridor, severing the country's link with the Baltic Sea. The Free City of Danzig was captured in the first few hours. Polish warships were sunk or driven into internment in Swedish ports. On September 3 the city of Czestochowa in the south was taken and the Warta River crossed. Cracow fell on September 6.

Units of the Polish Army fought with desperate courage, only to be overwhelmed. Przemysl was captured on September 15, the important center of Lwow overrun on the 21st. German forces under Gen. Gerd von Rundstedt reached the outskirts of Warsaw on September 8, but the inhabitants put up a vigorous defense; it was not until September 27 that they surrendered, with their city in ruins about them. Modlin fell the following day.

Russian troops with tanks and aircraft now appeared from the east to administer the *coup de grâce.* Germany and the Soviet Union divided the prostrate Polish nation between them, the Soviets retaining all territory east of the Bug River, comprising 75,000 square miles. Small sections of the conquered land were parceled out to Lithuania and Slovakia.

It was a major victory for Adolf Hitler and he took full credit for the brilliant tactical success of the blitzkrieg. He had won his gamble.

divisions must be used for the crucial breakthrough.

As for the time of the attack, Hitler told his reluctant generals, "The start cannot take place too early. It is to take place in all circumstances (if at all possible) this autumn." But despite his insistence on haste, delay after delay ensued, and then on January 13 the Nazi warlord postponed the onslaught indefinitely "on account of the meteorological situation." Weather may have played a part in the calling off of the attack, but we know today that plans for a daring German assault on two other little neutral states farther to the north had in the meantime been ripening in Berlin and now took priority. The phony war, so far as the Germans were concerned, was coming to an end with the approach of spring.

The innocent-sounding code name for the latest plan of German aggression was *Weseruebung*," or "Weser Exercise." It was the brainchild of the Navy. In fact, the Army High Command was not even consulted, much to its annoyance, and Goering was not brought into the picture until the last moment —a slight that infuriated the corpulent Chief of the *Luftwaffe*.

The Navy had long had its eyes on the north. Since Germany had no direct access to the wide ocean, the Naval officers felt they needed bases in Norway to forestall a British blockade (which during World War I had effectively bottled up the Imperial Navy in the North Sea). Such bases would be vitally useful in protecting vessels carrying shipments of Swedish iron ore, on which Germany's very existence depended.

It was concern for Germany's supply of the necessary ore that persuaded Hitler to adopt the plan. But when he hastily issued the order to "put units in readiness," no Army officer had yet been designated to lead the enterprise. Someone suggested Gen. Nikolaus von Falkenhorst, who had fought in Finland at the end of World War I, and Hitler immediately sent for him. Falkenhorst had never even heard of the proposed Norway operation.

"I was made to sit down," he recounted later. "Then I had to tell the Fuehrer about the operations in Finland in 1918. He said, 'Just tell me how it was.' And I did."

To his surprise, the General found himself appointed then and there Commander in Chief of the operation. The Army would put five divisions at his disposal. At noon the Fuehrer dismissed Falkenhorst and told him to report back at 5 p.m. with plans for the occupation of Norway!

"I went out and bought a Baedeker, a travel guide," Falkenhorst explained at Nuremberg, "in order to find out just what Norway was like. I didn't have any idea. Then I went to my hotel room and worked on this Baedeker. At 5 p.m. I went back to the Fuehrer."

The General's plans, although understandably somewhat sketchy, seemed to be satisfactory to Hitler; the next day, March 1, he issued the formal directive for "Weser Exercise." Denmark had now definitely been added to the list of Hitler's victims; the Air Force had its eyes on bases there to be used against Great Britain.

"Weseruebung" was ordered to begin at 5:15 a.m. on April 9, 1940. At precisely an hour before dawn on that day, the German envoys in Copenhagen and Oslo presented to the Danish and Norwegian governments a German ultimatum demanding that they accept on the instant, and without resistance, the "protection of the Reich." The ultimatum was perhaps the most brazen document yet composed by Hitler and Ribbentrop.

The Danes were in a hopeless position. Their pleasant, flat little country was incapable of defense against Hitler's panzers. The Army fought a few skirmishes, but by the time the Danes had finished their hearty breakfasts it was all over. The King, on the advice of his Government, capitulated and ordered resistance to cease.

But in Norway things were different. Although by noon on the first day of operations the five principal cities and ports and the one big airfield along the west and south coasts were in German hands, King Haakon VII refused to give up. Driven into exile from his capital, pressed to surrender and approve a government headed by the pro-Nazi traitor Vidkun Quisling, Haakon assembled the members of the Government and told them: "I cannot accept the German demands. If the Government should decide to accept them, abdication will be the only course open to me."

The Government, though there may have been some waverers, could not be less courageous than the King, and it quickly rallied behind him.

That evening from a feeble little rural radio station, the only means of communication to the outside world available, the Norwegian Government flung down the gauntlet to the mighty Third Reich and called upon the people to resist the invaders. There were only 3 million of them—but there was now hope that British troops might arrive to help them.

Great Britain had prepared a small expeditionary corps for Norway, but the British were unaccountably slow in getting troops under way. By late April the southern half of the country, comprising all the cities and main towns, had been irretrievably lost. But northern Norway seemed a little more secure. By May 28 an Allied force of 25,000 men had driven the Germans out of Narvik.

When the *Wehrmacht* struck with stunning force on the western front, every Allied soldier was needed to plug the gap. Narvik was abandoned, the Allied troops were hastily re-embarked and King Haakon and his Government were transported to London.

Despite his amazing successes, the Fuehrer had his bad moments during the Norwegian campaign. General Alfred Jodl's diary is crammed with entries recounting a succession of the warlord's nervous crises. Hitler had a fit of hysteria about the loss of Narvik, and for the first time the *Wehrmacht* commanders had a foretaste of how their demonic Leader cracked under the strain of even minor setbacks in battle. It was a weakness which would grow on him when, after a series of further astonishing military successes, the tide of war changed; and it would contribute mightily to the eventual debacle of the Third Reich.

Still, the quick conquest of Denmark and Norway had been an important victory. It secured the winter iron-ore route, brought Hitler air bases hundreds of miles closer to the main enemy and, perhaps most important of all, immensely enhanced the military prestige of the Third Reich. Nazi Germany seemed invincible.

But there was one military result of the Scandinavian adventure which could not be evaluated at once. German Naval losses were heavy: 10 out of 20 destroyers and 3 of 8 cruisers, plus 2 battle cruisers and 1 pocket battleship, were damaged so severely that they were out of action for several months. Hitler had no fleet worthy of mention when the time to invade Great Britain came, as it did shortly, and this proved an insurmountable handicap.

The possible consequences of the crippling of the German Navy, however, did not enter the Fuehrer's thoughts as, at the beginning of May, he worked with his generals on the last-minute preparations for what they were confident would be the greatest conquest of all.

Shortly after dawn on May 10, 1940, the Ambassador of Belgium and the Minister of the Netherlands in Berlin were informed that German troops were entering their countries "to safeguard their neutrality against an imminent attack by the Anglo-French armies"—the same hollow excuse that had been made just a month before with Denmark and Norway. A formal German ultimatum called upon the two governments to see to it that no resistance was offered; if it were, it would be crushed.

Great Britain and France were caught napping; London was preoccupied with a Cabinet crisis which was resolved only on the evening of May 10 with the replacement of Chamberlain by Winston Churchill as Prime Minister. Nevertheless, the Allied plan to meet the German attack in Belgium went ahead for the first couple of days almost without a hitch. A great Anglo-French army rushed northeastward to man the main Belgian defense line along the Dyle and Meuse rivers. As it happened, this was just what the German High Command wanted. Though the Anglo-French armies did not know it, they sped directly into a trap that, when sprung, would prove utterly disastrous.

As the battle began, the two sides were evenly matched in numbers—136 German divisions against 135 divisions of the French, British, Belgians and Dutch. The defenders had the advantage of vast defensive fortifications: the impenetrable Maginot Line in the south, the Belgian forts in the middle and fortified water lines in the Netherlands in the north. Even in the number of tanks, the Allies matched the Germans. But they had not concentrated them as had the latter, and, because of the Dutch and Belgian suicidal prewar policy of strict neutrality, there had been no staff consultations which would have enabled the defenders to pool their resources to the best advantage.

The Germans had a unified command, the initiative of the attacker, a contagious confidence in themselves and a daring plan. This was to launch the main German assault in the center, through the Ardennes, with a massive armored force which would then cross the Meuse north of Sedan, break out into the open country and race to the Channel at Abbeville.

Such a strike would hit the Allies where they least expected it, since their generals undoubtedly, like most Germans, considered this hilly, wooded country

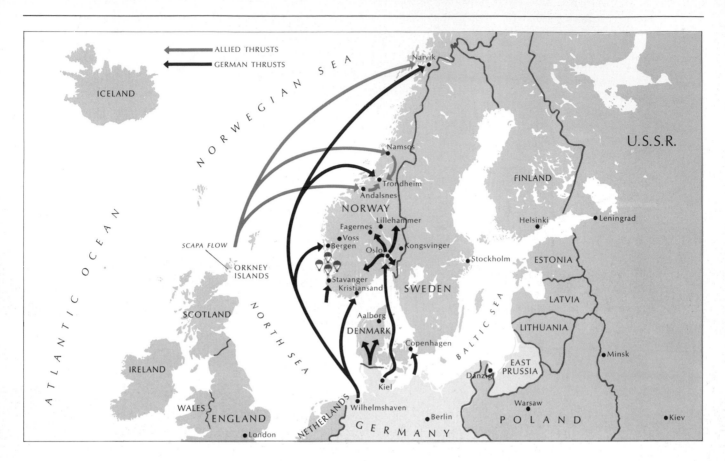

ALLIED THRUSTS
GERMAN THRUSTS

BLITZKRIEG IN SCANDINAVIA

For six months after the fall of Poland, Germany made no aggressive military moves in Europe. Then, early on the morning of April 9, 1940, troops of Hitler's *Wehrmacht* crossed the Danish border, and the little country was overrun so rapidly that resistance was impossible.

At the same time, Nazi warships appeared in the principal Norwegian seaports. Armed units were put ashore while more troops dropped from the skies on airfields and military bases. Radio stations, telephone exchanges, railway centers and government buildings were seized.

Narvik, Trondheim, Kristiansand, Bergen and Stavanger fell to the Germans. Oslo fought back with coastal defenses but was subdued.

The Allies rushed all the aid they could muster. Under the protection of the Royal Navy, landings were effected at Andalsnes and Namsos, where attempts were made to link up with portions of the Norwegian Army. Savage fighting developed at Trondheim, but the Germans' command of the air together with their superiority in numbers was overwhelming. The Allied force evacuated Andalsnes and Namsos on May 2 and 3. To the north, at Narvik, the British Navy sank ten enemy destroyers, with a loss of two of their own. British troops drove the Germans out of Narvik. They held the city until June 8 before being withdrawn.

Some units of the Norwegian Army retreated into Sweden and were interned; others were forced to surrender in the Lillehammer sector, at Kongsvinger, Voss and Fagernes. Operating from the new airfields, the German *Luftwaffe* was now able to force Great Britain to withdraw her major battleships from Norwegian waters.

In a matter of little more than three weeks Hitler had won another major victory. He had gained bases for his submarines and surface raiders to strike back at the British sea blockade. He had gained access to raw materials for his war machine, such as Norwegian and Swedish iron ore and timber, and had forestalled any idea the Allies might have had of using Scandinavia to mount an attack on the Reich.

A German raiding party, weapons ready, rides a mountain railroad in Norway, alert for snipers. Urged by their king, Haakon VII, to resist the invaders, Norwegian patriots conducted effective guerrilla warfare against the Nazis.

---

unsuitable for tanks. A feint by the right wing of the German forces would bring the British and French armies rushing pell-mell into Belgium. Then by cracking through the French at Sedan and heading west for the Channel, the Germans would entrap the major Anglo-French forces as well as the Belgian Army.

It was a daring plan, not without its risks, as several generals emphasized. But by now Hitler, who considered himself a military genius, practically believed that it was his own idea—it had actually been proposed by a gifted and imaginative staff officer of relatively junior rank (Gen. Erich von Manstein), against considerable opposition—and the Fuehrer's enthusiasm for it ensured its adoption.

The attack began along a front of 175 miles, from the North Sea to the Maginot Line. For the Germans everything went according to the book or even better than the book. Hitler's generals were confounded by the lightning rapidity and the extent of their own victories. As for the Allied leaders, they were quickly paralyzed by developments they had not faintly expected and could not comprehend.

Tanks—seven divisions of them concentrated at one point, the weakest position in the Western defenses, for the big breakthrough—that was what did it; that and the Stuka dive bombers and the parachutists and air-borne troops who landed far behind the Allied lines or on top of their seemingly impregnable forts and wreaked havoc.

By the time the Dutch surrendered on May 14, the die was cast for Belgium, France and the British Expeditionary Force (B.E.F.). Though it was only the fifth day of the attack, it was the fatal day. The previous evening German armor had secured four bridgeheads across the Meuse River, captured Sedan and gravely threatened the center of the Allied line and the hinge on which the flower of the British and French armies had wheeled into Belgium.

Winston Churchill himself, who had taken over as Prime Minister on the first day of battle, was dumfounded. He was awakened at 7:30 on the morning of May 15 by a telephone call from the new French Premier, Paul Reynaud, in Paris, who told him in an excited voice, "We have been defeated! We are beaten!" Churchill refused to believe it. The great French Army vanquished in less than a week? It was impossible. "I did not comprehend," he wrote later, "the violence of the revolution effected since the last war by the incursion of a mass of fast-moving armor."

It was on May 14 that the avalanche began. An army of tanks, unprecedented in warfare for size, concentration, mobility and striking power, broke through the French armies and headed swiftly for the Channel behind the Allied forces in Belgium. So enormous was the striking force that when it started through the Ardennes Forest from the German frontier on May 10, it stretched in three columns back for 100 miles behind the Rhine.

Preceded by waves of Stuka dive bombers, this phalanx of steel and fire could not be stopped by any means in the hands of the bewildered defenders. Around Sedan two tank divisions poured across a pontoon bridge and struck toward the west. By evening of that day the German bridgehead was thirty miles wide and fifteen miles deep, and the French forces in the vital center of the Allied line were shattered. The Franco-British armies to the north, as well as the twenty-two divisions of Belgians, were in dire danger of being cut off.

By the afternoon of May 16, German spearheads were sixty miles west of Sedan, rolling along the undefended open country. Nothing very much stood between them and Paris, or between them and the Channel. The French had only limited forces with which to stage a counterattack. Though the panzer divisions were ordered to do no more than proceed with "a reconnaissance in force," this was all they needed.

By the morning of May 19 a mighty wedge of seven armored divisions was only some fifty miles from the Channel. On the evening of May 20, to the surprise of Hitler's Headquarters, the 2d Panzer Division reached Abbeville, at the mouth of the Somme. The Belgians, the B.E.F. and three French armies were trapped. By May 24 the British, French and Belgian armies in the north were compressed into a relatively small triangle, and there was no hope of breaking out

(Left) *The Dutch had counted on their water defenses slowing down the invading Nazis. But these German troops have little difficulty crossing the expanse of the Meuse River in May 1940.*

(Right) *Parachutists played a key role in the conquest of the Low Countries and later of Crete. Here a Nazi soldier is about to follow his fellow troopers.*

(Below) *The Cathedral of Tournai stands miraculously unscathed amid the ruins of the Belgian city that was laid waste by the advance of Hitler's mighty army through the Low Countries.*

of the trap. The only hope, and it seemed a slim one, was possible evacuation by sea from Dunkirk.

It was at this juncture that the German armor, now within sight of Dunkirk and poised for the final kill, received a strange—and, to the soldiers in the field, inexplicable—order to halt their advance. It was the first of the German Fuehrer's major military mistakes in World War II, and it provided a vital reprieve to the Allies, leading to the miracle of Dunkirk (see pages 112–116).

But it did not save the Belgians. Although his Army fought magnificently, King Leopold III surrendered, against the unanimous advice of his Government, early on the morning of May 28.

Despite this additional setback, the British nation and its leaders were still determined to fight to the end. But Hitler and his generals, ignorant of the sea as they were—and remained—did not dream that the sea-minded British could evacuate a third of a million men from a small battered port and from the exposed beaches of Dunkirk right under their noses.

It was not until May 30 that the German High Command woke up to what was happening. For four days Nazi communiqués had been reiterating that the encircled enemy army was doomed. Yet by dawn of June 2 only 4000 British troops remained in the perimeter, protected by 100,000 French who now manned the defenses. The British Army escaped without its heavy arms and equipment, to be sure, but with the certainty that the men would live to fight another day.

The obvious determination of the British to fight on does not seem to have troubled Hitler's thoughts. He was sure they would see the light after he had finished off France, which he now proceeded to do. The morning after Dunkirk fell, on June 5, the Germans launched a massive assault on the Somme, and soon they were attacking in overwhelming strength along a 400-mile front across France. The French were doomed. Against 143 German divisions they could deploy only sixty-five, most of them second-rate, for the best units had been expended in Belgium. In victorious confusion, the German troops surged across France like a tidal wave. On June 14 undefended Paris was occupied. On June 16 Premier Reynaud resigned and was replaced by Marshal Henri Philippe Pétain, who the next day asked for an armistice.

Hitler replied that he would first have to consult his ally, Mussolini. For this strutting warrior, after making

sure that the French armies were beaten, had hopped into the war on June 10, to try to get in on the spoils.

The Duce's campaign was ludicrous. By June 18, when Hitler summoned his junior partner to Munich to discuss an armistice with France, some thirty-two Italian divisions, after a week of "fighting," had been unable to budge a scanty French force of six divisions, though the defenders were now threatened by assault in the rear from the Germans sweeping down the Rhone Valley.

Mussolini was unable even to get Hitler to agree to joint armistice negotiations with the French. The Fuehrer was not going to share his triumph with this Johnny-come-lately, and the Duce left Munich bitter and frustrated.

I followed the German Army into Paris that June, always the loveliest of months in the majestic capital, and on June 19 got wind of where Hitler was going to lay down his armistice terms. It was to be on the same spot where Germany had capitulated to France and her allies on November 11, 1918: in the little clearing in the woods at Compiègne. There the Nazi warlord would get his revenge, and the place itself would add to the sweetness of it for him. Late on the afternoon of June 19 I drove there and found German army engineers pulling the old *wagon-lit,* or railway car, in which the World War I armistice had been signed, out to the tracks in the center of the clearing, on the exact spot, they said, where it had stood at 5 a.m. on November 11, 1918.

And on the afternoon of June 21 I stood by the edge of the forest at Compiègne to observe the latest and greatest of Hitler's triumphs, of which I had seen so many over the last turbulent years. It was one of the loveliest summer days I ever remember in France. A warm June sun beat down on the stately trees, casting pleasant shadows on the wooded avenues leading to the little circular clearing. At 3:15 p.m. precisely, Hitler arrived in his big Mercedes.

"I observed his face," I wrote in my diary. "It was grave, solemn, yet brimming with revenge. There was also in it, as in his springy step, a note of the triumphant conqueror, the defier of the world. There was

Crushed and devoid of hope, a weary French soldier sinks down by the side of the road. The French Army, once reputed to be the strongest in Europe, was decisively smashed by the invading Germans, and the Government routed. In anguish, the French Premier, Paul Reynaud, told Churchill, "We are beaten!"

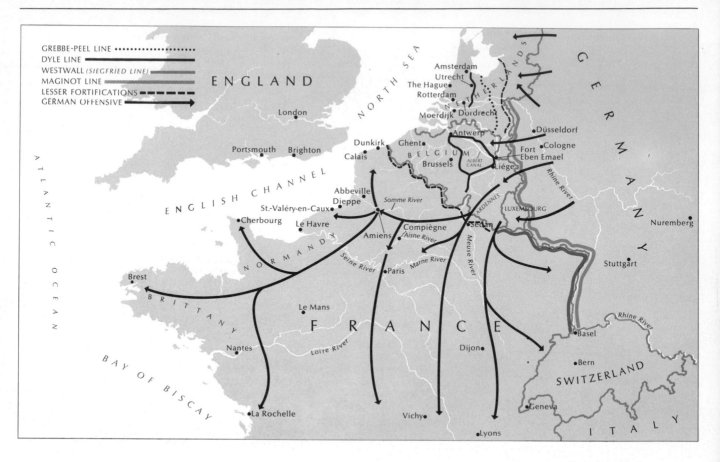

HITLER'S WAR MACHINE ROLLS OVER WESTERN EUROPE

After the fall of Poland, Hitler and his High Command secretly worked toward a greater triumph—the crushing of France and Great Britain. The offensive began on May 10, 1940. In the grayness of predawn, a massive force of eighty-nine divisions, with forty-seven in reserve, struck at the neutral Low Countries of Luxembourg, the Netherlands and Belgium.

Defenseless Luxembourg was quickly overrun. The Netherlands followed, the Germans bypassing the forts of the Grebbe-Peel Line with airborne troops.

Belgium, also, had vainly counted on a bulwark of fortifications, at Liége and along the Albert Canal. Here, too, wedges of Nazi armor hammered through with relative ease. Thirty-five divisions of the French Army and the British Expeditionary Force were rushed to support the hard-pressed Belgians, who had retired to their Dyle Line.

While Gen. Fedor von Bock's Army Group B was cutting through Belgium, troops of Gen. Gerd von Rundstedt's Army Group A had unexpectedly penetrated the rugged Ardennes country north of the Maginot Line and captured Sedan on the Meuse. Scarcely pausing, Rundstedt's armor crashed on, with the Channel ports as its objective.

The cause of the Allies, already bleak, became hopeless when King Leopold of Belgium surrendered his Army on May 28. Fighting a rearguard action all the way, close to 340,000 British and French troops retreated to Dunkirk on the English Channel, one of the few unoccupied seaports. There followed one of the greatest evacuations in the history of warfare (see pages 112–116).

Leaving the British to be dealt with later, Hitler turned to the task of finishing off Germany's ancient foe, France. The German offensive swept across France, from Brittany and Normandy to the Swiss border. The Maginot Line was encircled and its garrisons captured. On June 14 German troops entered Paris, and two days later Premier Paul Reynaud resigned. He was replaced by the aged Marshal Henri Philippe Pétain, who soon thereafter asked the Germans for an armistice.

With drums beating, German troops tramp past the Arch of Triumph. Paris fell to the enemy on June 14, 1940—scarcely one shot was fired in its defense.

something else, a sort of scornful inner joy at being present at this great reversal of fate."

When he reached the little opening in the forest and his personal standard had been run up, his attention was attracted by a large granite block.

"Hitler, followed by others, walks slowly over to it [I am quoting my diary], steps up and reads the inscription engraved in French in great high letters:

"HERE ON THE ELEVENTH OF NOVEMBER 1918 SUCCUMBED THE CRIMINAL PRIDE OF THE GERMAN EMPIRE—VANQUISHED BY THE FREE PEOPLES WHICH IT TRIED TO ENSLAVE.

"Hitler reads it and Goering reads it. I look for the expression in Hitler's face. I have seen that face many times at the great moments of his life. But today! It is afire with scorn, anger, hate, revenge, triumph.

"He steps off the monument and contrives to make even this gesture a masterpiece of contempt. He glances back at it, contemptuous, angry—angry, you almost feel, because he cannot wipe out the awful, provoking lettering with one sweep of his high Prussian boot. He glances slowly around the clearing, and now, as his eyes meet yours, you grasp the depth of his hatred. But there is triumph there, too—revengeful, triumphant hate.

"Suddenly, as though his face were not giving quite complete expression to his feelings, he throws his whole body into harmony with his mood. He swiftly snaps his hands on his hips, arches his shoulders, plants his feet wide apart. It is a magnificent gesture of defiance, of burning contempt for this place now and all that it has stood for in the twenty-two years since it witnessed the humbling of the German Empire."

Hitler and his party then entered the armistice railway car, the Fuehrer seating himself in the chair occupied by Marshal Ferdinand Foch in 1918. Five minutes later the French delegation arrived, headed by Gen. Charles Huntziger. They looked shattered, but retained a tragic dignity. They had not been told that they would be led to this proud French shrine to undergo such a humiliation, and the shock was no doubt just what Hitler had calculated.

Hitler and his entourage left the *wagon-lit* as soon as General Keitel had read the preamble to the armistice terms. The conditions were hard and merciless, and on the second day of the negotiations the French delegates continued to bicker and delay. Finally, at 6:30 p.m., Keitel issued an ultimatum: the French

must accept or reject the German armistice terms within an hour. Within the allotted time the French Government capitulated. At 6:50 p.m. on June 22, 1940, Huntziger and Keitel signed the treaty. France was now destined to become a German vassal.

A light rain began to fall as the delegates left the armistice car and drove away. Down the road through the woods you could see an unbroken line of refugees making their way home on weary feet, on bicycles, on carts, a few fortunate ones on old trucks. I walked out to the clearing. A gang of German army engineers had already started to move the old *wagon-lit*.

"Where to?" I asked.

"To Berlin," they said.

The Franco-Italian armistice was signed in Rome two days later. Mussolini was able to occupy only what his troops had conquered, which meant a few hundred yards of French territory, and to impose a fifty-mile demilitarized zone opposite Italy in France and Tunisia. The armistice was signed at 7:35 p.m. on June 24. Six hours later the guns in France lapsed into silence.

France, which had held out unbeaten for four years the last time, was out of the war after six weeks. German troops stood guard over most of Europe, from the North Cape above the Arctic Circle to Bordeaux, from the English Channel to the River Bug in eastern Poland. Adolf Hitler had reached the pinnacle. The former Austrian waif, this corporal of World War I, had become the greatest of German conquerors.

All that stood between him and establishment of German hegemony in Europe under his dictatorship was one indomitable Englishman, Winston Churchill (see pages 118–119), and the determined people he led, who did not recognize defeat when it stared them in the face and who now stood alone, virtually unarmed, their island home besieged by the mightiest military machine the world had ever seen.

ADOLF HITLER—TWISTED GENIUS OF WAR

For nearly seven years, from 1906 to 1913, a shabby young German named Adolf Hitler haunted the meaner streets of Vienna, glamorous capital of the Austro-Hungarian Empire—unknown, unnoted, a nobody. With a minor talent for drawing, he considered himself a coming artist. Meanwhile he did odd jobs, including house painting and sign painting, slept in flophouses and often went hungry. The young man was short and dark-haired, far removed from the stereotype of a blond Nordic. But he harbored a twisted vision of glory for Germany and himself—he could never think of the two apart—a vision that was destined to plunge Europe, then the world, into an appalling war in 1939.

Hitler was born into a lower-middle-class family on April 20, 1889, in Braunau, a small Austrian town on the frontier with Germany. His father, Alois, was a lowly customs official, and his mother, a Bavarian German, had worked as a servant. Until the age of thirty-nine, Alois had been known as Schicklgruber, his mother's name, but some years before Adolf's birth he legally adopted the surname "Hitler," presumably his father's.

Adolf was fairly good at his studies in his youth, but because his family moved so often he never completed his secondary education. At eighteen, several years after his father's death, he went to Vienna, determined to become an artist. In two successive years he failed in the examinations for enrollment in the Vienna Academy of Art. Knocking around the Austrian capital, lonely and embittered, young Hitler absorbed the prejudices of its lower middle class, especially hatred of socialists and Jews. At the same time the unsystematic reading of narrow-minded racist books, long brooding, plus his inborn tendency to self-delusion, turned him into a fanatic German nationalist of the blood-and-soil variety.

In 1913, when he was twenty-four, Adolf migrated to Munich, a great cultural center. As soon as World War I started, a year later, he volunteered and went to the front in a Bavarian regiment. Though he reached only the rank of *Gefreite* ("lance corporal"), he was twice decorated for bravery. Toward the war's end he was wounded and hospitalized.

In vanquished Germany, humiliated and in economic distress, the fairy tale that the country had been "stabbed in the back" by Social Democrats and Jews took hold on some German minds. It offered an alibi for defeat and a formula for revenge which was to be fearsomely carried out. Munich was a hot-bed of such extreme nationalism, and Hitler fitted readily into that political atmosphere, with its stress on enemies within, traitors and scapegoats.

An anti-democratic group calling itself the German Workers' Party had only six members. Hitler became the seventh. Before long he changed its name to National Socialist German Workers' Party—popularly known as the Nazi Party. His crusading zeal, his real talent as an organizer, a satanic gift for intrigue and slander in discrediting anyone who might dispute his claim to supreme leadership of the supernationalist movement and, especially, his power as a rabble-rousing orator quickly attracted thousands, then tens of thousands. From Munich and Bavaria the party spread to the rest of Germany and even to German communities beyond the nation's frontiers.

Hitler organized his followers along military lines, with brown-shirted *Sturmabteilung* ("Storm Troopers") as his private army of fanatics and bullyboys. He preached a strange amalgam of "master-race" pretensions, racist and political violence, national glory and vengeance—all of it soaked in hatred of real or imagined enemies of German greatness. What the doctrine lacked in logic, it made up in hysteria and blind faith in the Fuehrer.

In November 1923 Hitler, together with Gen. Erich von Ludendorff and other ultranationalists, tried to seize control of the Bavarian provincial government in Munich. Their putsch was a dismal failure. Put on trial, Hitler drew a five-year prison sentence, of which

Few men in modern times have matched Adolf Hitler in the art of rabble-rousing demagogy. Natural gifts for acting helped him manipulate the emotions of an audience, as his face mirrored his words—from reasonable pleading to hysterical fury, from irony to raging threats. Multitudes were swayed by his oratory.

he served merely nine months in the old fortress at Landsberg.

Sympathetic officials enabled him to use this time of incarceration to write the first volume of a bizarre book he was to call *Mein Kampf* ("My Struggle"), which he dictated to two fellow prisoners, one of whom was Rudolf Hess. It was an outpouring of his disordered philosophy, hatreds, and plans for himself and the Fatherland. Completed after he left prison, *Mein Kampf* was not taken seriously at first in Germany or in the rest of the world, but by 1928 it was selling enormously.

After Hitler's release his party marked time for a few years, solidifying its organization and training its armed divisions. The result was a kind of shadow government, geared to move into power in the future. Bloody clashes with the Communists, whose strength was also rising, became routine. Nazism appeared to thrive on violence. But it was the worldwide economic Depression, especially acute in Germany, that touched off its dramatic expansion. From twelve Reichstag deputies in 1928, the Hitler contingent rose to 230 in 1932—short of a majority, but the country's largest party.

In the elections of 1932 Hitler was narrowly defeated for president by Paul von Hindenburg, an aged hero of World War I. Under pressures of unemployment and general disorder, Hindenburg on January 30, 1933, appointed Hitler Chancellor in a new Cabinet in which the Nazis were a minority. But Hitler, backed by his brown-shirted armies, proceeded to rule the country single-handedly, in disregard of the President and the Cabinet. He forced the Reichstag to vote him extraordinary powers, which he applied without limit or mercy. His Storm Troopers and the new Gestapo (Secret Police) crushed all opposition parties, slaughtered hundreds, jammed thousands—ultimately millions—into inhuman concentration camps.

When Hindenburg died in 1934, Hitler took over the presidency while remaining Chancellor, and formally assumed the higher title of Fuehrer. His totalitarian state, the Third Reich, dominated Germany and proceeded, in contempt of the Versailles Treaty, to rearm for the domination of all Europe.

At that point the biography of Hitler became identical with the history of Germany, of Europe and of the world. Having been permitted to occupy the Rhineland in March 1936, Hitler believed that the democracies would not dare stop his further conquests. And he was right—up to a point. In March 1938 Nazi Germany annexed Hitler's native Austria. Seven months later, with the consent of Great Britain and France, it swallowed the Sudetenland, and in March 1939, without that consent, it took over all the rest of Czechoslovakia.

Then, with a Moscow-Berlin nonaggression pact as guarantee against a two-front war, Hitler on September 1, 1939, unleashed his first blitzkrieg—against Poland. It brought a declaration of war by both Great Britain and France. By May 1940 the awe-inspiring German war machine had rolled over the Low Countries and France to the English Channel, where it was stopped short by defeat in the Battle of Britain (see pages 120–129).

Frustrated in the West, Hitler turned on the Soviet Union, which he invaded on June 22, 1941. His forces reached the Volga and the Black Sea before Russia could slow up, and then reverse, their impetus.

The amazing career of Adolf Hitler reached its heights of triumph and empire in 1942, then began to decline sharply. It ended in his suicide and the burning of his body on April 30, 1945, as Soviet Russian troops in Berlin were breaking into his last headquarters, an underground bunker in the Chancellery building. Hitler was fifty-six years old. On the day before his death he married Eva Braun, long his friend and mistress; she joined him in death (see page 424).

Not since Napoleon Bonaparte had any man affected history as profoundly, and as disastrously, as the little Austrian-born would-be artist. In addition to military casualties from the war he started, Hitler, in pursuit of his sick delusions, was responsible for the murder of literally millions of innocents. The principal victims were Jews, an estimated 6 million of whom were transported from Nazi-held nations to scientifically equipped extermination centers.

Relying on intuition more than on reason, he was able to sway and manipulate huge crowds. Along with his fits of demonic temper and his bursts of hysteria, he had remarkable political instincts, especially in detecting and exploiting the fears and weaknesses of adversaries.

How much of Hitler's charisma was genius, how much madness? The question will be argued for generations and perhaps centuries to come, not only by historians but by psychopathologists.

MEIN KAMPF

BY ADOLF HITLER

The following excerpts from the book scored as the Nazis' satanic bible are typical of Hitler's schemes and beliefs.

[Mein Kampf ("My Struggle") was begun by Adolf Hitler in prison in 1924–25. While its historic importance as the key book of the Nazi movement is immense, its literary and intellectual value is nil. The book is poorly written and poorly organized: a hodgepodge of Hitler's thoughts on race, government, German, or "Aryan," destiny, his political party and methods, intermingled with biographical passages. Much of it seems to consist of memories of half-digested random reading.

The assumption that Mein Kampf *offered a detailed blueprint and timetable of Hitler's plans for conquest is not entirely true. The book reveals its author's character and psychology, but contains little guidance to his specific plans. At that stage he probably had hopes and visions rather than fixed intentions.—Ed.]*

The psyche of the great masses is not receptive to anything that is half-hearted and weak. Like the woman . . . who would rather bow to a strong man than dominate a weakling, the masses love a commander more than a petitioner and feel inwardly more satisfied by a doctrine tolerating no other beside itself, than by the granting of liberalistic freedom from which, as a rule, they can do little and are prone to feel that they have been abandoned.

I achieved an understanding of the importance of physical terror toward the individual and the masses. . . . Terror at the place of employment, in the factory, in the meeting hall and on the occasion of mass demonstrations will always be successful, unless opposed by equal terror.

Propaganda . . . for the most part must be aimed at the emotions and only to a very limited degree at the so-called intellect. All propaganda must be popular and its intellectual level must be adjusted to the most limited intelligence among those it is addressed to. Consequently, the greater the mass it is intended to reach, the lower its purely intellectual level will have to be.

The receptivity of the great masses is very limited, their intelligence is small, but their power of forgetting is enormous. In consequence, all effective propaganda must be limited to a very few points and must harp on these in slogans until the last member of the public understands what you want him to understand by your slogan.

All human culture, all the results of art, science and technology that we see before us today, are almost exclusively the creative product of the Aryan. This very fact admits of the not unfounded inference that [he] alone was the founder of all higher humanity, therefore representing the prototype of all that we understand by the word "man."

Those who want to live, let them fight, and those who do not want to fight in this world of eternal struggle do not deserve to live.

The nationalization of the broad masses can never be achieved by half measures, by weakly emphasizing a so-called objective standpoint, but only by a ruthless and fanatically one-sided orientation toward the goal to be achieved.

Anyone in this world who does not succeed in being hated by his adversaries does not seem to me to be worth much as a friend.

A folkish [National Socialist term for pure German, anti-Semitic] state must begin by raising marriage from the level of a continuous defilement of the race and give it the consecration of an institution which is called upon to produce images of the Lord and not monstrosities halfway between man and ape.

The folkish state . . . must see to it that only the healthy beget children; that there is only one disgrace: despite one's own sickness and deficiencies, to bring children into the world; and one highest honor: to renounce doing so. And conversely it must be considered reprehensible: to withhold healthy children from the nation.

A man of little scientific education but physically healthy, with a good, firm character, imbued with the joy of determination and willpower, is more valuable for the national community than a clever weakling.

No boy and no girl must leave school without having been led to an ultimate realization of the necessity and essence of blood purity.

It must be a greater honor to be a street cleaner and citizen of this Reich than a king in a foreign state.

The folkish state must free all leadership and especially the highest—that is, the political leadership—entirely from the parliamentary principle of majority rule—in other words, mass rule—and instead absolutely guarantee the right of the personality.

There must be no majority decisions, but only responsible persons, and the word "council" must be restored to its original meaning. Surely every man will have advisers by his side, but the decision will be made by one man.

The young [Nazi] movement, from the first day, espoused the standpoint that its idea must be put forward spiritually, but that the defense of this spiritual platform must, if necessary, be secured by strong-arm means.

Bear in mind the devastations which Jewish bastardization visits on our nation each day, and consider that this blood poisoning can be removed from our national body only after centuries, if at all. . . . This contamination of our blood, blindly ignored by hundreds of thousands of our people, is carried on systematically by the Jew today. Systematically these black parasites of the nation defile our inexperienced young blond girls and thereby destroy something which can no longer be replaced in this world.

"God has made me Fuehrer and ruler of every man and woman of German blood in every country on earth!" boasted Hitler. Here, with the streets of Nuremberg echoing to the thunder of the crowd's "Sieg Heil!" members of the Hitler Youth parade past their leader in stiff German precision.

JAPAN GIRDS FOR WAR
The Japanese Invasion of China

On July 7, 1937, the commander of a unit of Japanese troops engaged in night maneuvers near the Marco Polo Bridge at the junction of the Peiping–Tientsin and Peiping–Hankow railroads in north China reported that his men had been attacked by Chinese soldiers. Using this and similar "incidents" as a pretext, the Japanese warlords ordered an all-out assault on the Chinese provinces that they did not already occupy. (For an account of the events leading up to the Japanese attack, see pages 94–107.)

The Japanese seized city after city, forcing the Nationalist armies of Chiang Kai-shek into retreat. Tientsin was occupied in July 1937, as was Peiping, where a new provincial puppet government controlled by Japan was established. Shanghai and Hankow were taken. The great port city of Canton and the key railroad center of Tungshan (now Suchow) soon felt the grip of the conqueror. A concentrated Japanese drive was made against Nanking, already vacated by Chiang and his Government. The conquest of that city on December 13, 1937, was followed by a period of extreme violence and terror which has become known as the rape of Nanking. An estimated 40,000 helpless civilians were slaughtered in a week-long orgy of looting, burning, rape and murder.

The Nanking atrocities stiffened Chinese determination to resist the invader. The common cause brought together Communist and other factions in support of the Nationalists.

During the siege of Nanking, Japanese bombers on December 12, 1937, sank the U.S. gunboat *Panay*, which was anchored in the Yangtze River. It was engaged in evacuating foreign neutrals (see page 98). The attack on the *Panay* added to growing American sympathy for the Chinese and anger at the Japanese.

By the end of the year, Japan controlled a large proportion of northern China, much of inner Mongolia and most major inland and port cities. Besides conquering new territories, Japan had three goals in China: to annihilate the Chinese Army; to cut off all supplies from outside China's borders; and to force the collapse or capitulation of Chiang's Government.

Despite its early triumphs, Japan achieved none of these. Chiang's armies, battered but relatively intact, withdrew to the mountain fortress of Chungking near the headwaters of the Yangtze. Although a Japanese blockade succeeded in slowing vital supplies, they were never choked off completely. At first they were brought in by railroad from French Indochina, Hong Kong and the Soviet Union. When the Japanese severed these rail lines, the supply route was the British-built Burma Road that ran from Lashio in Burma to Kunming behind the Nationalist lines.

Finally, despite heavy losses of men and territory, Chiang's Government showed no sign of collapse; indeed, his hand was strengthened by the foreign invasion and particularly by the cruelties the invaders meted out to the civilian populace. Only such a threat from China's long-standing enemy could have united the Chinese people and induced Mao Tse-tung and his tough Communist guerrilla army to fight alongside the Nationalists, with whom they had been locked in combat for eleven years.

As months went by, the Japanese advance slowed; by the end of 1938 it had stalled completely. The invading army was stretched dangerously thin and could do little more than occupy the major cities and ports; the Chinese countryside was too vast to control and bands of wily guerrillas menaced units that dared stray beyond their outskirts. Chinese morale had never been as high since the war began. Industries were beginning to be rebuilt in the interior.

It was soon clear to the Japanese that neither force of arms nor blockade could crush Chinese nationalism. Japan's Chinese adventure had only served to alienate further the United States and to tie down large numbers of troops who might better have been used somewhere else.

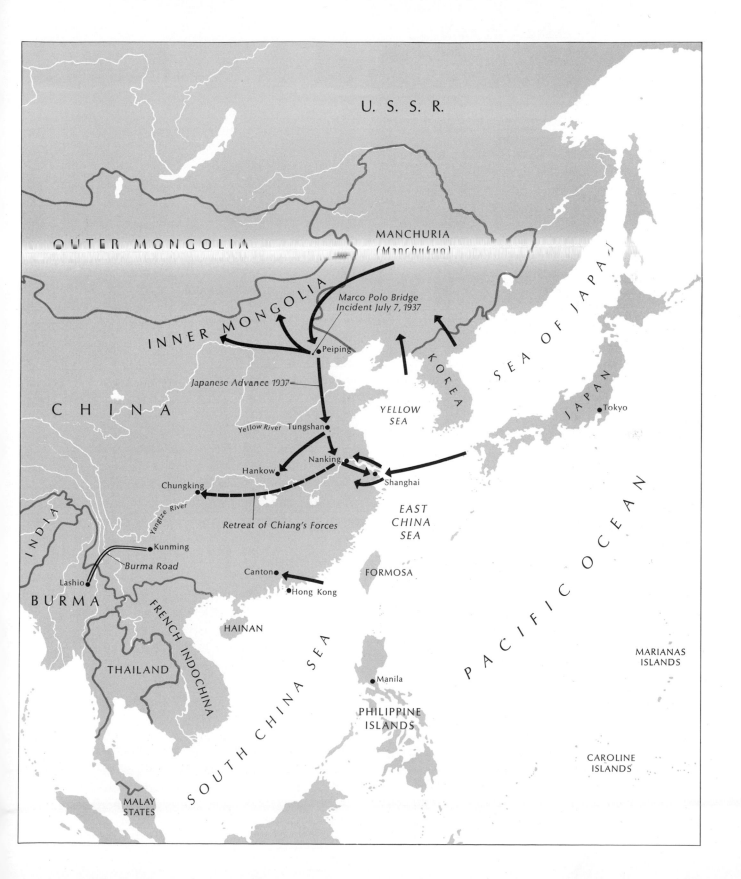

U. S. S. R.

OUTER MONGOLIA

MANCHURIA
(Manchukuo)

INNER MONGOLIA

Marco Polo Bridge
Incident July 7, 1937

Peiping

Japanese Advance 1937

CHINA

KOREA

SEA OF JAPAN

YELLOW
SEA

JAPAN

Tokyo

Yellow River   Tungshan

Hankow   Nanking

Shanghai

Chungking

Yangtze River

Retreat of Chiang's Forces

EAST
CHINA
SEA

Kunming

Burma Road

INDIA

Lashio

BURMA

FRENCH INDOCHINA

THAILAND

Canton

Hong Kong

FORMOSA

HAINAN

SOUTH CHINA SEA

MALAY
STATES

PACIFIC OCEAN

Manila

PHILIPPINE
ISLANDS

MARIANAS
ISLANDS

CAROLINE
ISLANDS

93

HOW AND WHY JAPAN PREPARED FOR WORLD WAR

BY REAR ADM. SAMUEL ELIOT MORISON, USNR (RET.)

A review of the tumultuous years in which Japan embarked on its disastrous mission to conquer the lands of Southeast Asia and the Pacific is offered by a famous naval historian.

[*In the 1920's a movement closely resembling Hitler's National Socialism was gaining strength in Japan. It envisioned a totalitarian state under Army control. Numerous secret societies, of which the Black Dragon was the most notorious, furthered its cause. It was sometimes called* Showa *("Enlightened Peace") Restoration, sometimes* Kodo-Ha *("the Way of the Emperor"). At home, its zealots aimed to destroy the power of big capitalists, liberalism and Western influences. Abroad, they wished to achieve absolute Japanese domination over the Far East, with a dream of* Hakko Ichiu *("the eight corners of the world under one roof"), the leading position among the nations, as the final goal. The movement was fanned to white heat by the limitations on Japanese Naval expansion attained by Great Britain and the United States in the treaties of 1921 and 1930, as well as the U.S. Immigration Act excluding Orientals. The* Showa *and* Kodo *fanatics were openly committed to desperate measures.–Ed.*]

Following the alleged attempt to explode a bomb on the tracks of the South Manchuria Railway on September 18, 1931, Gen. Senjuro Hayashi, a *Kodo* man who commanded the Japanese Armed Forces in Korea, moved his Kwantung Army into Manchuria (see map on page 17). Neither the Japanese Foreign Office nor the War Department knew anything about the "incident" until after it had supposedly occurred.

The Japanese Foreign Minister had to accept the accomplished fact and explain it as best he could to the world. A state of war with China followed, and this gave the military a legal and constitutional control over the Japanese Government.

Henry L. Stimson, Secretary of State in the Hoover Administration, promptly protested against the Japanese invasion of Manchuria; the League of Nations invoked the Kellogg-Briand Pact and appointed the Lytton Commission to study the situation and report. On January 7, 1932, Stimson announced what is known as the nonrecognition policy. The United States would not recognize any "situation, treaty or agreement" brought about by the use of force. And, in an open letter of February 23, 1932, he invited the nations of the world to follow suit.

Tokyo replied by formally recognizing the independence of Manchukuo (the Japanese name for the new state) and setting up a puppet Manchu Emperor. China countered with an anti-Japanese boycott.

During the early months of 1932 Japan landed sailors and soldiers in Shanghai, drove out Chinese forces with a maximum of savagery and destruction, and having saved her "honor," withdrew at the end of May. The Lytton Commission reported at the end of September, condemning the Japanese action in Manchuria. Japan replied by withdrawing from the League of Nations.

In the meantime, the Japanese militarists had consolidated their power by the simple means of getting rid of inconvenient persons; during the first half of 1932 the Minister of Finance, the chief manager of the Mitsui interests and the seventy-five-year-old Prime Minister, Ki Inukai, were assassinated. It was even planned to kill U.S. Ambassador Joseph C. Grew and Charlie Chaplin (then visiting Tokyo), in the hope of provoking a war with the United States and thus riveting military control on the Government.

Governments dominated by the military were in control during the next few years. When opposition began to develop, terrorists struck again. The refusal of Japan's Finance Minister in February 1936 to sanction a further increase of Army appropriations was a signal for his assassination by Army extremists, together with that of Adm. Makoto Saito, Lord Keeper of the Privy Seal, and Gen. Jotaro Watanabe, the Inspector General. The Prime Minister, Adm. Keisuke Okada, was also marked down, but the murderers shot his brother-in-law by mistake.

The spirit of the ancient samurai, *the warrior class, lived again in the Army of modern Japan. These grim-faced officers in bulletproof armor were photographed at Shanghai in 1932.*

Astride his favorite white horse, His Imperial Majesty Hirohito, Emperor of Japan, proudly rides in review of his troops with members of his military staff early in 1938.

The cruiser Idzumo *of the Japanese Navy steams into the captured port of Shanghai, her decks packed with fighting men, to the acclaim of flag-waving spectators. Renouncing Naval limitations in 1936, Japan began building a Navy to equal or surpass those of Britain and the United States.*

Uniformed against the cold, members of a Japanese regiment sink down to rest while making a strenuous forced march in Manchuria, which Japan began occupying in 1931. Spirited resistance put up by bands of Chinese guerrilla fighters failed to stop the invaders from conquering the country.

The Genro, the elder statesmen, chose the next Cabinet, Prime Minister Koki Hirota's, which took office in March 1936, and at once began preparations for full-scale war with China. When the Army was ready, it invaded China proper. That was the famous "China Incident" of July 7, 1937, a cooked-up clash between Japanese troops on maneuvers and a Chinese outpost on the Marco Polo Bridge near Peiping (now Peking).

For two years the U.S. Government concentrated on diplomatic efforts to "bring Japan to her senses" and restore peace in China. President Franklin D. Roosevelt might have declared that a state of war existed and so invoked the Neutrality Acts and prevented the export to Japan of scrap iron, aviation gas and other war munitions with which she was building up forces that were eventually to be used against us. But any such embargo must, according to the Neutrality Acts, be applied impartially; and if so applied, would have hurt China, whose war industries and merchant marine were rudimentary, far more than it would have hurt Japan.

No peaceful effort was neglected to stop the Chinese war; but peaceful efforts were insufficient. The United States with eighteen other nations took part in a conference at Brussels in 1937 to consider ways and means to end the war. Japan refused to participate. The conference proposed a suspension of hostilities and offered mediation to bring about a settlement. Japan replied that the "China Incident" was her exclusive affair.

Although the Japanese Foreign Office probably did its feeble best to dissuade the Army in China from molesting Americans and their property, these warnings were consistently disregarded. As Ambassador Grew wrote in 1941, American churches, hospitals, universities and schools throughout China had been bombed despite flag markings on their roofs; American missionaries and their families had been killed; and there could be no doubt that these attacks were planned, because the Japanese Army had been furnished with maps showing the locations.

Even the sinking of a U.S. ship and the deliberate shooting down of survivors failed to arouse the American people from their dream of peace. U.S.S. *Panay* was one of five small shoal-draft river gunboats that had been built about ten years earlier primarily for patrolling the Yangtze River in order to protect American nationals during the Chinese civil war.

On November 21, 1937, when Japanese forces were

(Top right) Meeting Chinese resistance, a Japanese machine-gun unit goes into action south of the Yellow River.

approaching Nanking, Chiang Kai-shek's Foreign Office notified the American Embassy that it must prepare to evacuate. The Ambassador and most of the personnel left next day in U.S.S. *Luzon;* the rest stuck it out for another week, when they decided to depart in the *Panay.* Ambassador Grew so notified the Japanese Government on December 1. On the 11th the gunboat embarked the American officials together with a number of civilians and started upriver, escorting three oil barges that also wished to escape. Two British gunboats and a few other British craft followed the same course.

At 11 a.m. the next day (December 12), the *Panay* and the three tankers anchored near Hohsien, upstream from Nanking. American flags were hoisted on their masts and painted on their awnings and topsides. The day was clear, sunny and still. No guns were manned or even uncovered.

Shortly after 1:30, three Japanese Navy bombing planes flew overhead and released eighteen bombs; immediately afterward, twelve more planes dive-bombed and nine fighters strafed, making several runs over a space of twenty minutes. The *Panay* replied with her .30-caliber machine guns. By 2:05 all power and propulsion were lost, the main deck was awash, and as the captain, Lt. Comdr. J. J. Hughes, saw that his ship was going down, he ordered her to be abandoned. Japanese planes strafed the boats on their way to shore and even combed the reeds along the riverbank for survivors. Two of the three oil barges were also bombed and destroyed. Two bluejackets and one civilian passenger died of their wounds; eleven officers and men were seriously wounded.

Ambassador Grew at first expected his country to declare war, but the promptness and apparent sincerity with which the Japanese Government and people apologized and expressed their readiness to make what reparation they could, turned away wrath. The Japanese official inquiry resulted in the face-saving explanation that the attack was all a mistake; ships emblazoned with American flags had been mistaken for

(Bottom right) Chinese troops help the wounded and clear the streets after a Japanese air raid has brought devastation to Chungking, where Chiang Kai-shek had moved his capital.

Chinese at 600 yards' range. A U.S. Naval Court of Inquiry at Shanghai brought out unmistakable evidence that the sinking was deliberate. But the United States was so anxious to avoid war that it accepted the "mistake" theory put forth by the Japanese, together with an indemnity.

The Japanese "rape of Nanking," following the sinking of the *Panay,* shocked the civilized world, but nothing was done about it. Almost every week news reached Ambassador Grew of fresh outrages against American persons and property in China. On June 11, 1938, Secretary of State Cordell Hull made a public statement reproving the air bombing of innocent civilians by the Japanese Air Force in China. And on July 1 he announced that the United States was "strongly opposed to the sale of airplanes or of aeronautical equipment" to any nation then making a practice of bombing civilians from the air.

Japanese ingenuity was able to cope with aeronautics, but not with oil or iron ore. In petroleum products particularly, Japan was exceedingly vulnerable; almost her entire supply had to be imported. Why, then, did the U.S. Government allow exports of oil and scrap iron to continue? For several reasons: On the legal level, any such restriction would have violated the existing commercial treaty with Japan. On the level of broad policy, any drastic action would have united Japan behind the militarists and destroyed our hope that the unexpectedly stout resistance of Chiang Kai-shek would discredit them and bring liberal elements back into power. Ambassador Grew warned his Government in 1938 that if Japan were deprived of oil, she would move south and take what she wanted in Borneo and Sumatra; consequently, neither an oil embargo nor any other economic sanctions should be imposed until and unless the United States was "prepared to see them through to their logical conclusion, and that might mean war."

Prince Fumimaro Konoye, the Japanese Prime Minister, announced on December 22, 1938, the basis on which Japan expected to make peace with China. China must accept the "independence" of Manchukuo, submit to Japanese military occupation and permit the establishment of an economic protectorate. Within a week Chiang Kai-shek refused.

Prince Konoye was then replaced by the zealous Kiichiro Hiranuma, who formed a Cabinet with two extremist generals in key positions. Hachiro Arita, the Foreign Minister, initiated negotiations with the European Axis (Germany and Italy) with a view to a definite military and political alliance in case either side came into conflict with the Soviet Union. That country was causing the Japanese militarists apprehension, because the Soviets had a military force ready and available for action. Several clashes had occurred on the border between Manchuria and Siberia in which the Japanese Army had been badly beaten by the Russians. Although the *Kodo* men in the Army were willing to provoke a war with the United States, of whose capacity to project power across the Pacific they were contemptuous, they feared the Soviet Union and wanted assurance of Axis support before starting the "New Order in East Asia."

In the spring of 1939 Japanese troops occupied the strategic island of Hainan in the South China Sea. Hainan contained a valuable deposit of iron ore and was a good jumping-off place for an attack on Malaya. Next, Japan announced that she had annexed small Spratly Island off Indochina, hitherto claimed by France. Both annexations suggested that the master militarists of Japan were contemplating a change of direction in their program of expansion.

These latest annexations probably had something to do with a quick transfer of U.S. Naval strength from the Atlantic to the Pacific. Following the annual Fleet Problem and concentration maneuvers held in the Caribbean, the Fleet departed for the West Coast en route to Hawaii.

It cannot be said that the return of the Fleet had any effect on the Japanese military. The last important conquests of the Japanese Army had been at Canton and Hankow in October 1938. Chiang Kai-shek's Government had retired to Chungking on the upper

Yangtze and was putting up a heroic and effective resistance. This led to a certain loss of face by the Japanese Army.

Most high Naval officers appear to have been opposed to the "China Affair." They believed that Japan's destiny lay on the sea and that she should get possession of the Netherlands East Indies, with their wealth in strategic resources and people, before attempting to bring so vast a country as China under control. But they had to admit that a southward expansion could only be carried out at the risk of war with Great Britain and probably with the United States. Accordingly, China was picked on as the first victim. Now that China was proving too obstinate to conquer, why not swing south and take the risk?

The first move in that direction came in 1938 when the Japanese Army in a series of amphibious operations occupied the shores of the South China Sea, seeking to shut China off from the ocean. In May and June 1939 the Japanese Army was active in the Shanghai International Settlement, trying to make life there intolerable for the American and European residents; and in June it began blockading the British and French concessions at Tientsin.

The Japanese Air Force stepped up its attacks on Chungking, Chiang Kai-shek's capital. In the air raids of July 6–7, 1939, bombs fell on an American church near the Embassy and close to the gunboat U.S.S. *Tutuila*. President Roosevelt believed that the time had come to impose economic sanctions. To clear the way, the 1911 Treaty of Commerce with Japan was denounced on July 26, 1939, which meant that after January 26, 1940, the President and Congress could dictate the terms upon which Japan might continue to trade with the United States. American public opinion

approved this step with hardly an important dissent. The Japanese Government, accustomed to merely verbal protests, was taken by surprise. Before the treaty expired in January 1940, Europe had gone to war.

In April 1939 Hitler went fishing for an unconditional military pact between Germany, Italy and Japan which would bring all three into any war that one of them started. General Seishiro Itagaki, War Minister in the Hiranuma Cabinet, and the *Kodo* men in general were all for it; but the Imperial Court, Big Business, Navy Minister Mitsumasa Yonai and Adm. Isoroku Yamamoto were against it. They foresaw that any such pact might involve Japan in war with Great Britain and the United States, and they succeeded in stalling the negotiations. Hitler and Ribbentrop, exceedingly annoyed at this outcome, threatened to find another ally; and Hitler's nonaggression pact of August 1939 with Stalin was, in part, his "answer" to Japan.

This desertion of the Anti-Comintern Treaty by Hitler, without even consulting his Far Eastern partner, was naturally resented in Japan. It exposed her to a greater concentration of troops on the Manchurian frontier and possibly to a Russian invasion of Mongolia.

On the other hand, strong forces pulled Japan into Hitler's orbit. There was an ideological affinity between Nazi doctrine and Japanese policy. The Army extremists were strong for a German alliance, thinking it would frighten America and Great Britain into keeping hands off East Asia, where Britain and France had valuable possessions that they coveted. So, on the whole, a German victory held out greater promise to the Japanese warlords.

There was no doubt as to where the interests of the

The American gunboat Panay, *bombed by the Japanese on the Yangtze River December 12, 1937, is shown sinking in progressive stages. Tokyo quickly apologized and paid an indemnity of slightly more than $2 million to keep U.S. trade channels open.*

United States lay. It was clearly our duty to prevent any formal alliance between Japan and the Axis which would give her the same opportunity to expand southward, at the expense of the Allies, as her alliance with the same Allies had afforded in 1915, at the expense of Germany. Ambassador Grew was instructed accordingly, and in confidential talks with Japanese statesmen urged that their country maintain a strict neutrality.

The Japanese generally countered with the hint that if the democracies wanted neutrality, they must give Japan a free hand in China and abandon Chiang Kai-shek to his fate. After all, the entire coast of China by 1940 was held by the Japanese Army, so that aid aid could no longer be sent to China except over the Burma Road. Why not be realistic and recognize Japan's "Monroe Doctrine of the Pacific"? In the meantime outrages against American persons and property in China continued, and every section of China seized by Japanese armies was at once closed to the trade of other powers.

On January 6, 1940, Adm. James O. Richardson became Commander in Chief of the United States Fleet and hoisted his flag on U.S.S. *Pennsylvania* at San Pedro Harbor in the Philippines. He was somewhat disturbed to find that a considerable detachment of the Fleet, consisting of cruisers and destroyers, had already been sent to Hawaii.

American newspapers of March 31, 1941, announced that the Fleet maneuvers that spring would take place in the Hawaiian area. The reception of this announcement in Japan was significant. Tokyo papers reacted in a resentful and defiant manner, declaring that the maneuvers were planned as a demonstration against Japan. The Navy Ministry spokesman announced that if the maneuvers crossed the international date line they would be regarded as a "brandishing of the big sword" near Japanese territory.

On April 2 the rest of the U.S. Fleet departed from West Coast ports for the Hawaiian Islands, where it conducted maneuvers well to the eastward of the 180th meridian. Although the Fleet was scheduled to return to its West Coast bases on May 9, the Chief of Naval Operations, Adm. Harold R. Stark, on the 7th ordered it to remain two weeks longer, and shortly afterward

Cheering and waving battle flags, invading Japanese troops cele-brate the breaching of the historic walls and the capture of the Chinese city of Nanking in December 1937.

informed Admiral Richardson that he would be based at Pearl Harbor until further notice.

In reply to Richardson's question from Pearl Harbor, "Why are we here?" Stark wrote on May 27, 1940, "You are there because of the deterrent effect which it is thought your presence may have on the Japs going into the East Indies."

The timing of this Fleet movement was determined by events in Europe and the repercussion in Japan. On April 15, 1940, Foreign Minister Arita, doubtless tipped off by the Germans on impending events, hinted that his country's policy had broadened out from a mere liquidating of the "China Incident" to a "Greater East Asia Co-Prosperity Sphere." What he grandiloquently termed "relations of economic interdependence and of coexistence and co-prosperity" between Japan and the Netherlands East Indies must be maintained, whatever happened to the home country.

Secretary of State Hull took prompt notice of this in a press release declaring that any armed intervention in the Dutch colonies "would be prejudicial to the cause of stability, peace and security" in the entire Pacific. The Japanese Government decided to commit no overt act, but sent economic missions to Batavia which became increasingly exigent and arrogant.

On May 10 German armies crashed into the Low Countries, and on the 14th swung on France. One month later they were in Paris, and within three days Marshal Pétain had surrendered.

General George C. Marshall, on June 7, 1940, warned Hawaii to be on the alert "against an overseas raid from the west by a hostile nation." Admiral Richardson instituted a plane patrol to the westward of Oahu that covered considerably more ocean than did the one subsequently set up by Adm. Husband E. Kimmel. Great Britain, momentarily expecting a German invasion, consented under pressure from Japan to close the Burma Road for three months on July 18. That was one of Chiang Kai-shek's two remaining connections with the outside world, the other being Hanoi, the port of French Indochina.

The fall of the Netherlands and of France opened up new opportunities for easy Japanese conquest. Immediately one began to hear more of the "Southward Advance" and of "Greater East Asia," which diverted public attention from the sorry mess that the Japanese Army had made of China.

The moderate Yonai ministry fell, and on June 22

a new one was formed under the smooth Prince Konoye. He at once set about organizing a "New Structure" in Japan. This was, in effect, the Japanese version of totalitarianism that had long been planned and promoted under the name *"Showa* Restoration." The Government gradually assumed complete control over operations and profits of the *zaibatsu,* the big financial and industrial interests. All political parties were suppressed on the theory that the entire nation was united in loyalty to the Emperor; laborers were required to work long hours in war industries; all luxuries and many pleasures were forbidden. Ambassador Grew interpreted all this as preparation for an early move on Indochina, whose northern provinces offered a new base of attack on Chungking.

He was right. As a result of heat applied by Hitler at Vichy, and under the feeble pretense of "protecting" Indochina from invasion, Marshal Pétain on August 30, 1940, consented to a Japanese military occupation of, and construction of airdromes in, northern Indochina. This was the first formal breach of the status quo in East Asia since the outbreak of war in Europe.

On September 27, 1940, Japan formally joined the Axis with the famous Tripartite Pact, a treaty of alliance with Germany and Italy. Japan recognized the Hitlerian "New Order in Europe"; Germany and Italy recognized "the leadership of Japan in the establishment of a New Order in Greater East Asia." Each would assist the other if "attacked by a power at present not involved in the European war or in the Sino-Japanese conflict." That power, of course, was the United States. By the threat of a two-ocean war, both governments hoped to frighten the United States into remaining neutral, and Foreign Minister Yosuke Matsuoka also expected that the Tripartite Pact would stifle American protests against Japanese expansionist policy.

Admiral Richardson regarded Japanese expansion and other events in the Orient as of slight concern to the United States. He had written to Admiral Stark before departing San Pedro that the Chief of Naval Operations should repeatedly impress on the President that a war with Japan would last five to ten years, and that our old war plan was defective and obsolete. He objected to basing the Fleet permanently at Pearl Harbor, not only because he regarded the security of the Western Hemisphere as "the paramount thing," but because he disliked Pearl for logistic reasons. An additional sea voyage of 2000 miles would be required for the inadequate fleet train to bring out recruits, equipment and supplies; morale would be impaired by keeping the men at a distance from their homes. If there were danger of war with Japan, the Fleet could be readied more promptly for combat through the superior facilities of Pacific Coast bases. The Admiral felt so strongly about this that he visited Washington in July and again in October 1940 to press his views on the President and the State Department.

Admiral Richardson was relieved on February 1, 1941, by Admiral Kimmel. On the same day the U.S. Fleet was renamed the Pacific Fleet, and that Fleet stayed at Pearl. Obviously, if Admiral Richardson's views had prevailed, the Pacific Fleet might not have been the victim of a surprise attack; the Japanese would hardly have sent their carrier force as far as the West Coast. Yet even though the Fleet was based at Pearl Harbor on December 7, 1941, it need not have been surprised there. The mere fact of having the Fleet there from May 1940 meant that this Hawaiian port was immensely improved as a fleet base and infinitely better prepared for hostilities.

The Tripartite Pact as good as told the world that Japan intended to pursue her southward advance, confident that Germany would come to her aid in the event of a head-on collision with the United States.

As soon as Hitler declared war on the Soviet Union in June 1941, his efforts in Japan were directed toward persuading her to invade Siberia. No Japanese Government wanted any part of that. From that time on, Hitler ceased to count in the formation of Japanese policy; the German Embassy in Tokyo was not kept informed about the last negotiations with the United States—and the attack on Pearl Harbor took it, too, by surprise.

In contrast to the Atlantic war, where the U.S. and Royal Navies cooperated as virtual allies before the German declaration and knew exactly what each had to do thereafter, the three future allies in the Pacific failed to cooperate before December 8, 1941, and did so "too little and too late" thereafter.

The first Anglo-American staff conversations respecting the Pacific were an indirect result of the "China Incident" and the completion of the Anti-Comintern Pact in October 1937. President Roosevelt and Secretary Hull, foreseeing the United States' being involved in a two-ocean war, instructed Adm. William D. Leahy, then Chief of Naval Operations, to draw up a war plan based on that contingency. At London in January 1938, U.S. and British representatives agreed to recommend cooperation in case of war, with the Royal Navy's basing a battle force on Singapore if the Japanese moved south, and the U.S. Fleet concentrating at Pearl Harbor.

In May 1939, when the British Government believed that war with Germany and Italy was close, it informed our War Plans Division that owing to the necessity of watching the Mediterranean, it would be impossible to send a battle force to Singapore. Nothing was then decided, but the Joint Planning Committee of the U.S. Army and Navy drew up a new war plan on the assumption that no Battle Fleet of the Royal Navy could be counted on in the Pacific.

The British believed that Singapore was essential to the defense of the Malay Barrier (the string of islands from the Kra Isthmus to Timor) and of the Empire; without it, the lifelines through the Indian Ocean to Australia and New Zealand would be severed. They were very insistent that the United States divide its Pacific Fleet in order to defend Singapore. The American delegation doubted the premise and resisted the demand. It believed that Singapore was not essential for the defense of the Malay Barrier or the Imperial lifeline; that Singapore could not be defended if Japan seized Indochinese airfields within bombing distance; and that to detach warships to Singapore would merely offer the Japanese Navy an opportunity to defeat the United States Navy in detail.

Finally the British agreed, in case of war with Japan, to send at least six capital ships to defend Singapore if the United States Navy would assist the Royal Navy in watching the Mediterranean. That arrangement was in the course of being carried out when the surprise attack on Pearl Harbor altered everything.

The United States was becoming more and more uneasy over her moral position. She was protesting against aggression in the Far East while selling the material means of conquest to Japan. She was allowing Japan to bid against U.S. Armed Forces in the home market for steel, oil and other strategic items.

Economic sanctions began with the "moral embargo" of July 1938 against the export of planes and their equipment to countries engaged in bombing civil-

ians. In early February 1940 Senator Key Pittman of Nevada introduced a resolution calling for an embargo on war materials to Japan; the following July Congress passed an "Act to Expedite the Strengthening of the National Defense." It authorized the President "to prohibit or curtail the exportation of any military equipment or munitions . . . or machinery, tools . . . or supplies necessary for the manufacture, servicing or operation thereof," whenever he determined such action to be "necessary in the interest of national defense."

In the same month Congress passed the Two-Ocean Navy Bill, such a law having was already before Congress; the destroyers-naval bases deal with Great Britain was just over the horizon (see page 39); and American industry, with much hesitation and reluctance, yet convinced of the necessity, began to convert from peace to war production.

While the main and declared purpose of the National Defense Act was to keep strategic materials and supplies at home, the broad powers that it gave the President made it possible for him to implement national policy by giving export licenses in favor of our friends and denying them to our prospective enemies. In practice the licenses were only accorded in favor of the British Commonwealth, China, the Netherlands East Indies and resistant groups in Europe. This saved Japan's face but was equally effective in gradually denying her access to American markets for war materials.

On November 8, 1940, the Emperor approved the appointment as Ambassador to Washington of Adm. Kichisaburo Nomura, a former foreign minister and man of high personal character who was known to be opposed to a breach with the United States. At the same time the Japanese began an intensive militarization of the Marshall and Caroline islands, building airfields, seaplane bases and fortifications.

On January 27 Ambassador Grew confided to his diary: "There is a lot of talk around town to the effect that the Japanese, in case of a break with the United States, are planning to go all out in a surprise mass attack at Pearl Harbor. Of course I informed our Government." Actually this was the very time when Admiral Yamamoto began planning the Pearl Harbor attack.

On February 7 Mr. Grew observed that Japan was continuing her "nibbling policy" to the south, on this occasion by turning to her advantage an undeclared war between Thailand and French Indochina. Japan mediated in the dispute and obtained, early in March 1941, a settlement much to her own interest. Thailand secured some of her "lost provinces," and Japan, as the price of saving the rest of them for France, exacted of Vichy a monopoly of the Indochinese rice crop and the right to occupy the airport at Saigon, within bombing distance of Singapore.

On April 13, 1941, Foreign Minister Matsuoka concluded a Russo-Japanese nonaggression pact with Vyacheslav M. Molotov, Soviet Minister of Foreign Affairs. Stalin consented because of the possibility of an attack by Germany; Japan wanted it to secure her Manchurian frontier and to release forces for the southward advance.

During the spring Japan poured troops into northern Indochina in preparation for taking the rest of that colony at one gulp. On July 2 the Government called up between 1 and 2 million conscripts, recalled all its merchant ships from the Atlantic and adopted other measures indicating warlike intentions. On July 25 the Japanese Minister of Foreign Affairs informed Ambassador Grew that Vichy had consented to admit Japan to a joint protectorate of French Indochina. This meant that Japan was free to extend her military occupation over the entire colony, which was done forthwith. It also completed the left curve of a strategic horseshoe around the Philippines.

This time the American reply came quickly, and in deeds, not words. On July 26, 1941, President Roosevelt issued an executive order freezing Japanese assets in the United States. His intention was to choke off Japanese-American trade, including the highly important oil exports. No Japanese vessels were allowed thenceforth to discharge cargo in United States ports, and those already in our ports had to depart with ballast.

Up to this time there had been only a "moral" restriction on the export of petroleum products to Japan other than high-octane gas and aviation lube oil. American shipowners had been "morally" dissuaded from carrying fuel oil to Japan, but immense quantities were still going there in Japanese and neutral tankers. Now all that stopped. And the freezing of Japanese assets, which was also done by Great Britain and the Dutch, had a restrictive effect on procurement of oil in the Netherlands East Indies. Deprived of cash for foreign exchange, Japanese tankers were forced to lay up for weeks in harbors on Borneo or Sumatra while their captains waited for money from home.

The oil embargo and assets-freezing order of July 26, 1941, made war with Japan inevitable unless one of two things happened: The United States might reverse its foreign policy, restore trade relations and acquiesce in further Japanese conquests; or the Japanese Government might persuade its Army at least to prepare to evacuate China and renounce the southward advance. There was small chance of that at a time when the Australians and the Dutch were virtually helpless, when the German Army, apparently irresistible, was sweeping into Russia, and, in North Africa, Rommel had pushed back the British to the suburbs of Alexandria.

No measure short of war could then have diverted the Japanese militarists from seizing their "golden opportunity" for expansion. Any temporary concession, however welcome to liberal Japanese civilians, would surely have been disregarded by the Army, which would accept no compromise that did not place America in the ignominious role of collaborating with conquest.

In any case Japan had to make up her mind quickly because the oil embargo and the freezing of her assets in the United States threatened a general impoverishment of her economy. Shortly she would lack fuel oil for normal domestic consumption, let alone naval operations.

Japan imported about 88 percent of all oil products consumed in the country, and about 80 percent of the total came from the United States. During the last few years the Government had been stockpiling oil as fast as possible, and in the year ending March 31, 1941, imports reached an all-time high with 22,850,000 barrels of crude oil and 15,110,000 barrels of refined products. This was about enough for one year of war.

Other strategic items such as rubber, scrap iron, tin and tungsten would dwindle; but oil was paramount. Japan must get more oil in order to conquer or conquer in order to get more oil; and the Roosevelt Administration had determined to shut off oil. The American people were tired of placating Japan with oil and scrap, conniving at an aggressive policy against friendly nations. There was no doubt about their feelings in the matter. But they did not yet understand, and of course the Administration could not tell them, that shutting off oil made one of two things inevitable: war with Japan, or an easy Japanese conquest of areas which, without doubt, would make that nation well-nigh invincible.

So, beginning with the assets-freezing order, both countries intensified their military preparations. On July 26, 1941, President Roosevelt signed an order nationalizing the Armed Forces of the Philippine Commonwealth and appointing Douglas MacArthur Commanding General, U.S. Army Forces, Far East. The Japanese Army planners were busy drafting plans for major strikes against the Malay Peninsula, the Philippines and Pearl Harbor, as well as minor ones against the British crown colony of Hong Kong, North Borneo, Guam and Wake. The U.S. Navy made no new war plan, but the country accelerated industrial and military preparation all along the line.

During the conquest and sacking of Nanking in 1937, thousands of the Chinese population were put to death by the Japanese invaders. Corpses littered the streets, as shown in this scene before the city wall. Although the Japanese warlords referred to the military campaign as the China Incident, it was in every respect a full-scale brutal war.

In the fall of 1940 Hitler's *Luftwaffe* flew into
England's skies laden with death and destruction. Rising to meet it
were the nation's finest young men in their Spitfires and Hurricanes.
The Royal Air Force shot down so many black-crossed
planes that the threat of invasion was thwarted.

AGAINST LONG ODDS

GREAT MOMENTS IN FREEDOM'S HOUR OF CRISIS

THE FLYING TIGERS

BY RUSSELL WHELAN

Experts said that the Flying Tigers would be quickly wiped out when they came up against the planes of the vaunted Japanese Air Force. Yet this small band of American pilots, led by a tough ex-U.S. Army officer nicknamed Old Leatherface, had other ideas.

It was Christmas Day 1941, but the thoughts of the American people dwelt not on the glad old memory of Bethlehem but on the shocking facts of the new war in the Pacific and Asia. Pearl Harbor was a taste strong and bitter in every mouth. It was a sickening thing to see Americans doubting their own strength. Then suddenly from far across the world came news of a significant victory over the forces of Nippon. The Flying Tigers had flown and struck.

The Flying Tigers? Who were they? They were American boys, fighting pilots trained in our own Army and Navy and now members of the new American Volunteer Group employed by the Government of Generalissimo Chiang Kai-shek to protect the lifeline of China, the Burma Road.

Early on Christmas Day a Japanese aerial armada had headed for Rangoon, the major seaport of Burma. There, awaiting transport to China, crowding the wharves and warehouses, were many million dollars' worth of American lend-lease supplies. The Japanese raiders came boldly, knowing that their enemies mustered only a skeleton air force for the defense of Burma. They flew in strength, sixty bombers escorted by thirty fighters, to blast Rangoon.

As the first bombardier studied his sight for the first blow, 12 little fighting planes raced down out of the sun onto the backs of the invaders. Joined by 16 planes of the Royal Air Force, the defenders raged through the sky, and soon 9 Japanese pursuit planes

and 15 bombers had fallen. At least 7 more crashed before the main Japanese force scattered. The Flying Tigers had gained a valiant victory.

They went on from there in smoke and blood and death to compose their epic. They helped save Rangoon and the Burma Road for sixty-five precious days.

In the spring of 1937, with the Japanese menace mounting, Chiang Kai-shek needed someone to reorganize and train his ramshackle air force. His agents plucked Col. Claire L. Chennault from his hometown of Waterproof, Louisiana.

Chennault, then forty-seven and retired from the U.S. Army Air Force for partial deafness, was a leather-faced, steel-eyed champion of air power. His book, *The Role of Defensive Pursuit* (1935), had stirred controversy with conventional military men.

In China he inherited a batch of obsolete aircraft and a grab bag of venturesome fliers. Because he lacked planes, men and money to put his ideas into practice, the years that followed were frustrating.

Then, in March 1941, Washington announced a policy of lend-lease aid to China. The only supply line on the ground still open was the Burma Road. To keep it open, Chennault proceeded to recruit and organize the American Volunteer Group for operation as a unit of the Chinese Air Force.

In late July the first members of the group reached the Toungoo base in southern Burma for intensive training by Chennault. Already 100 Curtiss P-40 pursuits had been acquired. On the noses of their planes, the pilots painted the red mouth and flashing teeth of a tiger shark, reputedly feared by the Japanese; this was soon displaced by a Bengal tiger with two wings flying through a V for victory. The Chinese called them Flying Tigers, and the name stuck.

By the time of the attack on Pearl Harbor, Chennault was geared for action. On December 18 two of his squadrons took off for the Kunming air base in Yunnan province, at the Chinese terminus of the Burma Road. On the 20th they fought their first battle, killing six of the ten enemy bombers. At dawn on Christmas Day the contingent in Burma scored its dramatic success in the skies over Rangoon.

At no time did the group have more than fifty-five combat planes capable of flight or more than seventy pilots capable of flying them. This slender strength was always divided between at least two bases. Yet

(Above) *The tiger-shark design on the Curtiss P-40 Flying Tigers accurately indicated the fighting ability of the air squadron.*

their exploits quickly made the Flying Tigers world famous and Chennault himself a living legend of triumphs against heavy odds.

In the summer of 1942 Chennault, now a Brigadier General, was put in command of all U.S. Air Forces in the Burma-China theater, and his Volunteer Group was incorporated into those forces.

This tiny U.S. formation had in less than seven months "exploded the myth of Japanese aerial invincibility," as one historian has put it. The Flying Tigers were officially credited with the destruction of 299 Japanese airplanes. At least 1500 Japanese airmen had lost their lives in encounters with this American unit.

Against these figures, the Volunteer Group lost 10 pilots killed in action, 2 pilots and 1 crew chief lost on the ground as the result of bombings and 3 pilots missing in action. Ten fliers were killed accidentally.

The record shows what the protection of the Flying Tigers meant to the cities of China and the transport over the Burma Road. But the true gold of their achievement lies hidden in the imponderables of the human spirit: the effect upon the long beleaguered and unaided Chinese; the inspiration to an America suddenly plunged into a worldwide war.

Major General Claire L. Chennault of the Flying Tigers.

THE MIRACLE OF DUNKIRK

BY WINSTON S. CHURCHILL

In his history of the war, from which the passages on these pages are excerpted, Prime Minister Churchill gives a succinct account of the epic Dunkirk evacuation (May 26 to June 4, 1940). He had taken office slightly more than two weeks earlier, and he personally directed the operations in the greatest military rescue in history. When withdrawal of the surrounded British and Allied forces from northern France offered the last hope, a plan for evacuation was set up under the code name "Operation Dynamo." Its chances of success were not rated high—what actually happened surpassed the most optimistic expectations. A decisive element in the "miracle" was the mobilization in a few days of a great fleet of small private boats to help embark the troops massed on the Dunkirk coast under withering enemy fire, and transport them across the English Channel. The country "should prepare itself for hard and heavy tidings," Churchill told the House of Commons as the evacuation got under way, but he expressed confidence that Britain would move "through disaster and through grief to the ultimate defeat of our enemies."

"In the midst of defeat," Churchill was to sum it up, "glory came to the island people, united and unconquerable; and the tale of the Dunkirk beaches will shine in whatever records are preserved of our affairs."

On the evening of the 26th an Admiralty signal put "Operation Dynamo" into play, and the first troops were brought home that night. After the loss of Boulogne and Calais, only the remains of the port of Dunkirk and the open beaches next to the Belgian frontier were in our hands. At this time it was thought that the most we could rescue were about 45,000 men in two days. Early the next morning, May 27, emergency measures were taken to find additional small craft "for a special requirement." This was no less than the full evacuation of the British Expeditionary Force. It was plain that large numbers of such craft would be required for work on the beaches, in addition to bigger ships which could load in Dunkirk harbor. On the suggestion of Mr. H. C. Riggs of the Ministry of Shipping, the various boatyards, from Teddington to Brightlingsea, were searched by Admiralty officers, and yielded upward of forty serviceable motorboats or launches, which were assembled at Sheerness on the following day. At the same time lifeboats from liners in the London docks, tugs from the Thames, yachts, fishing craft, lighters, barges and pleasure boats — anything that could be of use along the beaches—were called into service. By the night of the 27th a great tide of small vessels began to flow toward the sea, first to our Channel ports, and thence to the beaches of Dunkirk and the beloved Army.

Once the need for secrecy was relaxed, the Admiralty did not hesitate to give full rein to the spontaneous movement which swept the seafaring population of our south and southeastern shores. Everyone who had a boat of any kind, steam or sail, put out for Dunkirk, and the preparations, fortunately begun a week earlier, were now aided by the brilliant improvisation of volunteers on an amazing scale. The numbers arriving on the 29th were small, but they were the forerunners of nearly 400 small craft which from the 31st were destined to play a vital part by ferrying from the beaches to the off-lying ships almost 100,000 men. In these days I missed the head of my Admiralty Map Room, Captain Pim, and one or two other familiar faces. They had got hold of a Dutch *schuit* [canal boat], which in four days brought off 800 soldiers. Altogether there came to the rescue of the Army under the ceaseless air bombardment of the enemy about 860 vessels, of which nearly 700 were British and the rest Allied.

Meanwhile ashore around Dunkirk, the occupation of the perimeter was effected with precision. The

troops arrived out of chaos and were formed in order along the defenses, which even in two days had grown. Those men who were in the best shape turned about to form the line.

The enemy had closely followed the withdrawal, and hard fighting was incessant, especially on the flanks near Nieuport and Bergues. As the evacuation went on, the steady decrease in the number of troops, both British and French, was accompanied by a corresponding contraction of the defense. On the beaches among the sand dunes, for 3, 4 or 5 days scores of thousands of men dwelt under unrelenting air attack. Hitler's belief that the German Air Force would render escape impossible and that therefore he should keep his armored formations for the final stroke of the campaign, was a mistaken but not unreasonable view.

A factor which Hitler had not foreseen was the slaughter of his airmen. British and German air quality was put directly to the test. By intense effort Fighter Command maintained successive patrols over the scene and fought the enemy at long odds. Hour after hour they bit into German fighter and bomber squadrons, taking a heavy toll, scattering them and driving them away. Day after day this went on, till the glorious victory of the Royal Air Force was gained.

But all the prowess in the air would have been vain without the sea. . . . To and fro between the shore and the ships plied small boats, gathering the men from the beaches as they waded out or picking them from the water, with total indifference to the air bombardment, which often claimed many victims. The vast number of boats defied air attack. The Mosquito Armada as a whole was unsinkable.

On the 30th I held a meeting of the three Service Ministers and the Chiefs of Staff in the Admiralty War Room. We considered the events of the day on the Belgian coast. The total number of troops brought off had risen to 120,000, including only 6000 French; 860 vessels of all kinds were at work. A message from Admiral [William] Wake-Walker at Dunkirk said that

A miracle of deliverance, Churchill called the mammoth rescue operation at Dunkirk. John Masefield, British Poet Laureate, called it a Nine Days' Wonder. For the Allied troops, massed for evacuation along the twenty-five miles of French coast, the immediate task was survival. Here, one of the soldiers takes a shot at a low-flying German airplane.

Dunkirk evacuation: May 26–June 4, 1940. An armada of small boats from a myriad of southeastern coastal ports crossed the Channel to Dunkirk in order to rescue troops of the British Expeditionary Force, together with thousands of French and Belgian soldiers.

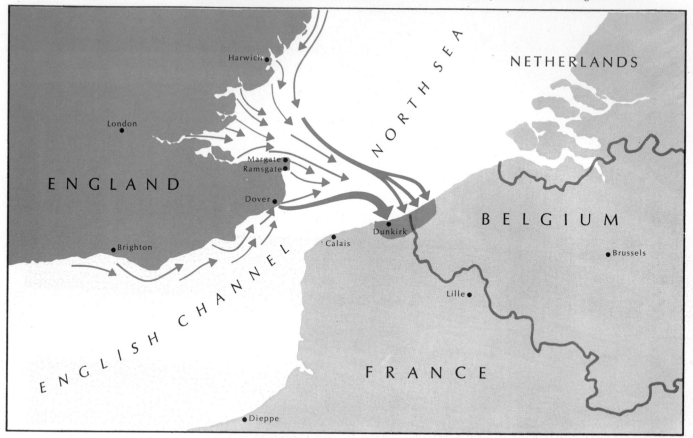

Grimly determined, the great statesman-soldier, Winston Churchill, leaves the Admiralty office after his designation as First Lord of the Admiralty in September 1939. Eight months later Churchill became Prime Minister in a coalition government that led the British to victory over Hitler.

total and unmitigated defeat." The Stalin-Hitler Pact drew his fiery denunciation.

On the day when Chamberlain declared war on Germany, he appointed Churchill, his outspoken critic, First Lord of the Admiralty. In the months of the "phony war" the country remained torpid and confused. But the Nazi invasion of the Netherlands in May 1940 awakened and alarmed the British people. Chamberlain resigned and Churchill became Prime Minister in a coalition government.

At an age when most men are winding up their careers—he was then in his sixty-sixth year—Churchill was on the brink of his most demanding and glorious period. His unique oratorical powers were at their zenith. In times of bitter defeat, when England stood alone, he rallied the people of his besieged island to heroic sacrifice and unquenchable faith in ultimate victory.

Churchill was at once the unflagging believer in ultimate victory and the embodiment of the spirit of freedom. He developed a fateful personal friendship with President Franklin D. Roosevelt. Perhaps his most significant achievement was to align the overwhelmingly isolationist United States against the Hitler Axis. What had been an informal Anglo-American collaboration, climaxed by American Lend-Lease, became a Grand Alliance on the day the Japanese attacked Pearl Harbor. Six months earlier, despite his long hostility to Communism, Churchill had accepted Soviet Russia as an ally, as had Roosevelt.

When the victory was won, ironically, Churchill was defeated by the Labour Party in 1945 and succeeded by Clement Attlee. He served again as Conservative Prime Minister from 1951 to 1955, then stayed on in the Commons until 1963.

But political offices no longer mattered. His prestige grew. He was the nearly deified hero of his own nation, of the American people and of free men everywhere. His monumental memoirs, *The Second World War,* completed in 1954, were followed in 1958 by *A History of the English-speaking Peoples.* In 1953 he was awarded the Nobel Prize for Literature. In 1963 President John F. Kennedy proclaimed him an Honorary Citizen of the United States.

His romantic, flamboyant lust for life was never impaired. When Sir Winston Churchill died on January 24, 1965, all humanity realized that one of history's immortals had passed from the scene.

THE BATTLE OF BRITAIN

BY WINSTON S. CHURCHILL

The Luftwaffe—*the powerful air arm of Hitler's blitzkrieg—had tasted its first reversal in the skies over Dunkirk. But its main strength had been deployed elsewhere. With France in his grasp, Hitler directed his full attention, and all the might of the* Luftwaffe, *to Britain. Churchill believed that the fate of Western civilization depended on the outcome of this battle. In his classic history of World War II, the Battle of Britain is recounted by the man who inspired his people to repel the Nazis.*

Our fate now [June 1940] depended upon victory in the air. The German leaders had recognized that all their plans for the invasion of Britain depended on winning air supremacy above the Channel and the chosen landing places on our south coast. The preparation of the embarkation ports, the assembly of the transports, the minesweeping of the passages and the laying of the new minefields were impossible without protection from British air attack.

For the actual crossings and landings, complete mastery of the air over the transports and the beaches was the decisive condition. The result, therefore, turned upon the destruction of the Royal Air Force [R.A.F.] and the system of airfields between London and the sea.

I did not myself at all shrink mentally from the impending trial of strength. I had told Parliament on June 4: "The great French Army was very largely, for the time being, cast back and disturbed by the onrush of a few thousand armored vehicles. May it not also be that the cause of civilization itself will be defended by the skill and devotion of a few thousand airmen?" And to [Jan Christiaan] Smuts, on June 9: "I see only one sure way through now—to wit, that Hitler should attack this country and in so doing break his air weapon." The occasion had now arrived.

The German Air Force had been engaged to the utmost limit in the Battle of France, and, like the German Navy after the Norway campaign, it required a period of weeks or months for recovery. This pause was convenient to us too, for all but three of our fighter squadrons had at one time or another been engaged in Continental operations.

During June and early July the German Air Force revived and regrouped its formations and established itself on all the French and Belgian airfields from which the assault had to be launched. By reconnaissance and tentative forays it sought to measure the character and scale of the opposition which would be encountered. It was not until July 10 that the first heavy onslaught began, and this date is usually taken as the opening of the battle.

There were three successive but overlapping phases in the attack. First, from July 10 to August 18, the harrying of British convoys in the Channel and our southern ports from Dover to Plymouth—whereby our Air Force should be tested, drawn into battle and depleted, and damage done to those seaside towns marked as objectives for the forthcoming invasion. In the second phase, August 24 to September 27, a way to London was to be forced by the elimination of the Royal Air Force and its installations, leading to the violent and continuous bombing of the capital. This would also cut communications with the threatened shores. But in [Hermann] Goering's view there was good reason to believe that a greater prize was here in sight, no less than throwing the world's largest city into confusion and paralysis, the cowing of the Government and the people, and their consequent submission to the German will. Their Navy and Army staffs devoutly hoped that Goering was right. As the situation developed, they saw that the R.A.F. was not being eliminated, and meanwhile their own urgent needs for the "Sea Lion" adventure [the cross-Channel invasion] were neglected for the sake of destruction in London.

And then, when invasion was indefinitely postponed for lack of air supremacy, there followed the third and last phase. The hope of daylight victory had

Firemen spray burning buildings in a London street after a blitz (air raid). The magnificent spirit of the capital was evident after the all-clear signal, as volunteers fought the fires, labored to restore electric, gas and telephone service, tended to the wounded—and removed the dead.

121

(Top left) *At a German operational headquarters, Hitler and a group of his generals inspect a war map. On the Fuehrer's right is Gen. Walther von Brauchitsch, and to his right stands Gen. Wilhelm Keitel. Brauchitsch disagreed with Hitler's decisions during the war with Russia and was vehemently overruled.*

---

faded, the Royal Air Force remained vexatiously alive, and Goering in October resigned himself to the indiscriminate bombing of London and the centers of industrial production.

In the quality of the fighter aircraft there was little to choose. The Germans' [planes] were faster, with a better rate of climb; ours more maneuverable, better armed. Their airmen, well aware of their greater numbers, were also the proud victors of Poland, Norway, the Low Countries, France; ours had supreme confidence in themselves as individuals and that determination which the British race displays in fullest measure when in supreme adversity. One important strategical advantage the Germans enjoyed and skillfully used: their forces were deployed on many and widely spread bases whence they could concentrate upon us in great strengths and with feints and deceptions as to the true points of attack.

By August the *Luftwaffe* had gathered 2669 operational aircraft, comprising 1015 bombers, 346 dive bombers, 933 fighters and 375 heavy fighters. The Fuehrer's Directive No. 17 authorized the intensified air war against England on August 5.

The continuous heavy air fighting of July and early August had been directed upon the Kent promontory and the Channel coast. Goering and his skilled advisers formed the opinion that they must have drawn nearly all our fighter squadrons into this southern struggle. They therefore decided to make a daylight raid on the manufacturing cities north of The Wash. The distance was too great for their first-class fighters, the Me. [Messerschmitt] 109's. They would have to risk their bombers with only escorts from the Me. 110's, which, though they had the range, had nothing like the quality, which was what mattered now.

Accordingly on August 15 about 100 bombers, with an escort of forty Me. 110's, were launched against Tyneside. At the same time a raid of more than 800 planes was sent to pin down our forces in

---

(Bottom left) *Field Marshal Hermann Goering and officers of his staff peer from the French shore of the English Channel toward the distant cliffs of Dover. Goering is the sixth figure from the right in the photograph (taken July 1, 1940).*

the south, where it was thought they were all gathered. But now the dispositions which [Air Chief Marshal Sir Hugh] Dowding had made of the Fighter Command were signally vindicated. The danger had been foreseen. Seven Hurricane or Spitfire squadrons had been withdrawn from the intense struggle in the south to rest in and at the same time to guard the north. These squadrons were able to welcome the assailants as they crossed the coast. Thirty German planes were shot down, most of them heavy bombers (Heinkel 111's, with four trained men in each crew), for a British loss of only two pilots injured. Never again was a daylight raid attempted outside the range of the highest-class fighter protection. Henceforth everything north of The Wash was safe by day.

August 15 was the largest air battle of this period of the war; five major actions were fought on a front of 500 miles. It was indeed a crucial day. In the south all our twenty-two squadrons were engaged, many twice, some three times, and the German losses, added to those in the north, were seventy-six to our thirty-four. This was a recognizable disaster to the German Air Force.

It must have been with anxious minds that the German Air Chiefs measured the consequences of this defeat, which boded ill for the future. The German Air Force, however, had still as its target the port of London, all that immense line of docks with their masses of shipping, and the world's largest city, which did not require much accuracy to hit. On August 20 I could report to Parliament:

The enemy is of course far more numerous than we are. But our new production already largely exceeds his, and the American production is only just beginning to flow in. Our bomber and fighter strengths now, after all this fighting, are larger than they have ever been. We believe that we should be able to continue the air struggle indefinitely, and as long as the enemy pleases, and the longer it continues, the more rapid will be our approach first toward that parity, and then into that superiority, in the air, upon which in large measure the decision of the war depends.

Up till the end of August, Goering did not take an unfavorable view of the air conflict. He and his circle believed that the English ground organization and the

(Above) *This is part of the inferno that was London in the great fire ignited by Goering's bombers in late December 1940. Taken from the top of St. Paul's Cathedral, the picture shows the instant ruin of Paternoster Square at the left. The conflagration blazed most fiercely in this famous business quarter, including Newgate Street, Paternoster Row and Warwick Lane.*

(Right) *Amid the horrors of the blitz, everyday life goes on. On a rubble-strewn street, a fruit vendor's homemade sign boasts: "Our oranges came through Musso's lake"—referring to Mussolini's Mediterranean where, even in those dark days, the British Navy had defeated Italy's Naval squadrons.*

(Far right) *At the first wail of sirens, people sought shelter wherever they happened to be. Here English children find it in a trench. City dwellers in southern England grew accustomed to the roar of bombers and the deafening explosions as the life-and-death air war was fought overhead.*

aircraft industry and the fighting strength of the R.A.F. had already been severely damaged. They estimated that since August 8 we had lost 1115 aircraft against the German losses of 467.

There was a spell of fine weather in September, and the *Luftwaffe* hoped for decisive results. Heavy attacks fell upon our airdrome installations around London; on the night of the 6th, sixty-eight aircraft attacked London, followed on the 7th by the first large-scale attack of about 300. On this and succeeding days, during which our antiaircraft guns were doubled in number, very hard and continuous air fighting took place over the capital, and the *Luftwaffe* was still confident through its overestimation of our losses. But we now know that the German Naval Staff ...wrote in their diary on September 10:

There is no sign of the defeat of the enemy's Air Force over southern England and in the Channel area, and this is vital to a further judgment of the situation.... We have not yet attained the operational conditions which the Naval Staff stipulated to the Supreme Command as being essential for the enterprise, namely, undisputed air supremacy in the Channel area and the elimination of the enemy's air activity in the assembly area of the German Naval forces and ancillary shipping.

As by this time Hitler had been persuaded by Goering that the major attack on London would be decisive, the Naval Staff did not venture to appeal to the Supreme Command; but their uneasiness continued, and on the 12th they reached this somber conclusion:

The air war is being conducted as an "absolute air war," without regard to the present requirements of the naval war, and outside the framework of "Operation Sea Lion." In its present form the air war cannot assist preparations for "Sea Lion," which are predominantly in the hands of the Navy. In particular, one cannot discern any effort on the part of the *Luftwaffe* to engage the units of the British Fleet, which are now able to operate almost unmolested in the Channel, and this will prove extremely dangerous to the transportation.... Up to now the in-

tensified air war has not contributed toward the landing operation; hence for operational and military reasons the execution of the landing cannot yet be considered.

In the fighting between August 24 and September 6, the scales had tilted against Fighter Command. During these crucial days the Germans had continuously applied powerful forces against the airfields of south and southeast England. Their object was to break down the day fighter defense of the capital, which they were impatient to attack. Far more important to us than the protection of London from terror bombing were the functioning and articulation of these airfields and the squadrons working from them.

In the life-and-death struggle of the two air forces, this was a decisive phase. We never thought of the struggle in terms of the defense of London or any other place, but only who won in the air. There was much anxiety at Fighter Headquarters at Stanmore, and particularly at the headquarters of No. 11 Fighter Group at Uxbridge. Extensive damage had been done to five of the group's forward airfields, and also to the six sector stations. If the enemy had persisted in heavy attacks against the adjacent sectors and damaged their operations rooms or telephone communications, the whole intricate organization of Fighter Command might have been broken down. It was therefore with a sense of relief that Fighter Command felt the German attack turn onto London on September 7, and concluded that the enemy had changed his plan.

This same period (August 24 to September 6) had seriously drained the strength of Fighter Command as a whole. The Command had lost in this fortnight 103 pilots killed and 128 seriously wounded, while 466 Spitfires and Hurricanes had been destroyed or seriously damaged. Out of a total pilot strength of about 1000, nearly a quarter had been lost. Their places could only be filled by 260 new, ardent, but inexperienced pilots drawn from training units, in many cases before their full courses were complete. The night attacks on London for ten days after September 7 struck at the London docks and railway centers and killed and wounded many civilians, but they were in effect for us a breathing space of which we had the utmost need.

We must take September 15 as the culminating date. On this day the *Luftwaffe,* after two heavy

The indomitable Winston Churchill inspects the ruins of historic Coventry Cathedral after the heavy German air bombing of November 14–15, 1940. The Cathedral, almost completely gutted by explosions and fire, was left in this state as a memorial of the war.

attacks on the 14th, made its greatest concentrated effort in a resumed daylight attack on London.

It was one of the decisive battles of the war, and, like the Battle of Waterloo, it was on a Sunday. I was at Chequers [the official country residence of British prime ministers, in Buckinghamshire]. I had already on several occasions visited the headquarters of No. 11 Fighter Group in order to witness the conduct of an air battle, when not much had happened. However, the weather on this day seemed suitable to the enemy, and accordingly I drove over to Uxbridge and arrived at the Group Headquarters. Number 11 Group comprised no fewer than twenty-five squadrons covering the whole of Essex, Kent, Sussex and Hampshire, and all the approaches across them to London.

My wife and I were taken down to the bombproof Operations Room, fifty feet below ground. All the ascendancy of the Hurricanes and Spitfires would have been fruitless but for this system of underground control centers and telephone cables. . . . In the south of England there were at this time No. 11 Group HQ and six subordinate fighter station centers. All these were under heavy stress.

The Group Operations Room was like a small theater, about sixty feet across, and with two stories. We took our seats in the dress circle. Below us was the large-scale map table, around which perhaps twenty highly trained young men and women, with their telephone assistants, were assembled. Opposite to us, covering the entire wall, where the theater curtain would be, was a gigantic blackboard divided into six columns with electric bulbs, for the six fighter stations, each of their squadrons having a subcolumn of its own, and also divided by lateral lines.

Thus, the lowest row of bulbs showed as they were lighted the squadrons which were "standing by" at two minutes' notice, the next row those "at readiness," five minutes, then "at available," twenty minutes, then those which had taken off, the next row those which had reported having seen the enemy, the next—with red lights—those which were in action, and the top row those which were returning home. On the left-hand side, in a kind of glass stage box, were the four or five officers whose duty it was to weigh and measure the information received from our Observer Corps, which at this time numbered upward of 50,000 men, women and youths. Radar was still in its infancy, but it gave warning of raids approaching our coast, and

the observers, with field glasses and portable telephones, were our main source of information about raiders flying overland. Thousands of messages were therefore received during an action.

On the right hand was another glass stage box containing Army officers who reported the action of our antiaircraft batteries, of which at this time in the Command there were 200. At night it was of vital importance to stop these batteries firing over certain areas in which our fighters would be closing with the enemy.

"I don't know," said Air Vice Marshal [Keith Rodney] Park [Commander of No. 11 Fighter Group] as we went down, "whether anything will happen today. At present all is quiet." However, after a quarter of an hour the raid plotters began to move about. An attack of "40 plus" was reported to be coming from the German stations in the Dieppe area. The bulbs along the bottom of the wall display panel began to glow as various squadrons came to "stand by." Then in quick succession "20 plus," "40 plus" signals were received, and it was evident that a serious battle impended. On both sides the air began to fill.

One after another signals came in, "40 plus," "60 plus"; there was even an "80 plus." On the floor table below us the movement of all the waves of attack was marked by pushing disks forward from minute to minute along different lines of approach, while on the blackboard facing us the rising lights showed our fighter squadrons getting into the air, till there were only four or five left "at readiness."

These air battles, on which so much depended, lasted little more than an hour from the first encounter. The enemy had ample strength to send out new waves of attack, and our squadrons, having gone all out to gain the upper air, would have to refuel after seventy or eighty minutes, or land to rearm after a five-minute engagement. If, at this moment of refueling or rearming, the enemy were able to arrive with fresh unchallenged squadrons, some of our fighters could be destroyed on the ground.

Presently the red bulbs showed that the majority of our squadrons was engaged. A subdued hum arose from the floor, where the busy plotters pushed their disks to and fro in accordance with the swiftly changing situation. Air Vice Marshal Park gave general directions for the disposition of his fighter force, which were translated into detailed orders to each fighter station by a youngish officer in the center of the dress circle, at whose side I sat. He gave the orders for the individual squadrons to ascend and patrol as the result of the final information which appeared on the map table.

The Air Marshal himself walked up and down behind, watching with vigilant eye every move in the game, supervising his junior executive hand, and only occasionally intervening with some decisive order, usually to reinforce a threatened area. In a little while all our squadrons were fighting, and some had already begun to return for fuel. All were in the air. The lower line of bulbs was out. There was not one squadron left in reserve. At this moment Park spoke to Dowding at Stanmore, asking for three squadrons from No. 12 Group to be put at his disposal.... This was done.

The young officer, to whom this seemed a matter of routine, continued to give his orders, in accordance with the general directions of his Group Commander, in a calm, low monotone, and the three reinforcing squadrons were soon absorbed. I became conscious of the anxiety of the Commander, who now stood still behind his subordinate's chair. Hitherto I had watched in silence. I now asked, "What other reserves have we?" "There are none," said Air Vice Marshal Park. The odds were great; our margins small; the stakes infinite.

Another five minutes passed, and most of our squadrons had now descended to refuel. In many cases our resources could not give them overhead protection. Then it appeared that the enemy was going home. The shifting of the disks on the table below showed a continuous eastward movement of German bombers and fighters. No new attack appeared. In another ten minutes the action was ended. We climbed the stairways which led to the surface, and almost as we emerged the all clear sounded.

It was evident that the enemy had everywhere pierced our defenses. Many scores of German bombers, with their fighter escort, had been reported over London. About a dozen had been brought down while I was below, but no picture of the results of the battle or of the damage or losses could as yet be obtained.

Although postwar information has shown that the enemy's losses on this day were only fifty-six [not 183, as was believed at the time], September 15 was the crux of the Battle of Britain. That same night our Bomber Command attacked in strength the shipping in the ports from Boulogne to Antwerp. At Antwerp, particularly heavy losses were inflicted. On September 17, as we now know, the Fuehrer decided to postpone "Sea Lion" indefinitely. It was not till October 12 that the invasion was formally called off till the following spring. In July 1941 it was postponed again by Hitler till the spring of 1942, "by which time the Russian campaign will be completed." This was a vain but an important imagining. On February 13, 1942, Admiral [Erich] Raeder had his final interview on "Sea Lion" and got Hitler to agree to a complete "stand-down." Thus perished "Operation Sea Lion." And September 15 may stand as the date of its demise.

Yet the Battle of London was still to be fought out. Although invasion had been called off, it was not till September 27 that Goering gave up hope that his method of winning the war might succeed. In October, though London received its full share, the German effort was spread by day and night in frequent small-scale attacks on many places. Concentration of effort gave way to dispersion; the battle of attrition began. Attrition! But whose?

In cold blood, with the knowledge of the aftertime, we may study the actual losses of the British and German Air Forces in what may well be deemed one of the decisive battles of the world.

[The following totals are from a detailed chart of aircraft losses in the Battle of Britain from July 10 through October 31, 1940:
British aircraft lost by R.A.F. (complete write-off or missing) 915
Enemy aircraft claimed by the R.A.F. and other British sources 2698
Enemy aircraft actually destroyed according to German records ....1733]

No doubt we were always oversanguine in our estimates of enemy scalps. In the upshot we got two to one of the German assailants, instead of three to one, as we believed and declared. But this was enough. The Royal Air Force, far from being destroyed, was triumphant. The stamina and valor of our fighter pilots remained unconquerable and supreme. Thus Britain was saved. Well might I say in the House of Commons, "Never in the field of human conflict was so much owed by so many to so few."

THE VOICE FROM LONDON

BY EDWARD R. MURROW

Both before and after the United States entered the war, millions of Americans saw the conflict from the vantage point of London—through the eyes of a great American radio reporter. Along with his gift for the vivid word and image, Edward R. Murrow brought to his broadcasts a rare dimension of understanding and compassion for the average person caught in the maelstrom of war.

September 3, 1939

Forty-five minutes ago the Prime Minister [Neville Chamberlain] stated that a state of war existed between Great Britain and Germany. Air-raid instructions were immediately broadcast, and almost directly following that broadcast, air-raid warning sirens screamed through the quiet calm of this Sabbath morning. There were planes in the sky—whose, we couldn't be sure. Now we're sitting quite comfortably underground. We're told that the all-clear signal has been sounded in the streets, but it hasn't yet been heard in this building. In a few minutes we shall hope to go up into the sunlight and see what has happened. It may have been only a rehearsal. London may not have been the objective—or may have been.

December 31, 1939

Tonight Britain says farewell without regret to this year of grace 1939. When the year began there seemed some reason for hope. Prime Minister Chamberlain was claiming that peace in our time was assured. He was preparing to go to Rome for conferences with Signor Mussolini. Editorial writers were telling us one year ago today that Britain had been near to war in 1938, but there were brighter prospects for 1939. The big news in London at this time last year was that Germany had decided to build more submarines, that she would seek parity with Britain. London papers told their readers that this action need cause no alarm. Germany was acting in accordance with existing treaties, and anyway she probably wanted more submarines to meet the threat of Russian Naval expansion.

One year ago today many writers were predicting a year of peace and prosperity. The new year was greeted with horns, sirens and bells. There were gay parties in London's hotels, and families were together. Of course, there was war news a year ago, but it all seemed very remote to Londoners. There were pictures of exploding mines in our papers, but they were halfway around the world—in the war between China and Japan. Franco's bombers raided Barcelona twice, Italian forces [aiding the Nationalists] south of Lérida were forced to retreat. But even the war in Spain seemed remote.

The end of 1939 finds Britain near the end of the fourth month of a war which has confounded the experts. Roughly 1 million men are under arms in Britain and hundreds of thousands more will probably be asked to register on Tuesday of next week. Homes have been broken up by evacuation. The cost of this war cannot be conveyed by mere figures. There are tens of thousands of men and women manning searchlights and antiaircraft guns, fire engines and ambulances, all over Britain. Many businesses have been ruined. Prices continue to rise. There are no bright lights this year, and there will be no sirens or horns sounded at midnight tonight, lest they be confused with air-raid warnings.

May 10, 1940

At nine o'clock tonight a tired old man spoke to the nation from No. 10 Downing Street. He sat behind a big oval table in the Cabinet Room, where so many fateful decisions have been taken during the three years that he has directed the policy of His Majesty's Government. Neville Chamberlain announced his resignation.

Winston Churchill, who has held more political offices than any living man, is now Prime Minister. He is a man without a party. For many years he sat in the

House of Commons, a rather lonesome and often belli-cose figure, voicing unheeded warnings of the rising tide of German military strength. Now, at the age of sixty-five, Winston Churchill, plump, bald, with mas-sive round shoulders, is, for the first time in his varied career of journalist, historian and politician, the Prime Minister of Great Britain. He now takes over the su-preme direction of Britain's war effort at a time when the war is rapidly moving toward Britain's doorstep. Mr. Churchill's critics have said that he is inclined to be impulsive and at times vindictive. But in the tradi-tion of British politics he will be given his chance. He will probably *take* chances. But if he brings victory, his place in history is assured

June 2, 1940

Yesterday I spent several hours at what may be, to-night or next week, Britain's first line of defense, an airfield on the southeast coast. The German bases weren't more than ten minutes' flying time away — across that ditch that has protected Britain and condi-tioned the thinking of Britishers for centuries. I talked with pilots as they came back from Dunkirk. They stripped off their light jackets, glanced at a few bullet holes in wings or fuselage, and as their ground crews were refueling motors and replenishing the guns with ammunition, we sat on the ground and talked.

I can tell you what those boys told me. They were the cream of the youth of Britain. As we sat there, they were waiting to take off again. They talked of their own work, discussing the German Air Force with all the casualness of Sunday morning quarterbacks talking over yesterday's football game. There were no nerves, no profanity and no heroics. There was no swagger about those boys in wrinkled and stained uni-forms. The movies do that sort of thing much more dramatically than it is in real life.

August 18, 1940

I spent five hours this afternoon on the outskirts of London. Bombs fell out there today. It is indeed sur-prising how little damage a bomb will do unless, of course, it scores a direct hit. But I found that one bombed house looks pretty much like another bombed house.

It's about the people I'd like to talk, the little people who live in those little houses, who have no uniforms and get no decorations for bravery. Those men whose only uniform was a tin hat were digging unexploded bombs out of the ground this afternoon. There were two women who gossiped across the narrow strip of tired brown grass that separated their two houses. They didn't have to open their kitchen windows in order to converse. The glass had been blown out. There was a little man with a pipe in his mouth who walked up and looked at a bombed house and said, "One fell there, and that's all." Those people were calm and courageous. About an hour after the all clear had sounded, people were sitting in deck chairs on their lawns, reading the Sunday papers. The girls in light cheap dresses were strolling along the streets. There was no bravado, no loud voices, only a quiet acceptance of the situation. To me those people were incredibly brave and calm. They are the unknown heroes of this war.

This afternoon I saw a military maneuver that I shall remember for a long time, a company of women dressed in Royal Air Force blue marching in close order. Most of them were girls with blond hair and plenty of make-up. They marched well, right arms thrust forward and snapped smartly down after the fashion of the Guards. They swung through a gate into an airdrome that had been heavily bombed only a few hours before. Some of them were probably frightened, but every head was up. Their ranks were steady and most of them were smiling. They were the clerks, the cooks and waitresses going on duty. I was told that three members of the Women's Aux-iliary Air Force had been killed in a raid there this morning.

September 13, 1940

This is London at 3:30 in the morning. This has been what might be called a routine night — air-raid alarm at about nine o'clock and intermittent bombing ever since. I have the impression that more high ex-plosives and fewer incendiaries have been used to-night. Only two small fires can be seen on the horizon. Again the Germans have been sending their bombers over singly or in pairs. The antiaircraft barrage has been fierce but sometimes there have been periods of twenty minutes when London has been silent. Then the big red buses would start up and move on till the guns began working again.

The silence is almost hard to bear. One becomes accustomed to rattling windows and the distant sound

English workmen dig trenches for air-raid shelters in London's Hampstead Heath during the Munich crisis of September 1938—a full year before the outbreak of World War II. Anticipating the eventual onset of hostilities, the British began early to organize the A.R.P. (Air Raid Precautions). Civil defense measures such as blackouts and air-raid wardens saved many lives when the bombs began to fall.

A mother and her young son sit in the ruins of their home in England after an air raid and manage to prepare a warm meal. The ability of the English people to withstand the terrors of the Nazi blitz proved to be a vital psychological factor in winning the Battle of Britain.

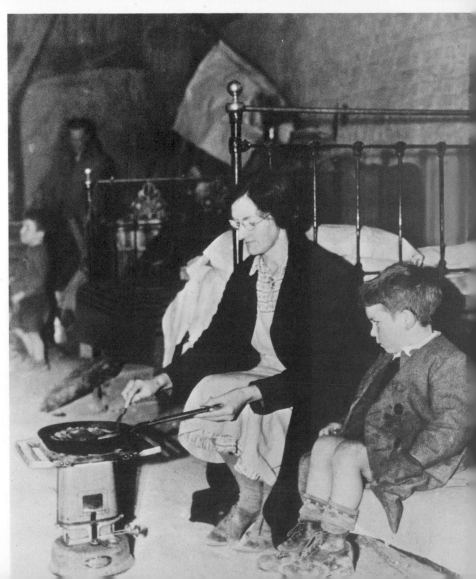

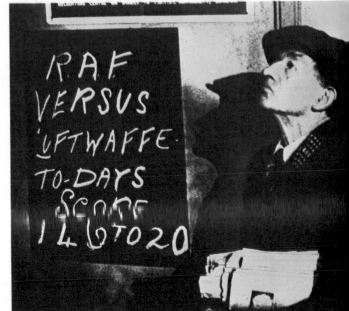

(Left) *Seeking scrap iron to help the war effort, Londoners remove gratings and fences.* (Below) *In proud defiance of the constant bombing, the people kept a daily score of the air fight: 146 enemy planes lost to only twenty R.A.F. aircraft.*

The grim aftermath of a raid: Londoners remove one of their dead from a devastated street.

of bombs, and then there comes a silence that can be felt. You know the sound will return. You wait, and then it starts again. That waiting is bad. It gives you a chance to imagine things. I have been walking tonight — there is a full moon, and the dirty-gray buildings appear white. The stars, the empty windows are hidden. It's a beautiful and lonesome city where men and women and children are trying to snatch a few hours' sleep underground.

October 10, 1940

This is London, ten minutes before five in the morning. Tonight's raid has been widespread. London is around the outskirts. People have been reported from more than fifty districts. Raiders have been over Wales in the west, the Midlands, Liverpool, the southwest and northeast. So far as London is concerned, the outskirts appear to have suffered the heaviest pounding. The attack has decreased in intensity since the moon faded from the sky.

All the fires were quickly brought under control. That's a common phrase in the morning communiqués. I've seen how it's done, spent a night with the London fire brigade. For three hours after the night attack got going, I shivered in a sandbag crow's nest atop a tall building near the Thames. It was one of the many fire-observation posts. There was an old gun barrel mounted above a round table marked off like a compass. A stick of incendiaries bounced off rooftops about three miles away. The observer took a sight on a point where the first one fell, swung his gunsight along the line of bombs and took another reading at the end of the line of fire. Then he picked up his telephone and shouted above the half gale that was blowing up there: "Stick of incendiaries — between one-ninety and two-twenty — about three miles away."

Five minutes later a German bomber came boring down the river. We could see his exhaust trail like a pale ribbon stretched straight across the sky. Half a mile downstream there were two eruptions and then a third, all close together. The first two looked as though some giant had thrown a huge basket of flaming oranges high in the air. The third was just a balloon of

fire enclosed in black smoke above the housetops. The observer didn't bother with his gunsight and indicator for that one — just reached for his night glasses, took one quick look, picked up his telephone and said, "Two high explosives and one oil bomb," and named the street where they had fallen.

There was a small fire going, off to our left. Suddenly sparks showered up from it as though someone had punched the middle of a huge campfire with a tree trunk. Again the gunsight swung around, the bearing was read and the report went down the telephone lines: "There is something in high explosives on that fire at fifty-nine."

There was peace and quiet inside for twenty minutes. Then a shower of incendiaries came down far in the distance. They didn't fall in a line. They looked like flashes from an electric train on a wet night, only the engineer was drunk and driving his train in circles through the streets.

One sight at the middle of the flashes, and our observer reported laconically: "Breadbasket at ninety covers a couple of miles."

Half an hour later a string of fire bombs fell right beside the Thames. Their white glare was reflected in the black lazy water near the banks and faded out in midstream where the moon cut a golden swath broken only by the arches of famous bridges. We could see little men shoveling those fire bombs into the river. One burned for a few minutes like a beacon, right in the middle of a bridge. Finally those white flames all went out.

December 25, 1940

Christmas Day began in London nearly an hour ago. The church bells did not ring at midnight. When they ring again, it will be to announce invasion. And if they ring, the British are ready. Tonight, as on every other night, the rooftop watchers are peering out across the fantastic forest of London's chimney pots. The antiaircraft gunners stand ready. And all along the coast of this island, the observers revolve in their reclining chairs, listening for the sound of German planes. The fire fighters and the ambulance drivers are waiting, too. The blackout stretches from Birmingham to Bethlehem, but tonight over Britain the skies are clear.

This is not a merry Christmas in London. I heard that phrase only twice in the last three days.

London's Underground (subway) network was used as a raid shelter and proved the most effective single life-saving element throughout the Battle of Britain. The Liverpool station, with 6000 bunks, even provided a children's playroom, a library and dance instruction. This scene shows the Elephant and Castle station.

THE HUNTERS AND THE HUNTED

Only the dogged persistence of the British Navy and a disabling torpedo hit by a carrier airplane brought an end to the greatest sea chase in naval history. These two accounts reveal from the British and the German viewpoints the dramatic pursuit and finish of the mighty German battleship Bismarck.

The Sinking of the "Bismarck"

BY CAPT. RUSSELL GRENFELL, R.N.

In the middle of May 1941, Great Britain's fortunes were low. At sea, sinkings had reached crisis proportions; the German Naval Command was attacking Britain's sea-lanes not only with U-boats and aircraft but also with surface vessels. And now word had come that two large German warships, heavily screened and accompanied by eleven merchant vessels, were steaming northward in the Kattegat. One of the warships was believed to be the powerful new battleship *Bismarck.*

Were the enemy warships planning to break out into the Atlantic? Since this offered the greatest possible menace, the British assumed that it would be attempted and based their own plans accordingly.

All the exits from the North Sea by which the Germans might break out must be guarded, a necessity which confronted the British with a vast complexity of search-and-chase operations, notoriously expensive of ships.

Sir John Tovey, Commander in Chief of the Home Fleet, had a force of 2 battleships (*King George V* and *Prince of Wales*), 2 battle cruisers (*Hood* and *Repulse*) and 1 aircraft carrier (*Victorious*) to give battle to the *Bismarck.* The odds of five ships to one look satisfactory. But the *Bismarck* was larger than any British battleship; she carried a main armament of eight 15-inch guns—one inch larger than those of the latest British battleships; and she was believed to be as fast as, or faster than, any British capital ship.

The British big ships were by no means of similar high quality. The *Repulse* was twenty-five years old, had two guns less than the *Bismarck* and was weakly armored and of short fuel endurance. The *Hood,* although powerful, was over twenty years old. The *Prince of Wales,* conversely, was too new. Two of her turrets had been installed just three weeks before, and there had not been time to work the ship's company up to battle efficiency. The *Victorious* had just taken on her aircraft, the first time that the reservist pilots had ever landed on a carrier's deck. Thus Admiral Tovey had only one ship, the *King George V,* that could be regarded as a fair match for the *Bismarck.*

The Admiral decided to divide his heavy ships into two forces to cover the exits into the Atlantic. The *Hood* and *Prince of Wales* would steam north; his own flagship, the *King George V,* the *Victorious* and the *Repulse* would cover the passages to the Faeroe Islands to the south.

There remained the question of when to send out these two squadrons. Fuel supplies might play a decisive part in a chase that could well cover many hundreds of miles. If the British interceptor forces sailed too early and patrolled fruitlessly while the *Bismarck* was still in harbor, they would be that much short of fuel when she did emerge. On the other hand, if they delayed sailing too long, she might get out before them, with too long a start to be caught.

At 1:15 p.m. on May 21, a pilot, searching the Norwegian coastline in a special Spitfire of the Coastal Command Photographic Reconnaissance Unit, sighted and photographed two warships in a secluded fjord near Bergen. One of them was identified as the *Bismarck,* the other was a cruiser which later proved to be the *Prinz Eugen.*

At midnight that night, since the *Bismarck* had not been sighted again, Admiral Tovey sent the *Hood* and her squadron on their way north. The following day, May 22, was one of bad flying weather and of suspense. But at 7:45 p.m., when the Admiral received an aerial-reconnaissance report that the *Bismarck* and her accompanying cruiser were no longer at Bergen, he prepared to take his own squadron to sea immediately. He also sent the cruiser *Suffolk* to reinforce the cruiser *Norfolk,* already on patrol in Denmark Strait.

At seven o'clock on the evening of May 23, Capt. R. M. Ellis was standing on the bridge of the *Suffolk*. Continuing bad weather had prevented any assistance from aircraft in his patrol. Most of Denmark Strait was covered in fog and mist, but there was a lane of clear water about three miles wide just below the edge of an Arctic ice pack. The *Suffolk* was steering southwestward in this lane, close to the mist. At 7:22 p.m. a lookout sighted the *Bismarck* and with her the cruiser *Prinz Eugen*. They were about 14,000 yards away, a dangerously close range to enemy guns that could shoot as far as 40,000 yards. Captain Ellis put his wheel over on the instant to make for the fog and sent out the enemy-report signal.

Keeping radar contact, he maneuvered in the mist to allow the *Bismarck* to pass him so that he would be able to take up a shadowing position behind her. Watching intently on the radar screen the white dots that represented the two enemy ships, he saw them cross his course to the northward, steaming fast. Captain Ellis then steered back into the open, saw the Germans fifteen miles ahead and set course to shadow them, sending out a string of wireless signals as he went.

Deep in the mist, the *Norfolk* took in those signals. Her commander, Capt. A. J. L. Phillips, ordered his ship's course altered to close with the enemy's reported position. At 8:30 p.m., after an hour's hard steaming, the *Norfolk* suddenly ran out of the mist and sighted the *Bismarck* and the *Prinz Eugen* about six miles away, steaming toward her on the port bow. Captain Phillips put the wheel hard astarboard to get back into the mist and made smoke to cover his withdrawal. This time the *Bismarck* was on the alert and opened a very accurate fire. Three 15-inch salvos straddled the *Norfolk*, and another came down in her wake. By immense good fortune she was not hit and got back into the mist undamaged.

After she had achieved this sanctuary, like the *Suffolk* she maneuvered to take a shadowing position well behind the enemy. She stationed herself off the German ships' port quarter, so that they could not slip away by turning in that direction. Thus the pursuit continued, chasers and chased rushing at nearly full speed through the icy waters of Denmark Strait in the half-light of the Arctic night, in and out of the fog banks, snow and rain squalls.

Meanwhile, Vice Adm. Lancelot Holland's squadron of the *Hood* and *Prince of Wales* with six destroyers had been steaming hard to cut the enemy off. At 5:35 a.m. on May 24, Holland sighted the two German ships and changed course to close with them. Officers and men, who had been at their battle stations since shortly after midnight, prepared to swing the big, silent turrets into action.

In the *Norfolk* and the *Suffolk* excitement mounted. Now that the big ships had arrived, the cruisers' object had been successfully achieved, and their tired officers and men prepared to watch the destruction of the enemy. Little did they realize what they were about to see.

From now on, things happened very quickly. When the range was down to 25,000 yards the *Hood* and the *Prince of Wales* opened fire on the *Bismarck*. The *Bismarck* and the *Prinz Eugen* at once replied. Those in the *Prince of Wales* noted, not without relief, that both German ships were firing at the *Hood*.

The principal guideposts in modern naval gun battles are the splashes made by shells hitting the water. These splashes leap up to a great height—in the case of large shells to about 200 feet—and are the means whereby gun-control officers know where their shots are going and make the appropriate corrections. What the control officer wants is a "straddle": that is to say, one or more splashes over and one or more splashes short. He then knows that he is on target and that there may be one or more hits. As a rule, he will not see those hits. With delayed-action fuses, a shell may penetrate deep into a ship's hull before exploding, and the flash will be invisible from outside.

The *Prinz Eugen* scored the first hit in less than a minute. A large fire broke out by the *Hood*'s mainmast, spread rapidly forward and blazed up high; then it died down a bit and seemed to pulsate up and down. The range meanwhile was coming down rapidly. The *Bismarck* had obtained several straddles on the *Hood*, and had very probably hit her.

Suddenly the horrified spectators in the British cruisers saw a vast eruption of flame leap upward between the *Hood*'s masts to a height of many hundreds of feet. The volcanic upshoot of fire lasted but a second or two; and when it disappeared the place where the Hood had been was covered by an enormous column of smoke. Through it the bow and stern of the ship could just be discerned, each rising steeply up as the central part of the ship collapsed. The *Hood* had blown up in the middle, broken in half, and in a couple of minutes the battle cruiser had completely disappeared.

The *Prince of Wales* now came in for the full blast of the enemy's ferocity. A towering wall of water leaped out of the sea close at hand, where a 15-inch salvo had landed. It was swiftly followed by salvos of the *Bismarck*'s secondary-armament, 6-inch shells which, mingling with the *Prinz Eugen*'s 8-inch shells, began to fall one on top of the other with whirlwind rapidity. The din was tremendous.

Every now and then the *Prince of Wales* shuddered as something hit her, and those in the after-control became aware of black smoke drifting past them from a fire farther forward. In the midst of this turmoil, a 15-inch shell came streaking down and smashed through the bridge, exploding just as it emerged on the other side. The bridge instantly became a shambles, every officer and man killed or wounded except Capt. John C. Leach and the Chief Yeoman of Signals.

To make matters worse, the newness of the ship was now telling against her. Small mechanical breakdowns kept occurring in the turrets, one gun and another missing a salvo. The ship continued to take hits. Two shells pierced her side at the waterline and a number of compartments were flooded. Captain Leach, who by now had moved to the lower bridge, decided to break off the engagement and wait for reinforcement. He retired out of action behind a smoke screen.

The *Bismarck* made no attempt to follow, although she did not show any sign of damage. The only evidence that suggested she might have been hit was a conspicuous pillar of black smoke that shot up out of her funnel after about three minutes of battle.

The loss of the *Hood* was a heavy blow to the British. A whole generation of Naval men had grown up to regard her as the most powerful ship in the world. And in her first battle she had disintegrated after having been under fire only a few minutes. Only three survivors were ever found.

The *Bismarck*'s shooting was brilliant, far better than the British Navy could then show. Her fire control was extremely good and her spread of salvos very small indeed. Her achievement was remarkable. Faced by a two-to-one enemy superiority, in five or six salvos she had blown up one ship and in twelve or so more had driven the other ship out of action.

The defeat of the *Hood*'s detachment changed the situation in an instant. If it had been necessary to sink the *Bismarck* before the catastrophe of the *Hood*'s de-

struction, it was doubly so afterward. Although the German battleship was later reported to be leaving a broad track of oil behind her, she was now continuing southwest at full steam, apparently unscathed. There were at this time ten convoys at sea in the Atlantic, some of which had only a screen of light vessels for protection. This potentially disastrous situation spurred the Admiralty on to more drastic action.

Vice Admiral Sir James Somerville's Force H—consisting of the battle cruiser *Renown,* the aircraft carrier *Ark Royal,* the cruiser *Sheffield* and six destroyers—was at Gibraltar, 1500 miles or so to the southward, to seal the western exit of the Mediterranean against the Italian Fleet. Now it was decided to bring Force H against the *Bismarck.* Hundreds of miles to the northwest in mid-Atlantic, the battleship *Ramillies* was ordered away from her convoy to close and intercept the enemy from the westward. About 500 miles from the Irish coast, the battleship *Rodney* was similarly detached from a convoy and ordered to intercept.

Within six hours of the *Hood*'s destruction, 2 additional battleships, 1 battle cruiser, 1 aircraft carrier, 3 cruisers and 9 destroyers had joined in the chase. A concentration was thus being arranged which, for its dramatic character and for the vastness of the area involved, had few, if any, rivals.

The *Norfolk* and *Suffolk* went on shadowing the *Bismarck* after the *Hood* had been sunk. The *Prince of Wales* was steaming near the *Norfolk,* and some 300 miles to the eastward Sir John Tovey on the *King George V* was pushing on toward the enemy at his squadron's best speed. With him were the aircraft carrier *Victorious* and the *Repulse.*

For some hours the weather was clear, and the cruisers kept the enemy ships in sight at fifteen to eighteen miles' distance. About 11 a.m., however, banks of mist were sighted ahead. Both cruisers closed in as much as they dared, but about noon they lost sight of the enemy in mist and drizzle. Since the radar then in use had a range of only about thirteen miles, contact during the afternoon was intermittent.

Captain Ellis of the *Suffolk* had been expecting that the *Bismarck* might endeavor to turn on one or the other of the shadowers under cover of low visibility and trap it at close range. Now at 6:30 p.m. his radar began to report the range as rapidly decreasing, and, alert against an ambush, he put his wheel over and increased to full speed. As his ship swung around, the

Bismarck appeared out of the mist and opened fire with all her guns. Captain Ellis ordered smoke to be made and managed to hide behind it.

This brief action took both ships over toward the *Norfolk* and the *Prince of Wales*. The latter opened fire in support of the *Suffolk,* whereupon the *Bismarck* made away at high speed. (It is now known that the *Bismarck*'s sally was made to cover the withdrawal of the *Prinz Eugen,* which was to make her separate way to an oiler for refueling, and then, eventually, to the port of Brest.)

Thus far the British had managed to follow the *Bismarck*'s course. But Sir John Tovey was worried lest she escape by the use of high speed during the night. The only means of slowing her up before darkness set in was to attack with the *Victorious*' aircraft. If they could only get some torpedoes into her and so inflict underwater damage, they might reduce her speed sufficiently to prevent any inconvenient spurts during the night.

Before dark, then, nine airplanes from the *Victorious* went after the *Bismarck* from a distance of 100 miles, almost the extreme limit of their range. This was the first occasion in history of a battleship at sea being attacked by carrier-borne aircraft. The crews, most of them untrained for sea work, pressed home their attack with great gallantry. All nine planes dropped their torpedoes, and all returned to the carrier. However, only one torpedo was seen to take effect, and the *Bismarck* was not slowed down.

Altogether, the day was one of painful defeat and frustration. Moreover, at midnight the *King George V*'s destroyers had to leave for Iceland. The long high-speed dash had depleted their fuel tanks too much for them to remain at sea. The *Repulse* would also soon have to leave for refueling. It was a grim reversal of fortune since the corresponding time the day before, when the *Bismarck*'s career seemed as good as over. But there was even worse to come. For at 3 a.m. on May 25 the shadowing cruiser *Suffolk* lost contact with the *Bismarck*. She was not resighted until 31½ hours later.

It was a period of mounting tension, of desperate speculation as to the *Bismarck*'s course, of worry over dwindling fuel supplies, above all of fear lest the British ships were steaming away from the enemy instead of toward her.

Finally the *Bismarck* was spotted at 10:30 a.m.

May 26 by aircraft of the Coastal Command. But meanwhile a long deviation toward the North Sea had cost the British much precious headway. From having been practically level with the enemy, they were now far behind her.

The *Bismarck* had a lead of about fifty miles over the *King George V* and, moreover, would soon be under German air cover. If she maintained her going speed of about twenty knots, she could be within German bomber range by daylight the next day. In order to bring her into action at all, her speed would have to be considerably reduced on this very day.

But how could this be done? Only by torpedoes. The one real hope lay in the *Ark Royal's* aircraft. Twenty-four hours or so earlier Force H had been 1500 miles away. Now pushing northward at full speed, this force might well be the only obstacle to the *Bismarck*'s arrival in harbor.

When the wireless message came that the *Bismarck* had been found again, fifteen airplanes on the *Ark Royal* were prepared for the torpedo strike. At 2:30 p.m. the fly-off began. The *Bismarck* was forty miles away. The crews were told that no other ship was anywhere near.

The weather had been deteriorating all day, and while the air strike was still in preparation, Admiral Somerville had ordered the cruiser *Sheffield* to find and shadow the *Bismarck*. The order was flashed by signal searchlight and went only to the *Sheffield*. The *Ark Royal* never noticed her departure.

The striking force flew off a little later. The crews, flying through rain and mist, picked up a ship on their radar in roughly the expected position. Assuming it was the *Bismarck,* they pressed home the attack. It is hardly surprising that in that tense moment they should have failed to recognize the *Sheffield*.

On the *Sheffield,* Captain Larcom had received Admiral Somerville's signals that the air striking force had taken off, so he was not startled when the planes came in sight. As he turned his glasses toward them, however, he realized suddenly that they were diving down to attack his ship. Instantly he rang for full speed and put his wheel over to confuse the attackers' aim. Not a gun was fired by the *Sheffield,* and her officers and men watched in silence as the torpedoes dropped toward the water.

The first fell into the sea with a heavy splash, and the impotent observers braced themselves. A moment later their attention was focused on something even more arresting. As the second torpedo touched the water, it detonated with a thunderous roar. The next did the same thing. The torpedo heads had been armed with magnetic pistols, and it was plain that these were going off on hitting the water.

Of the remaining torpedoes, three exploded innocuously. And three airplane crews realized that a mistake was being made and withheld their torpedoes. Thus there were only six or seven dangerous torpedoes in the water for the *Sheffield* to contend with. Captain Larcom swung the ship one way and another to avoid them, with such skill that all passed harmlessly by.

It was a gloomy set of airmen who returned to the carrier, but they were to have another chance at the *Bismarck*. The planes were refueled and more torpedoes made ready. By 7 p.m. the striking force was again up on deck and ranged for takeoff. It was still blowing hard. Visibility was variable, the cloud ceiling was at 600 feet or less, and large rainstorms were sweeping across the sea. As the planes took off, everyone on the *Ark Royal* knew the crews meant to succeed this time.

About forty minutes later the *Sheffield* sighted them. She signaled: ENEMY TWELVE MILES DEAD AHEAD; and they were seen climbing into the clouds. After an interval there came an outburst of gunfire, sharp on the starboard bow, and the bright winking of numerous shell bursts in the air.

The distant display of antiaircraft fire flashed and sparkled for some minutes and then died away. There was a pause, and then those on the bridge of the *Sheffield* saw one and then two more planes flying back. They came past low and on a level with the bridge. Their torpedoes were gone, and as one plane flew close by, the crew smiled broadly and held their thumbs up.

When the air striking force returned to the *Ark Royal,* it was found that five airplanes had been damaged by gunfire. Despite this and the failing light, only one plane crashed. After the crews were interrogated, it was established that one direct hit had been obtained on the *Bismarck.*

Presently reports to Admiral Tovey from the *Sheffield* and later from a shadowing airplane of the *Ark Royal* indicated that the *Bismarck* had turned about in her tracks and was now moving in a generally northward direction. Why was she behaving in this strange, and indeed suicidal, manner? Could it be that her rudders had been damaged and she was no longer under control?

A seeming confirmation of this heartening theory was received when the last straggling airplane shadowers got back to the *Ark Royal* with this important information: Immediately after the aircraft attack, the *Bismarck* had made two complete circles, then had apparently come to a stop heading north, and on this point of the compass she lay wallowing in the seas. Now the evidence was clear.

After the anxieties and disappointments of the past few days, when hope of catching the *Bismarck* had declined practically to zero, the enemy's evident disablement seemed almost too good to be true. The senior officers had realized that the air attack which did the vital damage was virtually the last hope of slowing up the *Bismarck* and thus preventing her escape. That such a last-minute attempt should be an overwhelming success was beyond reasonable expectation. Yet, the one forlorn chance had come off.

The next day, May 27, dawned with the poor visibility of a stormy horizon. At 8:15 a.m. the *Norfolk* sighted the *Bismarck* about eight miles ahead and signaled the news to the *King George V* and the *Rodney.*

At 8:47 the *Rodney*'s 16-inch guns opened the battle. Just as the salvo was due to fall, the *King George V*'s guns flashed. The *Bismarck* remained silent for two minutes; then she joined in. Her third salvo straddled the *Rodney* and nearly hit her. Captain Frederick Dalrymple-Hamilton altered course to bring more guns to bear and began to subject the *Bismarck* to heavier gunfire than she herself could develop.

At 8:54 the *Norfolk* opened fire with her 8-inch guns at 20,000 yards. The *King George V* and the *Rodney,* which had now come into even lesser range, brought their secondary armament into action. And at 9:04 the cruiser *Dorsetshire* joined in the action.

The enemy's gunnery efficiency was now noticeably falling off. During the next few minutes both British battleships went in closer, and details of the *Bismarck* were easily discernible through binoculars. Obvious signs of punishment were visible: a fairly large fire was blazing amidships; some of her guns seemed to have been silenced, and the others were firing only spasmodically.

At lessening range the two British battleships poured in a heavy fire from both main-armament and secon-

This close-up of the German battleship Bismarck *was taken from the Nazi cruiser* Prinz Eugen *during the* Bismarck's *bombardment of the British battle cruiser* Hood *off the coast of Greenland in the Denmark Strait. Minutes later the British ship was blown up. The* Bismarck *was chased far out to sea by several British warships and three days later sent to the bottom.*

dary-armament guns. A large explosion occurred just abaft the upper of the *Bismarck*'s two foremost turrets, which blew the back of it up over the bridge. The *Bismarck*'s speed had by now been reduced to an unsteady crawl, and the British battleships had to zigzag back and forth to keep their guns trained on her.

By 10 a.m. the *Bismarck* was a silent, battered wreck. Her mast was down, her funnel had disappeared, her guns were pointing in all directions and a cloud of black smoke was rising from the middle of the ship. Inside she was clearly a blazing inferno, for the bright glow of internal fires shone through numerous

shell and splinter holes in her sides. Her men were deserting their guns; parties of them could be seen running to and fro on the upper deck as the shells continued to rain in, and jumping over the side to escape by a watery death from the terror on board.

But the *Bismarck*'s flag still flew. Ostensibly, at least, she remained defiant. Powerless and surrounded by enemies, she did not surrender.

The British were determined to sink her, and as quickly as they could. At any moment long-distance German planes might appear, or torpedoes might come streaking in from U-boats that were already amazingly late in arriving on the scene; and nagging anxiety over the acute fuel shortage added to the urgency. The *Rodney* was now firing nine-gun broadsides at the *Bismarck* from the 16-inch guns, the huge shells hitting her three and four at a time. A torpedo from the *Rodney* hit the *Bismarck* amidships. The *Norfolk* believed she had obtained at least one torpedo hit. But still the *Bismarck* floated.

However, it was obvious that the burning hulk, lying deep and sluggish in the water, would never get back to harbor, whether she sank now or later. At 10:15 a.m. Sir John Tovey on the *King George V* signaled to the *Rodney* to take a position astern. He had already waited dangerously long, and now he was going home.

As he steered away, the *Dorsetshire* fired two torpedoes at the *Bismarck's* starboard side, one of which exploded right under the bridge. The cruiser then steered around to her port side and fired another torpedo, which also hit. The shattered leviathan, her colors still flying, silently heeled over to port and disappeared beneath the waves.

The great chase was over. The mighty *Bismarck* had been disposed of, after a gallant fight against superior forces. All that remained of her were several hundred swimming men, their heads visible on the surface of the breaking seas. The *Dorsetshire* and the destroyer *Maori* managed to pick up 110 of them. Then came a lookout's report of a submarine periscope, and the British ships withdrew.

The destruction of the *Bismarck* ended one of the longest continuous chases in naval history. In dramatic reversals of fortune, in the frequent alternation of high optimism and blank disappointment, in brilliant victory followed quickly by utter defeat, it is probably unique in warfare.

On Board the "Bismarck"

BY EDWIN MULLER

To every nook and corner of the *Bismarck* the news of the sinking of the *Hood* on the morning of May 24, 1941, ran swiftly. There were outbursts of wild cheering. The top deck, empty during the action, was now full of men singing and embracing each other. The *Bismarck* had paid a cheap price for the victory. She had been hit, but her injuries were trivial. A mere handful of men were wounded.

All that day the jubilation went on. The busiest men on board were the motion-picture operators from Dr. Joseph Goebbels' Propaganda Ministry. They had filmed the action with the *Hood,* now they were recording the victory celebration. Soon Berlin would see on the screen how Great Britain's rule of the ocean had been ended.

Most of the crew were young—in their early twenties. Also aboard were some 500 Naval cadets in their teens. This glorious victory was exactly what they had confidently expected. At their age they could hardly remember a world before Hitler. As Hitler Youth, unquestioning belief in the "master race" had been driven into their souls every waking hour: "Today we rule Germany, tomorrow the whole world." One thing they knew: Germans were invincible.

And the *Bismarck,* too, was invincible. It was, indeed, by far the strongest warship on the seas. No one outside the German High Command knew her actual tonnage. It is believed that it was far greater than the 35,000 tons to which she was limited by treaty. Some rate her at 50,000. In her trials she is said to have made thirty-three knots, faster than any British or U.S. battleship of the time.

On deck she looked much like any other battleship. But below she was unique. Beneath the waterline she had five steel skins, each enclosing watertight spaces. The crew had been told that the *Bismarck* was not only able to defeat any British ship but could defeat any combination that could be brought against her. She was literally unsinkable.

There were some on board, older men, who didn't believe it; for instance, the commanding officer, Captain Lindemann. He knew that German ships could be sunk like any others. He was a quiet and capable officer, an old-style German Navy man rather than a fervent party man.

But his superior officer was a Nazi of the Nazis. Vice Admiral Gunther Luetjens was slight of build—but he made up for it by truculence of look and violence of spirit. He was an emotional leader who roused his men to high fervor. That he had corresponding fits of depression was not then known to the crew.

Morale had been high despite cramped living

quarters. Besides the cadets and regular crew there were several hundred extra men on board, making a total of some 2400. Space that other ships use for living quarters was devoted to extra protection. The crew slept forward in hammocks swung so close together that they touched. Aft, the junior officers were crowded four to a tiny room. The mess deck was dark and airless.

There had been much speculation among the crew as to where they were going when the *Bismarck* first left port, accompanied by the new 8-inch-gun cruiser *Prinz Eugen*. Most of them thought it was a raiding expedition against British merchantmen, such as Luetjens had conducted so successfully with the *Scharnhorst* and the *Gneisenau*. The extra men made that credible; they might be prize crews for captured vessels. Some had heard that the *Bismarck* was going to capture the Azores for the Reich. Now the purpose was clear—they had been destined to destroy the *Hood*.

Both Admiral Luetjens and Captain Lindemann were quite aware that the *Bismarck* was then being hunted by an ever-increasing concentration of British warships. The weather had grown cold and overcast, with snow squalls, sleet and mist. Keeping herself concealed in the thickening fog banks, the *Bismarck* ghosted southwest under full steam. Once, toward evening of the 24th, she turned on her pursuers, opening fire on the *Suffolk*. The British cruiser immediately put up a smoke screen and vanished behind it. When the *Prince of Wales* opened up with her big guns, the *Bismarck* turned away and made off at top speed.

The encounter was brief, resulting in no damage to any ship. Although the British were not aware of it at the time, the action was a deliberate ruse on the part of the *Bismarck* to allow the *Prinz Eugen* to slip away and head south for refueling, then on to the safety of her home port at Brest.

That evening Admiral Luetjens mustered the crew on deck and delivered one of his fiery, triumphant speeches. The thunder of applause and the deep *"Sieg Heil!"* went rolling out across the waves. An exulting radio message came from Hitler. The Fuehrer awarded the Knight's Insignia of the Iron Cross to the First Gunnery Officer. Other decorations came over the radio.

The ceremonies were rudely interrupted by the sounding of the general alarm. Enemy planes had been sighted. There was a buzzing like a swarm of bees and nine Royal Navy Swordfish aircraft from the British carrier *Victorious* swept in on the German battleship. One after the other they swooped close to the water, released their torpedoes and banked away. One torpedo struck the *Bismarck*'s starboard bow. A column of water leaped higher than the masthead, and the ship was jolted from end to end. The damage-control crew found that a compartment had been penetrated and filled with water.

It was no crippling damage, yet it seemed to have a profound effect on Admiral Luetjens. Probably at this point he also received disturbing news by radio of even stronger British concentrations moving to intercept him. From elation he seemed to have swung to despair. The Admiral made an extraordinary speech to the crew. He said the *Bismarck* would have to do battle. He hoped that U-boats and planes would come to help meet the British onslaught. If not, the *Bismarck* would take more than one of her opponents to the bottom with her. "Men, remember your oath; be true to the Fuehrer to death."

The effect of this on the young men was devastating. They had been told that their ship was unsinkable. Now, suddenly, there was talk of dying! To repair the Admiral's blunder, a message was circulated among the men. Help, it said, was on the way. A flotilla of U-boats was approaching; planes were coming—soon there would be 200 of them overhead.

It is probable that this statement was made out of whole cloth. But the crew believed it. Their spirits went up.

There was no further contact with the enemy during the night and all the next day. As the hours passed, the feeling grew that perhaps they had given the slip to the British ships. . . . Then, on the morning of the 26th, a plane was heard. Soon an American-built Catalina appeared through a break in the clouds, almost overhead. Every antiaircraft gun began to hammer, putting up a terrific barrage, and the plane disappeared. But the crew had the feeling of long arms reaching toward them.

Then a disturbing rumor went around the ship. There had been a quarrel between Luetjens and Captain Lindemann. Through his closed door the Admiral was heard shouting angrily. Lindemann had pointed out that the British would now concentrate every available unit, that they would never rest until they had hunted down the *Bismarck*. He urged the Admiral to turn toward home at once. Luetjens angrily vetoed this suggestion. He announced to the crew that he was leading them on to more victories. They cheered and felt much better. Nevertheless, they began to watch the horizon, hoping for reinforcement, and as time passed and no German craft hove into view the tension noticeably increased. The cockiness and good humor of the crew vanished and was replaced by fear and anxiety.

Since the encounter with the *Hood,* the *Bismarck* had sailed southwest and then south. Now, two days after the battle, she was headed toward Finistère, hoping to reach the French coast and creep along it to a safe harbor. But as darkness settled down that evening, fifteen Swordfish planes, this time from the aircraft carrier *Ark Royal,* made another sudden attack, scoring three hits. Two torpedoes did little damage, but the third struck the steering gear, jamming the rudders at an angle. The great battleship began to turn in circles.

There was frantic activity on board. The Iron Cross was promised to the man who could repair the rudders. Engines were stopped and a diver went overside. He put forth immense efforts, but when the *Bismarck* resumed way she still moved in circles.

Now the organized life of the ship was disrupted. There was shouting and aimless running around. In the midst of the confusion came an ironic note, a radio message from the Fuehrer: ALL OUR THOUGHTS ARE WITH OUR VICTORIOUS COMRADES.

The crew tried desperately to steer with the engines. But the ship limped along slowly, yawing from side to side like a drunken man.

The ship's command tried to give the crew's morale another shot in the arm. This time the message was specific: "Early in the morning tugs will come to our assistance, and fourscore planes."

Some of the crew believed it. Luetjens didn't. He made one grand gesture, a message to Hitler: "We shall fight to the last shell. Long live the Fuehrer, the Chief of the Fleet." After that he cracked. He was heard through his door shouting hysterically: "Do what you like. I'm through."

The next morning was overcast, and a cold wind whipped the ocean into whitecaps. On the horizon appeared the heavyweights of Britain's Grand Fleet, the *Rodney* and the *King George V.* They opened with

their 16-inch guns at about eleven miles, then moved in to half that range. A 16-inch shell weighs 2100 pounds, travels half a mile a second. Every time one struck, the *Bismarck* rocked and shuddered. But for a while she fought back, firing salvo for salvo.

The break came when a shell wrecked the main control station. That ended the *Bismarck* as a coordinated fighting machine. Her crew still fought the individual turrets by local control, but the shooting was wild.

The *Rodney* and *King George V* moved in closer, within two miles. They sent every shell home with methodical precision. The riddled mast hung like a crazy tangle of vines until a shell cut it off at the base and it came crashing down on the deck. Flames erupted from amidships. One turret leaned over, its guns cocked toward the sky. No vessel had ever taken such punishment before and remained afloat.

Now morale went to pieces. The crew of one turret mutinied, ran away. After a moment's hesitation, their officer ran, too. In another turret, when the men refused to obey, the officer shot them down.

Soon the ship began to keel slowly to port, and water poured in through shell holes and sprung plates. It flooded deck after deck, sucking and gurgling through the labyrinth of chambers and passages. Some compartments were shut off and many men were drowned as water rose to the ceilings. Others fought their way up to the air, jamming the companionways.

The top deck became an inferno. Holes opened, men's clothes were ripped off by explosions. Wounded men and boys were shrieking, and the dead lay everywhere. The panic-driven mob tried to get back below decks. But the ladders were packed with men fighting their way up from the rising water below.

By now the ship was almost over on her beam. Many were already struggling in the water; others were crawling out over the black, glistening bulge of the hull. Slowly the *Bismarck* tilted over and slid beneath the surface.

The men rescued by the British were haggard and hollow-eyed, as if they had gone through months of torture. Days later, after they had been put to bed, rested, given restoratives, they were still dazed. They hardly spoke, even to each other. It was more than physical shock that they had suffered. There had been shattered the faith on which their lives had been built —the belief in their own invincibility.

144

BRITAIN RULES THE MEDITERRANEAN

BY BRIG. GEN. S. L. A. MARSHALL,
USAR (RET.)

In the darkest summer of the war—1940—the British Navy, aided by air power, met and defeated the Axis against strategic odds in the Mediterranean. This victory raised a barrier along the sea and air lanes between Hitler's Fortress Europe and his forces in North Africa. At a time when the Nazi advance threatened to sweep all the way to the Suez Canal and even beyond, the supply routes from the Fatherland to its North African vanguard were seriously curtailed.

Within five hours after Italy's entry into the war on June 11, 1940, Mussolini's bombers flew over Valletta on the island of Malta. Italy's first strike was only a glancing blow, though Malta was neither armed to fight nor supplied to survive a long siege.

The Italians might have taken Malta at once had they dared to move upon the island. By declining to take that action, they forfeited the fight even as it began. Before the war Great Britain had neglected Malta, and now the strengthening of other bases had priority.

Mussolini in that hour was directing his Navy to "assume the offensive at all points in the Mediterranean and outside." Prime Minister Winston Churchill was telling his Chief of Staff to take any measures that might make Britain's enemies "wonder where they were going to be next, instead of forcing us to wall in the island and roof it over."

The Mediterranean seemed the least likely area for such adventuring. Initiative there lay clearly with the Italian Fleet, with its bases in well-armed harbors. Malta was only twelve hours' steaming time from Taranto—the major Italian Naval base—and thirty min-

utes' flying time from airfields on the Italian peninsula. Class for class, type for type, Britain's fighting ships were slower than Italy's by two to six knots.

But this view of the situation did not deter the British Admiralty or Adm. Sir Andrew Cunningham, who had a small fleet based at Alexandria, Egypt, or Vice Adm. Sir James Somerville, who had another small fleet at Gibraltar.

Admiral Cunningham's opening operations took the form of using the fleet to convoy supply ships to Malta. The Italian Navy, hyper-cautious, was preoccupied with escorting troop and supply ships to North Africa. These movements, practically at right angles to one another, mutually threatened each other's right of way. The first engagement came at a great distance on July 9, 1940. After the battleship *Giulio Cesare* and the cruiser *Bolzano* each took a hit, the Italian Fleet turned and fled at high speed, covered by a smoke screen. Otherwise inconclusive, the brief action convinced Cunningham that his slower force had little or no prospect of meeting the Italian Fleet in a main surface action.

In September the new carrier *Illustrious* joined Cunningham. At that time Somerville's Force H, based at Gibraltar, was providing cover for Britain's sea traffic as far as the narrows south of Sicily, where it came under the guard of the warcraft from Alexandria. Successful enough, it was too tame a game for Cunningham once he had the *Illustrious.*

Early in November additional warships for the Mediterranean Fleet arrived at Gibraltar. Accompanied by Force H, the reinforced fleet steamed east to Malta, where guns and men were disembarked. The carrier *Ark Royal* had come along and at Malta was detached to execute her part of a twofold plan: Somerville's ships turned back west; Cunningham's ships, taking up the escort duty, moved east.

The night of November 11 was remarkably fair, the moon full, the sky slightly overcast with thin clouds at 8000 feet. The *Illustrious,* screened by four cruisers and four destroyers out of Alexandria, had proceeded to a position off the west coast of Greece.

Between 8:30 and 9:30 p.m. the carrier's two striking forces of Swordfish—twenty-one warplanes—were launched to attack the Italian Naval base at Taranto. A few minutes earlier, planes from the westward-steaming *Ark Royal* had opened their diversionary attack against Italian air bases on Sardinia.

In ninety minutes the British airplanes were over Taranto. The surprise was complete. Italy's new battleship *Littorio* was hit by three torpedoes and put out of action. The older battleships *Cavour* and *Duilio* each took torpedo hits, the *Cavour* being sunk. One cruiser and one destroyer were disabled by bombs, and there was extensive damage to port installations.

The raid cost the British fleet only two planes.

Admiral Cunningham called it a feat unsurpassed in history as an example of economy of force. Indeed, this brief fight changed the balance of naval power throughout the Mediterranean and compelled the German *Luftwaffe* to extend southward to protect Sicily.

The general pattern for the passage of convoys to Malta was continued, with Force H out of Gibraltar guarding as far as the Sicilian narrows, where the

Units of Britain's Royal Navy engage warships of the Italian Fleet in the Mediterranean while escorting an Allied convoy to Malta. One British cruiser lays down a smoke screen as another fires a broadside. In 1940 the Royal Navy won mastery of the Mediterranean.

fleet from Alexandria took over. At one such transfer during "Operation Excess" on January 10, 1941, eighty-seven German Junkers dive bombers concentrated their attack on the *Illustrious,* striking her with six bombs. Sorely wounded, she made harbor in Malta.

Finally, on March 28, 1941, the British Fleet under Admiral Cunningham caught two Italian squadrons off Cape Matapan, Greece. Planes from the carrier *Formidable,* aided by ship gunfire, damaged 1 battleship and sank 3 cruisers and 2 destroyers. Thereafter the Italian Navy remained in hiding.

Matapan clinched British Naval supremacy east of Malta, without which the struggle for Africa could not have been won. When at last the Italian battle fleet lowered its flag in surrender, the ceremony fittingly took place under the guns of Fortress Malta.

A British convoy, having run the gauntlet of enemy sea and air power, is greeted by a band in the harbor of Malta. In recognition of the courage of the island's people in withstanding heavy enemy bombing, King George VI of England awarded them the coveted George Cross.

THE GALLANT DEFENSE OF THE PHILIPPINES

BY LT. COL. WARREN J. CLEAR, USA

From the time the Japanese troops set foot on Philippine beaches, the American and Allied forces were faced with defeat. Largely cut off from reinforcement and supplies, they fought bravely and inflicted heavy casualties on the enemy. For five heroic months the defenders held out against overwhelming odds. The Philippines . . . Bataan . . . Corregidor—*these names, remote-sounding before Pearl Harbor, now stood for courage and endurance, and the hope for ultimate victory. This description of the defense of the Philippines is given by an American Army officer who took part in it.*

We sat in the little boat, riding the night tides of Manila Bay. It was May 1942, and I was waiting for the submarine that was to take me on the first lap of my journey to the United States with the Army's confidential documents. I had plenty of time to think back through all the tragedy and blood and fury of the Philippine campaign. Seldom if ever in all military history had men fought more magnificently than had our own soldiers, sailors, marines and Philippine Scouts in this desperate struggle which every one of them knew was, in the end, hopeless. I resolved that if I ever got back home I would do my best to tell the true story of their heroism for all Americans to remember proudly.

I did get back. Here is the story.

Memory brings the smell of hot steaming blood to my nostrils: American blood crimsoning the swamps and rice paddies, and Japanese blood flowing beside it; Bataan, that wild and desolate peninsula of savage jungle and rocky mountain slope, a primitive wilderness which few white men had ever penetrated before. Crocodiles and snakes and huge pythons, the world's largest, infested its solitary morasses.

Into the northern end of Bataan Peninsula poured 80,000 Japanese veterans, eager for the kill. They knew all the cunning strategies that meant survival, the techniques that only the experienced professional can command. And they had their quarry at bay—the men of Gen. Douglas MacArthur's Philippine Command, crouching in their jungle foxholes.

But the jungle, which for centuries had protected the pygmy and the wild animal from conquest, now helped our fighting men. Overhead, the interlacing trees sheltered them from the dive bomber; underfoot, the treacherous swampland bogged the tank. When the Japanese soldier advanced, he had to advance on foot.

First he would come up against a screen of Filipino riflemen hidden in the undergrowth; and they would take their toll. Beyond these he found himself in a murderous belt of barbed-wire tangles, foxholes manned by American Regulars, machine guns trained down jungle trails. In every step forward lay the menace of concealed trip-wire explosives, TNT land mines and tens of thousands of fire-hardened, pointed bamboo sticks implanted in the ground, so sharp they penetrated the thickest shoe soles. The Japanese had at last run up against a savage technique of jungle warfare as cunning and merciless as his own. In every foxhole, often shallowly scooped out by bare hands and a tin helmet, the Japanese met an implacable foe; either the Japanese or the defender died right there.

In this fighting, many a soldier came to realize that self-confidence alone was not enough to sustain the human spirit. I remember jumping into a hole during a particularly heavy bombing attack. A sergeant crouched lower to make room for me. Then all hell broke loose, and I wasn't surprised to find myself praying out loud. I heard the sergeant praying, too.

Back of the foxholes stood Maj. Gen. Edward P. King, Jr., and his artillery. Eddie King could get as much out of guns and gun crews as any commander who ever handled men. He hid his pieces as carefully as a miser might hide gold, with canopies of carefully renewed foliage constantly maintained above them. His outfit—poison to the Japanese—once knocked out forty of their field guns in three days and, another time, for a stretch of ten days kept up such deadly fire that the enemy field artillery hardly fired a shot. But that was while we had a plane or two left and could get some observation.

Back of General King and his guns were the field hospitals where toiled the unsung, unspectacular heroes of Bataan—the doctors, nurses and hospital corpsmen. The nurses were unbelievably brave. All day long they would be covered with blood from amputations and the dressing of dreadful wounds. It did not seem possible that women could stand up to what they did. But somehow they endured it all.

Their immaculate white uniforms gave way to government-issue khaki shirts and homemade khaki skirts, then to army slacks. They ate the same food as the soldiers, went on short rations when the men did, worked countless hours until they dropped from fatigue and slept under barrages of bomb and shell.

In the reserve area, too, was General Headquarters. Major General Jonathan M. Wainwright—known as Skinny Wainwright to his men—Brig. Gen. William F. (Bill) Marquat and the others were fighting generals. They took it with the men. I saw one of them—Brig. Gen. A. M. Jones—pick up a Browning machine gun and plunge across enemy lines with a sergeant to rescue three privates who were cut off and out of ammunition. He brought them in, too.

Yet it was not in battle but between battles, during the dreary, apprehensive intervals when the anxious mind can eat at the heart, that Bataan's defenders best showed the depth and strength of spirit of the American fighting man. They gathered in little groups and told simple anecdotes of their lives back home. There were long discussions about religion. The general consensus was: "There will be no purgatory for us—after Bataan we'll go right on through, without any local stops." But beneath the chaff and banter the listener felt that to these men religion was something real and definite and necessary, something to be respected, whether it was yours or the other fellow's. They talked of morals and manners, economics and philosophy, and often the simplest men among them etched the clearest images in quaint speech.

It was an unforgettable experience to have the soul of America laid bare around furtive campfires in a distant land; to hear a Coast Artillery private, standing on the parapet of a gun pit, quote from the Koran: "We created not the heavens and the earth, and that which is in between them, by way of sport."

Their rough American humor never deserted them. I remember walking by a battery pit and overhearing a conversation on that endlessly discussed question, Why doesn't the fleet come?

The gunner was saying: "Where in hell do you suppose that fleet really is?"

"That's easy," came the answer. "The last letter I got from a girl friend of mine was postmarked St. Louis, Missouri. She never lets the fleet get more 'n ten miles away from her, so it's up the Mississippi!"

On another occasion, during a particularly heavy bombardment, two soldiers were huddling in a slit trench. Suddenly one of them began to smile. "What's so funny?" asked his buddy. "Oh, came the answer, I was just thinkin' of how scared I used to be when one of those Army dentists got me in his chair!"

The Nips, as the soldiers called the Japanese, got many a taste of American courage and ingenuity. There was the Bataan Air Force, for instance, also named the Bamboo Fleet because it was so patched together with native wood. When General Wainwright called for air support, a couple of quivering, battered P-40's would rise to give battle to dozens of Japanese Zeros. Until every last one of them was destroyed, these crates operated from two hastily built airfields constructed and kept in repair by workmen under constant bombardment. The fields, standing out like bull's-eye targets in the surrounding jungle, were really only widened portions of road, and were plastered so regularly by the Japanese that our men called the enemy raiders the morning and afternoon mail planes. Our pilots almost had to fight their way off the ground, for the Japanese were so near they could hear the P-40's warming up for the takeoff. Every flight was practically a suicide mission, yet the pilots gunned their machines into the air several times a day, week after week. They used to talk big over the radio just before going up, hoping to scare the listening Japanese out of the air.

Every day Lt. Col. Reggie Vance would fly between Bataan and Corregidor in an old crate tied together with wire which the Japanese always tried to knock down. He carried a Winchester rifle across his knees and a big-bladed bolo knife by his side. The gun was his armament for aerial combat. The bolo was to cut himself out of his harness if he fell into the water, for the Japanese had a nasty habit of machine-gunning the white parachutes and bright orange life preservers

Japanese infantry attack on Bataan. Driven back from their defensive positions on the Philippine island of Luzon, the Americans and Filipinos retreated to Bataan, a peninsula of savage jungle and extinct volcanos. There they held out for months against superior enemy forces, hunger and disease.

whenever they spotted them floating on the waves.

A group of wobbly P-40's was sent out one day to escort the Filipino ace, Capt. Jesus Villamor, who was to photograph the Japanese artillery at Cavite. The P-40 pilots were given specific orders not to go after enemy fighters, but to stick with Villamor. The pilots managed to resist the temptation of attacking the Japanese planes swarming toward them. Then, photographs taken, they came down close to the field while Villamor landed. At once Capt. Ben Brown, the flight leader, radioed to ask if now, mission completed, he was in the clear. Receiving an affirmative answer, the P-40's zoomed up and, despite all the handicaps of altitude, superior enemy strength and numbers, eliminated six Zeros in the air, while our men cheered from the foxholes. Five of the six P-40's got back.

As long as they could pull a trigger or fix a bayonet, our men held their ground. Veterans of scores of bloody fights, many of them had been wounded once, twice, three times, and still had staggered back to stand again with their comrades.

But courage alone was not enough. Lack of food proved their undoing. Cut off from all supplies, the army on Bataan had to feed from its meager stocks nearly 100,000 people—the troops, the natives and the many thousands who had come over from Manila when it was evacuated. Just back of the fighting, the men of Brig. Gen. Charles C. Drake's Quartermaster Corps set up rice mills, bakeries which for a time produced 20,000 loaves of bread a day and slaughterhouses in which they butchered horses, mules, wild pigs and carabao—the water buffalo of the Philippines. They were even credited by the soldiers with slaughtering pythons and crocodiles and issuing them as food. But there was never enough food to go around.

The Quartermaster Corps also operated a fishing fleet that caught 10,000 pounds of fish a night until the Japanese discovered the boats and strafed them out of existence. Toward the end of January, when the

The great U.S. Naval base at Cavite on Manila Bay burns fiercely under a pall of smoke. As both Clark Field and Cavite were overrun in the opening days of the war, MacArthur's Philippine Command had neither the air nor naval support to defend the city of Manila.

rice gave out, a heroic merchant-marine captain sneaked his interisland steamer through the Japanese blockade into Manila Bay with 17,000 sacks of rice, 5000 bunches of bananas and 10,000 eggs. But it was the last island boat to get through. After that the fighters on Bataan went on half rations.

The daily serving of mule meat brought typical soldier comments. An artillery sergeant held up a piece of dubious-looking meat on a fork and philosophized: "Well, I beat hell out of these sons-of-guns for twenty years—but they're sure getting back at me now!" The men liked the carabao meat better. They made sandwiches of it which they called caraburgers, in an attempt to recapture dim memories of home.

As malnutrition weakened the men, they became more susceptible to malaria, dysentery, beriberi and scurvy. And with the increasing incidence of disease came an increasing scarcity of medicine. The number of sick in the hospitals rose day by day. When Bataan surrendered on April 9, most of the men in every regiment were weakened by disease; all were suffering from the ravages of hunger. In the last desperate days, the men who were withstanding the relentless twenty-four-hour onslaughts of the enemy were existing on a daily ration of a cup of rice and a few scraps of mule meat.

On the other side of the lines the picture was vastly different. Perhaps never before had a Japanese army eaten so well as did the invaders of Bataan, with their own supplies and the loot of Manila. Furthermore, most of the Bataan diseases were endemic in Japan, so that when the Japanese did contract them it was in mild form. Thus it was not the dive bombers or the slashing thrusts of infantry or the ceaseless pounding of heavy guns that brought the Japanese victory: our forces succumbed to the throttling fingers of starvation and disease.

Weeks of savage fighting in tropic heat, weeks without sleep, had made the youngest of these men "Bataan-faced"—the lines of old age etched deep; black circles of fatigue under weary, bloodshot eyes; the hollow at the base of the skull matching the sharp-ridged cheekbones.

In the words of General MacArthur, "Through the bloody haze of [Bataan's] last reverberating shot, I shall always seem to see the vision of grim, gaunt, ghastly men, still unafraid."

To understand and to feel something of the ordeal

151

that the city of Manila went through means going back to 12:45 on the afternoon of December 8, 1941 (December 7, U.S. time). In one fateful hour the Japanese had in effect captured the Philippines.

They came in over Clark Field at 10,000 feet—fifty-four two-motored Mitsubishi bombers from Formosa (Taiwan). They hit everything in sight—runways, hangars, shops, planes on the ground. Then eighty-six Zero fighters swooped in low. When they left, Clark Field was a bloody shambles of pilots and groundmen, shattered runways, flaming hangars—an inferno of red-glowing rubble. That raid and the simultaneous attack on other airfields near Manila sealed the fate of Luzon and Corregidor.

It wiped out more than half our air force almost before it had been able to get into action. The dreadful significance of the tragedy was not lost on any man, from private to general. From that moment on, they all knew they were fighting in a lost cause. But that knowledge did not weaken their resolve.

Two days later, sharp at noon, the Japanese struck Nichols and Nielson fields. It was the story of Clark Field all over again—strafed, blazing barracks; bomb-shattered runways and hangars; wrecked, flaming planes; torn and bloody bodies. Dive bombers wheeled over the adjacent rice paddies, searching out and strafing personnel with their murderous .50-caliber fire. Men were hunted down like wild animals as they sought refuge in the fields. Many a young soldier learned that it was death to take shelter in roadside ditches; the Zeros gave these plausible shelters their most searching fire.

Our men died because ten years of calculated preparation and the ability to concentrate superior force permitted the Japanese Empire to bring against them exactly as much as was needed to destroy them. Eighty dive bombers came over, that day—but 380 could have been assigned to the job if the Japanese General Staff had felt that number was necessary. No adequate defense was possible simply because we had not spent millions upon millions of dollars, through the years, to make our position tenable, and because we had lived up to the letter of treaties with Japan which forbade us to fortify the Philippines adequately.

At almost the same moment that Nichols and Nielson fields and the surrounding area were being strafed, Japanese planes attacked Cavite Navy Yard. I saw them, fifty-four heavy four-motored bombers in per-

fect V-formation, their silver wings and bodies shining in the sun. The dull roar of their motors was like the rumble before a storm. They circled the doomed base leisurely—there were no fighters to come up at them, no antiaircraft guns to break them up. When they were ready, they let go. In two hours the Cavite Yard was wiped off the map, and the Fleet had lost its only Asian base.

It was no surprise to us when the Japanese pushed seventy-six crowded transports into Lingayen Gulf, north of Manila Bay, on December 21. We had always figured they would make their main attack on this gulf, and we had held mimic warfare maneuvers there for years to get ready for it. They did just what was expected. But they had us without naval or air protection. They were able to swing in boldly with a line of cruisers and destroyers. These laid down a reduced-charge fire—lobbed big stuff into our beach defenses. Then, in their steel-armored barges which they slid out of the hulls of special carriers, they got 80,000 men ashore—minus plenty who bit the sand of the beach. Next came their miniature tanks, 10 feet by 5, weighing 3 tons and capable of 30 m.p.h.; and finally the larger 7-ton jobs.

Before this superior strength our troops fell back to Manila. And here the Japanese made a bad blunder. If they had landed in force on Bataan Peninsula—which was then almost undefended except for one small fort in Subic Bay—their campaign might have been quickly concluded without the loss of the thousands of men they subsequently sacrificed. But they counted on bottling up the American army in Manila, and General MacArthur outsmarted them. Instead of trying to keep Manila, he withdrew into Bataan, holding off the enemy forces converging from north and south long enough to slam the door in their faces.

I was on duty with General MacArthur's staff in Manila. One day, as the Japanese were closing in, I had to go south to Batangas on a mission. While I was there, the Japanese advance guard passed through; so when I finished my business, they were between me and Manila. There was nothing to do but drive up the Manila Road and see what would happen. Fortunately my Filipino driver, a Corporal of the Scouts, was as cool and capable as they come. We started off at 2 a.m. New Year's Day. With the help of a Jesuit priest we had picked up on the road, we succeeded in fooling Japanese soldiers into letting our car pass.

We made our way through darkened Manila toward the glow of flame that was the waterfront. The thunder of distant artillery fire shook the air. Close by, terrific explosions followed successive enormous flashes of blue flame—Air Corps demolition men were blowing up aviation gasoline. To the east the shambles of Cavite still glowed like a white-hot inferno. To the south great columns of black smoke, shot through with crimson flame, reached thousands of feet into the sky—the oil reservoirs at Pandacan. To the north, just 500 yards away, all the remaining boats that might be used for a Japanese assault on Corregidor were being fired by our demolition men. The leaping flames lighted up the shattered hulks of twenty other ships, themselves aglow, sunk by the Japanese that afternoon. Three piers nearby were aflame.

And directly across the street in front of me was the Manila Hotel. It, too, was ablaze—but not from explosives. A big New Year's Eve party was still going strong at 4:30 a.m. While Manila's solid citizens were at home preparing for the ordeal which would come in a few hours, the less stable element was engaging in one last, hysterical binge.

I went into the hotel. The gentlemen were in white ties and tails; their ladies wore formal evening gowns, gardenias, orchids. Mostly American, with some English, they were sipping tall cool drinks or swinging gracefully across the polished dance floor—while outside in a night of death and desolation, not five miles away, American boys were fighting in blood and filth to turn back the invading horde.

I passed between the tables looking for a friend who had a boat that might get me to Corregidor. Then I got out of there. I was glad to be outside. It was safer, I reflected—some irritated Japanese bomber might well drop a stick or two on the glitter and gaiety of the Manila Hotel.

I paced along the waterfront looking for anything that might float as far as Corregidor. I could see nothing. Then a welcome voice called out, "Hey, Colonel, we're shoving off—last boat!"

I got in. We looked around to see if there was anyone else we could pick up. All around us on the waterfront the flames were leaping higher. Silhouetted against the fire we could see gangs of Quartermaster Corps men still plunging into the warehouses and carrying out ammunition, medicine, foodstuffs and clothing. Under the endless strafing of Japanese planes they dumped them into battered trucks which came and went unceasingly all that night until the last split second, carrying precious loads into Bataan Peninsula.

As we watched, one of the gangs went into the long warehouse back of Pier 7 for another load. There was a blinding flash, a roar, and the warehouse disintegrated. No one came out.

We shoved off.

The Rock, as the island fortress of Corregidor was called, was a target the Japanese bombers couldn't miss, and it mattered little where they hit it. Every square yard was packed with personnel, food, ammunition or communications. The common conception of Corregidor as a huge impregnable rock labyrinthed with tunnels is entirely erroneous. There was one central tunnel, with lateral passages for hospital wards, supplies and ammunition. Of the 10,000 people on the island, only 600 could be sheltered in them. Most of these were the sick and wounded.

All the great 12-inch rifles and mortars and all but one of the 3-inch guns were out in the open, and there was no protection for the gun crews. Hiding the guns in galleries blasted out of Corregidor's rocky cliffs had often been recommended, but the provisions of our treaty with Japan, honorably observed, prevented this modernization of the island's defenses. From the captured Mariveles Mountains, at the southern end of Bataan, the Japanese were able to command all of Corregidor with their big guns. And our men, without observation planes, had to fight blindfolded against an enemy who had constant and complete observation.

After December, when the Japanese had destroyed all of the great barracks on Topside, the upper part of the island, the troops had to live, sleep and eat in the open. During bombings they ran from one foxhole to another, naked in their defenselessness. Major General George F. Moore, commander of Corregidor, and I were standing fifty yards away when a 500-pound bomb scored a direct hit on a 12-inch battery, killing a young Coast Artillery Captain and thirty-five of his gun crew. They were crushed to death in an improvised dugout.

But once we were able to give the Japanese a taste of their own medicine. They mounted six 9.4-inch guns on the southern peninsula, in an area plotted and calibrated years before by our farsighted Coast Artillery officers. Natives slipping in at night by canoe gave us their positions. We had them as surely as if they had

(Above) *After the fall of Bataan Peninsula in April 1942, the decimated American and Filipino forces under General Wainwright made a last stand on the offshore island of Corregidor. But on May 6, 1942, the Japanese, bayonets ready, moved in in overwhelming numbers. Corregidor had fallen.*

(Left) *Despite Corregidor's big guns, one of which is shown blasting away at the Japanese, the sheer force of enemy weapons and manpower finally prevailed, and the rugged rock in Manila Bay was surrendered. Five short months after the attack on Pearl Harbor, the Philippines were totally under Japanese occupation.*

(Right) *General Jonathan M. Wainwright broadcasts at a Manila radio station, reluctantly ordering his troops in the Philippines to lay down their arms. As he speaks a Japanese guard watches attentively. Guerrilla resistance by Filipino patriots and American survivors continued to harass the victors until the long-awaited return of American troops took place.*

been ten feet from our guns. General Moore waited patiently day after day until the enemy batteries had been completely established and personnel moved in to man them. Then, at three o'clock one fine morning, eight of our big howitzers began hurling 762-pound demolition and shrapnel shells into the enemy emplacements. We learned later that 600 Japanese were killed and hundreds of others wounded. The batteries were completely destroyed. In the Japanese-controlled newspapers in Manila, the Emperor's High Command protested "this brutal and treacherous killing of sleeping men."

One day, with another officer and a Quartermaster Corps Sergeant, I was down on the docks when fifty-four heavy bombers flew in suddenly from the South China Sea. For four hours they dropped 300-pound, 500-pound and 1000-pound eggs that shattered everything in the whole area. The blasting effect of the heavier bombs was so terrific that railroad rails near me were broken neatly into 6-inch lengths from the concussion.

Fifty bombers made a special effort to destroy General MacArthur and his staff. The dive bombers first strafed 100 cars parked about the administration building and set them afire. Then the heavy bombers began dropping 500-pounders. Four hit the corners of the big concrete building, making craters you could drop a house in. Two bombs tore through the three concrete floors above the room in which Maj. Gen. Richard K. Sutherland and two aides were crouching. The whole building heaved and shuddered like a ship in a storm. Chunks of ceiling and 50-pound pieces of shrapnel showered the lower floor. One end of the building was sucked out by the tremendous vacuum created by the bursting of a huge bomb a few yards away.

"I guess this is it," was General Sutherland's only comment. Many others died in the building that day, but the Chief of Staff and his aides escaped unhurt.

The great hospital on Topside was blasted off the face of the earth by sixty-seven Japanese bombers. Fortunately, the medical officers had removed all the patients a couple of days before and carried them down to the tunnel. Even there the patients were only relatively safe. In one of the laterals next to them were 250,000 pounds of black powder. In other laterals were 220,000 gallons of gasoline, thousands of rounds of 3-inch antiaircraft (AA) ammunition, giving off

explosive picric-acid fumes, and thousands of 8-inch, 10-inch and 12-inch shells. Nobody needed a NO SMOKING sign—to strike a match there would have meant death for everybody on the island. Every man there knew that he was living on top of a volcano.

The chapels on Topside were bombed. So the Christian Church once again had to take shelter in the catacombs. Every Sunday morning the chaplain would improvise an altar in the tunnel, using heavy cases filled with antiaircraft shells. Soldiers and nurses knelt on the concrete floor or sat on empty ammunition boxes. The wounded, most of whom insisted on attending, were wheeled from the hospital laterals or carried in on litters.

All through the endless days of hardship and horror, General MacArthur's courage and coolness contributed to the maintenance of morale throughout all ranks. The same is to be said for Mrs. MacArthur. Many a night she had to make a dash from the exposed frame house in which she slept to the shelter of the tunnel, carrying little Arthur, their son, in her arms. Arthur never came willingly—he wanted to stay out to see the bombs burst.

An impressive ceremony took place on the Rock one day—the second inaugural of President Manuel Quezon. To avoid the bombers, it was held in the tunnel mouth, with Chief Justice José Abad Santos of the Philippines giving the oath of office.

A tableau of a very different kind was enacted daily down at the beach. Officers and men, in shorts or less, dived into the water and came up firmly clasping what they obviously regarded as precious objects. The explanation was that two barges, one loaded with good Scotch whisky and the other with chocolate bars, prunes and raisins, had been sunk at this spot by a direct hit. The men gladly braved the shark-infested waters to bring up the salvage.

There was money to burn on Corregidor. I mean that literally. Millions of dollars had been brought from Manila, and to save it from the enemy it had to be destroyed. Great stacks and armfuls of $5, $10 and $20 bills were burned in bonfires, to the intense interest and wonderment of the soldiers standing by. One of the officers got a great kick out of lighting his cigar with a $100 bill.

The island's only defenses against the endless and merciless fleets of silver-colored bombers were a few 3-inch antiaircraft guns. The total amount of AA ammunition on hand at the start of the siege was 30,000 rounds; at an average daily expenditure of 1000 rounds, this would have lasted only a month. The air raids were so frequent, and it was so necessary to conserve ammunition, that Japanese bombers were able to dump their loads without being fired on. With the type of ammunition they had, the gun crews had to wait until the planes were directly overhead, the shortest range.

During the first days of February a submarine got through the Japanese blockade with a small quantity of modern 3-inch ammunition with mechanical fuses. The battery commanders doled it out as if each shell were made of solid gold. They saved their fire until large bomber formations came over and presented extremely favorable targets. With the new stuff, our gunners reached up 25,000 feet and knocked many an overconfident Japanese pilot out of the sky.

All these AA batteries were in the open with only a circle of sandbags around them. Often the burst of a 300-pound or 500-pound bomb near the gun emplacement blasted the sandbags, the weapons and the crew. But the men never flinched; they were always ready for more.

And so it went on to the inevitable end. I wasn't there for the final days, but I can see the big bombers searching out the few remaining guns, the dive bombers swooping down for the kill at exhausted gun crews. Day after day the enemy batteries on Bataan poured their screaming projectiles into the tunnel mouth, tearing away the face of cliffs, smothering the beach defenders in bloody debris. And then the steel barges, loaded with savage foes, loomed out of the darkness of the channel and spewed their crews ashore.

The island was on fire. Ammunition dumps were blowing up. Relentlessly the fresh hordes of attackers moved forward toward the tunnel. In the hospital laterals 100 white-faced women huddled, shuddering, against the walls. All was darkness and confusion, destruction and death. Into the black tunnel itself smashed the invaders. There was bloody work there with bayonet, knife and hand grenade. It had to come at last—the very end.

But some days before this, the morning came when General Sutherland called me aside. "Your transportation came in last night," he said. "The submarine is on the bottom now, but she'll come up at midnight. Be ready to go aboard. No personal baggage—no one is to know anything about it. Those are orders."

The day was spent seeing friends on the Rock for the last time, without being able to say good-bye. Perhaps a few hints were dropped that there might be a way to get precious letters home if given to me—I know I was a walking post office when I left.

That afternoon I climbed the narrow hogback crest of Malinta Hill with General Moore. Across the bay, Manila's shattered waterfront was caught in the bright rays of the descending sun. Through General Moore's glasses I could see an enormous Japanese flag flaunting atop the Manila Hotel. I wondered momentarily how the New Year's Eve party makers liked the invaders....

We turned toward the setting sun. A mile away, on Topside, the Stars and Stripes flew serenely from an oft-shattered, oft-mended pole. It looked pathetically small against the darkening sky.

Captain Ray, Rear Adm. Francis W. Rockwell's Chief of Staff, came up to me. "In five minutes," he said, "one of my officers will guide you to a boat which will take you to the rendezvous point in the bay." We went down to the beach, lugging the six mail sacks of confidential documents I was taking along.

A moment later the little boat slipped away from the beach. We reached the rendezvous and sat waiting, as I have related earlier. To the north, across the bay, the flashes of a tremendous artillery duel tore gashes in the purple-black sky. Gradually the flashes united into a sheet of flame fifteen miles long, the length of the front. The flame on our side appeared bright blue and yellow; on the Japanese side it was dull red. The roar of the guns and crash of the shells seemed to strike down upon us. Under those screeching shells were my friends and comrades of a quarter of a century of soldiering....

Then, off the port bow, a small blue light blinked twice. Cautiously our little craft edged forward. There was the submarine. A hand reached down, and I scrambled up the wet sloping side.

"Take a good look at the sky," the commander said. "It will be ten days before you see it again."

The hatch closed behind me, shutting out the flaming frenzy of battle, the last sight of doomed Corregidor. Silently the sub glided through the black waters, slowly we crept past the menacing minefields. Bataan and Corregidor slipped astern into the night.

DOUGLAS MacARTHUR— HERO OF THE PHILIPPINES

Very early in life Douglas MacArthur developed the conviction that he was a child of destiny. This crystallized into an ambition to become one of the great soldiers of history—an ambition that was amply fulfilled. He became not only one of the greatest generals in modern times but also the most dramatic of American military leaders.

MacArthur was born in 1880 at a U.S. Army post near Little Rock, Arkansas. His father, Gen. Arthur MacArthur, had won the Congressional Medal of Honor in the Civil War and later distinguished himself in the Philippine campaign of the Spanish-American War. He became the first Military Governor of the islands.

Douglas was deeply devoted to his mother, who constantly impressed upon him the glamour and ideals of military life. When he entered the U.S. Military Academy at West Point in 1899, both he and his mother took it for granted that he would be the top man there. He was. He stood at the head of the 1903 graduating class, with the highest scholastic record in the first 100 years of the Academy's history. He was manager of the football team, won his letter in baseball and was captain of the cadet corps.

In part because of his father, he always felt that his fortunes were bound up with the Philippines. And in fact he was assigned to the islands as soon as he had received his commission as a lieutenant of engineers. One of his first tasks was to make a survey of Leyte, on whose beaches, forty-one years later, he would land a great American army.

Douglas MacArthur emerged from World War I as the youngest divisional commander in the U.S. Army. He had a tour of duty as Superintendent of West Point, and in 1922 returned to the Philippines as Brigade Commander. From 1930 to 1935 he was Chief of Staff, U.S. Army—one of the youngest ever appointed to that post.

In 1935 he was back in the Philippines, assigned to organize and train the special army of the Philippine Commonwealth. When war came on December 7, 1941 (December 8, Philippine time), General MacArthur was in his sixty-second year, but in a sense his military biography was still ahead of him. As Commander in Chief in the Pacific theater, he would impose total surrender on Imperial Japan, then serve as Military Governor in that occupied country.

In the Philippines, MacArthur fought against superior forces and equipment, under the terrifying handicaps of dwindling manpower, weapons and matériel. Because high-level decisions assigned first priority to the Atlantic-European theater, he received virtually no reinforcements nor supplies. Indeed, there were highly placed men, especially in the Navy, who held that the Philippines should be bypassed, not defended. But MacArthur opposed surrender, even after Manila had fallen, and later events showed that his actions seriously delayed the enemy's schedule of conquest.

The American and Philippine forces absorbed murderous punishment, but they held out for five months. MacArthur was evacuated from Bataan in spite of his protests; his only desire was to stay with his men until the end. He left the Philippines in a PT (patrol-torpedo) boat on March 11, 1942, and after a hazardous trip through enemy-infested waters, reached Mindanao, where he was flown to Batchelor Field, south of Darwin, Australia. It was there that he made his celebrated promise that he would return.

In 1944 MacArthur stood at a microphone on the invasion beach at Leyte, in the midst of raging battle. "People of the Philippines," he said slowly, emotionally, "I have returned. By the grace of Almighty God, our forces stand again on Philippine soil. . . .The hour of your redemption is here. . . . Rally to me!"

This was Douglas MacArthur at his most dramatic: rhetorical, flamboyant, perhaps posing for history— but the successful leader. Much criticism came to him for his theatrical streak. It was the kind of posturing which can be condoned only if accompanied by genius, and that MacArthur had. He was aware of playing a leading role in great dramas of his time and uninhibited in making it known.

The camera catches Gen. Douglas MacArthur at a supreme moment of triumph after he has stepped ashore on the beach of the island of Leyte. The promise he had made in Australia many months before that he would return to the Philippines has been fulfilled.

159

DISASTER—
AND GLORY—
IN THE PHILIPPINES

BY GENERAL OF THE ARMY
DOUGLAS MacARTHUR, USA

These passages are drawn from Reminiscences, *the book Gen. Douglas MacArthur finished only weeks before his death in 1964. The Philippines, he affirmed, were ill-prepared for the sudden and vast Japanese attack. The reinforcements MacArthur was often promised did not arrive in time.*

Our air force in the Philippines contained many antiquated models and was hardly more than a token force with insufficient equipment, incompleted fields and inadequate maintenance. The force was in process of integration, radar defenses were not yet operative and the personnel was raw and inexperienced. They were hopelessly outnumbered and never had a chance of winning.

Actually, the ultimate usefulness of our air arm in the Philippines had become academic because of the crippling of the American Fleet at Pearl Harbor. We were operating under the provisions of a basic plan known as Rainbow 5. It provided that our supply lines —the sea-lanes—should be kept open by the Navy, and our ground forces should hold out for from four to six months. The Pacific Fleet would then move in with massive force, escorting relieving ground troops. The Navy, being unable to maintain our supply lines, deprived us of the maintenance, the munitions, the bombs and fuel and other necessities to operate our air arm. Our original supplies were meager and were soon exhausted. This naval weakness enabled the enemy to establish a blockade of the Philippines which, without other effort on his part, would shortly render our air power helpless. The strike at Pearl Harbor not only damaged our Pacific Fleet but destroyed any possibility of future Philippine air power. Our sky defense died with our battleships in the waves off Ford Island. It canceled "Rainbow 5" and sealed our doom.

A top-level decision had long before been reached that the Atlantic war came first, no matter what the cost in the Far East. President Roosevelt and Prime Minister Churchill, in a Washington conference after the Japanese attack on Pearl Harbor, reaffirmed a policy to concentrate first on the defeat of Germany. Until victory was won in Europe, operations in the Pacific would be directed toward containing the Japanese with the limited resources available. General [George C.] Marshall, the Army Chief of Staff, supported this policy. Unhappily, I was not informed of any of these vital conferences and believed that a brave effort at relief was in the making.

On December 10, 1941, the only two Allied capital ships in the whole western Pacific, the British battleship *Prince of Wales* and the battle cruiser *Repulse,* both commanded by my friend Vice Adm. Sir Tom Phillips, were sunk off the Malayan coast. Sir Tom went down with the *Prince of Wales*; and a whole naval era went down with him. Never again would capital ships venture into hostile waters without air protection; the early advocate of air power, Billy [Brig. Gen. William] Mitchell, had been right.

To allow my main bodies to be compressed into the central plain in defense of Manila by an enemy advancing from both directions could only mean early and complete destruction. By retiring into the peninsula, I could exploit maneuverability of my full forces to the limit and gain our only chance of survival. Our plan of defense, therefore, was that [Maj. Gen. Jonathan M.] Wainwright would fight a delaying action on successive lines across the great central plain from Lingayen Gulf on the north to the neck of the Bataan Peninsula in the south. Under cover of these delaying actions [Brig. Gen. Albert M.] Jones with his troops from Manila and from the central plain would all be withdrawn into Bataan, where I could pit my own intimate knowledge of the terrain against the Japanese superiority in air power, tanks, artillery and men.

The Japanese had not expected that our forces would be withdrawn from Manila, intending to fight the decisive battle of the campaign for control of the city. The devastating attack on Pearl Harbor and the subsequent thrusts in Asia left only this one important obstacle in the path of the Japanese onslaught in the Southwest Pacific. Our tenacious defense against tremendous odds completely upset the Japanese military timetable, and enabled the Allies to gain precious months for the organization of the defense of Australia and the vital eastern areas of the Southwest Pacific. Bataan and Corregidor became a universal symbol of resistance against the Japanese and an inspiration to carry on the struggle until the Allies should fight their way back from New Guinea and Australia, liberate the Philippines and thus press on to the Japanese homeland itself.

The Japanese themselves realized the important effect of protracted resistance in the Philippines. Their historical records state: "There was an influence, a spiritual influence, exerted by the resistance on Bataan. Not only did the Japanese at home worry about the length of the period of resistance on Bataan, but it served to indicate to the Filipinos that the Americans had not deserted them and would continue to try to assist them."

[*To the Filipinos and to many mainland American fighting men, the U.S. failure to provide the beleaguered islands with even minimal munitions and supplies was utterly bewildering. They felt themselves abandoned, even betrayed.–Ed.*]

If only help could have reached the Philippines, even in small form, if only limited reinforcement could have been supplied, the end could not have failed to be a success. It was Japan's ability to continually bring in fresh forces and America's inability to do so that finally settled the issue. . . . It seemed incredible to me that no effort was made to bring in supplies. I cannot overemphasize the psychological reaction of the Filipinos. They were able to understand military failure, but the apparent disinterest on the part of the United States was incomprehensible. Aware of the efforts the Allies were making in Europe, their feelings ranged from bewilderment to revulsion.

The Filipinos, even as the smoke pillars of their burning villages dotted the land, were being told that Europe came first. Angry frustration, for citizens and soldiers alike, irritated bruised nerves and increased the sense of heartache and loss. And the enemy, night after night, in the seductive voice of Tokyo Rose, rubbed raw the wounds by telling them over the radio that defeat and death were to be their fate while America's aid went elsewhere. President [Manuel] Quezon was stunned by the reports of the huge amounts of American supplies now being sent to Russia. His expression of bewildered anger was something I can never forget. As an evidence of assurance to these people suffering from deprivation, destruction and despair, I deemed it advisable to locate [my] headquarters as prominently as possible, notwithstanding exposure to enemy attack.

He [President Quezon] told Col. Charles Willoughby, my versatile G-2 [military-intelligence officer]: "For thirty years I have worked and hoped for my people. Now they burn and die for a flag that could not protect them. I cannot stand this constant reference to Europe. I am here and my people are here under the heels of a conqueror. Where are the planes that they boast of? America writhes in anguish at the fate of a distant cousin, Europe, while a daughter, the Philippines, is being raped in the back room."

Our troops were now approaching exhaustion. The guerrilla movement was going well, but on Bataan and Corregidor the clouds were growing darker. My heart ached as I saw my men slowly wasting away. Their clothes hung on them like tattered rags. Their bare feet stuck out in silent protest. Their long, bedraggled hair framed gaunt, bloodless faces. Their hoarse, wild laughter greeted the constant stream of obscene and ribald jokes issuing from their parched, dry throats. They cursed the enemy and in the same breath cursed and reviled the United States; they spat when they jeered at the Navy. But their eyes would light up and they would cheer when they saw my battered, and much reviled in America, "scrambled egg" cap. They would gather round and pat me on the back and say, "Mubuhay Macarsar" ["Long live MacArthur"]. They would grin—that ghastly, skeletonlike grin of the dying—as they would roar in unison, "We are the battling bastards of Bataan—no papa, no mama, no Uncle Sam."

They asked no quarter and they gave none. They died hard—those savage men—not gently like a

Man's inhumanity to man touched new depths, even for war-time, in the notorious March of Death. For six days (April 10–15, 1942) some 3000 prisoners of war, many of them severely wounded, were forced to walk 140 miles. Tortured by hunger, thirst and scorching heat, abused by their captors, hundreds dropped in their tracks or were murdered by their guards. (Above) Some of the victims, hands tied behind their backs, rest briefly. (Left) In a picture taken by their conquerors, Americans fly the white flag as Corregidor capitulates.

---

stricken dove folding its wings in peaceful passing, but like a wounded wolf at bay, with lips curled back in sneering menace, and a nerveless hand reaching for that long sharp machete knife. And around their necks, as we buried them, would be a thread of dirty string with its dangling crucifix. They were filthy and they were lousy and they stank. And I loved them.

[*On orders from President Roosevelt, MacArthur left Bataan for Australia, on March 11, 1942.-Ed.*]

I sent for General Wainwright, who was to be left in command, to tell him good-bye. A fine, soldierly figure, he had already done wonders in the campaign and was popular with both the officers and men. I told him, "Hold on till I come back for you." I was to come back, but it would be too late—too late for those battling men in the foxholes of Bataan, too late for the valiant gunners at the batteries of Corregidor, too late for General Wainwright.

I stepped aboard PT-41. "You may cast off," I said. Although the flotilla consisted of only four battle-scarred PT boats, its size was no gauge of the uniqueness of its mission. This was the desperate attempt by a Commander in Chief and his key staff to move thousands of miles through the enemy's lines to another war theater, to direct a new and intensified assault. Nor did the Japanese themselves underestimate the significance of such a movement. Tokyo Rose had announced gleefully that, if captured, I would be publicly hanged on the Imperial Plaza in Tokyo, where the Imperial towers overlooked the traditional parade ground of the Emperor's Guard divisions. Little did I dream that bleak night that five years later, at the first parade review of occupation troops, I would take the salute as Supreme Commander for the Allied powers on the precise spot so dramatically predicted for my execution.

When we arrived at Batchelor Field [Australia], reporters pressed me for a statement. I said: "The President of the United States ordered me to break through the Japanese lines and proceed from Corregidor to Australia for the purpose, as I understand it, of organizing the American offensive against Japan, a primary object of which is the relief of the Philippines. I came through and I shall return."

I spoke casually enough, but the phrase "I shall return" seemed a promise of magic to the Filipinos. It lighted a flame that became a symbol which focused the nation's indomitable will and at whose shrine it finally attained victory and, once again, found freedom. It was scraped in the sands of the beaches, it was daubed on the walls of the barrios, it was stamped on the mail, it was whispered in the cloisters of the churches. It became the battle cry of a great underground swell that no Japanese bayonet could still.

163

DEATH MARCH FROM BATAAN

BY LT. COL. WILLIAM DYESS, USA

Brutality in war is as ancient as is warfare itself. But the Bataan death march lives in the chronicles of World War II as a sustained atrocity whose savagery revealed the character of the enemy—the attitude of his Army toward captives taken in battle—and shocked the American public to an intensified dedication to the cause of democracy.

North of our narrow flying field stood Mount Bataan, its jagged crater rising 4700 feet above us into the clear cool sky. From these upper reaches came the drone of Japanese dive bombers, circling endlessly. To the south, smoke was still rising from the rubble which a few days before had been Mariveles.

The dust that enveloped the field was being stirred up by the wheels of trucks and gun carriages. Japanese artillery was preparing to open fire on Corregidor from the sunken rice paddies and nearby ridges. Out of the pall of smoke and dust new prisoners—American and Filipino soldiers—emerged in lines and groups to join those of us already there.

An urgent whispering came to us from all sides:

"Get rid of your Jap stuff, quick!"

"What Jap stuff?" we whispered back.

"Everything—money, souvenirs. Get rid of it!"

We did so without delay—and just in time. Japanese noncommissioned officers and three-star privates searched our persons, then went through our packs, confiscating personal articles now and then. I saw men shoved, cuffed and boxed. This angered and mystified us; we were not resisting. A few ranks away a Japanese soldier jumped up from a pack he had been inspecting. In his hand was a small shaving mirror.

"Nippon?" he asked the owner. The glass was stamped, "Made in Japan." The soldier nodded. The Japanese stepped back, then lunged, driving his rifle butt into the American's face. The Yank went down. The raging Japanese stood over him, driving crushing blows to the face until the prisoner lay insensible. A little way off a Japanese noncom was smashing his fists into the face of another American soldier. He, too, it seemed, had been caught with some Japanese trifle. We were shocked. Someone explained to me that the Japanese assumed that contraband articles had been taken from the bodies of their dead.

The 160 officers and men who remained of my 21st Pursuit Squadron were assembled with about 500 other American and Filipino soldiers of all grades and ranks. They were dirty, ragged, unshaven and exhausted. Many were half starved.

We stood for more than an hour in the scalding heat while the search, with its beatings and abuse, was completed. Then the Japanese guards began pulling some of the huskiest of our number out of line. These were assembled into labor gangs, to remain in the area. As the rest of us were marched off the field, our places were taken by hundreds of other prisoners who were to follow us on the death march from Bataan.

We turned eastward on the national highway, which crosses the southern tip of Bataan to Cabcaben and Bataan Airfield, then veers northward through Lamao, Balanga and Orani. Ordinarily the trip from Mariveles to Cabcaben Field is a beautiful one, but on this day there was no beauty. Coming toward us were seemingly interminable columns of Japanese infantry, truck trains and horse-drawn artillery, all moving into Bataan for a concentrated assault on Corregidor.

Our captors made no move to feed us. The march started on April 10, 1942. Few of us had had anything to eat since the morning of the day before. Many had tasted no food in four days. We had a little tepid water in our canteens, but nothing else. At intervals we saw mounds of captured American food, bearing familiar trademarks, on the sides of the road.

As we marched along, I rounded up the officers and men of my squadron. I didn't know yet what the score was, but I felt we would be in a better position to help one another and keep up morale if we were together.

The sun was nearing the zenith now. The penetrating heat seemed to dissipate the small stores of strength remaining within us. The road, which until this moment had been fairly level, rose sharply in a zigzag grade. We neared Little Baguio, then passed through it. In a short time we were abreast of the blackened ruins of Hospital No. 1, which had been bombed heavily a couple of days before.

Among the charred debris sick and wounded American soldiers were walking about dazedly, dressed only in hospital pajama suits and kimonos. Here and there a man was stumping around on one leg and a crutch. Some had lost one or both arms. They looked wonderingly at the column of prisoners.

When the Japanese officers saw them, these shattered Americans were rounded up and shoved into the marching line. All of them tried to walk, but only a few were able to keep it up. Those who fell were kicked aside by the guards. Those of us who tried to help these men were kicked, slugged or jabbed with bayonet points. For more than a mile these bomb-shocked cripples stumbled along with us. Eventually their strength ebbed and they began falling back through the marching ranks. I don't know what became of them.

About a mile east of the hospital we encountered a major traffic jam. On either side of the congested road, hundreds of Japanese soldiers were unloading ammunition and equipment. Our contingent of more than 600 American and Filipino prisoners filtered through, giving the Japanese as wide a berth as the limited space permitted. Eventually the road became so crowded we were marched into a clearing.

Here, for two hours, we had our first taste of the Oriental sun treatment, which drains the stamina and weakens the spirit. Our captors seated us on the scorching ground, exposed to the full glare of the sun. Many of us had no covering to protect our heads. When I thought I could stand the penetrating heat no longer, I was determined to have a sip of the tepid water in my canteen. I had no more than unscrewed the top when the aluminum flask was snatched from my hands. The guard who had crept up behind me poured the water into a horse's nose bag, then threw down the canteen. He walked among the prisoners, taking away their water and pouring it into the bag. When he had enough, he gave it to his horse.

Whether by accident or design, we had been put just across the road from a pile of canned and boxed food. It seemed worse than useless to ask the Japanese for anything. An elderly American Colonel did, however. He crossed the road, pointed to the food and then to the drooping prisoners. A squat Japanese officer grinned at him and picked up a can of salmon. He smashed it against the Colonel's head, opening the American's cheek from eye to jawbone.

As though waiting for just such a brutal display to end the scene, our guards ordered us to our feet and herded us back onto the road. Their ferocity grew as we marched on into the afternoon. They were no longer content with mauling stragglers or pricking them with bayonet points. The thrusts were intended to kill.

We had marched about a mile after the sun treatment when I stumbled over a man writhing in the hot dust of the road. He was a Filipino soldier who had been bayoneted through the stomach. Within a quarter of a mile I walked past another. The huddled and smashed figures beside the road eventually became commonplace to us. The human mind has an amazing faculty of adjusting itself to shock.

At sundown we crossed Cabcaben Airfield, from which our planes had taken off less than thirty-nine hours earlier. We were marched across the field and halted inside a rice paddy beyond. We had had no food nor water, and none was offered, but we were grateful of the chance to lie down and rest.

I was just dropping off when there came an outburst of yelling and screeching. The Japanese had charged in among us and were kicking us to our feet. They herded us back to the road and started marching us eastward again. During the brief respite leg muscles had stiffened. Walking was torture.

It was dark when we marched across Bataan Field, which with Cabcaben Field I had commanded two days before. It was difficult walking in the darkness. Now and again we passed the huddled forms of men who had collapsed from fatigue or had been bayoneted. The march continued until about 10 p.m. When we were halted, some naïve individual started a rumor that we were to be given water. Instead we were about-faced and marched back. For two more hours we stumbled over the ground we had just covered.

It was midnight when we recrossed Bataan Field and kept going. We were within a short distance of Cabcaben Field when the Japanese diverted the line into a tiny rice paddy. There was no room to lie down. Some of us tried to rest in a half squat, others drew up their knees and laid their heads on the legs of the men next to them.

The thirst had become almost unbearable by now.

(Top left) *American servicemen captured by the Japanese after the courageous defense of Bataan start the infamous March of Death to O'Donnell Prison Camp in the Philippines in April 1942. Thousands began the fearsome trek, but only a relative handful arrived at the prisoner-of-war compound. This photograph was made by the Japanese and later taken from them.*

Given almost no water nor food, the captured Americans had to carry their own sick and exhausted comrades. To leave a man behind on the trail meant his death.

(Bottom left) *Watched by a Japanese soldier, American prisoners sink down for a brief rest along the route to the prison camp. To add to the torment, the enemy forced their captives to go bareheaded under the blistering tropical sun. Any faltering prisoner was bayoneted or shot.*

A Japanese officer appeared surprised that we wanted water. He permitted several Americans to collect canteens from their comrades and fill them at a stagnant carabao wallow which had been additionally befouled by seeping seawater. We held our noses to shut out the nauseating reek, but we drank all the water we could get.

At dawn of the second day the impatient Japanese soldiers stepped among and upon us, kicking us into wakefulness. We were hollow-eyed and as exhausted as we had been when we went to sleep. The rising sun blinded us as we marched. The temperature rose by the minute. Noon came and went. The midday heat was searing. At 1 p.m. the column was halted and Japanese noncoms told American and Filipino soldiers they might fill their canteens from a dirty puddle beside the road. There was still no food. At 2 p.m. we were told it would be necessary to segregate the prisoners as to rank: colonels together, majors together, and so on. This separated all units from their officers.

The line of march was almost due north now. We reached Balanga, about twenty miles from Cabcaben Field, at sundown. We were marched into the courtyard of a large, prisonlike structure dating from the Spanish days, and were told we would eat, then spend the night there.

At one side of the yard, food was bubbling in great caldrons. Rice, soy sauce and sausage were boiling together. The aromatic steam that drifted over from those pots had us almost crazy. While we waited we were given a little water. After drinking we were ordered into the line for what appeared to be a routine search. Our guards lined us up in a field across the road. As we left, grinning Japanese held up steaming ladles of sausage and rice. The officer followed us to the field, then began spouting denunciations and abuse.

"When you came here you were told you would eat and be allowed to sleep," he said. "Now that is changed. We have found pistols concealed by three American officers. In punishment for these offenses you will not be given food. You will march to Orani [five miles to the north] before you sleep."

The accusation was undoubtedly a lie. If a pistol had been found, the owner would have been shot, beaten to death or beheaded on the spot. Besides, we knew that the original searchers hadn't overlooked even a toothbrush, to say nothing of a pistol.

Our guards had been increased for the night march, and rigid discipline was imposed. We were formed into columns of fours. A new set of guards came up on bicycles and we were forced to walk practically at double-quick to keep up. After two hours these guards were replaced by a group on foot. The change of gait cramped our leg muscles; walking was agony.

We had learned by rough experience that efforts to assist our failing comrades served usually to hasten their deaths and add to our own misery and peril. So we tried the next best thing—encouraging them with words. Talking had not been forbidden.

It was during a period of slow marching that an old friend, a Captain in the Medical Corps, began dropping back through the ranks. It was plain he was just about done in. I said, "Hello, Doc. Taking a walk?"

"I can't go another kilometer," he said slowly.

"Well, Doc, I'm about in the same fix," I told him. Nothing more was said until we had covered two or three kilometers. Every now and then Doc would begin to lag a little. When this happened, the fellow on the other side of Doc would join me in slipping back and giving him a little shove with our shoulders. Kilometer after kilometer crawled by, but Doc didn't fall out. If he had, his bones would have been left to bleach somewhere along that road of death.

The hours dragged by, and as we knew they must, the dropouts began. It seemed that a great many of the prisoners reached the end of their endurance at about the same time. They went down by twos and threes. I can never forget their groans and strangled breathing as they tried to get up again. Some succeeded. Others lay lifeless where they had fallen.

I observed that the Japanese guards paid no attention to these. I wondered why. The explanation wasn't long in coming. There was a sharp crackle of pistol and rifle fire behind us from a "clean-up squad" of Japanese buzzards. Bodies were left where they lay. On through the night we were followed by orange flashes and thudding shots.

At 3 a.m. of April 12—the third day—our group arrived half dead at Orani, in northeastern Bataan, after a twenty-one-hour, thirty-mile march from Cabcaben, near the peninsula's southern tip. Close to the center of the town the Japanese ordered us off the road to a barbed-wire compound a block away. It had been intended for 500 men. Our party numbered more than

600. Already in the compound, however, were some 1500 Americans and Filipinos.

The stench of the place reached us long before we entered it. Hundreds of the prisoners were suffering from dysentery. Human waste covered the ground. Maggots were in sight everywhere. There was no room to lie down. We tried vainly to sleep sitting up.

Japanese soldiers told us there would be rice during the morning. We paid no attention. We didn't believe them and were too miserable to care. As the sun climbed higher, Americans and Filipinos alike grew delirious. Their wild shouts and thrashing about dissipated their ebbing energy. They began lapsing into coma. For some it was the end. Brief coma was followed by merciful death. I had a blinding headache from the heat, glare and stench.

Japanese noncommissioned officers entered the compound and ordered the Americans to drag out the bodies and bury them. We were told to put the delirious ones into a thatched shed a few hundred feet away. Then the grave-digging began.

We thought we had seen every atrocity the enemy could offer, but we were wrong. The shallow trenches had been completed. The dead were being rolled into them. Just then an American soldier and two Filipinos were carried out of the compound. They were in a coma. A Japanese noncom stopped the bearers and tipped the unconscious men into the trench. The guards then ordered the burial detail to fill it up. As the earth began falling about the American, he revived and tried to climb out. His fingers gripped the edge of the grave. He hoisted himself to a standing position.

Two Japanese guards placed bayonets at the throat of a Filipino on the burial detail. When he hesitated, they pressed the bayonet points hard against his neck. The Filipino raised a stricken face to the sky. Then he brought his shovel down upon the head of his American comrade, who fell backward to the bottom of the grave. The burial detail filled it up.

During the long afternoon, stupor served as an anesthetic for most of the prisoners in the compound. There was no food. Toward evening the guards allowed Americans to gather canteens and fill them at an artesian well. It was the first good water we'd had. Night brought relief from the heat, though there still was no room to lie down, despite the number of dead and delirious removed from the compound.

Dawn of April 13—our fourth day since leaving Mariveles—seemed to come in the middle of the night. Its magnificent colors and flaming splendor meant to us only the beginning of new sufferings. The temperature seemed to rise a degree a minute.

At 10 a.m., just as I was wondering how I could get through another day, there was a stir at the gates. Guards filed in and began lining us up in rows. Out of one of the dirty buildings came kitchen corpsmen, dragging cans of sticky gray rice which they ladled out —one ladleful to each man. Those of us who had mess kits loaned the lids to men who had none. The portion given to each man was equivalent to a saucer of rice.

The food was unappetizing and was eaten in the worst possible surroundings, but it was eaten. It was our first in many a day. I began feeling stronger immediately, despite the growing heat. There was not enough of the rice, however, to stay delirium and coma for the weaker prisoners. There were those for whom it came too late. Scenes of the previous afternoon were repeated, and there were additional burials in shallow graves.

The rest of us passed the afternoon in a stupor. We continued to sit while the sun dropped behind the western mountains. In the twilight we were ordered to our feet. It was still light as we were marched out of the compound toward the road. About midnight rain started falling. It was chilling, but it cleansed some of the filth from our stinging bodies and relieved the agony of parched dryness. The rain lasted about fifteen minutes.

We were refreshed for a time, but as the grinding march continued, men began falling down. When I saw the first man go down I began wondering whether the buzzard squad was following us as it had been two nights before. A flash and the crack of a shot answered my question.

Just before daybreak the guards halted the column and ordered us to sit down. The ground was damp and cool. I slept. Two hours later we were prodded into wakefulness and ordered to get up. The sun had risen. Our course was northeasterly now, and we were leaving the mountains and Bataan behind. The country in which we found ourselves was flat and marshy. This was Pampanga Province.

Our stay on the damp ground had caused leg muscles to set like concrete. This was the cool of the morning, yet my throat was still afire with thirst. And just across the road bubbled an artesian well. Its splashing was plainly audible and the clear water was almost too much for my self-control. I thought if I could only reach that well and gulp all the water I wanted, the Japs could shoot me and welcome. The next minute I told myself I was balmy even to entertain such a thought.

The Japanese were aware of the well, and they must have known what was passing through our minds. A Filipino soldier darted from the ranks and ran toward the well. Two others followed him. Two more followed these, then a sixth broke from the ranks. Guards all along the line raised their rifles and waited for the six to scramble into the grassy ditch and go up on the opposite side, a few feet from the well. The guards fired again and again, until all six lay dead. Thus did our fifth day of the death march start with a bloodbath.

From then on I practiced detaching myself from the scenes about me. I have no doubt this saved my sanity on more than one occasion in the days to come. I remember little of the two miles we walked after the six murders at the well. We were at the outskirts of Lubao, a sprawling city of 35,000, before mutterings around me brought me back to earth to look upon a new horror. All eyes were directed toward the mutilated corpse of a Filipino soldier hanging on a barbed-wire fence. This was a ghastly Japanese object lesson, of course.

Our scarecrow procession began passing through the rough streets of Lubao. We were in a residential section. Windows of homes were filled with faces that bore compassionate expressions. Presently from the upper windows of a large house a shower of food fell among us. It was followed quickly by other gifts tossed by sympathetic Filipinos who stood on the sidewalks. There were bits of bread, rice cookies, lumps of sugar and cigarettes.

The guards went into a frenzy. They struck out right and left at the Good Samaritans, slugging and jabbing with bayonets indiscriminately. Then they turned their rage upon us. When the townsfolk saw their gifts were only adding to our misery, they stopped throwing them. Some Filipinos asked the Japanese officers if they might not help us, but they were warned to stay away. I recall a merchant who wanted to open his store to us. We could have anything we wanted free, he said. A Japanese officer warned him to keep his distance. This was at Santo Tomas or Santa Monica,

the two small settlements between Lubao and Guagua, about three miles to the northeast. In Guagua also the Filipino civilians tried to slip food to us. For that they were beaten and clubbed—as we were.

We neared San Fernando, Pampanga Province, during the afternoon of our fifth day's march. It was at San Fernando, according to rumor, that we were to be put aboard a train and carried to a concentration camp. From among the 600 and more American and Filipino military prisoners who had started with me from Mariveles, many familiar faces were missing. We had come almost eighty-five miles with nothing to eat except the one ladle of rice given to us more than twenty-four hours before.

We could now see the railroad tracks which ran alongside the highway at Guagua, amid the lush vegetation of the flat, marshy countryside. We could have entrained an hour before. I doubted, therefore, that the railroad figured in any plans for us.

Just ahead of me, in the afternoon heat, were two American enlisted men, stumbling along near the point of collapse. I wasn't in much better shape. At this moment we came abreast of a *calasa* (covered cart) which had stopped beside the road.

An American Colonel, who had also been watching the two enlisted men, observed that no guard was near us. He drew the two soldiers out of line and helped them into the cart, then got in also. The Filipino driver tapped his pony. The cart had moved only a few feet when the trick was discovered.

Yammering guards pulled the three Americans from the cart and dragged the Filipino from the driver's seat. A stocky noncommissioned officer seized the heavy horsewhip. The enlisted men were flogged first. They fell to the ground and lost consciousness.

The Colonel was next. He stood his punishment a long time. When he finally dropped to his knees his face was so crisscrossed with welts it was unrecognizable. Bleeding and staggering, the Colonel was kicked back into the line of American prisoners.

I don't know what became of the enlisted men. I never saw them again. During the remaining two miles we marched I listened for shots, but heard none. The soldiers probably were bayoneted.

The sun still was high in the sky when we straggled into San Fernando, a city of 39,000 population, and were put in a barbed-wire compound similar to the one at Orani. We were seated in rows for another sun treatment. Conditions here were the worst yet. The prison pen was jammed with sick, dying and dead Americans and Filipinos. They were sprawled amid the filth and maggots that covered the ground. Practically all had dysentery. Malaria and dengue fever appeared to be running unchecked. Guards had shoved the worst cases beneath the rotted flooring of some dilapidated building. Many of these prisoners had already died.

After sunset Japanese soldiers entered and inspected our rows. Then the gate was opened again, and kitchen corpsmen entered with cans of rice. We held our mess kits and again passed lids to those who had none. Our spirits rose. We watched as the Japanese ladled out helpings to the men nearest the gate. Then, without explanation, the cans were dragged away, and the gate was closed. It was a repetition of the ghastly farce at Balanga. The fraud was much more cruel this time because our need was vastly greater. We put our mess kits away and tried to get some sleep.

But the Japanese had something more in store for us. With an outburst of shrill whooping and yelling, guards poured into the compound with fixed bayonets. They feinted at the nearest prisoners with the sharp points. The Japanese outside the compound cheered the jokesters within. One made a running lunge and drove his bayonet through an American soldier's thigh. This stampeded several other prisoners, who trampled the sick and dying men to the ground. The Japanese left, laughing. There was little sleep that night. There were shouts of delirium. There was moaning. There were the pitiful sounds of men gasping their last.

At dawn of April 15, the sixth day of our ordeal, we were kicked to our feet by the guards and ordered to get out of the compound. They did not even make a pretense of giving us food or water.

Enough prisoners had been brought out of the compound to form five companies of 115 men each. In this formation we were marched to a railroad siding several blocks away where stood five ancient, ramshackle boxcars. None of these could have held more than fifty men in comfort. Now 115 men were packed into each car and the doors were pulled shut and locked from the outside.

There was no room to move. We stood jammed together because there wasn't sufficient floor space to permit sitting. As the day wore on and the sun climbed higher, the heat inside the boxcars grew to ovenlike intensity. There was little ventilation, only narrow screened slits at the ends of the cars. A large number of the prisoners were suffering from dysentery. Men began to faint. Some went down from weakness. They lay at our feet, face down in the filth.

After a seemingly interminable wait, the train started with a jerk. The ride lasted more than three hours. Later I heard that some men died in each of the five cars. When the doors were opened, someone said we had reached Capas, a town in Tarlac Province, and that we were headed for O'Donnell Prison Camp. When the prisoners tumbled out into the glaring sunlight, the wretchedness of their condition brought cries of compassion from Filipino civilians who lined the tracks.

We were marched several hundred yards down the tracks to a plot of bare scorching ground amid the tropical undergrowth. It was another sun treatment. The Japanese guards formed a picket wall around us to forestall the friendly Filipinos who had come to give us food and water. Some of these, however, hurled their offerings over the heads of the Japanese, hoping they would fall into our midst. Then they took to the bush, outrunning the guards who pursued them.

We sat for two hours in the little clearing before we were ordered to our feet. A seven-mile hike to O'Donnell Prison Camp was ahead of us. As we straggled on, we had ample reason to bless the kindly Filipinos of Capas. Having seen other prisoners pass that way, they had set out cans of water among the bushes and in high grass along the road. Our guards found many of these and kicked them over before our eyes. But some were overlooked and a few of us were able to take the edge off our thirst. One gaunt American said he believed that he owed his life to the thoughtful townsfolk.

My first good look at O'Donnell Prison Camp was from atop a rise about a mile off. I saw a forbidding maze of tumbledown buildings, barbed-wire entanglements and high guard towers from which flew the Japanese flag. As we stood, staring dazedly, there came to me a premonition that hundreds about to enter the prison this April day would never leave it alive. I wondered how long I could last. Sharp commands by the Japanese guards aroused me. We started moving.

DOOLITTLE BOMBS TOKYO

BY BRIG. GEN. S. L. A. MARSHALL,
USAR (RET.)

We are destined to win. *So the Japanese claimed, and so it appeared—from Pearl Harbor through the early months of 1942. Then, in April, came news that lifted the spirit of the entire nation: a group of U.S. planes had bombed Tokyo! We had hit the enemy's greatest city, the capital of the island empire! As a tactical strike, it had little impact on the military power of the Japanese, but for its effects on the psychology of America and her enemy in the Pacific, the Tokyo raid was a master stroke of offensive action.*

In late March 1942 the Japanese Government decreed a first full-dress air-raid drill for Tokyo. Starting at 9 a.m. on April 18 the city would stage a three-hour alert, and all the military planes based on Honshu would form a protective umbrella above Tokyo throughout the exercise.

The story was given to the Japanese press, but the event went unnoted elsewhere in the world. On April 2, while official word of the air-raid drill was getting around Japan, the U.S. carrier *Hornet* put to sea out of San Francisco; aboard her, along with the ship's company, were sixteen Army B-25's, Col. James H. Doolittle, thirty-one other Army pilots and forty-eight air crewmen. Their mission was to bomb Tokyo after dark on April 18. By merest chance the evening of the same day as Tokyo's first air alert had been chosen. Naming a firm date well in advance was imperative. The U.S. raiders had to home in on friendly fields in China and would risk being shot from the skies unless these bases were alerted to receive them at an appointed hour.

This amazing coincidence of alert and attack points

up the salient characteristic of possibly the most daring and spectacular operation in American military history. All that happened conformed to "Murphy's Law": "If anything can go wrong, it will." As blunder piled on blunder, one mistake compensated for another, and in the end came salvation, glory and immeasurable success.

The project, conceived in January 1942, was regarded as a small thing, hardly more than a gesture of American derring-do to lift hearts on the home front during the darkest days of the war. Pilots and air crewmen, assembled at Eglin Field, Florida, for a cram course in the technique of takeoff from a carrier in an Army medium bomber, were no collection of superstars. They were drawn on a volunteer basis from the 17th Bombardment Group, because it had the planes. Such was the training grind's intensity, with so much to be learned, that there was no time to instruct crewmen how to bail out. Only a few of the pilots had ever parachuted from a plane.

By the time Task Force Mike, under command of Vice Adm. William F. Halsey, had left the Hawaiian Islands behind, it was a considerable expedition, counting 2 carriers (*Hornet* and *Enterprise*), 3 heavy cruisers, 1 light cruiser, 8 destroyers and 2 oilers. The weather was foul all the way, and the same could be said for high-level communications.

In order to ensure secrecy, Gen. George C. Marshall and Gen. Henry H. Arnold used double-talk for their cabled exchanges with Generalissimo Chiang Kai-shek about the project. So guarded were these communications that neither side understood the other, although both assumed they did. Chiang thought it was a project for delivering to him forty or fifty bombers from India. As Task Force Mike moved over the international date line and into enemy waters, Chiang advised the expedition to make a slight diversion and take a crack at the Japanese in the Andaman Islands. Almost at the last minute he found out that Tokyo was to be bombed and that the raiders would fly on to his domain, and he was greatly alarmed at the news.

When they were well over the date line, Halsey's fleet suddenly found itself twenty-four hours ahead of schedule. Though no explanation of this error was ever made, the suspicion exists in some quarters that the Navy miscalculated the effect of the date line on the timing of the voyage.

At 3:10 a.m. on April 18 the *Enterprise*'s radar revealed two enemy surface craft 21,000 yards off, and two minutes later a light appeared on the same bearing. Halsey turned the Task Force (T.F.) almost due north for a time, then swung west again. Two more enemy vessels appeared on the *Enterprise*'s grid, and as the T.F. again evaded, Halsey realized that he was coping with successive screens of picket ships more than 700 miles east of the Japanese coast. At 7:15 one search plane returned and reported seeing an enemy patrol ship forty-two miles directly ahead. All ships turned left to avoid detection. Twenty minutes later another Japanese patrol ship of about 120 tons was sighted from the *Hornet* at 20,000 yards' range. Its radio was crackling.

Admiral Halsey, worried for the safety of the two carriers, was now certain that the T.F. had been sighted and that Tokyo had been warned. (It was a reasonable assumption, but a wrong one; no message got through to Tokyo.) He precipitately ordered the Doolittle Raiders to prepare to launch. The carriers would turn into the wind at twenty-six knots; all patrolling planes would land on the *Enterprise*. The cruiser *Nashville* would turn aside and sink the Japanese patrol ship with gunfire.

As the T.F. got under way, the *Hornet*'s position was 35° 45′ N., 153° 40′ E. The B-25's and their crews had been transported to within 620 miles of the closest promontory of Japan. The Army fliers were at breakfast when told that they must take off approximately twelve hours early. They heard the news unruffled and continued with their coffee while the planes were being readied; some missed the meal altogether. Except that they would depart in the sequence already agreed upon, the original plan was abandoned at this moment. It would be a daylight, instead of an after-dark, raid. They were still five hours' flight from Tokyo. There would not be fuel enough to get them to the Asian mainland, so they would have to ditch in the East China Sea. Fortunately they were spared the knowledge that they would be going against a fully alerted city under massive air cover.

Before the first B-25 cleared the *Hornet*'s flight deck, the *Nashville* had been left behind to accomplish her mission of destroying the Japanese patrol boat. After firing on the enemy vessel, the *Nashville* finally dispatched a boarding party to sink her.

Directly east of Tokyo on Honshu Island lies Cape Inubo, a pimple projecting from the mass of the Chiba Peninsula. South of Tokyo, along the west shore of Tokyo Bay, are Kawasaki and Yokohama. Some 150 miles west of Tokyo Bay is Nagoya, on Ise Bay. A hundred miles or so farther on are Osaka and Kobe, lying on the north shore of Osaka Bay. Since these six cities, all pretty much in line, were the targets to be attacked, the pilots of the sixteen B-25's had been directed to cross the Japanese coastline at Cape Inubo and from there on to fly the bombing mission at treetop level.

By the original plan, Colonel Doolittle, his B-25 loaded with incendiary bombs, would take off first, three hours before Lt. Travis Hoover in the second plane; Doolittle would set Tokyo ablaze to light the target for the follow-up planes. Once the early launch was ordered, it was too late for Doolittle to change his bombload, and the scheme no longer made sense. Hoover followed Doolittle by three minutes instead of three hours.

At 8:18 a.m. aboard ship (7:18 Tokyo time), Doolittle made his run down the *Hornet*'s flight deck, took off into the forty-knot wind, circled the carrier twice to get his exact heading, checked his compass and then, as Hoover's plane came alongside him, headed for Tokyo. Plane No. 3, piloted by Lt. Robert M. Gray, was in the air five minutes later. Plane No. 4, under Lt. Everett W. Holstrom, had trouble with the right engine from the moment of launching, but went on with none of the crew knowing that owing to a repairman's carelessness, the electrical lead to its gun turret was unconnected.

By 8:10 Tokyo time, or fifty-two minutes after the start, the first fourteen planes had taken off. Due to navigational mistakes, only two of them found Cape Inubo; most of them missed it by many miles. The pilots who hit the landfall right on the button were Lt. Harold F. Watson in Plane No. 9 and Lt. Richard O. Joyce in No. 10. From first to last, these were the only perfect performers.

Most of the others, losing their way, came at Tokyo from all points of the compass, some attacking north up the bay, others hitting from the west. An utterly bizarre and circumstantial pattern, contrived by faulty instruments, hard weather and human error, it turned miraculously into what seemed a stroke of genius. Because of these meanderings, the Japanese were wholly mystified and deceived about the source of the attack.

From the flight deck of the U.S. carrier Hornet, *a B-25 bomber heads for Japan—part of the Doolittle raid of April 18, 1942, which gave Tokyo its first taste of war, only four months after Pearl Harbor. The sortie shattered the myth of the impregnability of the Japanese homeland.*

So Task Force Mike was given a cushion, the Japanese flak was denied a line on which to aim and President Roosevelt made "Shangri-la" a household word, when he later facetiously named the mythical Tibetan refuge (from James Hilton's novel *Lost Horizon*) as the raiders' mysterious base.

Doolittle was fired on by a Japanese freighter when 600 miles out, and later he crossed over a camouflaged Japanese cruiser that took no note of him whatever. He reached the Honshu coast at 11:55 a.m., fifty miles north of Cape Inubo, having wasted that many miles edging into the teeth of a forty-knot wind. He had come along at the 150–166-m.p.h. speed at which the B-25 was able to achieve maximum economy of fuel, as did fourteen of the aircraft that were more or less following him. The one exception was Plane No. 8, piloted by Capt. Edward J. York, which was eating gas at such a rate that York figured he would never get beyond the Japanese islands after dropping his

bombload and headed for Vladivostok, U.S.S.R., where he was interned by the Russians for some months.

Twenty minutes after crossing the coast, Doolittle and Hoover were over Tokyo. On their direct southerly course, they had flown over hundreds of Japanese country folk who simply waved them on their way. In Tokyo the three-hour air-raid drill was just coming to an end. Barrage balloons at the mouth of the Tama River were being hauled down. Traffic had almost resumed its normal flow, except that pedestrians stopped to gawk at the Japanese fighter planes stunting directly overhead.

At the Sumida River that cuts across northern Tokyo, Hoover turned west to his target, while Doolittle went southwest, directly over the city. As Doolittle pulled up to 1200 feet to release the incendiary clusters, Hoover, by now miles away, went to 900 feet and let go the demolition bombs. By sheer ac-

The wreckage of Colonel Doolittle's bomber following the first air raid on Japan's home islands is investigated by curious Chinese villagers after the plane crashed in that mountainous country. The Colonel and members of his crew managed to parachute safely to earth.

cident, the hits from the two planes coincided at 12:15 p.m. Tokyo time, and by a sorry mischance several of the pellets from the first of Doolittle's fire clusters hit the largest hospital in Tokyo and burned it to the ground.

An alert Japanese antiaircraft (AA) crew fired a round uncertainly in Doolittle's direction, then broke off. Doolittle was at that moment so close to the Imperial Palace that he could have hit it more quickly than the Armory, his second target. But no one else fired at him. The already alerted city could not be realerted; the book didn't cover such a situation. The Japanese attack planes overhead, seeing the U.S. bombers come in below them, assumed they were part of the friendly air show.

By a strange irony, Tokyo's first air-raid exercise, staged by a people who boasted that their country would never feel the impact of an enemy bomb, had worked out as a gift to Doolittle and his men.

The Swiss Ambassador was lunching with Ambassador Joseph Grew at the U.S. Embassy.

"Sounds like the real thing," said His Excellency. "Must be your fellows."

"Impossible," said Grew. "Just the air show."

"Bet you a hundred dollars," said the Swiss.

"Taken," said Grew.

Hoover's assigned target had been a group of powder factories. Somehow he missed them, and just what he did hit neither he nor his bombardier, Lt. Richard E. Miller, could say later. They were over the right place, according to the map, and bombs were away when ordered, but the target certainly did not explode. Hoover flew on west, then changed his direction to south. He was under no more stress than if he had been delivering the mail.

There was a twenty-minute lapse after Doolittle and Hoover hit and got away. That was because the B-25's that followed had drifted too far north or south.

175

Lieutenant Gray, pilot of No. 3, reached the coast fifteen miles south of Cape Inubo, flew across the Chiba Peninsula and went at the city from the south. He was looking for a steel works, a gas works and a chemical plant. At 1450 feet he let go his bombs, and they seemed to be about where he wanted them. There was a little flak, but not enough to jar the twin-engined plane. He flew on west.

Plane No. 4, its entire flight marked by engine trouble, made its landfall on a small island, Mitake, eighty miles south of Tokyo. Though Lieutenant Holstrom now knew that his turret gun was out and had just been told that his left gas tank was leaking, he turned north up the coastline toward Tokyo. The city was partly aware that an attack was on; the AA guns began to react, as did the Japanese planes overhead. While still south of the bay, Holstrom saw Japanese pursuit ships maneuvering toward him as if about to peel off. He jettisoned his bombs in the ocean and winged west as fast as possible.

Lieutenant Dean E. Hallmark in Plane No. 6 had tailed Capt. David M. Jones in Plane No. 5 to the Honshu coast at a point thirty miles above Cape Inubo. Jones turned south and for twenty minutes was lost. Getting his bearing at the mouth of Tokyo Bay and then turning north again, Jones lost Hallmark, whose plane crashed in the ocean shortly after dropping its bombload. He and his surviving crew fell into Japanese hands. Charged with a war crime, the crew was imprisoned for forty months; Lieutenant Hallmark was executed.

Jones, noting too late that one of his gas tanks was only two thirds full, suddenly changed his mission and decided to bomb the first suitable-looking targets along Tokyo's southwestern bay shore. As he went at a nest of oil tanks and "a saw-toothed factory" resembling an aviation plant, AA batteries opened fire and churned the air all about him. His fourth bomb overshot the mark and exploded next to the corner of another factory.

Lieutenant Ted W. Lawson in No. 7 made a landfall near Kasumiga Lake and turned south along the Chiba Peninsula, intending to attempt a straight east-west run across the city. After dropping his bombs on his assigned targets he flew south, then west, to deceive the enemy, meeting with no interference; but as he approached the Chinese mainland with gas running low, he was forced to ditch a quarter of a mile offshore.

Watson and Joyce came along then for the only perfect runs of the attack. It was nearing one o'clock, the raid had been going forty-five minutes, and all the way from the coastline the two planes were under AA fire. Paying no heed, Watson barreled straight across Tokyo from the northeast to the southwest, the widest part of the city, flying at 300 feet. He passed directly above the Imperial Palace and the Diet building, where the flak flew thickest. Approaching Kawasaki, Watson rose to 2500 feet for his run. The bombs were dropped in train, and as the last one fell, a Japanese pursuit plane came up under the B-25's belly, firing from 100 yards away. Watson was certain he had hit his primary target—the Kawasaki Truck and Tank Plant. Instead he had bombed the heart out of the Tokyo Gas & Electric Engineering Co.

As Joyce came out of the clouds above upper Tokyo Bay to look for his target, a Japanese carrier steaming south to Yokosuka engaged him. At the same moment that the B-25 lurched from AA fire, he saw what he wanted—the main plant of the Japanese Special Steel Co.—and he went straight for it at 2500 feet altitude. His first two bombs exploded dead on target; Joyce was so heavily beset right afterward that he knew nothing of the third and fourth bombs. The Japanese crowd below waited for his plane to fall. One big hunk of metal tore through the fuselage just ahead of the automatic stabilizer. Joyce went into a steep dive, trying to shake off the ground fire; as he made the maneuver, nine Japanese pursuit planes came in above his plane and a little to his right front. Joyce quickly pulled away and continued up the Tama River toward the mountains. Twice more on its way west the bomber was attacked by fighter formations, and twice again it was hit by ack-ack (antiaircraft fire). Joyce, in the only U.S. plane hit during the raid, fought off more enemy aircraft than all the other B-25's combined.

Plane No. 11, piloted by Capt. Charles R. Greening and assigned to bomb Yokohama, never got there. Making his landfall well to the north of the city, Greening was attacked by four enemy fighters while flying down the Chiba Peninsula. Sergeant Melvin J. Gardner, the gunner, hit two of the pursuers, and one crashed in flames. With the two others still on his heels, Greening saw what first looked like a thatched village but proved to be a well-camouflaged tank farm. He let all four of his incendiaries go at this one target and turned back east to the sea to shake off the pursuit.

The crew heard tremendous secondary explosions, and when they rode west again, they could see black smoke filling the sky where they had made their run.

Lieutenant William M. Bower, Yokohama-bound in No. 12, by sheer accident followed Greening over the same route. Crossing the coast he was lost and flew south along the peninsula looking for a check mark, but instead ran into the blaze that Greening had lighted. That oriented him; he turned west to cross the bay. There were at least eight sausage balloons over his target, the Yokohama shipyard and docks. The flak steadily thickened; he saw three of the balloons shot down by fire meant for him and decided to get away in a hurry. So he turned north to bomb the Ogura Oil Refinery and several nearby factories.

Lieutenant Edgar E. McElroy, in No. 13, had trailed after Bower and Greening until reaching the coast. Where they maintained course and hence lost themselves briefly, he suspected he was too far north and turned left. His target was the Yokosuka Naval Base, and his run was favored by phenomenal good fortune. The bombardier, Sgt. Robert C. Bourgeois, dropped the first bomb in a way that he thought would ensure its hitting land. Instead, it exploded amidships through the deck of a Japanese carrier in dry dock— a fluke hit observed only by the gunner, Sgt. Adam R. Williams. The next two demolitions blew up a crane, set fire to a tied-up transport and blasted a repair shop. The incendiary fired a line of buildings used for administration. As the B-25 sped up and away, McElroy looked at his watch. The raid on the Tokyo area ended at 1:41 p.m. The way out was along the southern coast and past the southwest corner of Kyushu.

The three planes assigned to attack the more westerly cities were crossing the coast about the time the strikes were being made on Yokohama. Major John A. Hilger in No. 14 and Lt. Donald G. Smith in No. 15 flew together from the carrier to the mouth of Tokyo Bay, then on for another hour and a quarter to Ise Bay, where they parted company. Hilger dropped his incendiaries on the Nagoya Castle Barracks, the Mitsubishi Airplane Plant and a tank farm, while Smith bombed the Vyenoshita Steel Works, the Kawasaki Aircraft Factory and the Electric Machinery Works in Kobe. Both pilots made their runs without drawing fire; the earlier hits on Tokyo had failed to alert the cities to the west. Ten minutes after Smith flew on, Kobe sounded an alert.

For Lt. William G. Farrow in No. 16, fate had reserved its unkindest cut of the day. He didn't even hit the right city. He dropped his four incendiaries in a second attack on Nagoya, thinking he was making a run against Osaka—but this was not to be his worst break, by far.

So of sixteen B-25's aimed to strike Japan, fifteen actually bombed enemy installations, and only one failed to fly away westward, to clear the Japanese islands under its own power. No one was yet saved, however; none had enough fuel to reach his destination on the Asian mainland. With darkness came the storm and murk that blotted out the horizon and everything below. Still, the storm gave the aircraft the gift of a 125-mile tail wind and in so doing saved them for a while. But later, at midnight and in the small hours, they were doomed; so thick was the fog that no landings were possible. Most of the men got to earth by parachuting.

Gradually, with the aid of Chinese villagers and guerrillas, they gathered together and were brought to places where the injured could be treated and flown home. But in addition to York's and Hallmark's groups, Farrow's was also missing. They had made the longest flight of all, deep into the Chinese interior, and by the worst luck imaginable, they had landed in the great bend of the Yangtze River that the Japanese were holding. Farrow and a crewman were executed, but three others managed to survive forty months' imprisonment.

In the wake of the raid the people of Tokyo panicked. The press clamored for more protection. Dignitaries went on radio to soothe public fears and assure citizens that the situation would quickly be righted. Soon squadrons of Zeros were brought back from the fighting rim of Japan's mushrooming Pacific Empire, and AA batteries, withdrawn from the active war zones, blossomed from the roofs of Tokyo's more prominent buildings. It was a concession to the home front, but a move that Japan could ill afford to make, and the richest prize to come from Doolittle's audacious undertaking.

A young Sergeant, David J. Thatcher, had gone with the expedition as gunner for Lawson in Plane No. 7. In Chungking someone asked him how he accounted for the success of the show. He answered with words to which nothing need be added: "It was only by the hand of God that any of us came out alive."

THE BATTLE OF THE CORAL SEA

BY REAR ADM. SAMUEL ELIOT MORISON,
USNR (RET.)

By the end of April 1942, the tally of Japanese victories in the Pacific seemed unending. She had conquered all the Philippines save for the island bastion of Corregidor. The flag of the Rising Sun flew over Hong Kong, Thailand, Malaya, the Netherlands East Indies and a goodly part of Burma. Flushed with success, the Imperial High Command now reached out to take Tulagi in the Solomons and Port Moresby in Papua. This would mean the severing of Allied lines of communication with Australia and lead to the eventual conquest of that entire continent. How the Japanese plans were rudely upset is related by Samuel Eliot Morison in a detailed account of a vital naval battle—the first such encounter ever fought entirely by air, with surface ships of both American and Japanese fleets out of sight and never in contact with each other.

The Coral Sea is one of the world's most beautiful bodies of water. Typhoons pass it by; the southeast trade winds blow fresh across its surface almost the entire year, raising whitecaps which build up to long surges that crash on Australia's Great Barrier Reef in a 1500-mile line of white foam. Lying between the Equator and the Tropic of Capricorn, it knows no winter, and the summer is never uncomfortably hot. The islands on the eastern and northern verges—New Caledonia, the New Hebrides, the Louisiades—are lofty, jungle-clad and ringed with coral beaches and reefs. Here the interplay of bright sunlight, pure air and transparent water may be seen at its best. Only in its northern bight—the Solomon Sea—does the Coral Sea wash somber shores of lava and volcanic ash. That bight had been dominated by Japan since January 1942, from her easily won base at Rabaul. It was now time, in the view of her war planners, that she move into the dancing waters of the broad Coral Sea.

Cincpac [Commander in Chief, U.S. Pacific Fleet] Intelligence smoked out the gist of this plan by April 17, and Adm. Chester W. Nimitz saw to it that Task Force 17, a two-carrier group (*Lexington* and *Yorktown*) under Rear Adm. Frank Jack Fletcher, was there to spoil it. That is why the Coral Sea, where no more serious fights had taken place in days gone by than those between trading schooners and Melanesian war canoes, became the scene of the first great naval action between aircraft carriers.

The Japanese operation plan was not simple; her Naval strategists believed in dividing forces. There were three main divisions: (1) A left prong (Rear Adm. Kiyohide Shima), to occupy Tulagi in the lower Solomons and establish a seaplane base whence Nouméa could be neutralized; (2) a right prong (Rear Adm. Sadamichi Kajioka's Port Moresby invasion group, floating a sizable army in a dozen transports, covered by heavy cruisers and the light carrier *Shoho*), to start from Rabaul, whip through Jomard Passage in the Louisiades, and capture Port Moresby; and (3) Vice Adm. Takeo Takagi's big carrier striking force, including *Shokaku* and *Zuikaku*, veterans of Pearl Harbor, to enter the Coral Sea from the east and destroy anything the Allies might offer to interfere with this plan. The whole was to be directed from Rabaul by the Commander in Chief of the Fourth Fleet, Vice Adm. Shigeyoshi Inouye.

Admiral Nimitz did not have even half this force at his disposal; but he put together under Admiral Fletcher's command all he had and gave him no more specific orders than to stop the enemy. Fletcher in *Lexington*, familiar with the Coral Sea, came steaming west from Pearl Harbor. *Yorktown* was ordered to cut short a period of upkeep at Tongatabu, waltz over to the Coral Sea and rendezvous with "Lady Lex." Most of the ships of "MacArthur's Navy," not yet named Seventh Fleet, also joined. These were three cruisers—H.M.A.S. *Australia* and *Hobart*, U.S.S. *Chicago*—and a few destroyers, under the command of Rear Adm. J. G. Crace, R.N.

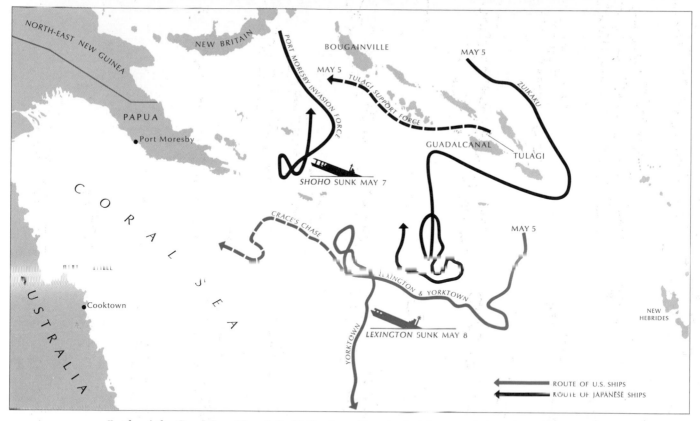

Battle of the Coral Sea: May 4–8, 1942. In a historic duel between Japanese and American carrier-based aircraft, an enemy attempt to transport an invasion force to Papua and occupy strategic Port Moresby was turned back. Both sides suffered serious losses in ships and planes.

The ensuing action was full of mistakes, both humorous and tragic, wrong estimates and assumptions, bombing the wrong ships, missing great opportunities and cashing in accidentally on minor ones.

The Japanese won the first trick. Admiral Shima's group occupied Tulagi, unopposed, on May 3. They took the second, too, on May 4, when *Yorktown*'s planes bombed Tulagi and did only minor damage. At the same time, however, Japan missed her best chance to win this game. To save an extra ferrying mission, *Shokaku* and *Zuikaku* were ordered to deliver nine fighter planes to Rabaul; this delayed the two big carriers two days, so that on May 4 they were too far away to counterattack Fletcher.

Nothing much happened on May 5 and 6, when each big carrier force was searching for its enemy without success. At one time they were only seventy miles apart. That 6th day of May, when Lt. Gen. Jonathan M. Wainwright surrendered Corregidor in the Philippines, marked the low point of the entire war for American arms. But the next day opened with a bright dawn. This transition from Corregidor to the Coral Sea is startling and dramatic.

At dawn on the 7th *Shokaku* and *Zuikaku* sent out a search mission for an enemy force they suspected to be in the Coral Sea. The search planes sighted Fletcher's retiring fueling group, fleet oiler *Neosho* and destroyer *Sims*, and made the second big mistake of this error-crowded battle by reporting them to be a carrier and a cruiser. Admiral Takagi promptly sank them both. This cost Rear Adm. Tadaichi Hara, the carrier division commander under Takagi, six planes and saved the American carriers from attack.

The American planes, however, were off on a similar wild-goose chase. That particular blunder had resulted from the report of a *Yorktown* search plane, at 8:15 a.m. on May 7, of "two carriers and four heavy cruisers" about 175 miles northwest of the American force. Fletcher, naturally assuming that this meant Takagi's Striking Force, launched full deckloads to go after it. When these aircraft were already airborne it was discovered that the "two carriers and four heavy cruisers," owing to a disarrangement of the pilot's code contact pad, should have been reported as "two heavy cruisers and two destroyers." Nevertheless, by good luck the *Lexington* and *Yorktown* fliers

encountered the light cruiser *Shoho,* piled in on her and put her under in a matter of ten minutes—a record for the entire war. "Scratch one flattop!" signaled *Lexington*'s dive-bomber commander.

It was not the right flattop, but the loss of *Shoho* so discouraged Admiral Inouye that he ordered the Port Moresby invasion group, instead of pressing on through Jomard Passage, to mill around at a safe distance north of the Louisiades. Thus our attack on the wrong carrier thwarted the enemy's main object.

More grim humor on the 7th was furnished by "Crace's Chase." Fletcher gallantly weakened his carriers' screen by detaching Rear Admiral Crace, R.N., with his two Australian cruisers, U.S.S. *Chicago* and a few destroyers, to find and attack the Port Moresby invasion force. Crace handled this mixed group so efficiently as to beat off thirty-one land-based bombers from Rabaul; and he also fought off three U.S. Army Air Force B-17's from the Townsville (Queensland) base, which thought his ships were Japanese. To cap this comedy, the thwarted Japanese planes claimed to have sunk two battleships and a heavy cruiser.

Toward evening of the same day, Takagi sent a search-attack mission to find and bomb Fletcher's carriers. They missed the flattops, but had a rough experience. First they were intercepted by Fletcher's fighter planes and lost nine of their number; then, after dark, six tried to land on *Yorktown,* mistaking her for Japanese; and eleven more were lost trying to make night landings on their own carriers.

On May 8 came the payoff. The two major carrier groups under Fletcher and Takagi (or, to name the officers in tactical command of the carriers, Aubrey W. Fitch and Hara), which had been fumbling for one another for the better part of three days and nights, finally came to grips. Each located the other and attacked. Never were forces more even. The Japanese Admiral had 121 planes; Fitch had 122. Hara had a screen of four heavy cruisers and six destroyers; Fitch, now Crace was away, had but one more of each type. Nature, however, gave the Japanese carriers one great advantage. They were in a belt of heavy overcast which

had moved into the Coral Sea from the Solomons, while the Americans were out in the clear under brilliant sunshine. Thus the *Yorktown* attack group, forty-one planes strong, missed *Zuikaku* under a rain squall, concentrated on *Shokaku* and obtained only two bomb hits; but one of these bent the flight deck so that she could no longer launch planes. Half of *Lexington*'s attack group failed to find the fog-enshrouded enemy; the other half gave *Shokaku* another bomb hit. Takagi, who by this time (noon) believed that both American carriers were sinking, decided he could dispense with the damaged carrier and sent her back to Truk.

His assumption was about half correct. The Japanese attack group, amounting to some seventy planes, gave both American carriers a severe working over. *Yorktown* took one bomb hit which killed sixty-six men; *Lexington* took two torpedoes and two bomb hits. The end of the battle found "Lady Lex" listing, with three fires burning but her power plant intact. There was every prospect of damage control quenching the fires, when suddenly she was wracked by two internal explosions which forced Capt. Frederick Sherman to abandon ship. This was done skillfully, some 150 wounded being lowered in basket stretchers into motor whaleboats, while the able-bodied slid down lines into the water, where they were picked up by destroyers. Rear Admiral Thomas C. Kinkaid, who handled these rescue operations, showed the qualities that helped him to emerge as one of our great flag officers.

"Lady Lex," beloved as few warships have been by her crew, some of whom had been on board since she was commissioned in 1927, finally had to be sunk by a friendly destroyer's torpedoes. Her loss gave the Japanese the winning score in tonnage sunk; but that does not register the effect of the battle. Admiral Inouye, fearful of risking the Port Moresby Invasion Force south of Papua without air cover, ordered it to retire to Rabaul; and never again in this war did the keel of a Japanese warship vex the Coral Sea south of the Louisiades. Thus the battle was really won by the Americans owing to their biggest mistake, the sighting and bombing of *Shoho;* her loss led Inouye to throw in the sponge. Even the big carriers' battle turned out ill for the Japanese, because *Shokaku* took two months to repair, and *Zuikaku* took over one month to replace her plane losses. Neither big flattop could take part in the great Battle of Midway (see pages 192–211) coming up. But *Yorktown* could and did.

The carrier Lexington, *the main American casualty in the victorious Battle of the Coral Sea, is shown immediately after the fatal explosion. United States losses also included a destroyer and a tanker. The enemy lost seven major warships and took heavy punishment on seven other ships. In this key battle of the Pacific theater, surface vessels did not exchange a single shot.*

DRESS REHEARSAL: THE STORY OF DIEPPE

BY QUENTIN REYNOLDS

To strike a blow at Hitler's Fortress Europe, to test the strength and weaknesses of its defenses and at the same time to throw a scare into the Nazi High Command—these were the goals of the August 1942 raid on the French coastal town of Dieppe. Whether the blow was successful or not is still debated today. As the first seaborne strike against the Germans in World War II, Dieppe did assuredly provide invaluable know-how that paid off later—and it gave the lie to the myth, fostered by Hitler and Goebbels, of the impregnability of the German-held coastline of Europe. But the casualties suffered by the British, Canadian and American forces (predominantly by the Canadians) were severe. Quentin Reynolds, one of the most celebrated correspondents of World War II, viewed the raid close at hand from the Headquarters ship. Here is what he witnessed on that historic day.

[*Early in the war, picked men from all British services were organized into Combined Operations, under Lord Louis Mountbatten, for special training in amphibious warfare, from small raids to assault landings. At the core of the new formation were the Commandos, hard men prepared for feats of daring and endurance. Because their courage and nonchalance caught the popular imagination, the entire organization, of which they were only a component, came to be known as the Commandos.*

Starting with raids on the Channel Islands, the Commandos carried their attacks to enemy strongholds from Norway to both coasts of the Mediterranean. Their most widely known adventure was a landing behind the German lines in Libya, North Africa, in November 1941, for an attack on Gen. Erwin Rommel's headquarters. Unfortunately, the "Desert Fox" was not at home, but a number of his top officers were killed, and the boldness of the undertaking made military history.

The principal arena of Commando interest, naturally, was the French coast on the Channel and the Atlantic. Raids on St.-Nazaire and Bruneval were accounted successful. The objectives of such raids, apart from harassment of the enemy and destruction of his installations, were to probe the character of German defenses, to bring back prisoners, to tie down the Luftwaffe and other forces—the enemy could not know when and where the British-led daredevils would strike next.

On August 19, 1942, the largest and most ambitious Commando operation up to that time—a reconnaissance in force—was carried out at Dieppe. This vital harbor was not only among the most strongly defended enemy points on the Channel but part of what is known as the Iron Coast, because of German fortifications in addition to the high, unscalable cliffs. To make matters worse, the British flotilla as it approached the French coast ran into a small German force of armed trawlers. The hope of surprise was canceled out. It was an assault in daylight against a fully alerted, thoroughly entrenched enemy: in Churchill's words, "a hard, savage clash."

In all, nearly 10,000 men were involved, at sea, on the ground and in the air. Canadian elements drawn from famous regiments such as the Royal, Essex Scottish, South Saskatchewan and Fusiliers Mont-Royal made up most of the ground forces. Of 5000 Canadians engaged, 3350 were killed, wounded or missing. Casualties in all other contingents—including the U.S. Rangers, for whom it was the first battle—were equally staggering.

The price paid was brutal, but measured by Commando objectives, the raid was adjudged a victory. In the perspective of later events Dieppe can be seen as a dress rehearsal for the invasion of North Africa eighty days later and for the assault on Fortress Europe on D day, June 6, 1944.—Ed.]

On the evening of August 17, Maj. Jock Lawrence phoned me at the Savoy Hotel in London. "Be at my office at ten in the morning in civilian clothes. Bring your uniform in a bag. Sweet dreams!"

Jock's "office" was the headquarters of Lord Louis Mountbatten, Commander in Chief of Combined Operations, which included the Commando detachments. I had long wanted to go along on a Commando raid, and now it had been arranged.

At Combined Operations Headquarters everybody was calm, unhurried. The secrecy in regard to raids was so well kept that very few even at Headquarters knew of them in advance. Jock took me to Lt. Col. Trolly Peck-Smith, who ordered me: "You will go to Jock's apartment and change into your uniform there. A car will pick you up at two o'clock and drive you to a port. There you will board the destroyer *Calpe*. Lieutenant Boyle will be expecting you. You will be the only correspondent on this ship, the Headquarters ship that directs the whole show."

At Lawrence's place we found his roommate, Lt. Col. Loren B. Hillsinger, an American officer, packing in a great hurry. He left, and Jock laughed. "He's going on the same show you are. There will be several American observers and a few American troops—just a token force."

When I had changed into my uniform, Jock said, "Take off those war-correspondent tabs. If people see them, they might figure there is some big show on. We'll use a pair of lieutenant colonel's silver leaves. Then you'll be merely another American officer."

Soon a car painted in dull brown squealed to a stop outside. I went out and climbed in the back with two officers—a Wing Commander and a British Major. The Wing Commander said to the driver, "Straight for Portsmouth."

Seventy-eight miles later our driver stopped at a concrete pierhead. A Warrant Officer politely asked us for identification cards and told us to wait for a few minutes. Soon we were joined by a Canadian Captain—a press officer. He asked us what ships we had been assigned to, and the Wing Commander and the Major said they were to go on the destroyer *Berkeley*. (A few hours later, when the *Berkeley* received a direct bomb hit, both of them were killed.)

"How come a Canadian press officer is in on the show?" I asked.

The Captain smiled. "It's pretty much of a Cana-

dian show. Our troops got awfully tired of sitting on their fannies these past two years. They want to fight. You should have heard them cheer this morning when Ham [Maj. Gen. J. H.] Roberts told them this was to be the real thing."

The *Calpe* looked very small and tired, but all destroyers look tired in their war paint. I climbed up the gangway and met a good-looking young man who introduced himself as Lieutenant Boyle.

"Shall we go to the wardroom?" he suggested. It is almost a rite on British warships that a visitor is first given the courtesy of the ship by the offer of a drink. Boyle ordered a drink for me, tea for himself.

Soon the ship shook herself like a puppy which had just come out of the water, and Boyle said calmly, "We're off. Now first of all I want to introduce you around."

We climbed two sets of iron ladders to a fairly large, pleasant room. Three men were doing things with radio instruments and headphones. But my eyes were on the big, smiling man who stood up as I entered. "Glad you're on board," he said. "I'm Roberts."

Boyle told me at last that we were headed for Dieppe. Minesweepers were ahead, trying to cut a lane through the German defense.

"Ever been to Dieppe?" young Boyle asked.

"Two weeks ago, with the night fighters," I told him nonchalantly, and his eyes popped out.

"You actually flew in combat with them?" He was really excited. "I've often wanted to do that. Those pilots are marvelous. And such kids—most of them."

"How old are you?" I asked, amused.

Boyle colored slightly. "I'll be twenty-one in about three hours. Tomorrow is my birthday."

A sailor stuck his head into the room. "Captain Hughes-Hallett would like to see you on the bridge, sir." Boyle and I climbed three sets of iron ladders to the bridge.

Captain John Hughes-Hallett, in charge of the Naval operations, would be complete boss until we arrived at Dieppe. Then General Roberts would take over in conjunction with Air Commodore Adrian T. Cole. Combined Operations meant just that: the Army, Navy and Air Force acting as a team in perfect harmony.

We were lying about two miles offshore, apparently at our rendezvous point. It was quite dark, but we could see ships all around us. There were fat transports, heavy-bellied, with small invasion barges on their decks. There were the long tank landing craft, low in the water, and occasionally the sleek form of a destroyer slithered by.

"Any cruisers or battle wagons with us?" I asked Hughes-Hallett.

He shook his head. "We have destroyers, but nothing larger. Every available fighter aircraft will be with us at dawn, however."

I suddenly realized that we were under way. Boyle and I went below to the wardroom again, and he spread out a map and several large photographs on the table.

"Here's a general view of Dieppe." He pointed to the map. "You'll notice various notations on it, such as 'possible light gun' or 'road block' or 'antitank obstacle' or 'house strengthened,' and a hundred others. The R.A.F. has been taking pictures of Dieppe for weeks; the last were taken yesterday."

The photographs looked as though they had been taken from 100 feet up. The amazing telescopic lenses used by the R.A.F. could "see" from terrific heights.

"And here," Boyle added, "is our timetable."

He handed me three sheets of typed paper. As I read them I realized the weeks of work that Mountbatten, Hughes-Hallett and Roberts had put in on planning this raid. Every ten minutes something was scheduled to happen. Zero hour, when landings would be made on the beaches, was 5:20 a.m.; at 5:10 our destroyers were to shell those beaches for ten minutes. Each had its particular target. Exactly 1780 shells were to be fired, and the three beaches to be shelled were exactly 1780 yards long.

"Entering the minefield," Joe Crowther, the little mess steward, broke in. "Better put on the Mae Wests and get on deck." Life jackets were called Mae Wests even in official language by then. We slipped into them and went on deck.

Ahead of us I saw a light. "The minesweepers dropped lighted buoys where they had cleared," Boyle explained. "One about every half mile."

We passed within twenty yards of the small green light and now we were in the minefield. We plowed along at a rather brisk pace. Far ahead I saw another one of the small lights. So far so good. A sharp breeze had sprung up, but I noticed that I was sweating. I peered ahead, looking for the next buoy, but there was nothing but darkness and beyond that the enemy. Not a voice broke the silence. The ship veered slightly to starboard and I was sure that we had missed the way. And then suddenly, 100 yards ahead, a tiny light

A trio of wounded and exhausted Canadian soldiers who took part in the daring daylight raid on the French port of Dieppe is forced to surrender to troops of the German garrison. The landing operation began at dawn on August 19, 1942, and lasted for nine hours.

showed. Always, in war, the suspense is more frightening than the actual combat.

On we went, hitting each little green light right on the nose. Then a bell clanged somewhere; voices were heard again; the ship seemed to breathe a sigh of relief. We were through the minefield.

Now the time for keeping secrets had passed. "Suppose everything goes according to plan," I asked Roberts, "is there any thought of establishing a permanent bridgehead?"

"No," he smiled. "We have food, medical supplies and ammunition for one day only. We want, if possible, to destroy shipping in the harbor, grab a radio detection finder, destroy the torpedo factories. More important, the raid will show the Hun that he can't relax his vigilance anywhere on the coastline; that he must, in fact, strengthen his defenses. He can only do that by withdrawing troops, planes and guns from Russia. Of course, we'd rather move in on a big scale and establish what is so foolishly called a second front; but you know as well as I do the difficulties of that."

I went up on the bridge and was surprised to find that we had practically stopped. Evidently we were almost there. Far ahead a light blinked.

"That's a lighthouse," one of the officers on the bridge told me. "It's good news, too. It means they don't expect us."

"Where are we now?" I asked.

"About ten miles off Dieppe."

The main force, which had Dieppe itself for its objective, would land to the right of the harbor. Commando No. 4 Unit was to land some six miles farther to the right and knock out a 6-inch gun battery. This was an absolute must; the night before, the unit's commander, brilliant young Lt. Col. Lord Lovat, had told his men simply, "Do it even at the greatest possible risk."

To the left of Dieppe there was another 6-inch gun battery, on high ground which commanded the beaches in front of the city. Commando No. 3 Unit was to knock this one out.

Obviously, we hadn't been detected yet. Closer our flotilla crept. It was just 3:47 a.m. And then . . . The night that had been sleeping awakened brilliantly in a riot of dazzling green and bright-red streaks that arched the sky, flashing vividly against the black velvet of the night. We stood there, stunned, on the bridge. These were tracer bullets, and they came from our left. Then the sharp bark of guns came across the water.

August 19, 1942: Forewarned, the Nazi garrison at Dieppe on the French coast exacted a heavy toll of life when Allied troops came ashore in what had been planned as a surprise raid. Tanks that had landed with the invaders were all disabled before the withdrawal.

Boyle returned from General Roberts' cabin. "A German tanker was going in, a few miles to the left of Dieppe, escorted by four or five E boats [motor torpedo craft]. They saw our Commandos' barges and started giving them hell. This," he added gloomily, "will upset our schedule."

I went into Roberts' cabin and sat on the floor close to the door, out of the way. Roberts and Cole talked calmly, and men with earphones and mouthpieces received reports and gave them to Roberts.

"The E boats have been dispersed. Three of them sunk. The tanker has been destroyed. Commando Number Three and the Royal Regiment are trying to find their rendezvous and proceed."

But the fire from the E boats had scattered the landing barges filled with Commandos and sunk some of them. Many of the Commandos died before ever reaching shore. Others turned back. One landing barge, however, managed to flank the E boats unobserved and touch down on the beach. The men in this barge were not actually combat Commandos. They had been trained in liaison and communication. But they carried guns. They waited for a few moments, and then twenty-four-year-old Maj. Peter Young said, "We got orders to put that six-inch battery out of action, didn't we?"

Someone said, "That's right."

"Then what the hell are we waiting for?" he growled.

There were only twenty men. They went inland a quarter of a mile, unobserved, and found the 6-inch battery. They scattered, Indian fashion, and opened fire with their little automatic rifles. They couldn't silence the battery, but they worried it so by their sniping that we, offshore, never got its full attention.

Now the dawn was growing brighter. The barrage opened as the second hand of my watch hit 5:10. The air seemed to tremble and vibrate with the sound. For ten minutes the guns thundered and golden flashes cut the half light of the dawn and then, as though it had all been rehearsed by a master director, the curtain of the night rolled up, and in front of us lay the city of Dieppe.

From the left flank came the dull boom of 6-inch guns. Then came the rattle of machine-gun fire. Cutting through it all I heard the high, singing sound of the Spitfires—twenty-four of them—two squadrons. Now they broke formation, swinging into flights of four each. They separated and hit different levels so that we would be protected from all sides.

Roberts kept getting reports—few of them good. Each beach, each objective, had been given a name.

"Report from Orange Beach, sir. Commando Number Four accomplished its mission—returning."

"What about Red Beach?"

The aide shook his head and repeated monotonously, "Calling Red Beach. Calling Red Beach." This was where Commando No. 3 was supposed to have landed.

"Purple Beach calling. Asks for more smoke on west cliffs. Being strafed badly."

"Henderson, tell Alfred," Roberts said.

Colonel Henderson, one of Roberts' aides, spoke into a microphone. "Calling Alfred. Calling Alfred. Lay smoke on west cliffs immediately. Are you getting me? Over."

"Alfred" today was R.A.F. Headquarters in England. Somewhere 300 miles away, orders were given. We had Douglas Bostons hovering over us, each equipped with two-way wireless. I walked on deck and saw two Bostons dive from nowhere, trailing white feathery smoke behind them. It settled on the cliffs. They banked sharply and retraced their flight, and now the tops of the cliffs were hidden by this artificial layer of cloud. Machine gunners there would not be able to see our men huddling behind the low seawall on the beach.

This was the essence of Combined Operations. Not two minutes had passed since General Roberts had asked for smoke on the cliffs—and now the cliffs were shrouded.

We had moved closer inshore now. Shells came from the shore batteries; one landed fifty feet from us and threw up a cascade of water. Boats of every kind stretched as far as the eye could see. Small motor launches dashed from ship to ship. Motor torpedo boats roared throatily by, and large barges filled with men and guns were moving toward the shore.

A landing craft approached us and tied up, and men climbed on board. They were dirty and grimy and their faces were streaked with black, but they were grinning. This was part of Lovat's No. 4 bunch. They hadn't been able to locate their own ship so they'd come to us.

"How was it?" I asked a big Commando as he climbed on deck.

"A piece of cake," he laughed. "We got close to them before they even knew we were there. We were shot with luck. A shell from our mortar hit their magazine and blew the whole bloody works up. Then we rushed in and finished them off."

And then the *Luftwaffe* came. From now on we were under constant pressure from enemy aircraft. Wherever you looked you saw dogfights as Focke-Wulfs and Dorniers tried to break through our protecting umbrella of Spitfires. I watched two Dorniers die, falling like balls of orange fire into the sea. A third met a shell squarely in midair and simply came apart, a mass of scattering debris.

A landing barge pulled alongside and delivered the first wounded. The doctor was waiting in a small room two decks below. He told the walking cases to sit down in the passageway while he took care of the two who were badly wounded. Both men lay there with eyes wide open, their faces drained of blood, expressionless, as though their pain had fashioned masks for them. One had been shot in the stomach. The doctor's expression didn't change as he stuck a needle into the man's arm. The second man had a leg wound. The doctor gave him an injection of something. Two orderlies hurriedly cut the man's trouser leg and bared the wound. Below his knee the leg held only by a shred.

"How did I get out?" The voice that came from the man was a dead monotone. "We touched down and stepped ashore and machine guns came from both sides. . . . Everyone was hit—except me. . . . They kept shooting at us. . . . They didn't hit me. . . . They were all killed—all except me. . . . They never hit me. . . ."

The voice trailed off into nothingness. The doctor swore under his breath. "Too late, damn it!" The man on the table was dead.

Our Oerlikon guns were barking angrily, which meant that the enemy planes were still coming. The wardroom was crowded now. At least a dozen men in soaking uniforms were in there, and the mess steward Joe Crowther was helping them to remove their wet clothes and get into warm blankets. Most of the wounds were shrapnel wounds, and those aren't so bad unless you are hit in the stomach.

Occasionally a bomb fell fairly close, and down below the waterline we were never sure whether we had received a direct hit or not. We'd hear an explosion and the ship would creak and list a bit, and we'd be quiet and then Joe Crowther would laugh and say, "Hell, that was half a mile away." Joe had been merely a Yorkshire accent a few hours before. Now he was

emerging as a personality. "This is a lucky ship," he said, wrapping a newcomer in blankets.

Someone stumbled down the iron ladder and a familiar form lurched into the wardroom. It was Wallace Reyburn of the Montreal *Standard*. His face was ashen. He took two steps into the room, then collapsed slowly to the floor. I lifted his head and forced some brandy down his throat. He choked, shook his head, opened his eyes and recognized me.

"This is a hell of a story, isn't it?" He grinned weakly. Then he added, "I'm not sure, but I think I got hit a couple of times."

"How was it on shore?" I asked.

"Bloody awful," he shivered. "I was with the Saskatchewans. There was a twelve-foot parapet on the beach and on top was very tough barbed wire. Our guys worked and worked and finally one of them cut through it and we went over. That's when they discovered us. We ducked through some machine-gun fire and got to a deserted house. But then they started dropping mortars on us and that wasn't good. So we started to go to the city itself.

"We had to cross a river and there was a bridge across it. The first men who started over were all mowed down. Then Lieutenant Colonel C. C. I. Merritt came up. What a man! A big, youngish guy. He just said calmly to his men, 'Don't bunch up. Here we go.' And then, carrying his tin hat in his hand, he walked across that bridge like he was taking a stroll. Last I saw of him, he was going toward Dieppe with a gun in each hand. I hope he gets back."

"How long were you on shore, Wally?"

"Over six hours. The last hour was the worst, just waiting for our boats to take us off. They came on the dot, but the tide was out and we had to run three hundred yards through machine-gun fire and mortar shells to reach them.

"It was what Dunkirk must have been—men lying there on the beach wounded or dead; men up to their knees in water waiting for boats; men aiming rifles at planes that passed so fast you could hardly see them.

"The boat I got in was stuck, but we shoved it off, and when we were out about fifty yards, so help me, it began to sink. Just went down under us. There was another boat about twenty yards away and we swam to that. Then that one started to sink. But the British sailors went from man to man grabbing helmets, guns, anything that was heavy, and threw it all overboard to lighten the boat, and we managed to get away."

Both our Oerlikons and our 4-inch guns were firing now, and the noise and vibration filled the small room. The lamp over the table began swinging from side to side crazily. We listed badly to port and then to starboard—we were zigzagging, zigzagging. Evidently the German planes were getting in on us.

I guess the lurch came first, a split second before the explosion. The ship heaved upward and lurched to port. And then the explosion came, and it was as though you'd hit a giant glass with a giant tuning fork, and the sound of it kept ringing in your ears long after the blow had been struck. From the pantry that adjoined the wardroom there was a mighty rush of water. We all hung onto tables and chairs, and then above all the noise came a hearty belly laugh. It was Joe Crowther.

"Hear that new eight-inch gun of ours?" his Yorkshire voice boomed. "Sounds just like a bomb hittin' us, don't it? Hell of a gun, that big eight-inch. Shakes the ship up a bit. Broke all the glasses in my pantry."

I looked at Joe's big, innocent, moonlike face and I blessed him. We were far below the waterline and there would be small chance of getting up the iron ladder if we started to sink. We had no 8-inch gun, but some of the tenseness which had gripped the wounded men left them.

Men were hurrying into the pantry with tools. The ship had righted itself, but we were still zigzagging. The planes hadn't been driven off.

I went on deck. Every ship was moving, so as not to present a stationary target. Flak ships (small craft carrying only antiaircraft guns) spouted lead into the skies. Spitfires darted here, there, everywhere. But sometimes, in pursuit of an enemy plane, they left openings, and Dorniers and Focke-Wulfs slashed through and bombed and strafed our ships.

A barge came alongside and discharged about thirty men—nearly all wounded. Our decks were crowded now with wounded. Some lay stretcher to stretcher, and others leaned against gunwales and ammunition boxes. Two of the men who had just come aboard were American Rangers. They looked very young.

"Who were you with?" I asked a tall, blond youngster.

"Commando Number Four," he said. "It was bad on shore, but, my God, how those Commandos can fight! We were after a six-inch battery, and there was

an orchard just before we came to it. Know what those Commandos did? They lay down and fired; then stood up, grabbed an apple off a tree and fired again."

His pal had a shrapnel wound in his arm, but he laughed at it. "I knew nothing could happen to me," he said, grinning. "I had a swell mascot with me—a Bible." He dug into his water-soaked clothes and came out with a sodden little book. "My father carried it all through the last war, and he never got hurt. So when I left he gave it to me, and believe me I'll always carry it."

I walked aft and saw where the bomb had hit. The debris had been cleared away, but some blood remained. Several stretchers lay together, and the faces of the men lying there were covered.

Then the *Berkeley* was hit. A large bomb landed amidships and broke her back. We didn't hear the bomb, although the *Berkeley* was only 400 yards from us. The noise from our own guns and from bombs landing nearby had swelled into one earsplitting symphony of sound, so that no one note could be distinguished.

We went to the help of the stricken ship. Motor torpedo boats and landing barges had surrounded her, and the British Navy was doing a job now. I doubt if any man stayed in the water for more than three minutes. Many were killed when that bomb hit, but the last of the wounded were taken off.

Young Boyle came in the wardroom. "The show is over," he said quietly. "Everyone is on the way home. Everyone but us. General Roberts is going in toward the beaches to pick up any men who may be in the water. We'll be here alone and we're sure to catch hell," he added cheerfully.

From the deck we could see the ships retreating. Our destroyer turned in toward the shore, steaming so close in that the Germans turned their machine guns on us. We stood behind gun screens and bulkheads, and the bullets rat-tat-tatted against them. Now and then someone spotted men clinging to rafts or wreckage, and we steamed slowly to them and hoisted them aboard. The shelling was bad now because they had us alone.

I was standing just outside the passageway amidships when suddenly, above the sound of our guns, came a new noise—a noise that having heard it once you never forget. A Focke-Wulf 190 had gotten through the umbrella of Spitfires and was hurling itself downward at us. I stood frozen and so did the four men around me. Boyle was there and Air Commodore Cole. The plane came from 5000 to 300 feet in a few seconds, then dropped a bomb. The air was full of roaring noise. I fell back through the passageway.

I lay there on my back, listening to the world coming to an end. I was dazed. I didn't know whether I'd been hit or not. Then I bit on something and spit out a gold inlay. I picked it up and put it in my pocket. Evidently the concussion had loosened it.

I got up shakily and walked the two steps to the deck. The two men who had been standing on either side of me lay there dead. A sailor helped Air Commodore Cole inside. The face was covered with blood. Young Boyle had been hit in the neck and the head.

I fingered the little gold inlay in my pocket. I'd been standing with four men; two of them were dead, the other two seriously wounded. I had only lost an inlay.

We'd been here nearly nine hours now and everyone was tired. There was no spontaneous shouting among the gun crews when they sighted a German plane. They merely loaded and fired automatically. We had about 500 wounded on board. The decks and wardroom were packed with silent men.

A body can take a terrible beating; it is practically indestructible. But nerves can stand only so much. When nerves get frayed, the strain on them over a period of time becomes too much. This has nothing to do with a man's inherent courage or stamina. The reaction is entirely involuntary.

"Let's go home, for God's sake!" A Lieutenant stood up suddenly. "I've had enough," he sobbed. "Let's go home!"

"Have a drink, man," Joe Crowther soothed. "We've all had enough, but the Skipper knows what he's doing."

The Lieutenant drank deeply from the bottle. The rest of the men looked away from him, as though not to notice his outburst. He had broken the rules.

The Chief Engineer stuck his head in the doorway. "We're headed for home," he said, and you could almost hear the relief exude from the men in the room.

Dorniers and Focke-Wulfs kept after us, and we had two more near-misses. But then we caught up with our flotilla and passed it. This was fine, we thought. We'd be home in a couple of hours. But that hadn't been General Roberts' idea. Oh, no. Once again he had to be first through that minefield.

Hours passed, and now the sun, having seen enough this day, balanced itself on the horizon. Far ahead we saw a thin line, and then there was England. We were home, but there was no jubilation on board. Everyone was too tired, and men were thinking of comrades who had been left behind.

General Roberts walked out on deck. He, too, looked tired now. He leaned over the rail, staring down into the water.

"It was tougher than you figured, wasn't it?" I asked.

He drew a deep breath. "Yes," he said slowly. "It was tougher than we figured."

The next day Lord Mountbatten talked to correspondents at a press conference.

"We did not accomplish all of our objectives," he said. "But we did accomplish our main purpose. We sent a fairly large naval force to Dieppe, and kept them there for more than nine hours. We lost only one destroyer. The R.A.F. lost ninety-eight planes, but saved thirty of the pilots. They officially downed at least ninety-one German aircraft, and two hundred others are listed as probables. The raid taught us a great deal which will be of value in subsequent operations."

About 10,000 men were engaged in the operation, including the Naval personnel and the R.A.F. pilots. More than a third were killed or wounded. But the fact that the raid was launched against perhaps the best-fortified spot on the coast meant that no other spot was immune. The Germans had to give up their hope of sending divisions from France to the eastern front.

The back of the *Luftwaffe* was broken that day in August. Our planes were able to make daylight sweeps over France with much less opposition than they had met before. The magnificent Focke-Wulfs and the well-trained German pilots lost that day were not expendables.

General Dwight D. Eisenhower studied every move of the Dieppe operation in planning the North African campaign. In fact, he was big enough to ask Lord Mountbatten and his staff to help him plan that venture. Three days after the Americans had landed in northern Africa, Eisenhower sent Mountbatten a cable of thanks for his help. By inference, he was thinking of the men who had died at Dieppe. It would be safe to say that many American lives were saved in North Africa because of lessons learned in the dress rehearsal by the Commando raid at Dieppe.

The long string of Japan's victories had at last run
its course, and for America and her Allies the retreating was over.
Now came the time to counterattack. U.S. infantrymen are
shown wading ashore on Makin Atoll. Here the
Japanese garrison was crushed in a few days.

ON THE ISLAND ROAD TO TOKYO
WE RETREAT NO MORE

MIDWAY: TURNING POINT IN THE PACIFIC

BY J. BRYAN III

A month after its setback in the Coral Sea, the Japanese Navy attacked the U.S. base at Midway. The battle was not just a turning point in the Pacific war but one of the most decisive in the history of warfare. J. Bryan III has recorded the blazing action that shattered Japan's dream of empire.

The Battle of Midway was one of the most furious in all history. Even before the last salute to its dead was fired, we and our Allies hailed it as a great American victory. So it was—but how great only became evident years afterward when documents were made available showing that it was the turning point of the war in the Pacific. They also showed how narrowly it missed being a defeat. If a certain Japanese scout had taken a longer look; if a young American cryptanalyst had been less acute; if a dive-bomber pilot from the *Enterprise* had guessed wrong; if the signal for an emergency turn had reached Capt. Akira Soji promptly—if any one of such seemingly trivial components had been different, years later the United States might still have been struggling to dislodge the Japanese from Hawaii.

Although Midway was fought on June 3–6, 1942 (June 4–7, U.S. time), it had been precipitated six weeks before, on April 18. At shortly before eight o'clock that morning, Vice Adm. William F. Halsey signaled from his flagship, the carrier *Enterprise,* then 620 miles off Tokyo, to Capt. Marc A. Mitscher of the carrier *Hornet,* nearby. The signal read: LAUNCH PLANES X TO COLONEL DOOLITTLE AND HIS GALLANT COMMAND GOOD LUCK AND GOD BLESS YOU.

Doolittle's raid (see pages 172–177) deceived the Japanese into assuming that the fliers had jumped off from a land base—Shangri-la, President Roosevelt called it jocosely. Officers of the Imperial General Staff measured their charts. Except for the sterile and unlikely Aleutians, the American outpost nearest Tokyo was Midway Atoll, some 2100 miles eastward. Not only must this be Shangri-la, the Japanese concluded, but it was additionally dangerous as "a sentry for Hawaii," 1150 miles farther east. They had long contemplated seizure of "AF," their code name for Midway. The Commander in Chief of their Navy, Adm. Isoroku Yamamoto, had only to designate the forces and set the date. This he now did. By the end of April the ships chosen for "Plan MI"—Midway Islands—were being mustered from the fringes of the empire.

Right then, a full month before the first gun was fired, Yamamoto lost the battle—for the same reason that precisely a year after the Doolittle raid, he would lose his life. (On April 18, 1943, U.S. planes shot down a Japanese bomber over Bougainville in the Solomons, sending Yamamoto, planner of the Pearl Harbor and Midway attacks, to his death.) Certain ingenious men in the U.S. Navy had broken Japan's most secret codes, and when Yamamoto flashed "Plan MI" to his subordinate commanders, these phantoms were eavesdropping at his shoulder.

The eavesdroppers' hearing was not quite perfect. They weren't entirely sure whether D day would be at the end of May or early in June—or whether "AF" was Midway or Oahu. Cominch (Commander in Chief, U.S. Fleet) Adm. Ernest J. King thought it was Oahu at first, but Cincpac Adm. Chester W. Nimitz thought it was Midway. He flew out there from Pearl Harbor on May 2, along the curve of those small, sparse wave breaks with the odd names: Nihoa, French Frigate Shoal, Gardner Pinnacles, Lisianski Island, Pearl and Hermes Reef and, finally, Midway.

The lagoon at Midway is about five miles across, and the two islets, Sand and Eastern, lie just inside the southern reef. Sand Island is about 850 acres; its highest point is thirty-nine feet. Eastern is less than half that size. Both are arid and featureless; yet they are far more important than many larger, lusher islands. The name of the atoll tells why: Midway across the Pacific, it is strategically invaluable.

Accompanied by Col. Harold D. Shannon, commanding the 6th Marine Defense Battalion, and Capt.

Cyril T. Simard, commanding the Naval air station, Admiral Nimitz inspected both islands. Each had its own galleys, mess hall, laundry, post exchange, powerhouse and dispensary. The chief difference was that all the aviation facilities except the seaplane hangars were on Eastern. For a whole hot day Nimitz strode and climbed and crawled through the establishment, peering at firing lanes, kettles, ammunition dumps, repair shops, barbed wire, underground command posts. He said nothing about his secret information, but he asked Shannon what additional equipment was needed to withstand "a large-scale attack." When Shannon told him, Nimitz emphasized the point again: "If I get you all these things you need, then can you hold Midway against a major amphibious assault?"

"Yes, sir."

Soon after Nimitz returned to Pearl Harbor, he wrote a letter addressed to Simard and Shannon jointly. The Japanese, Nimitz said, were mounting a full-scale offensive against Midway, scheduled for May 28. Their forces would be divided thus, and their strategy would be so. He was rushing out every man, gun and plane he could spare.

By now Nimitz knew for certain that Midway was the objective. A smart young officer, Comdr. Joseph J. Rochefort, in Combat Intelligence's ultrasecret unit at Pearl Harbor, had suggested instructing Midway to send an uncoded radio message announcing the breakdown of its distillation plant. Midway complied, and two days later cryptanalysts intercepted a Japanese dispatch informing certain high commands that "AF" was short of fresh water.

Nimitz' letter had a violent impact, but Midway was not dislocated. Although its war had been "cold" so far, the garrison had stayed taut. Every dawn, patrol planes fanned out westward over a million and a half square miles of ocean. The galleys served only two meals a day. The marines carried their rifles and helmets everywhere, even to the swimming beaches. At night everyone went underground except lookouts. So Simard and Shannon had to make no radical adjustments; they had only to assign priorities to their final efforts, and to absorb their reinforcements as smoothly as possible.

On May 25 they heard from Nimitz again: D day had been postponed until June 3. The reprieve let them put the last touches on their defenses. Shannon's garrison now numbered 2138 marines. Simard's fliers

and service troops numbered 1494, of whom 1000 were Navy personnel, 374 were marines and 120, Army men. Midway was a thicket of guns and a brier patch of barbed wire. Surf and shore were sown with mines—antiboat, antitank, antipersonnel. Every position was armed—some even had Molotov cocktails. Eleven motor torpedo boats would circle the reefs and patrol the lagoon, to add their antiaircraft (AA) fire to that of the ground forces and to pick up ditched fliers.

A yacht and four converted tuna boats were assigned to the sandspit islands nearby, also for rescues. Nineteen submarines guarded the approaches from southwest to north and eastward as far as 200 miles north of Oahu.

Defensively Midway was as tough as a hickory nut. Before a landing force could pick its meat, a bombardment would have to crack it open. That is what worried Simard and Shannon. If enough Japanese ships stood offshore, under a fighter umbrella and out of range of Midway's coast defenses, and began throwing in a mixture of fragmentation and semi-armor piercing shells, it would take a lot of planes to beat them off. On June 3, the first day of enemy contact, Midway had 120—thirty of them patrol planes, slow and vulnerable; and thirty-seven others, fighters and dive bombers, dangerously obsolete. Worse, some of their crews were Army, some were Navy and some Marine, and interservice liaison was little more than a wishful phrase.

Midway's fliers would write one of the most heroic chapters in the history of forlorn hopes. But if Midway's security had depended on its air arm alone, its ground arm might have had to resort to throwing Molotovs. Nimitz, however, in addition to fortifying the shores of his orphan island, also fortified its seas. Only a few ships were available, but he sent them all—the aircraft carriers *Enterprise* and *Hornet,* with six cruisers and nine destroyers, constituting Task Force 16; and the carrier *Yorktown,* with two cruisers and six destroyers, constituting Task Force 17. Rear Admiral Raymond A. Spruance, commanding T.F. 16, flew his flag on the *Enterprise.* Rear Admiral Frank Jack Fletcher, the overall commander, flew his on the *Yorktown.*

The two task forces sortied from Pearl Harbor and rendezvoused on June 2 at "Point Luck," 325 miles northeast of Midway. A signal searchlight on the *Yorktown* blinked, and Spruance's flag secretary made an entry in the war diary: "Task Force Sixteen [is]

193

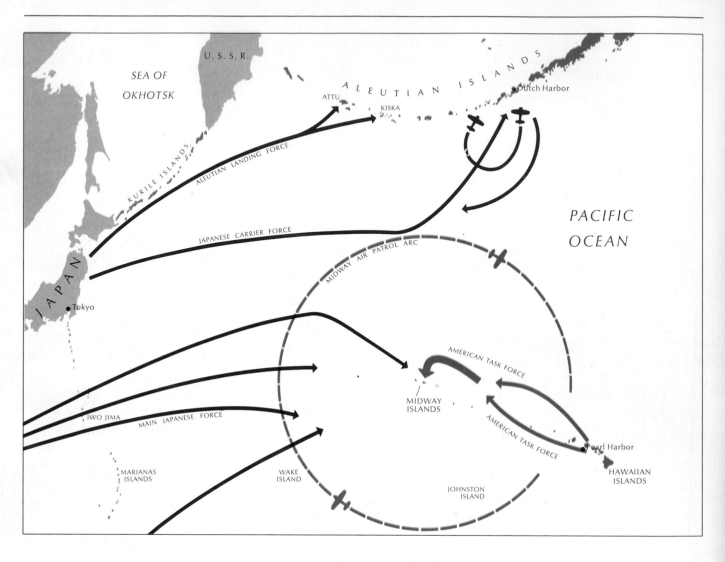

THE BATTLE OF MIDWAY

The Midway Islands—two tiny islets —loomed large in the grand strategy of the Japanese warlords following the Battle of the Coral Sea (see pages 178–181). Midway was to be captured and used as a base for the subjugation of Hawaii, little more than 1150 miles to the southeast.

As part of the plan, ships of the U.S. Pacific Fleet were to be lured north to the Aleutians by a diversionary Japanese attack on Dutch Harbor and the islands of Attu and Kiska. This maneuver was calculated to clear the way for a strong Japanese

striking force to capture Midway.

Admiral Yamamoto had no way of knowing that the United States had earlier cracked Japan's Naval code. Two American task forces with three large carriers were ready and waiting for the arrival of the main Japanese force in the Midway area on June 3, 1942 (June 4, U.S. time).

By the time the battle was over, Japan had been dealt the worst Naval defeat in her history: All four Japanese carriers and a heavy cruiser had been sunk, more than

250 planes had been lost, and more than 2000 men had been killed.

The United States had by no means escaped unscathed. The carrier *Yorktown* and a destroyer had been sent to the bottom. Some 150 planes had been wiped out, the installations on Midway severely pummeled and more than 300 Americans lost.

The Battle of Midway, vividly described in the story beginning on page 192, marked the end of the Japanese dream of naval domination of the Pacific Ocean.

A flight of Dauntless dive bombers races to meet the enemy fleet during th Battle of Midway. Their amazing feat in knocking out four enemy flattop brought about Japan's first naval defeat in three and a half centuries.

directed to maintain an approximate position ten miles to the southward of Task Force Seventeen . . . within visual signaling distance [so as not to break radio silence]." Next day he added, "Plan is for forces to move northward from Midway during darkness, to avoid probable enemy attack course." Then, "Received report that Dutch Harbor [off Unalaska Island] was attacked this morning."

Yamamoto had chosen Dutch Harbor for the opening scene of his "Plan AL" (Aleutians), which was parallel to "Plan MI" and had the dual purpose of seizing Aleutian territory and weakening Nimitz' strength by luring part of it north. Word of the attack was still flashing from command to command when another flash outshone it. Spruance's flag secretary logged it thus: "Midway search reports sighting two cargo vessels bearing 247 [degrees from Midway], distance 470 miles. Fired upon by antiaircraft."

The report was made by Ens. Jack Reid, who had lifted his Catalina from the Midway lagoon at 4:15 a.m., forty minutes before sunrise on June 3. Chance did not lead him to the enemy in that waste of water. Nimitz had written Simard, "Balsa's ["Balsa" was the Navy's code name for Midway] air force must be employed to inflict prompt and early damage to Jap carrier flight decks." Rear Admiral Patrick N. L. Bellinger put it otherwise: "The problem is one of hitting before we are hit." As Commander Patrol Wings Hawaiian Area, Bellinger had not merely to state the problem but to find the solution:

"To deny the enemy surprise, our search must ensure discovery of his carriers before they launch their first attack. Assuming that he will not use more than twenty-seven knots for his run-in [to the launching point], or launch from farther out than 200 miles, Catalinas taking off at dawn and flying 700 miles at 100 knots will guarantee effective coverage. With normal visibility of twenty-five miles, each Catalina can scan an 8° sector. It is desirable to scan 180° [the western semicircle], so twenty-three planes will be needed."

Nimitz gave them to him. Not all twenty-three were Catalinas. To share the patrol, the Army sent thirteen Flying Fortresses, Lt. Col. Walter C. Sweeney, Jr., commanding, from the 431st Bombardment Squadron; eight arrived on May 30 and more later. Simard assigned them to the southwest sector—the least likely source of attack—because their crews were compara-

tively unskilled in recognition of ships, and much depended on accurate reports of the enemy's power.

Meanwhile, one Catalina had met a direr threat than any enemy plane—a weather front, deep and wide, which developed 300 miles to the northwest and hung there, mocking Bellinger's calculations. Such a front would let the enemy creep up to its edge unseen and launch a night attack impossible to intercept. Midway's only comfort was the probability that the weather screening the enemy from observation would also screen the skies from the enemy, preventing accurate navigation and forcing postponement of his attack until dawn allowed him a position fix.

But even though—if this guess was good—bombs would not fall until 6 a.m. or perhaps 6:30, Simard could not risk an earlier attack catching him with sitting ducks. Accordingly, as soon as the search planes were airborne, the remaining Catalinas and Fortresses also took off, to cruise at economical speed until the search had covered the first 400 miles, by which time these heavy planes would have consumed enough gas to permit their landing on the cramped 5000-foot strip without jettisoning their bombs or burning out their brakes. The smaller planes did not take off, but they were manned and warmed up, ready to go.

The patrol crews' schedule was brutal. Midway had enough food, water and sleeping space for essential personnel only. Since maintenance crews were luxuries, the patrol crews were topping their fifteen-hour searches with hours more of repairing and refueling.

The hard grind was forgotten, however, when Ensign Reid reported, "Two cargo vessels . . ." and, twenty-one minutes later, "Main body bearing two-six-one, distance seven hundred miles. Six large ships in column." Reid was wrong. This was not Yamamoto's main body; it was only a small part of one task group in his occupation force.

The occupation force, approaching from the southwest, consisted of 2 battleships, 2 seaplane carriers, 1 light carrier, 8 heavy cruisers, 22 destroyers and various supply and patrol ships, escorting 12 transports. The invasion troops aboard them were 1500 marines for Sand Island; 1000 soldiers for Eastern; 50 marines for little Kure Island, sixty miles west of Midway; two construction battalions and various small special units. Vice Admiral Nobutake Kondo commanded from the battleship *Atago*.

The striking force, hidden by the weather front in

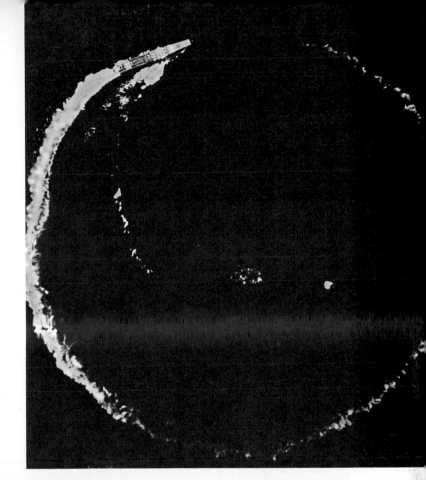

(Right) *The Japanese carrier* Kaga *maneuvers in a complete circle in a vain effort to escape the deadly attentions of American war planes during the Battle of Midway in June 1942. Hit repeatedly by U.S. dive bombers, the* Kaga *became a blazing torch; the intense heat set off explosions in her bomb storage compartment and among her planes. The ship burned from bow to stern all day, then plunged out of sight.*

(Below) *This photograph, taken by an American bomber from an altitude of 20,000 feet, shows the Japanese carrier* Akagi *attempting to evade American bombs. Like her sister carriers,* Kaga *(shown above) and* Soryu, *the* Akagi *was turned into a flaming wreck from bull's-eye hits by American dive bombers. Abandoned by officers and crew, the carrier that had been the flagship of the Commander of the Japanese striking force, Vice Adm. Chuichi Nagumo, stayed afloat until the following day, when it was finally sunk by torpedoes delivered by a Japanese destroyer.*

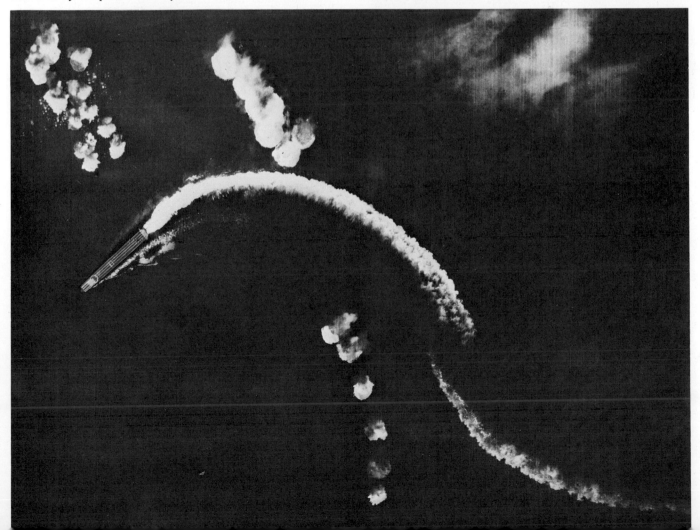

the northwest, consisted of 2 battleships, 4 carriers, 2 heavy cruisers, 1 light cruiser, 12 destroyers and 5 supply ships. Vice Admiral Chuichi Nagumo, who had commanded the striking force at Pearl Harbor, was in command again from the carrier *Akagi*.

The main body, far to the west, consisted of 7 battleships, 1 light carrier, 2 seaplane carriers, 3 light cruisers, 13 destroyers and 4 supply ships. Yamamoto commanded from the new battleship *Yamato*. She and her sister ship, the *Musashi*, were the most formidable in the world—63,700 tons (our Iowa-class battleships were 45,000) and mounting nine 18.11-inch guns (our ships mounted nine 16-inchers).

"Plan MI" could have been a plagiarism of Simard's and Shannon's fears. It called for the striking force to crush Midway's defenses with a three-day air attack, the main body to follow up with a big-gun bombardment and the occupation force to put its troops ashore on beaches where only maggots moved. The Japanese later admitted this much, but they disagreed on the plan's next provision. Some said there was none beyond holding on. Others said that Midway and Kure were to have been stepping-stones to Pearl Harbor.

All morning of June 3 radio reports crackled through Midway's earphones, as search pilots spotted the converging elements of the occupation force. Simard wanted to hit them with the Fortresses, but Nimitz had ordered "early damage to Jap carrier flight decks," and no carriers had been sighted. Then, at eleven o'clock, Ensign Reid sent a correction: There were eleven ships, not six. By now the Fortresses were back and refueled. Simard decided to attack.

Nine Fortresses, Sweeney leading, took off at 12:30 p.m. and four hours later sighted a force of "five battleships or heavy cruisers and about forty others." Sweeney broke his flight into three V formations and stepped them down at 12,000, 10,000 and 8000 feet. Extra fuel tanks in their bomb bays left room for only half a bombload, four 600-pounders apiece, but the bombardiers thought they hit a heavy cruiser and a transport. The Fortresses had not yet landed when four Catalinas with volunteer crews took off to make a night torpedo attack. Catalinas were not built to lug torpedoes, and their crews were not trained to drop them. Still, three pilots managed to find the enemy force—the same one the Fortresses had annoyed that afternoon. Lieutenant William L. Richards' torpedo blew a hole in the tanker *Akebono Maru*.

The weary crews were almost home when Midway radioed them that it was under air attack.

Reveille had sounded at three o'clock as usual on the morning of June 4, and at 4:15, as usual, the dawn search planes took off—eleven Catalinas, scouting for Nagumo's carriers. As soon as they were clear, the Fortresses—there were now fifteen—flew out to reestablish contact with the occupation force. The planes left behind were motley. Four were Army Marauders, normally a medium bomber, but rigged to carry torpedoes. Six more were Navy Avengers, torpedo planes of a brand-new type. The rest belonged to the two squadrons of Marine Aircraft Group 22, Lt. Col. Ira E. Kimes commanding. The fighter squadron, VMF 221, had some stubby little Buffaloes, so slow and vulnerable that they were known as Flying Coffins, and a few Wildcats, new and tough and fairly fast. The scout bombing squadron, VMSB 241, also was mixed, with new Dauntlesses and old Vindicators—so old that the marines called them Vibrators.

All had been manned since 3:15 a.m. Their crews watched the sun rise, grumbling that battle would be better than this everlasting waiting around. Even then battle was approaching, at 200 miles an hour. For more than half the men it would be the last battle.

The Japanese striking force had run from under its sheltering weather front shortly after midnight. Dawn gave Nagumo his position, 200 miles northwest of his target and just astride the international date line. At 4:30 a.m. he turned his four carriers into the southeasterly breeze and began to launch "Organization No. 5"—36 fighter Zeros, 36 dive-bomber "Vals" and 36 torpedo-bomber "Kates."

Midway received its first warning at 5:25 a.m., when a Catalina reported "in clear," uncoded: "Unidentified planes sighted on bearing three-two-zero, distance one hundred miles." The same Catalina reported again at 5:34: "Enemy aircraft carriers sighted one-five-zero miles, three-three-zero degrees." At 5:52 another Catalina corrected and elaborated this sighting: "Two carriers and battleships bearing three-two-zero, distance one-eight-zero, course one-three-five [toward Midway], speed twenty-five." The fourth report was from the radar station on Sand: "Many planes, eighty-nine miles, three-two-zero degrees."

Midway sounded the alarm, and even as its planes were taking the air, Simard radioed his flight leaders:

"Fighters to intercept, dive bombers and torpedo planes to hit the carriers, Fortresses to forget the occupation force and head north—your primary target is the carriers!" By a few minutes past six every combat plane that could leave the ground was airborne. Visibility was excellent, the sea calm.

Fighting 221's twenty-five operational planes were organized into five irregular divisions. The squadron's skipper, Maj. Floyd B. Parks, led a group of three divisions consisting of eight Buffaloes and four Wildcats. The executive officer, Capt. Kirk Armistead, led the other two, of twelve Buffaloes and one Wildcat. Parks's group made the first contact. They had climbed to 12,000 feet and had left Midway thirty miles astern when one of his pilots called, "Tallyho! Hawks at angels twelve [bombers at 12,000 feet], supported by fighters!" Parks pushed over. The time was 6:16 a.m.

The "Vals" were flying in two V-of-V's formations, one far behind the other, with the Zeros below both. Parks's group, then Armistead's, fell on the "Vals" like sheep-killing dogs, but the Zeros fell on the marines like wolves, slashing and springing back for another slash. Outnumbered as the marines were, and hopelessly outclassed, their only chance of escape was to dive at full throttle for the cover of ground fire. Few reached it. Zeros set ablaze one plane after another, then machine-gunned two of the pilots in their chutes.

The "Vals" closed their ragged ranks and pressed on. Midway was waiting. All guns were manned, and radar had tracked the flight steadily since 5:53 a.m., when it had been picked up. At 6:22 D Battery reported, "On target, fifty thousand yards, three-two-zero." And at 6:30 a.m. Colonel Shannon ordered, "Open fire when targets are within range." One minute later every AA battery was firing. The first wave had arrived exactly on the schedule that Shannon and Simard had hypothesized.

These were bombers at 14,000 feet. Of the original thirty-six, ground observers now counted only twenty-two. The opening bursts of AA fire were short, but the next scored direct hits on the leading plane and one other. The rest dropped their 533-pound bombs on Eastern and the northeast shore of Sand and left.

The second wave was composed of eighteen dive bombers. The flight leader dropped his huge 1770-pounder, followed it down, rolled onto his back and flew across Eastern at fifty feet, thumbing his nose. The AA crews shot him down almost regretfully. The

other "Vals" pulled out over the lagoon into the torpedo boats' fire. Several crashed. Zeros circled and strafed both islands, then followed the bombers home. Midway's only air attack of the war had lasted thirty-one minutes.

The AA gunners had shot down ten Japanese planes and they swore that if their visibility hadn't been cut by smoke from a burning oil tank, they'd have shot down ten more.

Lieutenant Joichi Tomonaga, commanding the strike, radioed Nagumo at 7 a.m.: "There is need for a second attack," but at 7:07 another report assured him, "Sand Island bombed and great results obtained."

Simard and Shannon had assayed the damage by then. Casualties were few—ten dead, eighteen wounded. Ground-defense equipment had suffered only slightly—one height finder had been damaged; but many of the less important installations were flat, sieved or in flames. On Sand, in addition to the oil tanks, which burned for two days, the seaplane hangars were afire.

Eastern lost its powerhouse, mess hall, galley and post exchange, but the airstrips, a dump of gasoline drums and all radio and radar facilities were untouched—the Japanese presumably intended using them.

As soon as the all clear sounded, Colonel Kimes broadcast the order: "Fighters land, refuel by divisions, Fifth Division first." No one landed. He broadcast again. Still no one landed. He changed the order to "All fighters land and reservice." Ten of the original twenty-five touched down, several blowing their tires on the jagged bomb fragments that littered the runway. Six of the pilots were wounded; only three of the planes were fit for further combat.

Fighting 221 had taken fearful punishment, but how much it had inflicted was uncertain. Since there was no way to reckon the missing pilots' scores, Intelligence accepted only the claims of the ten survivors, as verified by ground observers: 43 enemy "sures" for 13 Buffaloes and 2 Wildcats. The enemy's own preposterous figures at the time were 42 Marine sures for 4 "Vals" and 2 Zeros.

Even if the marines had known of this disparity, it is doubtful that they would have roused themselves to argue it. They were too dumfounded by the performance of the Zero. Its speed, climb and maneuverability surpassed anything they had ever seen. Fighting 221 would not engage the Zeros again until Guadalcanal; but the other squadrons' trials were just beginning, ordeals by fire that too often ended in ordeals by water.

When Simard radioed his flight leaders the bearing and distance of the enemy fleet, his intention was a simultaneous strike by all squadrons—by such a swarm of planes attacking from so many directions and elevations that although they would neither be coordinated nor have fighter cover, the enemy could not protect all his carriers against them. The plan was excellent in theory, disastrous in practice. The attacks were made separately, not simultaneously. As a result the enemy could focus his attention on one group at a time.

First to fly the gauntlet were the six Navy Avengers. The rest of their squadron was aboard the *Hornet*. These six crews had been detached for a special mission: to battle-test the new Avenger in comparison with the fleet's only other torpedo plane, the obsolescent Devastator. Their flight leader was Lt. Langdon K. Feiberling.

Before Midway faded astern, they saw the smoke of the first bombs. Then the enemy screen loomed ahead, with two big carriers in the distance. Zeros jumped them at once. Nagumo wrote in his log at 7:10 a.m., "Enemy torpedo planes divide into two groups," and at 7:12, "*Akagi* notes that enemy planes loosed torpedoes [and] makes full turn to evade, successfully. Three planes brought down by AA fire." Zeros continued to hammer the remaining three. Two wavered, then splashed in. The last, riddled and broken, and its pilot, Ens. Albert K. Earnest, bleeding from a shrapnel wound, somehow lurched on.

Earnest could not defend himself. His own guns were jammed; his turret was shattered, the gunner killed; and his tunnel gun, served by a wounded radioman, was blanked by the dangling tail wheel. Nor could he even dodge. His elevator control was cut and his hydraulic system smashed; the bomb-bay doors hung open, damping speed, and one landing wheel hung down, dragging the plane askew. The Zeros chased him for fifteen miles and turned back then only because their ammunition belts were empty. Earnest wiped the blood from his eyes, guessed his homeward course—his compass was splintered—and staggered in. The Avenger crashed when it landed, but Earnest crawled out alive, to make his report.

The citation for his Navy Cross praised his awareness of "the inestimable importance of determining the combat efficiency of a heretofore unproven plane." Admiral Spruance distilled the triumph—and sixteen men's epitaphs—into one crisp statement to Admiral Nimitz: "The new Avenger should be substituted for the Devastator as soon as possible."

Nagumo's respite was brief. He had hardly shaken off the Avengers when he was under torpedo attack again, by the four Marauders of the Army's 69th Medium Bombardment Squadron, Capt. James F. Collins commanding. They had been the last to leave Midway, beating the bombs by mere minutes, but their speed had overtaken the Dauntlesses and Vindicators, now trudging astern. Even as Collins sighted the enemy force, a line of Zeros swung toward him. He led his flight straight at them, then ducked toward the water. One pilot yelled, "Boy, if Mother could see me now!" A black wall of AA fire solidified ahead. Two Marauders crashed into it and fell, but Collins and Lt. James P. Muri broke through. Again the *Akagi* was the target. Collins dropped his torpedo at 800 yards; Muri closed to 450 and barely cleared her flight deck on his pull-up. Each thought he had scored, but Nagumo recorded at 7:15 a.m., "No hit sustained."

Zeros chased them out to the screen, wrecking Muri's turret and killing his tail gunner. Collins' turret could fire only in jerks, and his tail gun was jammed. Yet their two crews shot down three Zeros, maybe four, and the crippled Marauders—the landing gear of one had been shot away, and the other, burning, had more than 500 holes—held together just long enough. When they touched down at Eastern, they were nothing more than junk.

Meanwhile, Sweeney's fifteen Fortresses, heading westward since before dawn in search of the occupation force, had turned north as soon as they picked up Simard's six-o'clock relay of the position report on the striking force. They sighted it at 7:32 a.m., but Sweeney held his bombs. His primary target was the two carriers, and both were hidden by clouds. He began to orbit at 20,000 feet, hoping that they would venture out.

Actually, four of them were down there, all veterans of the attack on Pearl Harbor: the *Kaga* and *Akagi*, slightly smaller than our big Essexes; and the sisters *Soryu* and *Hiryu*, slightly smaller than our light Independence class.

In twenty minutes Sweeney had his hope. The *Soryu*

reported, "Fourteen enemy twin-engine planes over us at thirty thousand meters." Nagumo logged at 7:55: "Enemy bombs *Soryu* (nine or ten bombs). No hits." And a minute later: "Noted that the *Akagi* and *Hiryu* were being subjected to bombings."

The carriers fired a few bursts of AA fire, then ran back under the clouds, leaving further defense to their combat air patrol (CAP). The Zeros had no stomach for the stalwart Fortresses; their passes were cautiously wide. Sweeney was surprised: "Hell, I thought this was their varsity!"

As he resumed his watchful orbit, the marines poured in: Scout Bombing 241's first attack group, sixteen Dauntlesses, Maj. Lofton R. Henderson commanding. Ten of the pilots had not joined the squadron until the week before, and thirteen were totally inexperienced in Dauntlesses, so Henderson decided not to dive-bomb, but to glide-bomb, a shallower, easier maneuver. He was spiraling down from 9000 feet to his attack point at 4000 when the Japanese fighters caught them. The marines' rear-seat men splashed four, but the Japanese pilots and their ships' AA fire splashed six Dauntlesses, two in flames. One was Henderson's. Seeing him burn, Capt. Elmer G. Glidden, Jr., second in command, moved into the lead. Below him was a cloud bank. He dived for it to lose his pursuit and broke through dead above the *Akagi*. Three fighters had just left her deck. She had gone to battle speed when she first spotted the Dauntlesses, and now she was writhing in her course.

Glidden pushed over and dropped his bomb from 500 feet, with the nine other pilots strung out astern. All managed to get clear of the Japanese force, but on their way home damage dragged two more planes into the sea, and of those that landed, another two would never fly again. One crewman counted 259 holes.

Henderson's group reported that their 500-pounders scored two hits and a near-miss, and Captain Aoki of the *Akagi* later testified that this was the exact tally of her injuries, which proved fatal. However, there is also evidence that she suffered them in a subsequent attack. The *Akagi* would be a proud memorial, but the men of Scout Bombing 241 do not need her. They have another in the name of Henderson Field on Guadalcanal. Parks, Feiberling, Henderson—three flight leaders had been killed, and the battle was not yet two hours old.

Meanwhile, the carriers' evasive tactics were inter-mittently taking them under open sky, so the Fortresses, still at 20,000 feet, began to potshot. They reported three hits on two carriers, then turned homeward, their bombs exhausted.

That was at 8:24 a.m. Three minutes later Nagumo wrote: "Enemy planes dive on the *Haruna*." The marines were striking again. These were VMSB 241's second attack group, eleven lumbering Vindicators, led by Maj. Benjamin W. Norris. The pilots were as green as Henderson's—nine of them had never flown a "Vibrator" before May 28. They approached the enemy force at 13,000 feet and had just sighted it, twenty miles off, when three Zeros, doing graceful vertical rolls, ripped through their formation.

The concentrated .30-caliber fire of four rear-seat men knocked one Zero down. More Zeros joined in, and another went down. Norris headed for the clouds at top speed. When he burst out, at 2000 feet, he expected to find the carriers below. Instead, he was directly above the battleship *Haruna*, zigzagging in the van of the formation near her sister, the *Kirishima*.

Norris now faced a split-second decision. The carriers were his target, but his low altitude would make it suicidal to attempt taking these vulnerable planes—their skin was partly fabric—through the intense AA fire of the whole force. On the other hand, the *Haruna* not only was close below but might not be alert against attack, as the carriers certainly were. He chose the *Haruna*. The air was so rough with shell blasts that the marines could hardly hold their planes in a true dive. Geysers rose near the *Haruna*, and one splashed on the *Kirishima*'s fantail, but Nagumo wrote, "No hits."

The Zeros were waiting at the screen. They shot down two Vindicators and shot away another's instruments and elevator control; the pilot limped as far as possible, then ditched in the sea near Kure. The rest made it back as best they could, the last touching down at 10 a.m.

They had left Midway neat and taut. Now it was debris. The spring morning stank of ruin. Buildings were a jackstraw pile of charred timbers. The up-heaved sand, littered with thousands of dead birds, was still cold under foot. The once-buzzing airstrips were silent. Two thirds of the combat planes had been smashed or lost; half the aircrewmen were killed or missing. And the enemy's four deadly carriers were still intact to threaten further attack.

Ashore, the situation seemed grave. But afloat, our own carriers had joined the battle.

Dawn on June 4 found the American forces about 220 miles northeast of Midway. A four-knot breeze blew from the southeast. Clouds were low and broken, with visibility twelve miles. Admiral Fletcher's Task Force 17, built around the carrier *Yorktown*, was steaming ten miles to the north of Spruance's Task Force 16, built around the carriers *Hornet* and *Enterprise*. Admiral Fletcher, the Senior Officer Present Afloat and Officer in Tactical Command, knew that the enemy's occupation force had been sighted west of Midway, but he did not close its position. His target was the striking force, which was expected to approach from the northwest. The *Yorktown*'s scouts had searched that sector on the day before; half an hour before sunrise next morning, Fletcher sent them out again. An hour later, at 5:34, he intercepted the first of the reports that the Catalinas were flashing back to Midway, but not until 6:03 did they give him what he wanted: "Two carriers and battleships," with their bearing, distance, course and speed.

His staff laid out the data on a plotting board. The carriers were too far to be reached with an immediate strike. However, if the Japanese commander held his course—it was likely he would, to take advantage of the head wind—an intercepting course would soon bring him within range. At 6:07 a.m. Fletcher ordered Spruance: "Proceed southwesterly and attack enemy carriers when definitely located. I will follow as soon as my planes are recovered."

Spruance headed out at twenty-five knots. The range had closed sufficiently by seven o'clock. His task force swung into the wind, and the first plane roared down the *Enterprise*'s deck. Her Air Group 6 launched 57 planes in all: 10 fighters (Wildcats), 33 dive bombers (Dauntlesses) and 14 torpedo planes (Devastators). Nearby, the *Hornet*'s AG 8 was launching almost identically: 10 Wildcats, 35 Dauntlesses and 15 Devastators. Each group was ordered to attack one of the carriers, now an estimated 155 miles southwest. The launch was completed by 8:06. The task force swung out of the wind and the six squadrons sped away.

But if Fletcher blessed the scout who found Nagumo, the latter had one of his own to bless. At 7:28, halfway through Spruance's launch, Nagumo's scout sent back this message: "Sight what appears to be ten enemy surface ships in position bearing ten degrees, two-four-zero miles from Midway. Course one-five-zero, speed over twenty knots."

Nagumo at once ordered his force, "Prepare to carry out attacks on enemy fleet units!" Then he told the scout, "Ascertain ship types and maintain contact."

"Enemy is composed of five cruisers and five destroyers," the scout replied. Presently he added, "Enemy is accompanied by what appears to be a carrier."

By now the *Enterprise* had picked him up on her radar and had sent her combat air patrol to make the kill. He was still there, still transmitting: "Sight two additional enemy cruisers in position bearing eight degrees, distance two-five-zero miles from Midway. Course one-five-zero degrees, speed twenty knots"; but the CAP pilots could not find him. It made little difference; the damage was already done. A few minutes later he signed off: "I am now homeward bound." The time was 8:34 a.m., he had been in the air since five o'clock, and the needles of his fuel gauges were drifting toward Empty.

Major Norris' old Vindicators were swarming over the *Haruna* and *Kirishima* just then, and Nagumo had no leisure until 8:55, when he curtly ordered the scout: "Postpone your homing. Maintain contact with the enemy until arrival of four relief planes. Go on the air with your longwave transmitter [to give them a radio bearing]."

Nagumo then told his captains, "After completing homing operations [recovering the planes that had struck Midway], proceed northward. We plan to contact and destroy the enemy task force." They had built up speed to thirty knots when, at 9:18 a.m., a lookout sighted fifteen American planes, close to the water. They were the *Hornet*'s Torpedo 8, Lt. Comdr. John C. Waldron commanding—the rest of the squadron whose six Avengers had already flown to enduring glory.

It will never be known how, of the six squadrons launched, Waldron's plodding, 120-knot Devastators were the first by half an hour to find the enemy. It is known only that they did not rendezvous with the rest of the *Hornet*'s strike, as they should have.

Although the Japanese carrier force was now far from its predicted position (it had maneuvered radically to dodge Midway's planes, then had turned northeast to attack Spruance), Waldron flew a confident course, straight into its guns. He had lost his own fighters, and Zeros were ahead, astern and around him.

The AA fire was almost thick enough to screen the twisting ships; it gored huge holes in wings and fuselages, cut cables, smashed instruments, killed pilots and gunners. Plane after torn plane—fourteen of them —plunged into the sea, burned briefly and sank. A rear-seat man in another squadron, miles away, overheard Waldron's last words: "Watch those fighters! . . . How'm I doing? . . . Splash! . . . I'd give a million to know who did that! . . . My two wingmen are going in the water. . . ."

The rest of Torpedo 8 is silence, except for the voice of its sole survivor, Ens. George H. Gay. He heard Waldron, and he heard his own gunner cry, "They got me!" Then he was hit himself, in the left hand and arm. He turned and saw the Zero. He dropped his torpedo and flew down her flank, near the bridge: "I could see the little Jap captain jumping up and down, raising hell."

A 20-mm. shell exploded on Gay's left rudder pedal, ripping his foot and cutting his controls, and his plane crashed between the *Kaga* and the *Akagi*. He swam back to get his gunner, but strafing Zeros made him dive and dive again; the gunner sank with the plane. A black cushion and a rubber raft floated to the surface. Gay was afraid to inflate the raft; it might draw the Zeros. He put the cushion over his head and hid under it until twilight, peeking out to watch the battle. Tossed by the wash of Japanese warships, wounded, alone, he was the only man alive of thirty who had been vigorous a few moments before.

Gay was shot down at about 9:40 a.m. At 9:58 Nagumo wrote: "Fourteen enemy planes are heading for us." They were the *Enterprise*'s Torpedo 6, Lt. Comdr. Eugene E. Lindsey commanding. Not only had they, too, lost their fighter cover, but they were attacking an enemy alerted by the previous attack. Before a torpedo pilot can drop with any hope of a hit, he must maintain a steady course and altitude for at least two minutes. A full squadron of Zeros pounced on Torpedo 6 at this vulnerable time. Ten of the Devastators, including Lindsey's, were shot down at once, most with their torpedoes still in the slings. The other four escaped only because the Zeros were called away to meet a new threat, the *Yorktown*'s Torpedo 3.

The principal contact report had mentioned only two enemy carriers, but Intelligence had warned Fletcher that two more would be present. Rather than risk their planes' catching the *Yorktown* with hers on deck, he decided to send about half of them to reinforce the *Hornet*'s and *Enterprise*'s and to hold the rest until the two missing carriers were reported.

The *Yorktown* group—12 Devastators, 17 Dauntlesses and 6 Wildcats—was in the air by 9:06 a.m. For once the torpedo planes had the cover they needed so desperately; their fighters clung to them the whole way. Better yet, the *Enterprise*'s fighters, which had become separated from their own torpedo squadron, joined up in support. They sighted the enemy at ten o'clock, but they still had fourteen miles to go when Zeros caught them. The six Wildcats were outnumbered two to one. The fast Zeros splashed three, then sped after the Devastators. By now their commander, Lt. Comdr. Lance E. Massey, had worked his way within a mile of the *Akagi*. As he turned to make his run, a Zero shot him down in flames. Six more of his squadron fell. The remaining five made their drops, then the Zeros shot down another three. The last two escaped.

Of the forty-one torpedo planes which the American carriers had sent into battle, thirty-five had now been lost. Of the eighty-two men who flew them, sixty-nine had been killed, including the three squadron commanders. And of the torpedoes they dropped, not one had scored a hit. Yet these men did not die in vain. The valor that drew the world's admiration also drew the enemy's attention. His dodging carriers could not launch a new strike. And while every gun in his force trained on the torpedo planes, and every Zero fell on them, our dive bombers—unopposed—struck the *Kaga,* the *Akagi* and the *Soryu* their death blows.

The thirty-three Dauntlesses of Scout Bombing 6, led by Lt. Comdr. Clarence W. McClusky, commanding the *Enterprise*'s air group, had climbed up the estimated bearing of the enemy force until they should have been on top of it. McClusky cocked his wing and looked down. Visibility was perfect, except for a few small clouds. From his altitude of 19,000 feet, he could see more than 95,000 square miles of ocean. A hundred miles southeast of him was a tiny blur: Midway. But Midway was all he saw; the rest of the ocean was empty. He held on for another seventy-five miles. Still nothing, and time was running out. Merely finding the enemy carriers would not be enough. McClusky had to find them before they could launch a strike against our own carriers. Where were they? He had to guess fast and guess right.

When the *Hornet*'s group reached the estimated position and faced the same guess, their leader, Comdr.

(Top left) Struck repeatedly by Japanese bombs and aerial torpedoes, the U.S. carrier Yorktown *remains afloat while members of a salvage crew work to save her. Finally, two torpedo hits by an enemy submarine sent her to the bottom.*

Stanhope C. Ring, sent twenty-two of his bombers home and pressed forward with the rest: thirteen Dauntlesses and ten Wildcats. Like McClusky, he held southwest for half an hour, but then—with emptiness still ahead—he turned southeast, toward Midway, and then northeast. His determination to attack ignored the insistences of his fuel tanks, and when he finally abandoned the search, it was too late for most of his planes to make even Midway. The Wildcats gasped and ditched, one after another, all out of fuel; only eight of the pilots were rescued. Two of the Dauntlesses died over the Midway lagoon; their crews waded the few yards to the beach. The other eleven landed with their last pints at 11:20 a.m. Their welcome was something less than effusive. Not expecting the Dauntlesses, and seeing them jettison their bombs offshore, the marine lookouts mistook them for enemy planes. They sounded the air-raid siren and even scrambled one of Fighting 221's badly riddled fighters to intercept them.

But McClusky decided that the enemy had reversed his southeast course—Capt. George D. Murray of the *Enterprise* called it "the most important decision of the entire action"—so he headed his bombers northwest. They had already burned up nearly half their fuel; if he didn't find his target soon, our task forces would lose his planes as well as their ships. Fifteen minutes passed, twenty, twenty-five, before his eye caught a faint white streak below—the wake of a lone Japanese destroyer; and presently, far to the north, three carriers, veering and twisting among their escorts, slid out from the broken overcast: the *Soryu* in the lead, with the *Kaga* to the east and the *Akagi* to the west. The *Hiryu*, some distance ahead, stayed under the clouds and was never seen.

Nagumo's strike against the American carriers was just about to take off. The *Kaga* had thirty planes on her flight deck and thirty more on her hangar deck, all armed and fueled. They were awaiting the signal,

(Bottom left) Wounded in the furious fighting that characterized the Battle of Midway, an American seaman is moved from one ship to another. Winston Churchill was later to write: "This memorable American victory was of cardinal importance....At one stroke the dominant position of Japan in the Pacific was reversed."

when Lt. Comdr. Maxwell F. Leslie's squadron of seventeen Dauntlesses from the *Yorktown* dropped four bombs on her, shattering her bridge and killing every man on it, including Captain Okada. Explosions leaped from plane to plane, from deck to deck. A solid pillar of fire shot 1000 feet into the air. Smoke shrouded her, a black pall slashed with scarlet, and the blinded helmsman let her run wild.

Meanwhile McClusky split his attack: half for the *Akagi*, half for the *Soryu*. He took a last look around —still no Zeros—and pushed over. The enormous red "meatballs" on the yellow flight decks became as sharply defined as bull's-eyes. . . .

The *Soryu* also had sixty planes aboard. Three bombs spattered blazing gasoline fore and aft on her hangar deck. A magazine exploded; both engines stopped; she lost steerageway. Captain Yanagimoto shouted from the bridge, "Abandon ship! Every man to safety! Let no man approach me! *Banzai! Banzai!*" He was still shouting *banzai*'s when flames rose around him. Most of the company struggled to the forward end of the flight deck, out of the fire and smoke, and huddled there until a violent explosion blew them into the sea.

Since some of her Midway group had not yet returned, the *Akagi* had only forty planes aboard. Her fighters tried to get clear. As the first of them gathered speed, the first bomb smashed among them near the midships elevator, and another hit the portside aft. Damage did not seem severe, but when Captain Aoki ordered the magazine flooded, the after pumps would not function. The bridge took fire from a burning fighter below and the fire spread.

Nagumo summoned a destroyer to transfer himself and his staff to the light cruiser *Nagara*. Within an hour the *Akagi*'s flight deck flamed from end to end. When her engines stopped, an officer investigated. Her whole engine-room staff was dead.

The American torpedo attacks had drawn the Zeros to water level, so they needed only a short sprint to catch Bombing 6 after the pullout. Eighteen of McClusky's thirty-three Dauntlesses splashed in the water, but fuel exhaustion was to blame for some of them. He himself was wounded in the shoulder. Leslie's Bombing 3 returned intact to the *Yorktown*'s landing circle, only to have her warn them away. Before the *Enterprise* could take them aboard, two of the seventeen ran dry and ditched. Worse, a *Yorktown* fighter

205

pilot, shot in the foot, crash-landed on the *Hornet* without cutting his gun switches. His six .50's jarred off, and the burst killed five men and wounded twenty.

The *Yorktown* warned away her planes because her radar had picked up an incoming strike. Two hours before, at 10 a.m., Nagumo had reported Task Force 17's position to Yamamoto: "After destroying this, we plan to resume our 'AF' attack." At 10:50 he admitted, "Fires are raging aboard the *Kaga*, *Soryu* and *Akagi*," but added firmly, "We plan to have the *Hiryu* engage the enemy carriers." And at 10:54 the *Hiryu*'s blinker boasted: ALL OUR PLANES ARE TAKING OFF NOW FOR THE PURPOSE OF DESTROYING THE ENEMY CARRIERS.

"All" was an exaggeration; the strike consisted of only six fighters and eighteen bombers. As soon as they appeared on the *Yorktown*'s radar screen, at 11:50, her combat air patrol dashed to intercept them. Ten bombers went down at once and AA fire knocked down two more, but three bombs struck the ship, and one of them hurt her. It tore through to her third deck and exploded in the uptakes, blasting out the fires in two boilers and flooding the boiler rooms with fumes. It also set the paint on her stack ablaze and ruptured the main radio and radar cables. Steam pressure fell; she lost way and went dead in the water.

Admiral Fletcher took a quick turn around the flight and hangar decks. When he climbed back to the flag bridge, he found it wreathed in smoke so dense that his blinkers and flag hoists were blanketed. With all communications gone, he and the key men of his staff slid down a line and transferred to the heavy cruiser *Astoria*. Meanwhile, the *Yorktown*'s repair gangs patched her decks, and the engineering force coaxed her up to twenty knots. By 2 p.m. she was shipshape again—she even hoisted a bright new ensign to replace one stained by battle smoke. It had scarcely shaken out its folds when another ship's radar picked up a second attack group, thirty miles to the west—six fighters and ten torpedo planes from the *Hiryu*. Fletcher's task force was now alone. Spruance was thirty miles eastward, farther from the enemy, since launching and landing had kept the *Hornet* and *Enterprise* on an easterly course. However, Spruance had sent Fletcher two heavy cruisers and two destroyers as AA reinforcements. The *Yorktown*'s CAP and the combined AA batteries splashed five of the torpedo planes, but four broke through and made their drops at her. The heavy cruiser *Portland* tried in vain to in-

terpose herself. Two torpedoes struck the *Yorktown*'s port flank, almost in the same midships spot. A witness said, "She seemed to leap out of the water, then she sank back, all life gone." The time was 2:45 p.m.

Dead, dark, gushing steam, she drifted in a slowing circle to port. Her list increased to 26°; her port scuppers were awash, and she seemed about to capsize. Stretcher bearers threaded her steep passageways, collecting the wounded. At 2:55 Capt. Elliott Buckmaster ordered, "Abandon ship!" Destroyers stood in. Swimmers climbed aboard and clotted their decks in a whispering deathwatch, but the *Yorktown* floated on. The late afternoon was beautiful, with a calm sea and a flamboyant sunset.

So far, no American had seen more than three Japanese carriers at one time, and three were known to have been crippled by 10:30 a.m. However, this torpedo-plane attack, nearly four and a half hours later, strongly supported the prediction of a fourth carrier. Fletcher had not long to wait for positive corroboration. Even as the *Yorktown* still reeled, one of her scouts reported that 1 carrier, 2 battleships, 3 heavy cruisers and 4 destroyers were steaming due north, about 160 miles west of Spruance's task force.

Fletcher ordered the *Enterprise* and *Hornet* to strike immediately. The *Enterprise* completed her launch first. By 3:41 she had twenty-four Dauntlesses in the air, including ten refugees from the *Yorktown*. They had flown about an hour when they saw three large columns of smoke from the burning *Kaga*, *Akagi* and *Soryu*. A few destroyers were standing by them; the rest of the force was some miles to the north, fleeing with the surviving carrier, the *Hiryu*. The bombers swung westward in order to dive out of the blinding afternoon sun and pushed over from 19,000 feet. They lost three planes to Zeros, but they laid four heavy bombs on the *Hiryu*'s deck, starting such enormous

fires that the last pilots in line saw that she was already doomed and kicked over to bomb a battleship nearby. When the second half of the strike — sixteen more Dauntlesses, from the *Hornet* — arrived a half hour later, they ignored the *Hiryu* completely and dropped their bombs on a battleship and cruiser. All the *Hornet*'s planes returned.

The *Hiryu*'s forward elevator was blasted out of its well and hurled against the bridge, screening it and preventing navigation. She had only twenty planes aboard, but they were enough to feed the fires, which quickly spread to the engine room. Her list reached 15°. She began to ship water.

Of the four carriers, the *Soryu* was the first to sink. A picket submarine, the U.S.S. *Nautilus*, spied her smoke, crept within range and shot three torpedoes into her between 1:59 and 2:05 p.m. Her fires blazed up but died by twilight, and boarding parties were attempting to salvage her when she plunged at 7:20. Fifty miles away, Ensign Gay, under his black cushion, had been watching the burning *Kaga*. Several hundred of her crew were still huddled on her flight deck when an explosion tore her apart. She sank five minutes after the *Soryu*.

The *Akagi* and the *Hiryu* sank the next morning, June 5. The *Akagi* was stout. Her dead engines, staffed by dead men, suddenly came to life and turned her in a circle for nearly two hours, until they stopped forever. Still she would not sink. One of her destroyers torpedoed her at dawn.

The *Hiryu* was the flagship of Commander Carrier Division 2, Rear Adm. Tamon Yamaguchi, an officer so brilliant that he was expected to succeed Yamamoto as Commander in Chief. Burly, with a face like a copper disk, he was an alumnus of Princeton University and had been the chief of Japanese Naval Intelligence in the United States. When he and Captain Kaku of the *Hiryu* saw that she could not be saved, they delivered a farewell address to the crew, which was followed "by expressions of reverence and respect to the Emperor, the shouting of *banzai*'s, the lowering of the battle flag and command flag. At 3:15 a.m. all hands were ordered to abandon ship, His Imperial Highness' portrait was removed and the transfer of personnel to destroyers got under way. . . . The Division Commander and Captain remained aboard. They waved their caps to their men and with complete composure joined their fate with that of their ship." Two destroyers tried to

scuttle her with torpedoes at 5:10, but she continued to stay afloat until 7.

All four carriers were gone. With them went more than 2000 men. Spruance reported that we now had "incontestable mastery of the air."

To the top commanders at Midway, meanwhile, June 4 had been a day of deep anxiety. The reports that reached them during the morning of only one enemy carrier being damaged made the ruins around them prophetic of worse. Incredibly, Lieutenant Colonel Sweeney, commanding the Fortresses, had not yet been told of the two U.S. Navy task forces offshore. Believing that Midway was fighting alone and hopelessly, he sent seven of his planes, all that were ready for instant flight, back to Oahu, both to save them from destruction and to help defend the Hawaiian Islands against the invasion which he assumed would follow Midway's imminent fall. Although Lt. Comdr. Paul H. Ramsey, the Air Operations Officer, was better informed, even he thought it "quite possible that we would be under heavy bombardment from surface vessels before sunset."

Midway's air strength was now reduced to 2 fighters, 11 dive bombers, 18 patrol planes and 4 Fortresses, plus aircraft under repair. Sweeney led the four Fortresses against the scattered carrier force in the first strike of the afternoon. Two more, patched up, took off an hour later for the same target. At 6:30 p.m., as the pilots made their bombing runs, they sighted another six Fortresses a mile below—a squadron which had flown from Molokai, southeast of Oahu, straight into the battle. All three formations reported bomb hits, but Nagumo's log acknowledges none.

The marines tried next. Their eleven dive bombers, Maj. Benjamin W. Norris commanding, went out at dusk, but squalls thickened the moonless sky, and they had to abandon their search. Only the blue glare from their exhausts kept them together until Midway's oil fires guided them home. Ten returned safely; Major Norris did not return. Midway mounted one more strike that evening. Eleven torpedo boats dashed out at 7:30 p.m., hoping to cut down a straggling ship, but they, too, found nothing.

As the torpedo boats left, the Molokai Fortresses landed, with alarming news: Zeros had jumped them during their attack. Midway had learned by now that the enemy's fourth—and presumably last—carrier had been crippled at five o'clock, so Zeros aloft two hours later implied that a fifth carrier was present. Actually the Zeros were orphans from the burning *Hiryu,* but Midway could not know this. Nor did it know that a patrol craft's report at nine o'clock of a landing on Kure, sixty miles west, was derived from simple hysteria. On the contrary, each report strengthened the other. The possibility of invasion became a probability.

Midway radioed its picket submarines to tighten the line against the approaching enemy, and launched two Catalinas with torpedoes to support the interception. The Catalinas took off at midnight. At 1:30 a.m. on June 5 an enemy submarine suddenly fired eight rounds into the lagoon, then submerged. Midway's belief that this was a diversion to cover a landing party seemed confirmed at 2:15 a.m., when one of its own submarines, the U.S.S. *Tambor,* reported "many unidentified ships" only ninety miles westward.

The garrison already had done its utmost. There was nothing left now but the ceaseless servicing of the planes and waiting out the night.

Far northeast of Midway, the American warships were also waiting. Fletcher's task force, maimed by the loss of the *Yorktown,* now merely sheltered battleships behind Spruance's. The *Hornet* and the *Enterprise* were unimpaired, but Spruance was wary of the fast Japanese battleships and "did not feel justified in risking a night encounter. . . . On the other hand, I did not want to be far from Midway the next morning. I wished to have a position from which either to follow up retreating enemy forces or to break up a landing attack on Midway. At this time the possibility of the enemy having a fifth CV [carrier] somewhere in the area . . . still existed."

Spruance had cruised slowly east, then a few miles north, east again and a few miles south, when the *Tambor*'s sighting ended his aimlessness. He headed toward Midway at twenty-five knots.

There, as the morning of June 5 dawned, the Catalinas were off at 4:15 a.m., followed by the Fortresses. At six o'clock the first report came in: "Two battleships streaming oil," with the bearing, distance, course and speed. They were not battleships but heavy cruisers, the *Mogami* and *Mikuma.* The Catalina pilot's mistake in identification was excusable. These sister ships, together with the *Kumano* and *Suzuya,* were Japan's notorious "gyp cruisers"— professedly built to the conditions of the London Naval Confer-

ence, but really far larger and more powerful. They were longer than any battleship at Pearl Harbor.

The four, a vanguard for the occupation force, had been given a screen of destroyers and sent ahead to bombard Midway in preparation for the landing. They were steaming at full speed when a lookout spotted the *Tambor* even as she spotted them. An emergency turn was ordered, but the *Mogami* missed the signal. She knifed into the *Mikuma*'s port quarter, ripping it open and wrenching her own bow askew, so that neither ship could make more than fifteen knots. The collision occurred soon after 3:40 a.m.

At 2:55 a.m. Yamamoto's subordinate commanders had received an astonishing dispatch: OCCUPATION OF "AF" IS CANCELED. . . . RETIRE. . . .

Thus far, the enemy's motives and maneuvers at Midway have been reconstructed from official documents; but on this critical point—why Yamamoto decided to break off the battle—the files are silent. He himself is dead, so only conjectures are left.

At 6:30 the evening before, a scout pilot from one of Nagumo's ships had reported sighting "four enemy carriers, six cruisers and fifteen destroyers . . . thirty miles east of the burning and listing carrier. . . . This enemy force is westward bound." The pilot was myopic. The American force had only two operational carriers by then and was bound eastward. Still, Nagumo had no reason to doubt the sighting, and although his log does not say so, presumably he informed Yamamoto at once. Yamamoto seems not to have received the message, for at 7:15 p.m. he was broadcasting:

"One. The enemy task force has retired to the east. Its carrier strength has practically been destroyed.

"Two. The Combined Fleet units in that area plan to overtake and destroy this enemy, and, at the same time, occupy 'AF.'

"Three. The Mobile Force [Nagumo], Occupation Force and Advance Force [submarines] will contact and destroy the enemy as soon as possible."

Nagumo has written: "It was evident that the above message was sent as a result of an erroneous estimate of the enemy, for he still had four carriers in operational condition and his shore-based aircraft on Midway were active." Accordingly, at 9:30 p.m. he repeated the pilot's sighting, and again at 10:50. One of these messages must have reached Yamamoto. When it did, the shock of learning that the American force, which he believed crippled and quailing, was on the offensive and stronger by two unsuspected carriers—although neither statement was true—may have jolted him into ordering the retirement.

All this, it should be emphasized, is conjecture. But it is a fact that the Battle of Midway was over.

Midway's fighting was done, but its work was not—the work that had begun early on June 4, when the first American pilot parachuted from his flaming plane. All that day, the next, and for weeks afterward, Catalinas searched the ocean for rafts and life jackets. They found Ensign Gay on the afternoon of the 5th.

On June 6 they picked up another pilot, a Lieutenant (jg.) who had been clutching the bullet holes in his belly for two days. The Japanese had strafed him in his raft—to prove it, he brought in his splintered paddle. The Catalinas rescued more than fifty men. Thirty-five were Japanese from the *Hiryu*'s engine room. They had drifted thirteen days and 110 miles.

The biggest aftermath job was salvaging the *Yorktown*. It started auspiciously. The destroyer *Hughes*, standing by her on the night of June 4, rescued two wounded men, who had been overlooked when she was abandoned, and one of her fighter pilots, who paddled up in his raft. On the afternoon of June 5 the minesweeper *Vireo* took her in tow. About two o'clock the following morning, Captain Buckmaster and a

working party of 170 returned with three other destroyers. Repairs crept as slowly as the *Yorktown* herself, but by noon jettisoning and counterflooding had begun to reduce her list, and with the help of the destroyer *Hammann,* lashed to her starboard side and supplying power and water, her fires were being brought under control. Then, at 1:35 p.m., a lookout sighted four torpedo wakes to starboard. The *Hammann*'s gunners opened fire, hoping to detonate the warheads, and her Captain tried to jerk her clear with his engines, but nothing availed. One torpedo passed astern. One hit the *Hammann*. The other two hit the *Yorktown*. They were death blows for both ships.

Geysers of oil, water and debris spouted high and crashed down. The convulsive heave of the decks snapped ankles and legs. Stunned men were hurled overboard, then sucked into flooding compartments. The *Hammann*'s back was broken; she settled fast and sank by the head. Almost at once, her grave exploded. The concussion killed some swimmers outright; others slowly bled to death from eyes, mouth and nostrils.

The *Yorktown*'s huge bulk absorbed part of the two shocks, but her tall tripod foremast whipped like a sapling, and sheared rivets sang through the air. The rush of water into her starboard firerooms helped counter her port list at first, but Buckmaster knew that she was doomed. Too many safety doors had been sprung, too many bulkheads weakened. He mustered

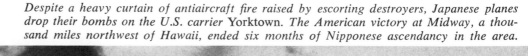

Despite a heavy curtain of antiaircraft fire raised by escorting destroyers, Japanese planes drop their bombs on the U.S. carrier Yorktown. *The American victory at Midway, a thousand miles northwest of Hawaii, ended six months of Nipponese ascendancy in the area.*

the working party to abandon ship. A few did not appear—the torpedoes had imprisoned them in compartments now completely submerged. An officer phoned one compartment after another. When a voice answered from the inaccessible fourth deck, he asked, "Do you know what kind of a fix you're in?"

"Sure," said the voice, "but we've got a hell of a good acey-deucey game down here. One thing, though . . ."

"Yes?"

"When you scuttle her, aim the torpedoes right where we are. We want it to be quick."

They did not need to scuttle her. Early the next morning, "she turned over on her port side [in Buckmaster's words] and sank in two thousand fathoms of water, with all her battle flags flying." As her bow slid under, men on the destroyers saluted.

So ended the Battle of Midway. The United States had lost 1 carrier, 1 destroyer, 147 planes and 307 men. Japan had lost 4 carriers, 1 heavy cruiser, 253 planes and 2300 men. It was a decisive American victory. Exactly six months after Pearl Harbor, naval balance in the Pacific was restored. It was also Japan's only Naval defeat since 1592, when the Koreans under Yi Sunsin, in history's first ironclad ships, drove Hideyoshi's fleet from Chinhae Bay.

Tactically, Japan's sunken carriers and dead combat pilots—some 100 of her finest, plus another 120 wounded—caused drastic changes in her whole Naval establishment. To replace the carriers, she had not only to convert seaplane tenders, thereby curtailing long-range reconnaissance, but to rig flight decks on two battleships. The pilots could never be replaced. Said Capt. Hiroaki Tsuda, "The loss affected us throughout the war."

Strategically, Midway canceled Japan's threat to Hawaii and the West Coast, arrested her eastward advance and forced her to confine her major efforts to New Guinea and the Solomons. Moreover, her efforts were no longer directed toward expansion, but toward mere holding.

The initiative that Japan dropped, the United States picked up. We moved forward from the "defensive-offensive," in Admiral King's phrases, to the "offensive-defensive," and thence to Tokyo Bay. What ended there had begun at Midway. Said Rear Adm. Toshitane Takata, "Failure of the Midway campaign was the beginning of total failure."

Our commanders may have recognized it at the time, but they restrained their optimism. Immediately after the battle, Admiral Nimitz announced only that "Pearl Harbor has now been partially avenged. Vengeance will not be complete until Japanese sea power is reduced to impotence. We have made substantial progress in that direction." Then his jubilation broke out in a pun: "Perhaps we will be forgiven if we claim that we are about midway to that objective."

ACTION AT GUADALCANAL, "ISLAND OF DEATH"

BY MAJ. FRANK O. HOUGH, USMC

The Guadalcanal campaign was the longest and the bloodiest in the whole Pacific War, with the jungle itself as much an adversary as the Japanese. For six agonizing months— August 1942 to February 1943—the fighting swayed back and forth between the fanatical defenders and the Americans. Major Hough, combat correspondent, spares no details in describing the savage fighting, as the United States began to regain ground.

Moving through empty, placid seas, some thousands of marines were learning a hundred dull details of life aboard the plodding Navy transport U.S.S. *Henderson*. The 1st Marine Division was going to war, though none of them, from the Commanding General down, expected that they would actually meet war in the very near future. Much of the personnel had been in training for more than a year, but the units had only recently been brought up to war strength by incorporation of many men fresh from boot camp, and the full combat teams had had little opportunity to work together as units. The plan was to set up training bases in New Zealand to remedy this deficiency.

The forward echelon, including Division Headquarters, had left Norfolk, Virginia, on May 20, aboard the *Wakefield* and two smaller ships, and reached Wellington, New Zealand, via the Panama Canal on June 14. The men worked hard and cheerfully at establishing their training base, anticipating a long period of abundant liberty among a hospitable, congenial populace; but on June 25 the division was ordered to prepare to move into combat as soon as possible.

It was a disgruntled and exhausted division that shoved off from Wellington on July 22 for a destination known only to the Division Command. Our smashing Naval victory at the Battle of Midway had set the stage for a quick American follow-up offensive, and the activities of the Japanese themselves provided the cue to where it should be launched.

The archipelago known as the Solomon Islands runs from a point about 5° below the Equator, adjacent to New Britain, for several hundred miles in a southeasterly direction. The several large islands and innumerable smaller ones lie in two parallel chains, separated by a wide channel which came to be known as the Slot. Guadalcanal is the next to the last island in the southern chain. Early in July it was verified that the Japanese were building a sizable airfield on Guadalcanal, with such dispatch that it might be expected to be operational by mid-August.

The beaches selected for the Marines' landing were about four miles east of the nearly completed airfield: fine wide beaches, backed by the evenly spaced trees of a big coconut plantation. The day—August 7, 1942 —was clear and calm, the surf running low.

The naval covering force and carrier-based aircraft had given the beaches a quick going over and had thoroughly plastered the airfield area. The assault waves formed with quiet efficiency and moved in to hit the beach at 9:10 a.m. While units assembled and moved inland to predetermined phase lines, the Higgins boats (personnel landing craft) returned to the transport area for more troops and supplies.

The initial assault troops consisted of two battalions of the 5th Marine Regiment. Their mission was to set up a perimeter defense some distance inland, thus covering further troop landings and obtaining dispersal areas for the supplies to be brought ashore. The 1st Marine Division began landing in column of battalions at 11 a.m. and advanced immediately inland through the perimeter in a generally westerly direction. The 1st Battalion thereupon moved up on their right, following the shore in the direction of Lunga Point, leaving beachhead security to the 3d Battalion.

Once through the coconut grove, the troops met the

Surprising the enemy: Marines rush ashore from a landing boat near Lunga Point, on north Guadalcanal. Their objective was an unfinished Japanese airstrip which, when completed by Seabees, was named Henderson Field. At first the marines met little resistance, a deceptive start to six months of desperate fighting.

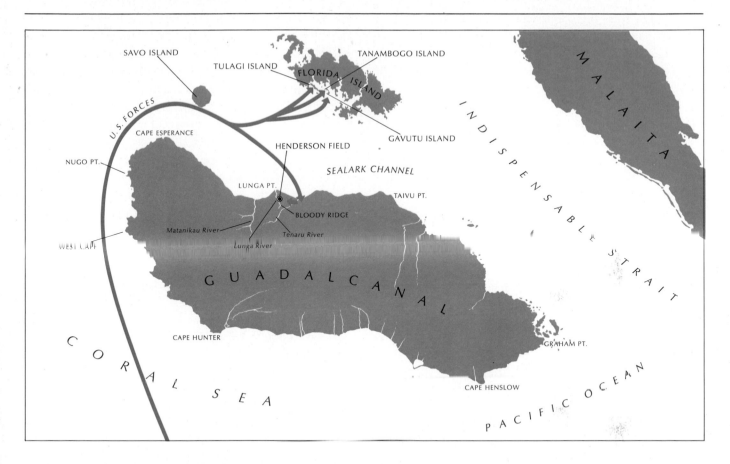

GUADALCANAL: First Stop on the Road to Tokyo

In July 1942 U.S. air reconnaissance revealed that the Japanese had begun constructing an airfield on Guadalcanal in the Solomon Islands —a serious threat to the Allies' supply line to Australia.

On August 7, 1942, the U.S. 1st Marine Division landed on Guadalcanal and on the islands of Tulagi, Tanambogo and Gavutu across Savo Sound. Sharp fighting on Tulagi and its neighboring islets continued for three days before the enemy was overpowered. On Guadalcanal, however, the airfield was captured with comparative ease. (The Americans renamed it Henderson Field to commemorate a Marine flier, Maj. Lofton R. Henderson, who had been killed at Midway.)

Determined to regain the airfield, the Japanese struck back by land, sea and air. Reinforcements were rushed from their base at Rabaul. Night after night, Japanese warships bombarded the land positions where the marines had dug in around the perimeter of Henderson Field, and attacked the supply ships of the Allied fleet. In the Battle of Savo Island (August 9), four Allied heavy cruisers were sunk and a fifth crippled. Several more naval engagements were fought during the six-month struggle for Guadalcanal. In the Battle of the Santa Cruz Islands (October 25), the carrier *Hornet* was sunk and the *Enterprise* disabled. The tables were turned in the Naval Battle of Guadalcanal

(November 13–15), when 11 Japanese troop transports, 2 battleships, 1 cruiser and 3 destroyers were sunk.

Meanwhile, Japanese land assaults continued. The beleaguered marines of the 1st Division ultimately began to get assistance from the men of the 7th Marine Regiment, to be followed by members of the Army American Division.

The grim fighting continued through December and into 1943. The struggle for Guadalcanal finally came to an end on February 7, when the last Japanese was evacuated from the island. The operation was the first American ground offensive in the Pacific and marked the end of Japanese territorial gains.

GI's slosh through ankle-deep water in a camp pitched in a soggy coconut grove. At Guadalcanal, Americans got their first taste of warfare in the jungle.

jungle. On this, their first meeting, it was an enemy, enigmatic and implacable, which impeded their progress, caused units to lose contact and direction, and filled them with a hundred unnamed fears as night closed in.

The jungle of the Solomons is the type known as rain forest. No air stirs here, and the hot humidity is beyond the imagining of anyone who has not lived in it. Rot lies just under the exotic lushness. The ground is porous with decaying vegetation, emitting a sour, unpleasant odor. Dampness, thick and heavy, is everywhere, result of the rains which give the forest its name—torrential in season, never ceasing altogether for more than a few days at a time. Mosquitoes—bearers of malaria, dengue and a dozen lesser-known fevers—inhabit the broad, deep swamps, which are drained inadequately by sluggish rivers where dwell giant crocodiles.

Through this steaming wonderland, marines of the 1st Division moved toward the airfield, hacking their way through the undergrowth, bogging down in swamps, fording sluggish streams, struggling through occasional "open" patches of tough kunai grass higher than a man's head. There was no determined opposition, only a few scattered snipers. Progress was described as satisfactory, and advanced units set up perimeter defenses for the night.

The 1st Marines reached the airfield late on the second day; the 5th continued along the shore to Kukum, a native village beyond the mouth of the Lunga River. Japanese bivouac areas showed every sign of having been precipitately abandoned. Later intelligence disclosed that the defenders had orders to take to the hills in case of attack, but this would not account for their failure to destroy the large stocks of food and building materials or the fine refrigerating and generating plants. The Guadalcanal attack can be rated among the great strategic and tactical surprises in the war.

Meanwhile, matters on the beach were anything but satisfactory. Both planning and personnel proved wholly inadequate to cope with the flood of supplies that poured ashore in the wake of the troops. As big tank lighters and ramp boats brought in the artillery, rolling stock and other heavy equipment, the scene on the beach passed through confusion to chaos.

As anticipated, the enemy's reaction was prompt and violent. The first air alert sounded about 1 p.m. on the first day, the Japanese having sent a flight down from Rabaul after receipt of the alarm. Fighter-escorted bombers swept in fearlessly through a sky blossoming with flak—and proceeded to ignore their main chance with a shortsightedness that seemed incredible. This flight and those that followed concentrated entirely on the convoy, ignoring the supplies piled all over the beach in plain view. Had those supplies been destroyed or even seriously harmed, the expedition would have been doomed at a single stroke. As it was, all the Japanese accomplished was to inflict minor damage on the shipping, including one destroyer. A heavier raid the following day caused a few casualties and set fire to the transport George F. Elliott, which burned brightly all night before sinking with a large quantity of much-needed supplies.

But at this stage we could still outblunder the Japanese. Throughout August 8 air reconnaissance had reported enemy naval units lurking to the west and northwest within striking distance of Guadalcanal. About dusk a delayed report came from a coast watcher of a heavy-cruiser task force on the move. In order to screen our vulnerable transports, two cruiser-destroyer groups, including both Australian and U.S. ships, were posted on either side of small Savo Island.

How the enemy was able to elude a force posted specially in expectation of his arrival has never been entirely explained. But approach he did, undetected, early the following morning. The loafing ships were suddenly blasted at point-blank range by the big guns of what was apparently a number of heavy cruisers. Silhouetted by flares and the light from the burning transport Elliott, our ships were so many sitting ducks. In approximately thirteen minutes from the opening salvo, the heavy cruisers U.S.S. Astoria, Quincy and Vincennes and H.M.A.S. Canberra were either sunk or sinking, and U.S.S. Chicago severely damaged.

Whereupon the Japanese, with a curious knack for losing opportunities, hurried back the way they had come without entering the transport area, where their attentions might well have been catastrophic.

When dawn came, our transports began weighing anchor. With what remained of their convoying warships in attendance, they silently stole away to the south, taking with them more than half of the cargoes—inadequate to begin with—which they had not had time to unload. By evening the marines were on their own. All that the marines ashore had to sustain them during the time that elapsed before another convoy arrived was the piled-up litter on the beach which the enemy aviators had not bothered to destroy; that and the rice and fish heads which the hurriedly departing Japanese had left in their bivouac area.

With the men and supplies available, it was obviously impossible to attempt any extensive mopping up of enemy remnants in this unfamiliar territory and still ensure the safety of the important ground already taken. Indeed, there were not enough men to form a continuous-perimeter cordon at a safe distance around Henderson Field, as the marines had named the captured airdrome. As planned by the Japanese, the original landing strip was 3778 feet long by 160 feet wide. At the time of its capture, it had been completely graded and all but 197 feet surfaced with coral, clay, gravel and dry cement. A defense system was set up with flanks resting on the sluggish Tenaru River to the east and a grassy ridge two miles short of the Matanikau River to the west.

There were no really heavy air attacks during the first two weeks on Guadalcanal, just repeated small raids: six or seven bombers cruising the field at leisure and unloading just about as they pleased. The airstrip had been completed within the first few days, yet no fighter protection arrived during those two weeks.

The enemy on shore also proved more of a nuisance than a menace during this period. After the first few days, increasing numbers of sad-looking characters began slinking out of the bush and giving themselves up in hopes of getting something to eat. We soon found out that these were not soldiers but laborers, most of them Korean.

Our Intelligence was able to piece together from their stories that there had been about 2000 of these people on the island when we had landed, guarded and supervised by some 600 troops. This force had evidently regained some semblance of cohesion following their inglorious flight on D day, and indications were that their point of assembly was Matanikau village, some three miles west of our perimeter.

Colonel Frank B. Goettge, Division Intelligence Officer, determined to lead a patrol into the Matanikau region. The project did not arouse much enthusiasm in other quarters, but he was insistent. "The way to get intelligence about the enemy is to go where the enemy is," he declared. And go he did, on the evening of August 12, taking a patrol of twenty-one enlisted

men and four officers, including a surgeon and an interpreter. The marines, fighting in a strange territory in total darkness, were ambushed soon after they moved inland. They did not have a chance. Only two sergeants and a corporal survived the massacre.

The fate of the Goettge patrol prompted the first really earnest efforts to wipe out the troublesome pocket of the enemy. Three company-strength patrols moved into the region immediately west of the Matanikau. Final results were inconclusive. Veteran jungle fighters with the great advantage of knowing the terrain intimately, the enemy's major parties were able to slip away from any enveloping movement we tried to throw about them.

The entire Marine force on the island at this time included only two infantry regiments with their reinforcing elements. With his inadequate means, Maj. Gen. Alexander A. Vandegrift, Commanding Officer 1st Marine Division, was still trying to eliminate the enemy to the west, when to the east the foe struck what was to prove his first major blow. This fell on the night of August 20. Only the previous afternoon, the first squadron of Marine fighter planes had, at long last, established itself on Henderson Field.

There were many features connected with this Battle of the Tenaru which were puzzling to people as slightly acquainted with Japanese military psychology as were our officers at that early stage. What, for instance, could the enemy reasonably hope to accomplish by attacking two reinforced regiments with a mere 1000 men? Perhaps they grossly underestimated our numbers. Perhaps they took their own propaganda too literally and honestly believed themselves supermen, each worth easily ten of us decadent democrats. This Japanese force had been landed within the past few days, apparently from destroyers, some distance to the east of our positions. It was commanded by Col. K. Ichiki.

On August 19 a marine patrol in the Koli Point region had surprised and annihilated an enemy patrol which was obviously the advance party of a much larger force. The dead were found to be clean, well dressed and splendidly equipped, obviously new to the island. Very evidently something was cooking. All hands were exhorted to remain especially alert.

The Japanese did not bother to bring up artillery. They did not call for a preliminary fire mission from their ships, which had been able to shell us with complete impunity for the past two weeks. Relying entirely on surprise, they moved as silently as possible, on the night of August 20, from their assembly area to the east bank of the Tenaru, then suddenly hurled an overwhelming force of infantry across the sandspit that completely blocked the mouth of that sluggish river at this season.

The marines opened up with everything they had. The carnage on the narrow spit was ghastly. But the impetus of their rush carried the Japanese forward over their own dead and dying—until they hit some newly installed wire. This seemed to take them completely by surprise, though a few actually got into marine foxholes; the rest milled around in bewilderment. High-pitched screams of pain, fury, frustration rose above the raving of the automatic weapons that were piling up their dead.

It was hot work for many minutes for the handful of marines at the point of contact. Japanese grenades reached the nearer foxholes, and men were killed and wounded there. Then the crazy tide receded, leaving its broken debris strewn across the sandspit.

The enemy attacked again and again, both across the spit and at other points just inland from the river's mouth. A hardy handful succeeded in reaching the western bank a couple of hundred yards farther inland, only to be pinned down there and eliminated at leisure when daylight came.

With the new day Colonel Ichiki, instead of drawing off his battered force while he still had time, chose to dig in among the widely spaced trees of the coconut plantation on a narrow point at the mouth of the river. He opened a fire fight with the marines on the opposite bank. It seemed incomprehensible that having failed to break through a thinly held line in the darkness, he really believed he had a chance of doing so in broad daylight, with the entire division alerted.

The 1st Battalion, 1st Marines, was brought up from its bivouac in the Lunga area. The men forded the Tenaru more than a mile above its mouth, deployed to cut off retreat inland or toward the east, and moved slowly through the jungle toward the coconut grove on the point. Downriver the unequal fire fight continued. In the afternoon the 1st Battalion debouched from the jungle, and the final trap was sprung. Colonel Ichiki wrote finis to his campaign by burning the regimental colors and shooting himself.

The first flight of Marine planes which moved in to base on Henderson Field on August 19 consisted of one fighter squadron and one dive-bomber squadron. None of the personnel had ever been in combat—a deficiency that was remedied in short order.

The Japanese had begun landing troops on the island in comparatively small contingents within the first few days of our occupation. Aside from the Ichiki detachment, their first—or first-known—attempt to bring in reinforcements on a large scale precipitated the Battle of the Eastern Solomons on August 24.

This occurred when a U.S. carrier task force intercepted an enemy convoy some distance short of Guadalcanal. The surface forces did not make contact; it was a case of planes versus ships on both sides, with the dive bombers from Henderson Field flying missions in support of the Navy carrier-borne planes.

The result was not especially conclusive, and the enemy losses were never fully verified. They are believed to have been considerable. At any rate for some time after this flight the Japanese showed a marked disinclination to risk their vulnerable heavy transports within range of our land-based bombers and resorted to methods of piecemeal reinforcement of their garrison: bringing the troops down in smaller craft traveling only by night along a chain of staging points on other islands; and carrying them as deck loads on destroyers and fast cruisers which could slip in under cover of darkness.

Perhaps this was not the fastest way to build up a formidable attacking force, but there were increasing indications that another major assault to recapture the field was impending. The persistent landings of the Japanese had been concentrated to the northwest, where a force of formidable dimensions was being built up in the Tassafaronga-Kokumbona region. On August 29, however, a convoy was spotted unloading troops near Taivu Point, some miles to the east. It was decided to strike there by land.

This assignment was given to the Raider Battalion, newly arrived from Tulagi, with the Parachute Battalion in reserve. There had been reports, subsequently verified, that the enemy force numbered up to 5000. Yet all that the Raiders encountered was disorganized and unusually ineffectual resistance from what turned out to be a small rear echelon. The main enemy forces had moved inland a day or two earlier, cutting a trail as they went, in a generally southwesterly direction.

218

The Raiders were to meet them a few nights later, however, when the whole howling mob boiled out of the jungle to hurl themselves against the south-central sector of the airfield perimeter.

The enemy attack called for a coordinated three-pronged drive against the east, center and west sectors of the inland perimeter, supported by heavy air bombing by day and naval gunfire by night. The effort ended in as complete frustration as Colonel Ichiki's, and on a considerably larger scale. So difficult were communications in that country that the three assaults were poorly coordinated. The eastern force, after days of cutting trail and lugging in a through the dense jungle, arrived in position late and too exhausted to attack with determination. The western force did not attack at all until the main effort, in the center, had been completely defeated, and it was beaten off with comparative ease.

There was nothing easy about the fight in the center, however. This action, known as the Battle of the Ridge —sometimes called Bloody Ridge, Raiders' Ridge or Edson's Ridge—turned out to be one of the hottest of its kind. It began in the evening of September 12, accompanied by heavy naval shelling, and lasted with varying intensity all that night and the following day, not to be definitely decided until shortly before dawn on the morning of the 14th. The defense line was breached at several points, some units were temporarily cut off, and there was wholesale infiltration. One small group of Japanese even penetrated to the Division Command Post, which had been placed dangerously far forward.

The ridge extended about 1000 yards due south from a point about a mile beyond the airstrip, which it commanded. Its crest and upper slopes were open and grassy, but the lower slopes and the valleys that flanked them were densely jungled. The defense line ran across the ridge itself and down into the jungle on either side.

The right bore the brunt of the first night's fighting and was forced back, necessitating a withdrawal all along the line in order to maintain contact. When daylight efforts on the 13th failed to drive the enemy from newly won positions, Col. Merritt A. Edson decided on a further strategic withdrawal. This shortened his lines to about 1500 yards, but they were still dangerously thin and not so well integrated as would have been desirable, owing to the rugged terrain.

The second night's attack was concentrated mainly on the ridge itself. The Japanese reached deep into the bag of tricks with which we were to become increasingly familiar as the war progressed. They talked in loud voices when approaching in order to draw fire that would reveal our position prematurely. They spread a smoke screen and shouted, "Gas attack!" They shouted other things in English—insults, threats, fake commands. They cut in on the wavelength of the portable radios to issue confusing reports. They charged down the length of the ridge and swarmed up out of the jungles that flanked it. They obliged Colonel Edson to contract his lines again. At one crucial point he had only sixty men holding the ridge proper. But they held it.

What made Bloody Ridge, and the Guadalcanal campaign in general, such a terrible experience was the unending pressure to which all hands were subjected. There were no rest areas or recreation facilities, nowhere a man could go and nothing he could do to recuperate nerves rubbed raw by the strain of what amounted to perpetual combat. There was scarcely a day or night during the four months the 1st Marine Division was on Guadalcanal when it was not attacking or being attacked by land, sea or air, and in many instances all three. Guadalcanal was a laboratory in which the techniques of future victories were developed by painful experimentation. The marines who landed on Guadalcanal were essentially assault troops; they were neither trained nor equipped for a protracted defensive action. Much of the equipment they had intended to bring ashore had been hauled away upon the premature departure of the first transport convoy. And the first Army troops did not arrive until mid-October: one regiment, which came as reinforcements, not relief.

The complete domination of air and sea which the Japanese had enjoyed at the outset had been considerably diminished by the arrival of our planes at Henderson Field. The enemy could harass and retard, but not seriously check, the arrival of our supplies and reinforcements, and we could do just about the same to him. During the two weeks' lull that followed the Battle of the Ridge, nightly parades of warships and landing craft poured Japanese into the Tassafaronga area to the northwest, while we in turn received an important reinforcement by the arrival, on September 18, of the last remaining regular element of the 1st

In the first big battle on Guadalcanal, Japanese attackers were beaten back with heavy losses on both sides. Enemy dead are strewn here on the sands of the Tenaru River.

The six-month struggle for Guadalcanal saw several major battles at sea. (Above) A U.S. destroyer fires at the enemy dug in on the island. (Below) The carrier Wasp, engulfed in flames and sinking, was torpedoed by a Japanese submarine September 15, 1942, while escorting a transport convoy to Guadalcanal. Despite enemy interference, the troops reached port safely.

Division: the 7th Marines, who had been in Samoa.

The Japanese had begun stepping up the intensity of their air attacks late in September, and the tempo continued to mount as October progressed. They were obviously trying to knock out Henderson Field and its planes in preparation for a major landing. They paid a staggering price in men and planes, but they came perilously close to succeeding. In a sense they did succeed.

On October 11 so heavy and continuous were the air attacks that our planes were too busy or too battered to go after a task force discovered approaching early in the afternoon. Fortunately, our Navy had a task force of its own in the vicinity and took over the job that night in a fierce half-hour engagement off Cape Esperance. They sank one heavy cruiser and one destroyer and damaged another cruiser and destroyer; later that night bombers from Henderson Field sank two destroyers. But still more enemy ships were coming.

The situation on the airfield was becoming critical. Although our plane losses had been ridiculously low in comparison with the enemy's, we could ill afford even that loss. Surviving planes were battered and badly worn, pilots and ground crews on the verge of exhaustion. We were scraping the bottom of our aviation gasoline barrel even before October 13, when two flights of enemy bombers caught our planes on the ground, set fire to one of our few remaining fuel dumps and made a shambles of the landing strip. A crisis came that night.

The Japanese heavy artillery had opened in the field early in the evening. Beyond the Matanikau enemy ground troops were throwing up signal rockets. All hands were expecting a land attack. This never materialized, but it was about the only thing that didn't. Later in the evening an air alert sounded again. It was Louie the Louse—as the marines had named the pilot of one Japanese plane. He dropped a flare over the airfield, and all hands dove for their dugouts. They had lived through many naval bombardments, but they had never lived through anything like that night.

This time the Japanese had battleships. For an hour and twenty minutes they lay off Savo Island, pouring in a steady stream of 12-inch and 14-inch shells. Cruisers added their 6's and 8's. Destroyers swung in close with their 5's, while bombing planes came over

in relays and the heavy artillery ashore contributed its bit to the general chaos.

Of ninety planes that had been operational the day before, only forty-two were in condition to leave the ground in the morning—after the strip had been repaired sufficiently for them to take off.

Late that afternoon one of these hardy survivors, scouting between more air raids, discovered the enemy's main troop convoy coming down the Slot: six large transports, escorted by destroyers. Four Dauntless dive bombers (all that were operational) and seven Army fighter planes attacked as evening was drawing on, but they merely damaged one destroyer. The ships plodded on and were soon lost in the closing night. At dawn they were calmly discharging troops and cargo about fifteen miles down the coast to the south.

The night's bombing and shelling had left us only three bombers in operating condition; the runway was so badly pitted that two of these were wrecked attempting to take off. The Wildcat fighters, which had been less hard hit, went at the transports with machine guns. More dive bombers were hurriedly put in shape. The Japanese responded with flights of Zeros, float planes, and a storm of antiaircraft artillery fire from the screening warships. Before the day was over, we had thrown in everything we could glue together. The Army sent over a flight of B-17 Flying Fortresses from their base at Espiritu Santo in the New Hebrides; 11 that morning found three enemy transports beached.

It was during this hectic period that the first U.S. Army troops (164th Infantry) reached the island, to be pitchforked at once into battle. They reached their bivouac area just in time for the naval shelling that the Japanese dished out the night of the 13th.

The Japanese attack now in the making was under Lt. Gen. Harukichi Hyakutake, Commanding General of the Seventeenth Army, recently arrived from Rabaul to take personal charge. Essentially it was similar to the one which had failed at Bloody Ridge more than a month before. Hyakutake had fresher men and more of them, that was the main difference: a full division, heavily reinforced.

Once more they moved deep into the jungle to the south, cutting trail and lugging gear. This time, at the cost of prodigious labor, they achieved a degree of tactical surprise: the trail went through so far below the perimeter that our patrols failed to discover it.

Japanese patrol activity increased along the lower Matanikau on October 20. During the following night, tanks could be heard moving up toward the west bank. Artillery chased them back, how far we did not know, and we took the hint to bring half-tracks and 37's into the area.

The Matanikau attack finally developed shortly after dark on the night of October 23, with Hyakutake trying to throw two full infantry regiments against the narrow front held by the 3d Battalion, 1st Marines. It was preceded by the closest equivalent of a barrage that the Japanese, with their odd ideas of using artillery, had yet put on. Then their tanks, which we had been hearing for some time, dashed out of the jungle and started for our positions. There were ten of them, in two waves: little 18-tonners, exceedingly vulnerable. The only practicable crossing was the sandspit at the river's mouth, narrow and without cover. Only one made it, overrunning a machine gun emplacement and several foxholes. A marine, crouching in one of the latter, calmly slipped a hand grenade under one tread, crippling its steering mechanism. It reeled around into the surf where a half-track 75 destroyed it.

Meanwhile, the 11th Marines had opened up with the heaviest massed fire the campaign had produced to date, saturating the area. They had been registered on this particular target for weeks. The carnage was terrible. The Japanese infantry, which had been grouped to follow the tanks, never left the cover of the jungle, where they could be heard yelling and screaming. When our patrols explored the region a few days later, they counted some 600 dead.

The main attack from the south developed about midnight of October 24, hitting a sector below and to the east of Bloody Ridge where the previous drive had been turned back. After ten days of being bombed, shelled and strafed, the soldiers were spoiling for a chance to fight back. They got it that night and handled it like veterans. The Japanese attack followed the familiar pattern: a power thrust against a narrow front. Our artillery quickly zeroed in on the ground it would have to cross and pounded the enemy assembly area in depth. A torrential downfall of rain hampered both attackers and defenders. The position, well wired in, stood firm as a rock. With the approach of dawn, the Japanese fell back silently to regroup.

The men at the front spent the day repairing wire and generally improving their positions, and with darkness the enemy to the south began to move again. This time their immediate objective was a little to the west of the previous night's attack—the sector under Lt. Col. Lewis B. Puller.

The first assault hit the defenders' wire about 10 p.m., and from then until after dawn the firing was almost incessant. By 5:30 the following morning Colonel Puller's command had withstood six separate assaults of undiminishing fury. Now a seventh, launched with final desperation, achieved a small breakthrough; but even this was to be short-lived. Before the Japanese could exploit their gain or even dig in to hold it, daylight came. Caught in a savage crossfire, the pocket became a deathtrap. Few, if any, of the enemy got back through the gap in our wire.

During the early morning hours of October 26, another enemy force launched a furious assault against the inland flank of the Matanikau sector, about four miles to the west. As a diversion this came at least two days too late to have any effect, but it did provide plenty of trouble while it lasted.

At Guadalcanal the Japanese threw at us everything that they had within reach. The island became a sinkhole, a bottomless pit into which they poured ships and planes and men. Before the end of the campaign 50,000 Japanese, by conservative estimate, had died either on Guadalcanal or on ships attempting to reach it. Dark rumors of the "Island of Death" seeped back to more remote posts of the Imperial Army.

As that bloody October drew to a close, the troops ashore knew that they had smashed the enemy, that they were deathly tired from heavy fighting and months of bombing and shelling, and that, instead of getting the rest they had so well earned, they were moving out to attack once more. The Japanese were coming again—coming in the greatest strength they had yet displayed. Several separate naval task forces were on the prowl. A transport convoy of twelve large ships lurked somewhere to the northwest, prepared to make the final dash. This time they planned to land two reinforced divisions to join the battered, scattered survivors of earlier catastrophes.

But we had received some additional troops ourselves, and air reinforcements had brought our strength on Henderson Field to 5 Marine squadrons, 4 Navy squadrons and 1 Army squadron. The ground forces shortened and strengthened their lines and waited with confidence.

The Japanese employed the same tactics which had so nearly succeeded in mid-October: to neutralize Henderson Field by intensive air and naval attack in order to permit the vulnerable transports to come in unmolested by our air force. The intensity of their bombing attacks was stepped up sharply on November 11 and 12. But now few of their bombers were able to get through to the field.

During the night of November 12 a powerful Japanese task force closed in for the kill. About 1 a.m. November 13, Louie the Louse flew over the field and dropped flares. But at this juncture something occurred that seems to have been quite outside the enemy's expectations.

The transports which had brought in our reinforcements had been escorted by a small task force of cruisers and destroyers in two groups, under command of Rear Adm. Daniel J. Callaghan and Rear Adm. Norman Scott, respectively. Admiral Callaghan hurled his force with stunning suddenness squarely into the enemy fleet south of Savo Island. He was ridiculously outnumbered and outweighed. The enemy was moving in three columns, and Callaghan led the American force straight down between them, blazing away to port and starboard. Within fifteen minutes practically every U.S. ship had been damaged. In approximately half an hour the survivors had passed through the entire enemy fleet, whereupon they broke off the action and slipped away into the darkness, leaving the enemy milling about in too great confusion to shell anybody ashore. What remained of the several columns were firing into each other long after their attackers had disappeared.

This exploit was not achieved without cost. A shell struck the bridge of the flagship U.S.S. *San Francisco,* instantly killing Admiral Callaghan and the ship's commander, Capt. Cassin Young. Admiral Scott went down with his flagship, the light cruiser U.S.S. *Atlanta;* another light cruiser and 4 destroyers were lost; and 2 cruisers and 3 destroyers were badly damaged. Japanese losses were 1 heavy cruiser, 1 light cruiser and 1 destroyer definitely sunk, and 1 battleship crippled. Two additional cruisers and at least three destroyers were left burning furiously and presumed sunk.

As usual when their preconceived plans were upset, the Japanese seemed incapable of adapting themselves to the altered situation. The bewildered task force limped off to the west to reorganize, its mission completely frustrated. Not a shell fell on Henderson Field that night.

The following night, however, a task force did get through and shelled the field. There was at least one battleship, plus cruisers and destroyers. Again the Japanese displayed that singular ineptness which characterized their operations throughout the Guadalcanal campaign. In October an intensive bombardment lasting an hour and twenty minutes had failed to knock out Henderson Field; now they shelled for only thirty-seven minutes and departed precipitately before the threat of a couple of PT boats, which were all we could muster to throw against them.

Our search planes were off with the dawn—and when they reported back, all hands knew that this was it. The Japanese transports were making their run for the island: 11 of them, crammed with troops and

Making use of the experience gained in jungle fighting during the Guadalcanal campaign, U.S. troops battled the Japanese from island to island in a steady advance up the Solomon Islands chain. (Above) American infantrymen flush out the enemy from a tropical wilderness.

equipment, convoyed by 5 cruisers and 6 destroyers. Our air arm hit them with everything we had. Marine, Navy, Army: dive bombers, torpedo bombers, scout bombers, even B-17's. They attacked in swarms, in relays, shuttling from the scene of action back to Henderson Field to refuel and rearm, then back to the slaughter. They blasted everything that floated, concentrating on the transports. One after another sank or caught fire. Late afternoon found the survivors, abandoned by their protecting escort, still staggering forward.

Under cover of darkness, four of them actually made the run and beached near Tassafaronga. It was a brave but futile gesture. With the coming of daylight on November 15, planes and long-range artillery destroyed them before they could unload.

But even as darkness was closing mercifully over the helpless transports, the Japanese Navy was rushing hell-bent toward another major disaster. A strong task force was hastening down from the north, evidently intending to shell the airfield into helplessness in order to save the surviving troop ships. This included a battleship in addition to the usual heavy and light cruisers and destroyers. But coming up from the opposite direction were the two much more powerful U.S. battleships *South Dakota* and *Washington,* escorted by four destroyers, under Rear Adm. Willis A. Lee.

The ensuing action did not last long. The Japanese succeeded in sinking three of the destroyers. While the *Washington* picked up survivors, both American battlewagons opened up with radar-directed fire from their 16-inch guns. In the roaring hour before the enemy scattered and fled, the Japanese lost one battleship and a destroyer, sunk; another battleship, cruiser and destroyer, heavily damaged.

These three days of diverse but almost continuous action became known as the Naval Battle of Guadalcanal. Its effect on the Japanese was crippling, temporarily, at any rate; it left them without the ships to send more troops into Guadalcanal, even if they had the troops to send after the terrible losses they had sustained in these attempts. The decisive phase of the Guadalcanal campaign had closed.

As far as Guadalcanal was concerned, the 1st Marine Division was through to all intents and purposes as November drew to a close. For four months they had fought in one of the foulest climates on earth; had been bombed, shelled and shot at between periods of actual fighting. Now, as American troops continued to pour in and Japanese troops were unable to reach the island, it was possible to start relieving these units on the lines. Soon they would be able to leave altogether.

Following the enemy's crushing naval defeat, the nature of ground operations underwent a marked change. This did not become apparent immediately. For nearly a month our activities were confined mainly to patrolling, punctuated by infrequent clashes with an enemy who, unable to attack, appeared to have withdrawn a considerable distance from our lines. Then the time appeared ripe to inaugurate the offensive which would drive them from the island.

It proved painfully slow going. As became evident, the Japanese, abandoning hope of resuming the attack with the resources at hand, had utilized the breathing spell to dig in defensively. They attempted to establish no continuous lines of resistance, no organized defense in depth. Instead, they prepared isolated strongpoints to take full advantage of the rugged, jungled ground—in ravines, on reverse slopes, in other areas in defilade from our artillery fire where often a single machine-gun nest could pin down an entire battalion. The consummate skill of the Japanese in the utilization of terrain and camouflage, which was a feature of all Pacific campaigns, now came conspicuously to the fore. And with it went that dogged persistence which caused men, without hope of escape or of gaining anything more than a little time, to fight grimly to the death. With equal grimness the marines and soldiers learned to contain the pockets of resistance and push on, leaving them for the reserve troops to clean out.

By the beginning of February 1943 organized resist-

ance on Guadalcanal had ceased. Radio Tokyo announced that the Japanese High Command, deeming Guadalcanal of little value anyway, had withdrawn its troops intact without interference from the badly beat-up Americans. We soon found out that Tokyo, for one of the few times during the war, had told the literal truth. On February 7 the last of the Japanese troops had been removed. The Japanese Navy had accomplished what hardly an American on Guadalcanal would have believed possible.

Using submarines, destroyers, any swift craft available, and taking full advantage of the moonless nights, which grounded our aircraft, to shuttle back and forth to the nearest island still in their possession, they had successfully evacuated not only their high officers but some 12,000 troops. Here was a truly brilliant achievement to crown their bungling and inept campaign.

The Guadalcanal campaign was the longest in the entire Pacific war. Ground fighting lasted for six months. It was far from being the bloodiest. Marine units listed 1242 killed in action, dead of wounds and missing; wounded numbered 2655. But if the number of men knocked out by sickness were counted, casualties would have been close to total. Very, very few of the marines who fought there—and not many of the later-arriving soldiers—failed to contract at least malaria.

The importance of the operation has a number of facets. It marked our assumption of the offensive, which we were never to relinquish, and by the same token, the end of the Japanese offensive. The strategic and tactical gains were obvious: guaranteed safety for our supply line to Australia; an air base and advanced staging area from which to strike toward the heart of the enemy's gains. It demonstrated clearly to the world at large that the Japanese soldier was something less than the superman he had been pictured on the strength of his early, easy conquests.

Following Guadalcanal, it would be our men's flesh and blood that were pitted against the emplaced weapons of the enemy. It might be said, without too great risk of contradiction, that Japan's greatest military achievement of the war was the conversion of a fighting force imbued for generations with the philosophy of attack into what were quite likely the most tenacious defensive fighters in all military history.

For that, unfortunately for us, is precisely what the Japanese became as the war moved westward.

FIGHTING BACK IN NEW GUINEA

BY GEORGE H. JOHNSTON

New Guinea was the first rung in the island ladder that would carry the Allies back across the Southwest Pacific to the Philippines. The main burden of the fight to force the Japanese to retreat over the Owen Stanley Range was borne by the Australians—long known for their skill in combat. George H. Johnston expresses the horror and the valor of this campaign in the battle of the Kokoda Trail.

The limit of the Japanese advance toward Port Moresby—the mountain ridge and village of Ioribaiwa—was captured today, September 28, 1942, and our troops are pushing ahead through a heavy rainstorm toward the scattered villages that line the Kokoda Trail.

The Japanese offered little resistance, although they had built up a high timber palisade across the top of the ridge in front of an involved system of weapon pits and trenches. Twenty-five-pounders blew great holes in the palisade and the Australians went in with bayonets and grenades. The Japanese invaders didn't wait for any more. They scuttled northward through the jungle, abandoning a stack of unburied dead and a great dump of equipment and ammunition. They left to us the steep ridge down which we had retreated a couple of weeks ago while they rolled stones and grenades down on us and plastered our rear guard with fierce mortar and machine-gun fire.

The Japanese have left a lot of graves on Ioribaiwa Ridge; trampled in the mud between the bodies of the dead is an elaborate shirt of scarlet silk with a black dragon embroidered on it. Most of the corpses are emaciated. Lieutenant General Sir Thomas Blamey, the Australian Field Commander, was right about letting the jungle beat the Japanese. The evidence scattered everywhere along the track and through the jungle is that this Japanese army was at the point of starvation and riddled with scrub typhus and dysentery. The stench of the dead and the rotting vegetation and the fetid mud is almost overpowering. One of our doctors carried out a couple of autopsies. Many of the Japanese, he said, had died because hunger had forced them to eat the poisonous fruits and roots of the jungle. It is clear now that the enemy stopped at Ioribaiwa Ridge because he was humanly incapable of thrusting ahead any farther.

The Australians are pushing on very cautiously, profiting by these grim reminders of an advance that went too fast, building up store dumps and medical posts, taking meticulous care about sanitation and hygiene, advancing in three prongs that are exploring every sidetrack and cleansing every yard of jungle as they go.

In this dense terrain of matted vegetation, half-hidden native tracks and steep gorges, there are ever present the threats of ambush, counter-infiltration and outflanking. But the Australians are climbing slowly and grimly up the southern flanks of the Owen Stanley Range with the knowledge that the only Japanese behind their thrusting spearheads are dead ones.

From the crest of Imita Ridge the vast valley of Ua-ule Creek lies like a bowl of tumbled green jungle held between the jagged purple peaks of the lower Owen Stanleys. The three-toothed ridge of Ioribaiwa guards the other side of the valley with an almost unbroken wall of jungle, clear in the tropical light. Beyond, the afternoon thunderheads are massing above and between the rising peaks of the range. The rolling clouds have beheaded the great bulk of Mount Urawa and scattered tufts and wisps of cotton wool across the flanks of distant Maguli.

The valley below is silent. The only sound is the soft hiss and drip of rain among the great jungle trees of Imita Ridge. But no sound comes from Ua-ule Valley, for no man lives there, and the only movement is the play of shadows across the matted trees.

Down the north wall of this valley came the Japanese one day last month. For three bitter weeks they had driven everything before them. They had fought courageously, fanatically, without mercy. Ragged,

exhausted, hungry Australians straggled through the silent valley on their retreat to Imita Ridge, while the rear guard fought to stem the Japanese tide on the crest of Ioribaiwa. Just as the enemy was hidden by that silent blanket of jungle so were the countless deeds of heroism.

In one tiny clearing a young Australian lay wounded by a sniper's bullet. His patrol was coming up behind him unaware of the hidden ambush. He could have feigned death and escaped when darkness came. Instead, he shouted warnings and directions to his comrades. The enraged Japanese pumped more bullets into him, but the Australian continued to direct his patrol. He was dead when his comrades returned after wiping out the Japanese.

On this same terrible slope, six soldiers from Victoria had squirmed to within a few yards of the Japanese positions to silence a troublesome enemy gun pit and had killed every man in it. Across this mysterious valley had shrieked the 25-pound shells from the Australian guns that held the Japanese and blasted them out of Ioribaiwa. For the Japanese never reached the foot of that valley of silence, never climbed the southern wall of Imita. Across this valley last week went the grim-faced, green-uniformed Australians on the terrible march back to the crest of the path through the Owen Stanleys—and beyond.

Five days ago the Japanese began their resistance again—on the wide shallow plateau of the Gap, the pass through the forbidding spurs of the main range. The weather is bad, the terrain unbelievably terrible, and the enemy is resisting with a stubborn fury that is costing us many men and much time. Against the machine-gun nests and mortar pits established on the ragged spurs and steep limestone ridges, our advance each day now is measured in yards. Our troops are fighting in the cold mists of an altitude of 6500 feet, fighting viciously because they have only a mile or two to go before they reach the peak of the pass and will be able to attack downhill—down the north flank of the Owen Stanleys. That means a lot to troops who have climbed every inch of that agonizing track, who have

American Douglas A-20 Havocs skip-bomb a Japanese freighter off New Guinea. Waterspouts indicate bombs already dropped—two by the plane taking the picture and two by the one just clearing the ship. The Japanese considered control of New Guinea and Guadalcanal essential for their planned offensive against Australia.

buried so many of their cobbers—their buddies—and who have seen so many more going back, weak with sickness or mauled by the mortar bombs and bullets and grenades of the enemy, men gone from their ranks in order to win back a few more hundred yards of this wild, unfriendly and utterly untamed mountain. Tiny villages which were under Japanese domination a few weeks ago are back in our hands—Ioribaiwa, Nauro Creek, Menari, Efogi, Kagi, Myola—and we are fighting now for Templeton's Crossing.

Your mental processes allow you to be conscious of only one thing: "The Track," or, more usually, "The Bloody Track." You listen to your legs creaking and stare at the ground and think of the next stretch of mud, and you wonder if the hills will ever end. Up one almost perpendicular mountain face more than 2000 steps have been cut out of the mud and built up with felled saplings inside which the packed earth has long since become black glue. Each step is two feet high. You slip on one in three. There are no resting-places. Climbing it is the supreme agony of mind and spirit. The troops, with fine irony, have christened it the Golden Staircase!

Life changes as you push up the track. Standards of living deteriorate. Thoughts become somber; humor takes on a grim, almost macabre quality. When men reach the nadir of mental and physical agony, there are times when sickness or injury or even death seems like something to be welcomed. Near Efogi, on a slimy section of the track that reeks with the stench of death, the remains of an enemy soldier lie on a crude stretcher, abandoned by the Japanese retreat. The flesh has gone from his bones, and a white bony claw sticks out of a ragged uniform sleeve, stretching across the track.

In this territory the Japanese are fighting, with a stubborn tenacity that is almost unbelievable, from an elaborate system of prepared positions along every ridge and spur. Churned up by the troops of both armies, the track itself is now knee-deep in thick black mud. For the last ten days no man's clothing has been dry, and all have slept—when sleep was possible—in pouring rain under sodden blankets. Each man carries his personal equipment, firearms, ammunition supply and five days' rations. Every hour is a nightmare.

The Australians have reconquered the Owen Stanley Range. Today, on November 2, they marched into

Kokoda unopposed, through lines of excited natives who brought them great baskets of fruit and decked them with flowers. They marched downhill through Isurava and Deniki, where many of them had fought the bloody rear-guard action of August. The Japanese troops had fled. Patrols cautiously went ahead to scout, squirmed their way through the rubber trees to test out Kokoda's defenses. But Kokoda was empty. There was no sound but the droning of insects and the noise of the rain pattering through the trees. Kokoda, key to the Owen Stanleys, had been abandoned by the Japanese without a fight. Their defense of Kokoda had been the pass through the range, and they had failed to hold that defense line.

Today Australian troops in ragged, mud-stained green uniforms, wearing charred steel helmets that had been used for cooking many a meal of bully beef on the Kokoda Trail, stood in ranks round the flagpole in front of the administrative building while an Australian flag (dropped with typical courtesy, friendship and thoughtfulness by an American fighter pilot) was slowly hoisted in the still air. There was no cheering. There was no band playing. There were merely the packed lines of these hundreds of weary Australians, haggard, half starved, disheveled, many wearing grimy stained bandages, standing silently at attention in the rain. For weeks their muttered "Kokoda or bust!" had been the most quoted saying of the track. Well, here was Kokoda, and lost in the rain clouds behind was the great blue rampart of the Owen Stanleys, with the shaggy 13,240-foot crest of Mount Victoria hidden by the afternoon thunderheads.

Within an hour the Australian spearhead was snaking down the narrow track leading from the little plateau to the flat jungle-choked plain below. They were marching on to try to catch the fleeing enemy.

The Allies are closing in from seven directions. The Americans went into action twenty-four hours earlier, and three columns of green-uniformed doughboys are even now assaulting the tough defense perimeter around Cape Endaiadère, Buna and Giropa Point. The Australians are pushing up the track to Sananda, and another force, advancing with staggering speed, has reached to within a mile of the north coast at Gona. The village of Soputa, south of Sananda, has just fallen to the Australians and Americans.

Back at headquarters are the senior generals—Douglas MacArthur, Blamey and George C. Kenney—established in New Guinea to direct operations on the spot. Blamey lives in a camouflaged tent lined with maps on which colored pins illustrate the inexorable advance of the troops under his command.

MacArthur miraculously retains complete privacy in a garrison area where there has never been privacy before, where even American and Australian nurses have had to avert their eyes from the spectacles of nude soldiers showering under roadside hydrants and naked men wandering carelessly everywhere.

MacArthur is just as remote, just as mysterious as he has been ever since he reached Australia eight months ago. He lives with Kenney in a white-painted bungalow surrounded by a riotous tropical garden of frangipani and hibiscus and flametrees. He is rarely seen. I remember how one American soldier came up to me in a state of great excitement because he had seen the great man. "I got a glimpse of him before breakfast," he said. "He was walking beneath the trees in a pink silk dressing gown with a black dragon on the back." Another man told me he had seen MacArthur in the afternoon with signal forms in one hand and a bunch of green lettuce which had been flown up from the mainland in the other. Between munches he doubtless analyzed the progress of the carefully prepared plan to take Papua back from the Japanese.

The Japanese, right now, are on the defensive everywhere. There are many problems that the Allies have had to overcome. The Australians call this a Q War—a quartermaster's war, in which supply and movement are everything that matters, except fighting courage. These problems have been largely solved by dynamic Major General Kenney, who has built up his air transport organization to an enormous scale. Almost every foot of our advance from Ioribaiwa across the Owen Stanleys and the northern plain to Buna has been made possible only by the endless work of innumerable young pilots, who have dropped or landed thousands of tons of food, equipment, munitions and guns. Many of them are American kids from flying schools who flew the great Douglases and Lockheeds across the Pacific and straight to New Guinea.

Along the narrow, winding Sananda track, flanked by swamps and thick jungle, both sides had dug in, in small pockets. Little isolated battles were raging to the noise of thudding mortars, chattering

FIGHTING BACK IN NEW GUINEA

machine-gun fire and the zip and whine of bullets. Sometimes our men advanced with bloodcurdling yells to rout out Japanese nests at bayonet point or with grenades. But the progress generally was pitifully slow.

Soon after we had smashed through the Japanese defenses at Soputa village, the enemy brought up a 75-mm. mountain gun, and for two days its shelling of the Allied forward positions held up any appreciable advance. An order was issued that the gun was to be silenced at all costs. The job was allotted to ninety men of an Australian Imperial Forces (A.I.F.) battalion which had been fighting with magnificent courage and determination in the slimy Papuan jungles for two and a half months.

Under the command of Capt. Basil Catterns of Sydney, the mud-stained, heavily armed men crept into the flanking underbrush at dawn. The enemy gun position was only two miles away, but the Australians had to make a wide detour to get around the deep, evil-smelling swamps.

For more than eight hours the men hacked and smashed their way through the entangling vines and rotten trees, their direction plotted and corrected by the noise of the enemy gun in action. Just before dusk Catterns saw ahead of him a Japanese camp with strong defenses all around and the mountain gun firing from a pit in front of the camp and sending shells over the trees into the Australian positions two miles away.

After a few moments' consideration, the Australians decided to launch their first assault on the camp to clean out the Japanese troops. They were drawn up in a wide sweeping curve. Zero hour was fixed at sunset, and they crouched in the jungle until the order to charge was given. Within a few seconds one of the most spectacular and bloody battles of the New Guinea war was raging in the tiny clearing.

The Australians tore their way through two barricades of plaited vines that the Japanese had erected and swept across three lines of trenches, with Bren guns and tommy guns blazing. Others lobbed showers of grenades into the Japanese posts.

The Japanese were taken completely by surprise, as thousands of bullets whacked into native huts. Screaming, they came pouring from the huts, but within a few seconds every exit had been blocked by a pile of Japanese dead. More were blown to pieces by Australian grenades, and others were mowed down like ripe corn

as the Australians continued their terrorizing rush through the camp. Grenades burst among the fires on which the Japanese evening meal was cooking, and in the great flash of flame some of the huts caught fire.

Some Australians were killed and many wounded. The enemy recovered from his surprise and hit back hard. The Australians circled around their wounded with blazing guns and slowly retreated into the jungle, carrying their wounded with them, behind the screen of gunfire. In the darkness the Australians dug defense positions as best they could while the wounded were attended to, and half the men fought a defensive action against more than 100 Japanese, who maintained a constant nightlong fire from machine guns, mortars and grenades. Other Japanese were pouring from a second camp nearby. By dawn the Australians were completely surrounded, and there was no way of getting a message through to inform their unit.

"We were holding a sausage-shaped perimeter sixty yards long and thirty yards wide," said Captain Catterns. "We had stacked our wounded around a large tree in the center of our position, but as the Japanese counterattacked throughout the day the wounded were systematically picked off one by one by snipers. The Japanese sniped at the slightest movement.

"Under the protection of heavy machine-gun fire, their grenade throwers would advance and concentrate on one of our weapon pits or trenches and plaster it until they were satisfied it was wiped out. Then they would turn to another Australian position. It was evidently their intention to whittle our defenses away one by one until we were exterminated."

Lieutenant Stewart Blakiston of Geelong, one of the few officers to survive, said: "Some of us almost cried with relief when just before sunset we heard the rattle of musketry as an Australian battalion advanced up the track toward us."

When the tide of battle had rolled on by dawn the next day, only four officers and twenty other ranks of the gallant ninety lived to march out from that terrible jungle clearing. But near the bodies of the sixty-six brave Australians were the bodies of more than 150 Japanese.

The Australians had done their job. They had silenced a dangerous enemy pocket; they had paved the way for an almost bloodless advance of two miles by the troops behind them. And buried in the mud beside the tangled jungle track was the abandoned 75-mm.

(Left) *Bodies of U.S. soldiers lie half buried in the sand on the beach at Buna, New Guinea. This picture—one of the first views of American dead to be released—shocked people at home who were unaccustomed to the grim realities of war.* (Above) *Marines wade through the surf at Cape Gloucester, New Britain, for the plunge into almost impenetrable jungles.*

Back from the front lines on Cape Gloucester after three weeks of intense jungle fighting, marines display Japanese flags captured on Hill 660, scene of some of the toughest action.

gun which the Australians had been ordered to put out of action.

The Japanese have been trying desperately to reinforce their last garrison in Papua. Under cover of darkness and bad weather several destroyers have succeeded in running the Allied air blockade and have landed reinforcements at Buna. Other formations of fresh enemy troops have been brought down the coast from Salamaua in small boats, landing barges and even native craft. Today they continued their plan of reinforcement with submarines, at least nineteen of which—including one big fellow of 3000 tons—were sighted heading for Buna on the surface in convoy formation. They crash-dived within sixty seconds when our planes came over.

Nevertheless, our forces are closing in everywhere. At Gona the Australians have cut their way through to the beach and are now trying to silence the immensely strong pillboxes and gun pits that the Japanese have established near Gona Mission. At Buna the Americans have driven a wedge to within 800 yards of the government buildings, where the Japanese apparently have their focal positions. But it's a tough job. Deep swamps of black mud in which a man could drown limit the terrain over which we can attack. Every logical and practical line of approach is covered by a network of fortifications on which the Japanese have been working for months.

Every weapon pit is a fortress in miniature. Some are strengthened by great sheets of armor and by concrete, but the majority are merely huge dugouts—several are 150 feet long—protected from our fire and bombs by sawed logs and felled trees which form a barrier 6, 10 and sometimes 15 feet thick. The logs are held in place by great metal stakes and filled in with earth in which the natural growth of the jungle has continued, providing perfect camouflage. Many of the pits are connected by subterranean tunnels or well-protected communication trenches. The pits are heavily manned and each is filled with sufficient food, water and ammunition to enable the enemy to withstand a long siege. From every trench or pit or pillbox all approaches are covered by wide fields of sweeping fire along fixed lines.

At the moment the most desperate fighting is taking place on the Gona beach sector, where the A.I.F. is gradually whittling away the enemy's grip in a series of ferocious but costly bayonet charges. One Private described a typical attack to me today:

"We'd been advancing for hours through stinking swamps up to our knees when we reached better country in the coconut groves, but when we pushed through the plantation to the beach we met heavy machine-gun fire from a strong Jap post on the beach. We attacked in a broad sweeping line, charging across the sand with fixed bayonets and grenades, and stormed our way right into the position.

"It was the wildest, maddest, bloodiest fighting I have ever seen. Grenades were bursting among the Japs as we stabbed down at them with our bayonets from the parapets above. Some of our fellows were actually rolling on the sand with Japs locked against them in wrestling grips. It was all over within a few minutes. A few of the Japs had escaped, but the bodies of thirty were tangled among their captured guns.

"A bayonet charge like that is a pretty terrible business when you see your cobbers falling, when you can only see a tree ahead of you. You can't see the Japs hidden among the roots until you're right on top of them, and they are still firing and yelling as you plunge the bayonet down. But it's the only way to clean them out. Those bastards fight to the last. They keep fighting until your bayonet sinks into them."

I was just behind the front line at Gona, crouched down in the kunai grass with a party of twenty-one A.I.F. infantrymen from South Australia. They had been in action almost constantly for two months. They were thin, haggard, undernourished, insect-bitten, grimy and physically near the end of their tether. They were fighting on fighting spirit alone. And because that spirit was good they were still superlative troops.

They were talking among themselves about a Japanese weapon pit which was concealed in the butt of a huge jungle tree at the end of a clearing which lay beyond the kunai patch. The pit had held them up for two hours. Two of their number had been killed and five wounded when they first pushed through the kunai and ran into a scythelike sweep of fire from the Japanese positions. A twenty-three-year-old Subaltern from Glen Osmond was talking quietly to the men.

"No use sitting round, I guess. We might as well get stuck into it!"

The men grinned. The Lieutenant—who wore no badges of rank and was clad in the same green jungle uniform as the troops—turned to a lanky Sergeant. "How much of that grass do you reckon they've cleared away between the post and the edge of the kunai?"

"Seventy or eighty yards, I'd say," replied the Sergeant. A couple of Privates nodded and a Lance Corporal estimated it as nearer 100.

"Well, there are twenty-one of us now," said a stocky little Private from Renmark. "Once we get up to the bloody pit it would only take about six of us to dig the little blighters out." He tossed a hand grenade a few inches into the air and caught it nonchalantly.

"You ought to be one of the six, sport," interjected another Private, lolling on his back with his not covered steel helmet over his eyes and a piece of yellow grass moving up and down rhythmically with the champing of his jaws. "You're so bloody short, Tojo'll never be able to get a sight on yer!" A soft ripple of laughter ran around the little group.

But even that little burst of laughter was heard. From the Japanese post came the *pap-pap-pap* of a short machine gun burst. The bullets zipped harmlessly high overhead. The man who was chewing grass tipped his helmet back and looked in the direction of the enemy post, invisible behind the screen of kunai. "Use 'em up, Tojo," he muttered. "You ain't got much longer to go."

The Lieutenant buckled his belt and looked around at his men. They grinned and reached for their rifles and Brens and tommy guns. "According to Shorty here, this job's going to mean fifteen of us won't get through," he said, as if it were a grand joke.

"Wouldn't count on that," said the lanky man, spitting out the well-chewed piece of grass. "He always was an optimist!"

Another ripple of laughter. "Well, some come back, they say," grinned the Lieutenant. He motioned to the men. They took a final look at their weapons, saw the grenades were ready and began to squirm slowly toward the edge of the long grass. As he moved past, the lanky man winked at me. "Give us a good write-up," he said.

The advance of the twenty-one men made little movement in the grass, and the occasional shaking of the thick blades might have been only the wind blowing in from the beach. They reached the edge of the kunai. A few yards out in the cleared area were the twisted bodies of their comrades killed a couple of

hours before. There was a sudden flash of steel as the Australians sprang to their feet and started running. They were yelling like madmen. For a split second there was no sound from the enemy position. Then it started. The wild *brrrppp-brrop* of machine guns firing with fingers tight on the triggers, the crack of grenades, once the scream of a man.

The Australians were running in a straight line. It's no use swerving or dodging when you're charging into machine-gun fire. Their bayonets were at high port. Men were falling. One threw up his hands, stopped dead and stumbled to one side. Another fell as he was running, rolling over and over like a rabbit hit on the run. Another was spun around like a top before he crumpled up and slid to the ground. The little man who had predicted that six would get through had almost reached the Japanese pit when he fell. He went over backward as if somebody had delivered a terrific uppercut.

He didn't live to find out, but his estimate was wrong. Nine of the Australians got through. They wiped out the post, killing every one of the nineteen Japanese inside.

The show is over. It is January 23, 1943. There remain but a few Japanese soldiers in Papua to be killed or taken prisoner. Buna station, Giropa Point and Cape Endaiadère, where the Japanese resisted stubbornly from their foxholes for two bitter months, were captured by Australian and American infantry charging behind Australian-manned and American-built light tanks. On the Sanananda track the last pockets have been crushed. Some of the Japanese gave themselves up. Others stayed in their foxholes to be killed or to die of starvation and disease. Yesterday all organized fighting ceased.

It was on this date twelve months ago that war in New Guinea became a threat, when Rabaul on New Britain succumbed to the furious onslaught of the men of Nippon. Much has happened since then. The nearly 16,000 men that Maj. Gen. Tomitaro Horii threw into the attempt to conquer Papua have been killed or wounded or captured. Mostly they have been killed. And General Horii himself is dead. So are many other uncounted Japanese, destroyed in their planes and in the scores of ships that have become twisted junk on the sea floor for the sake of Japanese aggression in the southern Pacific.

TARAWA: CONQUEST OF THE UNCONQUERABLE

BY ROBERT LECKIE

The Japanese had made the coral islet of Betio the heart of the defense of Tarawa Atoll. It was so heavily fortified with bombproof blockhouses, pillboxes and bunkers that its commander boasted, "A million men cannot take Tarawa in a hundred years." Yet, U.S. marines, surging through water often dyed red with their blood, fought their way onto the beaches and over the seawall and conquered "unconquerable" Betio in four days.

The invasion fleet stood off Tarawa Atoll on the morning of November 20, 1943. Sixteen dark shapes slid into position about a mile off the western entrance to the lagoon, a few miles above the islet of Betio. They were the transports.

Below the lagoon entrance were the fire-support ships, battleships *Maryland, Colorado* and *Tennessee*, with their cruisers and destroyers. Japan might have wished she had attacked the *Maryland* and *Tennessee* in the open sea—where they would have been lost forever—instead of in the shallow waters of Pearl Harbor. They had been salvaged, modernized and sent out to join the bombardment forces.

It was about 4 a.m. A half moon flitted in and out of fleecy clouds. It was cool. Marines going down cargo nets into waiting landing boats could feel the perspiration drying on their foreheads.

They came from stifling galleys in which they had dined on steak and eggs, french fried potatoes and hot coffee, a meal as sure to induce perspiration as it was to provoke dismay from the transport surgeons who would soon be sewing up some of these men.

"Steak and eggs!" a surgeon aboard the *Zeilin* exclaimed. "Hell, that will make a nice lot of guts to have to sew up—full of steak!"

The men were boated now, moving slowly away from the big ships in order to make the difficult transfer to the amtracs (amphibious track-driven vehicles). They did it without accident. The attack lines were forming a quarter mile off the lagoon entrance. The little minesweepers *Pursuit* and *Requisite* darted into the channel to sweep it clear. At 4:41 a.m. a red star shell swished into sight high above Betio, and a half hour later the Japanese shore batteries opened up in a deafening chorus.

The American battleships fired back. Aboard the *Maryland* the great long barrels of steel fingered the sky. One of them leaped, flame spouting from it. A streaking blob of red sailed toward Betio. Marines in their tiny churning boats could watch its progress. They saw no explosion on Betio: the shell was short. Again the great gob of orange flame and the speck of streaking red, and again no explosion. But then dawn seemed to burst like a rocket from western Betio. A great sheet of flame sprang 500 feet into the air, and the explosion which succeeded it sent shock waves rolling out over the water.

The old *Maryland* had hurled one of her 16-inch armor piercers into the ammunition room of the 8-inchers mounted on Betio's western tip. It was perhaps the greatest single bombardment feat of the war, for that shell of more than half a ton had killed hundreds of men, had detonated thousands of enemy shells and had utterly wrecked the 8-inchers' blockhouse. And then the *Tennessee* and *Colorado* began to thunder. All the battleships were firing in salvos, drifting in and out of their own gunsmoke as they shelled the Betio shoreline. Heavy cruisers belched flame and smoke from 8-inch muzzles. The lights roared away with 6-inchers. Destroyers ran in close to send 5-inch bullets arching ashore with almost the rapidity of automatic weapons.

Betio was aglow, a mass of fires. Great dust clouds swirled above her. Smoke coiled up, fusing with them. Fires towered high and lighted the clouds with a fluttering pink glare. It seemed that Rear Adm. Harry W. Hill had been right, that Betio would not greet another dawn: the islet was being torn apart. She was no longer visible beneath that pall, now frowning, now glowing.

Then, at 5:42 a.m., the American warships ceased firing. The American carrier planes were coming in, and it would be well to let the smoke clear so that the Dauntlesses and Avengers and the superb new Hellcat fighters could see their targets.

But the air strike did not arrive, and in the interval the "pulverized" Japanese began firing back. They shot at the transports with 5-inchers and those 8-inchers still operative. They drove the transports off, and plowing after them in flight went the amtracs and landing boats loaded with marines. For half an hour the fleeing transports duck walked among exploding shells, and then, because the air strike had still not arrived, the Americal naval barrage resumed fire.

For ten minutes the air was filled with their bellowing, and then, with the islet again glowing, the carrier planes came in. Hardly a bursting enemy antiaircraft shell or bullet rose to chastise these strafing, swooping planes, and it seemed that Betio was surely *zemmetsu* —"annihilated." Again she was swathed in smoke.

But as the *Pursuit* and *Requisite* entered the lagoon through the reef passage, shore batteries on the landing beaches lashed out at them. The minesweepers called for the *Ringgold* and *Dashiell*. The two graceful destroyers swept into the lagoon, firing as they came, with amtracs full of marines churning after them.

A shell struck the *Ringgold* to starboard, passing through the engine room. But it didn't explode. Another . . . again a dud. Through the smoke and fire ashore the *Ringgold*'s gunnery officer had spotted the flashes of her tormentor. Her 5-inchers swung around and gushed flame. There was a great explosion ashore. The enemy gun's ammunition dump had been hit.

At nine o'clock the motors of the amtracs were rising to full throttle. The swaying, clumsy craft were going into Betio. They were taking harmless airbursts overhead; long-range machine-gun bullets rattled off their sides. The wind was blowing Betio's smoke into the faces of the men, blowing the water flat and thin over the reef—but the amtracs were bumping over it and boring in. Now the marines were ducking low beneath the gunwales, for a volcano of flame and sound had begun to erupt around them and there were amtracs blowing up, amtracs beginning to burn, amtracs spinning around, slowing and sinking. Other amtracs ground ashore and rose from the surf with water streaming from their sides; helmeted figures in mottled green leaped from them and sprinted across the narrow beaches toward the treacherous sanctuary of the seawall, falling, falling, falling as they ran.

The Scout-Sniper Platoon went into Betio five minutes before the first wave. It was led by a Lieutenant named William Deane Hawkins, but hardly any of the platoon's thirty-four men could remember his first name. He was just "Hawk," lean and swift like a hawk, a man as convinced of victory as he was sure of his own death in battle. When Hawkins joined the Marine Corps, he told his closest friend: "I'll see you some day, Mac—but not on this earth." He had come up from the ranks—risen through his own achievement.

Hawkins and the Scout Snipers went in to seize the pier extending about 500 yards into the lagoon. It split the landing beaches, and from it the numerous Japanese latrines now filled with riflemen and machine gunners could rake the marine amtracs passing to either side.

Hawkins had his men in two landing boats, one commanded by himself, the other by Gunnery Sgt. Jared Hooper. In a third boat were the flame-throwing engineers of Lt. Alan Leslie.

They came in and hit the reef. They were held up there, just as enemy mortars began to drop among them and drums of gasoline, stacked on the pier, began to burn. Sniper and machine-gun fire raked the boats. Airplanes were called down on the enemy guns while Hawkins and his men awaited transfer to amtracs. They got them and rode in to assault the pier. They fought with flamethrowers, with grenades, with bayonets. They fought yard by yard, killing and being killed, while the pier still burned, and swept ashore to attack enemy pillboxes.

Like Hector in his chariot, Lieutenant Hawkins stood erect in his amtrac as it butted through barbed wire, climbed the seawall and clanked among the enemy spitting fire and grenades.

In another amtrac, called *The Old Lady,* was a stocky Corporal named John Joseph Spillane, a youngster who had a big-league throwing arm and the fielding ability which had brought Yankee and Cardinal scouts around to talk to his father. *The Old Lady* and Corporal Spillane went into Betio in the first wave, a load of riflemen crouching below her gunwales, a thick coat of hand-fashioned steel armor around her unlovely hull. Then she came under the seawall and the Japanese began lobbing grenades into her.

Marines rush the airstrip on the Tarawa islet of Betio. As the U.S. offensive drove northward it came to numerous coral islands similar to this one, with no vegetation usable for cover. The marine at the right carries a shovel for digging foxholes in the sandy surface.

238

The first came in hissing and smoking, and Corporal Spillane dove for it. He trapped it and pegged it in a single swift practiced motion. He picked off another in midair and hurled it back. There were screams. There were no more machine-gun bullets rattling against *The Old Lady*'s sides. Two more smoking grenades end-over-ended into the amtrac. Spillane nailed both and flipped them on the seawall. The assault troops watched him in fascination. And then the sixth one came in and Spillane again fielded and threw.

This one exploded. Johnny Spillane was hammered to his knees. His helmet was dented. There was shrapnel in his right side, his neck and right hip, and there was crimson spouting from the pulp that had once been his right hand.

But the assault troops had vaulted onto the beach and were scrambling for the seawall. Though Johnny Spillane's baseball career was over, he had bought these riflemen precious time, and he was satisfied to know it as he called to his driver, "Let's get outta here." The squat gray amphibian backed out into the water to take him to the transport, where the doctor would amputate his right hand at the wrist.

Private, first class, Donald Libby also came in on the first wave. He came in crouching in fear, grimacing in pain. Machine-gun fire had been sweeping his amtrac since it had lumbered up on the reef, and there were bullets in both of Libby's thighs. Then a mortar shell landed in the amtrac, killing all but two men, hurling Libby into the water.

He came to the surface with seven shrapnel fragments lodged in his flesh. He was bleeding heavily, but he hoped the salt water would stanch the flow. He dog-paddled toward his wrecked amtrac. It was canted on its side in the water. Libby grabbed the amtrac's wheel and hung onto it. A life preserver floated by. He seized it and squirmed into it, clenching his teeth against the pain of the movement. He floated behind the amtrac, hardly more than his nose above the surface. At night, if he still had strength, he would try to swim out to the ships.

Lieutenant Commander Robert A. MacPherson buzzed back and forth over Betio and the lagoon in his Kingfisher observation plane. He was acting as the eyes of Maj. Gen. Julian C. Smith, aboard the *Maryland*. Major General Holland M. ("Howlin' Mad") Smith, commander of the amphibious forces, was up at Makin with Vice Adm. Raymond A. Spruance, the overall commander.

MacPherson peered below him. The muzzles of *Ringgold*'s and *Dashiell*'s guns were spitting flame and smoke, and the little amtracs were bobbing shoreward. Some of them stopped and began to burn. Tiny dots of men leaped on the beach, clambered over the seawall and vanished beneath the pall of smoke still obscuring Betio.

The marines seemed to be attacking in little groups of three or four, rarely more than half a dozen, moving behind their NCO's. Here and there a loner struck at the enemy.

Staff Sergeant Bill Bordelon was such a loner. He was one of four marines to survive the gunning of their amtrac from about 500 yards out. He reached the beach, running low. Behind him were the remainder of his men, dead or dying or drowning. Bordelon had to get the pillboxes that filled the air around these men with whining invisible death.

He prepared his demolition charges. He sprang erect and went in on the pillboxes, running at them from their flanks because the Japanese were using very small gunports that reduced their field of fire. Twice Bordelon threw and sprinted for cover, and each time a pillbox collapsed with a roar. Bordelon primed more charges and ran against a third.

Machine-gun bullets hit him, but he stayed on his feet. He saw the white blocks of explosive sail into the gunport, and ducked. The third position was knocked out. Then he seized a rifle to cover a group of marines crawling over the seawall.

Bordelon pushed aside a medical corpsman who wanted to treat his wounds. He had heard the cry of "Help!" from the surf. A wounded man was there. Bordelon dragged him ashore. He ran back into the water to find another wounded man and bring him in. Then, because he was either oblivious of his own wounds or convinced that he was dying and there was so little time, S. Sgt. Bill Bordelon ran again at an enemy position. And the Japanese gunners saw him coming and shot him dead.

The first battalion to reach Betio was the 2d Regiment's 3d under Maj. John F. Schoettel. At 9:13 a.m. two companies led by Maj. Michael ("Mike") P. Ryan reached the seawall on the right, or western, beach. They crawled up under its lee, taking fierce machine-gun fire. Major Schoettel was still offshore with his

remaining troops. He couldn't get in, and in two hours the companies under the wall were cut in half.

At 9:22 a.m. Maj. Henry P. Crowe's battalion hit the beaches on the left, or eastern, flank. Two of Crowe's amtracs found a break in the seawall and rolled through, speeding all the way across the airfield's main strip before they were halted. But it was an isolated success. Seawall gunports began to spit death among the marines on the beach. Snipers picked off head after head raised above the wall. One of Crowe's men strolled down the beach, heedless of the Major's angry bellowing to stay low. He grinned impishly at a wildly gesturing buddy, and then a rifle spoke and the marine crumpled to the ground; when he rolled over, his eyes were bulging from the impact of the bullet which had passed behind them.

"Somebody go get that Jap son of a bitch," Major Crowe yelled. "He's right back of us here waiting for somebody to pass by."

A marine leaped up on the seawall. After him came a flame-throwing team, one marine with the twin cylinders of liquid fire strapped to his back and holding the nozzle out to spray, the other covering him with rifle fire. The marine beyond the wall hurled blocks of dynamite into a pillbox fifteen feet inland. There was a roar, and clouds of smoke and dust billowed out. A mushroom-helmeted figure darted out of the exit. The man with the nozzle squirted. A long hissing spurt of fire struck the Japanese soldier, and he flamed like a struck match, shivered, and was charred and still.

At the central beach, marked by the burning pier, Col. David M. Shoup was trying to come ashore to take command of the battle. With Shoup were Lt. Col. Evans F. Carlson of Makin and Guadalcanal, who had come to Tarawa as an observer; redheaded Maj. Tom Culhane, Shoup's operations officer; Lt. Col. Presley M. Rixey, commander of an artillery battalion; and Comdr. Donald Nelson, the regimental surgeon. They came to the reef in a landing boat. Shoup hailed an amtrac carrying wounded out to the transports. The wounded were transferred into the landing boat and Shoup's party boarded the amtrac.

It was about ten o'clock, and as the amtrac waddled shoreward, Colonel Shoup listened to radio reports of the carnage on the beaches. On his right Major Schoettel was still caught out on the lagoon, unable to reach the two companies being chopped up under the seawall.

The first message came out to the ships from the beach. No one could identify the sender. It said: "Have landed. Unusually heavy opposition. Casualties seventy per cent. Can't hold."

To the marines of the fourth, fifth and sixth waves waiting beyond the reef in landing boats and LCM's (landing craft, mechanized), this meant one thing: they must hurry ashore.

They rode in to the reef and found the water no higher than three feet and often only inches deep. They looked for the amtracs which were to take them into the battle. There weren't any.

Eight amtracs had been destroyed as the first wave attacked. Many more of them carrying the next two waves had been knocked out, and others were hit when they tried to back off the beach to return to the reef. Fifteen of them sank the moment they reached deeper water. Major Henry C. Drewes, commander of the amtrac battalion, had been killed; nearly all the amtrac gunners were dead. They had dueled the shore guns, but they had been visible and unprotected. The enemy had been neither.

The men waiting outside the reef would have to wade in. They clambered out of their boats, milled about on the reef while bullets keened among them, and then jumped off it and began to walk through waist-high water.

The Japanese gunners hung on grimly to their triggers, for now they understood why Rear Adm. Keiji Shibasaki had been so confident of repelling the invaders. The Americans were walking along a broad avenue of death. There were so many of them falling, they would surely stop coming.

But they waded on, from a quarter mile out, from a half mile out—unable even to fire their weapons, for they had to hold them overhead to keep them dry—sometimes stepping into coral potholes and going under, there to lose helmets and weapons.

"Spread out!" the officers cried. "Spread out!"

Private, first class, Richard Lund came in with a radio and screamed as a bullet struck him in the right chest and came out his right arm. It spun him around and knocked him under. He arose and walked on—with the radio.

Marines died in the deep water and in the shallow surf, where gentle waves rolled their bodies along the beaches. They fell like fanned-out decks of cards, once they had gained the leftward beach and blundered into the point-blank fire of weapons poked through seawall gunports. They were caught on barbed wire offshore and killed, and here Lt. Col. Herbert R. Amey, commander of the 2d Battalion 2d Regiment, met instant death.

Still they came on, even the wounded clinging to the burning pier, working their way in, hand over hand. Above them Lieutenant Commander MacPherson gazed in horror from his observation plane, watching the tiny figures wading through the water with rifles held high, watching them vanish, feeling tears of grief gathering behind his eyes.

But they got inshore, even the wounded, even the dying youth with his chest torn open who fell on the beach and cried for a cigarette.

"Here, I'll light one for you," a marine said.

"No," the stricken youth gasped. "No time . . . gimme yours. . . ."

The cigarette was thrust into his mouth and held there. The youth drew, the smoke curled out his chest—and he died.

There were rifles stuck in the sand of the beaches, and there were bottles of blood plasma hanging from them. The bottles were tied to rifle butts with gauze, and their little rubber tubes ran down into needles jabbed in the veins of wounded Americans. Corpsmen talked gently to the stricken men, waving the flies away.

The corpsmen and the doctors worked throughout the clamor of battle. They laid the men out on stretchers, giving them plasma and morphine. Marine riflemen guarded them as they worked, for sometimes the Japanese attempted to sneak down to the beaches and throw grenades in among the casualties.

They came out from under the pier or from the latrines or slipped into the water from the hulk of the *Saida Maru,* a freighter which had been knocked over on its side by an American destroyer in the preinvasion bombardments. The Japanese swam to shore through their own fire. One of them appeared in the central sector. He came out of the water brandishing a grenade. A marine sentry charged him and bayoneted him in the belly and then shot his bayonet free.

As the doctors worked on, corpsmen loaded the wounded aboard the amtracs, which then took them to the reef and the waiting landing boats. Men needing immediate care were draped over rubber boats and hauled to the reef by hand.

On the flat terrain of Betio and other Tarawa islets in the Gilbert Islands, invading *Americans* often fought behind hastily made sandbag entrenchments. Here, from back of such artificial cover, a marine rises up to throw a hand grenade against a Japanese pillbox.

Marines met ferocious resistance on Betio in Tarawa Atoll, stormed on November 20, 1943. The cost was ghastly—980 dead, 2101 wounded—but Betio fell in four days. Virtually all of the 4690 Japanese defenders were killed. (Above) *Assault on an enemy bombproof.* (Below) *A marine is placed on a rubber boat for transfer to a troop ship, then to the base hospital.*

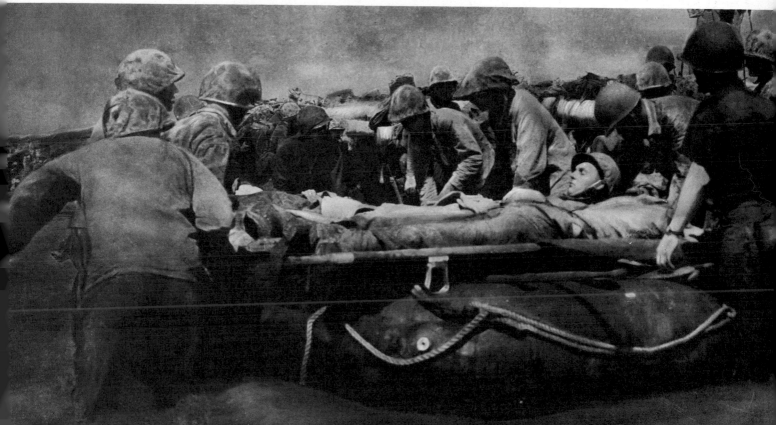

From the reef the wounded went to the transports; sometimes they were shelled en route, and there would be dead among them by the time they came alongside the ships. On one of these ships a landing boat with a gaping 5-inch shell hole in its side was hoisted on deck. The wounded were taken out. But there were three dead marines. Their bodies were placed in winding sheets and taken to the rail. Chaplain Harry Boer was called. He was a young minister who had never said the burial service before. Marines and sailors removed their helmets, and Chaplain Boer spoke:

"We are in the presence of the last enemy, death. We did not know these men personally, but God does —and therefore we commit them unto Him who is the righteous judge of the earth."

There was the screech of a plane diving to bomb a Japanese ammunition dump, and the chaplain paused, waiting for the explosion ashore. A sheet of flame rose into the air. The Dauntless had hit the dump. It had also knocked out a Marine tank, but no one aboard ship knew this. They bowed their heads again as the chaplain continued:

"It is for us, the living, in the presence of these dead, to devote ourselves more seriously to the task before us. 'I am the Resurrection and the Life, and he that believeth in Me, though he were dead, yet shall he live.'"

The white-sheeted figures went over the side. There was a splash. An impersonal voice blared over the bullhorn on the bridge: "The issue ashore is still in doubt."

Colonel Shoup, who was trying so hard to get ashore, was being struck by savage fire. Machine-gun bullets raked Shoup's amtrac as it neared the beach. The vehicle slewed around and retreated to the end of the pier. It circled to the east, or left, side and joined a wave of LCM's lightering dual-purpose medium tanks to Major Crowe's embattled battalion.

Then a pair of Japanese 75-mm.'s spoke. *Whang! Whang!* One LCM went under with all aboard and another withdrew, sinking.

Colonel Shoup's amtrac again returned to the pier. An exploding mortar shell wounded Shoup in the leg, all but knocking him unconscious. But he was still determined to get ashore, for now he was out of contact with Major Schoettel's battalion on the right.

Schoettel's battalion was attacking, though its leader was still unable to get ashore. Major Mike Ryan had reorganized the two shattered seawall companies and struck inland. They were slowly rolling up the enemy, and six Sherman tanks were coming in to help them.

The tanks left their LCM lighters on the reef and came on through water up to their turrets. Men walking with flags guided them around the treacherous potholes. The Shermans came slowly, leaving widespreading V's in their wake, rocking and lurching as their 75's roared. When they reached the beach, they found it so littered with dead and wounded that they could not pass. They would not crunch over the bodies of their buddies, dead or living, and they backed into the water again to make for the gap which the engineers had blown in Shibasaki's seawall.

Private Libby wondered if anyone would come for him. The battle had grown fiercer since he had been hurled into the water and had seized hold of his ruined amtrac. Now he could hear the clanging, tooth-rattling *whang* of a Japanese gun and hear the screams of stricken men. Libby was still alone in water now made chalky with dust. He swayed like a beached log, growing colder. . . .

Libby had heard the dreadful slaughter of the 3d Battalion 8th Marines, as they came to reinforce Major Crowe's battalion on the left. They came speeding up to the reef, five boats abreast. The landing ramps banged down. *Whang!* The boat farthest right vanished. It had been there, and then it was not there.

Whang! A second boat disappeared. One of the coxswains became terrified of approaching the reef. "This is as far as I go!" he cried. His ramp banged down and a full boatload of heavily laden marines charged off it into fifteen feet of water. Many drowned, but others were able to shuck their loads and swim to the reef, hauling themselves over it, oblivious of how it slashed their flesh.

Hardly a third of that first wave reached the beach. Then the second wave of Crowe's reinforcements started ashore. Colonel Shoup shouted at them from the pier, waving his arms and ordering them to come his way, to take shelter behind the pier and wade to the central beach. They did, but by the time the second wave got ashore it was badly disorganized.

At last Colonel Shoup reached the wall. He set up his command post in a hole dug in the sand behind a pillbox of Japanese. He was fifteen yards inland, but he could see almost nothing of the battle for the dust that hung over Betio.

It was everywhere, a cloying caking dust that was thick and clogged in the nostrils, coarse in the throat and clotted in the corners of the eyes. It swirled in dense clouds or sparkled in tiny jewels within those shafts of hot sunlight sometimes made visible by explosions that rent one cloud of dust only to start another.

Into this dust at about noon came the 1st Battalion 2d Regiment. Its men, under Maj. Wood R. Kyle, joined the attack in the central sector. They were also riddled, and many of them were deflected toward the right, or western, flank where Major Ryan still attacked and the tanks rolled toward the seawall gap.

Four of the tanks had foundered in potholes, but two of them reached Ryan as he re-formed for a flanking assault through the pillboxes on the western shore. The Shermans rolled over foxholes, blasted pillboxes open with their cannon, and machine-gunned the escaping survivors. Once Lt. Ed Bale's *China Gal* met a Japanese light tank in open combat and dueled her. The impact of the Japanese 37's on *China Gal*'s hide left the steel lemon yellow on the inside, but the 75's of the bigger Sherman made the Japanese tank a smoking wreck.

On the left side, a pair of 37-mm. guns had been dragged ashore. The boats carrying them had been sunk, but the gunners had rolled their heavy wheeled weapons through the water. They got them up on the beach, but there was still no way to get them over the seawall. Two Japanese light tanks were seen bearing down toward the lip of the wall.

"Lift 'em over!" came the cry. "Lift 'em over!"

The 900-pound guns were shoved over the wall. There they spoke with sharp authority. One enemy tank lurched around and gushed flame. The other fled.

The marines on the left had a Sherman tank of their own to force their way across Betio. It was a smoke-blackened, dented hulk called *Colorado,* commanded by Lt. Lou Largey. It was the lone survivor of the four which had come into Major Crowe's sector that morning.

One had been destroyed by an American dive bomber. Another had been set afire by enemy guns. A third had been hit by the Japanese and had fallen into a hole in which enemy ammunition was piled. It had been there when another American dive bomber

screeched down, and it had gone up with the exploding shells. The *Colorado* had also been hit and set aflame, but Largey had taken it back to the beach to put out the fire, and by early afternoon the tank was again charging pillboxes.

At 1:30 p.m., with all but a single battalion of the reserve committed, Maj. Gen. Julian Smith was convinced that the critical point had been reached. He asked Gen. Holland Smith up at Makin to release the 6th Marine Regiment to him. If Holland Smith said No, Julian Smith was prepared to gather this last battalion, to collect his bandsmen, specialists, typists and service people, and lead them into the battle himself. Howlin' Mad Smith said Yes. Assured now of a fresh and large reserve, Julian Smith notified the uncommitted 1st Battalion 8th Regiment to stand by for a landing. The men had been boated since before dawn, as had all the Marine combat teams. All that was required was to select the proper place to land. At 2:45 Julian Smith signaled Shoup to ask him if he thought a night landing possible. Shoup never got the message, and the 1st Battalion 8th stayed in their boats.

Someone had come for Private Libby.

The wounded marine had felt the tide going out and pushed himself away from his wrecked amtrac. He hoped to float out to the ships on the tide.

Just then someone waded toward him. He wore a marine's helmet and had a rifle slung across his back. He carried a bayonet in his hand. He came directly toward Private Libby, and he called out: "What state are you from?"

"Maine," Libby gasped. "Where you fr——?"

Private Libby came to his feet, for the bayonet this man was lifting was hooked at the hilt, Japanese style. The man lunged. Libby threw up his left hand. The bayonet pierced his palm. Libby grabbed the blade with his right hand and wrenched it away. The Japanese fumbled for his rifle. Libby swung and hit him behind the ear with the hilt. The soldier moaned and sank into the water. Libby hit him on the forehead as he fell, seized his head and held him under.

Private Libby let go and began paddling weakly toward the reef. Hours later an amtrac found him floating in his life preserver, 1000 yards offshore. Blood still flowed from his torn hands, but he was alive.

Colorado was on the left and *China Gal* was on the

right, between them were perhaps 3500 U.S. marines, and the sun was setting behind the tuft of the islet, which was shaped somewhat like a parrot.

Some 5000 assault troops had come ashore, and of these about 1500 were already dead or wounded. And now, between that pair of tanks, there were two separate and precarious holds on Betio. The left, or eastern, foothold (facing inland), in which Colonel Shoup's command post was located, began at about midway of the north coast and ran west for some 600 yards. It was 250 yards deep at its farthest penetration, roughly halfway across the airfield. Holding this, from left to right, were Major Crowe's 2d Battalion 8th Regiment; the riddled 3d Battalion 8th Regiment; and the 1st and 2d Battalions 2d Regiment. The right, or western, hold was a tiny enclave 200 yards deep and perhaps 100 yards wide which Major Ryan's reorganized 3d Battalion 2d Regiment had hacked out on the extreme western tip—the bird's beak. Between Ryan's toehold and Shoup's foothold was a gap fully 600 yards wide, stuffed with Japanese men and guns.

Out in the lagoon, still in boats, were the recently alerted 1st Battalion 8th Regiment and those waves of the 3d Battalion 8th Regiment which had been unable to get ashore.

Standing west of Tarawa in ships was the 6th Marine Regiment, just returned to Maj. Gen. Julian Smith. There was urgent need for artillery ashore, and Lieutenant Colonel Rixey was preparing to bring in some batteries under cover of darkness.

These were the lines of the 2d Marine Division as the dust began to settle and night fell on Betio. But there were no lines as such; there were groups of marines who had dug in here or fortified an abandoned pillbox there. There were gaps everywhere. Flanks were dangling. The inland advance of some units could be measured in hundreds of yards, others in scores of feet. Some troops were still trapped beneath the seawall. In some places the Japanese would need to go only thirty feet to drive the Americans into the sea.

It was a situation made for counterattack, and even the most rear-ranked private among all those embattled marines knew that just as the Japanese often defended at the water's edge, they often counterattacked at night.

Rear Admiral Shibasaki had planned to counterattack. He had always believed that his defenses would stop the Americans at the seawall, and that a strong nocturnal counterblow would finish them off.

But the terrible bombardment which had failed to slaughter Shibasaki's men had knocked out his communications. His men were scattered over the island in strongpoints and there was now no way of assembling them for the counterattack.

Admiral Shibasaki stayed within his huge bombproof command post. Though his men lobbed mortars into the marines on the beaches or swam out to the wrecked American boats or the capsized *Saida Maru* to harass them with sniper fire, they did not counterattack. They had killed many Americans that day; next day they would kill more. Admiral Shibasaki was not cast down by the loss of his communications. Obviously it was the Americans, not the Japanese, who were in a tight spot.

All through the day cries of "Corpsman!" "Corpsman!" had been raised above and below the seawall. Men who fought on although wounded were dying from loss of blood. And there was a shortage of blood plasma and of bandages.

"Doc" Rogalski had patched up the dozen or so who remained of the forty men Lt. Toivo Ivary had led against the central sector. Ivary's right leg had been shattered by a grenade, and he had been shot in the arm. Sergeant Jim Bayer had been shot in the head. Rogalski had fixed up the Lieutenant's leg with splints and sulfa and bandaged the Sergeant's head. And then, during the morning-long fight to knock out a pillbox looming over the seawall, he had used up the rest of his supplies.

In the afternoon, as more wounded were brought back to the beach, Rogalski was forced to take medical kits from the bodies of fallen fellow corpsmen. He waded into the lagoon to strip dead marines of the little first-aid pouches attached to their cartridge belts. At last Rogalski could find no more bodies in the black waters of the lagoon. The tide had floated them out.

Faint cries of "Corpsman" were still being raised along the beach that night as Rogalski sat, helpless, under the seawall. Suddenly four amtracs came out of the darkness and crawled up to the wall. Rogalski rose expectantly, but then slumped back. Marines jumping out of two of them had begun to unload artillery shells and were wrestling howitzer parts over the side. Then Rogalski saw stretcher-bearers and corpsmen jumping out of the other two amtracs, and he ran to join them, helping them put Ivary and Bayer and the other wounded into the amtracs for the trip to the reef and the waiting landing boats. The amtracs roared away, even as wading artillerymen emerged from the water.

Beyond the reef Lieutenant Ivary lay in the landing boat that was taking him to a transport. He could hear voices high above him. He felt the boat being lifted up in the air. And as the booms swung the landing boat onto the deck of the transport, ten short-snouted pieces of artillery were being made ready, hub to hub, under the seawall.

They would be firing at dawn.

The men of the 1st Battalion 8th Marines, who had spent the night on the lagoon, came up to the reef in landing boats. At 6:15 a.m. on the morning of November 21, the ramps of the landing boats banged down, and the marines began wading in. From blockhouses on the beach and from the wrecked hulk of the *Saida Maru* came a terrible steady drumming of machine-gun fire; the morning of the second day was worse than the first.

Out on the reef marines were rescuing wounded comrades and dragging them back to the landing boats. Private, first class, James Collins carried one stricken man back. He turned and seized another, a corpsman who had been shot in the shoulder. He lifted him. There was an explosion, and half the wounded man's head was blown off. Collins dropped the lifeless body and waded to the beach in tears. Only three of the twenty-four men who had been in his boat reached the shore. Only ninety of 199 men in the first wave ever got in.

But the wade-in continued, while marines of the 1st and 2d Battalions 2d Regiment attacked furiously against the blockhouses that were delivering that awful fire. The pack howitzers, lined up hub to hub on the beach, were leaping and baying in an attempt to silence enemy machine guns. The artillerymen were using shells with delayed fuses intended to explode once they penetrated the concrete, but the gunners were firing at a narrow front, and they could not get them all.

Carrier planes swooped down to strafe and bomb the blockhouses, yet the enemy fired on. Dive bombers pounded the *Saida Maru,* but it still crackled with fire. Marine mortars ashore hammered the *Saida Maru,*

but the bullets from it only slackened, they did not stop. It would eventually take a force of dynamite-throwing engineers covered by riflemen to clean out the ship infestation.

Sometimes the marines sought to veer away from the enemy's field of fire. One platoon slipped off to the right toward the sector held by Major Ryan. They waded into a cove, and they were shot down to a man.

It continued for five full hours, and when Maj. Lawrence Hays at last got his battalion ashore and reorganized, he found he had lost 110 men killed and 224 wounded. But 600 marines had survived the wade-in. They were now available for the desperate battle raging everywhere along the western half of Betio. As Colonel Shoup radioed Julian Smith at 11:30 a.m.: "The situation ashore doesn't look good."

Earlier that morning, just as the dreadful wade-in began, Shoup had ordered Lieutenant Hawkins to take his Scout-Sniper Platoon against a Japanese position holding five machine guns. It barred the way to the central sector attack with which Shoup hoped to cut Betio in two.

Hawk gathered his men. He had often said, "I think my thirty-four-man platoon can lick any two-hundred-man company in the world." Now he was going on a company-size mission to prove it. His men moved methodically from gun to gun, laying down covering fire while Hawkins crawled up to the pillbox gunports to fire point-blank inside or toss in grenades. The guns fell, but not before Hawkins had been shot in the chest. He had already lost blood from shrapnel wounds the day before, but he still resisted the corpsman's suggestions that he accept evacuation.

"I came here to kill Japs, not to be evacuated," Hawkins said. He and his men knocked out three more enemy positions, and then Hawkins was caught in a burst of mortar fire; when they carried him to the rear he was already dying.

But he and his men had opened the way for the cross-island attack, an assault which Colonel Shoup held as important as Major Ryan's drive to clear Betio's western beaches for the safe arrival of the reinforcing 6th Marines.

Still in charge of the battle so long as Julian Smith remained aboard the *Maryland*, Colonel Shoup crouched in his command post (CP) and listened to telephoned reports, his hand shaking slightly. His CP was still in front of the occupied Japanese pillbox, and it seemed to be crowned by a perpetual cloud of dust rising from the attack south across the airfield. Out of the dust just before noon limped the dirtiest marine Shoup had seen so far. A quarter inch of grime coated his beardless face, while a lock of limp blond hair hung from beneath his helmet. The youth's name was Adrian Strange, and he entered the Colonel's CP bawling, "Somebody gimme a pack of cigarettes. There's a machine-gun crew out there in a shell hole, and there ain't one of 'em's got a butt."

Someone threw him a pack of cigarettes. Imperturbable, impressed by neither the brass crouching below him nor the bullets buzzing above, Private Strange took one of the cigarettes and lighted it.

"I just got another sniper," he said, grinning. "That's six today, an' me a cripple." He blew smoke. "Busted my ankle steppin' in a shell hole yesterday." The bullets began buzzing as though coming in swarms, and Private Strange sneered, "Shoot me down, you son of a bitch!" before turning to limp back to the airfield.

Not all the marines on Betio that day were like Private Strange. A few minutes after he had limped off, a tearful young Major ran into Shoup's CP, crying: "Colonel, my men can't advance. They're being held up by a machine gun."

Dave Shoup spat in disgust.

"God a'mighty! One machine gun!"

The Major turned in confusion and went back to his men, and he had hardly disappeared before there was a sharp *crrrack!* in the CP and Cpl. Leonce Olivier yelped in pain. A Japanese in the pillbox had poked a rifle out an air vent and shot him in the leg. Someone dropped a grenade down the vent, but no one took comfort from the muffled explosion. The Japanese pillbox had walls three feet thick and was probably compartmented inside.

The confused young Major came back.

"Colonel, there are a thousand goddam marines out there on the beach and not one will follow me across the airstrip."

Shoup spat again.

"You've got to say, 'Who'll follow me?' And if only ten follow you, that's the best you can do—but it's better than nothing."

The Major departed—for good, this time—and the attack across the airfield to Betio's southern coast gained momentum. It reached its objective before dusk, after the marines had occupied abandoned enemy positions and beaten off two fierce counterattacks.

Betio was sliced in two and the marines had possession of most of the airfield, the base which would one day be known as Hawkins Field.

On the left flank, the marines under Major Crowe were making slow progress. They were trying to beat down the network of pillboxes and blockhouses surrounding Admiral Shibasaki's bombproof command post in their sector. It was slow because the men had to go in against an enemy concealed from view. The diving, strafing planes could not knock out these positions. Even Lieutenant Largey's thirty-two-ton *Colorado* was not heavy enough to crush most of them. Largey saw one of his own men fall from his fire and went back to report in grief to Crowe.

"I just killed a marine," he said. "Fragments from my seventy-five splintered against a tree and ricocheted off. Goddamn, I hate for that to happen."

"Too bad," Crowe muttered, "but it sometimes happens. Fortunes of war." He glanced upward at the American planes. "They do it, too. One fifty-caliber slug hit one of my men. Went through his shoulder, on down through his lung and liver. He lived four minutes." He shrugged. "Well, anyway, if a Jap ever sticks his head out of his pillbox the planes may kill him."

Over on the right flank, Major Ryan was calling for naval fire to knock out the Japanese positions. Lieutenant Thomas Greene, a naval gunfire spotter, signaled a destroyer and pinpointed Ryan's targets. The destroyer ran in and let go. Another destroyer followed. The men whom Shoup had already called fighting fools fanned out behind *China Gal* and another tank to begin their attack. The tanks stopped and one of the tank commanders called out: "Send us an intelligent marine to spot the pillboxes for us."

"Hell's fire!" a Sergeant snorted. "I ain't very smart, but I'll go."

He went, walking between the tanks, guiding them from pillbox to pillbox, and the western beaches began to fall.

To the east, Colonel Shoup heard the report of Ryan's progress with relief. At a few minutes before four o'clock, he turned to Major Culhane and said: "I think we're winning. But the bastards still have a lot of bullets left."

Then Shoup put his estimate into the language of official reports, concluding with that terse summary which would become historic: "Casualties many; percentage dead unknown; combat efficiency: we are winning."

Shoup's marines could have told him an hour earlier that the issue was no longer in doubt. The Japanese had begun to kill themselves. They had been told that Americans tortured their captives. Moreover, surrender meant disgrace to a man's family. So they had begun blowing themselves up, shooting or disemboweling themselves—choosing suicide as the means of immortalizing their spirits among Japan's warrior dead at Yasukuni Shrine.

Aboard the *Maryland* Maj. Gen. Julian Smith had given Col. Maurice G. Holmes of the 6th Marines his orders for a pair of landings. One was to be made on the newly cleared western beaches of Betio. The other would be on Bairiki, a little islet just east of Betio. Japanese had been reported attempting to reach Bairiki from Betio's tail. Smith also wanted to place artillery on the islet to batter Betio.

Shortly before five o'clock carrier planes began striking Bairiki, diving at the lone pillbox mounting two machine guns and held by fifteen Japanese. Passing through the gunports, .50-caliber bullets entered a gasoline can the Japanese had unwisely brought inside with them. Flames leaped from the position, and the 2d Battalion 6th Marine Regiment, commanded by big Lt. Col. Raymond L. Murray, occupied Bairiki without incident.

The other landing took place at about the same time. The 1st Battalion 6th Regiment, led by Maj. William K. ("Bill") Jones, rode rubber boats in to Betio's western tip. The men were embarrassed at the tearful welcome given them by Major Ryan's ragged remnant. They moved through them and dug in.

Up in the central sector, Col. Merritt A. Edson had come ashore. Julian Smith had sent "Red Mike" in to relieve the nearly exhausted Shoup. Edson took command at six o'clock, and Shoup resumed control of what remained of his 2d Marine Regiment. He had not slept for forty hours and his leg wound was paining him, but he had hung onto those two desperate holds and kept his scattered units fighting.

On the left flank, Major Crowe called for naval gunfire against Admiral Shibasaki's bombproof. His men were going to have to go up against it next morning, and he wanted them to go the easy way.

At dusk a destroyer ran in so close to Betio that it seemed it would scrape the bottom of the lagoon. Flame spouted from the muzzles of its 5-inchers. Four, five, six rounds—and then the answering crash and flame as the shells struck Admiral Shibasaki's command post. The graceful, slender ship was almost obscured in smoke. Chips of cement flew from the bombproof's five-foot walls, geysers of sand leaped from its roof, overgrown with palm trees. Some eighty rounds flashed around it like monster fireflies.

The destroyer stopped firing. Major Crowe shrugged.

"They never hit it squarely," he said, his outer gruffness masking an inner disquiet. "Just almost."

Within the bombproof Rear Admiral Shibasaki contemplated the shattered bits of the *Yogaki* Plan. He had gotten almost no help, nothing but a submarine or two which had harassed the enemy the night before the invasion. Last night a single plane had flown up from the Marshalls. Tonight he could expect no more. Obviously the Americans had neutralized the Marshalls. And Tarawa, he knew, was falling.

Having felt the lash of the American destroyer's 5-inchers, Shibasaki could guess that it would be his bombproof's turn tomorrow. He composed his last message for Tokyo. "Our weapons have been destroyed," it said, "and from now on everyone is attempting a final charge. . . . May Japan exist for ten thousand years!"

Abemama is truly called the Atoll of the Moon. She is the loveliest of all the Gilberts, a shimmering pale-green lagoon caught in a circlet of sun-bathed islets which are themselves clasped by the gleaming white of the beaches—and surrounding it all is the soft blue of the sea. To Abemama in 1889 came Robert Louis Stevenson as the guest of the philosopher-king Tem Binoka; to it three years later came representatives of the British Government; and to it after another half century came two companies of Japanese under a midget of a monocled colonel.

The colonel departed in 1943 with the airfield done and with some 1000 handsome, good-natured, lazy Abemamese introduced to the horrors of work. There were only an excitable captain and two dozen Japanese left when, in the early morning blackness of

(Above) *Having cleared a foothold on the sands of Betio, a large contingent of marines takes a short breather before plunging inland to wrest the vital Tarawa bastion in the Gilbert Islands from the Japanese. Despite saturation shelling by the U.S. Navy, which blew up nearly all the enemy's fuel and munitions dumps, the stubborn defenders were still firmly dug into pillboxes, blockhouses and reinforced concrete shelters that had to be taken the hard way, one by one.*

(Left) *Marines get ready to advance, under intense fire, from a narrow bridgehead in Tarawa. True to their bushido code, the Japanese fought literally to the death—scarcely one of the enemy was still alive when the best entrenched of the many islets, Betio, was taken on the fourth day. By the end of the first day of their landings, the invading Americans held only two beachheads some 250 yards deep, and 1500 of their 5000 assault troops had been killed or wounded.*

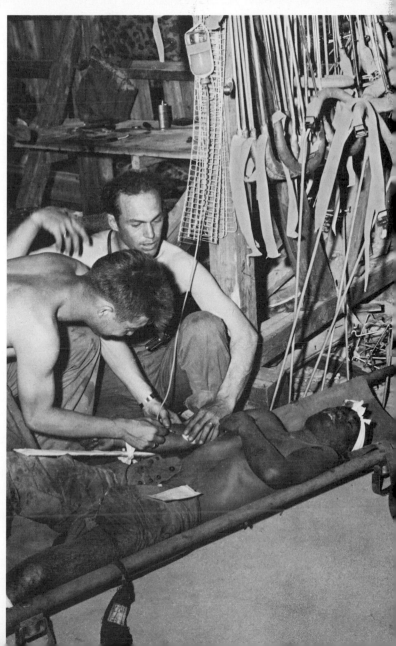

(Right) *Enemy wounded received the same medical care as American casualties. Here a seriously wounded Japanese soldier is being given a transfusion of blood plasma by U.S. Army medics. He is one of the few Japanese defenders at Tarawa who survived. Many committed suicide rather than surrender.*

November 21, sixty-eight marines led by Capt. James L. ("Jim") Jones came to Abemama to scout out the atoll's defenses for the November 26 invasion.

They came from Tarawa the night of November 20, making the eighty-five-mile run to the southeast aboard the big submarine *Nautilus*. Shortly after midnight the *Nautilus* heaved out of the sea and the marines came up on deck to inflate and launch rubber boats from her stern.

They were struck by rain squalls. Only three of the boats' outboard motors started. One conked out, and there were but two left to tow the remaining boats, all bobbing and wallowing in a wild cross sea of wind and wave, while the current pulled them toward the barrier reef. Two boats were carried off into the darkness. Aboard the others marines paddled frantically to avoid being cast up on the boiling reef.

An hour later the wind abated. The two missing boats rejoined the column. Now the only enemy was the current, and three hours later Captain Jones's men were paddling within the comparatively calm waters of the lee shore.

Jones began sending out patrols to scout the islets of Abemama. One of these scouting parties included Lt. George Hard, a short bald Australian who had lived in the Gilberts before the war and knew the people of Abemama. Minutes after the patrol set out, Lieutenant Hard saw and recognized two Abemamese wading to the marines' islet from another one to the right. Hard and the marines hid in the bushes, for the Australian had no notion of how the Gilbertese had reacted to Japan's "Greater East Asia Co-Prosperity Sphere." When the two men were almost on them, Hard jumped up and called a greeting in Gilbertese.

"Why, my word!" one of them replied in unruffled English. "It's Mr. Hard! But were you wise to come and visit us now, Mr. Hard? The Sapanese are here."

Hard grinned. So did the marines when they learned that the Gilbertese pronounce a *j* like an *s*. It was a pleasure to imagine the irritation of the numerous "Sapanese" who spoke English.

Mr. Hard's old friend explained that there were only twenty-five "Sapanese" now, but these were well entrenched around a radio station on another islet. They had heavy and light machine guns, mortars and much ammunition; their pillboxes on both ocean and lagoon beaches would not be easy to rush.

When Captain Jones heard the news, he decided to attack. That night he and his "Recon Boys" spotted the winking of blinker lights at sea. An enemy submarine had come to evacuate the atoll's garrison. But the Japanese couldn't get away. Jones's men had destroyed the motor-powered whaleboat that was to have been their getaway craft, and in the morning the "Recon Boys" would be out to destroy every member of the Japanese garrison as well.

The third day of battle on Betio—November 22—was businesslike and brutal. It had not the horror and transcending courage of the first day, when marines fought to rescue their stricken comrades and knock out the guns that struck them. Nor had it the desperation of the second, when men fought to avoid defeat. It had only the cold, wary precision of the cleanup. Men fought to exterminate an enemy gone to ground. They killed not to save or preserve, but to destroy. Such unexalted work requires professionals.

The marines were coldly efficient, as one battalion attacked east along Betio's spine, or southern shore, and another struck west into the Pocket.

The Pocket was that 600-yard gap which still separated the original Shoup beachhead from the one which Major Ryan had expanded on the west. At 7 a.m. the 1st Battalion 8th Regiment moved out of the Shoup beachhead to reduce it. The men attacked behind three light tanks, but a Japanese suicide soldier got under one of the tanks with a magnetic mine and blew himself and the vehicle apart. The 37-mm. guns of the light tanks were unable to do more than chip the pillboxes. By noon the attack had only succeeded in containing the Japanese strongpoints, and the half-tracks which had come up to relieve the tanks were driven back by machine-gun fire.

Meanwhile, the 1st Battalion 6th Regiment, which had landed on the western beaches the night before, moved rapidly toward the east. Major Bill Jones (whose brother Jim had led the "Recon Boys" ashore at Abemama) drove his men forward. They were as eager as men can be when attacking a maze of forts concealing a stubborn, skillful enemy. They also had three Shermans and the bulldozers of the engineers to accelerate their attack.

The tanks moved against a front about 100 yards wide. Fifty yards behind them came the riflemen, spread out and watching for suicide troopers with their magnetic mines. If a blockhouse or pillbox resisted the Shermans' shells, the tanks waddled on, leaving the position to the riflemen and flamethrowers. If individual assault would not storm the position, it could at least neutralize it while a bulldozer slipped in—its driver crouching behind the raised, sheltering blade—to seal it off with walls of sand.

At 11 a.m. the marines of Jones's group had reached the battalions of the 2d Regiment, which had fought to the southern shore, midway on the bird's back, the day before. Jones's men had killed 250 Japanese while taking very light casualties themselves. They moved out along the spine again. By nightfall they had reached the end of the airfield on the southern shore and were dug in looking eastward toward Betio's tail. Just to their left and rear, Major Crowe's men were moving toward them across the ruins of Admiral Shibasaki's bombproof.

The approaches to the bombproof, as it faced north toward Crowe's marines, were guarded on the right by a steel pillbox and on the left by a big emplacement made of reinforced coconut logs. At 9:30 a.m. Crowe's mortars had begun falling on the coconut-log structure.

It had blown up with a thundering detonation of flame and somersaulting logs. The puny 81-mm. mortars had scored a direct hit on what had been an ammunition warehouse as well as a bunker. Then jaunty, battered *Colorado* had rolled to the steel pillbox's right. It had fired twice, three times, and Shibasaki's bombproof had lain open to attack.

Crowe's men moved out, matching shot for shot with the bombproof's defenders but gradually coming in closer. Assault engineers crawled forward, led by a tall cheerful Lieutenant named Alexander Bonnyman. They gained the sides of the bombproof and forced their way to the top.

The Japanese counterattacked. They came in a fury, for the bombproof was the heart of their defenses. As they charged up the slopes of sand piled atop the building, they ran into Lieutenant Bonnyman. Though they should have overwhelmed him, they didn't. He raked them with carbine fire. They hesitated, and Bonnyman charged. "Follow me!" he shouted, and the engineers closed in after him. Bonnyman dropped and his marines went over him and beat the enemy back down the hill. Bonnyman died of his many wounds, but the top of the bombproof had been captured, and as the Japanese began to pour out of its eastern and southern exits they were cut down

by riflemen and the scything canister shot of the 37-mm. cannon. There were still about 200 Japanese left inside, among them Admiral Shibasaki.

Bulldozers heaped sand against the exits and sealed off the gunports. Marines poured gasoline down the air vents and dropped in hand grenades. There were muffled explosions and then screams. Crowe's men moved on toward Betio's tail to nail down the left flank of the marines of Major Jones.

Behind them, on the western beaches, the 3d Battalion 6th Marines had landed on Betio under Lt. Col. Kenneth F. McLeod. Also to their rear, at a rough cemetery in about the center of the 3houp beachhead, parties of their fellow marines were burying the dead.

Bulldozers scooped out long, long trenches three feet deep. Bodies were laid out in rows, without blankets or other covering, and the chaplains moved among them somberly, their lips moving with final prayers and the words of last rites. Bodies that had been identified were quickly placed in the trenches. When a trench was full, the bulldozers roared and butted against the piles of sand. It was soggy, wet sand, for it was impossible to dig more than four feet on Betio without striking water. The dead were covered over, the trench was rollered smooth—and a new one was dug. Many bodies were impossible to identify. One was brought in, headless, one-armed. Robert Sherrod, a war correspondent, turned away.

"What a hell of a way to die!" he exclaimed. But a big, redheaded marine gunner stared him in the eye and disagreed with him: "You can't pick a better way."

It was true. Any marine would prefer being blown apart to the languishing agony of shrapnel or bayonets in the belly, or to being left alone to perish in torment from wounds or exposure.

Many such solitary sufferers were being discovered this third day of battle. Corpsmen wading through the lagoon in search of bodies found live men lying within wrecked and blackened amtracs. In one of these they found a dozen dead marines and one who was still breathing. The man had shrapnel in his head, arms and legs. He had not had food or water since he went down the cargo nets early in the morning of November 20. He had lain in the sun for two days and been broiled like a lobster. His rifle lay with its muzzle pointing up toward his throat and the corpsmen could guess that he had tried to kill himself but had not had the strength to reach the trigger. They spoke to him gently, assuring him that his ordeal was over. He opened his cracked lips and mumbled: "Water—pour water on me."

Major General Julian Smith was on Betio. He had left the *Maryland* and boarded an amtrac with Brig. Gen. Thomas E. Bourke, his artillery commander. They went ashore at the western beach. They inspected defenses and then went back aboard the amtrac to move around to Colonel Edson's command post by water. As they passed the Pocket where Major Hays's men were battering enemy strongpoints, machine-gun fire struck the amtrac. The amtrac was knocked out. Smith and Bourke had to transfer to another, but they made it in to shore. At four o'clock Smith sent off this discouraging message to Brig. Gen. Leo D. Hermle, his assistant division commander:

Situation not favorable for rapid cleanup of Betio. Heavy casualties among officers make leadership problem difficult. Many emplacements intact on eastern end of the island. In addition many Japanese strongpoints to westward of our front lines within our position have not been reduced. Progress slow and extremely costly. Complete occupation will take at least five days more. Naval and air bombardment a great help but does not take out emplacements.

That night the Japanese themselves improved the situation for Smith, coming out of their emplacements in a boomeranging banzai charge.

They struck at Maj. Bill Jones's 1st Battalion 6th Regiment, as it held down the southern half of a 400-yard cross-island line. This line was drawn just east of the airfield, where the bird's body ends and the narrowing tail begins. The northern half was held by Major Crowe's men.

The attack was made skillfully at first. Some fifty Japanese slipped past an outpost line and by 7:30 p.m. had opened a small gap between two companies. They were obviously there to feel out the marine positions. They tried to draw fire.

But the marines did not shoot. They struck at the Japanese with bayonets and clubbed rifles and grenades, and while the beach guns and the howitzers on Bairiki converged in a hemming line of fire between the lines to bar a retreat, they killed them to a man.

In the interval between this thrust and the second attack, Major Kyle moved his company of marines into reserve behind Jones while Lieutenant Colonel McLeod leapfrogged a company forward to fill the gap this movement left. At eleven o'clock the Japanese came again, this time with two 50-man parties. They fired openly, shouting and throwing grenades aimlessly. A score of them came charging at a Browning automatic rifle (BAR) position held by Pfc. Lowell Koci and Pfc. Horace Warfield. They were clearly silhouetted in the glare of gasoline fires lighted behind them by marine mortars.

The marines fired. They ducked down to reload, and a Japanese soldier jumped into their hole, thrusting with his bayonet. It drove into Warfield's thigh. The Japanese strained to withdraw it, and Koci, a husky 200-pounder, seized his BAR by its muzzle and swung it around like a whip. The butt struck the man behind the head and brained him. His legs thumped the sand as he fell.

Again the artillery cut off retreat for these infiltrating Japanese, and the marines went about the work of destroying them.

At 4 a.m. on November 23, with the moon making a grotesquerie of the coral flats—humping the convex roofs of the pillboxes, squashing the squares of the blockhouses, catching the jagged stumps of coconut trees and drawing them out like giant corkscrews—some 300 more Japanese launched the counterattack that broke their own backs.

They flowed up against the marine lines yelling and jabbering, and for a time there seemed to be too many of them. Lieutenant Norman Thomas telephoned Major Jones and yelled: "We're killing them as fast as they come at us, but we can't hold much longer. We need reinforcements!"

There wasn't time for reinforcement; there was only time for what Jones was sternly commanding: "You've got to hold!"

While the destroyers *Schroeder* and *Sigsbee* hurled salvo after salvo into the Japanese assembly areas, while the shells of the marine artillery fell within seventy-five yards of the front lines, Thomas and his men fought with rifle, bayonet and grenade. By five o'clock the banzai charge was shattered. There were 200 dead Japanese within the marine lines, 125 more torn and broken corpses out where the artillery had fallen. Only 500 Japanese were left alive on Betio.

The men of the 2d Marine Division were rushing to victory on the morning of November 23. They were going downhill. The taste of triumph was in the air, and all those who pressed for it moved with a mastery that must have been annihilating to the souls of the enemy.

At seven o'clock the first of the carrier aircraft plunged to the attack. They bombed and strafed for half an hour. For another quarter hour, pack howitzers hurled their shells into the tail of Betio. Warships on both the ocean and lagoon sides thundered for the next fifteen minutes, and then it was eight o'clock and time for the riflemen to attack.

"Let's go!" called out McLeod, and the 3d Battalion 6th Regiment swept forward with crackling rifles. They were the freshest troops on Betio. They had not yet fought. They passed through the lines held by Maj. Bill Jones's marines—now exhausted from a day and night of constant fighting—and spread out on a two-company front to punch down the length of the narrowing tail. In front of them clanked *Colorado* and *China Gal*—those seemingly indestructible Shermans which were still capable of battle—while seven light tanks rolled to either flank.

The attack gathered momentum. It raced forward 150 yards within a matter of minutes. The Japanese defenders fired only fitfully at the onrushing Americans—and then turned their weapons on themselves.

On the left, or lagoon, side a system of supporting bombproofs slowed one company up. McLeod sent the other company racing down the ocean flank in a bypassing movement. Once they were past the bombproofs, the marines of this company spread out again. Behind them the bypassed company moved in on the bombproofs, while Lieutenant Largey brought *Colorado* into position. The liquid fire of the flamethrowers began to describe its fiery arc—disappearing through the mouths of the gunports. Suddenly a door flew open in the biggest of the bombproofs. Perhaps a hundred Japanese rushed out, tumbling over one another in their flight down a narrow exit channel.

Colorado's gun swiveled around and fired. Fifty, perhaps more, of the enemy were struck to the ground by that shattering shot, and soon resistance had ended among the bombproofs.

To the west, in the Pocket, the marines of Major Hays's battalion and the Ryan-Schoettel battalion were cleaning up. Half-tracks drove among the pillboxes and blockhouses blasting with their 75's, while kneeling riflemen picked off the fleeing enemy. Others hurled shaped charges and grenades. Flame-throwing teams darted up to the entrances and fire gushed from nozzles.

McLeod's marines were approaching Betio's eastern shore. *China Gal* rumbled among the blockhouses, taking on those that still fired cannon, while the light tanks went after the machine guns and rifles. The 3d Battalion 6th Regiment was making a slaughter of eastern Betio. The tail was lashing its last. The marines here killed 475 Japanese, with their own losses kept to 9 dead and 25 wounded. The enemy was too stunned to fight back.

At 1 p.m. a dusty, sweating marine waded into the sea between Betio and Bairiki and stopped to bathe his face in warm water.

Betio had fallen.

"The Saps are all dead," the tall young Abemamese said cheerfully on the morning of November 25, and asked for a cigarette. It was given to him, and he began to tell Capt. Jim Jones what had happened to the Japanese since Jones had attacked their radio station behind the shelling of the submarine *Nautilus,* only to be driven off with one marine killed and another wounded.

The following day, said the Abemamese, he had gone to the vicinity of the radio station. He had seen that the Captain of the atoll garrison was making a speech to about fifteen soldiers who had survived the shelling and the fight. He hid and watched.

The Captain waved his *samurai* saber and howled: "We shall kill the American devils!"

He yanked his pistol from its holster and brandished it in the air. It went off accidentally, striking the Captain and mortally wounding him. Then his men began killing themselves. They dug graves and lay down in them and placed the muzzles of their weapons in their mouths and pulled the triggers.

Captain Jones led his men to the radio station and found that this was so. The marines finished the burial job the enemy had begun, and the people of Abemama came out of hiding.

There were smiling young men, strong and athletic; eager youngsters, more than willing to shinny up trees and throw down coconuts to the marines; young girls

Time out: An American marine, his figure draped with hand grenades and extra clips of ammunition, pauses on a war-littered Tarawa beach to take a deep drink from his canteen.

with round bare breasts, straight black hair hanging to their waists, and skirts of sailcloth bound tightly around brown hips; and there were old people coming out of the hiding places where they had fled when the shooting began. They came back to their thatched huts to light cooking fires. Shyly and sweetly, some of the girls began to sing, "Brighten the Corner Where You Are."

The marines looked away. It was not that they were shy. It was just that they were embarrassed. They felt awkward in their clumsy habiliments of war. They felt heavy with themselves and their world, as though they had blundered into some Eden which had not known the serpent.

It was, of course, a romantic notion. But this was the Atoll of the Moon, that Abemama which the marines would prefer to remember as the "Land of Moonshine."

On November 24 the marines were preparing to leave Betio. The transports were already standing into the lagoon with deliberate slow majesty.

The 3d Battalion 6th Regiment would soon be sailing south to "invade" Abemama and gain a comic celebrity which marines do not value. The 2d Battalion 6th Regiment had already begun the long hot march up the atoll chain from Bairiki, driving all the Tarawa survivors before them until, at the northernmost islet of Buariki, they would destroy 164 Japanese against 4 of their own killed and 56 wounded.

But most of the 2d Division were departing the stench and heat and ruin of Betio. They had killed 4690 of the enemy, and 980 of their own comrades had died or were dying. They had suffered 2101 men wounded—and many of these would not be fit to fight again. But they had taken Tarawa the "untakable," they had done the thing Japan thought impossible. Yet, there was no thought of glory in their minds—of the posthumous Medals of Honor that would come to Hawkins, Bordelon and Bonnyman, or of the medal that Colonel Shoup would wear—as they came to the beach and stopped and blinked in astonishment.

There was no beach. The spring tides had come, and the sea flowed up against the seawall. For a moment there was wonder in the old eyes staring out of young faces. Then they shrugged and clambered aboard the boats. It was all one: high water on the reef would have meant high water at the seawall and no-

where to hide from the point-blank Japanese fire.

The boats took them out to the waiting ships while, overhead, roaring airplanes were already beginning to arrive on Hawkins Field. One of them carried Maj. Gen. Holland M. Smith. He had come from Makin, which had been taken by about 6500 soldiers of the Army's 27th Division. They had landed almost unopposed and killed 445 Japanese troops while capturing 104 laborers. They had lost 66 dead and 150 wounded. Howlin' Mad Smith was greeted at the airfield by Maj. Gen. Julian Smith.

The Generals Smith began to tour the island. Even Julian Smith, who had been on Betio since November 21, was stunned by what he saw. Both Generals understood at last why pillboxes and blockhouses which had withstood bombs and shells had eventually fallen. Within each of them lay a half dozen or more dead Japanese, their bodies sprawled around those of three or four marines. Julian Smith's men had jumped inside to fight it out at muzzle range.

Many of the pillboxes were made of five sides, each ten feet long, with a pair of entrances shielded against shrapnel by buffer tiers. Each side was made of two layers of coconut logs eight inches in diameter, hooked together with clamps and railroad spikes, with sand poured between each layer. The roof was built of two similar layers of coconut logs. Over this was a double steel turret, two sheathings of quarter-inch steel rounded off to deflect shells. Over this was three feet of sand.

"By God!" Howlin' Mad exclaimed. "No wonder these bastards were sitting back here laughing at us. They never dreamed the marines could take this island, and they were laughing at what would happen to us when we tried it. How did they do it, Julian?" he started to ask, and then, below and above the seawall, he found his answer.

Below it as many as 300 American bodies floated on that abundant tide. Above it, leaning against it in death, was the body of a young marine. His right arm was still flung across the top of the wall. A few inches from his fingers stood a little blue-and-white flag. It was a beach marker. It told the men following him where they should land. The marine had planted it there with his life, and now it spoke such an eloquent reply to that question of a moment ago that both Generals turned away from it in tears.

"Julian," Howlin' Mad Smith went on in soft amendment, "how can such men be defeated?"

ISLAND-HOPPING: PHASE I
August 1942 to December 1943

The initiative in the Pacific had now passed to the Americans, and the Joint Chiefs of Staff in Washington swung into action with a master plan for a two-pronged offensive aimed at the heart of the Japanese homeland. Co-commanders of the drive were Gen. Douglas MacArthur and Adm. Chester W. Nimitz. The directives: While MacArthur's arm fought its way up the northern New Guinea coast and then on to the Philippines, Nimitz' forces were to strike across the Pacific and overcome such strongholds as Tarawa, Kwajalein and Saipan, among the myriad islands and atolls.

Experience in tropical fighting had sharpened the Allied technique of amphibious warfare in which the target, first hammered by air and sea bombardment, was stormed by assault troops, followed in due course by the Seabees, the construction engineers who built roads, harbor facilities and the all-important airfields. Now a new strategy was developed—that of leapfrogging a strongly defended enemy position so that a more vulnerable target farther on might be attacked, leaving the first one cut off and isolated.

On February 21, 1943, U.S. Marines and Army troops, supported by Adm. William F. Halsey's fleet, stormed ashore to capture the Russell Islands in the Solomons. A pause in the offensive was called to bring in fresh troops and supplies; then Rendova was seized on June 30 and New Georgia invaded July 2. Here a Japanese garrison resisted until September.

Blazing sea engagements took place on July 6 and 13 in the Kula Gulf region, as the Japanese sought to reinforce New Georgia. Another free-for-all naval action was fought on August 6–7 in Vella Gulf, where the Japanese lost three destroyers. Overhead rival air fleets contested for mastery, the enemy taking major losses.

The heavily garrisoned island of Kolombangara was now leapfrogged, and Vella Lavella beyond it was taken on August 15. Two more enemy strongholds, Choiseul and the Treasury group, fell on October 27. The island-hopping advance had brought the offensive to the largest of the Solomon group, Bougainville. A landing party went ashore at Empress Augusta Bay on Novem-

ber 1. The battle for Bougainville was severe; resistance did not end until well into 1944.

While the Solomon campaign was in progress, American and Australian troops under MacArthur were punching their way up the New Guinea coast, their immediate target enemy bases at Lae and Salamaua on Huon Gulf. As in the Solomons, the Japanese began to bring in reinforcements from Rabaul. A fleet of eight transports escorted by eight destroyers was attacked by Allied planes in the Bismarck Sea on March 2, 1943. The battle lasted three days; when it was over twelve ships, including the transports, had been sunk.

Despite the defeat, the Japanese fought desperately to halt MacArthur's advance. Salamaua, threatened by a landing at Nassau Bay on June 30, managed to hold out until September 15 before it was overrun. The next day the Japanese base at Lae fell. Finschhafen surrendered to the Australians on October 2.

Efforts to isolate the Japanese base at Rabaul on New Britain had been made in June, when MacArthur's troops took Woodlark Island and the Trobriands in the Solomon Sea. This was followed on December 15 by the seizure of Arawe on the southern coast. Then, on December 26, U.S. Marines were put ashore on the western tip of New Britain to capture Cape Gloucester. On the same day Long Island, in the southern part of the Bismarck Sea, fell to the Americans.

Military action was by no means confined to the Southwest Pacific. On May 11, 1943, U.S. forces descended on the Aleutian island of Attu. After 2½ weeks of heavy fighting, the Japanese defenders died in a series of wild suicide charges at Chichagof Harbor on May 29–30. The following August 15 an American-Canadian force landed on Kiska, only to find that the Japanese had withdrawn their forces.

Admiral Nimitz' offensive fleet had been gathering strength in the Central Pacific. In mid-November Makin in the Gilberts fell, and Tarawa Atoll was overcome after a terrific struggle (see pages 236–257). The year 1943 ended for the Allies with their forces in the Pacific moving steadily forward.

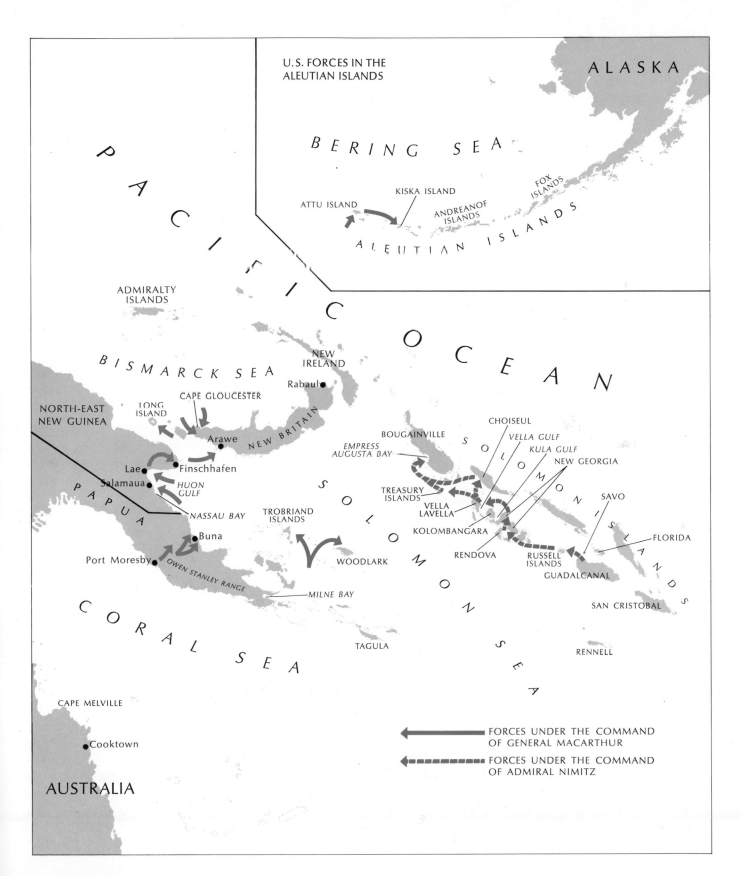

ALASKA

U.S. FORCES IN THE
ALEUTIAN ISLANDS

BERING SEA

KISKA ISLAND

ATTU ISLAND

FOX ISLANDS

ANDREANOF ISLANDS

ALEUTIAN ISLANDS

PACIFIC OCEAN

ADMIRALTY ISLANDS

BISMARCK SEA

NEW IRELAND

Rabaul

CAPE GLOUCESTER

LONG ISLAND

NORTH-EAST NEW GUINEA

Arawe

NEW BRITAIN

CHOISEUL

VELLA GULF

BOUGAINVILLE

KULA GULF

SOLOMON

EMPRESS AUGUSTA BAY

NEW GEORGIA

Lae

Finschhafen

Salamaua

HUON GULF

TREASURY ISLANDS

VELLA LAVELLA

SAVO

PAPUA

NASSAU BAY

TROBRIAND ISLANDS

SOLOMON

KOLOMBANGARA

RENDOVA

FLORIDA

Buna

Port Moresby

OWEN STANLEY RANGE

WOODLARK

RUSSELL ISLANDS

SOLOMON ISLANDS

GUADALCANAL

CORAL SEA

MILNE BAY

SEA

SAN CRISTOBAL

TAGULA

RENNELL

CAPE MELVILLE

Cooktown

AUSTRALIA

FORCES UNDER THE COMMAND
OF GENERAL MACARTHUR

FORCES UNDER THE COMMAND
OF ADMIRAL NIMITZ

259

The autumn of 1942 marked the beginning of the
end for Hitler and his Axis partners. British infantrymen
dramatize this reversal of fortunes as they advance on a German tank soldier
during the Battle of Alamein in North Africa in late October 1942.

THRUST AND COUNTERTHRUST
HITLER'S EMPIRE UNDER ATTACK

THE MARCH TOWARD MOSCOW

In July 1940, over the protests of military advisers who were apprehensive about fighting a war on two fronts, Hitler ordered his General Staff to draw up plans for invading the Soviet Union. This plan, "Operation Barbarossa," called for a massive attack along a wide front no later than May 1941; if it went smoothly, all of European Russia would be in Hitler's hands within five months, long before the start of the Russian winter.

But events elsewhere in Europe delayed the start of the invasion. Mussolini was determined to impress Hitler and the world with an Italian military triumph to rival Hitler's own. In October his Army attacked Greece from bases in Italian-occupied Albania. Caught off guard, its small Army outnumbered almost two to one, Greece seemed easy prey. But the Greek Army proved a stubborn foe, eventually driving the invaders out of Greece and back into Albania.

To his disgust, Hitler now had to bail out his inept ally. He was reluctant to divert troops from the invasion buildup on the eastern front and first tried diplomacy, urging the pro-Nazi government of Yugoslavia to aid the Italians. But two days after signing the agreement to intervene, the Yugoslavian regime of the Regent, Prince Paul, was overthrown, and young King Peter II, leading the new government, openly defied Hitler. The furious German dictator sent his divisions into both Greece and Yugoslavia, quickly crushing their hopelessly outnumbered armies. A British force sent to aid the Greeks was routed, first from Greece and then, in May, from the island of Crete to which it had retreated. The Axis powers now controlled the Aegean Sea, threatened the eastern Mediterranean and menaced Egypt, Turkey and the entire Middle East.

But Hitler had lost three weeks of precious time in launching his Russian invasion. Despite warnings from his generals, he was determined to go ahead, and at dawn on June 22, 1941, "Operation Barbarossa" was launched. One hundred and fifty divisions, almost 3 million men, poured across the Soviet border, spearheaded by armored columns and bombers. Taken completely by surprise, the Red Army fell back in confusion, its bewildered officers pleading for instructions from their superiors in Moscow. Thousands of Russian soldiers were killed, hundreds of thousands more taken prisoner. The overwhelming German onslaught seemed to sweep all before it, driving 200 to 400 miles into Russia in the first month. Once the Soviet defenses were breached, the attack divided into three parts: Army Group North, under the command of Field Marshal Wilhelm von Leeb, struck out for Leningrad along the Baltic coast; Army Group South, commanded by Field Marshal Gerd von Rundstedt, drove through the fertile Ukraine toward Kiev and the rich oil fields of the Caucasus mountains; and Army Group Center, led by Field Marshal Fedor von Bock, raced toward Moscow, as the ill-starred armies of Napoleon had done. Bock's force quickly took the lead, plunging two thirds of the way to the Russian capital in just 3½ weeks. By September 1941, Stalin had lost 2.5 million men, 22,000 guns, 18,000 tanks and 14,000 planes.

But the advance slowed in August as Hitler and his generals argued over how best to proceed. Bock's drive clanked to a halt, while some of his troops were moved indecisively to aid drives in the north and south. Hitler sought to destroy Russia's ability to wage war by controlling the Baltic, the Ukraine and the Caucasus. To do this, he was willing to divide his forces and pass up the chance to wipe out the scattered remnants of the Red Army. Several of his generals urged, instead, an all-out attack on Moscow, the hub of the sprawling railway system and the site of many arms factories.

While Hitler and his generals bickered, the battered Russians began to regroup, and the Russian people themselves commenced to rally to the defense of their country. The first German troops had been greeted as liberators by many Soviet peoples, such as the Ukrainians, who bore little love for the Communist regime in Moscow. But the German occupation, supervised by the dreaded *Schutzstaffel*, or S.S., was barbaric. Men, women and children were murdered, crops and homes burned and plundered, animals slaughtered. German cruelty united the Soviet people, who eagerly answered Stalin's call for a "Great Patriotic War." Hitler had sown the seeds of his own defeat.

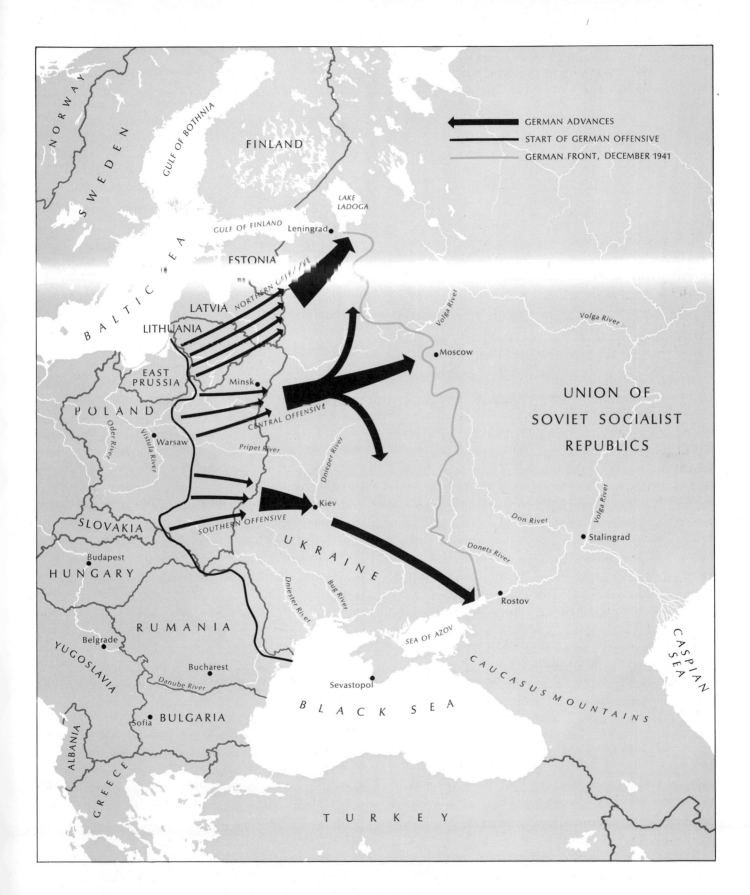

GERMAN ADVANCES

START OF GERMAN OFFENSIVE

GERMAN FRONT, DECEMBER 1941

NORWAY

SWEDEN

FINLAND

GULF OF BOTHNIA

LAKE LADOGA

GULF OF FINLAND

Leningrad

ESTONIA

BALTIC SEA

LATVIA

LITHUANIA

NORTHERN OFFENSIVE

Volga River

Volga River

EAST PRUSSIA

Minsk

Moscow

UNION OF
SOVIET SOCIALIST
REPUBLICS

POLAND

Oder River

Vistula River

Warsaw

Pripet River

CENTRAL OFFENSIVE

Dnieper River

SLOVAKIA

Kiev

Don River

Volga River

SOUTHERN OFFENSIVE

UKRAINE

Donets River

Stalingrad

Budapest

HUNGARY

Dniester River

Bug River

Rostov

RUMANIA

Belgrade

SEA OF AZOV

CAUCASUS MOUNTAINS

CASPIAN SEA

YUGOSLAVIA

Bucharest

Danube River

Sevastopol

BLACK SEA

ALBANIA

BULGARIA

Sofia

GREECE

TURKEY

THE GERMANS INVADE RUSSIA

BY WILLIAM L. SHIRER

Except for the Battle of Britain, Hitler's war machine had been undefeated and unchecked. He now sought to add the sprawling land of Russia to the empire he was building, as Napoleon had done. His armies, like those of the great French General, were finally brought to a halt by savage resistance, bitter cold, seas of mud and overextended supply lines.

On Sunday morning June 22, 1941, Adolf Hitler's armored, mechanized and hitherto invincible armies swept across the Niemen (now Neman) and various other rivers and penetrated swiftly into Soviet Russia. The Red Army, according to Gen. Franz Halder, Chief of the German Army General Staff, was "tactically surprised along the entire front." Within a few days tens of thousands of prisoners began to pour in; whole armies were encircled. By the beginning of autumn Hitler believed that Russia was finished.

So according to plan was the German progress along a 1000-mile front from the Baltic to the Black Sea, and so confident was the Nazi dictator that it would continue at an accelerated pace, that by the end of September he instructed the High Command to prepare to disband forty infantry divisions. This additional manpower would be utilized by industry.

Russia's two greatest cities, Leningrad and Moscow, seemed to Hitler about to fall. On September 18 he issued strict orders: "A capitulation of Leningrad or Moscow is not to be accepted, even if offered." What was to happen to them he made clear to his commanders in a directive of September 29:

The Fuehrer has decided to have St. Petersburg [Leningrad] wiped off the face of the earth.

...Requests that the city be taken over will be turned down, for the problem of the survival of the population and of supplying it with food is one which cannot and should not be solved by us. In this war for existence, we have no interest in keeping even part of this great city's population.

The same week, on October 3, Hitler said in an address to the German people: "I declare without any reservation that the enemy in the East has been struck down and will never rise again."

This boast was, to say the least, premature. In reality the Russians, despite the entrapment and loss of some of their best armies, had begun in July to put up a mounting resistance such as the *Wehrmacht* had never before encountered. The reports of frontline commanders began to be peppered, then laden, with accounts of severe fighting, desperate Russian stands and counterattacks. And there proved to be more Russians with better equipment than Hitler had dreamed was possible.

Fresh Soviet divisions of which German Intelligence had no inkling were continually being thrown into battle. "At the beginning," Halder wrote in his diary on August 11, "we reckoned with some 200 enemy divisions, and we have already identified 360. When a dozen of them are destroyed, the Russians throw in another dozen." Field Marshal Gerd von Rundstedt put it bluntly to Allied interrogators after the war:

"I realized soon after the attack was begun that everything that had been written about Russia was nonsense."

And now, to further complicate the Army's difficulties, there occurred the first great controversy over strategy in the German High Command. It led to a decision by the Fuehrer, over the protests of most of the top generals, that Halder considered "the greatest strategic blunder of the Eastern campaign." The issue was simple but fundamental. Should Army Group Center, the most powerful and successful of the three main German armies, push on to Moscow, 200 miles from its present position? Or should the original plan, which Hitler had laid down and which called for the main thrusts on the north and south flanks, be adhered to? In other words, was Moscow the prize goal, or were Leningrad and the Ukraine?

Moscow, the Army High Command pointed out to

Hitler, was a vital source of armaments production and, more important, the center of the Russian transportation and communications system. Take it, and the Soviets not only would be deprived of arms but would be unable to move troops and supplies to the distant fronts, which would weaken, wither and collapse.

But Hitler had his hungry eyes on the food belt and industrial areas of the Ukraine and on the Russian oil fields beyond in the Caucasus. Moscow could wait. The Fuehrer issued the orders to follow this course in a directive to his generals, and, adding insult to injury to those officers who did not appreciate his strategic genius, he sent what Halder called a "countermemorandum full of insults" such as that the Army High Command was largely composed of "minds fossilized in out-of-date theories."

"Unbearable! Unheard of! The limit!" Halder snorted in his diary. But in the end, of course, Hitler had his way.

In itself the offensive in the south was a great tactical victory. The Battle of Kiev ended on September 26 with the encirclement and surrender of 665,000 Russian prisoners, according to the German claim. To Hitler it was "the greatest battle in the history of the world," but although it was a singular achievement, some of his generals were more skeptical of its strategic significance. The army group in the center had been forced to cool its heels for two months; the autumn rains, which would turn the Russian roads into quagmires, were drawing near, and after them— the winter, the cold and the snow.

Reluctantly, then, Hitler gave in to the urging of his generals and consented to the resumption of the drive on Moscow. But too late! It was not until the beginning of October that the armored forces diverted to the southern drive could be brought back, refitted and made ready. On October 2 the great offensive was fully launched. "Typhoon" was the code name. A mighty wind, a cyclone, was to hit the Russians, destroy their last fighting forces before Moscow and bring the Soviet Union tumbling down.

The German drive along the road which Napoleon had taken to Moscow at first rolled forward with all the fury of a storm. By October 20 German armored spearheads were within sixty-five miles of Moscow, and the Soviet ministries were hastily being evacuated. Even the sober Halder now believed that Moscow could be taken before winter set in.

The fall rains, however, had commenced. *Rasputitza,* the period of mud, arrived. The great army, moving on wheels, was often forced to halt. As Gen. Guenther Blumentritt vividly described it: "The infantryman slithers in the mud. . . . All wheeled vehicles sink up to their axles in the slime. Even tractors can move only with great difficulty. A large portion of our heavy artillery was soon stuck fast. . . . The strain that all this caused our already exhausted troops can perhaps be imagined."

For the first time there crept into the reports of the German generals signs of doubt and then of despair. It spread to the lower officers and the troops in the field—or perhaps it ascended from them. The ghost of the *Grande Armée,* which had taken this same road to Moscow, and the memory of Napoleon's fate began to haunt the dreams of the Nazi conquerors.

Heavy snows and sub-zero temperatures came early that winter in Russia. General Heinz Guderian noted the first snow on the night of October 6, just as the drive on Moscow was being resumed. On October 12 he recorded that the snow was still falling. By November 7 Guderian was reporting the first severe cases of frostbite in his ranks, and on the 13th he wrote that the temperature had fallen to 8° below zero, and that the lack of winter clothing was becoming increasingly felt. The bitter cold affected guns and machines as well as men.

In retrospect Guderian added: "Only he who saw the endless expanse of Russian snow during this winter of our misery and felt the icy wind that blew across it, burying in snow every object in its path; who drove for hour after hour through that no-man's-land only at last to find too thin shelter with insufficiently clothed, half-starved men; and who also saw by contrast the well-fed, warmly clad and fresh Siberians, fully equipped for winter fighting . . . can truly judge the events which now occurred."

Those events may be briefly narrated. As November approached its end amid fresh blizzards and continued sub-zero temperatures, Moscow seemed within grasp to Hitler and most of his generals. North, south and west of the capital, German armies had reached points within twenty to thirty miles of their goal. To Hitler, poring over the map at his headquarters far off in East Prussia, the last stretch seemed no distance at all. His armies had advanced 500 miles; they had only a few

(Above) *The largest cannon used in World War II was the German gun "Dora." Successfully employed at Sevastopol, it was sent to aid in the Battle of Stalingrad, where Germany's Sixth Army was utterly destroyed by the Russians.*

(Right) *Nazi tanks rumble across the vast plains of the Ukraine. Germany launched its invasion of Russia on June 22, 1941, sweeping across the land on a 1000-mile front from the Baltic in the north to the Black Sea in the south.*

(Far right) *German troops reload weapons during their headlong thrust into Russia. The early weeks of the invasion—"Operation Barbarossa"—went so well for the Nazi forces that Hitler was convinced that a quick victory was inevitable.*

more miles to go. "One final heave," he said, "and we shall triumph." The final all-out attack on the heart of the Soviet Union was set for December 1, 1941.

The Nazi Army, comprising the greatest tank force ever concentrated on one front, stumbled on a steely resistance. By December 2 a reconnaissance battalion of the 258th Infantry Division had penetrated a suburb of Moscow, within sight of the spires of the Kremlin, but was driven out the next morning by a few Russian tanks and a motley force of hastily mobilized workers from the city's factories. This was the nearest the German troops ever got to Moscow.

By December 4 Guderian reported that the temperature had fallen to 31° below zero. The next day it dropped another 5°. His tanks, he said, were almost immobilized.

December 5 was the critical day. Everywhere along the front around Moscow the Germans had been stopped. At Fourth Army Headquarters it was realized that the outlook had changed completely. "Our hopes of knocking Russia out of the war in 1941," General Blumentritt wrote, "had been dashed at the last moment."

The next day, December 6, Gen. Georgi K. Zhukov struck. On the 200-mile front before Moscow he unleashed 100 divisions of troops equipped and trained to fight in the bitter cold and the deep snow. The blow delivered by this formidable force, which Hitler had not even faintly suspected to be in existence, was so sudden and shattering that the German Army never fully recovered from it. For a few weeks during the rest of that cold and bitter December and on into January it seemed that the beaten and retreating Germans, their front continually pierced by Soviet breakthroughs, might disintegrate and perish in the Russian snows, as had Napoleon's army just 130 years before. At several crucial moments it came very close to that. Perhaps it was Hitler's granite will and determination, and certainly it was the fortitude of the German soldier, that saved the armies of the Third Reich from a complete debacle.

But the failure was great. Moscow had not been taken, or Leningrad or Stalingrad or the oil fields of the Caucasus; and the lifelines to Great Britain and the United States, to the north and to the south, remained open. For the first time in more than two years of unbroken military victories, the armies of Hitler were retreating before a superior force.

That was not all, as Halder realized later on. "The myth of the invincibility of the German Army," he wrote, "was broken." There would be more German victories when another summer came around, but they could never restore the myth.

On Sunday, December 7, 1941, one day after Zhukov had launched his vast surprise counterattack, an event occurred on the other side of the earth that transformed the European war into a world war. Japanese bombers attacked Pearl Harbor. The next day Hitler hurried back by train to Berlin from his field headquarters in the East. He had made a solemn secret promise to Japan, and the time had come to keep it.

The Japanese onslaught on the U.S. Pacific Fleet at Pearl Harbor caught Berlin as completely by surprise as it did Washington. Though Hitler had made an oral promise to the Japanese Foreign Minister, Yosuke Matsuoka, that Germany would join Japan in a war against the United States, the assurance had not yet been signed, and the Japanese had not breathed a word to the Germans about Pearl Harbor. Besides, at this moment Hitler was fully occupied trying to rally his faltering generals and retreating troops in Russia.

But there is no doubt that Japan's sneaky and mighty blow against the American Fleet at Pearl Harbor kindled the Fuehrer's admiration—all the more so because it was the kind of surprise he had been proud of pulling off very often himself. He expressed this to Japanese Ambassador Hiroshi Oshima: "You gave the right declaration of war! This method is the only proper one."

The Fuehrer quickly decided to honor his unwritten promise to the Japanese. He was fed up with Roosevelt's attacks on him and on Nazism; his patience was exhausted by the warlike acts of the U.S. Navy against German U-boats in the Atlantic. Furthermore, he harbored a growing contempt for the United States and disastrously underestimated its potential strength. "I don't see much future for the Americans," he told his cronies at a conference a month later. "It's a decayed country. . . . My feelings against Americanism are feelings of hatred and deep repugnance."

At the same time he grossly overestimated Japan's military power, and he told some of his followers a few months later that he thought Japan's entry into the war had been "of exceptional value to us, if only because of the date chosen.

The Russian winter slowed the Nazi advance; the rains turned roads into rivers of mud. Men, horses and vehicles were quickly mired, and the German blitzkrieg ground to a halt.

269

After putting up a spirited fight with her antiaircraft guns, a German submarine is disabled and sunk near Ascension Island in the South Atlantic by bombs and depth charges from American planes. German U-boats took a heavy toll of Allied shipping before 1943.

"It was, in effect, at the moment when the surprises of the Russian winter were pressing most heavily on the morale of our people, and when everybody in Germany was oppressed by the certainty that sooner or later the United States would come into the conflict. Japanese intervention therefore was, from our point of view, most opportune."

At 2:30 p.m. on December 11, Germany formally declared war on the United States. Adolf Hitler, who a bare six months before had faced only a beleaguered Britain in a war which seemed to him as good as won, now, by deliberate choice, had arrayed against him the three greatest industrial powers in the world in a struggle in which military might depended largely, in the long run, on economic strength. Moreover, those three enemy countries together had a great preponderance of manpower over the three Axis nations. At the time, neither Hitler nor his generals nor his admirals seem to have weighed these sobering facts.

Although the Fuehrer's folly in refusing to allow the German armies in Soviet Russia to retreat in time had led to heavy losses, there is little doubt that Hitler's fanatical determination to hold on and fight also helped to stem the Soviet tide. The traditional courage and endurance of the German soldiers did the rest.

By February 20 the Russian offensive had run out of steam, and at the end of March the season of deep mud set in, bringing a relative quiet to the front. Both sides were exhausted. A German Army report of March 30, 1942, revealed what a terrible toll had been paid in the winter fighting: of a total of 162 combat divisions in the East, only 8 were ready for offensive missions. The 16 armored divisions had among them only 140 serviceable tanks—less than the normal number for 1 division.

While the troops were resting and refitting, Hitler was busy with plans for the coming summer's offensive. "If I do not get the oil of the Caucasus," he told Gen. Friedrich von Paulus, commander of the ill-fated Sixth Army, just before the summer offensive began, "then I must end this war."

Stalin could have said almost the same thing. He, too, had to have the Caucasian oil to stay in the war. That was where the significance of Stalingrad came in. German possession of it would block the last main route, via the Caspian Sea and the Volga River, over which the oil—as long as the Russians held the wells —could reach central Russia.

Besides oil to propel his planes and tanks and trucks, Hitler needed men to fill out his thinned ranks. Total casualties at the end of the winter fighting were 1,167,835, and there were not enough replacements to make up for such losses. The High Command turned to Germany's allies—or, rather, satellites—for additional troops. Hitler himself appealed to Mussolini for Italian formations, but the Duce was concerned about his ally's defeats on the eastern front. Hitler decided it was time for another meeting, to explain how strong Germany still was.

The Fuehrer, as always, did most of the talking. "Hitler talks, talks, talks," Count Galeazzo Ciano, the Italian Foreign Minister, wrote in his diary. "Mussolini suffers—he who is in the habit of talking himself, and who, instead, practically has to keep quiet. On the second day, after lunch, when everything had been said, Hitler talked uninterruptedly for an hour and forty minutes. He omitted absolutely no argument: war and peace, religion and philosophy, art and history. . . . The Germans—poor people—have to take it every day, and I am certain there isn't a gesture, a word or a pause which they don't know by heart. General [Alfred] Jodl, after an epic struggle, finally went to sleep on the divan. [General Wilhelm] Keitel was reeling, but he succeeded in keeping his head up. He was too close to Hitler to let himself go."

Despite the numbing avalanche of talk, or perhaps because of it, Hitler got the promise of more Italian cannon fodder for the Russian front.

At first, that summer of 1942, the fortunes of the Axis prospered. Even before the jump-off toward the Caucasus and Stalingrad, a sensational victory had been scored in North Africa by Gen. Erwin Rommel (see pages 278–281). He had resumed his offensive and by the end of June was sixty-five miles from the Nile, but Hitler, obsessed with his Russian campaign, refused to reinforce him adequately, and Rommel met defeat at Alamein.

Still, by the end of the summer, Hitler seemed to be on top of the world. German U-boats were sinking 700,000 tons of British and American shipping a month in the Atlantic—more than the Allied shipyards could replace. On the map, at least, the sum of Hitler's conquests by September looked staggering. German troops stood guard from the Arctic Ocean to Egypt, from the Atlantic Ocean to within 100 miles of the Caspian Sea.

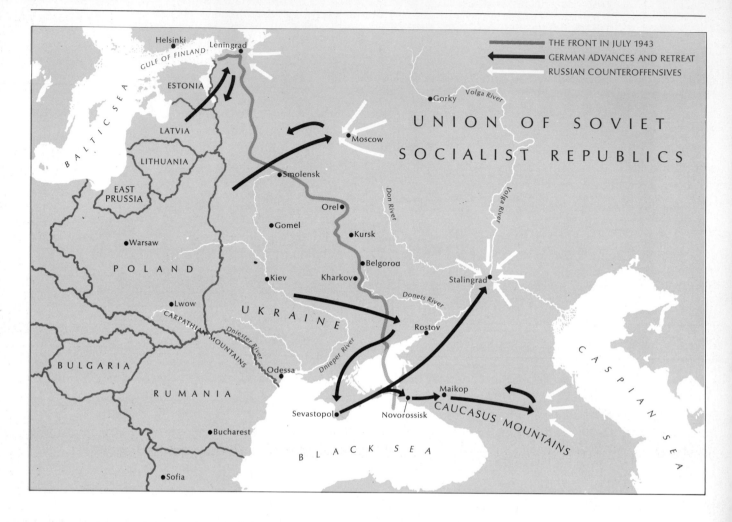

THE FRONT IN JULY 1943
GERMAN ADVANCES AND RETREAT
RUSSIAN COUNTEROFFENSIVES

END OF THE BLITZKRIEG

On December 6, 1941, a massive Soviet counteroffensive was launched in the Moscow area which hurled the Germans back fifty to 100 miles. In the south Rundstedt had seized Rostov, the "Gateway to the Caucasus," in November, but was checked by bad weather. Soviet counterattacks drove Rundstedt's troops back.

By March 1942 the Germans had retreated 150 miles along much of the front. To regain the initiative, Hitler planned a summer offensive, with the oil fields of the Caucasus as the objective.

This offensive started well with the recapture of Rostov and the tak-ing of Sevastopol, Novorossisk and the Maikop oil fields. Some esti-mates claim 5 million Russian men were killed, wounded or captured. An elated Hitler ordered the army split in two. Army Group A went on toward the Caucasus. Army Group B swung northward with Stalingrad as its aim.

The depleted Caucasus force continued to make rapid gains for a while, but fuel shortages and the mountainous terrain soon slowed the advance, and winter snows later stopped it. Meanwhile, Army Group B, driving toward Stalingrad, also met fierce resistance.

Hitler had now lost more than 1.5 million men on the Russian front and had failed to gain any of his original objectives. With the Sixth Army trapped in Stalingrad —and eventually destroyed there— Hitler ordered his Caucasus force to retreat in January 1943. The Ger-mans facing Moscow also fell back.

Hitler resolved to try one more major assault in the summer of 1943. The Russians, commanded by General Zhukov, saw the attack coming, beat it off and reclaimed Orel, Belgorod, Kharkov, the coal-fields along the Donets River and the eastern shore of the Black Sea. By November the Germans were in full retreat.

Soviet infantrymen in white uniforms creep toward the German lines near Moscow during the Russian counteroffensive of the winter of 1941–42.

A MARCH TO OBLIVION

BY BRIG. GEN. S. L. A. MARSHALL, USAR (RET.)

Stalingrad, the appalling five months' battle that wiped out nearly 300,000 of Nazi Germany's best troops, was Adolf Hitler's most terrible defeat. S. L. A. Marshall looks from a historian's perspective on a struggle that has been compared by many to Napoleon's debacle in Russia in the winter of 1812.

One of the deepest penetrations of Russia by an enemy in many centuries began as a victory march into a void. Mark the date: August 23, 1942. One panzer and one motorized division rolled unopposed to the edge of the wide and placid Volga River. Here they took positions above and below Stalingrad (now Volgograd), an industrial city sprawling some thirty miles north and south on the Volga's western bank. This force was but the advance guard of a mighty Nazi host that finally numbered close to 300,000 men.

Summer heat enveloped the desert land, traversed by deep ravines (*balkas* in Russian). There were few Red Army soldiers in evidence, so the Germans chose to rest after their practically unopposed march. It made the weather seem less oppressive. Rarely in history had a savage battle started so calmly. Although they had been unable to capture Moscow and Leningrad, the Germans held a third of the Soviet population in their power. A sense of confidence permeated the invaders.

Where the spearpoint of their 3d Motorized Division approached the river, one hill and one *balka* were defended by a few Russians. It was no more than a dot on the broad sector, and the German advance waited for the division to come up and wipe it out. The division arrived and did nothing, though there were less than 400 Red infantrymen on the hill. Stalingrad at that moment seemed cut off from the rest of the country, to be taken at leisure.

Here was the epitome of the Stalingrad drama, the reason why resistance within the city was not crushed early, when Hitler's legions were drawn up around it in overwhelming strength. It was not so much contempt for the enemy—the Russians had proved their mettle in their defense of Moscow—as the hypnosis which besets an army when its field power is fully arrayed, with nothing to challenge it on the horizon. Normal caution becomes drugged.

The two-division front quickly swelled to an armed camp stretching for leagues. The offensive, as planned, was to be the *Wehrmacht*'s masterpiece. Massive bombardment reduced three quarters of the city to rubble in a single day. Then the headquarters of 5 army corps and 13 infantry, 3 panzer, 3 motorized divisions and 1 antiaircraft division moved into Stalingrad. They comprised the Sixth German Army under General von Paulus—the weightiest phalanx ever advanced by Nazi Germany. Admittedly dangerously far forward, it was still, in German eyes, perfectly secure because of its immense might and its two-year record of brilliant victories. In addition it had an armed corridor linking it with the rear.

Weeks went by. The weather stayed pleasant. Meanwhile more Soviet troops were fed into the city, making the passage across the river and from the bare steppes by night. Resistance capacity within Stalingrad was mounting.

The debris of wrecked buildings and rotting corpses blocked the streets to tanks and motorized forces. Already it should have been evident that a house-to-house, man-to-man, rifle-and-bayonet battle was shaping up. But Paulus, lulled by the quiet which too often betrays commanders, was not yet alarmed, or worried about his army's rear.

Then Hitler began to press impatiently for strong attacks to finish the job. As a result the major formations became irretrievably committed forward, presenting concentrated targets for the Soviet counteroffensive which was being organized on the periphery; and the best German troops were being sacrificed in bitter hand-to-hand fighting within the city against desperate, death-defying Soviet soldiers and armed civilians.

In late September, Russian armored attacks from the north hit Paulus' perimeter, a prelude to the larger counterblow made possible by the several weeks of dawdling. One German corps commander, Gen. Gustav von Wietersheim, did become uneasy and urged that all forces on the Volga be withdrawn beyond the Don River, only some fifty miles from the Volga at its closest point. His foresight should have merited the thanks of his country; instead he was relieved of his command and disgraced.

In the following months, as the battle inside the city became an appalling contest of mutual slaughter in which thousands died daily, other commanders pleaded for retreat while it was still possible. Hitler refused to listen.

On November 19 the first Red Army blow fell in thunderous warning. General Konstantin Rokossovsky's Tank Army struck in overwhelming strength out of its bridgehead at Serafimovich on the north turn of the Don River bend and within four days reached Kalach on the south turn of the bend. There it joined up with General Yeremenko's army attacking toward the northwest out of a beachhead south of Stalingrad. In making this juncture, the Red forces had collapsed two Rumanian armies covering Paulus' rear and flank. General Georgi K. Zhukov was in overall command of the operation.

Thereafter, the question was whether the Sixth Army could be relieved by German forces to the west, or would fight its way out alone. No one then believed that it would be left in the ever-tightening trap to perish. Hitler's orders were to stand and fight, and Paulus dared not resist the Fuehrer while there was still time to save his dwindling army. Hitler now insisted on taking personal charge of the campaign—from 1300 miles away.

Cut off, too massive to be adequately supplied by air, the Sixth Army was being drained of strength as food, medicine, ammunition, arms and hope gradually ran out. The savage struggle in the city, in which the Soviet troops had the advantage, was bleeding the Nazi forces.

Meanwhile, since the end of October, the Lower Volga winter of big snows and convulsive storms had been growing more brutal. Tanks and armor were frozen to a standstill, German soldiers disabled or killed by icy winds.

In early December, Hitler finally consented to a relief operation. From the Fourth Panzer Army below the Don, Gen. Hermann Hoth sent his 57th Panzer Corps to attack eastward and cut a corridor toward the Stalingrad inferno. The Sixth Army was not to attack toward the approaching corps until it got to about twenty miles from Paulus' lines.

There was never a vainer hope. Still thirty-odd miles short of the ground where the convergence was to begin, the 57th Panzer Corps met its Waterloo. There is a small river, tributary to the Don, named the Askay, to which history has paid little or no heed. Yet along its banks the last and decisive battle for Stalingrad was fought. The German corps was met by superior Red Army forces, hit from both sides, riven and wracked. The rescue mission was too late and too weak.

Everything that followed was a Russian mop-up. The redoubtable Sixth Army became a legion of the doomed, though the ranks, denied any information, still clung to hope. From then to the end of January 1943, they gradually awakened to the bitter truth that they were caught in an ever-narrowing circle, doomed to physical and mental torments, on the slow march to degradation, hunger, despair and death.

On January 30 the Fuehrer promoted Paulus to Field Marshal—and on January 31 he was captured by the Russians. Two days later the pitiful remnants of his once magnificent army, by then a starved shadow, capitulated.

Some of the soldiers, after years as prisoners, made it back home. Far more of them died. Stalin later said that 146,700 Germans were picked up on the field and burned, but the actual casualties were much greater. Soviet dead and wounded also mounted to more than a hundred thousand. Stalingrad was a grotesque jungle of destruction, its great factories shattered, its air heavy with the stench of death.

The Nazis had suffered their most calamitous defeat. Hitler's hysterical anger was directed against the officers who surrendered and who had not committed suicide.

"What hurts me most," he wailed, "is that I still promoted him [Paulus] to Field Marshal. . . . A man like that besmirches the heroism of so many others at the last moment." He admitted to no guilt for the crushing disaster at Stalingrad.

(Top right) *Weeping women search for their loved ones among slaughtered civilians in a Russian village. The German occupation of western Russia ranks as one of the cruelest events in the war. Countless civilians died at the hands of the invading Nazis.*

Tally of destruction: The small Russian unit shown here fighting in the defense of Stalingrad had destroyed 6 German tanks, 8 cars and 11 supply vans when the photograph was taken. In the desperate struggle every backyard was a savagely contended battleground.

(Bottom left) *Soviet troops take shelter in a battered dwelling at Stalingrad.*
(Bottom right) *Germans man a machine gun in a Stalingrad street. During the battle the city sewers, cellars and ruins of buildings were bitterly contested.*

ERWIN ROMMEL—
THE "DESERT FOX"

Field Marshal Erwin Rommel was the only German military leader in World War II who was not only idolized by his own men but immensely admired by his enemies. Winston Churchill described him as a great general whose "ardor and daring inflicted grievous disasters upon us." The famous English war analyst, B. H. Liddell Hart, called him a military genius, who in North Africa "became a hero of the Eighth Army troops who were fighting him." In centuries of warfare, he added, "only Napoleon has made a comparable impression on the British."

The sobriquet "Desert Fox" which Rommel won among his adversaries was not disparaging, but a tribute to his cunning, speed and power of improvisation. The reports of Rommel's dramatic boldness captured the imagination of a world at war. The fact that in the end he paid with his life for turning against Hitler added dimensions to his romantic legend.

Erwin Johannes Eugen Rommel was born at Heidenheim, in the state of Württemberg, on November 15, 1891, the son of a schoolmaster. An officer cadet in 1910 and second lieutenant in 1912, he won the Iron Cross in France in World War I and fought also on the Italian and Rumanian fronts. Between the wars he held various regimental commands and taught in elite military schools. He had little interest in political movements, and although he admired the Fuehrer until the final years of the war, he never joined the Nazi Party.

It was a book he had written on infantry tactics that first brought Rommel to the attention of Hitler, and before long he was widely regarded as the Fuehrer's favorite military man. In 1938 Rommel, then a Colonel, was placed in command of a bodyguard battalion responsible for Hitler's personal safety. In that capacity he accompanied Hitler on the Nazi march into the Sudetenland, into Prague, then into occupied Poland.

Raised to Major General just before the war, Rommel was given command of a key panzer division in February 1940. He had had no experience or training in armored warfare. Yet three months later the brilliant performance of his "iron cavalry" in the sweep across France lifted him to fame almost at once. Clearly it was a type of combat ideally suited to his dynamism and mastery of surprise thrusts.

Meanwhile, Mussolini's armies were being wrecked in North Africa. To retrieve the losses, Germany assembled and sent into the area an *Afrika Korps,* in February 1941, with Rommel commanding its own and the Italian forces. He was under orders to submit a plan by April 20 for the recapture of Cyrenaica. Instead, without waiting for permission, he attacked the British at El Agheila on March 24, and fulfilled the mission before the deadline for the plan. The fourteen months of savage fighting which followed gained for him the accolade of "Desert Fox." Despite occasional reverses, he drove the Eighth Army steadily eastward. So formidable was his reputation that a British commander felt it necessary to warn his troops that Rommel was not a magician or superman.

On June 21, 1942, the *Afrika Korps* neared the frontiers of Egypt. A grateful Hitler made Rommel a Field Marshal—the youngest in the German Army. By the end of the month Rommel was deep inside Egypt. Having routed the disheartened British at Mersa Matruh, he battered his way to the Alamein line and was set for the final push to Alexandria, only sixty miles away—then an open road to Suez, Palestine, the Mideast oil fields. This was the climax of his dazzling advance—and its end.

Alamein, a forty-mile passage hemmed in by the Mediterranean on one side and an impassable canyon on the other, proved to be a bottleneck the *Afrika Korps* could not uncork. Being essentially a fixed front, it ruled out the wide flanking movements that had brought Rommel his victories. General Sir Claude Auchinleck, Commander in Chief for the entire Middle East, had assumed personal command of the Eighth Army. In what some have called the first Battle of Alamein, July 1 to 17, he finally stopped Rommel.

Then, in mid-August, Lt. Gen. Bernard L. Montgomery took command of the Eighth Army and prepared at leisure for the second and more celebrated

General Erwin Rommel and his staff officers map German strategy during the North African campaign. Rommel's reputation for skill and daring soon spread far beyond Germany, as his early victories in the desert dealt heavy blows to Allied morale.

Battle of Alamein. Time worked for the British. Rommel recognized that his acute shortages in fuel, equipment and planes—at a time when the strength of the opposing army was being massively expanded—precluded a breakthrough. He pleaded with the High Command in Berlin for large-scale reinforcements but they never arrived.

When Montgomery launched his offensive on October 23, 1942, Rommel was decisively outnumbered and outweaponed, under skies held by enemy air power. He favored immediate disengagement to salvage his depleted forces. Hitler, however, ordered resistance until "victory or death." Though he considered the order sheer madness, Rommel accepted battle and devastating losses before deciding to retreat on November 4. In fifteen days he fell back 700 miles. Allied armies under General Eisenhower had by that time invaded French North Africa, trapping Rommel in the longest pincers in history, from the Nile Valley to the Atlantic. Fighting hopeless rearguard actions against the British, he in due time confronted Eisenhower's fresh forces in Tunisia. In March 1943, seriously ill, he returned to Germany.

By July Rommel was sufficiently recovered to command an army group in northern Italy, and in January 1944 he was made Commander in Chief of the German armies from the Netherlands to the Loire. The successful Allied invasion of western Europe came in June, and he again faced General Montgomery. Rommel's strategy for meeting the invasion had been disregarded by the High Command—a major Nazi mistake, according to most military historians.

From the posthumous *Rommel Papers* it is evident that Rommel was increasingly disillusioned with Hitler's leadership while still in Africa. As the Allied armies cut more deeply into the European Continent, he recognized that the war was lost, made no secret of his conclusion, and urged the Fuehrer in vain to seek negotiations before it was too late.

While Rommel did not join the "Generals' Plot" against Hitler, he knew of it and did not discourage it. He favored the Fuehrer's arrest and trial rather than

Massive clouds of black smoke from burning gasoline stores fill the sky above the port of Tobruk, Libya. Captured by British troops on January 22, 1941, Tobruk yielded 25,000 Italian prisoners and the great number of military vehicles shown in the foreground. Shortly thereafter Hitler set up the Afrika Korps *to recover Axis territory that had been lost to the Allies.*

assassination. On July 15, 1944, he wrote Hitler, demanding that Germany seek an immediate armistice. Two days later, while motoring near Livarot, France, he was strafed by low-flying planes and seriously injured—the suspicion that these were not Allied but Nazi planes trying to kill him persists to this day. In any case, Rommel was out of the war.

Had the July 20 assassination attempt against Hitler succeeded, Rommel might well have become interim chief of state. But it failed. From the hospital he re-

tired to his home at Herrlingen, near Ulm, to convalesce. There on October 14 two Nazi Generals arrived. They gave him the choice of suicide or arrest, a trial and probable destruction of his family. Rommel told his wife and son: "In a quarter of an hour I shall be dead." He swallowed poison. Eager to conceal from the Germans the fact that their great hero had plotted against him, Hitler proclaimed national mourning for Rommel and gave him a state funeral.

The Rommel Papers, published in English in 1953,

was based on his wartime diaries, notes and more than 1000 letters to his wife and their teen-age son Manfred. He had written his wife nearly every day, even in the midst of furious battle. B. H. Liddell Hart, who edited the volume, declared that Rommel "was a born writer as well as a born fighter." Desmond Young, a British Brigadier who in 1950 published a biography of the "Desert Fox," summed up Rommel as "the perfect fighting animal, cold, cunning, ruthless, untiring, quick of decision, incredibly brave."

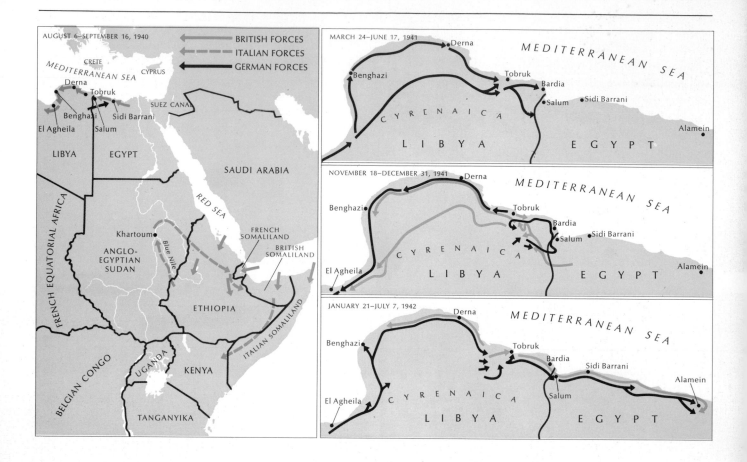

THE WAR IN AFRICA

To satisfy his dream of a new Roman Empire, Mussolini sent great armies against the British in Africa in 1940. They managed to enter the Anglo-Egyptian Sudan, seize French and British Somaliland and move into Kenya. Another Italian force attacked Egypt from Libya. Though outnumbered four to one, the British Army of the Nile, commanded by Gen. Sir Archibald Wavell, not only managed to contain all attacks but liberated Ethiopia (Italian East Africa), restoring Haile Selassie to his throne, and drove the Italians out of French, British and Italian Somaliland. By May 17, 1941, Mussolini's East African empire collapsed; it had lasted less than ten months.

In the north, along the Mediter-ranean coast, the Italian invasion halted at Sidi Barrani. On December 9, 1940, Wavell's defending forces counterattacked, driving the foe 500 miles into Cyrenaica and capturing the supply ports of Salum, Bardia, Tobruk, Derna and Benghazi.

Hitler now had to come to Mussolini's rescue. He sent an air wing, the *Afrika Korps* (an elite tank corps especially trained for desert combat) and a commander, Gen. Erwin Rommel. Combining the remnants of the Italian army with his German troops, Rommel attacked at El Agheila on March 24, 1941, forcing Wavell's small army out of the port cities it had so recently won. Only Tobruk remained in British hands.

Prime Minister Churchill replaced Wavell with Gen. Sir Claude Auchinleck. In November Auchinleck counterattacked, throwing the Germans back into Libya, relieving besieged Tobruk and regaining all of the ground Wavell had lost.

The seesaw war continued when Rommel launched a major drive toward Egypt in January 1942. Tobruk was at last captured, and Rommel crossed the Egyptian border on June 24. When Auchinleck seemed unable to cope with the latest Axis attack, Churchill replaced him with Gen. Hon. Harold Alexander and appointed Lt. Gen. Bernard L. Montgomery commander of the Eighth Army. Montgomery's task—to stop Rommel—was effectively carried out (see pages 286–299).

(Left) *Soldiers of the Australian 9th Division charge through a thick smoke screen at Alamein. Following a massive artillery barrage to soften up the German defenses, assault units poured forward, cutting wide gaps in the enemy lines. Constant pressure by Allied troops of the Eighth Army finally forced Rommel's army into retreat.*

(Below) *German infantrymen attached to General Rommel's once-triumphant Afrika Korps sit on the desert sand for a brief rest during a lull in their withdrawal before the forces of Montgomery. In the background smoke pours up from shelled German positions in the area of Tobruk.*

BERNARD LAW MONTGOMERY— THE "SPARTAN GENERAL"

The Army of the Nile (Eighth Army) was deployed along the forty-mile Alamein line, only a morning's drive from Cairo, facing Rommel's *Afrika Korps*, when Lt. Gen. Bernard Law Montgomery arrived in Egypt on August 13, 1942, to take over its command. His orders from Prime Minister Churchill had been crisp and clear: Rommel must be destroyed.

Seven months later that mission was completed. Rommel's Italo-German forces had been soundly defeated in late October—the first great victory scored against the Germans in the war—then pulverized in a slow but relentless pursuit. And Montgomery, previously little known outside British military circles, was being acclaimed as a remarkable commander in all Allied countries.

Montgomery was born in London on November 17, 1887, into the big and poor family of an Anglican vicar of North of Ireland origin. Two years later, his father having been made Bishop of Tasmania, the Montgomerys moved to Australia, where the boy spent the next twelve years of his life. It was an unhappy childhood, by his own account, because of a "clash of wills" between himself and his mother. His father, whom he considered "a saint on this earth," hoped Bernard would become a clergyman, but at a very early age the boy fixed on soldiering as his career.

The family returned to London in late 1901 and Bernard was sent to St. Paul's School. He excelled in sports, becoming captain of the rugby team, but not in his studies. However, he succeeded in entering the Sandhurst Royal Military Academy, from which he graduated, thirty-sixth in his class, in 1908. His first five Army years were spent in India, on the North-West Frontier and in Bombay.

During World War I Montgomery began as a Platoon Commander and ended, at thirty-one, as Chief of Staff of a division. After a year at the Staff College in Camberley, he saw service in Ireland and held a variety of staff appointments in Egypt, Palestine, India and England.

At the age of thirty-nine, in 1927, he was married. What he would describe as the happiest time of his life lasted only ten years. His wife died in 1937, leaving him to care alone for their nine-year-old son, David.

In 1938 Montgomery, now a Major General, was sent to Palestine to quell Arab rebellion. A few days before war was declared on Germany, he assumed command of the 3d Division in England, which became part of the ill-starred British Expeditionary Force evacuated through Dunkirk.

From December 1941 until his fateful assignment to Egypt, Montgomery headed the Southeastern Army, with primary responsibility for defending the Channel coast against the expected German invasion. His zeal for intense training, stern discipline and physical fitness was almost fanatic, giving him an Army reputation as a martinet and a bit of an eccentric.

He did not smoke, drink or swear. He rose at 6 a.m. and went to bed at 9 p.m., often even during battle. His recipe for fitness, which he sought to impose on his staff from generals down, was to run a long course before breakfast, whatever the weather, and to read the Bible daily. Devout and austere, he also had a flamboyant side to his character and self-assurance to the point of vanity.

Montgomery had seen no fighting since Dunkirk and chafed under the restraint. Then, almost accidentally, in the summer of 1942, came his supreme opportunity. General W. H. E. ("Strafer") Gott, appointed to head the Eighth Army, was killed when his plane was shot down, and Montgomery was named in his place.

Tidings of the scrawny, ascetic disciplinarian—the "Spartan General"— had preceded Montgomery to Egypt. But before long the battle-scarred veterans took "Monty" to their hearts. Wearing a gray sweater and corduroy slacks, his black beret at a cocked angle, he brought confidence and drew cheers wherever he appeared.

The *Afrika Korps* had been held on the Alamein line since July. On August 31 Rommel made his last attempt to break through, at the Alam Halfa Ridge, and was repulsed in a week of bloody battle. His already limited fuel, equipment and manpower were further depleted. Though pressed to follow up the victory at once, the cautious Montgomery waited for reinforcements, especially the American-made Sherman and Grant tanks being unloaded at Suez.

When he finally launched the offensive on October 23, the advantages were overwhelmingly on the British side: more men, control of the air, immense superiority in armor. Montgomery said: "It is now mathematically certain that I will eventually destroy Rommel." He did, in the slow, systematic warfare that was his style.

The German Field Marshal would have been wiser to retreat at once, but Hitler's orders were to stand at Alamein. Only on the twelfth day of fighting against impossible odds did he break off the battle. Despite rapidly dwindling Axis strength, it took the Eighth Army more than four months to obliterate the *Afrika Korps* in a 1400-mile chase.

Montgomery was knighted and made a full General in November 1942, while the pursuit was in progress. After North Africa was secured, he led the Eighth Army in the Allied invasion of Sicily, then of Italy.

Returning to England in January 1944, he was assigned command, under General Eisenhower, of all land forces for the invasion of western Europe on June 6. He directed land operations until August, when commands were reshuffled in view of the preponderance of American troops. Thereafter Montgomery headed the British-Canadian 21st Army Group, holding the northern end of the Allied lines in the Netherlands and Belgium.

While engaged in these operations he was promoted to Field Marshal, the highest rank in the British Army. In May 1945 Montgomery accepted the surrender of 500,000 German troops in his area, and then was placed in command of the British occupation forces in Germany. Raised to the peerage in 1946, Montgomery chose to style himself Viscount of Alamein. From June of that year until 1948 he served at the War Office as Chief of the Imperial General Staff. In his *Memoirs* (published in 1958) the chapter on this interval is titled, typically and accurately, "I Make Myself a Nuisance in Whitehall."

Field Marshal the Viscount Montgomery of Alamein was named permanent military chairman of the Western European Union, resigning in 1951 to serve as deputy to General Eisenhower, Supreme Commander of the North Atlantic Treaty forces. He held that post until his retirement seven years later.

Lieutenant General Bernard L. Montgomery, wearing his famous beret, surveys the terrain from the turret of a tank during the desert war. A self-assured and able leader, Montgomery and his British Eighth Army thoroughly defeated Rommel's elite Afrika Korps.

TWO BATTLES THAT STOPPED ROMMEL

BY FIELD MARSHAL THE VISCOUNT MONTGOMERY OF ALAMEIN

The man who led the British Army to victory over Rommel and the vaunted Afrika Korps *tells how he planned the tactics that turned the tide, and how he dealt with the crises that arose during the key battles of the desert war.*

The Battle of Alam Halfa

In the Eighth Army, orders had generally been queried by subordinates right down the line; each thought he knew better than his superiors and often it needed firm action to get things done. I was determined to stop this state of affairs at once. Orders no longer formed "the base for discussion," but for action.

What I now needed was a battle which would be fought in accordance with my ideas and not those of former desert commanders; furthermore, it must be a resounding victory and would have to come before our own offensive, so that confidence of officers and men in the High Command would be restored and they would enter on the stern struggle which lay farther ahead with an enhanced morale. They must come to believe.

I had taken command of truly magnificent material; it did not take me long to see that. The Eighth Army was composed of veteran fighting divisions. But officers and men were bewildered at what had happened and this had led to a loss of confidence. "Brave but baffled," the Prime Minister had called them.

This loss of confidence, combined with the belly-aching which went on and which was partly the cause of it, was becoming dangerous and could only be eradicated by a successful battle; a battle in which Rommel was defeated easily, and must be seen to have been beaten, and with few casualties to the Eighth Army.

I could not myself attack; Rommel must provide that opportunity for me. But in order to reap the full benefit, I must correctly forecast the design of his expected attack and determine in advance how we would defeat it. This was not difficult to do.

My intelligence staff were certain the break-in to our positions would be on the southern flank; this would be followed by a left wheel, his armored forces being directed on the Alam Halfa and Ruweisat ridges. I agreed, and my plans were based on this forecast. We were pretty clear about the timing, the direction and the strength of his attack.

I decided to hold the Alam Halfa Ridge strongly with the 44th Division and to locate my tanks just south of its western end. Once I was sure that the enemy main thrust was being directed against the Alam Halfa Ridge, I planned to move the armor to the area between the west of the ridge and the New Zealand positions in the main Alamein line. I was so sure that this movement of my own armor would take place that I ordered it to be actually rehearsed; and when it *did* take place on the morning of the 1st of September I had some 400 tanks in position, dug in and deployed behind a screen of 6-pounder antitank guns. The strictest orders were issued that the armor was not to be loosed against Rommel's forces; it was not to move; the enemy was to be allowed to beat up against it and to suffer heavy casualties.

It was obvious to me that Rommel could not just bypass my forces and go off eastward to Cairo; if he did so, I could have descended on his rear with 400 tanks and that would have been the end of his army.

I then decided that my extreme south flank should be mobile; the 7th Armored Division would hold a wide front and, as the attack came, would give way before it. When the attack swung left-handed toward the Alam Halfa Ridge, the 7th Armored Division would harry it from the east and south, and generally "shoot it up."

[Lieutenant] General [Brian G.] Horrocks had by now arrived from England to command XIII Corps on my left flank, and the details of the plan were placed in his very capable hands. I insisted that in fighting his battle he was not to allow XIII Corps, and particularly 7th Armored Division, to get mauled. They would have a part to play in our own offensive in October, and I outlined to him the ideas which were forming in my mind about that offensive. He entered into it with his characteristic enthusiasm.

The design of Rommel's attack was exactly as had been forecast to officers and men of the Eighth Army; we fought the battle as I had laid down. Once Rommel's forces had beaten up against our strong positions from the New Zealand Division area eastward, they became unable to move. We then concentrated on shooting them up from all directions and the Desert Air Force on attacking them from the air. This was very successful and after a few days the enemy losses in tanks and soft-skinned vehicles were so severe that he had to consider a withdrawal.

A most important factor which forced his eventual withdrawal was the action of the Desert Air Force under Air [Vice] Marshal [Arthur] Coningham. Army and Air Force worked on one plan, closely knit together, and the two headquarters were side by side. It had seemed to me when I arrived in the desert that the two services were tending to drift apart and that the true function of air power was not appreciated by commanders in the Eighth Army. This battle

brought us close together again and for the rest of my time in the Eighth Army we remained so.

A major factor in the overall air plan was [Air Chief Marshal Arthur W.] Tedder's decision to send his Wellingtons to bomb Tobruk behind Rommel's attack, so that his last quick hope of resupply vanished. This was the operative point in Rommel's decision to call off the attack; he was already beaten, and lack of petrol meant that he simply could not possibly resume the attack.

Once the plan to deal with the expected attack had been made and preparations begun, I had turned my attention to a consideration of our own offensive.

Rommel's attack came on the night of the [30th–] 31st of August. I had given instructions that I was to be woke up, but was asleep when the attack began soon after midnight. [Brigadier Francis] de Guingand tells his own story about that night. He decided he should wake me up and tell me the news; he said I merely replied, "Excellent, couldn't be better," and went to sleep again at once, and had breakfast at the usual time in the morning. I don't remember but am prepared to believe him. I was confident that if everyone obeyed orders, we must win this battle; my main preoccupation was to

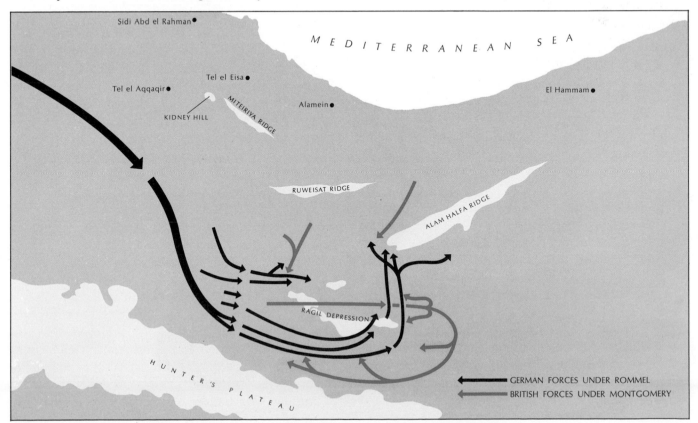

Battle of Alam Halfa: August 31, 1942. Masking his Eighth Army strength at Alamein, Lt. Gen. Bernard L. Montgomery lured the Afrika Korps into attacking near Alam Halfa. There, trapped by mines and sand, Rommel's panzers were pounded by British planes and artillery.

287

see, in this my first battle with the Eighth Army, that it was fought in complete accord with my master plan.

When I saw that Rommel's forces were in a bad way, I ordered a thrust southward from the New Zealand Division area to close the gap through which they had entered our positions. The enemy reaction was immediate and violent; they began to pull back quickly to the area of our minefield through which they had originally come. We left them there and I called off the battle. Moreover, it suited me to have their forces in strength on the southern flank since I was considering making my main blow, later on, on the northern part of the front. I remember Horrocks protesting to me that the enemy remained in possession not only of our original minefields but also of some good viewpoints from which to observe his corps area. I replied that he should get busy and make new minefields for his corps. As regards the observation points, such as Himeimat, it suited me that Rommel should be able to have a good look at all the preparations for attack we were making on our southern flank: they were a feint.

I have sometimes been criticized for not following up Rommel's withdrawal by launching the Eighth Army to the attack. There were two reasons why I did not do so. First, I was not too happy about the standard of training of the Army and also the equipment situation was unsatisfactory; time was needed to put these right. And secondly, I was not anxious to force Rommel to pull out and withdraw "in being" back to the Agheila position. If we were to carry out the mandate, it was essential to get Rommel to stand and fight and then to defeat him decisively. This had never happened to him before; he had often retreated, but it was always for administrative reasons. It was obvious that we would prefer to bring him to battle, when we were ready, at the end of a long and vulnerable line of communications—with ours short. Such would be his situation if he stood to fight at Alamein.

Thus the Battle of Alam Halfa ended in the way we wanted. The action of XIII Corps on the southern flank was all that could be desired. Horrocks fought his battle in full accord with the master plan and he deserves great credit for his action that day. He tells a story of how I congratulated him when it was all over, and then proceeded to tell him what he had done wrong and to give him a talk on how to command a corps in battle.

I was interested to read in 1955 a book called *Pan-zer Battles* by [F. W.] von Mellenthin, who was on the operations staff of Rommel at this time. He describes Alam Halfa as "the turning point of the desert war, and the first of a long series of defeats on every front which foreshadowed the defeat of Germany."

On reflection, certain important lessons emerged from this battle. It was an "Army" battle. The power of the Eighth Army was developed on a definite Army plan and a firm grip was kept on the battle at all times by Army HQ. This led to a recognition among officers and men of the necessity for one guiding mind which would control their destinies, and after this battle they accepted me as that one mind.

The Eighth Army consisted in the main of civilians in uniform, not of professional soldiers. And they were, of course, to a man, civilians who read newspapers. It seemed to me that to command such men demanded not only a guiding mind but also a point of focus; or to put it another way, not only a master but a mascot. And I deliberately set about fulfilling this second requirement. It helped, I felt sure, for them to recognize as a person—as an individual—the man who was putting them into battle. To obey an impersonal figure was not enough. They must know who I was. This analysis may sound rather cold-blooded, a decision made in the study. And so, in origin, it was; and, I submit, rightly so. One had to reason out the best way to set about commanding these men, to bring out their best, and to weld them into an effective and a contented team which could answer the calls I was going to make on them; and these were going to be increasingly arduous. But I readily admit that the occasion to become the necessary focus of their attention was also personally enjoyable. For if I were able thereby to give something to them—and it was a sense of unity which I was trying to create—I gained myself from the experience by the way it enabled me to get to know them, too, to sense their morale and, as time went on, to feel the affection which they generously extended to me. I started in the Alam Halfa battle by wearing an Australian hat—first of all because it was an exceedingly good hat for the desert, but soon because I came to be recognized by it—outside the Australian lines, anyway! Later, as readers may know, I took a black beret, again for utilitarian reasons in the first place.

And the twin badges on the beret were, in origin, accidental; but I quickly saw their functional result, and what started as a private joke with the tank regiment which gave it to me became in the end the means by which I came to be recognized throughout the desert. I soon learned that the arrival of the double-badged beret on the battlefield was a help—they knew that I was about, that I was taking an intense and personal interest in their doings and that I was not just sitting about somewhere safe in the rear issuing orders. The beret was functional in the way a "brass hat" could never have been. It became, if you like, my signature. It was also very comfortable.

Then again I think the battle is noteworthy as heralding a reversal of the previously accepted doctrine of "loosing" our own tanks at Rommel's armor directly he attacked. With an imperfectly trained army and inferior equipment it is necessary to adjust the tactics accordingly. I refused to exploit our success as such action did not suit my long-term plans.

And finally there was the raising of morale which follows a successful battle in which the High Command has foretold what will happen. It had happened, and we had won with few casualties. In this case the effect on morale was of tremendous importance. In my first few days in the desert we had removed uncertainty by taking a tight grip from Army Headquarters and announcing a reorganization which was to hold our prospects of victory in the desert war. All this had caused a feeling of relief. But the general atmosphere was: it looks good, it sounds good, but will it work? There was of course a great willingness to try and make it work, and a growing belief as the days passed. But it was Alam Halfa which produced the final belief in me and my methods—if you like, my prophecies—which was to make Alamein possible.

The Battle of Alamein

The basic problem that confronted us after the Battle of Alam Halfa was a difficult one. We were face to face with Rommel's forces between the sea and the Qattara Depression, a distance of about forty miles. The enemy was strengthening his defenses to a degree previously unknown in the desert, and these included deep and extensive minefields. There was no open flank. The problem was: First, to punch a hole in the enemy positions. Second, to pass X Corps, strong in armor and mobile troops, through this hole into enemy territory. Third, then to develop operations so as to destroy Rommel's forces.

This would be an immense undertaking. How could we obtain surprise?

It seemed almost impossible to conceal from the enemy the fact that we intended to launch an attack. I decided to plan for tactical surprise, and to conceal from the enemy the exact places where the blows would fall and the exact times. This would involve a great deception plan and I will describe later some of the measures we took.

Next, a full moon was necessary. The minefield problem was such that the troops must be able to see what they were doing. A waning moon was not acceptable since I envisaged a real dogfight for at least a week before we finally broke out; a waxing moon was essential. This limited the choice to one definite period each month. Owing to the delay caused to our preparations by Rommel's attack, we could not be ready for the September moon and be sure of success. There must be no more failures. Officers and men of the Eighth Army had a hard life and few pleasures; and they put up with it. All they asked for was success, and I was determined to see they got it this time in full measure. The British people also wanted real success; for too long they had seen disaster or at best only partial success. But to gain complete success we must have *time;* we had to receive a quantity of new equipment, and we had to get the army trained to use it, and also rehearsed in the tasks which lay ahead. I had promised the Eighth Army on arrival that I would not launch our offensive till we were ready. I could not be ready until October. Full moon was the 24th of October. I said I would attack on the night of October 23, and notified [Gen. Hon. Harold] Alexander accordingly. The comeback from Whitehall was immediate. Alexander received a signal from the Prime Minister to the effect that the attack must be in September, so as to synchronize with certain Russian offensives and with Allied landings which were to take place early in November at the western end of the North African coast ["Operation Torch"; see pages 300–310]. Alexander came to see me to discuss the reply to be sent. I said that our preparations could not be completed in time for a September offensive, and an attack then would fail: if we waited until October, I guaranteed complete success. In my view it would be

(Above) *Battle-hardened veterans of Montgomery's "Desert Rats" stride along a desert track. The British troops who defeated Rommel in North Africa came from virtually every corner of the Empire. Englishmen fought alongside wiry Gurkhas from Nepal and bearded Sikhs from India, as well as Scots, Canadians, Australians, South Africans and New Zealanders.*

(Right) *British Eighth Army infantrymen race past a damaged German tank left behind in the Libyan desert by one of Rommel's fleeing columns. After the Battle of Alamein, Montgomery's army nipped at the Germans' heels for three months, occasionally drawing blood but unable to bring to bay the "Desert Fox," who made good his escape into Tunisia.*

madness to attack in September. Was I to do so? Alexander backed me up wholeheartedly as he always did, and the reply was sent on the lines I wanted. I had told Alexander privately that in view of my promise to the soldiers, I refused to attack before October; if a September attack was ordered by Whitehall, they would have to get someone else to do it. My stock was rather high after Alam Halfa! We heard no more about a September attack.

It was becoming apparent to me that the Eighth Army was very untrained. The need for training had never been stressed. Most commanders had come to the fore by skill in fighting and because no better were available . . . few were good trainers. By the end of September there were serious doubts in my mind whether the troops would be able to do what was being demanded; the plan was simple but it was too ambitious. . . . The Eighth Army had suffered some 80,000 casualties since it was formed, and little time had been spent in training the replacements.

The moment I saw what might happen I took a quick decision. On October 6, just over two weeks before the battle was to begin, I changed the plan. My initial plan had been based on destroying Rommel's armor; the remainder of his army, the unarmored portion, could then be dealt with at leisure. This was in accordance with the accepted military thinking of the day. I decided to reverse the process and thus alter the whole conception of how the battle was to be fought.

My modified plan now was to hold off, or contain, the enemy armor while we carried out a methodical destruction of the infantry divisions holding the defensive system. These unarmored divisions would be destroyed by means of a "crumbling" process, the enemy being attacked from the flank and rear and cut off from their supplies. These operations would be carefully organized from a series of firm bases and would be within the capabilities of my troops. I did not think it likely that the enemy armor would remain inactive and watch the gradual destruction of all the unarmored divisions; it would be launched in heavy counterattacks. This would suit us very well, since the best way to destroy the enemy armor was to entice it to attack *our* armor in position. I aimed to get my armor beyond the area of the "crumbling" operations. I would then turn the enemy minefields to our advantage by using them to prevent the enemy armor from interfering with our operations; this would be done by closing the approaches through the minefields with our tanks, and we would then be able to proceed relentlessly with our plans.

The success of the whole operation would depend largely on whether XXX Corps could succeed in the break-in battle and establish the corridors through which the armored divisions of X Corps must pass. I was certain that if we could get the leading armored brigades through the corridors without too great delay, then we would win the battle. Could we do this? In order to make sure, I planned to launch the armored divisions of X Corps into the corridors immediately behind the leading infantry divisions of XXX Corps *and before I knew the corridors were clear*. Furthermore, I ordered that if the corridors were not completely clear on the morning of D plus 1, October 24, the armored divisions would fight their own way out into the open beyond the western limit of the minefields.

It will be seen later how infirmity of purpose on the part of certain senior commanders in carrying out this order nearly lost us the battle.

There was a Maj. E. T. ("Bill") Williams on my Intelligence staff who appeared to me to be of outstanding ability. In a conversation one day, about this time, he pointed out to me that the enemy German and Italian troops were what he called "corseted"; that is, Rommel had so deployed his German infantry and parachute troops that they were positioned between, and in some places behind, his Italian troops all along the front, the latter being unreliable when it came to hard fighting. Bill Williams' idea was that if we could separate the two we would be very well placed, as we could smash through a purely Italian front without any great difficulty. This very brilliant analysis and idea was to be a major feature of the master plan for the "crumbling" operations, and it paved the way to final victory at Alamein.

The object of the deception plan was twofold: (a) To conceal from the enemy as long as possible our intention to take the offensive; (b) when this could no longer be concealed, to mislead him about both the date and the sector in which our main thrust was to be made.

This was done by the concealment of real intentions and real moves in the north, and by advertising false signs of activity in the south.

The whole deception was organized on an "Army"

basis; tremendous attention to detail was necessary throughout, since carelessness in any one area might have compromised the whole scheme. To carry out such a gigantic bluff in the time available required detailed planning, considerable quantities of labor and transport, mass production of deception devices at the base, a large camouflage store with trained staff, and the coordinated movement of many hundreds of vehicles into selected areas. Because all these essentials were provided the scheme was entirely successful, and great credit is due to the camouflage organization in the Middle East at the time.

A feature of the visual deception was the creation and continued preservation of the layout and density of vehicles required for the assault in XXX Corps sector in the north; this was achieved by the 1st of October by the placing in position of the necessary dummy lorries, guns, ammunition limbers, etc. During the concentration of attacking divisions just before the day of the attack, the dummies were replaced at night by the actual operational vehicles. The rear areas, from which the attacking divisions and units came, were maintained at their full visual vehicle density by the erection of dummies as the real vehicles moved out. The reason for all this visual deception was that enemy air photographs should continue to reveal the same story.

In preparation for the offensive, dumps had to be made in the northern sector. For example, a large dump was created near the station of Alamein. This was to contain 600 tons of supplies, 2000 tons of P.O.L. [petrol, oil, lubricants] and 420 tons of engineer stores. It was of the utmost importance that the existence of these dumps should not become known to the enemy. The site was open and featureless except for occasional pits and trenches. Disguise provided the most satisfactory method of hiding the dumps, and the whole endeavor was a triumph for the camouflage organization.

Another example I will quote was the dummy pipeline in the south to cause the enemy to believe the main blow would be delivered on that flank. It was started late in September and progress in the work was timed to indicate its completion early in November. The dummy pipeline was laid for a length of about twenty miles, from a point just south of the real water point at Bir Sadi to a point four miles east of Samaket Gaballa. The pipe trench was excavated in the normal way. Five miles of dummy railway track, made from petrol cans, were used for piping. The "piping" was strung out alongside the open trench. When each five-mile section of the trench was filled in, the "piping" was collected and laid out alongside the next section. Dummy pump houses were erected at three points. Work began on September 26 and ceased on October 22; it was carried out by one section of 578th Army Troops Company.

There were of course other measures, such as the careful planting of false information for the enemy's benefit, but I have confined this outline account to visual deception in which camouflage played the major part. The whole plan was given the code name "Bertram," and those responsible for it deserve the highest praise: it succeeded.

The R.A.F. was to play a tremendous part in this battle. The A.O.C. [Air Officer Commanding] aimed to gain gradual ascendancy over the enemy fighters, and to have that ascendancy complete by October 23. On that day the R.A.F. was to carry out blitz attacks against enemy airfields in order to finish off the opposing air forces, and particularly to prevent air reconnaissance. At zero hour the whole bomber effort was to be directed against the enemy artillery, and shortly before daylight on October 24 I hoped the whole of the air effort would be available to cooperate intimately in the land battle, as our fighter ascendancy by that time would be almost absolute.

I issued very strict orders about morale, fitness and determined leadership.

It was clear to me that we could not inform the troops about our offensive intentions until we stopped all leave and kept them out in the desert. I did not want to create excitement in Alexandria and Cairo by stopping leave with an official announcement.

On October 21 unit commanders were to stop all leave, quietly and without publishing any written orders. They were to give as the reason that there were signs the enemy might attack in the full moon period, and that we must have all officers and men present.

What it amounted to was that by October 21, everyone, including the soldiers, would be fully in the operational picture; no one could leave the desert after that.

There was one exception. I ordered that the troops in the foremost positions who might be raided by the enemy and captured, and all troops who might be on patrol in no-man's-land, were not to be given any

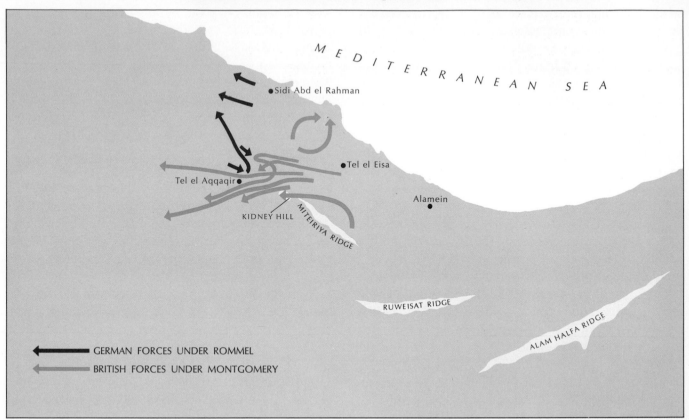

word about the attack till the morning of October 23.

This was to be an "Army" battle, fought on an Army plan and controlled carefully from Army HQ. Therefore every commander down to the lieutenant-colonel level must know the details of my plan, how I proposed to conduct the fight and how his part fitted into the master plan. Only in this way could perfect cooperation be assured. I issued the following personal message to the officers and men of the army:

1. When I assumed command of the Eighth Army I said that the mandate was to destroy ROMMEL and his Army, and that it would be done as soon as we were ready.

2. We are ready NOW.

   The battle which is now about to begin will be one of the decisive battles of history. It will be the turning point of the war. The eyes of the whole world will be on us, watching anxiously which way the battle will swing.

   We can give them their answer at once. It will swing our way.

3. We have first-class equipment; good tanks; good antitank guns; plenty of artillery and plenty of ammunition; and we are backed up by the finest air striking force in the world.

   All that is necessary is that each one of us, every officer and man, should enter this battle with the determination to see it through—to fight and to kill—and finally, to win.

   If we all do this there can be only one result —together we will hit the enemy right out of North Africa.

4. The sooner we win this battle, which will be the turning point of this war, the sooner we shall all get back home to our families.

5. Therefore, let every officer and man enter the battle with a stout heart, and with the determination to do his duty so long as he has breath in his body.

   AND LET NO MAN SURRENDER SO LONG AS HE IS UNWOUNDED AND CAN FIGHT.

   Let us all pray that the Lord mighty in battle will give us the victory.

   B. L. Montgomery
   Lieutenant General,
   G.O.C.-in-C., Eighth Army
Middle East Forces, 23-10-42

After briefing the press on the morning of October 23, I went forward that afternoon to my Tactical HQ established near XXX Corps HQ. In the evening I read a book and went to bed early. At 9:40 p.m. the barrage of over 1000 guns opened, and the Eighth Army, which included some 1200 tanks, went into the attack. At that moment I was asleep in my caravan; there was nothing I could do and I knew I would be needed later. There is always a crisis in every battle when the issue hangs in the balance, and I reckoned I would get what rest I could, while I could. As it turned out, I was wise to have done so: my intervention was needed sooner than I expected.

Throughout the war I kept a very precise diary and what follows is taken from notes made each day during the battle.

Saturday, October 24. The attack had gone in on the 23d of October in accordance with the plan I have just described. The whole area was one enormous minefield and the two corridors in the north had not been completely opened for the armored divisions of X Corps by 8 a.m. on October 24. In accordance with my orders, I expected the armored divisions to fight their way out into the open. But there was some reluctance to do so and I gained the impression during the morning that they were pursuing a policy of inactivity. There was not that eagerness on the part of senior commanders to push on and there was a fear of tank casualties; every enemy gun was reported as an 88-mm.—an antiaircraft gun used as an antitank gun, and very effective. The X Corps Commander was not displaying the drive and determination so necessary when things begin to go wrong and there was a general lack of offensive eagerness in the armored divisions of the corps. This was not the sort of battle they were used to. It was clear to me that I must take instant action to galvanize the armored divisions into action; determined leadership was lacking. I therefore sent for [Lt. Gen. Herbert] Lumsden and told him he must "drive" his divisional commanders, and if there was any more hanging back I would remove them from their commands and put in more energetic personalities. This action produced immediate results in one of the armored divisions; by 6 p.m. that evening the armored brigade of 1st Armored Division in the northern corridor was out in the open; it was then attacked by 15th Panzer Division, which was exactly what I wanted.

Farther south the New Zealand Division began its movement to the southwest as part of the "crumbling" operations. And farther south still, XIII Corps was playing its part according to plan.

Sunday, October 25. I have always thought that this was when the real crisis in the battle occurred. At 2:30 a.m. X Corps reported that the breakout of 10th Armored Division in the southern corridor in XXX Corps's sector was not proceeding well and that minefields and other difficulties were delaying progress. The Divisional Commander had said he did not feel happy about the operation, and that even if he did get out he would be in a very unpleasant position on the forward slopes of the Miteiriya Ridge. His division was untrained and not fit for such difficult operations; he wanted to stay where he was. Lumsden was inclined to agree. In the northern corridor, 1st Armored Division was out in the open and was being furiously attacked by the enemy armor, which was exactly what the doctor ordered, so long as I was the doctor in question. De Guingand rightly decided it was necessary for me to see the two corps commanders concerned and grip the situation; he issued orders for a conference at my Tactical HQ at 3:30 a.m. and then came and woke me and told me what he had done. I agreed. [Maj. Gen. Sir Oliver] Leese and Lumsden arrived on time and I asked each to explain his situation.

I discovered that in the 10th Armored Division one of the armored regiments was already out in the open and that it was hoped more would be out by dawn. The Divisional Commander wanted to withdraw it *all* back behind the minefields and give up the advantages he had gained; his reason was that his situation out in the open would be very unpleasant and his division might suffer heavy casualties. Lumsden agreed with him; he asked if I would personally speak to the Divisional Commander on the telephone. I did so at once and discovered to my horror that he himself was some 16,000 yards (nearly ten miles) behind his leading armored brigades. I spoke to him in no uncertain voice, and ordered him to go forward at once and take charge of his battle; he was to fight his way out, and lead his division from in front and not from behind.

I then told both corps commanders that my orders were unchanged; there would be no departure from my plan. I kept Lumsden behind when the others had left and spoke very plainly to him. I said I was determined that the armored divisions would get out of the minefield area and into the open where they could maneuver; any wavering or lack of firmness now would be fatal. If he himself, or the Commander 10th Armored Division, was not for it, then I would appoint others who were.

By 8 a.m. all my armor was out in the open and we were in the position I had hoped to have achieved at 8 a.m. the day before.

At noon I had a conference of corps commanders at 2d New Zealand [N. Z.] Division HQ. It became clear that the movement southwest of the N. Z. Division would be a very costly operation and I decided to abandon it at once. Instead, I ordered the "crumbling" operations to be switched to the area of the 9th Australian Division, working northward toward the coast; this new thrust line, or axis of operations, involved a switch of 180° which I hoped might catch the enemy unawares.

Wednesday, October 28. Hard fighting had been going on for the previous three days and I began to realize from the casualty figures that I must be careful. I knew that the final blow must be put in on XXX Corps's front, but at the moment I was not clear exactly where. But I had to get ready for it. So I decided to turn my southern flank (XIII Corps) over to the defensive except for patrol activities, to widen divisional fronts and to pull into reserve the divisions I needed for the final blow. The N. Z. Division I had already got into reserve.

We now had the whole of Rommel's Panzer Army opposite the northern corridor and I knew we would never break out from there. So I made that area a defensive front and pulled 1st Armored Division into reserve.

I also decided that for the moment I would use only XXX Corps to fight the battle in the north; so I pulled X Corps HQ into reserve, to get it ready for the breakout.

I ordered that operations by 9th Australian Division toward the coast be intensified, my intention then being to stage the final breakout operation on the axis of the coast road.

Thursday, October 29. During the morning it became increasingly evident that the whole of Rommel's German forces were grouped in the northern part of the front. The action of 1st Armored Division in the northern corridor, and the operations of 9th Australian Division northward toward the coast, had clearly made

him think that we intended to break out in the north along the coast, which was indeed my design at the time.

But we had now achieved what Bill Williams had recommended. The Germans had been pulled against our right and were no longer "corseting" the Italians. The Germans were in the north, the Italians together in the south; and the dividing line between them appeared to be just to the north of our original northern corridor.

I at once changed my plan and decided to direct the final blow at this point of junction, but overlapping well onto the Italian front. I took this decision at 11 a.m. October 29.

When could we stage the blow?

I knew that "Operation Torch," mounted from England, was to land in the Casablanca-Oran area on the 8th of November. We must defeat the enemy, and break up his army, in time to be of real help to "Torch." Quite apart from wanting to get to Tripoli first! But more immediately, the timing was affected by the need to get the Martuba airfields so as to assist by giving air cover to the last possible convoy to Malta, which was short of food and almost out of aviation fuel. The convoy was to leave Alexandria about the middle of November.

I decided that on the night of October 30 the 9th Australian Division would attack strongly northward to reach the sea; this would keep the enemy looking northward. Then on the next night, October 31, I would blow a deep hole in the enemy front just to the north of the original corridor; this hole would be made by the 2d N. Z. Division which would be reinforced by the 9th Armored Brigade and two infantry brigades; the operation would be under command of XXX Corps. Through the gap I would pass X Corps with its armored divisions.

We already had the necessary divisions in reserve and they had been resting and refitting.

What, in fact, I proposed to do was to deliver a hard blow with the right, and follow it the next night with a knockout blow with the left. The operation was christened "Supercharge."

During the morning I was visited at my Tactical HQ by Alexander and by Richard Gardiner Casey, who was Minister of State in the Middle East. It was fairly clear to me that there had been consternation in Whitehall when I began to draw divisions into reserve on October 27 and 28, when I was getting ready for the final blow. Casey had been sent up to find out what was going on; Whitehall thought I was giving up, when in point of fact I was just about to win.

I told him all about my plans and that I was certain of success; and de Guingand spoke to him very bluntly and told him to tell Whitehall not to bellyache. I never heard what signal was sent to London after the visit and was too busy with "Supercharge" to bother about it. Anyhow, I was certain the C.I.G.S. [Chief of the Imperial General Staff] would know what I was up to.

Friday, October 30. I spent the morning writing out my directive for "Supercharge." I always wrote such orders myself, and never let the staff do it. This was the master plan and only the master could write it. The staff of course has much detailed work to do after such a directive is issued. This procedure was well understood in the Eighth Army (and later, because of the experience in the Mediterranean, in 21st Army Group).

Saturday, October 31. It was clear to me that the stage management problems in connection with "Supercharge" were such that if launched on this night it might fail. I therefore decided to postpone it for twenty-four hours to deliver the blow on the night of November 1. This delay would help the enemy. To offset this, I extended the depth of penetration for a further 2000 yards, making 6000 yards in all—the whole under a very strong barrage.

I should add there were doubts in high places about "Supercharge," and whisperings about what would happen if it failed. These doubts I did not share and I made that quite clear to everyone.

Monday, November 2. At 1 a.m. "Supercharge" began and the attack went in on a front of 4000 yards to a depth of 6000 yards. It was a success and we were all but out into the open desert. By dusk we had taken 1500 prisoners.

Tuesday, November 3. There were indications the enemy was about to withdraw; he was almost finished.

Wednesday, November 4. At 2 a.m. I directed two hard punches at the "hinges" of the final breakout area where the enemy was trying to stop us widening the gap which we had blown. That finished the battle.

The armored car regiments went through as dawn was breaking and soon the armored divisions got clean away into the open desert; they were now in country clear of minefields, where they could ma-neuver and operate against the enemy rear areas and retreating columns.

The armored cars raced away to the west, being directed far afield on the enemy line of retreat.

The Italian divisions in the south, in front of XIII Corps, had nothing to do except surrender; they could not escape as the Germans had taken all their transport. I directed Horrocks to collect them in, and devoted my attention to the pursuit of Rommel's forces which were streaming westward.

A mass of detailed lessons will always emerge from any battle. In the British Army we are inclined to become immersed in details, and we often lose sight of the fundamentals on which the details are based.

There were three distinct phases in this battle, and operations were developed accordingly.

First: The break-in. This was the battle for position, or the fight for the tactical advantage. At the end of this phase we had to be so positioned and "balanced" that we could begin immediately the second phase. We must in fact have gained the tactical advantage.

Second: The "dogfight." I use this term to describe what I knew must develop after the break-in, and that was a hard and bloody killing match. During this we had so to cripple the enemy's strength that the final blow would cause the disintegration of his army.

Third: The breakout. This was brought about by a terrific blow directed at a selected spot. During the dogfight the enemy had been led to believe that the breakout would come in the north, on the axis of the coast road. He was sensitive to such a thrust and he concentrated his Germans in the north to meet it, leaving the Italians to hold his southern flank. We then drove in a hard blow between the Germans and Italians, with a good overlap on the Italian front.

Determined leadership is vital throughout all echelons of command. Nowhere is it more important than in the higher ranks.

If your enemy stands to fight and is decisively defeated in the ensuing battle, everything is added unto you. Rommel's doom was sounded at Alam Halfa; as Mellenthin said, it was the turning point of the desert war. After that, he was smashed in battle at Alamein. He had never been beaten before though he had often had to "nip back to get more petrol." Now he had been decisively defeated. The doom of the Axis forces in Africa was certain—provided we made no more mistakes.

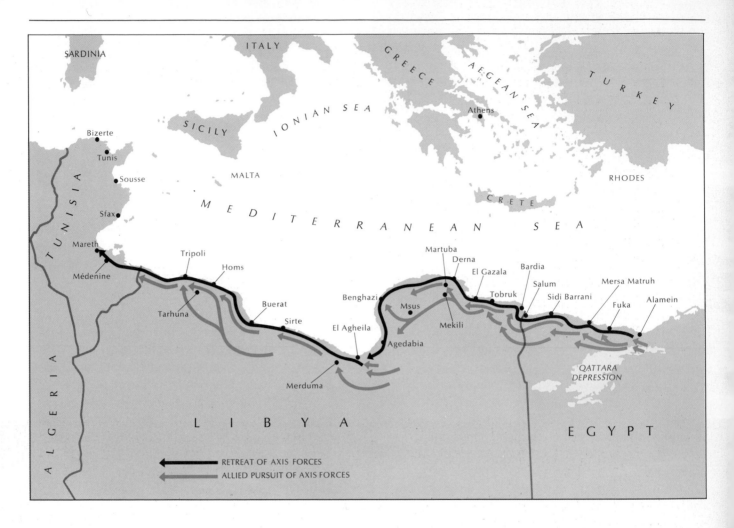

ROMMEL'S RETREAT TO TUNISIA

Rommel began his flight from Alamein on November 5 with Montgomery's armored columns in hot pursuit. The retreat almost became a rout, as undisciplined Italian infantry milled about the coastal road that Rommel had chosen for his escape. British air and naval bombing wreaked havoc among the fleeing troops, and everywhere the road was littered with smashed and broken-down vehicles.

At Mersa Matruh an armored column raced ahead to encircle the Axis army and seemed about to halt its headlong flight when a torrential downpour made impassable the

sandy desert track it was forced to follow. Somehow, under cover of the storm, Rommel slipped through the British trap and made good his escape, moving his troops quickly along the comparatively dry coastal road.

Montgomery never again came so close to capturing Rommel's army, but he continued to pursue it, destroying tanks and vehicles that strayed from their path or fell behind. Thousands of exhausted enemy surrendered, preferring imprisonment to further flight.

The chase continued for three months and covered 1400 miles.

During his retreat, Rommel lost 59,000 men, 1000 guns and 500 tanks, but he succeeded in bringing the rugged fighting core of his army out of Egypt, across Libya and into Tunisia on February 4, 1943. Here he hoped to link up with fresh Axis forces and turn upon his relentless pursuer.

But events beyond his control had already conspired to spoil his plan. On November 8, 1942, only three days after Rommel began his retreat, Allied forces had landed in French North Africa and were fighting their way toward his exhausted army from the west.

(Left) *Australian soldiers attached to the Eighth Army hug the ground as an enemy shell blasts a captured German tank in the Libyan desert. Breaking through the hastily set up German defensive lines at El Agheila and at Buerat, Montgomery's army smashed Rommel's rear guard.*

(Below) *A British armored car exchanges fire with elements of Rommel's Afrika Korps while an infantry patrol waits to go into action. From the beginning of the Alamein offensive, British forces advanced 1400 miles in ninety-two days, to capture Tripoli on January 23, 1943.*

"OPERATION TORCH"

BY COL. KARL DETZER

"The Allies have landed in North Africa"—the news electrified the American public. For the first time our troops were meeting the Nazis on the battlefield. The road to Berlin started on the shores of North Africa. Colonel Karl Detzer, who wrote this account of the campaign, from first landings in Morocco and Algeria to victory in Tunisia, is now a roving editor of the Reader's Digest.

"Operation Torch"—an Allied invasion of the western flank of North Africa—was destined to change the complexion of the war. The sharp arrows on the battle maps which had for so many months been pointing from Germany toward the western shores of North Africa were suddenly blunted. The campaign was also important for another reason: on the coasts of Morocco and Algeria, green American soldiers had their first experience with large-scale landing operations under enemy fire. The word "amphibious" was taken out of the military textbooks and put into history.

While Gen. Erwin Rommel was being held up by the British, led by Lt. Gen. Bernard L. Montgomery, at Alamein in the late summer of 1942, preparations for "Torch" were rushing to a climax in England. There had been some debate between the American and British strategists on just where the landings should take place. The British, wanting a shorter route to the fighting in Libya and along the Egyptian border, argued that the invaders should land at Algiers. The Americans pointed out that such a landing undoubtedly would result in the immediate occupation by Germany of all southern France, and that the *Wehrmacht* might even march through Spain and overwhelm Gibraltar. This would seal off our forces in the Mediterranean, leaving open only the long route around the Cape of Good Hope.

Besides, Americans were thinking of Dakar, in French West Africa, closest Old World port to South America. The Germans had been eyeing Dakar as a jump-off place for an attack on our own southern neighbors. The French officers in command at Dakar were openly pro-Nazi. It was a danger spot, whether or not the Germans chose to occupy it. It was the American contention that we must take the Atlantic coast of Morocco at the same time that we landed on the north shore.

There were not enough men or enough munitions in England to strike at both points simultaneously. The combined British and American staffs decided at last that the troops from England should strike along the Mediterranean and that other Americans, mounting their invasion from New York, should cross 3100 miles of the Atlantic and land on the west coast of Morocco at the same time.

Working against the clock, the planners sought to anticipate every need, to make sure that not a single one of the million items necessary for invasion would be missing on the morning our troops splashed ashore. Never before in history had so large a mechanized army attempted to land on hostile coasts. The very size of the operation made it necessary to reach quick decisions of tremendous importance.

For example, the matter of trucks versus men; only 700 ships would be available for the landings. Should we take a chance that the French forces in North Africa would surrender at once? If so, the wise decision would be to send fewer men and more trucks to carry them to the German battlefront. Or should we prepare for the worst on the beaches, plan definitely that the French would make a determined stand? In that case we should pour in more men and let the trucks follow on another convoy after we had secured a foothold in Africa.

The decision finally favored more men, fewer trucks. It wouldn't do to take a chance on being pushed back into the sea. (As it turned out, the French battled only five days at the most heavily defended port, after which all resistance collapsed. And there we stood, hundreds of miles from the Germans we wanted so desperately to attack, with no means of transportation.)

In London, the Allied armies were building their organization. Lieutenant General Dwight D. Eisenhower would command the invasion forces. Major

General Mark W. Clark would head the ground troops. The General Staff would consist of both British and American officers.

We had built up our army in England and Northern Ireland to nearly a quarter of a million men. We would take 126,000 of these for the invasion of Africa; 65,000 others would come from the United States. The British, landing to the east of us, would have a force of about 100,000. These numbers covered the original landings only. Other thousands would pour in after them, serving as reserve, finally taking their places in battle.

The date for "Torch" was set. We would land at dawn on the morning of November 8, 1942. That would be eleven months and one day after Pearl Harbor. We were moving fast.

One question kept popping up at staff meetings in London and Washington. Would the French Army in Africa fight with everything it had, put up only a token resistance or come over wholeheartedly to our side? There was no doubt about the rank and file or about the junior officers. They didn't like the Germans and despised the Italians.

Admiral Jean François Darlan, however, commanded all French Army and Navy forces in Africa. Darlan was a Vichy appointee. No doubt he would stand out against us, no matter what his juniors wanted. On the other hand, we knew through our Intelligence Division that other French officers would attempt to join us and bring their units along.

While the matter was being debated, a message from Robert D. Murphy, President Roosevelt's special representative to the French in Africa, arrived in London and sent General Eisenhower in a hurry to 10 Downing Street.

There the General and Prime Minister Churchill went over the details of a suggestion, brought by Murphy from a friendly group of French officers, that an American officer at once come secretly to Africa and talk to them. The friendly French knew the disposition of the French troops, they claimed; in fact they had all the information any attacking commander would want the most. The Frenchmen explained that they were loyal to the French Republic, not to Vichy and Hitler, and hoped to avoid bloodshed on either the Allied or French side in the proposed landings.

The Prime Minister fell in at once with the plan. No one knew, of course, whether the offer was gen-

uine. It could be a trick by the Germans, anxious to know what our plans were. The Prime Minister tossed prudence out the window. There was only one way to discover its authenticity. That was to go and find out.

Who, then, should have the dangerous and delicate assignment? Eisenhower chose Major General Clark. Long and lanky, sharp-eyed, with an eagle nose, broad shoulders and narrow hips, he even looked the exciting and romantic part he was about to undertake. Arrangements were made quickly. On a certain night a lamp was to be set in the seaward window of a lonely farmhouse on the bluffs above the Mediterranean not far from Algiers. This would be the signal that Eisenhower's representative should come ashore.

Clark and a small, hand-picked group of officers flew to Gibraltar, boarded a submarine, and with kayaks to paddle ashore, put out for the rendezvous. The submarine surfaced at dusk and Clark and his staff climbed quickly to the deck. A heavy sea was running. Off to the south the African coast lay in flat silhouette against the desert evening sky. There on the cliff stood the farmhouse. Not until it was quite dark did the signal lamp glow in the seaward window, as promised.

Clark was impatient to go ashore at once, in spite of the sea, but the submarine commander persuaded him not to attempt a landing that night. The kayaks, he insisted, couldn't stand up in the surf that was breaking along the dark beaches. So the submarine spent the night offshore, submerged at dawn and remained out of sight until evening.

On the second night the party did get ashore. There they met Murphy and Ridgeway Knight, a member of Murphy's staff, and the French officers who had the information that was needed. They turned over to the Americans and British the complete troop disposition of the French. Furthermore, they warned the Allies that the French Navy, rather than the Army, would put up the stiffest fight. Real trouble could be expected at Casablanca, where the giant French battleship *Jean Bart* lay in harbor, along with cruisers and several smaller craft.

Two Arab servants at the farmhouse had been dismissed for the day and the night, in anticipation of the meeting. They had gone at once to the Vichy police in the nearest town with the story that smuggling was to be attempted along the coast that evening. When the police arrived Clark and his fellow officers hid in an abandoned wine cellar, and the French conspirators took to the woods. The police search failed to find any trace of smuggling. The owner of the house and several of the civilian guests acted very happy, pretending that it was a drinking party. The policemen chuckled and went away.

The sea rolled ashore in heavier surges; darkness finally drained out of the African sky, and the sun came up. The submarine stayed below the surface all that day, and Clark and his party hid in their cellar. Once more the police came back, again found nothing, again returned to the village. Clark fretted to get away. Invasion day was drawing dangerously near; if the information gathered here was to be of any value to Eisenhower, he must get back to London fast. In spite of the surf, they launched their kayaks the second night. Clark was met by a plane in mid-Mediterranean and flown back to London. What he had learned was included in last-minute changes in the invasion plans.

On October 24, 1942, the fleets sailed out of British ports at the same time that another convoy, loaded with men and munitions, left New York Harbor. Never before had so much firepower, so many well-armed soldiers, so much material, been assembled for an attack by sea against an enemy-held continent. The 700 ships carried 22 million pounds of food, 38 million pounds of clothing, 10 millions gallons of gasoline and more than 1 million copies of 10,100 different maps. In addition, there were big guns by the thousand, tanks and bulldozers, and tons and tons of ammunition.

On both sides of the Atlantic the few high-ranking officers who knew the secret plans waited eagerly for news from the Mediterranean.

A radio news program was just finishing. It was nine o'clock Eastern war time on Saturday evening, November 7, 1942. Then the commentator said suddenly, with surprise in his voice: "Stand by, please, for an important announcement from Washington."

All over America men and women leaned closer to their radios. Then it came, the news which had been awaited impatiently by many fireside strategists who did not realize what it requires in labor and planning and supplies to take the offensive anywhere.

"Our troops at this minute are landing in North Africa," the radios flashed. This was it. This was the second front. Stalin did not recognize it as such—the second front he was demanding was in Europe.

It was 3 a.m. November 8 off the coast of North Africa. There 700 ships of a combined British-American Fleet had broken into smaller fleets and were turning their noses toward the shore. At Algiers, where the greatest Allied naval strength was concentrated, the British aircraft carrier *Argus* and the battleships *Nelson* and *Rodney* headed the big parade.

Three o'clock. Late-sitting radio listeners in southern Europe and northern Africa heard a familiar voice speaking in an unfamiliar tongue. The voice covered all the broadcast bands, French, Moroccan, Algerian and Tunisian. The President of the United States was speaking to all Frenchmen, civilians and soldiers and sailors alike. On Allied battleships and cruisers all along the coast, recordings of the President's speech, made ten days earlier in Washington, were being put on the air, aimed at North Africa.

"Mes amis," he began. There it was, the old, familiar "My friends," in stilted Groton French. But the voice was resolute and firm. "Have faith in our words. Help us where you are able." The broadcast was brief, to the point. It asked all loyal Frenchmen, all men who hated tyranny, to join with the liberators who at this moment were about to land on their shores. It ended in an upward sweep, almost Churchillian in its drama: *"Vive la France éternelle!"*

Off the coast of Africa, stretched along 1000 miles of shoreline from southwestern Morocco to Algiers, the landing craft were bouncing on the ground swell. Even before the landing craft headed shoreward, the planes had taken off from the carriers, and other planes were winging from battered airstrips on Malta. The first bombs they dropped contained not explosives but friendly little leaflets, with the scrawled signature of General Eisenhower. He repeated the President's plea for cooperation. He insisted that we came not as aggressors but as liberators.

The startled watchers along the coast realized slowly what was happening. Argument started among some isolated companies of French soldiers aboard the battleships and the cruisers of the French Fleet, crewmen awakened their officers and bugles sounded general quarters.

In the long white building of the French Admiralty just back of the quays in Algiers, Admiral Darlan was startled by the thunder of cannon down at the harbor mouth and by the *rat-tat* of machine guns on the Naval pier. There a company of American Rangers, emulating their British Commando cousins, had leaped swiftly ashore from a destroyer which backed away. They set fire to the warehouses and planted dynamite charges where they would do the most good, but were soon captured by overwhelming numbers of French marines.

British battleships offshore began to shell the city. In a few hours they accomplished the swiftest job of slum clearance on record; for some reason the newer districts came through unscathed. Before noon the Casbah was riddled; great fires blazed in the filthier districts. But the white city of Algiers, on its half-moon of green hills, glistened almost undamaged in the sun. At 7 p.m., after a day in which defense was only half hearted at best, Admiral Darlan and Gen. Alphonse Juin surrendered the capital city of Algeria.

At Oran, Algeria, we made three landings. Our troops went ashore first on the point northwest of the city called Mers-el-Kebir. There we encountered only light defense, but Americans died on the beaches, even so. Twenty odd miles northeast of Oran, around the corner of Cape Carbon, our men stormed up the shingle in the little landlocked harbor of Arzew. Farther west, at Cape Sigale in front of the village of Bou-Sfer, other doughboys were landing. At the same time, our troops were encountering heavy fire along the Atlantic seaboard of Morocco when they ran up the long, gently sloping beaches near Port-Lyautey and Rabat, northeast of Casablanca, and at Agadir, far to the south. These Atlantic landings were commanded by a General known then to very few Americans, a tough, hard-swearing tankman named George Patton.

Whereas Algiers had surrendered after only a brief show of force, the defenders of Casablanca held on. The *Jean Bart* in the harbor was ripped by the guns of our fleet almost immediately, but she lay on bottom in shallow water and bombarded our fighting ships and landing craft day after day, until direct hits silenced her guns.

A pair of French cruisers with destroyers scampering at their heels moved out of the narrow artificial harbor to give battle to the invaders, fought stubbornly and were overwhelmed at last by our superior naval forces. Shore batteries held out longer than anyone had expected.

On the second day our infantry regiments, many of which had been pinned helplessly to the beaches by French mortar fire, managed to break out of their narrow footholds and plunged inland to the coast road. With the few tanks and artillery pieces that they were able to drag ashore, they fought their way southward along this road toward Casablanca.

French resistance was spotty, depending on the temper and the conviction of individual commanders. Some units gave up easily. Some came over to our side. Others fought fiercely, manning strongpoints in stone houses and culverts and digging shallow trenches. Much of the French Army in Africa was made up of French settlers, Senegalese, Moroccans and half-civilized native tribesmen from the Atlas Mountains; they did what their commanders asked them to do.

Our losses were heavy on the beaches and on the flat shelf of seaside desert which lies along the ocean between the surf and the hills. Green American troops recovered from the early shock of combat in time, however, to overrun the ancient fishing town of Fédala before the French could bring up reinforcements.

The town itself was an unimportant huddle of native mud houses with narrow streets. But it was here that curious American GI's first came face to veiled face with that strange and exotic creature they had read about so avidly in the "Guide to North Africa" they carried in their packs: here were the ladies of the mysterious East. But when the Americans actually looked at the ladies, they were distinctly unimpressed. Someone back home was to write a bit of doggerel about *Dirty Gertie of Bizerte* which was to become famous — at home. But it was the Joes here in Africa who made up the song heard most often on the dusty marches and in the sunbaked camps beside the roads. The heroine was Stella the Belle o' Fédala, whose mother was nothing to talk about in polite society.

The battle for Casablanca raged for several days. The wide naked beaches, the scant shrubbery, the empty desert stretching flat to the distant blue foothills of the mighty Atlas, all gave little shelter. American casualties were heavy. Casablanca itself had a normal peacetime population of a quarter of a million, but refugees from France and Germany and Spain had swelled the number to twice that.

Admiral Darlan was captured early in the fight, and after listening to American officers, agreed to call off the battle. He immediately sent out word to his commanders to lay down their arms and to cooperate with

U.S. troops wade ashore from Higgins landing boats at Fédala, Morocco, during the opening phase of "Operation Torch," November 8, 1942. Resistance by the Vichy French varied; invasion forces met with fierce opposition on this beach, while on others there was little or none.

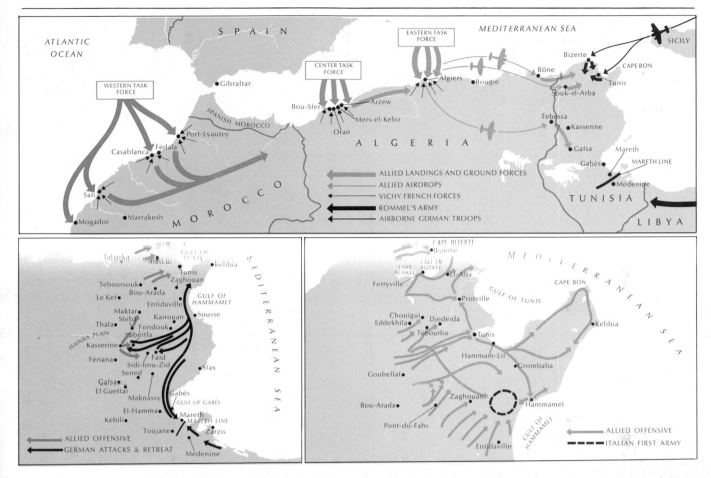

THE ALLIES CONQUER NORTH AFRICA

On November 8, 1942, British and American forces, under the command of Lt. Gen. Dwight D. Eisenhower, landed at Casablanca, Oran and Algiers in "Operation Torch" (see pages 300–310). Opposition by troops of Vichy France was overcome after four days of combat.

Meanwhile, Rommel's battered *Afrika Korps,* retreating before Montgomery's British Eighth Army, managed to reach the Mareth Line, a French-built fortification stretching some twenty miles southwest from the Gulf of Gabès. Here Rommel joined a larger force of Nazi troops fresh from Germany. Together they formed an army of some 175,000 men.

Faced with a combined British-American force on the west and the Eighth Army on the east, Rommel, with characteristic boldness, launched a sudden offensive against his foes. Spearheaded by Tiger tanks, he struck through the Faïd Pass and on westward to Kasserine Pass. Defending American troops were hurled back fifty miles and more before British and American reinforcements were able to stop the breakout and force Rommel back to his original position.

Thwarted on his western flank, the German commander turned savagely on his tormentor, the Eighth Army. On March 6, 1943, he sent his tanks hurtling toward Médenine, the main British supply center. They never reached it. Eighth Army anti-tank gunners destroyed fifty German tanks without a single British tank being lost.

A heavy assault by Montgomery on March 21 caused the Germans to retreat toward the Cape Bon Peninsula to escape encirclement. This was followed on April 6 by a joint attack by eastern and western Allied forces through the mountains toward Tunis and Bizerte. The Germans put up a stiff struggle, but in a lost cause. The Eighth Army took Tunis on May 7, and the Americans seized Bizerte on the same day.

The mauled Axis army now had no choice but to surrender, and on May 12 German and Italian commanders gave up, along with 275,000 men.

the Americans. He had collaborated with the Nazis and wasn't to be trusted, but in American hands he could and did save many lives in those first few days. On the third morning the tricolor of Republican France was flying again from government buildings, with the American flag on one side, the British on the other.

Almost as soon as the fighting ceased there, spearheads of American columns hurried east in the scant transportation they had brought ashore in their landings. If they could take and hold Tunisia before German reinforcements arrived from Europe, they would have Rommel's army in a nutcracker between our forces in the west and Montgomery's Eighth Army, advancing from Egypt. This is where our lack of transportation turned up to plague us. We did not have enough trucks, enough vehicles of any kind. So the spearheads rode swiftly into the east and the foot soldiers followed them, slogging along at too slow a rate to be of much help.

The distance from Algiers to Tunis by road was upward of 400 miles. Oran lay some 200 miles farther west, and Casablanca was another 500 miles farther on. Those of our troops who had landed at Agadir, Safi and Mogador, down the Atlantic coast, had a march of nearly 1500 miles to get to the fighting. There we were, afoot on a strange continent, we Americans who had boasted that we were going to ride to this war.

As soon as it was certain there would be no interference with our supply lines in Algeria and Morocco, the British landed from their troopships in the vicinity of Bône, about thirty miles from the Tunisian frontier, and at Bougie, farther up the coast. This was part of the strategy worked out at the meeting in June when Prime Minister Churchill had flown to Washington to talk about the menace of Rommel in Africa and to suggest a landing there. The British First Army and the American spearheads advanced boldly on the ports of Tunis and Bizerte.

Major General James H. Doolittle's planes covered the advance. There were not many planes — not enough, as it turned out. General Henri Giraud quickly organized a French brigade and hurried to get into the fight on the Allied side. His horse-drawn artillery rattled past plodding American columns and caused humorous comment up and down the line. Later, when the Americans saw the French cannoneers in

action, they learned to say, "I don't care where I fight if I've got those French guns backing me up."

There were some 10,000 German and Italian troops in Tunisia at the beginning of the campaign. Everyone wanted to get a whack at them before they collapsed. For the job looked easy: it would be a walkaway. But at headquarters the generals were worried. They feared that it would take more artillery, more tanks, more planes, more trucks than we had to dislodge the Nazi garrisons. Supplies and reinforcements were on the way, although it might be weeks before they arrived. Inexperienced American doughboys and most of their officers in the field didn't realize this. Seventy-six hours after Darlan's capitulation, they stormed across the Tunisian border.

Our sudden thrust to the south into Africa had caught Hitler and his staff completely by surprise. The secret had been well kept. In England press correspondents who were to be taken along to Africa received "inside information" that the convoy then making up was headed for Norway and they hurried out to buy heavy winter clothing. To aid in the deception, our Army Engineers in London had run off a huge printing of maps of the Norwegian coast and of the coast of the Netherlands and Belgium. German spies managed to get the false information back to the Continent.

When the radio told of our attack on Africa, the Nazis went into furious action. German emissaries rushed to Vichy. S. Pinkney Tuck, President Roosevelt's special representative there, knocked on Marshal Pétain's door shortly after dawn on invasion morning and presented a message from the President. Its tone was friendly. It explained that we came not as conquerors, but to keep French Africa free. We dared not permit the Germans to take over Algeria and Morocco. We should welcome French help.

Pierre Laval, dancing to Hitler's tune, was in the driver's seat. He brushed aside the President's explanation, and within a few hours the Vichy puppet government broke diplomatic relations with the United States. In Vichy old Pétain heard again the tramp of the *Wehrmacht* as it marched south to occupy the rest of France. It would take over the entire south coast, just as American and British generals had expected. It planned, also, to take the French Fleet in Toulon, and to turn its guns against the Allies.

At dawn, as the Germans descended on the port, the French Admirals gave the order which they had dreaded ever since the day they had formulated it in secret many months before. Dynamite charges were laid quickly on all the vessels, close to the magazines. Fuses were lighted. The sailors got ashore as best they could. Most of the officers still were at their posts when the explosions began. The French Fleet died by its own hand, there in the smoky harbor—battleships, cruisers, destroyers, small craft, sixty-two of them in all, blew up and sank at their moorings.

The U.S. Army announced its casualties in the campaign in Morocco and Algeria. They totaled 860 dead or missing and 1050 wounded.

On the morning of November 14 our troops crossed the frontier of Tunisia. Almost at once they ran into small stubborn Nazi units assigned to guard the border. These they overwhelmed and then continued to press on. Newspaper maps back home showed the enemy being crowded into smaller and smaller space, up in the northeast corner near Bizerte and Tunis. Any day, now, people said hopefully, the Germans must give in.

But the weather turned bad all along the front, and the brief season of winter rain brought mud to the hillsides of Tunisia and filled the wadis with brown and yellow water. Fog spread over the wet land and the nights turned cold. It was the mud that slowed our advance, held down the infantry, bogged the guns and for a time almost halted the trucks bringing up ammunition and food from the rear. It gave the Germans and Italians the time they desperately needed to prepare for a stand. Fast fleets of troopships and cargo vessels put out each evening from Sicily and Naples and from the occupied ports along the south coast of France, filled with German and Italian soldiers, guns and tanks. Axis planes, hurriedly brought back from combat on the Russian front, joined the battle.

Two weeks before Christmas, after a few days of comparative quiet on the front, the enemy struck. He hit us hard all along our thinly occupied line. He broke off and captured our spearheads, even overrunning some of our precious forward dumps.

General Montgomery's battle-hardened Eighth Army was charging west across the Libyan coastal deserts, driving Rommel's *Afrika Korps* ahead of it.

In a message to his troops Montgomery had promised good hunting in Libya, and they were getting it. The going was slower than the American generals, anxiously waiting for Montgomery's men to reinforce them, had hoped.

Back in Algiers, Casablanca and Oran, our ships at last were pouring supplies ashore in great quantity. The long single-track railway which followed the coast had been bombed and wrecked. Our Transportation Corps put it back in working order and ran the trains at express speed from the ports to the front. The operation of that line was our first railway experience overseas in this war. (Later the Army Service Forces were called upon to furnish engines and cars in six different gauges, with the crews to run them, for six different parts of the world.)

The trucks were coming ashore in ever-increasing numbers. At Casablanca, under the bright sun, an African version of Detroit came to life, and others followed it at Oran and Algiers. It was called the TUP plant, "TUP" being the initials for Twin Unit Pack. That's how the trucks came off the ships—knocked down in twin units, two motors, two bodies, two cabs, boxed together to save shipping space. GI's from Ford and General Motors, from Brooklyn filling stations and from Kentucky crossroad shops bossed thousands of Arabs in burnouses and turbans, who bolted thousands of trucks together on assembly lines fashioned from the crates themselves.

Ordnance and quartermaster companies on the docks filled the trucks with munitions and food and started them on the long road to the east. German planes strafed the convoys all along the coast; the quartermaster companies hauling rations along that road suffered serious casualties.

All through January the battle line seesawed over the Tunisian hills. Native tribesmen, grazing their sheep and camels on the new winter grass, watched impassively as the fighting ebbed and flowed. When artillery fire pockmarked a field where their flocks were grazing, they merely moved on to another field. A few of them died. Most of them seemed utterly bored.

In February the situation in Tunisia was decidedly no better. We had managed to bring up some reinforcements, but not enough of them. The 1st Infantry Division was in action, earning another battle star, taking heavy losses, winning the reluctant respect of

the enemy. The 1st, under Maj. Gen. Terry Allen, with Brig. Gen. Theodore ("young Teddy") Roosevelt as second in command, was a tough outfit even then and would grow more so as time went on. The men gloried in their toughness and in their scars. They resented the word "doughboys"—they had a new name for themselves: "dogfaces." They were proud of being dogfaces. Still, the Nazis had the preponderance of firepower, armor and air cover. They pressed even harder and we continued to fall back.

Not until March did America first hear of Kasserine Pass—"Kerosene Pass" to the GI's. This obscure fold in the African landscape had almost eluded our cartographers when they made their battle maps of Africa. They had marked it with three little dots, to represent ancient ruins, on Highway 20 between Sbeitla and Fériana. It was in Kasserine that our troops met their worst defeat in Africa.

The rolling land to the north and south of Kasserine and the narrow valleys hedged in by steep, rocky cliffs, had been a battleground for 3000 years. Here Carthaginians and Vandals, Caesar's legions, the horsemen of old Arab civilizations and, in later years, French soldiers had fought and died.

On Sunday afternoon, February 14, Kasserine Pass lay behind the Allied lines. Our troops had romped through and around it, driving the Germans eastward to the sea. We halted a little way beyond and the French XIX Corps gave up its place in the line to the Americans. The Frenchmen had been only half equipped, and casualties had worn their ranks too thin. The Americans took over the sector about noon.

Ahead lay a narrow gap between two steep mountains. The Americans looked it up on their maps and found that it was called Faïd Pass. There was no sign of the enemy. It promised to be a quiet day. Our tanks had been scattered among our various battalions, nowhere in great enough strength to turn back a sustained and heavy armored blow. And that's what came.

First the Stukas dived low, scooting down from the eastern hilltops, machine-gunning our infantry and bombing our artillery positions. Wave after wave, they poured out of the east in the heaviest aerial blow Americans had faced in Africa. Then out of the pass roared the German tanks. They were big Tigers, and on each of the forward machines was mounted a new 88-mm. cannon, heavier than anything the Allies could throw against them.

Our men fought bravely. But they had little air support, not enough guns of their own, not enough tanks concentrated anywhere to meet the furious assault. So they fell back to Kasserine. There they held for six days, dug into the hillside, with not enough food or water, not enough of anything except courage and the will to win. On Tuesday we attempted a counterattack with infantry but it failed almost before it began. We tried again on Thursday, with less success, and once more dropped back.

The Germans, when we finally were able to hold our line, had retaken 4000 square miles of territory. They had inflicted heavy losses on us in men and material. They had overwhelmed and captured many of our tanks and guns, some of our munitions dumps; other ammunition stores we had destroyed as we fled.

We made our stand in Hatnra plain, west of Kasserine, and there, while the enemy paused to gather new strength for a further drive, our reinforcements rolled out of the west. New tanks and trucks, guns and ammunition, tank destroyers—and a strange new weapon, then still listed as secret by the War Department. It was called a bazooka. It looked like a stovepipe with some gadgets hung on it and it cost less than $50 to build. It launched a rocket. One man could pack the wallop of a 75-mm. cannon. First used by American infantry against a pillbox near the coast, the bazooka terrified the enemy.

From January 14 to 24, 1943, Prime Minister Churchill, President Roosevelt and their military leaders met at Anfa, a seaside resort a few miles south of Casablanca, to plan the further prosecution of the war. The complexion of the conflict had so changed by then that it was safe to talk in terms of offensive strategy. The leaders of the free nations also felt secure enough by that time to speak out boldly to the Axis. So they announced their policy in dealing with Hitler, Mussolini and the Japanese. They would accept nothing less than unconditional surrender.

After the conference, Gen. George C. Marshall and other American military leaders flew to Algiers, to

*ritish soldiers with Bren-gun carriers make their way down the
de of a dry stream bed near Kasserine Pass. These rocky wadis,
id for all but a few weeks of the year, crisscrossed much of the
orth African desert and were an important factor in making
any of the Allied military movements difficult.*

where General Eisenhower had set up his headquarters in a hotel on the hills behind the terraced town. Everywhere the cry for more transportation was heard. If we only had enough trucks and enough trains to transport enough men and munitions fast enough, we could bring greater pressure to bear upon the enemy and speed victory in the African campaign. General Eisenhower needed tents, aerial bombs, spare parts for tanks. The largest single order the Army Service Forces ever received was cabled home.

Major General Wilhelm D. Styer received the message at his Pentagon desk, gasped once and began to punch buzzers. The experts gathered in his office, got out pencils and paper and commenced to figure how, once again, to do the impossible.

The order went out of the Pentagon Building to depots and ports on January 28. Three days later the first of the special convoy of twenty ships began to load. On February 15, 2½ weeks after the machinery was put in motion, the naval escort picked up the convoy and headed for Casablanca and Oran. Aboard was 235,000 tons of cargo, the difference between quick victory with smaller casualties, and a long-drawn-out, expensive decision. It arrived in Africa safe and on time.

We had stopped the Germans west of Kasserine and held them there. Now we were ready for the counterblow. Eisenhower put everything he had into the punch. Our Grant and Sherman tanks in overwhelming numbers spearheaded the attack.

The Germans were not ready for the added punch. For three bloody days we drove them back through Kasserine. Trucks and jeeps carried the infantry replacements straight up to our front lines, heedless of enemy fire. Our planes for once dominated the battlefield. Our tanks cut up the German armor, sliced it into small pieces and destroyed it.

At the same time the British Eighth Army charged out of Libya and around the corner of the sea, and halted to get its breath at the well-fortified positions of the Mareth Line. Rommel's forces were being squeezed steadily into an ever-smaller space.

The Germans fought furiously. Eventually, Rommel decided to attack in the north. The British regiments were not too strong up there—one extra corps thrown into the battle could turn the day. And Lieutenant General Patton, for once far behind the fighting, 200 miles away, decided to provide it.

It is written down in all the military textbooks that even a single division cannot travel any distance across the supply lines of an army in combat without disrupting those lines. Patton had four divisions. He had one narrow African road. He had three days. He had moonlit nights which would give the enemy advantage in watching his moves. It couldn't be done. Patton did it. Old soldiers like to tell about the miracle of Lieutenant General Patton's march—for a miracle it surely was.

He collected all the trucks of all the services and packed them with men and supplies. He cleaned up the American camps down to the last tent pin. He put the Transportation Corps in charge of the move and sent for the Military Police.

"We've got to cross the British supply lines," he said. "We've got to move fast. Yet we don't dare hold up a single British truck of food or ammunition. Get out there and handle traffic over the crossroads. Keep it moving."

The divisions traveled at night, hid in wadis and olive groves and under the shadows of the hills by day. The truckers and tankmen drove like madmen as soon as dark came down, bumper to bumper over frightening mountain roads. The British supplies kept coming through. In three days Patton's armor spearheaded the American thrust. That added power, precisely when it was needed, won the battle and won the war in Africa. It put the American 1st Armored and the American 1st, 9th and 34th Infantry Divisions into the final battle where they could share in the muddy glory of victory.

On May 12 Axis resistance ended on Cape Bon, east of Tunis and Bizerte. We were ready now for the long job that lay ahead on the Continent of Europe. The menace of the arrows pointing west in Africa was over. Instead, the arrows were pointing to the heartland of Germany.

It was on the deserts and in the hills of Tunisia and Algeria and along the Moroccan coast that the United States learned through hard experience how to fight the Nazis. What we learned there would pay big dividends in the invasion of Sicily and Italy.

GI's with the U.S. Army Air Corps pray during an open-air church service in the Algerian desert early in January 1943. Within six weeks American troops were to experience a savage baptism of fire during a battle with the Nazis at Kasserine Pass.

DWIGHT D. EISENHOWER— LEADER OF THE ALLIES

On Pearl Harbor day the fifty-one-year-old Dwight David Eisenhower, promoted to brigadier general only two months before, was well known and highly esteemed in strictly Army circles—but unknown to the American people. Yet six months later, in June 1942, he took command of U.S. forces in Europe and soon thereafter, in November, headed the combined Allied forces in the invasion of North Africa.

In less than a year, a relatively obscure Army officer thus emerged as one of the topmost figures in the great conflict. A moderately successful military career, but slow and routine, suddenly zoomed to spectacular heights.

As a small-town schoolboy in Abilene, Kansas, he somehow came to be called Ike, and it was as Ike that the American people took him to their hearts when he burst from obscurity to glowing fame. The simple nickname fitted both his homespun personality and the intimate affection he inspired.

Eisenhower was born into a poor, hard-working family on October 14, 1890, in Denison, Texas, the third of seven sons. The Eisenhowers had moved to Texas from Hope, Kansas, after the failure of their small general store. Two years after Dwight's birth they returned to Kansas, settling permanently in Abilene. Both his parents were of old colonial stock, of German descent on the father's side, Swiss on the mother's side.

Ike grew up in a deeply pious home. He was a good student and a good athlete. To add to the family income, he dropped out of high school and went to work in a creamery for one year. On graduating from high school in 1909 he returned to the creamery, later becoming night foreman. In June 1911, however, having qualified in a competitive examination, he entered the U.S. Military Academy at West Point. Although his academic record was only fair—he was the sixty-first in a graduating class of 164—he shone as a football star.

While stationed at Fort Sam Houston, Texas, he met Mamie Geneva Doud, the daughter of a prosperous Denver family. They were married within a month, on July 1, 1916, the same day that he was made a first lieutenant. Subsequent to the U.S. entry into World War I, Eisenhower commanded the first tank training center, at Camp Colt, Gettysburg, Pennsylvania, with the temporary rank of lieutenant colonel. The war ended as he was about to leave for France; he was among the few awarded a Distinguished Service Medal for services within the United States.

Promoted to major in 1920, he held a string of routine posts in the next ten years, broken by two periods of higher military education. He graduated from the Army Command and General Staff School at Fort Leavenworth, Kansas, in 1926, at the head of his class, and three years later completed a course at the Army War College. He then did a brief tour of duty in France, studying the terrain of the First World War, an experience that in due time would prove useful to him in planning the invasion of captive Europe.

From 1929 to 1932 he served as an aide in the offices of the Assistant Secretary of War, and then was transferred, as senior aide, to Chief of Staff Gen. Douglas MacArthur. He went with MacArthur to the Philippines in 1935, where he helped to organize the military establishment of the islands. In 1936 he was again given the temporary rank of lieutenant colonel.

Reassigned to mainland duties with the troops in 1940, he was stationed successively at several military posts. In the 1941 large-scale maneuvers in Louisiana, his strategy was credited for the "victory" and drew the favorable attention of Gen. George C. Marshall, then Chief of Staff.

Marshall had met Eisenhower only twice, eleven years apart and both times briefly. In 1930 he had chatted with the younger man in the office of the American Battle Monuments Commission in Washington and made a complimentary note about the unassuming officer in his personal notebook. They renewed the acquaintance in 1941 during the Louisiana maneuvers. It tells a lot about Eisenhower's ability to impress people that when the war started Marshall immediately called him to the capital, where he arrived one week after Pearl Harbor. Marshall consulted him on the strategic position in the Pacific theater and assigned him at once to responsible duties.

Soon after the Japanese attack, Eisenhower was appointed chief of the War Plans Division, then of the Operations Division which replaced it, with temporary rank of major general. In May 1942 Marshall sent him to England to study the problem of setting up a second front, and on his return he was chosen to command U.S. forces in Europe. He reached England in June.

From that point forward the story of Eisenhower is the story of the war in the Atlantic-European theater. He demonstrated a high talent for strategic planning and organization and, no less vital in a coalition war, for reconciling differences among the military leaders of the countries involved. He was entrusted with and executed successfully the invasion of North Africa in late 1942, then the invasion of Sicily in July and of Italy in September of 1943. He was made a full general in February 1943.

On Christmas Eve 1943 President Roosevelt announced Eisenhower's appointment as Supreme Commander of Allied Expeditionary Forces. His assignment was to plan and direct "Operation Overlord," the assault on Hitler's Fortress Europe. The final drive to liberate the Continent came on D day, June 6, 1944. In December of that year he attained the rank of five-star general. His grandiose mission was accomplished with Germany's formal surrender on May 8, 1945.

In November 1945 Eisenhower was recalled to Washington to succeed Marshall as Chief of Staff. He received a hero's welcome. With the possible exception of MacArthur, he was the most popular American military leader in the victorious war.

Eisenhower resigned from the Army to assume the presidency of Columbia University in 1948, but was recalled to active service at the end of 1950 to help organize the North Atlantic Treaty Organization (NATO). He remained in France as the first commander of the integrated Allied Forces at Supreme Headquarters Allied Powers, Europe (SHAPE).

In 1948 Eisenhower had turned down a bid by both Democratic and Republican leaders to run for President of the United States. Four years later, his political views more clearly defined, he agreed to answer "a clear-cut call to political duty" from the Republican Party. He was nominated on the first ballot

and elected, after running against Gov. Adlai Stevenson of Illinois, by the second largest popular majority ever received by a presidential candidate. In September 1955 Eisenhower suffered a serious heart attack. He recovered and returned to the White House in January. The following November he was reelected to a second term. Since the Republicans lost control of both houses of Congress in the same election, this was more a personal victory for Eisenhower than a victory for his party.

When he left office in January 1961, Eisenhower had won still another high rank: a top place among the U.S. Presidents most deeply loved and admired by the American people. He died March 28, 1969, after a prolonged illness.

Dwight D. Eisenhower commanded Allied forces from the invasion of North Africa in 1942 to the unconditional surrender of Germany two and one half years later. His qualities of leadership and his personal charm enabled him to gain unity and tactical cooperation among armies of many nations. In recognition of their achievements, he and General MacArthur were made the first five-star generals in the U.S. Army.

THE AMERICAN SOLDIER IN NORTH AFRICA

BY ERNIE PYLE

"What is it like to be there?" "How goes the war?" "How are our boys?" Ernest Taylor Pyle, better known as Ernie, answered these questions in a flow of syndicated columns from the battlefronts that won him the affection of U.S. civilian and soldier alike. No matter how close he was to danger and suffering, he saw and expressed the hearts of men, not just troops, at war. On April 18, 1945, Ernie Pyle was slain on the Pacific island of Ie Shima in the Ryukyus by a Japanese sniper.

In the spring of 1943 I was away from the front lines for a while, living elsewhere with other troops, and considerable fighting took place while I was gone. When I got ready to return to my old friends at the front, I wondered if I would sense any change in them. I did, and definitely.

The most vivid change was the casual and workshop manner in which they talked about killing. They had made the psychological transition from their normal belief that taking human life was sinful over to a new professional outlook where killing was a craft. No longer was there anything morally wrong about killing. In fact, it was an admirable thing.

I think I was so impressed by this new attitude because it hadn't been necessary for me to make the change along with them. As a noncombatant, my own life was in danger only by occasional chance or circumstance. Consequently, I didn't need to think of killing in personal terms, and killing to me was still just one thing—murder.

Even after a winter of living with wholesale death and vile destruction, it was only spasmodically that I seemed capable of realizing how real and how awful the war was. My emotions seemed dead and crusty when presented with the tangibles of war. I found I could look on rows of fresh graves without a lump in my throat. Somehow I could look on mutilated bodies without flinching or feeling deeply.

It was only when I sat alone away from it all or lay at night in my bedroll re-creating what I had seen, thinking and thinking and thinking of nightmare, that at times I felt I couldn't stand it and would have to leave.

But to the fighting soldier that phase of the war was behind. It was left behind after his first battle. His blood was up. He was fighting for his life, and killing now for him was as much a profession as writing was for me.

He wanted to kill individually or in vast numbers. He wanted to see the Germans overrun, mangled, butchered in the Tunisian trap. He spoke excitedly of seeing great heaps of dead, of our bombers sinking whole shiploads of fleeing men, of Germans by the thousands dying miserably in a final Tunisian holocaust of their own creation.

In that one respect the frontline soldier differed from all the rest of us. All the rest of us—you and me and even the thousands of soldiers behind the lines in Africa—wanted terribly, yet only academically, for the war to be over. The frontline soldier wanted it to be terminated by the physical process of his destroying enough Germans to end it. He was truly at war. The rest of us, no matter how hard we worked, were not. Say what you will, nothing can make a complete soldier except battle experience.

In the semifinals—the cleaning out of central Tunisia—we had large units in battle for the first time. Frankly, they didn't all excel. Their own commanders admitted it, and admirably they didn't try to alibi. The British had to help us out a few times, but neither American nor British commanders were worried about that, for there was no lack of bravery. There was only lack of experience. They all knew we would do better the next time.

The 1st Infantry Division was an example of what our American units could do after they had gone through the mill of experience. These boys did themselves proud in the semifinals. Everybody spoke about it. Our casualties included few taken prisoner. All the other casualties were wounded or died fighting. "They never gave an inch," a General said. "They died right in their foxholes."

I heard of a high British officer who went over the battlefield just after the action was finished. American boys were lying dead in their foxholes, their rifles still grasped in firing position in their dead hands. And the veteran English soldier remarked time and again, in a sort of hushed eulogy spoken only to himself, "Brave men. Brave men!"

A salute to the infantry—the goddam infantry, as they like to call themselves. I loved the infantry because they were the underdogs. They were the mud-rain-frost-and-wind boys. They had no comforts, and they even learned to live without the necessities. In the end they were the guys without whom the Battle of Africa could not have been won.

I wish you could have seen one of the unforgettable sights I saw. I was sitting among clumps of sword grass on a steep and rocky hillside that we had just taken, looking out over a vast rolling country to the rear. A narrow path wound like a ribbon over a hill miles away, down a long slope, across a creek, up a slope and over another hill. All along the length of that ribbon there was a thin line of men. For four days and nights they had fought hard, eaten little, washed none and slept hardly at all. Their nights had been violent with attack, fright, butchery; their days sleepless and miserable with the crash of artillery.

The men were walking. They were fifty feet apart for dispersal. Their walk was slow, for they were dead weary, as a person could tell even when looking at them from behind. Every line and sag of their bodies spoke their inhuman exhaustion. On their shoulders and backs they carried heavy steel tripods, machine-gun barrels, leaden boxes of ammunition. Their feet seemed to sink into the ground from the overload they were bearing.

They didn't slouch. It was the terrible deliberation of each step that spelled out their appalling tiredness. Their faces were black and unshaved. They were young men, but the grime and whiskers and exhaustion made them look middle-aged. In their eyes as they passed was no expression of hatred, no excitement, no despair, no tonic of their victory, there was just the simple expression of being there—as if they had been

there doing that forever and ever—and nothing else.

The line moved on, seemingly endless. All afternoon men kept coming around the hill and vanishing eventually over the horizon. It was one long tired line of antlike men. There was an agony in your heart and you felt almost ashamed to look at them.

They were just guys from Broadway and Main Street, but maybe you wouldn't remember them. They were too far away now. They were too tired. Their world can never be known to you, but if you could have seen them just once, just for an instant, you would know that no matter how hard people were working back home, they could never keep pace with those infantrymen in Tunisia.

On one unforgettable Tunisian day, between 3000 and 4000 shells passed over our heads. True, most of them were in transit, en route to somewhere else, but enough of them were intended for us to make a fellow very somber before the day was over. And just as a sideline, a battle was going on a couple of hundred yards to our left, mines were blowing up jeeps on our right, and German machine-gun bullets were zinging past with annoying persistency.

All day we were a sort of crossroads for shells and bullets. All day guns roared in a complete circle around us. About three eighths of that circle was German, and five eighths of it American. Our guns were blasting the enemy's hill positions ahead of us, and the Germans were blasting our gun positions behind us. Shells roared over us from every point of the compass. I don't believe there was one whole minute in fourteen hours of daylight when the air above us was silent.

The guns themselves were close enough to be brutal in their noise, and between shots the air above us was filled with the intermixed rustle and whine of traveling shells. You couldn't see a shell unless you were standing near the gun when it was fired, but its rush through the air made such a loud sound that it seemed impossible it couldn't be seen. Some shells whined loudly throughout their flight. Others made only a toneless rustle. It was an indescribable sound. The nearest I can come to it is the sound of a stick being jerked through water.

Some apparently defective shells got out of shape and made queer noises. I remember one that sounded like a locomotive puffing hard at about forty miles an hour. Another one made a rhythmic knocking sound as if turning end over end. We all had to laugh when it went over.

They say a man never hears the shell that hits him. Fortunately I don't know about that, but I do know that the closer they hit, the less time there was to hear them. Those landing within a hundred yards were heard only about a second before they hit. The sound produced a special kind of horror that was something more than mere fright. It was a confused form of acute desperation.

Each time it seemed certain that was the one. Ducking was instinctive. Whether I shut my eyes or not I don't know, but I do know I became so weak that my joints felt all gone. It took about ten minutes to get back to normal.

Shells that came too close made veterans jump just like neophytes. Once we heard three shells in the air at the same time, all headed for us. It wasn't possible for me to get three times as weak as usual, but after they had all crashed safely a hundred yards away, I knew I would have had to grunt and strain mightily to lift a soda cracker.

Sometimes the enemy fire quieted down, and we thought the Germans were pulling back, until suddenly we were rudely awakened by a heinous bedlam of screaming shells, mortar bursts and even machine-gun bullets.

I lived, of course, just as the men did. Our home was on the ground. We sat, ate and slept on the ground. We were in a different place almost every night, for we were constantly moving forward from hill to hill. Establishing a new bivouac consisted of nothing more than digging new foxholes. We seldom took off our clothes, not even our shoes. Nobody had more than one blanket, and many men had none at all. For three nights I slept on the ground with nothing under or over me. Finally I had one blanket and my shelter tent sent up.

We had no warm food for days. Each man kept his own rations and ate whenever he pleased. Oddly enough I was never conscious of the lack of warm food. Water was brought to us in cans, but very little washing was done.

Sometimes we were up all night on the march, and then we slept in the daytime till the hot sun made sleep impossible. Some of the men slept right in their fox-

holes, others on the ground alongside. Since rocks were so abundant, most of us buttressed our foxholes with little rock walls around them.

We were shot at by 88's, 47's, machine guns, tanks. Despite our own air superiority, we were dive-bombed numerous times, but the Germans were always in such a hurry to get it over and get home that usually their aim was bad, and the bombs fell harmlessly in open spaces. We could always count on being awakened at dawn by dive-bombing.

After being both shelled and bombed, I decided an artillery barrage was the worse of the two. A prolonged artillery barrage came very close to being unbearable, and we saw many pitiful cases of anxiety neurosis.

The nights were sometimes fantastic. The skies flashed all night from the muzzle blasts of big guns. Parachute flares shot from the ground and dropped from planes hung in the sky. Armored vehicles rumbled across country all night. German planes thrummed through the skies, seeking some flash of light on the ground.

At dusk groups of litter-bearers set out to carry the wounded from forward companies. Just after dawn each morning the stretchers and the walking wounded came slowly downhill from the night's fighting. Ammunition carriers in long lines toiled up to us, carrying triple clusters of heavy mortar shells on their shoulders.

A couple of miles behind us the engineers worked day and night without cease, digging and blasting and bulldozing passes through the hills so that our wheeled vehicles could follow the advance.

Sometimes we didn't sleep at all for thirty hours or more. At first the activity and excitement kept me awake. I didn't want to go to sleep for fear of missing something. At first, too, the noise of the artillery was terrific. But on my last two nights in the lines, I slept eight hours solid and never heard a thing.

During all the time we were under fire I felt fine. The catch-as-catch-can sleep didn't seem to bother me. I never felt physically tired even after the marches. The days were so diverse and so unregimented that a week sped by before I knew it. I never felt that I was excited or tense except during certain fast-moving periods of shelling or bombing, and those were quickly over. When I finally left the line just after daylight one morning, I had never felt better in my life.

And yet, once I was safe back in camp, an intense

weariness came over me. I slept almost every minute of two days and nights. I just didn't have the will to get up, except to eat. My mind was as blank as my body was lifeless. I felt as if every cell in my makeup had been consumed. It was utter exhaustion such as I have never known. Apparently it was the letdown from being uncommonly tense without realizing I was tense. It was not until the fourth day that I began to feel really normal again, and even then I was afraid I thought too much about the wounded men.

When they were about to go into battle, some men were very introspective and thoughtful. Other men carried on as if everything were normal. I remember one night when chow had come up just after dusk, and a dozen or so of us were opening tin cans to the tune of constant shellfire. Somebody started singing a parody of some song. Others joined in, and for five minutes there in the night they sang funny songs.

Another time we were sitting in the darkness on a rocky ledge, waiting to start a night march that would culminate in an attack in which some of the men would die before dawn. As we sat there, the officers who were to lead the attack got into a long discussion comparing the London and New York subways. The sum total of the discussion was that the London subways were better than ours. After that the conversation drifted off onto the merits and demerits of the Long Island Railroad. The only "warlike" aspect of the discussion was that somebody expressed a hearty desire to be riding on the Long Island Railroad that very minute.

The thing that Americans in Africa had fought and worked six months to get was finally achieved. When it did come, it was an avalanche almost impossible to describe. The flood of prisoners choked the roads. There were acres of captured material.

It was a holiday, though everybody kept on working. We all felt suddenly free inside, as if personal worry had been lifted. It was the way we used to feel as children on the farm, when our parents surprised us by saying work was finished and we were going to the state fair for a day. And when we had looked all day goggle-eyed at more Germans than we had ever expected to see in our lives, we really did feel as if we had been to a fair.

We saw Germans walking alone along highways. We saw them riding stacked up in our jeeps with one lone American driver. We saw them by hundreds, crammed as in a subway, in their own trucks with their own drivers. And in the forward areas our fairgrounds of mile after mile contained more Germans than Americans. Germans were everywhere. It made me a little light-headed to stand in the center of a crowd, the only American among scores of German soldiers, and not have to feel afraid of them. Their 88's stood abandoned. In the fields dead Germans still lay on the grass. By the roadside scores of tanks and trucks still burned. Dumps flamed, and German command posts lay littered, where they had tried to wreck as much as possible before surrendering.

But all these were sideshows—the big show was the mass of men in strange uniforms, lining roads, swamping farmyards, blackening fields, waiting for us to tell them where to go. High German officers were obviously down in the mouth over the tragic end of their campaign. We saw some tears. Officers wept over the ghastly death toll of their men during the last few days. Officers were meticulously correct in their military behavior, but otherwise standoffish and silent.

Not so the common soldiers. I mingled with them all day and sensed no sadness among them. Theirs was not the delight of the Italians, but rather an acceptance of defeat in a war well fought—why be surly about it? They were friendly, very friendly. Being prisoners, it obviously paid them to be friendly; yet their friendliness seemed genuine. Just as when the French and Americans first met, the Germans started learning English words and teaching us German words.

But circumstances didn't permit much communion between them and our troops. Those Americans who came in direct contact with them gave necessary orders and herded them into trucks. All other Americans just stared curiously as they passed. I saw very little fraternizing with prisoners. I saw no acts of belligerence and heard neither boos nor cheers. But I did hear a hundred times, "This is the way it should be. Now we can go on from here."

German boys were as curious about us as we were about them. Every time I stopped, a crowd would form quickly. In almost every group was someone who spoke English. In all honesty I can't say their bearing or personality was a bit different from that of a similar bunch of American prisoners. They gave us their cigarettes and accepted ours, for curiosity's sake. They

(Above) *A moment to relax: GI's break out a deck of cards under the palm trees at an oasis in southern Tunisia and, for a short while, forget the rigors of war. The American soldier soon learned the necessity of relieving the tensions of battle whenever possible, by any means at his disposal.*

(Left) *Triumphant Allied troops, their tanks festooned with tree branches, parade past jubilant crowds in Tunis on May 7, 1943. The Allied victory in North Africa was completed six days later when the last Axis troops surrendered. Rommel and some 700 of his men managed to escape to Europe.*

(Right) *While one American soldier uses his spare moments to read, a companion prefers a well-earned rest. U.S. veterans of the North African war could be proud of themselves: they arrived in the desert totally inexperienced in warfare, met a hard, resourceful foe and ultimately defeated him.*

examined the jeep and asked questions about our uniforms. If I passed one walking alone, usually he would smile and speak.

One high American officer told me he found himself feeling sorry for them—until he remembered how they had killed so many of his men with their sneaking mines, how they had pinned him down a few days before with bullets flying; then he hated them.

I am always a sucker for the guy who loses, but somehow it never occurred to me to feel sorry for these prisoners. They didn't give the impression of needing any sorrowing over. They were loyal to their country and sorry they lost but, now it was over for them, they seemed glad to be out of it.

I'd like to say something about the jeep. Good Lord, I don't think we could have won the campaign without the jeep. It did everything, went everywhere, was as faithful as a dog, as strong as a mule and as agile as a goat. It consistently carried twice what it was designed for and still kept going. I didn't even think it rode so badly after I got used to it. I drove jeeps thousands of miles, and if I had been called upon to suggest changes for a new model, I could have thought of only one or two little things. One was the handbrake. It was perfectly useless—it wouldn't hold at all. And in the field of acoustics, I wish they could have somehow fixed the jeep so that at certain speeds the singing of those heavy tires didn't sound exactly like an approaching airplane. That little sound effect caused me to jump out of my skin more than once. But except for those two trivial items, the jeep was a divine instrument of wartime locomotion.

We found out one thing about baths at the front—if we didn't bathe for a long time, the fleas didn't bother us. Apparently we either built up a protective coating that they couldn't get through, or else we became too revolting even for fleas. Whatever the reason, I knew of rash people who took an occasional bath and were immediately set upon by fleas.

What I have seen in North Africa has altered my own feelings in one respect. There were days when I sat in my tent alone and gloomed with the desperate belief that it was actually possible for us to lose the war. I don't feel that way anymore. Despite our strikes and bickering and confusion back home, America is producing, and no one can deny that. Even here at the far end of just one line, the trickle has grown into an impressive stream. We are producing at home, and we are hardening overseas. Apparently it takes a country like America about two years to become wholly at war. We had to go through that transition period of letting loose of life as it was, and then live the new war life so long that it finally became the normal life to us. It was a form of growth, and we couldn't press it. Only time can produce that change. We have survived that long passage of time, and if I am at all correct, we have about changed our character and become a war nation. I can't yet see when we shall win, or over what route geographically or by which of the many means of warfare. But no longer do I have any doubts at all that we shall win.

The men over here have changed, too. For a year, everywhere I went, soldiers inevitably asked me two questions: "When do you think we'll go home?" and "When will the war be over?" The home-going desire was once so dominant that I believe our soldiers over here would have voted—if the question had been put to them—to go home immediately, even if it meant peace on terms of something less than unconditional surrender by the enemy.

That isn't true now. Sure, they all still want to go home. So do I. But there is something deeper than that, which didn't exist six months ago. I can't quite put it into words—it isn't any theatrical proclamation that the enemy must be destroyed in the name of freedom; it's just a vague, but growing, individual acceptance of the bitter fact that we must win the war or else, and that it can't be won by running excursion boats back and forth across the Atlantic carrying homesick vacationers.

A year is a long time to be away from home, especially if a person has never been away before, as was true of the bulk of our troops. At first homesickness can almost kill a man. But time takes care of that. It isn't normal to moon in the past forever. Home gradually grows less vivid, the separation from it less agonizing. There finally comes a day—not suddenly but gradually, as a sunset-touched cloud changes its color —when a man is living almost wholly wherever he is. His life has caught up with his body, and his days become fully war days, instead of American days simply transplanted to Africa.

That's the stage our soldiers are in now—the ones

who have been over since the beginning, I mean. It seems to take about that long. It's only in the last few weeks that I've begun to hear frequent remarks, said enthusiastically and sincerely, about the thrill it will be to see Paris and to march down the streets of Berlin. The immediate goal used to be the Statue of Liberty; more and more it is becoming Unter den Linden.

Our men can't make this change from normal civilians into warriors and remain the same people. Even if they were away this long under normal circumstances, the mere process of maturing would change them, and they would not come home just what they had been. Add to that the abnormal world they have been plunged into, the new philosophies they have had to assume or perish inwardly, the horrors and delights and strange, wonderful things they have experienced, and they are bound to be different people from those who went away.

They are rougher than they were. Killing is a rough business. Their basic language has changed from mere profanity to obscenity. More than anything else, they miss women. Their expressed longings, their conversation, their whole conduct show their need for female companionship, and the gentling effect of femininity upon man is conspicuous here, where it has been so long absent.

Our men have less regard for property than they were raised to have. Money value means nothing to them, either personally or in the aggregate; they are fundamentally generous, with strangers and with each other. They give or throw away their own money, and it is natural that they are even less thoughtful of bulk property than of their own hard-earned possessions. It is often necessary to abandon equipment they can't take with them; the urgency of war prohibits normal caution in the handling of vehicles and supplies. One of the most striking things to me about war is the appalling waste that is necessary. At the front there just isn't time to be economical. In war areas, where things are scarce and red tape still rears its delaying head, a man learns to get what he needs simply by requisitioning. It isn't stealing, it's the only way to acquire certain things. The stress of war puts old virtues in a changed light. We shall have to relearn a simple fundamental or two when things get back to normal. But what's wrong with a small case of requisitioning when murder is the classic goal?

Our men, still thinking of home, are impatient with the strange peoples and customs of the countries they now inhabit. They say that if they ever get home, they never want to see another foreign country. But I know how it will be. The day will come when they'll look back and brag about how they learned a little Arabic, and how swell the girls were in England, and how pretty the hills of Germany were. Every day their scope is broadening despite themselves, and once they all get back with their global yarns and their foreign-tinged views, I cannot conceive of our nation ever being isolationist again. The men don't feel very international right now, but the influences are at work and the time will come.

I can't say truthfully that they are very much interested in foreign affairs, outside of battle affairs, at this time. Of course, by digging, a person could find plenty of politically and internationally minded men in our Army—all the way from generals to privates—who do spend considerable time thinking of what is to come after the victory, and how we are to handle it. But the average guy's thoughts on the peace can be summed up, I believe, in a general statement that after this war is won, he wants it fixed so that it can't happen again, and he wants a hand in fixing it. He has no more conception of how it should be done than to say he supposes some kind of world police force is the answer.

The men have been well cared for in this war. I suppose no soldiers in any other war in history have had such excellent attention as our men overseas. The food is good. Of course we're always yapping about how wonderful a steak would taste on Broadway, but when a soldier is pinned right down he'll admit ungrudgingly that it's Broadway he's thinking about more than the steak, and that he really can't kick on the food. Furthermore, cooking is good in this war. Last time good food was spoiled by lousy cooking, but that is the exception this time. Of course, there are times in battle when the men live for days on nothing but those deadly, cold C rations out of tin cans, and even go without food for a day or two, but these are the crises, the exceptions. On the whole, we figure by the letters from home that we're probably eating better than you are.

A good diet and excellent medical care have made our Army a healthy one. Statistics show the men in the mass healthier today than they were in civilian life back home.

Clothing, transportation, mail, Army newspapers,

these are well provided for our men. Back of the lines they have Post Exchanges where they can buy cigarettes, candy, toilet articles and all such things. If they are in the combat zone, all these things are issued to them free.

Our fighting equipment is the only thing that at first didn't stand head and shoulders above everything issued to soldiers of any other country, and that is only because we weren't ready for war, and for two years we have been learning what is good and what is bad. Already many of our weapons are unmatched by any other country. Give us another year, and surely it can be said that our men are furnished better weapons, along with better food, medical care and clothing, than any other army.

Now we are in a lull and many of us are having a short rest period. I tried the city and couldn't stand it. Two days drove me back to the country, where everything seemed cleaner and more decent. I am in my tent, sitting on a newly acquired cot, writing on a German folding table we picked up the day of the big surrender. The days here are so peaceful and perfect they almost give us a sense of infidelity to those we left behind beneath the Tunisian crosses, those whose final awareness was a bedlam of fire and noise and uproar.

Here the Mediterranean surf caresses the sandy beach not a hundred yards away, and it is a lullaby for sleeping. The water is incredibly blue, just as we have always heard it was. The sky is a cloudless blue infinity, and the only sounds are the birds singing in the scrub bushes that grow out of the sand and lean precisely away from the sea. Little land terrapins waddle around, and I snared one by the hind leg with a piece of string and tied it in photographer Chuck Corte's tent while he was out, just for a joke. Then I found myself peeking in every few minutes to see how the captive was getting along, and he was straining so hard to get away that I got to feeling sorry for the poor little devil, so I turned him loose and ruined my joke.

An occasional black beetle strolls innocently across the sandy floor. For two hours I've been watching one of them struggling with a cigarette butt on the ground, trying to move it. Yesterday a sand snake crawled by just outside my tent door, and for the first time in my life I looked upon a snake not with a creeping phobia but with a sudden and surprising feeling of compassion. Somehow I pitied him because he was a snake instead of a man. I don't know why, for I feel pity for all men, too, because they are men.

It may be that the war has changed me, along with the rest. It is hard for anyone to analyze himself. I know that I find more and more that I wish to be alone, and yet contradictorily I believe I have a new patience with humanity that I've never had before. When you've lived with the unnatural mass cruelty that mankind is capable of inflicting upon itself, you find yourself dispossessed of the faculty for blaming one poor man for the triviality of his faults. I don't see how any survivor of war can ever be cruel to anything, ever again.

Yes, I want the war to be over, just as keenly as any soldier in North Africa wants it. This little interlude of passive contentment here on the Mediterranean shore is a mean temptation. It is a beckoning into somnolence. This is the kind of day I think I want my life to be composed of, endlessly. But pretty soon we shall strike our tents and traipse again after the clanking tanks, sleep again to the incessant lullaby of the big rolling guns. It has to be that way.

It may be I have unconsciously made war seem more awful than it really is. It would be wrong to say that it is all grim; if it were, the human spirit could not survive two and three and four years of it. There is a good deal of gaiety in wartime. Some of us, even over here, are having the time of our lives. Humor and exuberance still exist. As some soldier has said, the Army is good for one ridiculous laugh per minute.

I don't attempt to deny that war is vastly exhilarating. The whole tempo of life steps up, both at home and on the front. There is an intoxication about battle, and ordinary men can sometimes soar clear out of themselves on the wine of danger-emotion. And yet it is false. When we leave here to go on into the next battleground, I shall go with the greatest reluctance.

On the day of final peace, the last stroke of what we call the big picture will be drawn. I haven't written anything about the big picture because I don't know anything about it. I only know what we see from our worm's-eye view, and our segment of the picture consists only of tired and dirty soldiers who are alive and don't want to die; of long darkened convoys in the middle of the night; of shocked silent men wandering back down the hill from battle; of chow lines and Atabrine tablets and foxholes and burning tanks and Arabs holding up eggs and the rustle of high-flown shells; of jeeps and petrol dumps and smelly bedding rolls and C rations and cactus patches and uniforms greasy black from months of wearing; and of laughter, too, and anger and wine and lovely flowers and constant cussing. All these it is composed of; and of graves and graves and graves.

That is our war, and we will carry it with us as we go on from one battleground to another until it is all over, leaving some of us behind on every beach, in every field. We are just beginning with the ones who lie back of us here in Tunisia. I don't know whether it was their good fortune or their misfortune to get out of it so early in the game. I guess it doesn't make any difference, once a man has gone. Medals and speeches and victories are nothing to them anymore. They died and others lived and nobody knows why it is so. They died and thereby the rest of us can go on and on. When we leave here for the next shore, there is nothing we can do for the ones beneath the wooden crosses, except perhaps to pause and murmur, "Thanks, pal."

White crosses and a Star of David in an American cemetery near Béja, Tunisia, mark the final resting places of some of the first U.S. soldiers to fall in battle against Nazi Germany.

RAID ON REGENSBURG

BY LT. COL. BEIRNE LAY, JR., USAF

The copilot of one of the planes tells what it was like to take part in a long-range bombing mission, clash with enemy fighters and endure the suspense of the flight to a North African airfield in a damaged plane.

In the briefing room the Intelligence Officer of the bombardment group pulled a cloth screen away from a huge wall map. Each of the 240 sleepy-eyed combat-crew members in the crowded room leaned forward. There were low whistles. I felt a sting of anticipation as I stared at the red string on the map that stretched from our base in England to a pinpoint deep in southwestern Germany, then south across the Alps, through the Brenner Pass to the coast of Italy, then past Corsica and Sardinia and south over the Mediterranean to a desert airdrome in North Africa.

"Your primary," said the Intelligence Officer, "is Regensburg. Your aiming point is the center of the Messerschmitt One Hundred and Nine G aircraft- and engine-assembly shops. This is the most vital target we've ever gone after. If you destroy it, you destroy thirty percent of the *Luftwaffe*'s single-engine-fighter production. You fellows know what that means to you personally."

There were a few hollow laughs.

After the briefing I climbed aboard a jeep bound for the operations office to check up on my Fortress (B-17) assignment. The stars were dimly visible through the chilly mist that covered our blacked-out bomber station, but the weather forecast for a deep penetration over the Continent was good. In the office I looked at the crew sheet, where the lineup of the lead, low and high squadrons of the group was plotted for each mission. I was listed for a copilot's seat. While I stood there, and on the chance suggestion of one of the squadron commanders who was looking over the list, the Operations Officer erased my name and shifted me to the high squadron as copilot in the crew of a steady Irishman named Lieutenant Murphy, with whom I had flown before. Neither of us knew it, but that Operations Officer saved my life right there with a piece of rubber on the end of a pencil.

At 5:30 a.m., fifteen minutes before taxi time, a jeep drove around the five-mile perimeter track in the semidarkness, pausing at each dispersal point long enough to notify the waiting crews that poor local visibility would postpone the takeoff for an hour and a half. I was sitting with Murphy and the rest of our crew near the *Piccadilly Lily*. She looked sinister and complacent, squatting on her fat tires with scarcely a hole in her skin to show for the twelve raids behind her. The postponement tightened rather than relaxed the tension. Once more I checked over my life vest, oxygen mask and parachute, not perfunctorily, but the way you check something you're going to have to use. I made sure my escape kit was pinned securely in the knee pocket of my flying suit, where it couldn't fall out in a scramble to abandon ship. I slid a hunting knife between my shoe and my flying boot as I looked again through my extra equipment for the mission: water canteen, mess kit, blankets and English pounds for use in the Algerian desert, where we would sleep on the ground and might be on our own from a forced landing.

Murphy restlessly gave the *Piccadilly Lily* another once-over, inspecting ammunition belts, bomb bay, tires and oxygen pressure at each crew station. Especially the oxygen. It's human fuel, as important as gasoline, up where we operate. Gunners field-stripped their .50-calibers again and oiled the bolts. Our top-turret gunner lay in the grass with his head on his parachute, feigning sleep, sweating out his thirteenth start.

We shared a common knowledge that grimly enhanced the normal excitement before a mission. Of

---

German aircraft factories in the town of Regensburg go up in smoke after fierce bombing by Flying Fortresses of the U.S. 8th Air Force. Regensburg is located at the juncture of the Regen and Danube rivers in southern Germany.

the approximately 150 Fortresses who were hitting Regensburg, our group was the last and lowest, at a base altitude of 17,000 feet. That's well within the range of accuracy for heavy flak. Our course would take us over plenty of it. It was a cinch also that our group would be the softest touch for the enemy fighters, being last man through the gauntlet. Furthermore, the *Piccadilly Lily* was leading the last three ships of the high squadron—the tip of the tail end of the whole shebang. We didn't relish it much. Who wants a Purple Heart?

The minute hand of my wristwatch dragged. I caught myself thinking about the day, exactly one year ago, on August 17, 1942, when I watched a pitifully small force of twelve B-17's take off on the first raid of the 8th Air Force to make a shallow penetration against Rouen, France. On that day it was our maximum effort. Today, on our first anniversary, we were putting thirty times that number of heavies into the air—half the force on Regensburg, the other half on Schweinfurt, both situated inside the German Reich. For a year and a half, as a staff officer, I had watched the 8th Air Force grow under Maj. Gen. Ira C. Eaker. That's a long time to watch from behind a desk. Only ten days ago I had asked for and received orders to combat duty. Those ten days had been full of the swift action of participating in four combat missions and checking out for the first time as a four-engine pilot.

At 7:30 a.m. we broke out of the cloud tops into the glare of the rising sun. Beneath our B-17 lay English fields still blanketed in the thick mist from which we had just emerged. We continued to climb slowly, our broad wings shouldering a heavy load of incendiary bombs in the belly and a burden of fuel in the main and wing-tip tanks that would keep the Fortress afloat in the thin air of the upper altitudes for eleven hours.

From my copilot's seat on the right-hand side, I watched the white surface of the overcast, where B-17's in clusters of six to the squadron were puncturing the cloud deck all about us, rising clear of the mist with their glass noses slanted upward for the long climb to base altitude. We tacked onto one of these clutches of six. Now the sky over England was heavy with the weight of thousands of tons of bombs, fuel and men being lifted four miles straight up on a giant aerial hoist to the western terminus of a 20,000-foot elevated highway that led east to Regensburg. At intervals I saw the arc of a sputtering red, green or yellow flare being fired from the cabin roof of a group leader's airplane to identify the lead squadron to the high and low squadrons of each group. Assembly takes longer when you come up through an overcast.

For nearly an hour, still over southern England, we climbed, nursing the straining Cyclone engines in a 300-foot-per-minute ascent, forming three squadrons gradually into compact group stagger formations—low squadron down to the left and high squadron up to the right of the lead squadron—groups assembling into looser combat wings of two to three groups each along the combat-wing assembly line, homing over predetermined points with radio compass, and finally cruising along the air-division assembly line to allow the combat wings to fall into place in trail behind Brig. Gen. Curtis E. LeMay in the lead group of the air division.

Formed at last, each flanking group in position 1000 feet above or below its lead group, our fifteen-mile parade—unwieldy, but dangerous to fool with—moved east toward Lowestoft, point of departure from the friendly coast. From my perch in the high squadron in the last element of the whole procession, the air division looked like huge anvil-shaped swarms of locusts—not on dress parade, like the bombers of the *Luftwaffe* that died like flies over Britain in 1940, but deployed to uncover every gun and permit maximum maneuverability.

The English Channel and the North Sea glittered bright in the clear visibility as we left the bulge of East Anglia behind us. Up ahead we knew that we were already registering on the German radio-direction-finder screen, and that the sector controllers of the *Luftwaffe*'s fighter belt in western Europe were busy alerting their squadrons of Focke-Wulfs and Messerschmitts. I stole a last look back at cloud-covered England, where I could see a dozen spare B-17's, who had accompanied us to fill in for any abortives from mechanical failure in the hard climb, gliding disappointedly home to base.

I fastened my oxygen mask tighter and looked at the little ball in a glass tube on the instrument panel that indicated proper oxygen flow. It was moving up and down as I breathed, like a visual heartbeat, registering normal.

Already the gunners were searching. Occasionally the ship shivered as guns were tested with short bursts.

I could see puffs of blue smoke from the group close ahead and 1000 feet above us, as each gunner satisfied himself that he had lead poisoning at his trigger tips. The coast of Holland appeared in sharp black outline. I drew in a deep breath of oxygen. In the making was a death struggle between the unstoppable object and the immovable defense, every possible defense at the disposal of the Reich, for this was a deadly penetration to a hitherto inaccessible and critically important arsenal of the German Fatherland.

At 10:08 a.m. we crossed the coast of Holland, south of The Hague, with our group of Fortresses tucked in tightly and within handy supporting distance of the group above us, at 18,000 feet. But our loosely linked column looked too long, and the gaps between combat wings too wide. As I squinted into the sun, gauging the distance to the barely visible specks of the lead group, I had a recurrence of that sinking feeling before the takeoff—the lonesome foreboding that might come to the last man about to run a gauntlet lined with spiked clubs. The premonition was well founded.

At 10:17, near Woensdrecht, I saw the first flak blossom out in our vicinity, light and inaccurate. A few minutes later, at approximately 10:25, a gunner called, "Fighters at two o'clock low." I saw them, climbing above the horizon ahead of us to the right—a pair of them. For a moment I hoped they were P-47 Thunderbolts from the fighter escort that was supposed to be in our vicinity, but I didn't hope long. The two F.W. 190's turned and whizzed through the formation ahead of us in a frontal attack, nicking two B-17's in the wings and breaking away in half-rolls right over our group. By craning my neck up and back, I glimpsed one of them through the roof glass in the cabin, flashing past at a 600-mile-an-hour rate of closure, its yellow nose smoking and small pieces flying off near the wing root. The guns of our group were in action. The pungent smell of burned cordite filled the cockpit and the B-17 trembled to the recoil of nose and ball-turret guns. Smoke immediately trailed from the hit B-17's, but they held their stations.

Here was early fighter reaction. The members of the crew sensed trouble. There was something desperate about the way those two fighters came in fast right out of their climb, without any preliminaries. Apparently our own fighters were busy somewhere farther up the procession. The interphone was active

for a few seconds with brief admonitions: "Lead 'em more". . ."Short bursts". . ."Don't throw rounds away" . . ."Bombardier to left waist gunner, don't yell. Talk slow."

Three minutes later the gunners reported fighters climbing up from all around the clock, singly and in pairs, both F.W. 190's and Me. 109-G's. The fighters I could see on my side looked like too many for sound health. No friendly Thunderbolts were visible. From now on we were in mortal danger. My mouth dried up and my buttocks pulled together. A coordinated attack began, with the head-on fighters coming in from slightly above, the nine- and three-o'clock attackers appearing from about level and the rear attackers from slightly below. The guns from every B-17 in our group and the group ahead were firing simultaneously, lashing the sky with ropes of orange tracers to match the bursts squirting from the 20-mm. cannon muzzles in the wings of the German single-seaters.

I noted with alarm that a lot of our fire was falling astern of the target—particularly from our hand-held nose and waist guns. Nevertheless, both sides got hurt in this clash, with the entire second element of three B-17's from our low squadron and one B-17 from the group ahead falling out of formation on fire, with crews bailing out, and several fighters heading for the deck in flames, with some pilots lingering behind under the dirty yellow canopies that distinguished their parachutes from ours.

As we swung slightly outside with our squadron, in mild evasive action, I got a good look at that gap in the low squadron where three B-17's had been. Suddenly I bit my lip hard. The lead ship of that element had pulled out, on fire, and exploded before anyone bailed out. It was the ship to which I had been originally assigned.

I glanced over at Murphy. It was cold in the cockpit, but sweat was running from his forehead and over his oxygen mask from the exertion of holding his element in tight formation and from the strain of the warnings that hummed over the interphone and of what he could see out of the corners of his eyes. He caught my glance and turned the controls over to me for a while. It was an enormous relief to concentrate on flying instead of sitting there watching fighters aiming between your eyes. Somehow, the attacks from the rear, although I could "see" them through my ears via the interphone, didn't bother me. I guess it was because there was a slab of armor plate behind my back, and I couldn't watch them, anyway.

I knew that we were in a lively fight. Every alarm bell in my brain and heart was ringing a high-pitched warning. But my nerves were steady and my brain working. The fear was unpleasant, but it was bearable. I knew that I was going to die, and so were a lot of others. What I didn't know was that the real fight, the bombardment of *Luftwaffe* 20-mm. cannon shells, hadn't really begun. The largest and most savage fighter resistance ever yet encountered was rising to stop us at any cost, and our group was the most vulnerable target.

A few minutes later we absorbed the first wave of a hailstorm of individual fighter attacks that were to engulf us clear to the target in such a blizzard of bullets and shells that a chronological account is difficult. It was at 10:41, over Eupen, that I looked out the window after a minute's lull and saw two whole squadrons, twelve Me. 109's and eleven F.W. 190's, climbing parallel to us as though they were on a steep escalator. The first squadron had reached our level and was pulling ahead to turn into us. The second was not far behind. Several thousand feet below us were many more fighters, their noses cocked up in a maximum climb. Over the interphone came reports of an equal number of enemy aircraft deploying on the other side of the formation.

For the first time I noticed an Me. 110 sitting out of range on our level out to the right. He was to stay with us all the way to the target, apparently radioing our position and weak spots to fresh enemy formations waiting farther down the road.

At the sight of all these fighters, I had the distinct feeling of being trapped—that the enemy had been tipped off or at least had guessed our destination and was set for us. We were already through the Germans' fighter belt. Obviously, they had moved a lot of squadrons back in a fluid defense in depth, and they must have been saving up some outfits for the inner defense that we didn't know about. The life expectancy of our group seemed definitely limited.

Swinging their yellow noses around in a U-turn,

This B-24 Liberator bomber of the U.S. 15th Strategic Air Force has burst into flames after a direct hit by enemy flak while on a mission over northern Italy. Seconds later a wing crumpled, and the plane plunged to earth. Two crewmen managed to bail out of the burning plane before it crashed.

328

the twelve-ship squadron of Me. 109's came in from twelve to two o'clock in pairs. The main event was on. I fought an impulse to close my eyes, and overcame it.

A shining silver rectangle of metal sailed past over our right wing. I recognized it as a main-exit door. Seconds later, a black lump came hurtling through the formation, barely missing several propellers. It was a man, clasping his knees to his head, revolving like a diver in a triple somersault, shooting by us so close that I saw a piece of paper blow out of his leather jacket. He was evidently making a delayed jump, for I didn't see his parachute open.

A B-17 turned gradually out of the formation to the right, maintaining altitude. In a split second it completely vanished in a brilliant explosion from which the only remains were four balls of fire—the fuel tanks—that were quickly consumed as they fell earthward.

I saw blue, red, yellow and aluminum-colored fighters. Their tactics were running fairly true to form, with frontal attacks hitting the low squadron and rear attackers going for the lead and high squadrons. Some of the Germans shot at us with rockets, and an attempt at air-to-air bombing was made with little black time-fuse sticks dropped from above, which exploded in small gray puffs off to one side of the formation. Several of the F.W.'s did some nice deflection shooting on side attacks from 500 yards at the high group, then raked the low group on the breakaway at closer range with their noses cocked in a sideslip, to keep the formation in their sights longer in the turn. External fuel tanks were visible under the bellies or wings of at least two squadrons, shedding light on the mystery of their ability to tail us so far from their bases.

The manner of the assaults indicated that the pilots knew where we were going and were inspired with a fanatical determination to stop us before we got there. Many pressed attacks home to 250 yards or less, or bolted right through the formation wide out, firing long twenty-second bursts, often presenting point-blank targets on the breakaway. Some committed the fatal error of pulling up instead of going down and out. More experienced pilots came in on frontal attacks with a slower rate of closure, apparently throttled back, obtaining greater accuracy. But no tactics could halt the tight formations of our Fortresses, nor save the single-seaters from paying a terrible price.

Our airplane was endangered by various debris. Emergency hatches, exit doors, prematurely opened parachutes, bodies and assorted fragments of B-17's and enemy fighters breezed perilously past us in the slipstream.

On we flew through the cluttered wake of a desperate air battle, where disintegrating aircraft were commonplace and the white dots of sixty parachutes in the air at one time were hardly worth a second look. The spectacle registering on my eyes became so fantastic that my brain turned numb to the actuality of the death and destruction all around us. Had it not been for the squeezing in my stomach, I might easily have been watching an animated cartoon in a movie theater.

The minutes dragged on into an hour. And still the fighters came. Our gunners called coolly and briefly to one another, dividing up their targets, fighting for their lives with every round of ammunition—and our lives and the formation. The tail gunner called that he was out of ammunition. We sent another belt back to him. Here was a new hazard. We might run out of .50-caliber slugs before we reached the target.

I looked to both sides of us. Our two wingmen were gone. So was the element in front of us—all three ships. We moved up into position behind the lead element of the high squadron. I looked out again on my side and saw a cripple, with one prop feathered, struggle up behind our right wing with his bad engine funneling smoke into the slipstream. He dropped back. Now our tail gunner had a clear view. There were no more B-17's behind us. We were the last.

I took the controls again for a while. The first thing I saw when Murphy resumed flying was a B-17 turning slowly out to the right, its cockpit a mass of flames. The copilot crawled out of his window, held on with one hand, reached back for his parachute, buckled it on, let go and was whisked back into the horizontal stabilizer of the tail. I believe the impact killed him. His parachute didn't open.

Still no letup. The fighters queued up like a breadline and let us have it. Each second of time had a cannon shell in it. The strain of being a clay duck in the wrong end of that aerial shooting gallery became almost intolerable. Our *Piccadilly Lily* shook steadily with the fire of its .50's, and the air inside was wispy with smoke. I checked the engine instruments for the thousandth time. Normal. No injured crew members yet. Maybe we'd get to that target, even with our re-duced firepower. Seven Fortresses from our group had already gone down, and many of the rest of them were badly shot up and shorthanded because of wounded crew members.

Almost disinterestedly I observed a B-17 pull out from the group preceding us and drop back to a posi-tion about 200 feet from our right wing tip. Her right wing-tip tanks were on fire, and had been for half an hour. Now the smoke was thicker. Flames were lick-ing through the blackened skin of the wing. While the pilot held her steady, I saw four crew members drop out the bomb bay and execute delayed jumps. Another bailed from the nose, opened his parachute prema-turely and nearly fouled the tail. Another went out the left waist-gun opening, delaying his opening for a safe interval. The tail gunner dropped out of his hatch, apparently pulling the rip cord before he was clear of the ship. His parachute opened instantane-ously, barely missing the tail, and jerked him so hard that both his shoes came off. He hung limp in the harness, whereas the others had shown immediate signs of life, shifting around in their harnesses. The Fortress then dropped back in a medium spiral and I did not see the pilots leave. I saw the ship, though, just before it trailed from view, belly to the sky, its wing a solid sheet of yellow flame.

Now that we had been under constant attack for more than an hour, it appeared certain that our group was faced with extinction. The sky was still mottled with rising fighters. Target time was thirty-five minutes away. I doubt if a man in the group visualized the possibility of our getting much farther without 100 percent loss. Gunners were becoming exhausted and nerve-tortured from the nagging strain—the strain that sends gunners and pilots to the hospital. We had been the aiming point for what seemed to be most of the *Luftwaffe*. It looked as though we might find the rest of it primed for us at the target..

Near the initial point, at 11:50 a.m., 1½ hours after the first of at least 200 individual fighter attacks, the pressure eased off, although hostile planes were still in the vicinity. A curious sensation came over me. I was still alive. It was possible to think of the target. Of North Africa. Of returning to England. Almost idly, I watched a crippled B-17 pull over to the curb and drop its wheels and open its bomb bay, jettisoning its bombs. Three Me. 109's circled it closely but held

their fire, even when being shot at by a B-17 from which the crew was bailing out. But I doubt if sports-manship had anything to do with it. They hoped to get a B-17 down fairly intact.

And then our weary, battered column, short twenty-four bombers but still holding the close formation that had brought the remainder through by sheer air dis-cipline and gunnery, turned in to the target. I knew that our bombardiers were grim as death while they synchronized their sights on the great Me. 109 shops lying below us in a curve of the winding Danube, close to the outskirts of Regensburg. Our B-17 gave a slight lift and a red light went out on the instrument panel. Our bombs were away. We turned from the target toward the snow-capped Alps. I looked back and saw a beautiful sight—a rectangular pillar of smoke rising from the Me. 109 plant. Only one burst was over and into the town. Even from this great height I could see that we had smeared the objective. The price? Cheap. Two hundred airmen.

A few more fighters pecked at us on the way to the Alps and a couple of smoking B-17's glided down toward the safety of Switzerland, about forty miles distant. A town in the Brenner Pass tossed up a lone burst of futile flak. Flak? There had been lots of flak in the past two hours, but only now did I recall having seen it, a sort of side issue to the fighters. Brigadier General LeMay, who had taken excellent care of us all the way, circled the air division over a large lake to give the cripples, some flying on three engines and many trailing smoke, a chance to rejoin the family. We approached the Mediterranean in a gradual de-scent, conserving fuel. Out over the water we flew at low altitude, unmolested by fighters from Sardinia or Corsica, waiting through the long hot afternoon hours for the first sight of the North African coastline. The prospect of ditching, out of gasoline, and the sight of other B-17's falling into the drink, seemed trivial mat-ters after the vicious nightmare of the long trial across southern Germany. We had walked through a high valley of the shadow of death, not expecting to see another sunset, and now I could fear no evil.

With red lights showing on all our fuel tanks, we landed at our designated base in the desert, after eleven hours in the air. I slept on the ground near the wing and, waking occasionally, stared up at the stars. My radio headset was back in the ship. And yet I could hear the deep chords of great music.

"OPERATION HUSKY": THE SICILY CAMPAIGN

This record of the Allies' victory in Sicily, the first step in the fight to drive Hitler and his Nazi armies from Europe, has been edited by S. L. A. Marshall from U.S. Army files.

Following the victory in Tunisia, Allied forces prepared for two months (May 13–July 9, 1943) to invade and conquer Sicily. "Operation Husky" was aimed, as Prime Minister Churchill said, at "Axis-held Europe's soft underbelly along the Mediterranean," and its purpose was to knock Italy out of the war. Sicily was defended by ten Italian divisions and two German, the 15th Panzer and Hermann Goering Panzer Divisions.

General Dwight D. Eisenhower, in supreme command, assigned the mission of invading Sicily to the Allied 15th Army Group composed of the British Eighth and the American Seventh Armies, under Gen. Hon. Sir Harold Alexander. The Seventh, commanded by Lt. Gen. George S. Patton, was formed of the 1st, 3d, 9th and 45th Infantry, the 82d Airborne and 2d Armored Divisions. The Eighth Army, commanded by Gen. Sir Bernard L. Montgomery, was composed of six infantry divisions, three brigades and an airborne division. A Canadian infantry division was brought in to keep liaison between British and American armies.

The final plan of attack called for the Americans, sailing from North Africa, to land on the south central coast of Sicily, mop up the western half of the island and swing east along the northern coast to Mount Etna, where the British would join them after landing on the southeast and advancing up the eastern coast. Then the Allied armies would trap the enemy in the northeastern corner of Sicily, cutting off any escape to Italy through the Strait of Messina. British and American airborne infantry, equal to a division in strength, were to land in rear areas and seize enemy airfields. Because of weather and pilot error, these troops were dropped thirty to fifty miles from their objectives (July 9–10), and failed to capture the airfields.

The night of D day, July 10, 3000 vessels carried 160,000 men with 1800 artillery pieces and 600 tanks from Africa to Sicily. The American troops, seasick in choppy waters, landed under cover of naval artillery and secured beachheads at Licata, Gela and Scoglitti (July 11). Next day around Gela 100 Nazi tanks, spearheads of a counterattack on three sides, threatened to drive the Americans into the sea; the resistance of the 1st Infantry Division repulsed the counterattack. East of Gela the 45th Division captured the Acate airfield. This defeat cost the enemy eighty planes and control of the skies over Sicily.

The British landed from Cape Passero to Syracuse on July 10, on the eastern end of a 100-mile front. Two days later they occupied the port of Syracuse, then advanced north along the coast, slowing down as they neared Catania. The Canadians fanned westward to link with the Americans at Ragusa.

Opposition to the Americans declined after their push north to Canicatti. The enemy held the British on his left and fell back toward Mount Etna in the northeast from his right and center, leaving only one division to cover the withdrawal. This was the strategy the Germans had adopted in Tunisia. Their aim was to delay and contain the Allies in Sicily and thus prevent attacks elsewhere in the Mediterranean.

The American forces moved rapidly over difficult country. Infantry and tanks pushed west to take Agrigento on July 22, and swept north across Sicily to seize Palermo on July 30. The 2d Armored and 3d Infantry Divisions, spearheaded by the 45th Division, moved east along the northern coast to the enemy's main line of resistance, which ran southeast from a point just west of Santo Stefano di Camastra to Troina.

Meanwhile the U.S. 1st Infantry Division and the Canadians advanced over the hills of central Sicily to capture Nicosia and Agira on July 29. Here the mountains rose to 5000 feet, and the ridge of Troina lay behind a valley in which the enemy had demolished the road and built numerous blocks. Across this valley and up the slopes the 1st Infantry Division attacked Troina in the bitterest assaults of the Sicilian campaign, lasting from July 29 to August 5. Bombings

An American armored car—its crew on the alert for trouble—rolls down a war-torn street in the dock area of Palermo, Sicily. Elsewhere in the city, wildly cheering crowds greeted the men of the U.S. Seventh Army as liberators rather than conquerors. Palermo surrendered without a fight.

(Below) An American medic gives blood plasma to a wounded GI in Sant' Agata, Sicily. Sadness, apprehension and despair are reflected on the faces of the townspeople huddled in the doorway. A hard fought rearguard action by the retreating Germans caused many Allied casualties.

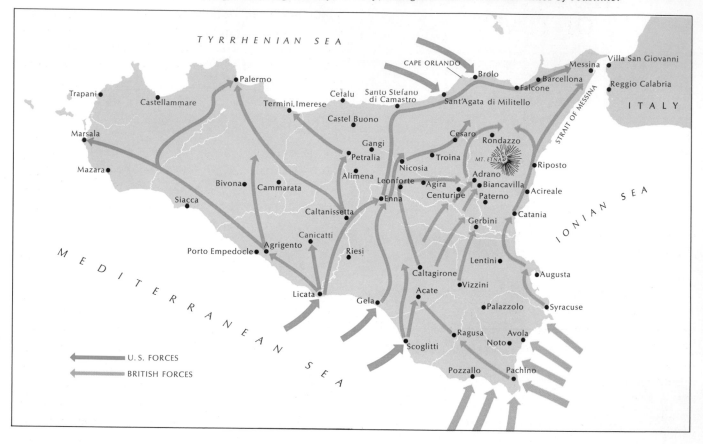

and heavy shelling compelled the enemy to withdraw. At the same time, the British outflanked Catania on the eastern coast with the capture of Paterno. The Axis center broke at Adrano and enemy forces fell back into a triangle whose apex was Messina.

The German withdrawal was hastened by a new strategy that contributed to the subsequent surrender of Italy. Hitler and Mussolini had been told by their generals on July 19 that because the Italian peninsula could not easily be defended against Allied naval power, the Axis must evacuate Italy to the Po Valley, where a defense could be erected for the industrial north. The enemy forces were therefore ordered to withdraw from Sicily across the Strait of Messina.

Toward this point American and British forces pressed from the west and south. Twice an American force landed in the enemy rear along the northern coast. The first time, the German line was cracked in a surprise assault by the units which captured Sant' Agata di Militello on August 11–12. Another amphibious assault in battalion strength was made around Cape Orlando to cut the enemy off from his communi-

cations with Randazzo. Our troops suffered heavy losses until the rest of the regiment drove through to their support at Brolo. Meanwhile American units pressed northeast from the interior to capture Randazzo on August 13.

It was now a race to trap the Nazis before they could evacuate all their forces. Combat teams leapfrogged one another along three routes to Messina. Our air and naval forces harassed the enemy's attempt to cross the narrow four-mile Strait of Messina. But the Germans evacuated some 100,000 troops. When the American 3d Infantry Division reached Messina, followed quickly by British units, the enemy had departed into Italy, leaving behind large stores of matériel.

Sicily was conquered in thirty-eight days. About 100,000 prisoners were taken, and 12,000 of the enemy were killed or wounded. Among the weapons captured or destroyed were 267 planes and 188 tanks. Allied casualties were some 25,000, including 7400 American losses. The conquest of Sicily sped the collapse of Italy and made the Mediterranean Sea more secure for Allied convoys. Italy lay open to invasion.

THE INVASION OF ITALY

BY MAJ. GEN. J. F. C. FULLER

The grim, inch-by-inch battle of the Allies to occupy the "boot" of Italy is told by one of the foremost analysts of military strategy.

Of all the greater Continental powers, Italy is the nearest, strategically, to being an island. Size for size, her coastline is the longest and her land frontier the most secure of any; therefore she is more open to sea than to land attack. Clearly, then, it is more profitable for an invading sea power operating from the west or south to land in Liguria than in Calabria, because the great natural obstacles protecting the valley of the Po—Italy's vital area of operations—are the Ligurian and Etruscan Apennines, some thirty miles in breadth. An invasion by way of Calabria, on the other hand, means that the invader will have to advance up the entire length of the Apennines, a distance of 600 miles. Further, as nearly every river, gully, ravine and spur runs at right angles to this central backbone, each forms a natural line of defense, which, if held, will have to be stormed frontally.

Though it would appear that General Eisenhower realized the advantages of the Ligurian line of approach, shortage of aircraft carriers and landing craft forced the Calabrian line upon him. Even then, as Gen. George C. Marshall, Chief of Staff of the U.S. Army, informs us, throughout the campaign which followed, "shortage of assault shipping and landing craft continued to haunt operations." The result was a long-drawn-out and exhausting campaign.

General Hon. Sir Harold Alexander was given command of the expedition, which comprised two armies, the British Eighth, under Gen. Sir Bernard L. Montgomery, and the Fifth, part British and part American, under Lt. Gen. Mark W. Clark. The Eighth was to land at Reggio Calabria, and when it had drawn the Germans into the toe of Italy, the Fifth was to land behind the Germans at Salerno and cut them off. Salerno was selected because it lay just within range of fighter air cover. If enough aircraft carriers had been available, the whole operation could have been rendered far more elastic; but as this was not the case, the Germans could not fail to gauge their enemy's plan. The invasion of the Eighth Army, which was prepared by a sustained air assault on the enemy's lines of communication and railway stations, was fixed for one hour before dawn on September 3, 1943. But the Germans, having fathomed their enemy's plan, were already rapidly retreating up the toe.

On the evening of September 8, the Italian Government formally surrendered, and the main elements of the Italian Fleet sailed for Malta. The naval base at Taranto was occupied by the British 78th Division and 1st Airborne Division on the 9th. And at 4 a.m. the same day, after a heavy preliminary bombardment and strongly supported by aircraft and naval gunfire, the Fifth Army began to land on the Salerno beaches. On the 11th it was heavily attacked by the Germans, powerfully supported by the *Luftwaffe,* and the situation became critical; the American cruisers *Philadelphia* and *Savannah* and the British battleship *Warspite* were hit by glider bombs.

One reason for this failure was that fighter planes based on Sicily could carry only sufficient gasoline to permit them to fight for fifteen minutes over the beachheads. Another was that, in the words of General Marshall, "the shortage of shipping made it impossible for General Alexander to bring his own heavy armor into the fight until the British 7th Division started to unload on D plus 5 [September 14]." At this time General Eisenhower informed General Marshall, "We are very much in the touch-and-go stage of this operation. . . . We have been unable to advance and the enemy is preparing a major counterattack. . . . I am using everything we have bigger than a rowboat. . . . In the present situation our great hope is the Air Force. . . ."

During the next three days—September 12–14—the entire tactical and strategical air forces were turned on the enemy. His troop concentrations were broken up and his columns raked heavily by machine-gun fire. On the 15th the crisis was over, and it is not too much to say that air power saved the Fifth Army. On the 16th the British Eighth Army linked up with the

(Above) *A Negro company keeps pressure on the enemy by a stream of mortar fire. This unit eliminated a number of Nazi machine-gun nests during the fighting near Massa, Italy.*

(Right) *U.S. B-25 bombers, on their way to batter German positions near Cassino, fly over clouds of volcanic smoke and ash from Mount Vesuvius during an eruption in March 1944.*

Fifth at a point some forty miles southeast of Salerno.

On September 27 Foggia was captured, and on October 1 Naples was occupied. Thereupon Field Marshal Albert Kesselring withdrew his army to the Volturno. On September 20 Sardinia had been evacuated by the Germans, as was Corsica on October 4. In the middle of October, Kesselring, abandoning the Volturno, fell back on the Garigliano River.

From now on the campaign developed into what Gen. Sir Henry Maitland Wilson describes as a "slow, painful advance through difficult terrain against a determined and resourceful enemy, skilled in the exploitation of natural obstacles by mines and demolitions." The main reason for the slowness was the inability on the part of the Allied armies to turn their enemy's flanks. On this question, General Wilson writes: "After the juncture of Fifth and Eighth Armies below Salerno, several small amphibious operations to turn the enemy's flanks had been considered; one such operation executed on the Eighth Army front at Termoli had proved encouragingly successful." But, "The position of landing craft within the theater was most difficult. Distribution and availability of craft had by now become a permanently limiting factor in planning all amphibious operations, not only in the Mediterranean but throughout all the Allied theaters of war."

There was another reason for this stalemate. Two campaigns were being fought at the same time, one on the ground and the other in the air. The building up at Foggia of the strategic bombing force, which was not under the command of General Eisenhower, consumed approximately 300,000 tons of shipping, during what, General Marshall points out, "were the most critical months of the Italian campaign. So heavy were the shipping requirements of the 15th Strategic Air Force . . . that the buildup of our ground forces in Italy was considerably delayed."

So long as the Germans did not intend to do more than delay their enemy, position after position was methodically taken. First the Volturno, next the Trigno, then the Sangro, until, on the Garigliano, Kesselring decided to stand.

The position he occupied was one of the strongest in Italy, and General Eisenhower rightly decided, while the Germans were pinned down by a frontal attack on the Garigliano, to turn their position by landing the American VI Corps in the Anzio-Nettuno area, some thirty miles south of Rome. From there a

successful advance inland would cut Kesselring's communications, and force him either to retire or surrender. Then, on December 24, Eisenhower, as well as General Montgomery, Air Chief Marshal Sir Arthur W. Tedder and Lt. Gen. Omar N. Bradley, was ordered to England to take over preparations for the invasion of France. Eisenhower was replaced by General Wilson; Lt. Gen. Sir Oliver Leese assumed command of the Eighth Army; and Lt. Gen. Ira C. Eaker took over the Mediterranean Allied Air Forces.

On the night of January 17 the Battle of the Garigliano was launched. Soon after the river was crossed, the left of the attack petered out around the village of Castelforte. The right, finding it impossible to establish its bridges, failed altogether.

On January 22, when the battle was in its last stage, the VI Corps—50,000 American and British troops—under command of Maj. Gen. John P. Lucas, landed, virtually unopposed, on the Anzio beaches at 2 a.m. The invasion came as a complete surprise; for although Kesselring knew that an expedition was in preparation at Naples, apparently he thought it was destined for Civitavecchia, Gaeta or Terracina. Instead of pushing on toward the Alban Hills, to magnify the initial surprise and create a scare epidemic in the rear of the German front on the Garigliano, Lucas set to work to consolidate his beachheads. The inevitable result was that Kesselring, realizing that his communications were not immediately threatened, contained the flanks and spearheads of the VI Corps and built up a strong counterattack force. Thus, within a few days of its landing the Allied expedition was bunkered, and would remain so for many months.

This dismal failure was followed by a series of three battles, all fought to gain the small town of Cassino, which was dominated by Monastery Hill, upon which stood the famous Benedictine Abbey of Monte Cassino.

The first of these battles was launched on January 29 and by February 4 was fought to a standstill. The blame for the failure was debited to the Abbey instead of to the hill upon which it stood; therefore it was decided to destroy the building. The decision was made public and freely discussed, with the inevitable result that when the blow fell, the Germans were fully prepared to meet it. Because the Abbey was so obviously a bomb trap and because Monastery Hill provided the Germans with innumerable observation posts, it is highly probable that Kesselring, an able soldier, would occupy the Abbey itself. Since then, it has been stated by the monks who lived there that the Abbey was never used by the Germans as an observation post.

On February 14 Allied aircraft scattered leaflets on the Abbey, warning the monks and refugees to leave it. The next day 229 bombers dropped 453 tons of bombs upon the Abbey and destroyed it. But all that this bombing did was to turn the Abbey from a building into a fortress, because the defense of a rubble heap mixed with ruins is an easier and more comfortable operation than the defense of a building. Not only is there plenty of material at hand to construct strongpoints with, but there are no roofs and floors to fall upon the defenders.

Next day Cassino and its surroundings were bombed again; yet it was not until the early hours of February 18 that the infantry attack was launched. The artillery bombardment opened at nine o'clock on the night of the 17th, and for five hours shells were poured on the rubble heaps at the rate of 10,000 per hour. At 2 a.m. February 18 the infantry went forward. Having made little progress, General Alexander wisely decided on the 19th to cut his losses and break the battle off.

Had the lesson been learned that saturation bombardments are seldom a shortcut to victory? No! For as Christopher Buckley, *Daily Telegraph* war correspondent, informs us: "The air attack on the Abbey had failed to produce the expected results; therefore the number of bombers and the weight of the bomb load must be increased. . . . The sledgehammer must be larger this time. Like the plagues of Egypt our assault upon Cassino was to gather in intensity until Pharaoh Kesselring saw fit to yield." This is corroborated by General Wilson himself. He states that "the Combined Chiefs of Staff were concerned over the influence which prolongation of the present situation in Italy might have on the overall strategic position. They felt that the concentration of nearly 3000 bombers and fighters on vital restricted areas would have a determining effect on the enemy provided it was related to vigorous offensive action on land."

Therefore, in the face of all evidence, the dogma that weight of metal could so stun the defenders that all the ground forces would have to do was merely to occupy the paralyzed target held the field. This is endorsed by General Eaker, for on March 15, the day the third battle of Cassino was launched, he is reported

to have said: "The efficiency of the bombing would be determined by the extent of the ground forces' advance." And not waiting for proof, he added: "Let the Germans ponder that what we have done on the Ides of March to the fortress of Cassino we will do to every stronghold where they elect to stand."

This time we will leave it to Lt. Gen. Jacob L. Devers, Deputy Allied Commander, to describe in a letter, written on March 24, the attack which took place on March 15:

"On March 15 I thought we were going to lick it by the attack on Cassino and advance up the Liri Valley. We used air, artillery and tanks, followed closely by infantry. I witnessed the attack from across the valley. It got off to a start with excellent weather. The bombing was excellent and severe, and the artillery barrage which followed it and lasted for two hours was even more severe and accurate, with 900 guns participating. Two groups of medium bombers, followed by eleven groups of heavies, followed by three groups of mediums, started on the minute at 8:30 a.m. and closed at noon, the groups coming over every ten minutes up to nine o'clock and thereafter every fifteen minutes. In spite of all this, and with excellent support all afternoon with dive bombers and artillery fire, the ground forces have not yet gained their first objective. . . .These results were a sobering shock to me. The infantry had been withdrawn in the early morning hours five miles to the north of Cassino. When they arrived back in the town of Cassino at approximately one o'clock close behind the barrage, the Germans were still there, were able to slow up their advance and even to reinforce themselves during the night by some unaccountable means."

One of the main items in the plan was to drop during the first three hours 1400 tons of bombs in an area of about a square mile; but such is the inaccuracy of bombing on even so large a target that the Eighth Army commander's caravan headquarters, standing three miles from Cassino, was demolished. More extraordinary still, an entire formation of heavy bombers dropped the whole of its load on the French Corps headquarters at Venafro, which it mistook for Cassino, though the two towns are twelve miles apart!

For eight days the battle continued. Then, little having been accomplished, a halt was called. This fiasco was followed by a period of true strategic bombing, directed by and in the main carried out by the

Tactical Air Force, against the German road and rail communications. By the end of March, twenty-five cuts on an average were made daily, and by mid-May they rose to seventy-five and even more. There can be no doubt that this sustained attack on the enemy's supply system, which not only interrupted his traffic but restricted him to night movements, did him far more damage than had any of the saturation bombing.

The Second Battle of the Garigliano was mounted and launched on May 11. This time Cassino itself was left alone.

The battle was opened by a night artillery bombardment of forty minutes of extreme intensity on a front of from thirty to forty miles. This time the infantry assault succeeded, partly on account of the air preparation and partly because the German winter line had now served its purpose; and, no longer supported by his ally, bad weather, Kesselring saw that the time to withdraw had come. On the night of May 16 he began to disengage his army; on the 17th, Cassino, turned from the rear, passed into British hands; and on the 18th, Monastery Hill was occupied by the Poles. On June 4 the Allied forces entered Rome, and two days later the news was flashed around the world that France had been invaded by the Americans and the British—a strategic second front had been opened.

Struggle for Italy: September 3, 1943. Successful Allied landings were made at Reggio Calabria, Taranto and Salerno. Stiff resistance by German defenders together with the rugged terrain combined to slow up the Allied advance. The fighting lasted twenty months.

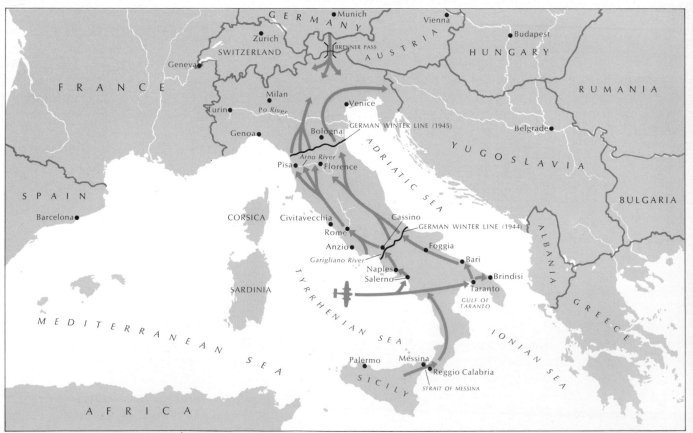

(Right) *The town of Cassino lies in ruins after a pounding by Fifth Army artillery on February 6, 1944, while on the heights the ancient Benedictine monastery stands unharmed. The Abbey was later flattened by Allied air bombing.*

(Left) *The liberation of Rome: Tanks of the U.S. Fifth Army form an incongruous scene as they lumber past the ancient Coliseum on June 4, 1944. Rome was the first of the Axis capital cities to fall; its capitulation moved President Franklin D. Roosevelt to remark, "One down and two to go."*

(Right) *Day of reckoning: Within hours of the liberation of Rome, local Fascist leaders are rounded up and brought in for trial by armed members of the resistance movement. The infamous Regina Coeli prison was stormed, and while prison guards stood aside, political prisoners were released.*

(Below) *Jubilant Italians give these GI's a joyous welcome as they gather around the Americans' jeep. Fascism was dead in the southern half of Italy, and the Germans were on the run. But many more months of hard fighting for the Americans and their Allies were to pass before Italy was finally free.*

The Germans had been driven from North Africa and pushed
up the boot of Italy. But the rest of Hitler's European empire
remained to be conquered. Here the armies of the Free World met
an enemy who fought hard and well. American soldiers are shown
blasting a German pillbox on the Cotentin Peninsula in France.

ASSAULT ON FORTRESS EUROPE
END OF THE THIRD REICH

OVERLORD: THE ALLIES' TRIUMPH IN NORMANDY

BY KENNETH S. DAVIS

The 6th of June, 1944—the date marks the crossing of the English Channel by the greatest seaborne invasion force the world has ever known. Kenneth Davis, assigned to the campaign as special correspondent, tells the story of the planning, the vast buildup of supplies, the crucial decisions and the action as the Allied armies stormed ashore on the beaches of Normandy. On that fateful day, all America and her Allies waited breathlessly for the first news of the secured landing.

Despite Allied victories in Italy in May and early June of 1944, the major focus of the war in Europe was upon a theater where none save air battles were fought but where impended perhaps the greatest battle, all things considered, in the history of the world. Everyone knew that it was coming. Concrete evidence of it weighed so heavily upon the British Isles that they would have been sunk into the sea, according to a wisecrack of the time, if they had not been held up by masses of barrage balloons.

In hundreds of hedge-bordered English fields, by late spring, were parks of camouflaged tanks, trucks, bulldozers, ducks (amphibious trucks), jeeps and self-propelled guns. Dozens of airfields were jammed with planes lined up beside the runways—more than 10,000 war planes in all. Dozens of ports large and small were jammed with shipping—well over 5000 ships and landing craft, including six battleships, twenty-two cruisers, and hundreds of destroyers, gun-boats, corvettes and other fire-support craft. Moved or moving into staging areas and embarkation ports were more than 1 million picked troops especially trained for the forthcoming operation, half of them American and half British or Canadian, organized in thirty-seven divisions for the amphibious assault.

Awesome indeed was this unprecedented concentration of power, and everyone saw it as the outward manifestation of what would be by far the most complicated plan ever made for a single operation of war. Eight hundred typewritten pages were required for a terse summary of the overall naval plan alone. A complete set of actual naval orders, with the necessary maps, weighed 300 pounds. Equally bulky were the plans for ground, air and logistic operations.

The final plan, "Operation Overlord," called for landings on five beaches, each three or four miles in length, each consisting of gentle slopes of hard sand or gravel up which wheeled and tracked vehicles could easily move—along some sixty miles of Normandy shore from near the mouth of the Orne River north of Caen to the eastern coast of the Cotentin Peninsula, at whose northern tip was Cherbourg, the first major Allied objective. The three eastern landings, on beaches designated Sword, Juno and Gold, immediately north of Caen and Bayeux, were to be made by troops of the British Second Army. The two western landings, on beaches designated Omaha (north of the village of Trévières) and Utah (due east of Ste.-Mère-Église), were to be made by troops of the American First Army. These landings were to be made at dawn. Preceding them by several hours, in the darkness of night (though it was to be a moonlit night), would be landings by airborne troops at either end of the assault front—British glider and parachute forces along the Orne River in tactical support of Sword and the general operation against Caen; Americans of the 82d and 101st Airborne Divisions in the vicinity of Carentan and Ste.-Mère-Église, in tactical support of Utah and the general offensive toward Cherbourg.

To deceive the enemy as to the time and place of the main assault, pinning down significant numbers of his troops far from the Normandy battleground, an elaborate cover plan was worked out. It centered on the creation of a fictitious U.S. Army group, assembled along the southeastern coast of England for assault across the narrowest part of the Channel, the Pas de Calais (Strait of Dover). False information concerning this group was fed into German espionage channels through known enemy agents; dummy landing craft appeared in large numbers in the Thames estuary and along the eastern coast; hundreds of dummy tanks were placed where German air reconnaissance could photograph them; huge though actually deserted tent encampments were laid out in East Anglia; a radio network was set up to simulate the traffic of an army group preparing to invade; and the pattern of air bombardment of France was carefully arranged to indicate that the Pas de Calais area was being softened up for the impending assault. Thus the Germans were to be led to believe for weeks after the initial landings that the Normandy operation was in the nature of a large-scale feint and that the main blow was yet to fall in the north. The German Fifteenth Army, nineteen divisions strong, would sit in watchful idleness on the Calais coast while German forces in Normandy were gradually overwhelmed.

Once the lodgments were made on the Normandy shore, the Allied troops were to move inland as rapidly as possible, linking up the five landing areas behind a continuous and expanding front. Victory along this front must then depend upon victory in the battle for reinforcement (all thirty-seven of the initial Allied divisions were to be on the Continent within seven weeks after D day) and for supply (a single division in battle must be furnished with at least 600 tons of supplies per day).

For this last, elaborate preparations were made, including the creation of two artificial prefabricated harbors, twenty underwater pipelines to pump 1 million gallons of gasoline a day from England to France and the building of a complete railway system to be transported across the Channel and set up in a remarkably short time in replacement of air-shattered systems of northern France. There was detailed planning, also, to make the most efficient use of the French road system for the movement of troops and supplies, transforming major highways into one-way traffic arteries of limited access and egress. An outcome of this planning would be the "Red Ball Express," soon to be the most famous traffic movement in the world—trucks rolling at high speed from Normandy toward Paris and beyond in all kinds of weather day and night, undeterred, almost unslowed, by the blackout.

Nor was gigantic buildup the sole source of superior material strength soon to be exerted over the enemy in France. The process of building up within the Allied fighting organism was accompanied by an accelerated process of tearing down within the Nazis'—and this, too, was a result of the plan as it began to be applied in early April. For two months thereafter, on every day of permissible weather, Allied air forces conducted sweeping raids upon the French railroad system in the north, with devastating effect. Railroad marshaling yards were ruined. Bridges were destroyed. (Of the two dozen bridges across the Seine between Paris and the sea, eighteen were completely broken and three more damaged.) Some 1500 of 2000 engines in northern France were immobilized. The whole region by the end of May had become a "railway desert."

Simultaneously the coastal radar network designed to give the Nazis warning of an Allied approach to France had been virtually paralyzed, some five sixths of the installations between the Pas de Calais and the Gulf of St.-Malo having been destroyed from the air. Moreover, the *Luftwaffe,* already weakened and forced again into battle against great odds, had been further reduced in strength—so much so that its operations were no longer a serious hazard to the invasion. Thus as Allied arteries of supply and reinforcement were opened and expanded, those of the Nazis were closed and severed; and as Allied eyes and ears were increased in their range of perception, those of the Nazis were blinded and deafened.

This might have gravely hampered the defensive strategy believed to be favored by German Field Marshal Gerd von Rundstedt, commander of all enemy forces in the West. Rundstedt had no faith in the efficacy of such fixed defenses as the much-touted "Atlantic Wall," decreed by Hitler in 1942 for construction from Norway to Spain. Even if it had been completed—and it yet remained in considerable part a propaganda myth, though construction on it had been rushed fanatically and frantically along the French Atlantic coast these last months—it could not defeat a truly determined effort by the Allies to establish a beachhead or beachheads and to expand them inland for several miles. Rundstedt was said to be convinced of this. His strategy was said to concede it. What he would count on, if he had his way, was a large mobile strategic reserve. This, held back in the interior in a position to strike in any of several directions, could be used to fight the decisive battle, not at the time and place of the initial landings (the Anglo-Americans, after all, were at liberty to choose these), but later, when enough troops and matériel were ashore to make their destruction catastrophic.

Despite his position at the top of the Western command, Rundstedt was not in actual control of German strategy in this theater. Nominally under him as Commander in Chief of German Army Group B was Gen. Sir Bernard L. Montgomery's old antagonist of the desert, Field Marshal Erwin Rommel, the most popular and audacious of German generals, who had been sent to France the previous November to reorganize the Channel defenses. Rommel not only disagreed completely with Rundstedt's strategic ideas, he had also obtained Hitler's approval of his own.

It was Rommel's conviction that Allied dominance of the air, coupled with the immense weight of naval and artillery bombardment which the Allies could lay down behind the lines, would deny to a strategic reserve the mobility it must have to be effective. Indeed, this reserve might be almost destroyed from the air as it was strung out along roads leading to the front under skies from which the *Luftwaffe* had been driven. Hence every available ounce of German strength must be massed at or immediately behind the coast, ready to be hurled at the invader while he was yet straddled and vulnerable between the two elements of water and earth. Later would be too late; later the enemy would be invincible. "The war will be won or lost on the beaches," Rommel declared. "The first twenty-four hours of the invasion will be decisive."

Direction of the final planning, preparation and execution of by far the greatest amphibious operation in the history of the world was vested in an organization remarkable in all respects and unique in some, though precedence for most of its features was provided by the Allied Force Headquarters (AFHQ) through which Gen. Dwight D. Eisenhower had commanded Mediterranean operations. Eisenhower had been actually functioning as Supreme Commander in England for nearly a month before he received, on February 12, 1944, the directive from the Combined Chiefs of Staff that formally assigned to him this command.

"You will enter the Continent of Europe," the directive said, "and, in conjunction with the other United Nations, undertake operations aimed at the heart of Germany and the destruction of her Armed Forces." The following day Eisenhower issued his first General

Men and supplies pour ashore on Omaha Beach for the Allied assault on the Cotentin Peninsula. Anchored offshore are some of the ships in the gigantic Allied fleet that made D day possible, while barrage balloons provide limited protection against Luftwaffe *attack.*

Order, which established the Supreme Headquarters, Allied Expeditionary Force (SHAEF), and on the day after that, he publicly announced the names of his principal subordinates. Deputy Supreme Commander was British Air Chief Marshal Sir Arthur W. Tedder. General Montgomery, Commander of the British Ground Forces, was scheduled for top operational command during the opening phase in Normandy; under him would be Lt. Gen. Omar N. Bradley, Commander of the American Ground Forces. British Adm. Sir Bertram H. Ramsay was commander of the combined naval forces, with Adm. Harold R. Stark commanding U.S. Navy forces in the theater. The combined air forces were commanded by British Air Chief Marshal Sir Trafford Leigh-Mallory; under him, U.S. Lt. Gen. Carl Spaatz commanded U.S. Air Forces, with Lt. Gen. James H. Doolittle commanding the powerful U.S. 8th Air Force. Eisenhower's Chief of Staff was (as in the Mediterranean) U.S. Lt. Gen. Walter Bedell ("Beetle") Smith.

By May 30 every contingency that could be foreseen and controlled by human prescience and ingenuity and by vast material resources had been prepared for. Every known risk deemed unavoidable had been

carefully calculated and accepted. D day was set for Monday, June 5, with the understanding that it might be postponed to June 6 or 7. H hour was to vary from 6:30 a.m. to 7:45 a.m. on the five beaches, depending on the tides. The day and hour were determined by a balancing of tidal and moonlight conditions. Moonlight was wanted for the night drop of airborne units: experience had shown that utter darkness decreased the efficiency of such operations. A relatively low tide was wanted to facilitate the clearance of paths through mines and obstacles that would be too deep under water for such work as the tide rose. Landing troops must move up over a greater width of beach under fire than they would have had to do at higher tide, but this was among the risks accepted.

There yet remained one great factor to condition all the rest in this enterprise—one difficult to predict with accuracy and wholly impossible to control. That factor was the weather.

The long-range forecast, generally optimistic on May 29, was pessimistic by Friday, June 2, though the Supreme Commander on that day ordered some invasion units to set sail on the following morning from ports on the Irish Sea. They must do so if they

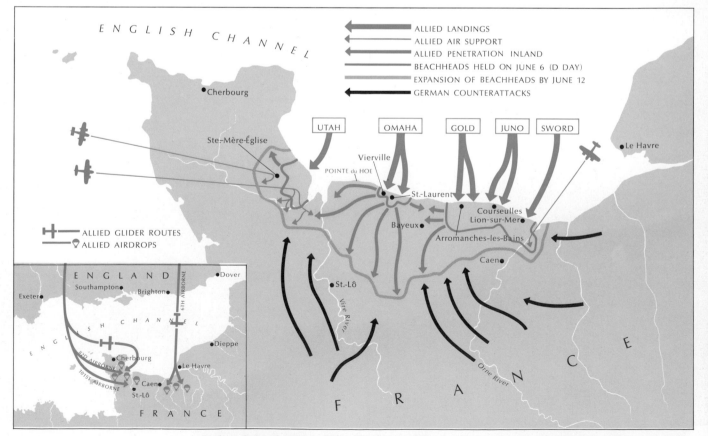

D day: June 6, 1944. The Allied invasion of France began at 1:30 a.m. when a massive airdrop was made behind Hitler's coastal defenses, followed some five hours later by the landing of Allied assault troops on five bullet-swept Normandy beaches.

were to reach rendezvous points for a June 5 D day.

On Saturday evening it appeared almost certain that D day must be postponed. There was developing (in early June!) a "typical December depression"—a series of low-pressure areas marching eastward across the North Atlantic, bringing with them high winds and rough seas and low clouds which would make landings difficult, naval fire support inaccurate and air support impossible. These conditions would prevail through the next forty-eight hours, and there appeared little chance that a "benevolent high" would move in to improve things during the twenty-four hours after that. Nevertheless, it was decided not to make the final decision on postponement until the four o'clock meeting on the morning of June 4. At that meeting Eisenhower moved D day forward to Tuesday, June 6, and ordered a meeting at 9:15 that evening for review of this decision.

The crucial conference began with a gloomy report on conditions prevailing on the coast of France. These were precisely what the Meteorological Committee had predicted they would be; had the June 5 date been adhered to, despite the forecast, a major disaster would almost certainly have resulted. But then the weather-man made a surprising announcement. There had been "some rapid and unexpected developments in the situation," he said; they permitted a ray of hope to lighten the darkness. A high-pressure area, previously stationary off the coast of Spain, was beginning to push northeastward. It should produce a gradual clearing of the skies and a moderation of the wind over Channel and assault areas throughout the next day, and clear or only partly cloudy skies over moderate seas on the morning of June 6. In all probability this interruption of foul weather would be brief, however. The skies would probably again be cloudy by noon of June 6, presaging a resumption of rain and wind on June 7.

Quick, nervous discussion followed. If the American Naval Task Force sailing for Omaha and Utah Beaches was to reach its destination by H hour of a June 6 D day, its commander, Rear Adm. Alan G. Kirk, must receive firm sailing orders within half an hour; moreover, a further postponement must be for a minimum of forty-eight hours, because of the necessity to refuel ships.

The actual decision must be made at once, and General Eisenhower alone had to make it. He sat in silence for what seemed to the others a long time.

Men of the U.S. 1st Division, part of the first D-day assault wave, wade toward Omaha Beach. Troops on the shore are pinned down by fire. Enemy mines, mortars and machine guns took a fearful toll.

When he spoke it was as if he talked, at first, to himself.

"The question is," he said, "how long can you hang this operation on the end of a limb and let it hang there?"

If he postponed for forty-eight hours, the weather, according to present indications, might be just as bad. Nor would conditions of tide and moon be quite right on June 8. Tidal conditions would not be right again, as a matter of fact, until June 19—and then, even if the weather was good, and no one could predict this, the airborne troops would have to drop in darkness instead of in the light of the moon. Nor was it reasonable to conclude that security could be maintained much beyond the present hour.

Again Eisenhower spoke, his face drawn. "I am quite positive we must give the order," he said slowly. "I don't like it, but there it is." He glanced at the clock on the wall, and at the faces of his commanders. "I don't see how we can do anything else." And so the orders went out to Kirk and the other Naval commanders. The mighty movement toward France began.

But even this was not the absolutely final decision. Another conference, to review weather conditions and confirm or retract the earlier orders, was set for four o'clock next morning, June 5.

The caravan that was Eisenhower's living quarters shuddered in gusts of wind, and rain needled into his face as if shot from a gun, when the Supreme Commander came down the aluminum steps and gravel path toward his waiting car. But when he arrived at Allied Headquarters he and the others found that the weather was developing as predicted six hours before.

"OK," Eisenhower said. "We'll go. . . ."

Of all the words in the English language, one of the least widely known in 1944, though destined for a considerable popular currency in 1945, was the word "implosion" (it is defined as a bursting in rather than a bursting out). The reverse of "explosion," it may be used to describe the kind of movement of forces that occurred in the storm-tossed English Channel from early morning until after dark on June 5, 1944. Energies originally scattered over thousands of miles—shaped into active or passive agencies of war in myriads of factories, farms, forests, mines, oil fields, mills, shipyards and military and naval installations throughout the United States and Great Britain—had been brought within the confines of this island, then gathered more closely together in southern England and at last focused as concentrated units of power in Plymouth, Dartmouth, Torquay, Portland, Southampton, Portsmouth and some fifteen or twenty other ports on England's southern shore and along the Bristol Channel. From these ports the power units were thrust out upon the sea in more than 2700 ships organized into fifty-nine convoys sailing through carefully mine-swept lanes into a rendezvous area of five miles' radius, nicknamed Piccadilly Circus, south of the Isle of Wight. Thus the implosion.

In "Piccadilly Circus" the mighty armada was formed into five powerful task forces, one for each of the assault beaches, and each provided with a buoy-marked minesweep lane that became two lanes halfway across the Channel, one lane for the fast convoys and one for the slow. Down these, in the brief darkness comprising night in that latitude at that season, the ships sailed over rough seas under a wrack of cloud that, flying in the wind, was torn asunder every now and then to permit the moon to show her face. A lucky moon, thought many who saw her in glimpses from the decks of pitching, rolling ships that night. A silver goddess who smiled upon this enterprise and blessed it. For the whole of this vast and intricate crossing was going almost precisely according to the plan, veritable miracles of seamanship were being accomplished, and no sign appeared that the enemy had any inkling of what was going forward.

With few and minor exceptions, every transport and cargo vessel ticketed for the initial assault—every LST (landing ship, tank) and LCT (landing craft, tank)—was in its designated place off the coast of Normandy by the assigned hour in the darkness before the dawn of June 6. Landing craft were lowered and net ladders slung over the sides of bucking ships. Down these clambered heavy-laden engineers and signalmen and infantrymen—down into waiting boats which, loaded, began to circle as their crews awaited the signal to head for shore. The preliminary naval bombardment began; German batteries replied tentatively, searchingly, then vehemently as definite targets were found. The predawn twilight was full of ominous noise.

Dawn came. The signal came. The tempo of naval gunfire increased, shells now bursting so thickly on and immediately behind the beaches as to hide the French coastal landscape with thick curtains of smoke and dust. The landing craft ceased their circling; they pushed forward in straight lines and at carefully regulated speeds against the vaunted, the long-feared "Atlantic Wall."

These first events were essentially the same before every landing area. Thereafter events differed as the landing areas differed in physical feature and in quantity and quality of defense. Let us look briefly at each in turn.

First, the westernmost landing, at Utah Beach, made by the U.S. VII Corps. The Utah landing, because the Germans could so easily block the beach exits (four causeways across a two-mile-wide flooded area), appeared in prospect the most difficult and hazardous of the five. In retrospect, it became the easiest and least costly. For this, two things were chiefly responsible— one of them an element of the plan, the other a happy accidental deviation from the plan. By the time the first seaborne units touched down in the shallow waters and upon the yellow sand at Utah's edge, American soldiers of the 82d and 101st Airborne Divisions had been fighting for hours upon the soil of France (see pages 357–361). The paratroopers had quickly dominated the countryside for as far as seven miles inland from the beach, drawing upon themselves defensive fire which would otherwise have been concentrated upon the seaborne landings.

The first infantry assault wave, elements of the 4th Division brought in by twenty landing craft, waded ashore at 7 a.m., receiving scarcely any enemy fire. This surprised them. So did their failure to recognize any of the terrain features designated on their maps, in terms of which their tactics had been planned. It was Brig. Gen. Theodore Roosevelt, Jr., who first realized that the landing craft had somehow slipped well over a mile south of the site aimed for—a site where, they later learned, the Germans had built strong defenses, including two casemated batteries that might have slaughtered the initial assault with an enfilading fire. Still without a field command following his relief in Sicily as Second-in-Command of the 1st Division, Roosevelt had requested and obtained permission to go ashore with the first wave. He quickly helped battalion commanders to adjust tactics to the terrain actually facing them and saw to it, a little later, that incoming landing craft were diverted from designated beach segments then under heavy fire to this safe one. Thus there was full capitalization of a fortunate error. The causeway exits were soon reached, their in-

land ends later secured by the airborne troops, and by nightfall of D day nearly all units had achieved their D-day objectives. Some thirty-six square miles of French soil had been liberated at a cost of less than 200 infantry casualties.

Far different was the story of Omaha Beach (see pages 362–371). It had been carefully prepared for maximum defense by the Germans, aided by a coastal terrain eminently suited to their purpose. A gently sloping strip of sand some 300 yards in width was bounded landward by a natural shingle seawall topped, a few yards farther on, by an artificial seawall—of concrete through half its three-mile length, of piling through the rest, above which ran a level, grassy stretch 200 yards wide, ending in moderately high bluffs. On the level stretch were two tiny villages whose houses, those the Germans had not demolished, were transformed into defensive strongpoints. The bluffs, edging a plateau extending inland, were much too steep to be climbed by wheeled or tracked vehicles, so that the only exits from the landing area were four ravines, up each of which ran an unsurfaced road or dirt track. The roads had been heavily mined; they were covered by rifle and machine-gun emplacements.

Since tactical surprise was here essential to the prevention of overwhelming enemy reinforcement, preliminary air and naval bombardment had not been long or intense enough to silence prepared defenses. From these defenses the enemy poured a withering fire upon landing craft as they touched down and upon the troops who floundered out of them into shallow water, where many not killed by shot or shell or mine were drowned when they were wounded or stumbled under their heavy burdens. All seemed chaos and confusion.

Most of the tanks that were supposed to precede the first infantry wave ashore and cover it with their guns never made it: they sank when canvas "bloomers," designed to float them in, collapsed or were destroyed by German shells. Wave organization was disrupted; units hit the beach as much as two miles from the segments assigned them. In consequence of these and other misfortunes, nearly all the Americans who survived the bloody approach spent all D-day morning huddled helplessly, fearfully, under the seawall and behind beach obstacles and stalled vehicles. There was no forward movement at all. For long hours of agony the issue was in doubt. By noon, Bradley, aboard U.S.S. *Augusta,* was seriously considering the possibility that the troops would have to be withdrawn and the Omaha force diverted to Utah.

But even as he considered this dire possibility, the issue was beginning to be decided against it, not by plan or high command, but by the naked courage of a few individual men. Small groups of these men began to blast holes in the barbed wire and, often with their mangled bodies, cleared lanes through the minefields until at last, in the late afternoon, infantrymen managed a general advance up the bluffs and vehicles began to move off the beach up the ravines. Even then a determined German counterattack would have liquidated the beachhead. Instead, by nightfall the German shore defenses were liquidated, the invasion front had been pushed a mile to a mile and a half inland, and reinforcements and supplies were coming onto Omaha in massive quantities. It became evident that V Corps (the 1st and 29th Infantry Divisions) would stay ashore. The cost had been high: some 2000 men killed, wounded or missing.

In the British sector things went better than at Omaha, though considerably less easily than at Utah. The British 6th Airborne Division—5300 paratroopers and airborne infantry—dropped on moonlit fields, woods and marshes northeast of Caen at the same time as the American 82d and 101st Airborne dropped on the Cotentin Peninsula. Their mission was to seize bridges over the Caen Canal and Orne River and knock out a formidable battery that ranged on Sword Beach. It was only partly accomplished, owing to badly missed paratrooper drop zones and the failure of some portions of the glider supply buildup. Nevertheless, at the price of 650 casualties, the division was approximately as successful as its American counterparts in easing the seaborne landings. These last began about an hour later than at Omaha and Utah because there were, before Gold in the west, Juno in the center and Sword in the east, reefs and patches of quicksand that had to be submerged by a higher tide to permit the passage of boats and amphibious vehicles and men afoot wading the shallows from sea to shore. The extra time was well employed by the Royal Navy. The British warships had two full daylight hours (instead of half an hour of full daylight, as the American Navy had) in which to shell shore installations before the first assault wave touched down. The shelling, to which rocket fire was added immediately after the first landing, proved effective; and on the British beaches, in

marked contrast to Omaha, a majority of the tanks assigned to support the infantry got ashore with the initial wave and fulfilled their assignment.

This was a three-division infantry assault—the British 50th Infantry, the Canadian 3d Infantry and the British 3d—incorporating some Free French units. It encountered less resistance and suffered fewer casualties than had been feared. Later, resistance stiffened. But the only determined German counterattack of the day failed (it was made by the 21st Panzer Division), and by nightfall the British 50th and Canadian 3d were linked up in a continuous front four to six miles inland from Gold and Juno. The British 3d had driven inland approximately the same distance from Sword and had made contact with the 6th Airborne at its left, though it remained separated from the Canadians at its right by a thin wedge—a single German battalion driven to the sea by the otherwise fruitless counterattack. All this was satisfactory. It was not, however, as deep a penetration as had been hoped for. Bayeux, a D-day objective, yet remained in German hands (it would be taken the next day, virtually undamaged). So did Caen, which General Montgomery had confidently predicted he would take before D day's sun went down.

But the overall picture was bright from the Allied point of view. Complete tactical surprise had, after all, been achieved. Rommel, the Allies were soon to learn, had not even been in France at the beginning of the twenty-four hours he had said would be decisive for the war. On the assumption that the predicted weather would make a major cross-Channel operation impossible, he had gone to Germany on June 4 to celebrate his wife's birthday and to confer with Hitler. He did not arrive back at his headquarters until six o'clock in the evening of D day.

Some 156,000 Allied fighting men had been established on nearly eighty square miles of Normandy soil at a total casualty cost of about 11,000; and Allied dominance of the skies, immediate shipping capacity, and prepared buildup made it unlikely in the extreme that the Germans could push this force back into the sea. "Operation Overlord," with all its fantastic risks and dangers, was succeeding.

Rows of wounded Allied troops lie on stretchers on the open deck of a U.S. Coast Guard LCT (landing craft, tank) off the Normandy shore. These troops were later transferred to a transport ship for the trip across the Channel to England.

Glider-borne U.S. assault troops, their faces blackened for night camouflage, tensely await a landing behind the German lines in the predawn hours of D day. Some 14,600 air sorties were flown during the first day of the Allied invasion of the Normandy beaches.

AIRDROP: BEGINNING OF THE LONGEST DAY

BY CORNELIUS RYAN

At a few minutes past midnight on D day, the first wave of Allied assault troops touched down on French soil by parachute and by glider. Hitler's fortress had been penetrated by men who had vaulted, airborne, over its wall. The story of this remarkable airdrop is told by Cornelius Ryan, who was aided in the preparation of his book The Longest Day *by Reader's Digest researchers and editors.*

Although the Germans didn't recognize it, the appearance of paratroopers on the Cotentin Peninsula was the clue to the fact that D day had begun. These first American troopers—120 of them—were pathfinders. They had been trained in a special school set up by Brig. Gen. James M. ("Jumpin' Jim") Gavin, Assistant Division Commander of the 82d Airborne. Their mission was to mark drop zones in a fifty-square-mile area back of Utah Beach for the full-scale American paratrooper and glider assault that would begin one hour later. "When you land," Gavin had told them, "you will have only one friend: God."

The pathfinders ran into difficulties at the very beginning. German flak was so intense that the planes were forced off course. Only thirty-eight of the 120 pathfinders landed on their targets. The remainder came down miles off.

Private Robert Murphy of the 82d landed in a garden in Ste.-Mère-Église. As he headed out of the garden and started toward his drop zone, lugging his portable radar set, he heard a burst of firing off to his right. He was to learn later that his buddy, Pvt. Leonard Devorchak, had been shot at that moment. Devorchak,

who had sworn to "win a medal today just to prove to myself that I can make it," may have been the first American to be killed on D day.

All over the area pathfinders tried to get their bearings. Moving silently from hedgerow to hedgerow, bulky with guns, mines, lights and fluorescent panels, they set out for rendezvous points. They had barely one hour to mark the drop zones for the full-scale American assault.

Fifty miles away, at the eastern end of the Normandy battlefield, six planeloads of British pathfinders and six R.A.F. bombers towing gliders swept in over the coast. The sky stormed with vicious flak, and antiaircraft batteries at Caen hung ??? ??? when the jumps began.

Two of the British pathfinders plunged out of the night sky squarely onto the lawn before the headquarters of Lt. Gen. Josef Reichardt, commanding officer of the German 711th Division. Reichardt was playing cards when the planes roared over, and he and the other officers rushed out—just in time to see the two Britons land.

It would have been hard to tell who were the more astonished, the Germans or the pathfinders. Reichardt could only blurt out, "Where have you come from?" To which one of the pathfinders, with all the aplomb of a man who has just crashed a cocktail party, replied, "Awfully sorry, old man, but we simply landed here by accident."

Reichardt hurried into his headquarters and picked up the phone. "Get me Fifteenth Army Headquarters," he said. But even as he waited for the call to be put through, the drop-zone lights in both the British and American sectors began to flash on. Some of the pathfinders had found their zones.

In St.-Lô, at the headquarters of the German LXXXIV Corps, the next level of command below Seventh Army Headquarters, the staff had gathered in Gen. Erich Marcks's room to honor him with a surprise birthday party. Standing in a little group around their stern-faced, one-legged general (he had lost a leg in Russia), the officers came to attention. Stiffly raising their glasses, they drank his health, blissfully unaware that, as they did so, thousands of British paratroopers were dropping on French soil.

For most of the paratroopers it was an experience they would never forget. Private Raymond Batten landed in a tree. His chute caught in the branches and he hung there slowly swaying back and forth in his harness, fifteen feet from the ground. It was very still in the wood, and as Batten pulled out his knife to cut himself down he heard the abrupt stutter of a Schmeisser machine pistol nearby. A minute later there was a rustling of underbrush beneath him. Batten had lost his Sten gun and he hung there helplessly, not knowing whether it was a German or another paratrooper moving toward him. "Whoever it was came and looked up at me," Batten recalls. "All I could do was to keep perfectly still and he, probably thinking I was dead, as I hoped he would, went away."

Batten got down from the tree as fast as he could and headed toward the edge of the wood. On the way he found the corpse of a young paratrooper whose parachute had failed to open. Next, as he moved along a road a man rushed past him shouting crazily, "They got my mate! They got my mate!" And finally, catching up with a group of paratroopers heading toward the assembly point, Batten found himself beside a man who seemed to be in a state of complete shock. The soldier strode along, looking neither to left nor right, totally oblivious of the fact that the rifle which he gripped tightly in his right hand was bent almost double.

Weird things happened to these early invaders. Lieutenant Richard Hilborn, of the 1st Canadian Battalion, remembers that one paratrooper crashed through the top of a greenhouse, "shattering glass all over the place and making a hell of a lot of noise," but he was out and running before the glass had stopped falling. Another landed, with pinpoint accuracy, in a well. Hauling himself up hand over hand on his shroud lines, he set out for his assembly point as though nothing had happened.

The most sinister enemy in these opening minutes of D day was not man, but what man had done with nature. In the British zone, at the eastern end of the Normandy battlefield, Rommel's anti-paratroop precautions paid off well: he had caused the Dives Valley to be flooded, and the waters and swamps were death-traps. The number of men who died in these wastes will never be known. Survivors say that the marshes were intersected by a maze of ditches seven feet deep, four feet wide and bottomed with sticky mud. A man plunging into one of these ditches, weighed down with guns and heavy equipment, was helpless. Many drowned with dry land only a few yards away.

In the square of Ste.-Mère-Église everybody looked up, transfixed. Then the German guns in the town began firing and the roaring was on top of them. The aircraft swept in through a crisscrossing barrage of fire. The planes' lights were on. They came in so low that people in the square instinctively ducked and the airplanes cast "great shadows on the ground and red lights seemed to be glowing inside them."

In wave after wave the formations flew over—the first planes of the biggest airborne operation ever attempted: 925 planes carrying 13,000 men of the U.S. 101st and 82d Airborne Divisions, heading for six drop zones all within a few miles of Ste.-Mère-Église. Lieutenant Charles Santarsiero was standing in the door of his plane as it passed over. "We were about four hundred feet up," he remembers, "and I could see fires burning and Krauts running about. All hell had broken loose. Flak and small-arms fire were coming up and our guys were caught right in the middle of them."

The troopers tumbled out of their planes, one after the other. Caught by a heavy wind, Pvt. John Steele saw that instead of landing in a lighted drop zone, he was heading for the center of a town that seemed to be on fire. Then he saw German soldiers and French civilians running frantically about. Most of them, it seemed to Steele, were looking up at him. The next moment he was hit by something that felt "like the bite of a sharp knife." A bullet had smashed into his foot. Then Steele saw something that alarmed him even more. Swinging in his harness, unable to veer away, he was heading straight toward the church steeple at the edge of the square.

Above Steele, Pfc. Ernest Blanchard saw the maelstrom of fire coming up all around him. The next minute he watched, horrified, as a man floating down beside him "exploded and disintegrated before my eyes," presumably a victim of the explosives he was carrying. Blanchard began desperately to swing on his risers, trying to swerve from the mob in the square below. But it was too late. He landed with a crash in one of the trees. Around him men were being machine-gunned to death. There were shouts, yells, screams and moans—sounds that Blanchard would never forget. Frantically Blanchard sawed at his harness. Then he dropped out of the tree and ran in panic, unaware that he had also sawed off the top of his thumb.

Steele now hung just under the eaves of the church, his parachute draped over the steeple. He heard the shouts and the screams. He saw Germans and Americans firing at each other in the square and the streets. And he saw, on the roof only a few yards away from him, German machine gunners firing at everything in sight. Steele decided that his only hope lay in playing dead. He hung so realistically "dead" in his harness that Capt. Willard Young of the 82d, who passed by during the height of the fighting, would never forget "the dead man hanging from the steeple." Steele was to dangle there for two hours before being taken captive by the Germans.

The mighty airborne armada was still droning ceaselessly overhead. Thousands of men were jumping for the drop zones northwest of the town, and between Ste.-Mère-Église and the Utah invasion area. On them hung the fate of the whole Utah Beach operation.

The Americans worked against staggering odds. The two divisions were critically scattered. Only one regiment—the 505th—fell accurately. Sixty percent of all equipment was lost, including most of the radios, mortars and ammunition. Worse still, many of the men were lost. The route of the planes was from west to east across the north-jutting peninsula and it took just twelve minutes to cross the peninsula. Hundreds of men, heavily weighted with equipment, jumped too early and fell into the treacherous swamps. Many drowned—some in less than two feet of water. Others, jumping too late, fell into the English Channel.

Corporal Louis Merlano landed on a sandy beach in front of a sign reading, ACHTUNG MINEN! He had been the second man in his group to jump. As he lay on the beach trying to get his breath he heard screams in the distance—they came from the last eleven men from his plane, who were at that moment drowning in the Channel.

Merlano got off the beach fast, ignoring mines. He climbed over a barbed-wire fence and ran for a hedgerow. Someone else was already there; Merlano didn't stop. He ran across a road and started to climb a stone wall. Just then he heard an agonized cry behind him. He whirled around. A flame thrower was hosing the hedgerow he had just passed, and outlined in the flame was the figure of a fellow paratrooper.

Americans came together in the night in countless small fields and pastures, drawn by the sound of a toy cricket. Their lives depended on a few cents' worth of metal fashioned in the shape of a child's snapper. One snap of the cricket had to be answered by a double snap. Two snaps required one in reply. On these signals men came out of hiding, from trees and ditches, around the sides of buildings, to greet one another. Major General Maxwell D. Taylor, commander of the 101st, and a bareheaded rifleman met at the corner of a hedgerow and warmly hugged each other. Some paratroopers found their units right away. Others saw strange faces in the night and then the familiar, comforting sight of the tiny American flag stitched above the shoulder patch. Lost men joined with small groups made up of men from different companies, battalions and regiments. Many troopers of the 82d were led by 101st officers and vice versa.

Hundreds of men found themselves in small fields, surrounded on all sides by tall hedgerows. The fields were silent little worlds, isolated and scary. In them every shadow, every rustle, every breaking twig was the enemy. Lieutenant Jack Tallerday moved down along the side of a hedgerow with his little group of men fanning out behind him. Soon they heard and then saw a group coming toward them. Tallerday snapped his cricket twice and thought he heard an answering click. "As our two groups approached each other," Tallerday says, "it was quite evident by their helmets that they were Germans." And then there occurred one of those curious incidents that happen in war. Without firing a shot, each group silently walked past the other, in a kind of frozen shock, until the darkness obliterated the figures as though they had never existed.

All over Normandy this night, paratroopers and German soldiers met unexpectedly. Three miles from Ste.-Mère-Église, Lt. John Walas almost tripped over a German sentry who was in front of a machine-gun nest. For a terrible moment, the men stared at each other. Then the German fired a shot at Walas at point-blank range. The bullet struck the bolt mechanism of the Lieutenant's rifle, which was directly in front of his stomach, nicked his hand and ricocheted off. Both men turned and fled.

Major Lawrence Legere talked his way out of trouble. Legere was leading a little group of men toward the rendezvous point. Suddenly he was challenged in German. He knew no German but he was fluent in French. In the darkness of the field he posed as a young farmer and explained in French that he had been visiting his girl and was on his way home. As he talked, he was fingering a grenade. He yanked

(Top left) A U.S. combat team vaults out the door and rushes into action after the glider has landed on French farmland. Their mission is to attack the Germans from the rear, disrupt their communications, seize strategically important roads and bridges, and cause as much general havoc and confusion as possible.

---

the pin, threw the grenade and killed three Germans.

These were crazy moments for everyone—particularly the generals. They were without staffs, without communications, without men. General Taylor found himself with a number of officers but only three enlisted men. "Never," he told them, "have so few been commanded by so many."

In an apple orchard outside Ste.-Mère-Église, Lt. Col. Benjamin H. Vandervoort, who was to hold the northern approaches to the town, was in pain and trying not to show it. His battalion surgeon, Captain Putnam, later recalled his first sight of Vandervoort: "He was seated with a rain cape over him, reading a map by flashlight. He recognized me and, calling me close, quietly asked that I take a look at his ankle with as little demonstration as possible. His ankle was obviously broken, but he insisted on replacing his jump boot, and we laced it tightly." Then, as Putnam watched, Vandervoort picked up his rifle and, using it as a crutch, took a step forward. He looked at the men around him. "Well," he said, "let's go." He moved out across the field. Vandervoort was to fight on his broken ankle for forty days, side by side with his men. When the battle of Normandy was over, Maj. Gen. Matthew B. Ridgway of the 82d said, "Vandervoort was one of the bravest, toughest battle commanders I ever knew."

Already the first reinforcements had reached the invasion troops. In the British area sixty-nine gliders had landed—forty-five of them on the correct landing strip near Ranville. On the other side of the Normandy battlefield, four miles from Ste.-Mère-Église, the first American glider trains were just coming in, lurching from side to side through "flak thick enough to land on." Sitting in the copilot's seat of the 101st's lead glider was the assistant division commander, Brig. Gen. Don F. Pratt. He was, reportedly, "as tickled as a schoolboy" to be making his first glider flight. Strung

(Bottom left) Once on the ground, British glider troops dig in close to the field where they came down. Other troops were to link up with them and consolidate positions. Glider units sustained some of the heaviest casualties of the Normandy operation; many of the aircraft crashed on landing, killing all aboard.

out behind was a procession of fifty-two gliders in formations of four, each glider towed by a Dakota. The train carried jeeps, antitank guns, an entire airborne medical unit, even a small bulldozer.

Surgical technician Emile Natalle was in the glider right behind General Pratt's. It overshot the zone and crashed into a field studded with "Rommel's asparagus"—heavy posts embedded in the ground as antiglider obstacles. Sitting in a jeep inside the glider, Natalle gazed out through one of the small windows and watched with horrified fascination as the wings sheared off and the posts whizzed past. Then there was a ripping sound and the glider broke in two—directly behind the jeep in which Natalle was sitting. "It made it very easy to get out," he recalled.

A short distance away lay the wreckage of Glider No. 1, smashed against a hedgerow. Natalle found the pilot lying in the hedgerow with both legs broken. General Pratt had been killed instantly, crushed in the crumpled cockpit. He was one of the few casualties in the 101st's landings, the first general officer on either side to be killed on D day.

It was nearly dawn—the dawn that 18,000 paratroopers had been fighting toward. In less than five hours they had more than fulfilled the expectations of General Eisenhower and his staff. The airborne armies had confused the enemy, disrupted communications and now, holding the flanks at either end of the Normandy invasion area, they had to a great extent blocked the movement of enemy reinforcements.

In the British zone, glider-borne troops were firmly astride the vital Caen and Orne bridges, which they had captured in a daring attack just after midnight, and paratroopers were in position on the heights overlooking Caen. By dawn the five German-held crossings over the Dives River would be demolished. Thus the principal British assignments had been completed and as long as the various arteries could be held, German counterattacks would be slowed down or stopped.

At the other end of the invasion beaches the Americans, despite more difficult terrain and a greater variety of missions, had done equally well. The men of the Allied airborne armies had invaded the Continent and secured the initial foothold. Now they awaited the arrival of the seaborne forces with whom they would drive into Hitler's Europe. For U.S. ground troops, H hour—6:30 a.m.—was exactly one hour and forty-five minutes away.

FIRST WAVE AT OMAHA BEACH

BY BRIG. GEN. S. L. A. MARSHALL,
USAR (RET.)

While the fighting at Normandy still raged, S. L. A. Marshall began reconstructing the events of D day by interviewing men who took part. His blow-by-blow, almost minute-by-minute, account of Americans at one segment of Omaha Beach is an unforgettable chronicle of death and daring, panic and heroism.

Few of the decisive battles of World War II have been as thoroughly reported for the official record as Omaha Beach on D day, June 6, 1944. While our troops were still fighting in western France, what happened to each unit in the Normandy landing was ascertained through eyewitness testimony of survivors. This research by field historians established where each company had hit the beach and by what route it had moved inland. Because every unit but one had been mislanded, the work was necessary in order to determine where each had fought, how it had fought, and what it had suffered.

The Army historians who wrote the first book about Omaha Beach, based on this field research, necessarily did a job of sifting and weighting the material. Normandy was an American victory; the primary task was to trace the twists and turns of fortune by which the success was won. But the effect of that emphasis was to slight the story of Omaha as an epic human tragedy which, in the early hours, came close to total disaster. The passing of the years has further tended to obscure the memory of shocking losses, failures and chaos in the Omaha landings that were the anguished prelude to victory.

On this two-division-front landing, only six rifle companies were relatively effective as units. They did better than others mainly because they had the luck to touch down on a less deadly section of the beach. Three times that number were shattered or foundered before they could begin to fight. Several units did not contribute a man or a bullet to the actual battle for the high ground, the steeply graded and heavily fortified bluff beyond a strip of sand which was fifty to 300 yards wide.

The ordeal of these ill-fated companies, the more wretched and blood-chilling individual experiences, were largely overlooked or toned down in the official accounts. In most of what has been written about Omaha there is less blood and iron and death than in the original field notes on battalion landings in the first wave. My own fading Normandy notebook, which covers the landing of every Omaha company, leaves little doubt on this score. Let's follow along with the Able and Baker Companies, 116th Infantry, 29th Division, as recorded in my notes.

Able Company, riding the tide in seven Higgins boats (personnel landing craft), is still 5000 yards from the beach when it first comes under enemy artillery fire. The shells fall short. But at 1000 yards Boat No. 5 takes a direct hit and founders. Six men drown before help arrives. Second Lieutenant Edward Gearing and twenty others paddle around until picked up by Naval craft, thus missing the fight at the shoreline. The other six boats ride unscathed to within 100 yards of the shore, where a shell into Boat No. 3 kills two men. Another dozen, taking to the water as their boat sinks, are drowned. That leaves five boats.

Lieutenant Edward Tidrick in Boat No. 2 cries out, "My God, we're coming in at the right spot, but look at it! No shingle, no wall, no shell holes, no cover. Nothing!" His men are at the sides of the boat, straining for a view of the target. At 6:36 a.m. ramps are dropped along the line of boats, and the men jump off into water anywhere from waist-deep to higher than a man's head. This is the signal awaited by the Germans on top of the bluff. Already pounded by mortars, the floundering assault line is now swept by crossing machine-gun fire from both ends of the beach.

Able Company has planned to wade ashore in three files from each landing craft, the center file going first, then flank files peeling off to right and left. The first men out try to do this, but they are ripped apart before they can make five yards. The mortally wounded sink at once, and even the lightly wounded—doomed by overloaded and waterlogged packs—are drowned.

From Boat No. 1 all hands jump off in water over their heads, and most of them are instantly carried down. Ten or so manage to clutch at the sides of the boat in an effort to stay afloat. The same thing happens to the men in Boat No. 4. Half of them are lost to gunfire or tide before anyone can get ashore. All order has vanished from Able Company before it has touched ground or fired a shot.

Already the churning sea runs red. Most of those who jump into shallow water are quickly knocked down by a bullet. Weakened by fear and shock, they cannot rise again and drown in a few feet of water. Some drag themselves ashore and collapse from total exhaustion, only to be overtaken by the waves and drowned. A few move safely through the rain of bullets to the beach, realize that they cannot hold there and retreat to the water for cover. With faces turned upward to keep their nostrils out of the water, they creep toward the land as the tide rises. That is how most of the survivors make it. The less rugged or less resourceful seek the cover of enemy obstacles moored along the upper half of the beach and are finished off by machine-gun fire.

Within seven minutes after the ramps drop, Able Company is inert and leaderless. At Boat No. 2 Lieutenant Tidrick takes a bullet through the throat as he jumps into the water. He staggers onto the sand and flops down ten feet from Pfc. Leo J. Nash. The Private hears the words gasped by the dying Lieutenant: "Advance with the wire cutters!" The order is futile—Nash has no cutters. Tidrick has raised himself up on his hands for an instant. Nash, burrowing into the sand, sees him ripped by bullets. From the cliff above, German machine-gunners are shooting into the survivors as from a rooftop.

Captain Taylor N. Fellers and Lt. Benjamin R. Kearfoot never make it. They are loaded with a section of thirty men in Boat No. 6. No one saw the craft go down. How each man on board met death remains unreported. Half of the drowned bodies were later found along the beach and it is assumed that the others, too, were claimed by the sea.

Along the beach only one Able Company officer still lives, Lt. Elijah Nance. He is hit in the heel as he quits his boat and hit again in the belly as he reaches the sand. By the end of ten minutes every sergeant is either dead or wounded. To the eyes of some survivors,

this clean sweep suggests that the Germans have spotted all the leaders and concentrated fire on them. Among the men who are still moving in with the tide, rifles, packs and helmets have already been cast away in the interests of survival.

To the right of where Tidrick's boat is adrift, its coxswain lying dead next to the shell-shattered wheel, the seventh craft noses toward the beach. It carries a medical section of one officer and sixteen men. The ramp is dropped. In that moment, two machine guns concentrate their fire on the opening. Not a man is given time to jump; all aboard are cut down where they stand.

By the end of fifteen minutes, Able Company still has not fired a weapon. No one gives any orders. The few able-bodied survivors move or not, as they see fit. Merely to stay alive is a full-time job. Yet a few men are remembered for their valor.

The first-aid man, Thomas Breedin, stands out among all others in Able Company. Reaching the sands, he strips off pack, blouse, helmet and boots. For a moment he stands there, so that others on the beach will see what he's about to do and follow suit. Then he crawls back into the water to pull in wounded men before they can be drowned by the tide.

The deeper water is still spotted with "tide walkers" advancing at the same slow rate as the rising water. But now, moved by Breedin's example, the stronger among them risk making themselves more conspicuous targets—they pick up fallen comrades and float them to the shore, raftwise. Machine-gun fire is raking the water. Burst after burst wrecks the rescue attempts, shooting the floating soldier from the hands of the walker, or killing both of them. But Breedin for this hour leads a charmed life and stays with his work indomitably.

By the end of half an hour, approximately two thirds of the company is gone forever. There are no precise casualty figures for this first half hour or for the first day. Whether more Able Company riflemen died from fire than from water was never ascertained.

By the end of the first hour, a number of survivors have crawled across the sand to the foot of the bluff, into a narrow sanctuary out of the line of fire. There they lie all day, some wounded, all exhausted and unarmed, too shocked even to talk to one another. No one happens by to offer water or succor. D day at Omaha Beach provides neither time nor space for

Assault troops leave their Coast Guard landing barges and struggle through the surf toward the Normandy shore. All during D day the barges ran a dangerous shuttle service between the savagely contested beaches and troop-filled transports, threading their way through minefields and sunken obstacles that threatened instant destruction.

Heavy Nazi machine-gun fire pins down U.S. soldiers behind steel "hedgehog" obstacles in the choppy surf off Omaha Beach. These obstacles, intended to sink or disable landing craft, were only the outermost rampart of the "Atlantic Wall" which the Germans had built along the northern coast of France. Once ashore, Allied soldiers still had to break through a maze of concrete bunkers, barbed wire and pillboxes before they could begin to fight their way inland.

such missions—every landing group is overwhelmed by its own assault problems.

By the end of one hour and forty-five minutes, six survivors from the boat section on the extreme right have worked their way to a shelf some yards up the face of the cliff. Four fall exhausted from the short climb. They stay there through the day, seeing no one else from their company. The other two, Pvts. Jake Shefer and Thomas Lovejoy, join a group from the 2d Ranger Battalion, which is attacking Pointe du Hoe to the right of the company sector, and fight with the Rangers throughout the day. Two men, two rifles—the sum total of Able Company's firepower on D day.

Baker Company is scheduled to land twenty-six minutes after Able, on the same sector, to bring support and reinforcement. A full load of trouble on the way in destroys the schedule. The sea is so rough that the men of Baker must bail furiously with their helmets to keep its six boats from swamping. Thus preoccupied, they do not see the disaster overtaking Able until they are almost on top of it. What they behold is either so limited or so horrible that discipline withers, the assault wave begins to dissolve, the chaos induced by fear virtually cancels out the mission. Great clouds of smoke and dust raised by the enemy fire have almost closed a curtain around the agony of Able Company. Outside this pall nothing is to be seen but lines of corpses adrift, a few heads bobbing in the water and the crimson-running tide. The British coxswains raise the cry: "We can't go in there. We can't see the landmarks. We must pull off."

In the Baker command boat, Capt. Ettore V. Zappacosta pulls a Colt .45 and shouts, "By God, you'll take this boat straight in!" His display of courage compels obedience, but it is still a questionable order. Those of the Baker boats that try to proceed suffer the fate of Able Company. Three times during the approach, mortar shells break right next to Zappacosta's command boat but leave it unscathed, thus sparing its men a few more moments of life. At seventy-five yards from the sand, Zappacosta yells, "Drop the ramp!" The end goes down—and a storm of bullet fire comes in.

Zappacosta jumps from the boat first, reels ten yards through the elbow-high tide and yells, "I've been hit!" He stumbles on a few more steps. The first-aid man, Thomas Kenser, yells, "Try to make it. I'm coming." But the Captain falls face forward into the waves, and his equipment and soaked pack pin him

to the bottom. Kenser jumps toward him and is shot dead in the air. Lieutenant Tom Dallas of Charley Company, who has come along for reconnaissance, is the third man. He makes it to the edge of the sand strip, where a machine-gun burst blows his head apart before he can flatten.

Private, first class, Robert L. Sales, who is lugging Zappacosta's radio, is the fourth to leave the boat, having waited long enough to see the others die. His heel catches on the end of the ramp, and he falls sprawling into the tide, losing the radio but saving his life. Every man who follows him is either killed or wounded before reaching dry land.

Sales alone gets to the beach unhit. To traverse those few yards takes him two hours. First he crouches in the water, waddling forward on his haunches just a few paces. He collides with driftwood—a floating log. In that moment a mortar shell explodes just above his head, knocking him groggy. But he hugs the log to keep from going down, and the effort seems to clear his head a little. Then one of Able Company's tide walkers hoists him aboard the log and, using his sheath knife, cuts away Sales's pack, boots and assault jacket.

Feeling stronger, Sales returns to the water and using the log as cover, pushes in toward the shore. Private Mack L. Smith of Baker Company, hit several times in the face, joins him, and an Able Company rifleman named Kemper, his right leg badly wounded, also comes alongside. They follow the log until at last they roll it to the farthest reach of high tide. Then they flatten behind it, staying there for hours after the flow has turned to ebb. The dead of both companies wash up to where they lie and then wash out to sea again. If any of them recognizes the face of a comrade, Sales and his companions, disregarding the fire, join in dragging the body onto the sand beyond the reach of water. So long as the tide is full, they stay at this task. Later, a first-aid man comes crawling along the beach and dresses Smith's face wounds, then moves on. Sales, as he finds the strength, bandages Kemper's leg. The three huddle behind the log until night falls. There is nothing else to report on any member of Zappacosta's boat team.

Only one other Baker Company boat tries to come straight in to the beach. Somehow the boat founders. Somehow all of its people—one British coxswain and about thirty American infantrymen—are killed. There is no one to take note and report where they perished.

Frightened coxswains in the other four craft take one look, instinctively draw back, then veer right and left away from Able Company's shambles. In this they dodge their orders. But such is the shock to the boat-team leaders, such their feeling of relief at the turning movement, that not one utters a protest.

Lieutenant Leo A. Pingenot's coxswain swings his boat far to the right toward Pointe du Hoe. Then, spying a small and deceptively peaceful-looking cove, he heads directly for the land. Fifty yards out, Pingenot orders, "Drop the ramp!" The coxswain freezes on the rope, refusing to lower. Staff Sergeant Odell L. Padgett jumps him and bears him to the bottom of the boat. Padgett's men lower the ramp and rush into the water. In two minutes they are all in up to their necks and struggling to avoid drowning. That quickly Pingenot is already far out ahead of them. Padgett comes even with him, and together they cross to dry land. The beach of the cove is heavily strewn with giant boulders. Bullets seem to be pinging off every rock.

Pingenot and Padgett dive behind the same rock. Glancing back, they are horrified to see that not one person has followed them. Quite suddenly smoke has half blanked out the scene beyond the water's edge. Pingenot moans, "My God, the whole boat team is dead." Padgett sings out, "Hey, are you hit?" Back come many voices from beyond the smoke. "What's the rush?" "We'll get there." "Who wants to know?" The men are still moving along, using the water as cover. Padgett's shout is their first information that anyone else has moved up onto the beach. They all make it to the shore, twenty-eight strong. Pingenot and Padgett manage to stay ahead of them, coaxing and encouraging. Padgett keeps yelling, "Come on, things are better up there!" Two men are killed and three wounded while they are crossing the beach.

In the cove the platoon latches onto a company of Rangers, fights all day as part of that company and helps destroy the enemy entrenchments on Pointe du Hoe. By sundown that mop-up is completed. The platoon bivouacs at the first hedgerow beyond the cliff.

Another Baker Company boat which turns to the right has less luck. Staff Sergeant Robert M. Campbell, who leads the section, is the first man to jump out when the ramp goes down. He drops into deep water, and his load of two bangalore torpedoes takes him straight to the bottom. He jettisons the bangalores and then, surfacing, cuts away all his equipment for good

measure. Machine-gun fire brackets him, and he submerges again briefly. Though not a strong swimmer, he heads out to sea. For two hours he paddles around, 200 or so yards from the shore. He hears and sees nothing of the battle, but somehow gets the impression that the invasion has failed and that all other Americans are dead, wounded or prisoners. In despair, strength fast going, he moves ashore rather than drown. Beyond the smoke he quickly finds the fire. He grabs a helmet from a dead man's head, crawls on hands and knees to the seawall and there finds five of his men, two of them unwounded.

Like Campbell, Pfc. Jan J. Budziszewski is carried to the bottom by his load of two bangalores. He hugs them half a minute before realizing that he must either let loose or drown. Next, he shucks off his helmet and pack and drops his rifle. Then he surfaces. After swimming 200 yards, he sees that he is moving in the wrong direction. So he turns about and heads for the beach, where he crawls ashore under a rain of bullets. In his path lies a dead Ranger. Budziszewski takes the dead man's helmet, rifle and canteen and crawls up to the seawall. The only survivor from Campbell's boat section to get off the beach, he spends his day walking to and fro along the foot of the bluff, looking for a friendly face.

In Lt. William B. Williams' boat, the coxswain steers sharp left and away from Zappacosta's sector. Not having seen the Captain die, Williams doesn't know that command of the unit has now passed to him. Guiding on his own instinct, the coxswain moves along the coast 600 yards, then puts the boat straight in. It's a good guess; he has found a little vacuum in the battle. The ramp drops on dry sand, and the boat team jumps ashore. Yet it's a close thing. Mortar fire has dogged them all the way; and as the last rifleman clears the ramp, one shell lands dead center of the boat, blows it apart and kills the coxswain.

Momentarily the beach is free of fire, but the men cannot cross it at a bound. Weak from seasickness and fear, they move at a crawl, dragging their equipment. By the end of twenty minutes, Williams and ten men are over the sand and resting in the lee of the seawall. Five others are hit by machine-gun fire crossing the beach; six men, last seen while taking cover in a tidal pocket, are never heard from again. More mortar fire lands around the party as Williams leads it across the road beyond the seawall. The men scatter. When the

(Left) *Architects of the D-day invasion: Allied Supreme Commander Dwight Eisenhower (center) and Air Marshal Sir Arthur W. Tedder (right), chief of Allied Air Forces, listen to Gen. Sir Bernard L. Montgomery, Deputy Supreme Commander of ground forces, during the invasion buildup.*

(Lower left) *A German sentinel sits in his concrete-reinforced machine-gun nest atop a Normandy cliff, his eyes searching the waters of the English Channel for the first sign of enemy activity. Unsure of where the Allies would strike, the Nazis were obliged to guard a 1200-mile stretch of coastline.*

(Top right) *Preinvasion photograph taken by a low-flying R.A.F. plane shows German labor troops scurrying for cover. They had been busily constructing, during low tide, a network of obstacles — called Rommel's asparagus — to protect the Normandy coast against Allied invasion forces. At high tide, the obstructions were concealed underwater.*

(Lower right) *Their hands above their heads, dazed German soldiers emerge from their bunkers overlooking the invasion beaches. After they had been hurried down the side of the cliff, they were put aboard waiting ships and transported to prisoner-of-war centers across the Channel.*

shelling lifts, three of them do not return. Williams leads the seven survivors up a trail toward the fortified village of Les Moulins on top of the bluff. He recognizes the ground and knows that he is taking on a tough target. Les Moulins is perched above a draw, up which winds a dirt road from the beach, designated on the invasion maps as Exit No. 3.

Williams and his crew of seven are the first Americans to approach it D-day morning. Machine-gun fire from a concrete pillbox sweeps over them as they near the brow of the hill, moving at a crawl through thick grass. Williams says to the others, "Stay here; we're too big a target!" They hug earth, and he inches forward alone, moving through a shallow gully. Without being detected, he gets to within twenty yards of the gun, downslope from it. He heaves a grenade; but it explodes in air, just outside the embrasure. His second grenade hits the concrete wall and bounces right back on him. Three of its fragments hit him in the shoulders. Then, from out of the pillbox, a German potato masher (hand grenade) sails down on him and explodes just a few feet away; five more fragments cut into him. He starts crawling back to his men; en route, three bullets rip his rump and right leg.

The seven are still there. Williams hands his map and compass (symbols of command) to S. Sgt. Frank M. Price, saying, "It's your job now. But go the other way—toward Vierville." Price starts to look at Williams' wounds, but Williams shakes him off, saying, "No, get moving." He then settles himself in a hole in the embankment, stays there all day and at last gets medical attention just before midnight.

On leaving Williams, Price's first act is to hand map and compass to T. Sgt. William Pearce, whose seniority the Lieutenant had overlooked. They cross the draw, one man at a time, and some distance beyond come to a ravine; on the far side they bump into their first hedgerow, and as they look for an entrance, fire comes against them. Behind a second hedgerow, not more than thirty yards away, are seven Germans, five rifles and two burp guns (machine pistols). On exactly even terms, these two forces engage for the better part of an hour, with no one getting hit. Then Pearce settles the fight by crawling along a drainage ditch to the enemy flank. He kills the seven Germans with a Browning automatic rifle.

For Pearce and his friends, it is a first taste of battle and its success makes them giddy. Heads up, they walk along the road into Vierville, disregarding all precautions. They get away with it only because the village is already in the hands of Lt. Walter Taylor of Baker Company and twenty men from his boat team.

Taylor is a luminous figure in the story of D day, one of the forty-seven survivors of the landings on Omaha who, by their dauntless initiative at widely separated points along the beach, save the mission from total stagnation and disaster. Courage and luck are his in extraordinary measure.

The Taylor story begins when Baker Company's assault wave breaks up just short of the surf where Able Company is in ordeal. Taylor's coxswain swings his boat sharp left, then heads toward the shore about halfway between Zappacosta's boat and Williams'. For a few seconds after the ramp drops, this bit of beach next to the village called Hamel-au-Prêtre is clear of fire. No mortar shells crown the start. Taylor leads his section, crawling across the beach and over the seawall, losing four men killed and two wounded in this brief movement. Some yards off to his right, Taylor has seen Lts. Harold Donaldson and Emil Winkler shot dead. But there is no halt for reflection; Taylor leads the section by trail straight up the bluff and into Vierville, where his luck continues. In a two-hour fight he whips a German platoon without losing a man.

The village is quiet when Pearce joins him. Pearce says, "Williams is shot up back there and can't move."

"I guess that makes me company commander," says Taylor.

"This is probably all of Baker Company," Pearce remarks and takes a head count; they number twenty-eight, including Taylor.

Taylor says, "That ought to be enough. Follow me!"

Inland from Vierville about 500 yards lies the Château de Vaumicel, imposing in its rock-walled massiveness, its hedgerow-bordered fields all entrenched and interconnected with artillery-proof tunnels. To every man but Taylor, the target looks prohibitive. Still, they follow him. German fire stops them 100 yards short of the château. The enemy is behind a hedgerow about fifty yards in front of them. Taylor's men flatten, open fire with rifles and toss a few grenades, though the distance seems too great.

By sheer chance one grenade glances off the helmet of a German squatting in a foxhole. He jumps up, shouting, *Kamerad! Kamerad!* Thereupon twenty-four of the enemy walk from behind the hedgerow with their hands in the air. Taylor pares off one of his riflemen to march the prisoners back to the beach. The brief fight has cost him three wounded. Within the château he takes two more prisoners, a German doctor and his first-aid man. Taylor puts them on a "kind of a parole," leaving his three wounded in their keeping while moving his platoon to the first crossroads beyond the château.

Here he is stopped by the sudden arrival of three truckloads of German infantry, who deploy into the fields on both flanks of his position and start an enveloping movement. The manpower odds, about three to one against him, are too heavy. In the first trade of fire, lasting not more than two minutes, a rifleman lying beside Taylor is killed, three others are wounded and the Browning automatic is shot from Pearce's hands. That leaves but twenty men and no automatic weapons.

Taylor yells, "Back to the château!" They crawl as far as the first hedgerow; then they rise and trot along, supporting their wounded. Taylor is the last man to go, having stayed behind to cover the withdrawal with his carbine until the hedgerows prevent fire against the others. So far the small group has had no contact with any other part of the expedition, and for all its members know, the invasion may have failed.

They make it to the château. The enemy moves in closer. The attacking fire builds up. But the stone walls are fire-slotted, and through the midday and early afternoon these ports serve the American riflemen well. The question is whether the ammunition will outlast the Germans. It is answered at sundown, just as the supply runs out, by the arrival of fifteen Rangers, who join their fire with Taylor's, and the Germans fade back.

Already Taylor and his force are farther south than any element of the right flank in the Omaha expedition. But Taylor isn't satisfied. The battalion objective, as specified for the close of D day, is still more than one half mile to the west.

So he leads them forth, again serving as first scout. Eighteen of his own riflemen and fifteen Rangers follow in column. One man is killed by a bullet while they are getting away from the château. Dark closes over them, and they prepare to bivouac. Having almost reached the village of Louviers, they are by this time nearly a half mile in front of anyone else in the U.S. Army. There a runner reaches them with the message that the remnants of the battalion are assembling 700 yards closer to the sea; Taylor and his party are directed to fall back to them. It is done.

Later, still under the spell, Staff Sergeant Price pays the perfect tribute to Taylor. He says, "We saw no sign of fear in him. Watching him made men of us. Marching or fighting, he was leading. We followed him because there was nothing else to do."

Thousands of Americans were spilled onto Omaha Beach. The high ground was won by a handful of men like Taylor who on that day burned with a flame bright beyond common understanding.

Their landing craft sunk off the coast of Normandy by a German mine, these two Americans, exhausted and suffering from shock, are rescued by the U.S. Coast Guard.

Aftermath of battle: An elderly French woman of Angirey sits in the doorway of her house and stares at the devastation left by German troops, who burned the village before retreating toward the Rhine River ahead of the fast-moving Allied columns.

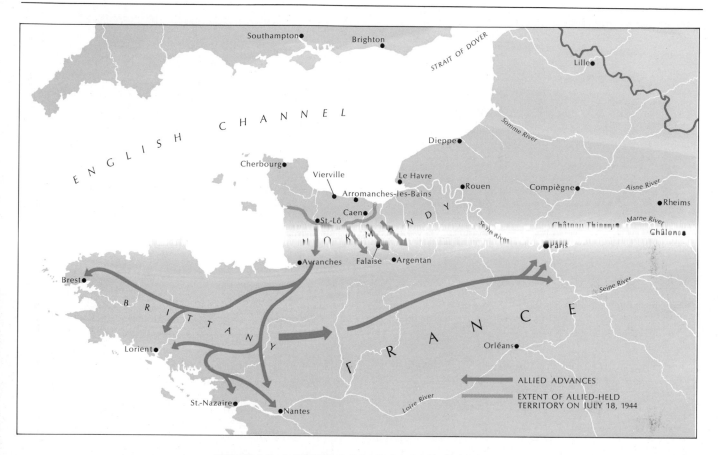

ALLIED ADVANCES

EXTENT OF ALLIED-HELD TERRITORY ON JULY 18, 1944

FROM NORMANDY TO PARIS

By June 13, 1944, a week after the D-day landings, the Allies had driven some twenty miles inland and had linked up to form a strong eighty-mile front. The U.S. First Army under Lt. Gen. Omar N. Bradley sealed off the Cotentin Peninsula and on June 27 captured the city of Cherbourg at its tip.

Bradley's forces then began to drive southeastward toward St.-Lô, protected by the British Second Army, whose task it was to keep Nazi armored divisions pinned down in the north near Caen.

The British had seized Caen and the roads that led from it by July 18, the same day that armored columns of General Bradley's First Army reached St.-Lô. The U.S. Third Army,

led by Lt. Gen. George S. Patton, plunged south of Avranches. By August 13 Patton had entered Nantes, isolating Axis forces in the ports of Lorient, St.-Nazaire and Brest. Then he turned east toward Laval, while British and Canadian forces pushed south from Caen.

The embattled German Seventh Army was in danger of encirclement. Hitler turned down the request by Field Marshal Gunther von Kluge, now in command of the German forces, for a strategic withdrawal and, instead, ordered a counter-attack. The Allies, pushed back at first, rushed in reinforcements and stopped Kluge, destroying almost 100 tanks. The Germans' only hope of escape now lay through a narrow

opening in the Allied noose between Falaise and Argentan. One third of Kluge's army made it through the gap. The fleeing Germans withdrew across the Seine, disorganized but determined to halt Patton's drive on Paris. Actually, Patton had orders to concentrate on annihilating the rest of the German Army in the field, and he hoped to bypass the French capital altogether. He had turned south of the city intending to cross the Seine when word came that the people of Paris had risen against their Axis masters.

On August 25 the capital of France was liberated by a two-division assault on the city, and Paris' four years of hated occupation were ended.

French children in Paris dig up cobblestones from a street to help build a barricade, after the FFI (French Forces of the Interior) rose up against the Nazis on August 24, 1944. The insurrection was inspired by the Allied advance on Paris.

(Below) *A captured German soldier, surrounded by angry Frenchmen, leans dejectedly on an armored vehicle in the Place de l'Opéra. Four summers after France had fallen to Hitler, Parisians were fighting for their city's freedom.*

(Above) *General Charles de Gaulle proudly leads a victory parade from the Arch of Triumph to the Cathedral of Notre Dame on August 26, 1944, the day after Paris was liberated.*

(Left) *Men of the U.S. 28th Infantry Division, veterans of the Normandy landings and the ensuing cross-country fighting, march along the Champs Élysées, the great Paris boulevard.*

THE PLOT TO KILL HITLER

BY GEORGES BLOND
(Translated by Frances Frenaye)

Of several wartime conspiracies to assassinate Hitler, the "Generals' Plot" was the last and the most nearly successful. Its organizers, German patriots all, had hoped that with the Fuehrer dead they could negotiate a surrender to spare their country its last agonies. The bomb was exploded—on July 20, 1944—in a conference room at Hitler's Headquarters, according to plan. Though several of his Generals were killed, Hitler himself escaped with only slight wounds. In the frightful vengeance which followed, thousands were arrested, hundreds executed. Published accounts of the plot that failed differ on many details. But the essential facts, on which there is general agreement, are presented vividly in this segment from a book by Georges Blond, well-known French novelist and journalist.

By July 1944 Berlin had received an immense tonnage of bombs. Many sections were completely destroyed, gaping craters were everywhere. Almost every night there was another raid; buildings crumbled, fire engines rushed vainly from one conflagration to another.

The morning of July 20 was unusually hot, with a feeling of storm in the air. But the guards at the Ministry of War in the Bendlerstrasse were fully uniformed. The Ministry was bearing up with equal stolidity under the heat and the melancholy war news. Order and punctiliousness reigned on every floor. In his office, Gen. Friedrich Fromm, Chief of the Army

of the Interior, was busy with urgent requests for reinforcements. Available troops were few.

In a nearby office three officers were parting after a long conversation: behind his own desk, Gen. Friedrich Olbricht, Fromm's deputy chief, and facing him, Col. Count Klaus von Stauffenberg, Chief of Staff, and Lt. Werner von Haeften. These two were about to set off to the airfield, where a Junkers was waiting to fly them to Hitler's Supreme Headquarters at Rastenburg, in East Prussia.

Stauffenberg, a powerfully built man covered with decorations, made this trip whenever telephone communication was considered inadvisable, and the Lieutenant went with him. Each of them carried a briefcase. Stauffenberg held in his left hand a handkerchief with which he was mopping his brow. This hand had only three fingers, and the right hand, which had been blown off by a mine in Tunisia, had been replaced by one of flexible metal.

His perspiring face produced a painful impression —the left eye was missing, the features hollow and strained. Moreover, he was under almost unbearable nervous tension. *The briefcase in his artificial hand contained a bomb intended to blow up Hitler at Rastenburg that very day.*

By July 20, 1944, German troops and their allies were retreating all along the eastern front, from the Baltic Sea to the Carpathian Mountains. The situation in the west, six weeks after the Allied invasion, was also alarming. A number of German generals went so far as to conclude, "Sooner or later, military defeat is inevitable. Only a decision on the political level can change the course of events."

In the airplane carrying him to Rastenburg, Stauffenberg sat with his briefcase on his lap. Despite his injuries, he had been chosen for the task because of the vehemence with which he had begged for it. He insisted that while he lay wounded in his bed, he had seen a vision and received from on high the mission of freeing his native land. Once the choice was made, the leaders of the plot had secured him a job which would enable him to make frequent visits to Hitler's Headquarters.

Very few people had access to the Fuehrer, and an attempt on his life was far from easy. It is impossible, even today, to know how many plots of the same kind were organized before this one of July 20, 1944.

The most definite and best known is the one of

376

March 13, 1943. At that time Hitler was on the eastern front near Smolensk, at the headquarters of Field Marshal Gunther von Kluge. On the plane that was to fly him back to Germany, one of Hitler's companions accepted a small parcel containing two bottles of cognac for delivery to a general at Rastenburg. Actually the parcel contained a time bomb, its detonator set for thirty minutes after the scheduled departure. The conspirators of Smolensk waited impatiently for news of disaster from an escorting plane. Finally a code message came through indicating that the Fuehrer was safe. The bomb had not exploded.

Stauffenberg knew that the bomb in his briefcase was identical to the one that had failed to go off on March 13, 1943, but the fact did not discourage him. The detonator had been carefully tested, and everything seemed to be in good order. This was the most efficient bomb that could be obtained, and it had the advantage of being both small and silent. There was no time to produce a better mechanism—already too many people were in the know, and there was the danger of the secret's being discovered by the Gestapo.

There was another reason for Hitler's enemies to hurry. If they delayed much longer, they would have nothing to gain. The provisional government slated to take power after Hitler's elimination would appeal to the Anglo-Americans in these terms: "We have freed Germany from National Socialism and are petitioning for peace. Treat us generously." They could not hope to be heard unless their plan was carried out well before complete defeat, when the Allies might still give up their demand for unconditional surrender.

Colonel Stauffenberg was well aware of these necessities and impatient to go ahead. Although he had been at the Ministry of War less than three weeks, he had already carried a bomb aboard an airplane three times. He had gone first, on July 11, 1944, to Berchtesgaden, where Hitler was spending a few days. For half an hour he had been in the same room with the Fuehrer, but had not pressed the detonator. Why not? Because Heinrich Himmler and Hermann Goering, whom it had been decided to kill at the same time, had not been present.

A second chance had come on July 15, this time at Rastenburg. But once again neither Himmler nor Goering had been in the conference room with Hitler. What was Stauffenberg to do? He had left the room and telephoned to his accomplices in Berlin. In code

language he had asked whether he should go ahead. "Yes," had been the answer. But by the time he had returned to the conference room, Hitler had gone.

"We simply can't muff it a third time," the Colonel said to himself as he sat in his plane on this morning of July 20. Whether or not Himmler and Goering were present, he was determined to set off the bomb. The main thing was to kill Hitler; he was sure to be there because he had himself summoned Stauffenberg.

On July 5 Field Marshal Kluge, former Commander of the Central Army Group in Russia, had appeared at Field Marshal Erwin Rommel's Headquarters at La Roche Guyon, He had come to replace Field Marshal Gerd von Rundstedt. In two weeks of intensive lecturing by Hitler, Kluge had been persuaded that if the Allies had not been thrown back into the sea, Rundstedt and Rommel were to blame.

"Your excessive pessimism and individualism have caused the Fuehrer to lose some of his confidence in you," he told the hero of the *Afrika Korps*.

"Are you quite mad?" Rommel retorted. "My advice to you is not to pass judgment on the situation here in the west until you have seen it yourself."

Kluge went off on a tour of inspection, and forty-eight hours later he presented Rommel with a spontaneous apology: "Things are exactly as you told me. . . . In spite of all the information that reaches him, the Fuehrer is living in a dream. When he is pulled out of it sufficiently to be told that something is going wrong, he can think only of finding a scapegoat."

After this Kluge somberly returned to the main headquarters at St.-Germain-en-Laye. Now, on the early morning of July 20, he was back at La Roche Guyon, rereading a memorandum from Rommel dated July 15. Here is the gist of this paper:

The situation on the Normandy front is increasingly difficult and is moving in the direction of a crisis. Because of the bitterness of the combat, the enemy's extraordinarily powerful matériel and his mastery of the air, our losses are rapidly weakening our fighting power. . . . After the loss of 97,000 men (including 2360 officers, 28 of them generals and 354 unit commanders) we have received only 6000 reinforcements. Our losses of matériel are equally severe. Under these circumstances, we must expect that within two to

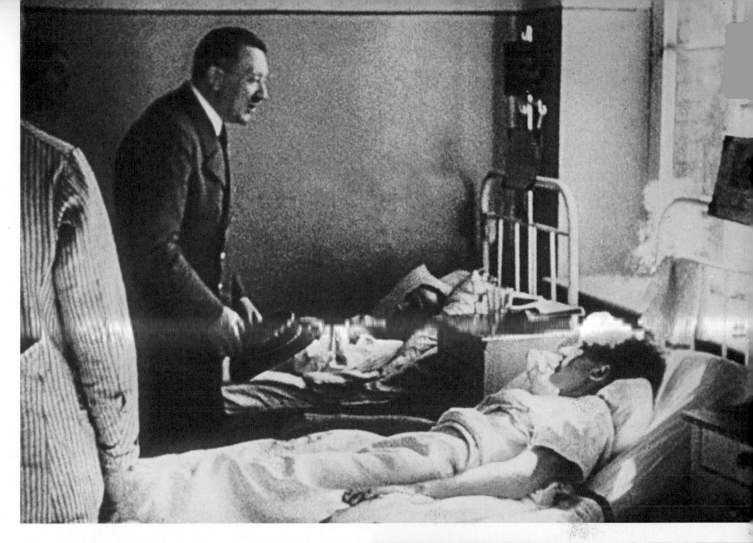

(Upper left) *The bomb-shattered house at Wolf's Lair, Adolf Hitler's East Prussian Headquarters, which was the scene of an assassination attempt on the Fuehrer. Three of those present were killed and twenty wounded, but Hitler escaped.*

(Lower left) *Hitler, only slightly injured by the explosion—his left arm remained stiff for the rest of his life—poses shortly afterward with Mussolini, Martin Bormann (behind the Italian dictator), Adm. Karl Doenitz and Hermann Goering.*

(Upper right) *Hitler made a point of having himself photographed visiting his officers who were wounded by the bomb explosion. His survival of the blast deepened his conviction that he was ordained by fate to lead his nation to victory.*

(Lower right) *The brother of the man who planted the bomb, Count Berthold von Stauffenberg, is shown at his trial, surrounded by guards. He was convicted and executed, as were most of the plotters, along with many innocent persons.*

three weeks the enemy will pierce our weakened front and fan out into France. The consequences of this breakthrough are incalculable.

And at the end Rommel had added a few lines in his own hand: "I must ask you to draw all the implications of the situation described above. As Commander of this Army Group, it is my duty to tell you this quite frankly."

The memorandum was addressed not to Kluge but to Hitler, and it was in Kluge's hands simply because it was passing through normal channels. He had held this text for three days without forwarding it, for two reasons. First, Rommel had been seriously wounded and was now in a hospital bed at Bernay. On July 17 his car had been machine-gunned by three fighter-bombers on the road near Livarot. Rommel was thrown out of the car bloody and unconscious, and it was not certain that he would survive. Second, Kluge could not forward the memorandum without adding a comment of his own, which was a thorny and indeed dangerous matter. Let us describe his predicament in the first person, as he might have seen it himself:

"So this is Rommel's ultimatum. I must say he gave me due warning. On July 12 when I asked, 'In your opinion, how long can we hold fast in Normandy?' he answered: 'Let us ask the field commanders and the generals just over them. If the answers are as I expect, let us tell Hitler our findings and ask him firmly to end the war in the west. We can be sure that he will violently reject this suggestion. And then the people who want to remove him from power can go ahead and carry out their plan.'

"Rommel spoke to me very frankly about the conversations he had held with emissaries of the conspirators of Berlin. I didn't conceal the fact that I too favored the destruction of National Socialist tyranny, but I insisted that political action was not my affair. Finally, in response to a direct question, I told him that my decision would depend upon how the field commanders answered our questionnaire.

"Rommel personally undertook the investigation, on July 13, 14 and 15. The answers he got are all deeply pessimistic. The memorandum is remarkably precise, and its predictions seem to me reasonable. Now, before sending it on, I must add a few lines of my own. In all conscience, I must approve the report and its conclusions, without making myself respon-

sible for the veiled ultimatum which it contains. And that's no easy matter. And yet to disavow the ultimatum may be a mistake, in case events take a different turn." He allowed himself twenty-four more hours to think it over.

Kluge was not the only tepid advocate of the conspiracy. A wide range of attitudes existed among the high officers of the *Wehrmacht*. Those chiefly involved in the plot were: the resigned Gen. Ludwig Beck, Field Marshal Erwin von Witzleben, Gens. Kurt von Hammerstein, Olbricht, Erich Hoepner, Henning von Tresckow, Hemuth Stieff, Erich Fellgiebel, and Georg Thomas, Colonels Stauffenberg and Fabian von Schlabrendorff.

Beck was the presumptive head of the successor government. As former Chief of Staff, he had left the Army in 1938, after having openly opposed Hitler's dismissal of Gens. Werner von Blomberg and Freiherr Werner von Fritsch, and he was the prime organizer of the conspiracy. By July 1944 he admitted to being physically and spiritually tired. However, he did not shirk responsibilities, for he thought that because his opposition to Hitler dated from before the war, he would inspire a maximum of confidence in the Allies.

Military men made up the shock battalion of the plot and its actual executors, but they did not expect to monopolize a successor government. The post of chancellor was reserved for Karl Friedrich Goerdeler, former conservative Mayor of Leipzig. Wilhelm Leuschner, a Social Democrat, was to be vice chancellor. The allotment of portfolios was an incredibly laborious job, for the post-Hitler government was supposed to contain representatives of every shade of political opinion participating in the conspiracy.

Colonel Stauffenberg could imagine, second by second, every step he would take from the landing of the airplane until the bomb exploded.

The seat of General Headquarters, known as Wolf's Lair, was half a dozen miles outside Rastenburg. It occupied three square miles of forest and was composed of three concentric zones to which a single road gave access. The outer zone contained the railway station and a miniature airfield. Here, too, were the barracks of the S.S. guards. The second zone was occupied by General Staff officers. A circle of land, mined in its entirety and surrounded by two rows of electrified barbed wire, protected the central zone. At intervals of 100 feet, inside and outside this inner circle, were S.S. guards. There was only one entrance, manned by S.S. and security men who examined all passes, and the passes were good for only a single visit.

Hitler's house—a concrete-lined air-raid shelter, with small windows in the part above ground—stood in the center of this zone, and around it, painted dark green and hung with moss and nets for camouflage, were the quarters of the officers of his personal staff. Hitler had a secondary frame house at his disposal, but apparently he very seldom made use of it.

Stauffenberg had visited Wolf's Lair only once, but every detail of what he had seen was etched upon his mind. Hitler's conferences began about 12:30. As soon as he had read his report and answered the Fuehrer's questions, Stauffenberg was to excuse himself to make a telephone call. Having set the detonator, he was to leave his briefcase, which contained the bomb, upon the table. The bomb was the equivalent of a 150-mm. shell, and its explosion within the closed walls was bound to be particularly effective.

As soon as the shelter was destroyed and the Fuehrer dead, he would telephone to the Ministry in Berlin, where Beck, Olbricht and other conspirators were waiting to hear from him. Then General Fellgiebel, Chief of Headquarters Communications, would cut off the complex of telephone lines connecting Wolf's Lair with Germany, the fighting fronts and the occupied territories.

Meanwhile, Olbricht would tell Fromm that Hitler had been killed and the time was ripe to put into operation the plan prepared for such an emergency. Fromm would then convey to all bureau chiefs the order: "Open the 'Valkyrie' envelope." The "Valkyrie Plan" had been prepared by the conspirators. According to its provisions, the Army was to take over, all S.S. troops were to be confined to barracks and their leaders kept under watch. Orders to this effect were to be sent to all Army generals.

Infantry and tank regiments stationed in the vicinity of Berlin were to move into the city and surround the most important public buildings, while the Guard Battalion commanded by the thirty-five-year-old Maj. Otto Remer was to defend the Ministry of War against assault from S.S. troops.

The new Chancellor, Goerdeler, was to go on the air. His speech, approved by Beck, would enlarge upon the following themes: The members of the new Government had never wanted war, and their primary aim was to promote peace; because no purpose could be achieved by imposing further sacrifices upon any of the belligerent peoples, the new Government contemplated an immediate armistice; moral standards must be restored, but only those who had given criminal orders must be punished; a federal state must be set up and general elections held as soon as possible.

The plane landed in the small airfield in the outer zone. Stauffenberg and Haeften were picked up by a waiting car. Now the road wound among the trees. They passed through a ring of guards, the second zone and a second ring of guards. The S.S. men saluted, examined their passes and let them go by. Shortly after this the two officers got out of the car and walked off with an S.S. officer who had come to receive them.

The officer led them, not to the Fuehrer's shelter but to his larch-wood house, which had been his original dwelling. The conference was to be held there, contrary to the usual procedure, on account of the heat wave. This did not alter Stauffenberg's plan. In the stump of his right arm he could feel the weight of the bomb. Within an hour, perhaps thirty minutes, everything would be over, and the destiny of Germany would take a new turn.

"Just a minute," said their guide, as they reached the antechamber.

He opened a door, disappeared and then came back, accompanied by Field Marshal Wilhelm Keitel and several other ranking officers. Keitel greeted Stauffenberg and said, "Come along. The conference has just begun."

It was 11:40. Keitel, Stauffenberg and the others went into the conference room, leaving Haeften in a room next door where there was a row of telephones. Maps were spread out on the conference table, more maps hung on the walls. Generals and admirals stood all around, with six stenographers among them, and Hitler was at one end. Stauffenberg at once noticed that both Goering and Himmler were missing.

General Adolf Heusinger was making a report on the eastern front. After this Hitler asked Stauffenberg to read the papers he had brought with him and posed questions to which the Colonel replied. Then it was another man's turn.

Stauffenberg set his briefcase down against a leg of the table, three feet from where Hitler was standing.

Just then an S.S. officer came to tell Stauffenberg that he was wanted on the telephone, a prearranged maneuver by which Haeften was making it possible for him to leave the room. Stauffenberg leaned over and, on the pretext of searching for a paper in his briefcase, set the mechanism of the time bomb. The deed was done. He got up and left the room. He found Haeften in the antechamber. Together they went out the front door and walked toward the car, not far away.

Suddenly there was a burst of fire followed by a deafening explosion. The roof of the frame house had caved in. Flames and bodies were being hurled into the air. After a few seconds of frozen silence, S.S. men ran shouting to the scene. Some of them carried stretchers right into the smoke. When the smoke fell away they could be seen coming out of the ruins of the house bearing bodies. They passed close to the car.

"I've just seen Hitler's corpse go by," Stauffenberg said excitedly. "Let's get out of here quickly."

He and Haeften got into the car and drove out on the same road by which they had come. At the first ring of guards they came to a stop. The S.S. men had obviously heard the explosion; perhaps they were suspicious. Stauffenberg leaned out the door.

"Urgent mission," he said firmly.

His mutilated face, furrowed with emotion, had never been more impressive. The S.S. men stared at the ribbons strung across his chest. An urgent mission. Surely this war hero, who had been seen on his way to a conference with the Fuehrer an hour before, was above suspicion.

"Pass," said the guard in charge.

The second ring of guards was passed with the same ease. Now they were at the airfield, where the plane was waiting. "We're taking off right away," Stauffenberg said to the pilot. "Just give me time to make a telephone call."

He went into a booth, asked to be connected with the Ministry of War and got General Olbricht on the line. Stauffenberg recognized Olbricht's voice. Very distinctly, he pronounced the code sentence which signified that the Fuehrer was dead, that the machinery of succession was to be put in motion.

Berlin, one o'clock. Olbricht walked into General Fromm's office and said, "There's been an attempt upon the Fuehrer's life at Headquarters. The Fuehrer is dead. We must proceed with the 'Valkyrie Plan.'"

Fromm: "Where did you get the news that the Fuehrer is dead?"

Olbricht: "Over the telephone from Stauffenberg."

Fromm (after a few seconds of hesitation): "I can't declare martial law on the grounds of what one Colonel has to say. I'll have to put in a call to Rastenburg myself."

Olbricht: "You won't be able to get through. The telephone exchange there has probably been destroyed by now."

But Fromm asked for the connection and almost immediately obtained it. Meanwhile Olbricht had picked up an auxiliary receiver. "Keitel speaking," said a voice from the other end.

Fromm: "There's a rumor here in Berlin of an attempt upon the life of the Fuehrer."

Keitel: "That's correct. But the attempt was a failure. The Fuehrer is very much alive and only slightly wounded. Where is Stauffenberg?"

Fromm: "He hasn't yet returned."

Putting down the receiver, Olbricht said, "Keitel's lying!"

He left Fromm's office and went back to join Beck. "Well?" Beck asked him.

"Fromm got Keitel on the wire. Keitel claims that the Fuehrer is no more than wounded, but I'm sure that's a lie. Stauffenberg was positive about it."

Beck and Olbricht finally decided to await the Colonel's return. Hours went by. Nothing happened. The situation was strange indeed!

Four o'clock. Stauffenberg walked into the office, his face streaming with perspiration.

"We decided to wait for you," Beck told him.

"What? You've taken no further steps? I can't believe it! You got my call, didn't you? The explosion was tremendous! I saw the bodies blown up into the air. Not a single man can have survived—"

Beck and Olbricht interrupted him.

"Keitel isn't dead. He answered the telephone."

"Then Fellgiebel didn't destroy the exchange!"

"Keitel claims that the Fuehrer's alive!"

"If Keitel survived, then he's lying!" the Colonel exclaimed. "I saw the Fuehrer's body with my own eyes! Hitler's dead and you haven't stirred a finger!"

The two others looked hard at each other. The Colonel had spoken with absolute assurance. Why should they believe Keitel rather than this man, who had risked his life in their cause? Perhaps Keitel was simply trying to gain time. He might be working out a counter-putsch with Himmler at this very moment.

"We must do something at once," Stauffenberg insisted. "Get the 'Valkyrie Plan' started. Pay no attention to Fromm and send out your orders!"

Olbricht telephoned to his Chief of Staff. Two minutes later the 800 telephone lines inside the Ministry were cleared for a priority message. Telegraph and teletype machines clicked, and the mechanism of the putsch was in motion. Olbricht and Stauffenberg went to Fromm's office.

"Hitler's dead," said the Colonel. "I placed the time bomb myself."

"The 'Valkyrie Plan' is under way," Olbricht added. "Orders have gone out already."

"It's not true!" exclaimed Fromm, bringing his fist down on the desk. "Who sent the orders?"

"Colonel von Quirnheim, my Chief of Staff."

Fromm summoned this officer, who confirmed his superior.

"In that case you are under arrest," said Fromm. And turning to Stauffenberg, he added: "Your attempt was a failure. There's nothing for you to do but take your own life."

"Not a bit of it!" said Olbricht. "We are arresting you!"

There followed a minute or two of confused interjections and some scuffling. Then Fromm was led into an adjoining room and the door locked behind him.

Hitler was not dead. He had been thrown against the wall in such a way as to hurt his right arm and hand; he had burns on his head and face; his clothes were in shreds; and he was in a state of mild shock. Keitel picked him up and carried him to his apartment in the shelter. The slightness of his injuries was proved by the fact that two hours after the explosion he decided to receive Mussolini, who had arrived at Rastenburg for a conference with him.

Just before the explosion, he had left the table to examine a map, and had thus put more distance between himself and the bomb. But others who were at an equal distance were not spared. There were thirteen victims. Hitler's secretary, three Generals and a Colonel were dead or mortally wounded; Gen. Alfred Jodl and seven Army and Navy officers were seriously injured. The survivors owed their luck to the fact that the conference was held in a frail wooden building. The

explosion tore off the roof instead of spending its full force inside, as it would have done in the concrete shelter.

The security officers launched an investigation at once. The bomb had not been thrown through a window, for no one had heard or seen any such thing. It had not been hidden under the floor, for the floor was crumbled rather than raised up. Therefore it must have been left in the room. It was recalled that an officer had left the conference two minutes before the explosion. And the guards outside admitted that he had seemed to be in a great hurry to get away.

Berlin, 4.30. The Ministry was besieged by telephone calls from the Generals who had received "Valkyrie Plan" orders and wanted confirmation and further details. The same answer was given to them all: "The Fuehrer is dead, and the Army has taken over. Everything is under control."

Conspirators kept pouring in. But many of them seemed to be unsure and in search of news. The leaders tried to infuse some spirit into them. After all, the "Valkyrie Plan" was in action. But not even the leaders had much conviction in their voices. Finally Beck made a statement: "My function as head of the government prevents me from taking part in the proceedings. I wish to maintain an umpire's neutral role. It is up to Generals Olbricht, Hoepner and Witzleben and Colonel Stauffenberg to go ahead according to plan."

An officer came in to say that various field commanders seemed incredulous and were hesitant to carry out the plan as directed. Why not make the radio announcement?

"Yes, Goerdeler must make his speech. He simply can't delay any longer. Where is Goerdeler, anyhow? Has anybody seen him?"

No one seemed to know where the future Chancellor could be. (Later it was learned that he had fled Berlin, in fear of arrest.)

"If he can't be found, then someone else can read his speech."

Of course! Why hang back? This carefully formulated text must be given to the German people! Who had a copy? Nobody. And who knew where one could be found? Nobody. Certainly, the organization of the putsch left a great deal to be desired. The morale of the conspirators was beginning to collapse. There was no alarm in the street. The troops and tanks that were supposed to surround all public buildings were nowhere to be seen. Not a single tank was in view.

At 6 p.m. the radio announced that there had been an unsuccessful attempt upon the life of the Fuehrer. But the Fuehrer had just received the Duce, and would go on the air later in the evening.

"They're bluffing!" said Stauffenberg. "Keitel and the rest are still trying to gain time."

A few minutes later Fellgiebel called in from Headquarters with the news that Hitler was alive. Stauffenberg shrugged his shoulders.

"He had to make the call. Probably they were holding a gun against the small of his back."

Several of the conspirators began to think that if the putsch had included the immediate seizure of all the radio stations, they would have found themselves considerably better off. With these in their hands, even if Hitler were alive, they might still have put it over. But what now? Beck proceeded to call up Kluge.

"Here, we've done everything according to plan," he began, "and there's been no serious resistance. I am calling to ask you to come out in our favor and issue appropriate orders."

"Haven't you heard the radio?" asked Kluge. "The Fuehrer isn't dead at all."

"That's not the question. We must carry off the putsch. There isn't really a Fuehrer anymore, since events prove the existence of a decisive opposition."

Kluge remained silent at his end of the wire. Finally he said, "We're up against a new and unexpected situation. I'll call you back after I've consulted my staff."

At this point Witzleben arrived at the Ministry. Surely he would pick up the telephone and call the hesitant Generals to order. He walked briskly into Beck's office and summoned Stauffenberg to talk to him behind closed doors. The other conspirators waited silently, straining their ears to overhear. Suddenly they all stared at one another. The voices inside were raised in violent argument. Then the door opened and Witzleben appeared with an angry look upon his face. He threw a glance at those present, shrugged his shoulders and declared, "I'm going home."

All of them felt as if they had been struck over the head by a crowbar. Didn't Witzleben's departure signify that the game was up? Some men went away. Just then Olbricht appeared at the door.

"All's well!" he exclaimed. "The 'Valkyrie Plan' is beginning to work. The Guard Battalion is moving in to protect our building. Look! Just as we planned it!"

Through the windows they could see troops moving into place on the Bendlerstrasse. Men who had been ready to give up the struggle a few minutes before now felt comfortably warm inside. In reality, everything was lost. A few minutes later they were to learn that the Guard had come not to protect the Ministry but to besiege it. They were prisoners, every one of them.

When Major Remer, the commander of the Guard Battalion, received those orders from the "Valkyrie Plan" which directly concerned him, his stomach turned over. The Fuehrer was dead, the Army had taken over and his first assigned job was to arrest Propaganda Minister Goebbels. He summoned Lieutenant Hager from the Ministry of Propaganda.

"Go slow," the Lieutenant advised him. "The radio hasn't announced the Fuehrer's death. We'd better find out for sure."

"Where can we do that?"

"From Goebbels himself. If the Fuehrer is dead, he'll know it."

Remer proceeded with Hager to the Propaganda Ministry, taking his Battalion. Thus he was prepared for any eventuality. While the Battalion stood below, Remer went straight to Goebbels' office.

"It's all a hoax," Goebbels told him coldly. "Hitler is only slightly wounded. Shall I call Headquarters?"

A few moments later his call was put through to Rastenburg; he said a few words and then handed the telephone to Remer. "Major Remer, do you recognize my voice?" These words registered like so many bullets upon Remer's brain. He was listening to the voice of the master of all Germany. Moved by a reflex of his whole being he answered: "Yes, Fuehrer."

"Are you convinced that I'm not dead?"

"Yes, Fuehrer."

That settled it. Major Remer marched his Battalion to the War Ministry.

From then on, things moved fast. Some of the officers inside the Ministry, who were only halfheartedly for the putsch anyhow, made up their minds quickly enough when they saw the S.S. troops move in. Lieutenant Colonel von der Heyden shouted, "Treason!" and fired the first shot of the day, at Stauffenberg, who limped into Beck's office with a bullet in his back. Fromm was released and came into the office where the conspirators were now trapped.

"I take it upon myself to constitute a special court-martial and to sentence five of you to death. Throw down your arms!" And he pointed to the five: Quirnheim, Olbricht, Stauffenberg, Haeften and Beck.

"I should like to keep my revolver in order to take upon myself the consequences of the situation," Beck told him.

"Then hurry up about it."

Beck placed the barrel of his revolver against his forehead. The revolver went off, and he fell onto a chair with his head bloody, but he was still alive.

"I give you exactly five minutes in which to write to your families," Fromm said to the others.

He went out of the room, while his prisoners sat down at a round table to write their farewell letters. The office was deathly silent, but heavy footsteps rang out through the rest of the building. In five minutes Fromm reappeared, accompanied by S.S. troopers, who took away all the prisoners except Beck.

"Give me another gun," Beck pleaded. And he shot himself in the head, again unsuccessfully. Fromm had him finished off a few minutes later.

Down in the courtyard the headlight of an army truck threw a bright spot upon a wall. The firing squad was lined up in the shadows. The first man to die was stood against the wall with his eyes blinded by the light. Before he could open them, there was a salvo. S.S. men dragged the body aside, while the squad proceeded with its work.

"Long live eternal Germany," Stauffenberg shouted before he fell.

It was all over. "A small clique of ambitious, conscienceless and criminally stupid officers"—this was how Hitler referred to the conspirators in his midnight radio address. Beginning the next day a secretly organized police network went to work throughout the nation. Some of the Marshals and Generals who were not involved, such as Rundstedt, demanded that the accused officers be brought before a court-martial. On August 7 eight of the accused, including Field Marshal Witzleben and General Hoepner, appeared before such a court, in closed session. All acknowledged their participation in the conspiracy. They were hanged, and photographs of the hanging were sent all over the world.

Meanwhile the press and radio announced a prize of a million marks for Goerdeler's head. The man slated to be chancellor hid out first in Berlin and then in East Prussia. Eventually he was recognized, reported, arrested, and executed on February 2, 1945. Fromm was sentenced for "cowardice," because he had acted too slowly in repressing the conspiracy, and was executed on March 19. General Karl von Stulpnagel, who had tried to put a bullet through his brain on the day after the conspiracy's failure but succeeded merely in blinding himself, was executed also. The executions—by firing squad, gallows, garrote and shot in the back of the neck, almost all within prison walls —went on until March 1945. Only the spectacular hangings were made public. The total number is not known. Some Allied investigators put the figure for arrests at more than 4000.

Many of the conspirators escaped reprisal by committing suicide. Kluge took poison while traveling by airplane to Berlin at the end of August in order to explain what he knew. Given the choice between poison and the "People's Court," Field Marshal Rommel chose to poison himself at his home near Ulm on October 14, 1944. For reasons which it is easy to understand, he was officially reported to have died of his wounds and to have taken his place in history as "one of the greatest of all German generals."

In the chaos that marked the end of the war, prisoners were transferred from one jail or camp to another; there were air raids everywhere and communications were disrupted, while many jailers fled, setting their captives free or leaving them behind. In this way several of the conspirators survived, bearing witness to the facts from which the story could be pieced together.

The drama of July 20, 1944, was the curtain-raiser of the larger drama of the death of Hitler's Germany. A small number of men, persuaded that only the elimination of Hitler could ward off further catastrophe, failed in their attempt. Shortly after midnight Hitler went on the air.

"I suffered no wounds, but merely a few burns, scratches and bruises, and I consider this fact a confirmation of the mission which Divine Providence has entrusted to me. I thank Providence and my Creator, not for saving my life, but for making it possible for me to endure my cares and pursue the task which my conscience commands me."

Absolute power was more than ever in his hands. Himmler was named Chief of Staff, and all officials suspected of being the least bit lukewarm were superseded. Most ranking Army officers sent protestations of loyalty to Hitler's Headquarters.

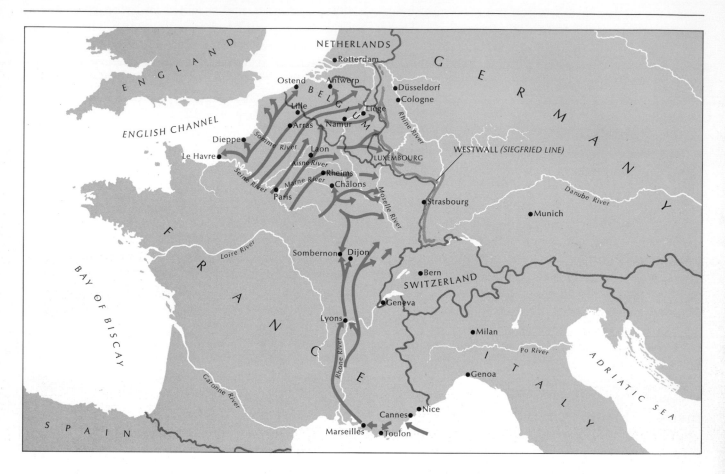

THE ALLIES' THRUST TOWARD THE WESTWALL

For three days, August 15 to 17, 1944, U.S. and Free French forces landed between Cannes and Toulon, in an assault known as Operation Anvil-Dragoon. The Allied invaders advanced northward in two spearheads, and by September 11 had captured Toulon, Marseilles, Lyons and Dijon, linking up with Patton's right flank at Sombernon.

Meanwhile, the Allied armies' drive toward Germany continued. The Canadian First Army captured a large German force near Le Havre, then the Nazi garrison at Dieppe, and advanced to Ostend.

Earlier, on September 4, the British Second Army had seized the Belgian port of Antwerp. The U.S. First Army, headed by Lt. Gen. Courtney

H. Hodges, took Laon, France, and Namur and Liége, Belgium, and liberated Luxembourg. In the south, Patton's Third Army swept over the Marne and captured Rheims and Châlons.

The veteran Rundstedt, commander of the Nazi forces, moved to strengthen the Westwall, or Siegfried Line, along Germany's western border with as many fresh divisions as he could find. Hitler had lost 2 million men since June—540,000 of them on the western front—and 200,000 more were bottled up in Atlantic and Channel ports far behind the Allied lines. Continued Allied bombing was battering the German war machine and destroying much of the all-important

oil without which it could not run.

But the Allied armies were encountering problems of their own. As they raced farther and farther inland, they became more and more difficult to supply. Thirty-six divisions were now ashore—more than 2 million men. Each division required between 400 and 600 tons of supplies every day, all of which had to be landed on the Normandy beaches and then brought up to the ever-more-distant front by train and motor convoy. Despite heroic efforts by the drivers of the Army Transportation Corps, the flow of supplies to the front was reduced to a trickle, and the Allied advance slowed, then stalled, as it neared the German border.

(Right) The sky above the French Riviera is filled with planes and parachutes as troops of the U.S. Seventh Army float down in an invasion of southern France, August 15, 1944.

(Right) *Mercy takes no sides: A U.S. medical jeep, carrying both American and German wounded, finds the going rough as it proceeds to the rear through the waters of the Moselle River. The first-aid unit is met by a group of American troops en route to the battle zone, themselves possible candidates for similar evacuation.*

(Below) *End of treachery: This Frenchman, who has been found guilty of collaborating with the enemy, pays with his life before a firing squad of his own countrymen. The photograph shows the victim's body falling as bullets sever the rope which has tied him to the stake. Wooden splinters are cascading through the air.*

(Left) *Under the white flag: A Nazi soldier gives the time-honored signal of surrender when overtaken by an American tank, whose gun is seen jutting into the foreground. The German soldier, a medical corpsman, was engaged with his comrades in bearing a wounded man to a first-aid station in Belgium, and all the group were eager to capitulate.*

(Below) *Stigma of guilt: A group of French women, their heads shorn of hair as the penalty for consorting with the enemy, have been loaded aboard a truck and are paraded through the streets in an exhibition of public shame. In some cases the foreheads of women judged guilty of collaborating with the Nazis were painted with swastikas by their countrymen.*

Paratroopers charge through shellbursts from German 88's during an attack in the Netherlands. "Operation Market-Garden," a daring airborne attempt to outflank the enemy's
Westwall in September 1944, was ultimately turned back with heavy Allied losses.

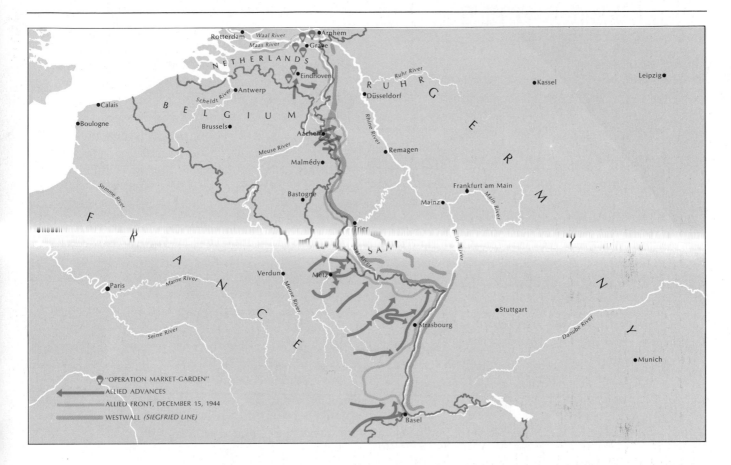

Map legend:

⏺ "OPERATION MARKET-GARDEN"
← ALLIED ADVANCES
ALLIED FRONT, DECEMBER 15, 1944
WESTWALL (SIEGFRIED LINE)

ADVANCE ON THE RHINE: Autumn of Costly Gains

On September 17, 1944, "Operation Market-Garden" was launched. Under Field Marshal Montgomery's command, 20,000 airborne troops were dropped over the Netherlands. Their mission was to seize crucial bridges across the Waal, Maas (Meuse) and Lower Rhine rivers and then link up with the British XXX Corps driving from the south. If successful, the way to the Ruhr and Berlin would lie open.

At first all seemed to go well. The 101st Airborne Division seized the bridge at Grave and made contact with the advancing British land forces. But at Arnhem on the Lower Rhine, the British 1st Airborne met disaster. Already plagued by bad weather which forced a delay in the massive drop, the 8000 men of the colorful "Red Devils" had the misfortune to come to earth where two divisions of veteran German panzer troops were freshly deployed. Only about one fourth of the "Red Devils" got out of the trap.

It was now clear that the Allies would have to blast their way through the German defenses to get to Berlin. Accordingly, toward the end of September 1944, Canadian troops captured the sealed-off Channel ports of Boulogne and Calais.

After weeks of fierce fighting, British and Canadian forces flushed the Germans from the banks and islands of the vital Scheldt estuary that runs for fifty-five miles from the great Belgian port of Antwerp to the sea. With these ports at last open to them, the Allies could reinforce and resupply themselves quickly.

All along the line the Allies now began again to press forward toward their two objectives, the industrial basins of the Saar and the Ruhr. In October, Hodge's First Army captured Aachen—the first German city to fall into Allied hands. Patton's Third Army seized Metz on October 3 and secured three bridgeheads across the Saar River, while, farther south, the U.S. Seventh Army under Lt. Gen. Alexander M. Patch overran Strasbourg on October 23 and reached the western bank of the Rhine.

THE BATTLE OF THE BULGE

BY BRIG. GEN. S. L. A. MARSHALL, USAR (RET.)

Some years ago a monument to the victory in the Battle of the Bulge was erected on Mardesson Hill near Bastogne, where besieged Americans fought a costly and strategically vital engagement. An inscription on the memorial recounting the course of the battle was written by S. L. A. Marshall, at the request of the Belgian and American governments— unique recognition of the military historian's knowledge and understanding of the crucial event. News of the German breakthrough in the Ardennes in December 1944 took General Marshall from Paris to the scene of battle, where he remained to the end. A quarter of a century afterward, General Marshall here describes and analyzes the Battle of the Bulge, the story of how Hitler's last desperate attempt to turn the tides of defeat posed a stunning challenge to the advancing Allies.

At midnight on December 17, 1944, there was a long ring on my telephone in the headquarters at the Majestic Hotel, Paris—that monument to the rococo which many years later would be the base for truce negotiators in the Vietnam war.

The voice on the other end, speaking for G-3 (operations and training section) of the Supreme Command, said, "There's a battle going on up front."

I replied, "Yes, I know all about it."

The man went on, "We need to name it for operational purposes."

I said, "Call it the Battle of the Ardennes."

He objected, "But there have been other battles of the Ardennes."

I said, "Wrong. In the past, much fighting in the Ardennes, but never a Battle of the Ardennes."

He tried again, asking, "Why not make it the Ardennes Defensive?"

I said, "Wrong again. Suppose we ultimately take the offensive and score big, which is almost certain to happen; then you will have the battle misnamed."

At that point he tossed in the towel. Officially, the Battle of the Ardennes it became. Still, man proposes, but labels, like events, take form through millions of men doing what comes naturally. That battle would be known to history under a quite different name.

With my opposite number from the War Department, Col. John A. Kemper, I had pored over maps in the war room for eight hours, trying to figure what the Germans were doing and how far they would get with it.

By luck more than inspired sweat, our guesswork proved perfect. The limits of the enemy advance were as we outlined them, within less than ten miles. Our purpose was to shift field historians from flank to flank so that we would cover every main fighting unit playing a role in stopping the attack.

John and I saw that night that a great enemy bulge was developing and coming our way. We did not foresee that the name of the action would become vulgarized as the Battle of the Bulge, as if it were a fat man's struggle against his obesity, simply because several million GI's so willed it. Nor could we then guess that in duration, ferocity and cost in life, the unfolding battle would be second only to the Meuse-Argonne of World War I, the worst bloodbath in our history.

Even as we toiled, the people at SHAEF (Supreme Headquarters, Allied Expeditionary Forces) in those same hours were beginning to understand the magnitude of the threat and were coming to grips with it. During the first thirty-six hours, they had not been sleepwalking as if transfixed by the shock of the surprise; the trouble was that only wisps of information were feeding back from the shattered front. Communication lines were down, and so were men, and while panic was not general, it occurred.

In Tennyson's words, "Someone had blundered," and "All the world wondered." Later, the oversimplifiers of history, ever ready to explain every mystery that heaven never intended mortals should understand fully, would cite a failure by Intelligence. It seemed a likely story.

The Supreme Command had gambled on a thinned-to-breaking-point defense of almost 100 miles of front in the Ardennes, a rugged and forest-grown region in France, southeast Belgium and Luxembourg, with few good roads and many defiles. The sector held by U.S. VIII Corps was manned only by two green divisions and two others so battle-weary that they required rest and refitting. The enemy buildup opposite these divisions had not gone on undetected. Most of the incoming German divisions had been spotted as they arrived by Maj. Gen. Kenneth Strong, the SHAEF G-2 (Military Intelligence Officer), and he had alerted his commanders. But on the operations side, the G-3's, Maj. Gen. Harold R. ("Pinky") Bull, the American, and Maj. Gen. John F. M. ("Jock") Whiteley, the Briton, had advised General Eisenhower to view the buildup as something to be watched but not as a cause for alarm, in which judgment they were supported by the Chief of Staff, Lt. Gen. Walter Bedell Smith.

They reasoned that the Germans were comfortably quartered and their main chance was to prolong the war in hope of better terms. It was a first-class reading of the logic of the German General Staff mind. The flaw was that now they were dealing strictly with the mind of Hitler, who after the failure of the July bomb plot (see pages 376–385) had closed his grip on the control and direction of all German military commands. In the Allied camp, Hitler's ascendancy over the General Staff, growing out of his misfortunes, was not known—or even guessed at.

The enemy campaign opened at 5:30 a.m. on December 16 with an attack by three German field armies that ripped the length of the U.S. VIII Corps front. It was a morning of dense fog, pierced at the start only by the flashes of a brief artillery preparation. Then came the infantry assault, its weight falling most heavily on the unseasoned 106th Division and the bone-tired 28th Division.

By midday the defending line was breached in at least three places beyond possibility of swift repair, though no general alarm was sounded. The onslaught was mistaken for a number of strictly local attacks, possibly meant to spoil an offensive then being launched by U.S. V Corps out of the northern flank of VIII Corps's sector. Correctly reading something more formidable out of the enemy movement, the V Corps commander, Maj. Gen. Leonard T. Gerow, asked to have his offensive thrust canceled, but was denied permission by the U.S. First Army at Spa.

That night the Supreme Commander, Gen. Dwight D. Eisenhower, felt a premonition and directed that the 7th Armored Division, out of Lt. Gen. William H. Simpson's Ninth Army to the north, and the 10th Armored, out of Lt. Gen. George S. Patton's Third Army to the south, be sent immediately to strengthen the VIII Corps front. Elsewhere there was little alarm. To the rear of the threatened front, men continued on their routine rounds. In Paris and Brussels life was as gay as the onset of wintry weather, not yet softened by snowfall, permitted.

One of America's ablest battle commanders, Maj. Gen. Maxwell D. Taylor, had departed on a brief mission to Washington, certain that he would miss nothing of importance. Field Marshal Sir Bernard L. Montgomery was preparing to leave for London to spend Christmas with his son.

The German enemy had been as careful in planning his attack as he was skillful in concealing it. The plan was conceived, in early September 1944, by Hitler. In that month, his forces were withdrawing from these same mountains of the Ardennes, and, except around the seaward approaches to Antwerp, were being driven from Belgium by the liberating armies. It was then that Hitler decided that a supreme effort in the upland, if staged in the most favorable season, might reverse the tide of war. His thinking was only partly guided by his two closest military advisers, Field Marshal Wilhelm Keitel and Gen. Alfred Jodl, the two men in whom he confided almost exclusively at this stage.

The far objective was to be the port of Antwerp. The far hope was that its capture would split the Allied armies, strip them of their supplies and cause Great Britain to quit the war. In line with such hopes, the German High Command husbanded its reserves during the fighting of the autumn, raised fresh divisions, withdrew others from the Italian and Russian fronts to refit them and intensified the production of tanks, motor fuel, ammunition and all other matériel essential to the last great lunge. What was achieved by the military planners and by the civilian directors and workers—under the pressure of Hitler's determination—must be termed nothing less than prodigious.

Gradually, very gradually, the commanders who would direct the battle were admitted to the secret, a few at a time. An early confidant was Field Marshal Walther Model, who would direct the fighting; later came Field Marshal Gerd von Rundstedt, the overall commander. Later still the army, corps and division commanders got the word. As opportunity afforded, the generals voiced their objections, contending that the plan was too ambitious. All of them failed to influence Hitler. His dream of what might be done prevailed, and his scheme to make surprise absolute succeeded phenomenally. To call it a masterpiece marred in the doing is not too much. Yet, there was never a chance that he would finally succeed. Hitler expected—or hoped—to see his panzers possess bridgeheads over the Meuse River by the second night of the battle. He dreamed of closing Belgium within his hands before its defenders could react to his daring.

Germany's High Command had brought together twenty-five divisions for the breakthrough, seventeen of which were used at the beginning. The infantry attack, strongly supported by antitank and antiaircraft formations, would block north and south of the penetration, trying to hold and extend the flanks as the armor drove through in the center.

Under Hitler's lash the German architects of the attack had proved their genius. An essential of the German plan, put there by Hitler himself, was that the crumbling Allied rear would be beset by continued mystery, terror and confusion. One column, led by a ruthless Colonel, Jochen Peiper, and a paratroop pack under a notorious character, Otto Skorzeny, were instruments to these ends. (In September 1943 Skorzeny had led the German rescue of Mussolini from Monte Corno, Italy, where he was held prisoner by his countrymen.) English-speaking, some wearing U.S. uniforms, these troops were to hit sensitive points, spread false reports, cut communications and kill at will.

As it happened, the impression they created of being in all places and threatening everything was much greater than they had hoped, though the physical damage they caused was far less than they had planned. Through early capture of some of these men, the Allied command got an exaggerated idea of the threat. One consequence was an almost ludicrous tightening of security measures throughout the theater, resulting in waste motion and heightened tension.

On December 17 Peiper's force intercepted and captured a large group of U.S. artillerymen driving south with the 7th Armored Division. The captives were herded into a meadow and gunned down. This massacre at Malmédy, discovered the same day by another American force, is still remembered as the most outrageous episode of that month of slaughter.

The 17th was in other ways a red-letter day for the Allied side, when the vanquishing of doubts gave rise to great decisions. In the nick of time the Supreme Command realized it was challenged by a full-scale German offensive and correctly estimated the size of the threat.

The total reserves of SHAEF within France were two badly worn U.S. Airborne Divisions, the 82d and 101st, refitting at Mourmelon le Grand. The decision of where and when to commit them was made by the Chief of Staff, Lieutenant General Smith, with the two G-3's advising. That night they were rushed toward the front in truck convoys with all lights blazing, the 82d to Werbomont, the 101st to Bastogne.

Bastogne and St.-Vith were to become the fulcrums of defense in the central Ardennes, each being the hub of a radial highway net. Deny the panzer forces use of the roads, either permanently or for a sufficient interval, and the enemy's drive to the Meuse must fail.

Around Monschau, Germany, in the north and Echternach, Luxembourg, in the south, the shoulders of the penetration—it was not yet a bulge—were holding steady. They would continue to do so mainly because of the accuracy and intensity of the 99th Division artillery around Monschau and the rocklike stand of the 2d Infantry Division on nearby Eisenborn Ridge. Chief guardian of the south shoulder was the 4th Infantry Division.

The most cheering, steadying factor in the thinking of the Supreme Commander was the stand of the 2d Division. General Eisenhower believed that the primary enemy objective was Liége, and he knew that this force at Eisenborn barred the way.

Other great decisions and countermoves were made or in the making. The U.S. Third Army, which was attacking eastward to the south of the First Army, was turned 90° to attack northward against the enemy's left flank. Men said later that only its great commander, Lieutenant General Patton, could have brought off such a complicated maneuver so quickly.

Because the First Army's front had been broken, its forces and communications parted as by a wedge, General Eisenhower put U.S. forces (previously com-

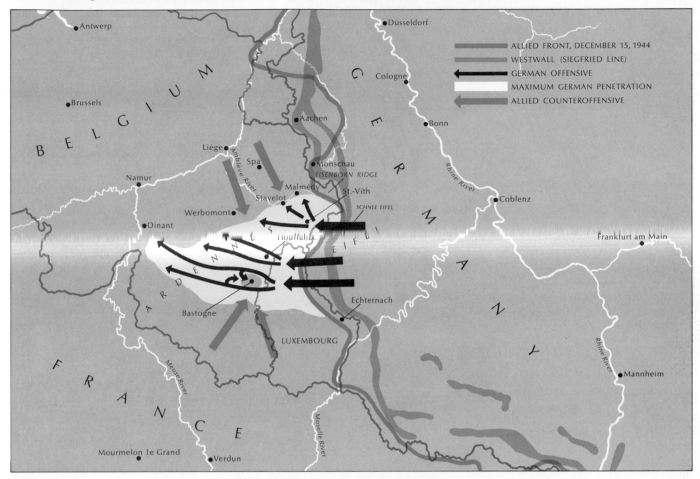

Battle of the Bulge: December 16, 1944–January 16, 1945. In an attempt to break through to Liége, then on to Antwerp, thus splitting the Allied armies, a German counterattack was launched through the Ardennes. Allied resistance, notably at St.-Vith, turned back the enemy.

manded by Lt. Gen. Omar N. Bradley) to the north of the expanding salient, under British Field Marshal Montgomery of the 21st Army Group. The decision, essential to ensure adequate control of fighting forces, was objected to by General Bradley and many other American officers.

By the third day the equivalent of more than two Allied field armies was converging on the battleground, either to serve as blocking forces at the road hubs in the central Ardennes or to engage along the flanks of the salient as the German armor and infantry fought on to widen and deepen their penetration.

It was clear from the start that the 101st Division would be surrounded at Bastogne by the German XLVII Panzer Corps. The latter's divisions had not been thrown off schedule in crashing the defenses of the U.S. 28th Division and were now racing the Americans for the town, a radio intercept having told the Germans who was coming. The question was whether the U.S. paratroopers, one combat command of the

10th Armored and a destroyer battalion would be able to hold, if enveloped.

St.-Vith, the other citadel, was a different problem. The enemy was already menacing it in superior strength as one combat command of the 7th Armored closed on the town to open its defense, helped by what remained of the broken 106th Division. Here the question was how long the Allied defense could withstand the hammering.

Much depended on the weather. The land was fogbound at the start and the ground unfrozen but not mushy, the ideal conditions Hitler had wished for so that Allied air power could not intervene. A little snow had fallen around the Schnee Eifel, the composite of low-ranging hills to the east, where the heaviest enemy concentration had been seated. Elsewhere the Ardennes lay bare and ugly. The Allies desperately needed fair weather, and within the week the first great snowstorm would whiten the landscape as a preliminary to clearing skies.

(Left) *S.S. Col. Jochen Peiper, commander of a panzer group, reads a road sign during the Ardennes breakthrough. Peiper and his men were accused of executing captive American soldiers.*

(Below) *The bodies of American soldiers who had been shot down by the Nazis after they had been taken prisoner were discovered under a layer of snow in a field near Malmédy. The numbers showing in the photograph are tags placed on each of the bodies as a means of identification.*

(Top right) *German infantrymen advance on the run past burning American vehicles at the height of the Battle of the Bulge. During the first three days, German spearheads penetrated sixty-five miles.*

(Bottom right) *Hampered by deep snow, men of the U.S. First Army prepare to launch a counterattack on the northern flank of the Bulge, in an attempt to turn back Hitler's last offensive.*

Americans within the Ardennes did not all react valiantly. In one large headquarters there was near-panic for several days. One artillery battalion retreated from Bastogne as the enemy came on. One corps commander, who stood as steady as Stonewall Jackson at the First Battle of Manassas, found himself in crisis deserted by most of his staff.

Such failures were the exception. Recovery came swiftly only because the vast majority of Americans did their duty or beyond. Right under the guns, many oddments joined the firing line—repairmen, clerks, police and drivers of trucks. They picked up arms and moved to a threatened crossroads or blew a bridge or guarded the precious stores. Generals and colonels at times served as traffic policemen to speed the troop flow into the danger area.

In Great Britain newly arrived U.S. formations, such as the 17th Airborne Division, were alerted to go by air to defend the line of the Meuse. The zone of supply in France was reorganized to feed the battle; its convoys going elsewhere were halted and faced about. Along the general front running from the Netherlands to Switzerland, the Allied armies shifted weight toward the battle. In the United States, where the alarm blighted the Christmas holidays, there was swift reapportionment of training forces to provide replacements for the wasting infantry line. In France scratch rifle companies were formed from airmen and rear-area soldiers.

Thus the Allies gained unity of action, and the signals were called for the month-long struggle ahead. In the Supreme Command and other headquarters vagueness had given way to steadiness. Great decisions had been taken. There remained the weeks of execution, in which deeds would match thoughts and courage would prove equal to the plan.

The spearpoint of the 101st Division—one battalion —beat the enemy to Bastogne by eight hours. Still, the German armor came up in such strength next morning that it could have stormed and taken the city had not one Nazi division commander, usually intrepid, apparently lost his nerve at the decisive moment. He halted his attack, hid in a cave all day, then signaled his higher command that Bastogne was held in such strength by the Americans that the entire panzer corps would have to be committed there, instead of flanking it to race for the Meuse. The message got to Hitler. He agreed. This was his first fatal deviation from plan.

Major General Anthony McAuliffe is decorated with the Distinguished Service Cross by Lt. Gen. George S. Patton.

The airborne division, fully closed in a tight ring around Bastogne, and soon thereafter wholly enveloped by the XLVII Panzer Corps, stayed light on its feet, fenced with the enemy and made superb use of its artillery, employing the guns only to stop direct attack. As the snowstorm hit heavily, forbidding air resupply, ammunition dwindled to less than five rounds per gun per day. Yet the surrounding Germans gained no impression of any shortage within the perimeter.

On December 22 came the high drama of the closed siege. The German corps commander, Gen. Heinrich von Luettwitz, called on the Bastogne garrison to surrender. The U.S. commander, Brig. Gen. Anthony C. McAuliffe, replied, "Nuts!"—a message considered by some to be as famous as "Don't give up the ship!" or "I have not yet begun to fight."

That same day the skies cleared. An airdrop supplied the needs of the Bastogne garrison, and Allied attack planes swarmed over the Ardennes, hunting down the German panzers. On the day after Christmas a spearpoint of the 4th Armored Division, Third Army, broke through from the south to relieve Bastogne. It was commanded by a youngster named W. Creighton Abrams, who later would command an army in Vietnam.

St.-Vith was a wholly different kind of show, a thunderous affair of blood and iron and pitched battle, with enemy numbers and weight of artillery ever increasing. The American defenders under Brig. Gen. Bruce C. Clarke had finally to back away to escape destruction. Their losses had been mournful, but they had fought back long enough to doom Hitler's hopes.

In the north, around Monschau and Eisenborn Ridge, the enemy attack foundered in the first week. The two German divisions in line had been pounded into immobility. The reserve division was committed and fared no better. On Christmas Eve the corps commander signaled the German High Command that he was defeated beyond recovery. Hitler knew then that the plan had failed.

Even so, the fighting flamed higher on Christmas Day and for some weeks thereafter. At Bastogne the enemy persisted in the siege and tried vainly to cut the corridor opened by Abrams' troops. The period of surprise long since past, the panzer armies were now committed to the vain task of trying to batter their way through. Instead of beginning a withdrawal, more men and more guns were sent forward to the Bulge in an effort to hold what had been gained and to expand the front if possible. The part of the battle that followed the passing of the American crisis was the bloodiest of all. None of the ground of the Ardennes was given back by the Germans. There was no sudden strategic retreat. Every hill and roadway had to be re-won by firepower and by paying the price in lives.

The weather at last turned bitter cold; there were gales and deep-drifting snows. A general change was wrought on the battlefront. The loss from exposure grew as great as the loss from fire. Attacking in white suits, the enemy could scarcely be seen. Villages became the chief prize in the daily struggle, as men fought for shelter and warmth. The folk of the Ardennes opened their hearts and hearths to the American fighters. They shared their food, blankets and fuel. They nursed the wounded and helped to comfort the ill.

During early January Lieutenant General Patton directed first the 101st Division and then the 17th Airborne to attack out of the narrow Bastogne salient in the hope of winning through to the north shoulder and

bagging the German armies within the Bulge. Each try ended in a bloody repulse. The German armor and artillery were in too great strength on the surrounding heights.

North of the Bulge, the U.S. VII Corps commander, Maj. Gen. J. Lawton Collins, was champing at the bit, straining to strike south and close the bag on the Germans. But Field Marshal Montgomery was biding his time and for his procrastination being roundly criticized by Americans at Spa and other headquarters. It remains an open question whether Montgomery did not at this stage have a better grasp of the situation and of the hard realities than did Patton at the south shoulder.

The spearhead of the panzer army in the north had rolled on past Stavelot. Then in the defiles beyond the Amblève River it was held and trapped by the new forces of the counterattack. The fighting went on within twenty miles of Liége. The spearpoint of the army in the west reached almost to the door of Dinant before it was stopped by the fire of the new American line.

When at last toward the middle of January the enemy could stand no more and the advance of Allied troops from both shoulders of the Bulge threatened a general envelopment, surviving German units backed away, still fighting with utmost desperation. But the power which they carried away with them was small indeed compared with what lay scattered and broken on the ground of the Ardennes. The storms which had beaten upon the upland throughout the battle had at last quieted; so had the fury of the German tempest. The campaign ended with the meeting of two U.S. task forces from north and south at the small village of Houffalize on January 16.

The full story of the fighting can never be told. There is hardly a town or village in the Ardennes that has not served as a shield and fortress for troops of the United States. The scars of the fight are still marked on the land, the forest, the bridges and the dwelling places. In the battle, 76,890 Americans were killed, wounded or marked missing. The number of Belgians who died, were wounded or suffered privation helping our troops cannot be known. They were wonderful friends in time of need.

With the troops, these countryfolk share the true glory, though many of the heroes of the Bulge were unsung and some of the bravest deeds were unseen.

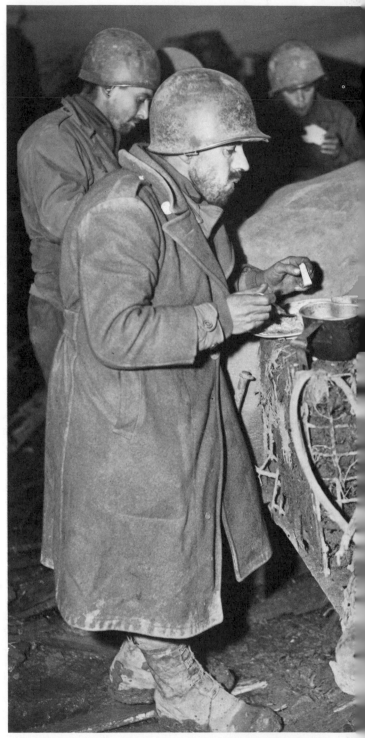

(Left) *For this sullen, battle-weary German soldier, captured after weeks of bitter fighting in the Hürtgen Forest, the end has come. The Hitlerian dream of world conquest by the "superrace" has ended in galling defeat and a prison camp.*
(Above) *Equally exhausted by the strain and danger of combat is the American fighting man, who is at the moment more interested in his first hot meal in weeks than in the victory he and his Allied comrades-in-arms have won.*

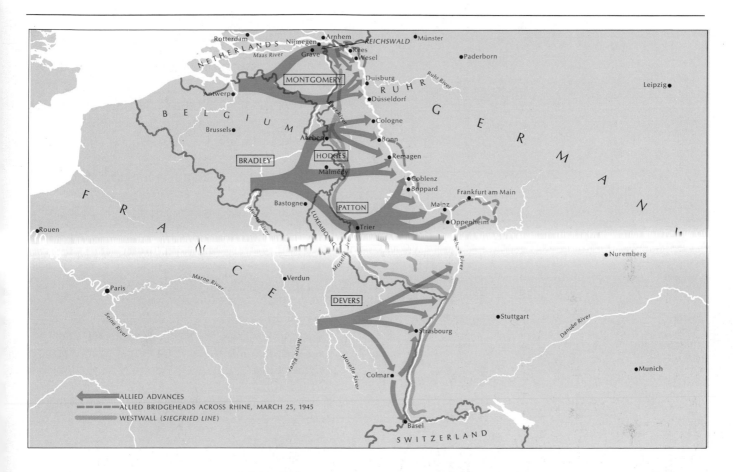

CONQUEST OF THE RHINE

With the Ardennes once again in Allied hands, Eisenhower set out to destroy the battered remnants of the German Army. The German defenders on the western front now numbered eighty-two divisions on paper, but only about twenty-seven were actually up to full strength.

In early February 1945 Eisenhower ordered three massive coordinated thrusts toward the Rhine. In the north, Montgomery's 21st Army Group split in two. The Canadian First and British Second Armies struck southeast toward the Ruhr, while the U.S. Ninth Army drove northeast. Between them they were to hurl the Germans out of the region between the Meuse and the Rhine and then clear the Rhine's

west bank, facing the Ruhr basin. Both forces won their objectives after overcoming unexpected obstacles: the British and Canadians, their armor bogged down by heavy rains, faced savage opposition in the dense Reichswald forest, while the U.S. Ninth Army was delayed two weeks by enemy action and the overflowing Roer River, deliberately flooded by the fleeing Germans.

In the center, Bradley's 12th Army Group (the U.S. First and Third Armies) drove north of the Moselle and, spearheaded by Patton's 4th Armored Division, reached the Rhine near Coblenz. Then veering southeast they captured an entire German force trapped in the mountainous Hunsrück region.

In the south, Lt. Gen. Jacob L. Devers' 6th Army Group (the U.S. Seventh and French First Armies) destroyed a major German force near Colmar, cleared the Rhine's west bank from Strasbourg to the Swiss border and then linked up with southern elements of Patton's force.

Meanwhile, the retreating Germans streamed across the Rhine, destroying bridges as they went—except at Remagen. Here the pursuing Americans took the Ludendorff railroad bridge and held it for ten days (until it collapsed), while five divisions crossed and established a twenty-mile bridgehead along the eastern bank (see pages 402–410). Ever-increasing Allied forces were now within the Rhine wall.

THE CAPTURE OF REMAGEN BRIDGE

BY LT. COL. KEN HECHLER, USAR

To the Germans the romantic Rhine had always been capable of being turned into a vast defensive moat simply by blowing up its bridges. Not since the time of Napoleon in 1806 had an invading army managed to cross its waters. Now, in the early months of 1945, with the armies of the Allied forces moving steadily toward the heart of the Fatherland, final preparations were made to transform the famous river into an impregnable barrier. As the last Nazi troops retreated beyond the Rhine, bridge after bridge was destroyed. There would be no easy way across for the invaders.

Then came one of the strangest and most dramatic moments of World War II. When troops of the 9th Armored Division of the U.S. First Army reached the town of Remagen on the west bank of the Rhine midway between Cologne and Coblenz, they found, to their astonishment, a bridge still standing, still spanning the waters of the mighty Rhine.

This is the story of the capture of the Ludendorff Bridge, the first Allied bridgehead across the Rhine. It is the story of a small band of American GI's who dared to venture across the heavily mined structure. Particularly it is the story of 2d Lt. Karl Timmermann of West Point, Nebraska, the first Allied officer to set foot on the east side of the Rhine. Combat historian Ken Hechler gives the details.

Late in the forenoon of March 7, 1945, a gray drizzly day, a little group of American soldiers on a road high above the town of Remagen was talking excitedly. Second Lieutenant Karl Timmermann and his second-platoon leader, Lt. James Burrows, were peering through field glasses at the Ludendorff Bridge over the Rhine River more than a mile away. They had not dreamed the structure would still be standing when they reached it.

"Jim, look at those damn Krauts going over," said Timmermann.

"And look at the cows and horses, too," Burrows said. "With all those people trying to cross over, that bridge would make a good target."

Burrows glanced around quickly for his mortar squad. "Amick," he yelled, "you and Mercadante set up and prepare to fire on that bridge." There was a hasty scuffling with the heavy base plates and stovepipe tubes as the men adjusted their mortars.

"Tim, I'm not so sure about this," Burrows said to his company commander. "Do you think our mortars will do the trick?"

"It sure tempts me."

"Let's plaster 'em, Lieutenant," one of the mortarmen called out.

"Well, we've got some heavy stuff back of us, and there's no sense in sticking a pin in their tail just to see 'em jump. Let's do it this way: get hold of Colonel Engeman, and he can bring up his tanks and call for some artillery."

A runner took off to alert the task force commander about the big bonanza that Timmermann had found.

A few minutes later Lt. Col. Leonard Engeman roared up, followed by Maj. Murray Deevers, the commander of the 27th Armored Infantry Battalion, and Deevers' operations officer, Maj. Don Russell. They watched the procession of German troops, vehicles and animals far below, making their antlike way across.

"Let's lower the boom," Engeman decreed. A radio message flew out, and presently somebody shoved a reply into his hand.

"Damn. They won't fire the artillery. Claim there are friendly troops in the vicinity." Engeman turned to Deevers. "Murray, we've got to take that town, and it looks like the doughs ought to go down fast and clean it out. I'll bring up my tanks to cover you. Let me know how you want to plan your attack."

The minutes ticked by. The stream of traffic across

402

the bridge slowed down. There was frustrating delay on top of the hill, as the debate proceeded on how to seize this tiger by the tail without inciting him to bite. Deevers spoke to the commanders of A and C Companies, Lieutenants Timmermann and William E. McMaster: "Tim and Mac, you make a reconnaissance down into town and give me a report on how to go in there."

Timmermann and McMaster made their way a little over 500 yards down the hill along a footpath into Remagen. They met no enemy fire, but they saw a lot of activity near the bridge and on the opposite side of the river.

When they returned from their reconnaissance, Timmermann got the nod from Deevers for the all-important task of breaking into Remagen. Lieutenant Jack Liedike's B Company followed, its mission to clear the southeastern part of town while protecting the right flank of the advance. Lieutenant McMaster's C Company was assigned to clear the northwestern part and protect the left flank.

Timmermann held a quick conference with his platoon leaders to issue the attack order and singled out Lieutenant Burrows to point the assault with his second platoon. It was about 1 p.m. He told Burrows to take the main road and work his platoon through the center of Remagen, hugging the buildings because of snipers. Sergeant Joseph DeLisio's platoon was to fan out along the river road on the left flank, crouching low because the Germans could observe clearly from the east bank. Sergeant Michael Chinchar's platoon was to capture the railroad station and move through town on the right flank of A Company before heading for the bridge.

Once Timmermann's men had started for Remagen, a further series of developments put new life and speed into the attack. Major Ben Cothran, Brig. Gen. William M. Hoge's operations officer, had charge of moving the command post (CP) for the combat command on the morning of March 7. Because the main effort of the 9th Armored Division was to capture bridges over the Ahr River, Hoge had stayed with the south column of his combat command and turned over to Cothran the job of moving his CP from Stadt Mechenheim to Birresdorf, three miles west of Remagen. After seeing the combat command's bag and baggage to Birresdorf, Cothran hopped into his jeep to find out how close to the Rhine Colonel Engeman's task force had come.

He got the same tingling sensation in his spine as everyone else when he emerged from the woods and saw the Rhine and the intact bridge below. He looked just long enough to see the German vehicles streaming across and several locomotives on the other side of the river getting up steam.

"Don't you think we ought to bring some artillery down on all that?" asked Colonel Engeman.

"My God, I've got to get the Old Man," yelled Cothran, scarcely aware of the question.

He radioed to General Hoge, who tore across the countryside to the scene, arriving shortly after one o'clock. Things began to happen fast. The General stormed at the delay in taking Remagen. He told everybody in sight to take the town immediately. Then he put his field glasses to his eyes and quietly studied the procession of troops and vehicles crossing the river.

"You know," he said in rather subdued tones to Colonel Engeman, "it would be nice to get that bridge, while we're at it. We might lose a battalion but. . . ."

Hoge continued to stare for another moment, then abruptly lowered his glasses and barked, "Engeman, Deevers, Russell, get those men moving into town!"

"Already on their way," the three replied, almost in unison. It was true—Timmermann had already led his men down the hill and into Remagen.

Burrows' platoon had its biggest scuffle in the main square near the city hall, where an automatic weapon momentarily slowed down the advance. As Burrows started to maneuver his men to flank the German gun, two of Lt. John Grimball's tanks rumbled up and fired several 90-mm. rounds into the square. The machine gun shut up suddenly. Grimball's tanks then intermingled with Burrows' second platoon of infantry and they pushed toward the bridge.

Timmermann's old platoon, the first, did not have too much trouble. Sergeant Chinchar proved an excellent interpreter of the frenzied remarks of Polish and Russian displaced persons and prisoners who were anxious to reward their liberators by indicating where the German soldiers were hiding.

The third platoon, headed by DeLisio, moved out rapidly under the aggressive leadership of the little Sergeant. "C'mon, you guys, just another town," De-Lisio cried, waving his arm and giving a hitch to his M-1 rifle. His men fixed bayonets as they moved slowly down the hill in single file past the church. They crept carefully along, squeezing close against the walls of buildings and keeping their submachine guns and M-1's cocked for trouble.

DeLisio came to a roadblock which the Remagen *Volkssturm* ("People's Army") had set up and then neglected to close. He posted four men at the roadblock and positioned a machine gun 100 yards farther inside the town. It was a perfect trap, in which they caught a number of German soldiers trying to slip through town to get across the Rhine. All were taken prisoner.

At several points civilians ran out and stopped Americans to point out cellars where German soldiers were hiding. Thoroughly demoralized, the Germans invariably surrendered without a shot; many of them realized the futility of resistance, and some had even sent civilians to bring in the Americans. Still, it was not an easy job to clean out the town. Sniper fire rattled from unseen locations, some 20-mm. German fire was landing in the town, and each quiet street carried the threat of a deathtrap at every corner.

Shortly after 2 p.m. Timmermann's men had cleaned out enough of Remagen to turn their rifle fire directly on the bridge. Before they actually reached the bridge, the men saw a volcano of rocks and dirt erupt into the air—the Germans had exploded the preliminary demolition which gouged a crater thirty feet wide in the approach to the bridge.

Gradually DeLisio, Burrows and Chinchar worked their platoons up to the bridge approach where they were joined by the tanks which had helped to clear out the town. "Look at that hole," grumbled Grimball. "It's not enough that they want to blow the bridge, they won't even let us get near it."

Timmermann came up for a brief conference with his platoon leaders. "Well, what're we goin' to do?" Burrows asked.

Across the river, they could see the German troops making frantic preparations to blow up the bridge. Timmermann glanced along the bridge and clearly saw the wires and the telltale charges, ready to go off. Turning to his platoon leaders, he said: "They'll probably blow it any minute now. Watch this—it ought to be good." He put his field glasses to his eyes and scanned the far bank. "They look like they want to get us out on the bridge before they blow it."

By three o'clock most of the infantrymen of A Company and the supporting tanks had taken up positions near the bridge. Myron ("Pluto") Plude, one of DeLisio's machine gunners, set up his gun and started

(Right) *A U.S. soldier of the 9th Armored Division surveys the intact Ludendorff railroad bridge across the Rhine River at Remagen, March 7, 1945. A dozen other Rhine bridges had been destroyed by the retreating Germans, and the Allies had expected a long and costly fight to cross the great river into Germany.*

throwing a few tracers across. The regular *thwump* of the tank cannon echoed against the high hills across the river. Looking back at the top of the hill from which he had first seen the bridge, Timmermann could observe more tanks belching smoke as they threw their shells across the Rhine. Everybody was tense, waiting for the Germans to deliver the inevitable *coup de grâce* to the shaky bridge.

Meanwhile, just south of Remagen at Sinzig on the Ahr River, an incident occurred which had a profound effect on the tankers and infantrymen in Remagen. About the time that Timmermann's men were approaching the Ludendorff Bridge, a task force under Lt. Col. William R. Prince, making the main effort of the 9th Armored Division, was meeting considerably tougher opposition in its attempt to seize the bridge over the Ahr. Prince's task force succeeded, nevertheless, in rushing the bridge before the Germans could blow it up. This notable feat was accomplished almost two hours before Timmermann led his men through Remagen to the bridge.

Colonel Prince's task force captured about 400 prisoners among the rabid defenders of Sinzig. His men also rounded up some *Volkssturmers* and civilians who were making menacing gestures. A couple of the civilians indicated that they had information "of great importance" which they would like to transmit to the American authorities. They told Lt. Fred de Rango that the German command planned to blow up the Remagen Bridge at four o'clock on the dot.

De Rango received this information about 2:30 p.m. Acting swiftly, he sent a priority radio message to Combat Command B Headquarters, alerting them to this new intelligence. The message had an authoritative ring, and the combat command forthwith relayed it to Engeman's task force. De Rango, feeling there was not a minute to lose and fearing that his radio message might have to pass through too many

(Right) *Tanks and infantrymen of the U.S. First Army traverse the Remagen Bridge. The twin stone towers at the German end were occupied by Nazi machine gunners until U.S. soldiers dislodged them. During the ten days the bridge remained standing five U.S. divisions managed to cross and fan out into Germany.*

channels, also dispatched a special messenger to carry the news to Colonel Engeman. Soon the messages started to ricochet around Remagen as everyone hurried to inform everyone else.

The German troops at the bridge later swore that their plan to blow up the bridge had no set time schedule but hinged on the appearance of American forces. Furthermore, it seems scarcely plausible that civilians in a neighboring town would have detailed information on a secret military plan of this nature. Authentic or not, the news spurred the American commanders and troops to quicker action in order to cross the bridge before it was blown up.

It was 3:15 when General Hoge received the message that the bridge was to be blown up at 4. He immediately stormed down to give the word to Colonel Engeman.

"Put some white phosphorus and smoke around the bridge so the Krauts can't see what we're doing, cover your advance with tanks and machine guns, then bring up your engineers and pull out those wires on the bridge, because we're going to take that bridge," General Hoge roared.

He directed Majors Deevers and Russell to get down to the bridge and order their men across. He turned again to Colonel Engeman: "I want you to get to that bridge as soon as possible."

Engeman started down the road in his jeep. On the way he cut open his radio and called Grimball: "Get to that bridge." Grimball's rich South Carolina accent clearly pierced the static: "Suh, I am *at* the bridge."

Engeman told him to cover the bridge with fire and keep the Germans off it. He then sent a messenger to summon Lt. Hugh Mott, a platoon leader in Company B, 9th Armored Engineer Battalion. The pair met in the rear of one of the big resort hotels about 200 yards from the bridge.

These were Engeman's orders: "Mott, General Hoge wants you to get out onto that bridge and see if it's mined or loaded with TNT, and whether it'll hold tanks. I'll give you fire support from my tanks, and you'll have infantry scouts out there too." It was a tough assignment.

Lieutenant Mott, a tall, dark and cool-headed twenty-four-year-old from Nashville, swiftly got hold of the two most reliable men in his platoon—Eugene Dorland, a big Kansas stonemason, and John Reynolds, a little North Carolina textile worker. On their way up to the bridge, they saw the crater blown at the bridge approach, and when the smoke had cleared they jumped into the crater for protection. They also saw Majors Deevers and Russell talking with Timmermann and pointing at the bridge. Mott waved his two men forward with him.

Deevers and Russell had made their way independently to the bridge, and both of them made contact with Timmermann to give the tall Nebraskan the order to take his men across.

On the surface, Karl Timmermann tried to treat his mission as if it were a big lark. This was part of his art of leadership. While giving orders to his three platoon leaders, he casually passed out some candy he had "liberated" in Remagen. "Here, try one of these Kraut rock candies, and don't break your teeth," he said with a flip to Forrest Miner, an assistant squad leader at the edge of the group. "Now, we're going to cross this bridge before—"

A deafening rumble and roar swallowed up the rest of Timmermann's sentence. The Germans had set off an emergency demolition two thirds of the way across the bridge. Able Company watched in awe as the huge structure lifted up and steel, timbers, dust and thick black smoke mixed in the air. Many of the GI's threw themselves to the ground or buried their faces in their hands.

Timmermann, who was trying to make out what was left of the bridge through the thick haze, yelled: "Look—she's still standing!"

Most of the smoke and dust had cleared away, and the men followed their commander's gaze. The sight of the bridge still spanning the Rhine brought no cheers from the men. It was like an unwelcome specter. The suicide mission was on again.

A thousand feet away, the German soldiers were working frantically around the far end of the bridge. They looked as if they were going to make another attempt to blow it up.

"Maybe they're just teasing us to get us out there and then blow us all to kingdom come," Carmine Sabia said. "I tell you, it's a trap."

Timmermann's casual air had disappeared. The grin was gone from his face as he strode up to the bridge. He saw at one glance that although some big holes had been blown in the flooring, the catwalks were clear for infantrymen to walk on. He quickly circled his arm in the air to call his platoon leaders together.

Other men clustered around, eager and apprehensive. "OK, Jim, Mike and Joe, we'll cross the bridge—order of march, first platoon, third platoon and then second platoon."

There was a moment of silence.

Timmermann turned to Burrows, cupped his hand and said in a low tone: "Jim, I want your platoon to bring up the rear so we have an officer in charge of the last platoon across." Then, in a louder tone which everybody could hear, "And when you get over, Jim, take your platoon up that high hill on the other side. You know, the old Fort Benning stuff: take the high ground and hold it."

There was no audible response to the challenge. To the tired, dirty, unshaven men it looked like sudden death. As Timmermann moved tentatively up to the bridge, a chattering of machine guns from the towers made him duck. Jack Berry ran up to one of the Pershing tanks, located Lieutenant Grimball and pointed at the towers.

Grimball did not hesitate. His Pershing let loose a blast. The tank shell opened a big crack in the tower, and the German machine-gun fire let up.

"Dammit, what's holdin' up the show? Now git goin'!" Timmermann yelled.

At this point, the battalion commander, Major Deevers, called out: "I'll see you on the other side and we'll all have a chicken dinner."

"Chicken dinner, my foot. I'm all chicken right now," one of the men in the first platoon shot back.

Major Deevers flushed. "Move on across," he yelled sharply.

"I tell ya, I'm not goin' out there and get blown up," the GI answered. "No sir, Major, you can court-martial and shoot me, but I ain't going out there on that bridge."

With that, Lieutenant Timmermann moved onto the bridge, and suddenly the man who had been arguing with Major Deevers joined the group from the first platoon which was starting across.

Timmermann's men had just advanced onto the bridge when Lieutenant Mott and Sergeants Dorland and Reynolds of the engineers ran out to join them and started cutting wires connected to the demolition charges. The engineers were a doubly welcome sight, because the infantrymen had not expected them. When the big German emergency charge had gone off on the bridge, Mott had decided that the main job of his en-

gineers would be to locate and cut the wires to the other demolition charges. The three men joined Timmermann and his lead scouts just as they were starting across the bridge, and there was no time to coordinate any plans as the whole group surged forward.

The right side of the bridge had been torn up by the German blasts, and so Chinchar's platoon started down the left catwalk. Here the men had some protection, because most of the German rifle and machine-gun fire was coming from the stone tower on the far right end of the bridge. The fire had quieted down after Grimball's tank blast, but it started up again as the first infantrymen picked their way across.

When Chinchar's men were about a third of the way over, they came to a halt as the machine-gun fire intensified. The American tanks were still firing, but the German return fire from both the towers and the tunnel was growing stronger. Nobody dared move ahead.

From a half-submerged barge about 200 yards upstream, the lead troops were getting more fire. It was not heavy and constant, but two snipers on the barge were beginning to zero in. There were no American tanks on the bridge, and so Timmermann ran back to yell to one of the General Sherman tanks at the bridge approach: "How about putting something on that barge?"

The tank found the range and blasted the barge with its 75-mm. gun until a white flag began to flutter.

"That's one thing they never taught us at Fort Knox," said a member of the tank crew later in reviewing his naval exploit.

Even with the barge menace removed, Timmermann faced a crisis. He ran forward to find that his old first platoon was frozen. The tank support was not silencing the opposition. The Germans were still running around on the far side of the river as though they were going to blow up the bridge with the American troops on it. Timmermann waved for Sergeant De-Lisio, leader of the third platoon.

"Joe, get your platoon up there and get these men off their tail," he yelled above the clatter of tank and machine-gun fire.

The little Bronx Sergeant with the mustache started weaving and bobbing across the bridge. One of the motionless figures hugging the flooring of the bridge grumbled as he passed: "There goes a guy with more guts than sense."

If DeLisio heard him, he gave no sign. Soon the rest

of his platoon was starting over, and in a minute a few men from Burrows' second platoon had moved forward also. The reinforcements fired at the tunnel and the towers, and soon the enemy fire began to lessen.

Above all the noise came Timmermann's constant: "Git goin', git goin'." The company commander was everywhere, encouraging and leading his men.

DeLisio worked his way up to the first man on the bridge, a third of the way across, and shouted: "What's the trouble?"

"Trouble? Can't you see all that sniper fire?"

"Why worry about a coupla snipers?" DeLisio laughed. "If this bridge blows up, we've got a whole battalion on it. Let's get off. C'mon, guys."

DeLisio, of course, was exaggerating—there wasn't a whole battalion on the bridge, only part of A Company; but the psychology worked. He helped uncork the attack. Other men with "more guts than sense" started to get up and weave and bob behind him.

Across the river a German train steamed into view, chugging south. Colonel Engeman, back in Remagen with his tanks, spotted the train and joyfully exclaimed: "Hallelujah! I've always wanted to fire a tank at a locomotive." Four or five tanks opened up. The firebox of the engine exploded. German troops started pouring out of the train and quickly set up positions to begin firing at their tormentors on the bridge and in Remagen.

DeLisio waved back for his support squad, led by Joe Petrencsik and Alex Drabik. Then he edged forward. Heavy fire started to come down on the bridge—20-mm. shells from German antiaircraft guns. Petrencsik with a sudden hunch yelled: "Duck!" DeLisio crouched, and something swooshed over his head and took a piece out of one of the stone towers.

In the middle of the bridge, Mott, Dorland and Reynolds of the engineers found four packages of TNT, weighing twenty to thirty pounds each, tied to I beams underneath the decking of the bridge. They climbed down and worked their wire cutters hot until the charges splashed into the Rhine. Above them they heard the heavy tramp of the infantrymen and the hoarse cry of Timmermann which everybody had now taken up: "Git goin'."

Back on the bridge, Dorland started to hack away at a heavy cable. He finally put the muzzle of his carbine up against the cable and blasted it apart.

By this time DeLisio had traveled two thirds of the

way across the bridge. The little Sergeant had a theory that if you advanced fast enough you wouldn't get hit, so instead of hugging the bridge when the Germans fired on him from the towers, he simply ran on until he got behind the towers on the German side of the bridge. DeLisio chortled to himself at his good luck, until he looked back and saw that the German fire from the towers was still pinning down the men who were supposed to be following him.

Somebody yelled: "Who's gonna clean out that tower?" DeLisio took the question as a challenge and ran back to the tower where most of the fire was coming from.

He pushed aside a few bales of hay blocking the door to the tower. Just as he started inside, a stray bullet went into the stone wall and ricocheted off. Sabia came up and yelled: "You're hit, Joe."

"You're crazy, Sabia. I don't feel nothin' at all."

Sabia insisted: "I saw that bullet, I tell ya I seen it go right through ya."

DeLisio ran his hands quickly around his field jacket and finding no blood he brushed Sabia away and went on up into the tower. Chinchar, Anthony Samele and Artis Massie entered the left tower. Everybody else moved forward.

DeLisio started running up the circular staircase. There were three floors in the tower, and he couldn't take anything for granted. He heard machine-gun fire above him, and then it suddenly stopped. Had the Germans heard him coming, and was he heading into a trap?

He slapped open a steel door with the heel of his hand and burst in on three German soldiers. They were bending over a machine gun as though it were jammed. There was an agonizing second as the three men jerked their heads around. DeLisio pumped out a couple of shots with his carbine, firing from the hip.

"Hände hoch!" he yelled.

The three Germans wheeled around with their hands in the air. DeLisio motioned them to one side with his carbine, and seizing the gun they had been using, he hurled it out of the window. Men starting across the bridge saw the gun plummet from the tower and began to move with more confidence.

In his pidgin German and his sign language, DeLisio tried to find out if there were any more soldiers left in the tower. His captives assured him that there weren't. But DeLisio was skeptical, and he motioned for the three of them to precede him up the stairs.

On the top floor of the tower, DeLisio pushed the three Germans into a room, where he found a German Lieutenant and his orderly. The Lieutenant dived for the corner of the room, but DeLisio stopped him with a couple of shots. He took away the Lieutenant's pistol. Then he marched all five prisoners down the stairs and told them to proceed unescorted over the bridge to Remagen. They were the first in a long parade of German prisoners taken near the bridge.

Over in the left tower, Chinchar, Samele and Massie also tossed a German machine gun out the window, and captured one cowering soldier. The flushing of the machine gun crew from the tower at being had across the Rhine.

Drabik had not seen DeLisio go into the tower and started looking for him. He asked several people on the bridge, but nobody seemed to know. He made up his mind that there was only one thing to do.

"Let's go!" he shouted. "DeLisio must be over there on the other side all alone."

Drabik took off for the east bank, weaving and wobbling. Just before he got across the bridge, he jounced so much that he lost his helmet. He did not stop to pick it up, but kept running at top speed until he reached the southeast bank of the Rhine. He was the first man over, followed closely by eight others. A few seconds afterward Timmermann, the first officer over, set foot on the farther side.

Once over the bridge Drabik wheeled to the left, still looking for DeLisio, and raced about 200 yards up the river road. The rest of his squad followed close behind, and he hastily set up a skirmish line in a series of bomb craters to ward off a possible German counterthrust.

The bridge itself was still a big question mark for the Americans. Every man that crossed it wondered if the Germans had yet played their final card, or if they were saving up a more devastating stroke that would at any moment topple the entire structure into the Rhine. The three engineers—Mott, Dorland and Reynolds—methodically searched for the master switch that controlled the German demolitions. Near the eastern end of the bridge, Dorland finally located the box that housed the switch, went to work on the heavy wires leading from it and blasted them apart with a few rounds from his carbine. A few minutes later the three engineers came upon a large unexploded 500- to 600-pound charge with its fuse cap blown. Mott and

his men examined it closely and found it correctly wired and prepared for detonation. Cutting all attached wires, they made it harmless.

At the Remagen end of the bridge, Colonel Engeman, Capt. George Soumas and Lt. C. Windsor Miller drove their men hard to clear the way for tanks and vehicles. While Mott and his two Sergeants were ripping out demolition wires and determining whether the bridge could hold traffic, other engineers checked the approaches for mines and pondered the problem of filling up the tremendous crater at the bridge approach. Miller finally called up Sgt. Lawrence Swayne, whose tank was equipped with a blade like a bulldozer, and Swayne began pushing dirt and debris into the big hole.

On the east bank DeLisio, who had stepped off the bridge shortly after Drabik, had already been sent by Timmermann on another trouble-shooting assignment. With four of his best men, the little Sergeant crept forward to investigate the menacing railroad tunnel at the end of the bridge. None of the Americans knew how strong a force the Germans had hidden in the blackness of the tunnel. All they knew was that it gave the enemy excellent cover and concealment, and that from it the occupants had ideal observation over the entire length of the bridge.

The five men moved forward cautiously, hugging the ground as shots rang out of the dark. When they reached the entrance, DeLisio fired two shots into the tunnel, and several German engineers quickly ran out, hands high above their heads, as if they had been eagerly awaiting this chance to give themselves up. Misled by the easy capture of this handful of the enemy, DeLisio failed to realize that there was a much stronger force deep in the tunnel. Moving his prisoners back, he reported to Timmermann that the tunnel looked clear and then joined Drabik along the river road.

Inside the tunnel, a German Major and Captain had received word shortly before four o'clock that the Americans had crossed the bridge. The news spread immediately through the milling throng of soldiers and civilians, and it became almost impossible to maintain even a semblance of order. Tank shells were bursting inside the tunnel, rifle fire was ricocheting off the walls, and three railroad tank cars were dripping gasoline that formed pools of potential destruction at the feet of the miserable tunnel occupants. Panic-stricken civilians were clawing at the soldiers to stop resistance. Except for the prudent engineers near the entrance who had made the most of their opportunity to surrender to DeLisio's patrol, few of the terrified Germans were even aware that five Americans had come and gone.

By a little after four o'clock Timmermann had only about 120 men on the east bank. As an experienced infantryman, he had recognized immediately from the other side of the river that the Erpeler Ley, the highest point in the immediate area, had to be taken fast. Summoning Lieutenant Burrows, he ordered him to take the second platoon up the precipitous slope. The heights of the Erpeler Ley, as well as the tunneled depths, had become crucial.

Burrows later said, "Taking Remagen and crossing the bridge were a breeze compared with climbing that hill." The lower slope was very steep, and the face of the cliff was covered with loose rock. Footing was slippery, and several men were severely injured when they fell. About halfway to the summit the Americans began receiving 20-mm. fire. Silhouetted against the face of the black cliff, the climbing men were easy targets for the German antiaircraft gunners.

At first the fire seemed to come from the west bank. Colonel Engeman sent one of his light tank platoons, under Lt. Demetri Paris, to clean out the pocket; but the antiaircraft fire continued with such intensity that Burrows' men soon became convinced it was coming from the northern part of the bridgehead. Some of them crawled around the bluff to the right to get out of the line of fire. Others slid to the base of the cliff.

Burrows' casualties mounted. His platoon Sergeant, Bill Shultz, was severely wounded in the leg by a 20-mm. shellburst. A mortar shell burst close to Frankie Marek and sent a piece of shrapnel through him. Those men who finally managed to reach the top saw only a few small sheds across a field about 100 yards away and a handful of German soldiers wandering around unconcernedly. Jim Cardinale, one of the American machine gunners, called excitedly, "Come on, lemme paste those guys, but good."

"Shut up or we'll shoot you, by God," one of the other men threatened in low but urgent tones. "We'll shoot you and push you off the cliff—you want to give our position away?"

Cardinale calmed down, and the Americans atop the cliff began a period of cautious and worried waiting. They could see numerous German infantrymen and vehicles in neighboring towns. At the base of the hill and along the side, the firing got heavier. The enemy seemed to be moving in for a counterattack.

The advance guard of the Remagen crossing was in a precarious position. With no weapons more powerful than light machine guns, Timmermann called for his antitank platoon under Lt. Dave Gardner to come to the east bank, instructing them to bring as many of their .50-caliber machine guns as they could and deploy them on ground mounts covering the roads into the bridgehead. Gardner's men also brought four rocket launchers and set them up with the machine guns.

Timmermann then appealed for more men, more weapons and more support. Major Deevers sent over Lieutenant McMaster's C Company, followed about 4:30 by Lieutenant Liedike's B Company. Their arrival eased the situation, but the battalion was still woefully weak and too strung out to present a very firm defense against a counterattack. Had German tanks struck at the flimsy American force between four and five o'clock, the Remagen bridgehead would certainly have been wiped out.

This possibility troubled Timmermann a great deal as he took stock of his thin line of men. It also troubled the men and weighed heavily on the minds of the B and C Company reinforcements that came across the bridge. Everybody was either asking about the arrival of American tanks or fearing the arrival of German tanks. The sound of German vehicles came from neighboring villages. Patrols on the edge of the bridgehead confirmed the suspicion that German forces were moving up for a counterattack.

On the Remagen bank Lieutenant Mott and the engineers were doing everything possible to make the bridge serviceable for tank traffic. Makeshift repairs were made in the shattered planking, and by dusk the bridge could support tanks. Reinforcement of the bridgehead was resumed, and from then on throughout the night an almost steady stream of men crossed the bridge to bolster the defenses on the east bank.

At 7 a.m. on March 8, one of the first jeeps driven across the bridge was manned by Chaplain William T. Gibble. At the entrance to the tunnel, Chaplain Gibble set up a simple field altar. Not many soldiers could get out of their foxholes to participate in this first service east of the Rhine, but those who did gave quiet thanks to God for the miracle of Remagen.

Beneath the comforting shelter of a U.S. tank gun, a wary GI covers two surrendering Germans in a rubble-strewn French courtyard. Seconds after this photograph was taken, a hidden Nazi sniper opened fire. Caught by surprise, the GI managed to scurry for cover unharmed, but the photographer was shot and killed instantly.

ROOSEVELT'S DEATH

BY JOHN TOLAND

"President Roosevelt is dead." The news flashed to all the capitals of the world—Allied and Axis alike. The tragedy brought grief to America and its friends—and to those in Axis nations who longed for an end to the war. To Adolf Hitler and his Nazi coterie, there was a flash of false hope that the alliance of their enemies would now collapse in disunity. These critical moments in the last days of World War II are re-created here.

In Warm Springs, Georgia, it was 11 a.m. on April 12, 1945. At the six-room clapboard cottage called the Little White House, two miles from the Warm Springs Foundation, President Franklin D. Roosevelt was trying to relax. Bad weather had grounded the courier plane from Washington, and the morning mail would not arrive until noon. With no work to do, Roosevelt decided to stay in bed and read the Atlanta *Constitution*.

"I don't feel any too good this morning," he told Lizzie McDuffie, an elderly Negro maid, and laid the *Constitution* on top of the paperback mystery he was reading. It was *The Punch and Judy Murders* and was opened at a chapter entitled "Six Feet of Ground."

An hour later he was sitting in his leather armchair chatting with two cousins, the Misses Margaret Suckley and Laura Delano, and an old friend, Mrs. Winthrop Rutherfurd. He wore a dark gray suit, a vest and a red Harvard four-in-hand tie. He disliked vests and preferred bow ties, but was intending to have his portrait painted. His secretary, William Hassett, brought in the outgoing mail, and the President started to sign letters. One prepared by the State Department tickled him. "A typical State Department letter," he told Hassett. "It says nothing at all."

A tall, dignified woman began to set up an easel near the windows. She was Mme. Elizabeth Shoumatoff, and she had already painted one watercolor of the President. She was doing another which Roosevelt planned to give to Mrs. Rutherfurd's daughter.

She draped a navy blue cape around the President's shoulders, and began to paint. At 1 p.m. Roosevelt said, "We've got just fifteen minutes more."

While Miss Suckley continued crocheting, and Miss Delano was filling vases with flowers, Roosevelt lighted a cigarette. Suddenly he touched his temple with his left hand; then the hand flopped down.

"Did you drop something?" asked Miss Suckley.

Roosevelt closed his eyes and said so quietly that only she heard it, "I have a terrific headache." He slumped over and lost consciousness. It was 1:15 p.m. The fifteen minutes were up.

Moments later Comdr. Howard Bruenn, the Navy doctor attending the President, arrived and ordered Roosevelt carried to the bedroom. He was breathing heavily; his pulse was 104, his blood pressure above the last mark of 300. Bruenn knew it was a cerebral hemorrhage. He injected aminophylline and nitroglycerin into Roosevelt's arm.

At 2:05 p.m. Bruenn phoned Adm. Ross T. McIntire, the President's personal physician, in Washington and reported that Roosevelt was still unconscious after what looked like a cerebral stroke. McIntire phoned Dr. James E. Paullin, former president of the American Medical Association, in Atlanta and asked him to rush to Warm Springs at once.

It was about then that Laura Delano phoned Eleanor Roosevelt at the White House and said that Franklin had fainted while sitting for his portrait. A moment later McIntire also phoned the First Lady. He was not alarmed, he said, but thought they should both go to Warm Springs that evening. He advised her, however, to keep her afternoon engagements, since a last-minute cancellation to go to Georgia would cause too much comment. As scheduled, Mrs. Roosevelt was driven to the Sulgrave Club to attend the annual benefit for the Thrift Shop.

Dr. Paullin raced over the back roads he knew so well, and at 3:28 p.m. he reached the Little White House. He found the President "in a cold sweat, ashy gray and breathing with difficulty." His pulse was barely perceptible, and by 3:32 p.m. his heart sounds disappeared completely. Paullin administered an

The "Big Three," Churchill, Roosevelt and Stalin, meet at Yalta, February 1945. Behind them stand their top foreign-policy advisers: (left to right) British Secretary of State for Foreign Affairs Anthony Eden, U.S. Secretary of State Edward R. Stettinius, Jr., Soviet Foreign Commissar Vyacheslav M. Molotov and U.S. Ambassador Averell Harriman. Many crucial decisions were made at the Yalta Conference: an agreement to hold a meeting in San Francisco for the organization of the United Nations; the division of Nazi Germany into zones of occupation; the establishment of a new Polish Government. In addition, Soviet Russia secretly agreed to enter the war against Japan following the surrender of Germany. On August 8, 1945—two days after the dropping of the first atomic bomb on Hiroshima by the United States—the Soviet Union fulfilled this agreement.

intracardiac dose of adrenalin. The President's heart beat two or three times, then stopped forever. It was 3:35 p.m. Central time.

In Washington it was 4:35 p.m. Mrs. Roosevelt was still at the Sulgrave Club, sitting at the head table listening to a pianist, Evalyn Tyner. At 4:50 someone whispered that she was wanted on the telephone. It was Stephen ("Steve") Early, the President's press secretary. In an agitated voice he said, "Come home at once."

Mrs. Roosevelt didn't ask why. She knew in her heart "that something dreadful had happened." But she felt "the amenities had to be observed" and went back to the party. After the pianist had finished her piece, Mrs. Roosevelt applauded, then announced that she had to leave, since something had come up at home. As she was driven back to the White House she sat with clenched hands.

She went to her sitting room where Early and Dr. McIntire told her that the President had died in a coma. Reacting automatically, she at once sent for Vice President Harry S Truman and then made arrangements to fly to Warm Springs that evening.

Truman was at the Capitol Building, presiding at a session of the Senate. Bored with a long speech by Senator Alexander Wiley of Wisconsin, he wrote a letter to his mother and sister:

Dear Mamma & Mary:

I am trying to write you a letter today from the desk of the President of the Senate while a windy Senator —— is making a speech on a subject with which he is in no way familiar. . . .

I have to sit up here and make parliamentary rulings—some of which are common sense and some of which are not. . . .

Turn on your radio tomorrow night at 9:30 your time, and you'll hear Harry make a Jefferson Day address to the nation. I think I'll be on all the networks, so it ought not to be hard to get me. It will be followed by the President, whom I'll introduce.

Hope you are both well and stay that way.

Love to you both. Write when you can.

HARRY

The Senate adjourned at 4:56 p.m. and Truman stepped into the office of Sam Rayburn for a drink. The House Speaker handed him a glass of bourbon and water, and suddenly remembered that Steve Early had just phoned and wanted Truman to call the White House. A minute later Early told Truman in an agitated voice, "Please come right over, and come in through the main Pennsylvania Avenue entrance."

That was all Truman remembered Early saying, and later he wrote that he was not at all upset—he only imagined that Roosevelt had unexpectedly returned from Warm Springs. But Rayburn thought his face paled abruptly, and a clerk in Truman's office claimed that he burst in, greatly agitated, and said, "I'm going to the White House."

Truman arrived at the White House at about 5:25 p.m. and was immediately taken up to Mrs. Roosevelt's second floor study. It was only when he saw the President's daughter, Mrs. Anna Boettiger, and Early that he finally realized, as he wrote later, "something unusual has taken place."

Eleanor Roosevelt stepped forward with calm, graceful dignity and put an arm gently around Truman's shoulder. "Harry," she said quietly, "the President is dead."

The Vice President couldn't speak for a moment. Finally he said, "Is there anything I can do for you?"

"Is there anything *we* can do for *you?*" she said. "For you are the one in trouble now." She told him how sorry she was for him and for the people of America.

Then she cabled her sons:

FATHER SLEPT AWAY. HE WOULD EXPECT YOU TO CARRY ON AND FINISH YOUR JOBS.

At 5:45 p.m. Attorney General Francis Biddle, Secretary of the Navy James Forrestal and Secretary of State Edward R. Stettinius, Jr., were in a meeting nearby when a message came for the latter to go to the White House. It was his duty as Secretary of State to proclaim the death of the President. By the time he walked into Mrs. Roosevelt's study, tears were flowing down his drawn cheeks. Truman told Stettinius and Early to summon the Cabinet immediately, and again asked Mrs. Roosevelt if he could do anything. She wondered if it was proper to fly to Georgia in a Government plane. Truman assured her it was.

He walked to the Presidential Office at the west end

of the building, where he telephoned his wife and daughter to come to the White House. He also phoned Chief Justice Harlan Fiske Stone, asking him to come at once to swear him in as President.

By now Secretaries Stettinius, Henry A. Wallace, Henry L. Stimson, Henry Morgenthau, Jr., Frances Perkins, Harold L. Ickes, Claude R. Wickard and Forrestal, as well as Foreign Economic Administrator Leo T. Crowley, Speaker Rayburn, House Majority Leader John W. McCormack, House Minority Leader Joseph W. Martin and several others, had gathered in the Cabinet Room of the White House.

A few minutes after six, Truman called the Cabinet to order and told them that it was his sad duty to report that the President was dead. "Mrs. Roosevelt gave me this news, and in saying so she remarked that 'he died like a soldier.' I shall only say that I will try to carry on as I know he would have wanted me and all of us to do. I should like all of you to remain in your Cabinet posts and I shall count on you for all the help I can get. In this action I am sure I am following out what the President would have wished."

All America was stunned that afternoon and shared a momentary disbelief. When Robert E. Sherwood, a playwright and Presidential adviser, heard that FDR was dead, he stayed by the radio "waiting for the announcement—probably in his own gaily reassuring voice—that it had all been a big mistake, that the banking crisis and the war were over and everything was going to be 'fine—grand—perfectly bully.'"

At the White House hasty preparations for swearing in the new President were made. A few minutes after 7 p.m. a Bible was found and placed near the end of the large, odd-shaped table given to Roosevelt by Jesse Jones. Truman, his wife and daughter at his left, faced Chief Justice Stone, who was wearing a blue serge suit. Mrs. Truman's eyes were red, and she looked frightened as her husband picked up the Bible with his left hand. But Truman failed to raise his right hand, and the Chief Justice calmly reminded him to do so. Under the circumstances, Forrestal thought, Stone's firmness gave dignity to the scene.

Repeating after Stone, Truman said, "I, Harry S Truman, do solemnly swear that I will faithfully execute the office of President of the United States, and will, to the best of my ability, preserve, protect and defend the Constitution of the United States." The brief ceremony was over. It was now 7:08 p.m.

All left but the new President and his Cabinet. They took seats around the table in an atmosphere that seemed unusually subdued. Truman was about to speak when Early came in and said the press wondered if the San Francisco Conference would take place as scheduled on April 25.

"The conference will be held as President Roosevelt has directed," Truman replied unhesitatingly. Peering levelly through his thick glasses, he told the Cabinet that he intended to "continue both the foreign and the domestic policies of the Roosevelt Administration." Characteristically, he added that he was going to be President in his own right and would assume full responsibility for his decisions. He hoped they wouldn't hesitate to give their advice, but all final policy judgments would be his alone. Within the space of a few minutes Truman had shown that he was a man unafraid to declare himself. After the short meeting Stimson remained; he said he had to discuss a most urgent matter. "I want you to know about an immense project that is under way—a project looking to the development of a new explosive of almost unbelievable destructive power" (see pages 500–514). Stimson said this was all he felt free to say at the time, and when the President left a few minutes later for his apartment at 4701 Connecticut Avenue, he was still puzzled.

The all clear had just sounded in Berlin the night of April 12, when Press Secretary Rudolf Semmler got a call at the air-raid shelter of the Propaganda Ministry. Someone from the Deutsches Nachrichtenbüro, the official German news agency, said, "Hello, listen, something incredible has happened. Roosevelt is dead!"

"Are you joking?"

"No, here's what the Reuters message says: 'Roosevelt died today at midday.'"

Semmler loudly repeated the message. The drowsy occupants of the shelter jumped to their feet, suddenly wide awake, and cheered. People laughed and shook hands. The Ministry cook crossed herself and cried, "This is the miracle that Dr. Goebbels has been promising us so long!"

Semmler called Ninth Army Headquarters and was told Goebbels had left and should be in Berlin soon. Then the Reich Chancellery phoned and asked Goebbels to call the Fuehrer as soon as he arrived. Fifteen minutes later Goebbels' car pulled up to the Ministry in the glow of fires from the recently bombed Adlon

Hotel and Chancellery. Several staff members hurried down the steps to meet Goebbels. "Herr Reichminister," a reporter said, "Roosevelt is dead."

Goebbels jumped out of the car and stood transfixed for a moment. At last he turned to Frau Inge Haberzettel and others from the office who had gathered excitedly around him, and said in a voice shaking with emotion, "Now, bring out our best champagne, and let's have a telephone talk with the Fuehrer!"

As he stepped into his office, Semmler couldn't resist shouting the news at him. Goebbels, face pale, said, "This is the turning point!" Then he asked, incredulous, "Is it really true?"

Some ten people hung over him as he telephoned Hitler. "My Fuehrer," he said feverishly, "I congratulate you! Roosevelt is dead. It is written in the stars that the second half of April will be the turning point for us. This is Friday, April the thirteenth! [It was just past midnight.] Fate has laid low your greatest enemy. God has not abandoned us. Twice he has saved you from savage assassins. Death, which the enemy aimed at you in 1939 and 1944, has now struck down our most dangerous enemy. It is a miracle!" He listened to Hitler for a while, and then mentioned the possibility that Truman would be more moderate than Roosevelt. Anything could happen now!

Goebbels hung up, his eyes shining, and began to make an impassioned speech. Semmler had never seen him so excited; it was as if the war were nearly over.

Lieutenant General Patton was just getting ready for bed in his trailer after a long evening with Generals Eisenhower and Bradley. His watch had stopped, so he turned on the radio to get the BBC time signal; what he heard was the announcement of Roosevelt's death. He rushed into the house where the others were sleeping and knocked at Bradley's door.

"Anything wrong?" Bradley asked.

"Better come with me to tell Ike. The President has died."

The two went to Eisenhower's room, and the three of them sat there until two in the morning, gloomily wondering what effect Roosevelt's death would have on the future peace. They doubted that any other man in America was as experienced as FDR in dealing with Stalin and other leaders, and agreed it was a tragedy that America had to change leaders at such a critical point. Finally they filed off to bed, still depressed.

When Churchill first heard that the President was dead, he felt as if he'd been "struck a physical blow" and was "overpowered by a sense of deep and irreparable loss." He telephoned Bernard Baruch at the Claridge, and in a deeply grieved voice asked, "Do you think I ought to go to Washington?"

"No, Winston, I think you ought to stay here on the job." Baruch promised to see Churchill before he flew back to Washington, and when he arrived at No. 10 Downing Street, Churchill was still in bed, looking greatly upset. "Do you think I ought to go?" he asked again.

Once more Baruch assured him it would be wiser to stay at home. He himself was leaving on *The Sacred Cow* with Judge Samuel Rosenman and others. It was noon by the time the plane took off on its long, sad trip to Washington. None of the passengers felt like talking, all were too occupied with their own memories of the President. Baruch remembered meeting Roosevelt first in Albany—he was a young, somewhat haughty State Senator then. And he recalled the great moment at the 1928 Democratic Convention when Roosevelt propelled himself on crutches up to the podium and made his gallant "Happy Warrior" nomination speech for Al Smith. Whatever his defects and errors, Baruch thought—and they had disagreed a number of times—FDR "believed deeply in the ideas and ideals of democracy" and "thought of liberty, justice, equality of opportunity, not in abstract terms, but in terms of human beings."

When Count Lutz Schwerin von Krosigk, Hitler's Minister of Finance, was told about Roosevelt he "felt the flutter of the wings of the Angel of History rustle through the room," and wondered if this could be "the long-desired change of fortune." He telephoned Goebbels and advised him to "take the press into tow at once." It should neither revile the new President nor praise him and, above all, there should be no mention of the feud between Roosevelt and Goebbels. "New possibilities may now arise, and the press must not spoil them by clumsiness."

Goebbels agreed. "This news will provoke a complete change in the entire German people's morale, for one can and must consider this event a manifestation of fate and justice!"

The Count was so stimulated that he immediately sat down and wrote to Goebbels as follows:

. . . I myself see in Roosevelt's death a divine judgment, but it is also a gift from God that we shall have to earn in order to possess. This death eliminates the block that has obstructed all roads leading to contacting America. Now they'll have to exploit this God-sent opportunity and do everything to get negotiations started. The only promising way, it seems to me, is through the intermediary of the Pope. As the American Catholics form a strong, united block—in contrast to the Protestants, who are split into numerous sects—the Pope's voice would carry great weight in the U.S.A. Considering the seriousness of the military situation, we must not be silent. . . .

At a conference late that morning, Friday the 13th, Goebbels counseled the press to write very objectively and noncommittally about Truman; to say nothing to irritate the new President; and to hide any rejoicing at Roosevelt's death. But by afternoon the Propaganda Minister's elation was already beginning to wane. When Gen. Theodor Busse called to ask if Roosevelt's death would truly bring about the turning point in Germany's fortunes, Goebbels replied halfheartedly, "Oh, we don't know. We'll have to see."

Certainly the first reports from the front indicated that the change of Presidents had not at all affected the enemy's operations, and later in the day Goebbels told Semmler and others on his staff, "Perhaps fate has again been cruel and made fools of us. Perhaps we counted our chickens before they were hatched."

All Germans, however, did not rejoice at the President's death. Edward W. Beattie, Jr.—a captured American war correspondent imprisoned in Stalag IIIA at Luckenwalde, some thirty miles south of Berlin—thought a few guards seemed genuinely sorry. Beattie had never before realized what Roosevelt meant to the oppressed people of Europe. All day Poles, Norwegians and French sought out Americans and shook their hands in sympathy. Major General Otto Ruge, the former Norwegian Commander in Chief, wrote the senior American officer, Lt. Col. Roy Herte, "The world has lost a great man, and my own country a true friend." And the senior British officer, Wing Comdr. Maurice A. Smith, wrote, "We of the British Empire have lost an ardent and loyal friend. . . . Had our desires been granted, he would have lived to see the fruits of the labor for which he strove so whole-

heartedly and gallantly." At the American barracks Colonel Herte ordered the announcement of death read. As the men stood at attention for one minute, several wept openly.

It was a full day for Truman. On his way to the White House he gave Tony Vaccaro of the Associated Press a ride. "Few men in history," the President said, "equaled the one into whose shoes I'm stepping, and I silently prayed to God that I could measure up to the task."

He summoned Secretary of State Stettinius and told him to prepare an outline of the problems with Soviet Russia, then went to the Capitol and asked a group of Congressional leaders if they would arrange a joint session of the Senate and House so that he could address them in person on April 16.

"Harry," said one Senator, "you were planning to come, whether we liked it or not."

"You know I would have," he replied in his tart Midwestern twang. "But I would rather do it with your full and understanding support and welcome."

Page boys and reporters lined up outside the Senate office, and the President shook hands with everyone.

"Boys," he said, "if you ever pray, pray for me now. I don't know whether you fellows ever had a load of hay fall on you, but when they told me yesterday what had happened, I felt like the moon, the stars and all the planets had fallen on me. I've got the most terribly responsible job a man ever had."

"Good luck, Mr. President," a reporter called out.

"I wish you didn't have to call me that."

All day he received messages of condolence and encouragement; the cable from Stalin read:

. . . THE AMERICAN PEOPLE AND THE UNITED NATIONS HAVE LOST IN THE PERSON OF FRANKLIN ROOSEVELT A GREAT STATESMAN OF WORLD STATURE AND CHAMPION OF POSTWAR PEACE AND SECURITY. . . .

In Moscow, Roosevelt's death had caused genuine grief as well as apprehension for the future; the front pages of all newspapers were edged with wide black margins, black-bordered flags were displayed and the Supreme Soviet stood in silence. (Even an enemy, the Japanese Prime Minister, Adm. Kantaro Suzuki, expressed his "profound sympathy" to the American people for the loss of a man who was responsible for "the Americans' advantageous position today." Some Japanese propagandists, however, started a story that Roosevelt had died in agony—and changed his last words from "I have a terrific headache" to "I have made a terrific mistake.")

Truman acknowledged Churchill's message of sympathy and added that he was about to cable his "views and suggestions on this Polish matter." At three o'clock he received Stettinius and Charles Bohlen, a State Department official, who briefed him on the Polish question. Truman began to compose another cable to Churchill:

STALIN'S REPLY TO YOU AND TO PRESIDENT ROOSEVELT MAKES OUR NEXT STEP OF THE GREATEST IMPORTANCE. ALTHOUGH WITH A FEW EXCEPTIONS HE DOES NOT LEAVE MUCH GROUND FOR OPTIMISM, I FEEL VERY STRONGLY THAT WE SHOULD HAVE ANOTHER GO AT HIM.

While Truman was still working on the message, Stettinius brought in a cable from W. Averell Harriman. The Ambassador had just seen Stalin, who hoped he could work as closely with Truman as he had with Roosevelt. Harriman had suggested to Stalin that the best way of assuring everyone of Soviet desire to continue collaboration would be to send Vyacheslav M. Molotov, the Russian Foreign Minister, to San Francisco. Stalin told Harriman that this would be done if Truman made a formal request to have Molotov visit Washington and then San Francisco.

The President asked Stettinius to draft the request.

Harry L. Hopkins, Roosevelt's chief adviser, was telephoning Robert Sherwood from St. Mary's Hospital in Rochester, Minnesota, just to talk about FDR. "You and I have got something great that we can take with us all the rest of our lives," he said. "It's a great realization. Because we know it's *true*, what so many people believed about him, and what made them love him." The President sometimes seemed to be making too many concessions to expediency, he admitted. "But in the big things—all of the things that were of real, permanent importance—he never let the people down."

Mrs. Roosevelt was riding on a Washington-bound train with her husband's body. It had been "a long and heartbreaking day." All night long she lay in her berth, looking out at the passing country and "watching the faces of the people at stations, and even at the crossroads, who came to pay their last tribute all through the night."

At ten o'clock on the morning of April 14, the train arrived at Union Station in Washington. Anna Boettiger, accompanied by her brother Brig. Gen. Elliott Roosevelt and his actress wife, Faye Emerson, entered the car that was carrying the body. Then Truman, Henry Wallace and James F. Byrnes, Director of War Mobilization, went aboard to pay their respects to Mrs. Roosevelt.

A caisson drawn by six white horses carried the flag-draped coffin down Constitution Avenue toward the White House as hundreds of thousands watched. No President's death since Lincoln's had so affected the American people. Many wept quietly; some were grim and stoic or just stood staring in a daze. It was still hard for Americans to accept the fact that the man who had been their President since 1933 was dead. Truman noticed an old Negro woman, apron held to her eyes, sitting on the curb crying as if she had lost a son.

As Judge Rosenman and his wife passed under the White House portico, she whispered, "This is the end of an epoch in our lives!" It was the end of an epoch for the United States, too, and for the entire world, thought Rosenman, and remembered the Jefferson Day address Roosevelt was to have made the previous day—particularly the last sentence, which was in his own handwriting: "Let us move forward with strong and active faith."

Just before four o'clock Truman, his wife and daughter went to the East Room of the Executive Mansion for the funeral service. Flanked by flowers, the casket had been placed in front of the French doors. Nobody stood when Truman entered, and one of the 200 mourners, Robert Sherwood, felt sure "this modest man did not even notice this discourtesy or, if he did, understood that the people present could not yet associate him with his high office; and all they could think of was that the President was dead."

The horse-drawn caisson bearing the body of President Roosevelt proceeds down Delaware Avenue on its way to the U.S. Capitol, then to the White House for funeral services. While Allies mourned, Goebbels exulted to Hitler: "My Fuehrer, I congratulate you! Roosevelt is dead! . . . It is the turning point!"

THE BATTLE FOR BERLIN

BY CORNELIUS RYAN

In the spring of 1945 two huge Russian army groups were poised east of Berlin for an all-out assault on the German capital. One, led by Marshal Georgi K. Zhukov, was assembled at Küstrin on the Oder, fifty miles to the east; the other, commanded by Marshal Ivan S. Konev, was seventy-five miles to the southeast, on the eastern bank of the Neisse. Both men were determined to get to Berlin first. The advance of the Allied forces from the west had been ordered by General Eisenhower to halt at the Elbe River.

Cornelius Ryan, aided by a team of Reader's Digest reporters and researchers, worked for more than three years to reconstruct the whole grim story—the military tactics, the human drama and the race to capture Berlin.

At a few minutes before 4 a.m. on Monday, April 16, 1945, there was complete silence in the darkness of the forests along the front occupied by Marshal Zhukov's 1st Belorussian Army Group, composed of 768,100 men. Beneath the pines and camouflage netting the guns were lined up, mile after mile. The mortars were in front. Behind them were tanks, their long rifles elevated. Next came self-propelled guns and, following these, batteries of light and heavy artillery. Along the rear were 400 *Katyushas*—multi-barreled rocket launchers capable of firing sixteen projectiles simultaneously. And massed in the thirty-mile-long Küstrin bridgehead on the Oder's western bank, now jammed with troops, were searchlights aimed directly at the German lines.

In a bunker built into a hill overlooking the bridgehead, Marshal Zhukov stood gazing impassively into the darkness as he waited for zero hour—4 a.m. He was determined to take Berlin by himself. He had no intention of letting anyone get there before him—especially not Marshal Konev, whose 1st Ukrainian Army Group was scheduled to launch a second major Russian assault at 6 a.m. from the south across the Neisse River. Zhukov looked at his watch. Seconds ticked away. Then Zhukov said quietly to his staff officers, "Now, comrades. Now."

Three red flares soared into the night sky. For one interminable moment the lights hung in midair, bathing the Oder in a garish crimson. The phalanx of searchlights flashed on. With blinding intensity the 140 huge antiaircraft lights, supplemented by the lights of tanks, trucks and other vehicles, focused directly on the German positions.

With an earsplitting, earthshaking roar the front erupted in flame, as more than 20,000 guns of all calibers poured a storm of fire into the German positions. Pinned in the merciless glare of the searchlights, the German countryside beyond the western Küstrin bridgehead seemed to disappear before a rolling wall of bursting shells. Whole villages disintegrated. Earth, concrete, steel and parts of trees spewed into the air and in the distance forests began to blaze.

The tempest of sound was stupefying. Rocket projectiles whooshed off the launchers in fiery batches and screeched through the night, leaving long white trails behind them. Amid the tumult Zhukov's shock troops began to move out.

In the ranks were men who had stood at Leningrad, Smolensk, Stalingrad and before Moscow; men who had fought their way across half a continent to reach the Oder. There were soldiers who had seen their villages and towns obliterated by German guns, their crops burned and their families slain by German soldiers. They had lived for this moment of revenge.

After thirty-five minutes the bombardment ended abruptly, leaving a stunning silence. In Zhukov's command bunker, staff officers suddenly became aware of the sound of the telephones. How long they had been ringing, no one could say. Officers began taking the calls from field commanders.

At first Zhukov did not believe the reports. The first objectives had been captured, but Nazi artillery fire from the heavily defended Seelow heights lying just beyond the western banks of the Oder was now pinning down the advancing Russians. In the streams and marshes Soviet tanks were churning helplessly.

At exactly 6 a.m. the forces of Marshal Konev's 1st Ukrainian Army Group attacked across the Neisse River. Konev's massed artillery was as merciless as Zhukov's had been. Konev was leaving nothing to chance. In order to beat Marshal Zhukov to Berlin, he knew he had to overwhelm the enemy within the first few hours. At 7:15 he got good news: a bridgehead had been seized on the western bank of the Neisse.

As time wore on, the Marshal had every reason to be in high spirits. His attack had moved with unforeseen speed, although the fighting had been brutally hard. By noon of the 17th his tanks had been crossing the Spree River and were by now approaching Lübben, the terminal point of the boundary line laid down by Stalin, separating Zhukov's front from his own. For Konev the moment had come to ask Stalin for permission to swing his tanks north toward Berlin.

Near Cottbus, in a medieval castle overlooking the Spree, Marshal Konev waited for his telephone call to go through to Moscow. An aide handed him the radiotelephone. It was Stalin. Konev reported his tactical situation, giving his precise position. "I suggest that my armored formations move immediately in a northerly direction, Comrade Stalin."

"Zhukov is having a difficult time," Stalin said. "He is still breaking through the defenses on the Seelow heights. Enemy resistance there appears stiff. Why not pass Zhukov's armor through the gap created on your front and let him go for Berlin from there?"

"Comrade Stalin," Konev said quickly, "I have adequate forces, and we are in a perfect position to turn our tank armies toward Berlin."

There was a pause. Finally Stalin said, "Very well. I agree. Turn your tank armies toward Berlin."

By nightfall of April 22, Konev's armies had cracked Berlin's southern defenses and had beaten Zhukov into the capital by more than a full day. (Stalin's order that was issued the next day—April 23—divided up the city between Zhukov and Konev. Although he could not complain publicly, Konev was crushed. Zhukov had been given the prize. The boundary line, which ran straight through Berlin, placed Konev's forces roughly 150 yards *west* of the Reichstag—which the Russians had always considered the city's prize plum, the place where the Soviet flag was to be planted.)

Now Berlin began to die. In most places, water and gas services had stopped. There were no newspapers. All transportation within the city was grinding to a halt as streets became impassable, and vehicles were crippled. On April 22 the city's 100-year-old telegraph office closed down for the first time in its history. The last message it received was from Tokyo: "Good luck to you all."

The Russian forces, after breaking the outer ring of the city's defenses, gouged their way into the second ring. They crouched behind the tanks and guns and fought up the streets, the roads, the avenues, and through the parklands. Leading the way were the battle-toughened assault troops of Konev's and Zhukov's Guards, and with them the soldiers of four great tank armies. Behind were line upon line of infantry.

They were a strange soldiery. They came from every republic of the Soviet Union. There were so many languages and dialects among them that officers often could not communicate with elements of their own troops. In the ranks were Ukrainians and Karelians, Georgians and Kazaks, Armenians and Azerbaijanis, Bashkirs, Tatars, Mongols and Cossacks. They came on horseback, on foot, on motorcycles, in horse carts and in captured vehicles of every sort.

Berlin was a holocaust. Its defense forces, supplemented by old men of the Home Guard and boys of the Hitler Youth, had been pushed back into the very heart of the city. There was fighting all through the Tiergarten area and in the zoo. Russian artillery was bombarding the city from the east-west axis, and a fierce battle was taking place within the Reichstag. Finally Gen. Karl Weidling, recently appointed Commandant of the city, could see nothing to do but surrender, and a little before 1 a.m. on May 2 the Red Army's 79th Guards Rifle Division picked up a radio message.

"Hello, hello," said the voice. "This is the Fifty-sixth Panzer Corps. We ask for a cease-fire. At twelve-fifty hours Berlin time we are sending truce negotiators to the Potsdam Bridge. Recognition sign: a white flag. Awaiting reply."

On receipt of the message, Gen. Vasili I. Chuikov ordered a cease-fire. Later that morning powerful loudspeakers all over the city announced the end of the hostilities. Although sporadic firing would continue for days, the Battle for Berlin was officially over, and people who ventured into the Königsplatz that morning saw the Red flag fluttering over the Reichstag.

THE END OF A TYRANT

BY H. R. TREVOR-ROPER

Twenty-three years after the event, new light was thrown on Hitler's suicide in a book by a former Soviet Intelligence Officer, Lev A. Bezymenski, published in the West in August 1968, titled The Death of Adolf Hitler. *His account, allegedly based on official Soviet documents, appears authentic, although the book was not published in the U.S.S.R.*

According to Bezymenski, a Soviet medical team, eight days after Hitler's death, performed an autopsy on the charred remains of the body and established that he had died by swallowing poison. Splinters of a cyanide capsule, the doctors reported, were found in the mouth. This contradicts the conclusions reached by Prof. H. R. Trevor-Roper and other historians that Hitler shot himself. However, the fact that part of the skull was torn away, presumably by gunfire, suggests that both a revolver and poison may have been involved in the suicide. Bezymenski does not explain the reason why Moscow had not divulged the Hitler autopsy findings for so many years.

Other than the ambiguity about the actual suicide method, the Russian's book does not differ essentially from the account that follows, drawn from the book, The Last Days of Hitler. *The author is Regius Professor of Modern History at Oxford University.*

In his Berlin bunker at midnight on April 29, 1945, Hitler was preparing for the end. During the day the last news from the outside world had come in. Mussolini was dead. Hitler's partner in crime, the herald of Fascism, who had first shown to Hitler the possibilities of dictatorship in modern Europe, and had preceded him in the stages of disillusion and defeat, had now illustrated in a signal manner the fate which fallen tyrants must expect. Captured by partisans during the general uprising of northern Italy, Mussolini and his mistress, Clara Petacci, had been executed and their bodies suspended by the feet in the marketplace of Milan to be beaten and pelted by the vindictive crowd. If the full details were ever known to them, Hitler and Eva Braun, whom he had married earlier in the day, could only have repeated the orders they had already given. Their own bodies were to be destroyed so that nothing remained.

In the afternoon Hitler had had his favorite Alsatian dog, Blondi, destroyed. Professor Werner Haase, his former surgeon, who was now tending the wounded in his clinic in Berlin, had come to the bunker and killed it with poison. After this, Hitler had given poison capsules to his two secretaries, for use in extremity.

In the evening, while the inhabitants of the two outer bunkers were eating in the general dining passage of the Fuehrerbunker, they were visited by one of the S.S. guards, who informed them that the Fuehrer wished to say good-bye to the ladies and that no one was to go to bed till orders had been received. At about 2:30 a.m. on April 30 the orders came. They were summoned by telephone to the bunker and gathered again in the same general dining passage, officers and women, about twenty persons in all. When they were assembled, Hitler came in from the private part of the bunker. His look was abstracted, his eyes glazed over with moisture. He walked in silence down the passage and shook hands with the women. Some spoke to him, but he said nothing or mumbled inaudibly.

When he had left, the participants in this strange scene remained for a while to discuss its significance. They agreed that it could have one meaning only. The suicide of the Fuehrer was about to take place. Then

---

The photographs to the right, made in the spring of 1945, are among the last ever taken of Hitler. (Top) The Fuehrer, slumped in an ill-fitting greatcoat, is accompanied by a group of aides. (Bottom) With an adjutant at his side, the German leader peers uncertainly from the doorway of his Berlin bunker.

there happened an unexpected thing. A great and heavy cloud seemed to roll away from the spirits of the bunker dwellers. The terrible sorcerer, the tyrant who had charged their days with intolerable melodramatic tension, would soon be gone, and for a brief twilight moment they could play. In the canteen of the Chancellery, where the soldiers and orderlies took their meals, there was a dance. The news was brought, but no one allowed that to interfere with the business of pleasure. A message from the Fuehrerbunker told them to be quieter; but the dance went on. A tailor who had been employed in the Fuehrer's headquarters, and who was now immured with the rest in the Chancellery, was surprised when Brigadefuehrer Johann Rattenhuber, the head of the police guard and a general in the S.S., slapped him cordially on the back and greeted him with democratic familiarity. In the strict hierarchy of the bunker the tailor felt bewildered. It was as if he had been a high officer. "It was the first time I had ever heard a high officer say 'Good evening,'" he said, "so I noticed that the mood had completely changed." Then from one of his equals he learned the reason of this irregular affability. Hitler had said good-bye and was going to commit suicide.

Later in the morning, when the new day's work had begun, the generals came as usual to the bunker with their military reports. Brigadefuehrer Wilhelm Mohnke, the Commandant of the Chancellery, announced a slight improvement—the Schlesischer railway station had been recaptured from the Russians—but in other respects the military situation was unchanged. By noon the news was worse again. The underground railway tunnel in the Friedrichstrasse was reported in Russian hands; the tunnel in the Vossstrasse, close to the Chancellery, was partly occupied; the whole area of the Tiergarten had been taken; and Russian forces had reached the Potsdamer Platz and the Weidendammer Bridge over the River Spree. Hitler received these reports without emotion. At about two o'clock he took lunch. Eva Braun was not there; evidently she did not feel hungry, or ate alone in her room. Hitler shared his meal, as he usually did in her absence, with his two secretaries and the cook. The conversation indicated nothing unusual. Hitler remained quiet and did not once speak of his intentions. Nevertheless, preparations were already being made for the approaching ceremony.

In the morning the guards had been ordered to col-

(Top right) *In more carefree days, Hitler poses with Eva Braun, his longtime mistress. She never attended the great Nazi rallies and was rarely seen publicly with the Fuehrer. On April 29, 1945, the two were married in the Fuehrerbunker, deep beneath the smoking rubble of the German capital.*

lect all their rations for the day, since they would not be allowed to pass through the corridor of the bunker again; and about lunchtime Hitler's S.S. adjutant, Sturmbannfuehrer Otto Guensche, sent an order to the transport officer and chauffeur, Sturmbannfuehrer Erich Kempka, to send 200 liters (211.4 quarts) of gasoline to the Chancellery garden. He found about 180 liters and sent it around. Four men carried it in and placed it at the emergency exit of the bunker. There they met one of the police guards, who demanded an explanation. At this moment Hitler's personal servant, Heinz Linge, appeared. He reassured the guard and dismissed the men. Soon afterward all the guards except those on duty were ordered to leave the Chancellery and to stay away. It was not intended that any casual observer should witness the final scene.

Meanwhile Hitler had finished lunch, and his guests had been dismissed. For a time he remained behind; then he emerged from his suite, accompanied by Eva Braun, and another farewell ceremony took place. Martin Bormann, head of the Party Chancery, and Paul Joseph Goebbels were there, with a group of others, including four women. Hitler and Eva Braun shook hands with them all and then returned to their suite. The rest were dismissed, all but the high priests and those few others whose services would be necessary. These waited in the passage. A single shot was heard. After an interval they entered the suite. Hitler was lying on the sofa, which was soaked with blood. He had shot himself through the mouth. Eva Braun was also on the sofa, also dead. A revolver was by her side, but she had not used it; she had swallowed poison. The time was half past three.

Shortly afterward, Artur Axmann, head of the Hitler Youth, arrived at the bunker. He was too late for the farewell ceremony, but he was admitted to the private suite to see the dead bodies. He examined them and stayed in the room for some minutes, talking

(Bottom right) *Hitler pats a boy's cheek as he awards Iron Crosses to members of the Hitler Youth for making a courageous last-ditch stand against the might of the advancing Russian Army. Still believing that fate was on his side, the Fuehrer, rather than surrender, ordered children to the front in the last days of the war.*

with Goebbels. Then Goebbels left, and Axmann remained there alone for a short while. Outside, another ceremony was being prepared: the Viking funeral.

After sending the gasoline to the garden, Kempka had walked across to the bunker by the subterranean passage which connected his office in the Hermann Goering Strasse with the Chancellery buildings. He was greeted by Guensche with the words, "The Chief is dead." At that moment the door of Hitler's suite was opened, and Kempka too became a participant in the funeral scene.

While Axmann was meditating beside the corpses, two S.S. men, one of them Hitler's servant Linge, entered the room. They wrapped Hitler's body in a blanket, concealing the bloodstained and shattered head, and carried it out into the passage, where the other observers easily recognized it by the familiar black trousers. Then two other S.S. officers carried the body up the four flights of stairs to the emergency exit and out into the garden. After this, Bormann entered the room and took up the body of Eva Braun. Her death had been tidier, and no blanket was needed to conceal the evidence of it. Bormann carried the body into the passage, and then handed it to Kempka, who took it to the foot of the stairs. There it was taken from him by Guensche; and Guensche in turn gave it to a third S.S. officer, who carried it upstairs to the garden. As an additional precaution, the other door of the bunker, which led into the Chancellery, and some of the doors leading from the Chancellery to the garden, had been hastily locked against possible intruders.

Sometimes the most careful precautions are unavailing; and it was as a direct result of this precaution that two unauthorized persons witnessed the scene from which it was intended to exclude them. One of the police guards, Erich Mansfeld, happened to be on duty in the concrete observation tower at the corner of the bunker, and noticing through the opaque, sulfurous air a sudden suspicious scurrying of men and shutting of doors, he felt it his duty to investigate. He climbed down from his tower into the garden and walked around to the emergency exit to see what was afoot. In the porch he collided with the emerging funeral procession. First there were two S.S. officers carrying a body wrapped in a blanket, with black-trousered legs protruding from it. Then there was another S.S. officer carrying the unmistakable corpse of Eva Braun.

Behind them were the mourners: Bormann, Gen. Wilhelm Burgdorf, Goebbels, Guensche, Linge and Kempka. Guensche shouted at Mansfeld to get out of the way quickly; and Mansfeld, having seen the forbidden but interesting spectacle, returned to his tower.

After this interruption, the ritual was continued. The two corpses were placed side by side, a few feet from the porch, and gasoline from the cans was poured over them. A Russian bombardment added to the strangeness and danger of the ceremony, and the mourners withdrew for some protection under the shelter of the porch. There Guensche dipped a rag in gasoline, set it alight and flung it out upon the corpses. They were at once enveloped in a sheet of flame. The mourners stood at attention, gave the Hitler salute and withdrew again into the bunker, where they dispersed. Guensche afterward described the spectacle to those who had missed it. The burning of Hitler's body, he said, was the most terrible experience in his life.

Meanwhile yet another witness had observed the event. He was another of the police guards, and he too came accidentally upon the scene in consequence of the precautions which should have excluded him. His name was Hermann Karnau. Like others of the guard who were not on duty, Karnau had been ordered away from the bunker by an officer of the S.S. Escort, and had gone to the Chancellery canteen; but after a while, in spite of his orders, he had decided to return to the bunker. On arrival at the door of the bunker, he had found it locked. He had therefore made his way out into the garden, in order to enter the bunker by the emergency exit. As he turned the corner by the tower where Mansfeld was on duty, he was surprised to see two bodies lying side by side, close to the door of the bunker. Almost at the same instant they burst, spontaneously it seemed, into flame.

Karnau watched the burning corpses for a moment. They were easily recognizable, though Hitler's head was smashed. The sight, he says, was "repulsive in the extreme." Then he went down into the bunker by the emergency exit. In the bunker he met Sturmbannfuehrer Franz Schedle, the officer commanding the S.S. Escort. He was distracted with grief. "The Fuehrer is dead," he said. "He is burning outside."

Mansfeld, on duty in the tower, also watched the burning of the bodies. As he had climbed the tower, after Guensche had ordered him away, he had seen through a loophole a great column of black smoke

Shattered symbol of Nazi power: A squad of Soviet infantrymen charge into what remains of the building that at one time had housed the Reichstag, the former legislative assembly of Germany. A short while later, the red banner of Soviet Russia fluttered from its rooftop.

rising from the garden. The smoke diminished and he saw the same two bodies which he had seen being brought up the stairs. They were burning. After the mourners had withdrawn, he continued to watch. At intervals he saw S.S. men come out of the bunker and pour more gasoline on the bodies to keep them alight. Some time afterward he was relieved by Karnau, and when Karnau had helped him to climb out of the tower, the two went together to look at the bodies again. By now the lower parts of both bodies had been burned away and the shinbones of Hitler's legs were visible. An hour later Mansfeld visited the bodies again. They were still burning, but the flame was low.

Late that night Brigadefuehrer Rattenhuber entered the dog-bunker (guards' rest room), where the guards were spending their leisure, and spoke to a Sergeant of the S.S. Escort. He told him to report to his com-

manding officer, Schedle, and to pick three trustworthy men to bury the corpses. Soon afterward Rattenhuber returned to the dog-bunker and addressed the men there. He made them promise to keep the events of the day a secret. Anyone talking about them would be shot. Shortly before midnight Mansfeld returned to duty in the tower. Russian shells were still falling, and the sky was illuminated by flares. He noticed that a bomb crater in front of the emergency exit had been newly worked upon, and that the bodies had disappeared. He did not doubt that the crater had been converted into a grave; no shell could have piled the earth around it so neatly. About that time, Karnau was on parade with other guards in the Vossstrasse, and one of them said to him: "It is sad that none of the officers seems to worry about the Fuehrer's body. I am proud that I alone know where he is."

427

NAZI DEATH FACTORY AT BUCHENWALD

BY EDWARD R. MURROW

The atrocities of war were well known to people "back home"—those in America and other Western nations whose lands had not been scarred by war. The press had told these stories vividly. But the horror of war had never been so shockingly revealed as in the accounts of the Nazi death camps that were reported as soon as Allied troops occupied them. Here is a transcription of a broadcast from infamous Buchenwald by Edward R. Murrow.

I have just driven more than a few hundred miles through Germany . . . most of it in the Third Army sector, Wiesbaden, Frankfurt, Weimar, Jena and beyond. . . . The tanks on the concrete road sound like a huge sausage machine, grinding up sheets of corrugated iron. . . . The power moves forward, while the people, the slaves, walk back, pulling their small belongings on anything that has wheels.

The Germans are well clothed, appear well fed and healthy, in better condition than any other people I've seen in Europe.

In the large cities there are many young men of military age in civilian clothes, and in the fields there are a few horses; most of the plows are pulled by cows, for the ghosts of horses dead in Russia and in Normandy will not draw plows. Old men and women work in the fields. There are cities in Germany that make Coventry and Plymouth appear to be merely damage done by a petulant child. But bombed houses have a way of looking alike, wherever you see them.

This is no time to talk of the surface of Germany. Permit me to tell you what you would have seen and heard, had you been with me on this trip. It will not be pleasant listening. If you are at lunch, or if you have no appetite to hear what Germans have done, now is a good time to switch off the radio.

For I propose to tell you of Buchenwald. It's on a small hill, about five miles outside Weimar.

This was one of the largest concentration camps in Germany . . . and it was built to last. As we approached it, we saw about a hundred men in civilian clothes, with rifles, advancing in open order across the fields.

There were a few shots. We stopped to inquire. We were told that some of the prisoners had a couple of S.S. men cornered in there. We drove on, reached the main gate. The prisoners crowded up behind the wire. We entered. And now let me tell this in the first person, for I was the least important person there, as you can hear. There surged around me an evil-smelling crowd; men and boys reached out to touch me. They were in rags and the remnants of uniforms. Death had already marked many of them, but they were smiling with their eyes. I looked out over that mass of men to the green fields beyond, where well-fed Germans were plowing.

A German, Fritz Kirchenheimer, came up and said, "May I show you around the camp? I've been here ten years." An Englishman stood to attention, saying, "May I introduce myself? Delighted to see you. And can you tell me when some of our blokes will be along?" I told him, "Soon," and asked to see one of the barracks. It happened to be occupied by Czechs. When I entered, men crowded around, tried to lift me to their shoulders. They were too weak. Many of them could not get out of bed. I was told that this building had once stabled eighty horses. There were 1200 men in it, five to a bunk. The stink was beyond all description. When I reached the center of the barracks, a man came up and said, "You remember me, I'm Peter Zenkl, onetime Mayor of Prague." I remembered him, but did not recognize him. He asked about Eduard Benes and Jan Masaryk.

I asked how many men had died in that building during the last month. They called the doctor. We inspected his records. There were only names in the little black book . . . nothing more. Nothing to show who had been where, what he had done or hoped. Behind the names of those who had died, there was a cross. I counted them. They totaled 242—242 out of 1200, in one month.

Starving inmates of Auschwitz, liberated by Allied troops, huddle on the ground, too weak to rise or comprehend that deliverance has come at last. Auschwitz was the grimmest of the concentration camps; between 3 and 4 million people were murdered or allowed to die here.

As I walked down to the end of the barracks, there was applause from the men too weak to get out of bed. It sounded like the handclapping of babies—they were so weak. The doctor's name was Paul Heller. He had been there since 1938. As we walked out into the courtyard, a man fell dead. Two others, they must have been over sixty, were crawling toward the latrine. I saw it, but will not describe it.

In another part of the camp they showed me the children, hundreds of them. Some were only six. One rolled up his sleeve, showed me his number. It was tattooed on his arm. B-6030, it was. The others showed me their numbers. They will carry them until they die. An elderly man standing beside me said, "The children . . . enemies of the State!" I could see their ribs through their thin shirts. The old man said, "I am Professor Charles Richer, of the Sorbonne." The children clung to my arms and stared. We crossed to the courtyard. Men kept coming up to speak to me and to touch me—professors from Poland, doctors from Vienna, men from all Europe, men from the countries that made America.

We went to the hospital. It was full. The doctor told me that 200 had died the day before. I asked the cause of death. He shrugged and said, "Tuberculosis, starvation, fatigue, and there are many who have no desire to live. It is very difficult." Dr. Heller pulled back the blanket from a man's feet to show me how swollen they were. The man was dead.

Most of the patients could not move.

As we left the hospital, I drew out a leather billfold, hoping that I had some money that would help those who lived to get home. Professor Richer from the Sorbonne said, "I should be careful of my wallet, if I were you. You know there are criminals in this camp too." A small man tottered up, saying, "May I feel the leather, please. You see, I used to make good things of leather in Vienna." Another man said, "My name is Walther Roede. For many years I lived in Joliet, came back to Germany for a visit, and Hitler grabbed me."

I asked to see the kitchen. It was clean. The German in charge had been a Communist, had been at Buchenwald for nine years, had a picture of his daughter in Hamburg, hadn't seen her for almost twelve years . . . and if I got to Hamburg, would I look her up?

He showed me the daily ration: one piece of brown bread about as thick as your thumb, on top of it a piece of margarine as big as three sticks of chewing gum. That, and a little stew, was what they received every twenty-four hours. He had a chart on the wall—very complicated it was. There were little red tabs scattered through it. He explained the tabs were there to indicate each ten men who died. He had to account for the rations, and he added, "We're very efficient here."

We went again to the courtyard, and as we walked, we talked. The two doctors, the Frenchman and the Czech, agreed that about 6000 had died during March. Kirchenheimer, the German, added that back in the winter of 1939, when the Poles began to arrive, without winter clothing, they died at the rate of approximately 900 a day. Five different men asserted that Buchenwald was the best concentration camp in Germany. They had had some experience in the others.

Dr. Heller, the Czech, asked if I would care to see the crematorium. He said it wouldn't be very interesting, because the Germans had run out of coke some days ago and had taken to dumping the bodies into a great hole nearby.

Professor Richer said perhaps I would care to see the small courtyard. I said Yes. He turned and told the children to stay behind. As we walked across the square, I noticed that the Professor had a hole in his left shoe and a toe sticking out of the right one. He followed my eyes and said, "I regret that I am so little presentable, but what can one do?"

At that point, another Frenchman came to announce that three of his fellow countrymen outside had killed three S.S. men and taken one prisoner.

We proceeded to the small courtyard. The wall was about eight feet high. It adjoined what had been a stable or garage. We entered. It was floored with concrete. There were two rows of bodies stacked up like cordwood. They were thin and very white. Some of the bodies were terribly bruised, though there seemed to be little flesh to bruise. Some had been shot through the head, but they bled but little. Only two were naked. I tried to count them as best I could and arrived at the conclusion that all that was mortal of more than 500 men and boys lay there in two piles. There was a German trailer, which must have contained another fifty, but it wasn't possible to count them. The clothing was piled in a heap against the wall. It appeared that most of the men and boys had died of starvation; they had not been executed.

But the manner of death seemed unimportant.

Murder had been done at Buchenwald. God knows how many men and boys have died there during the last twelve years. I was told that there were more than 20,000 in the camp. There had been as many as 60,000. Where are they now?

I pray you to believe what I have said about Buchenwald. I reported what I saw and heard, but only part of it. For most of it, I have no words.

Dead men are plentiful in war, but the living dead—more than 20,000 of them in one camp. . . . The country round was pleasing to the eye, and the Germans were well fed and well dressed. American trucks were rolling toward the rear filled with prisoners. Soon they would be eating American rations, as much for a meal as the men at Buchenwald had received in four days.

If I have offended you by this rather mild account of Buchenwald, I'm not in the least sorry.

Many men and many tongues blessed the name of Franklin D. Roosevelt. For long years, his name had meant the full measure of their hope. These men who had kept close company with death for many years did not know that Roosevelt would, within hours, join their comrades who had laid their lives on the scales of freedom.

Back in 1941, Winston Churchill said to me, with tears in his eyes, "One day the world and history will recognize and acknowledge what they owe to your President." I saw and heard the first installment of that at Buchenwald when I was there. It came from men all over Europe.

Their faces, with more flesh on them, might have been found anywhere at home. To them the name "Roosevelt" was a symbol, a codeword for a lot of guys named Joe, who were somewhere out in the blue with the armor, heading east. At Buchenwald they spoke of the President just before he died. If there be a better epitaph, history does not record it.

Hundreds of Nazi victims lie in grotesque heaps in a mass grave at a concentration camp. Some 10 million men, women and children died in these camps, which were scattered throughout Germany and neighboring occupied countries.

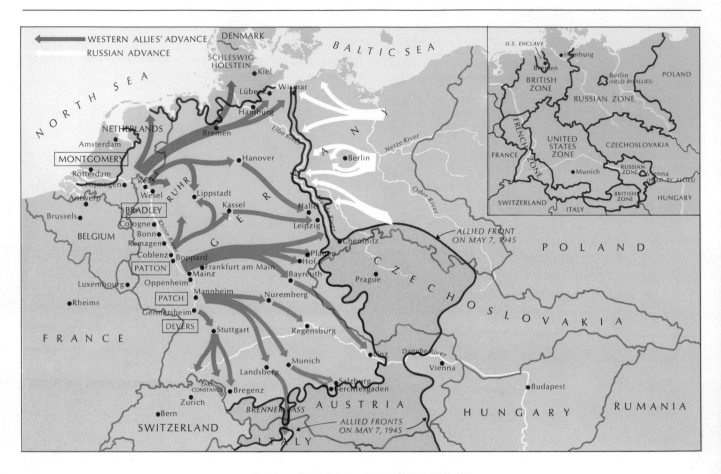

THE FINAL OFFENSIVE

Montgomery's 21st Army Group crossed the Rhine at Wesel on March 23, 1945, and then divided, as the Canadian First Army veered northward into the Netherlands and the British Second Army headed for Schleswig-Holstein and Denmark.

Following a Rhine crossing by Bradley's 12th Army Group, the U.S. First and Ninth Armies swiftly encircled the Ruhr, meeting at Lippstadt. The 300,000 Nazi troops caught in the envelopment were forced to surrender by the middle of May, thus freeing the two U.S. armies to plunge eastward, taking Kassel, Hanover, Leipzig and Halle before arriving at the east bank of the Elbe. Patton's swift-moving

Third Army captured Bayreuth, Hof and Plauen, then halted near the Czechoslovak border.

In order to forestall the rumored establishment of a Nazi "National Redoubt" in the Bavarian Alps, Patch's Seventh Army (part of Devers' 6th Army Group) seized Nuremberg, Munich, Berchtesgaden and Salzburg. Elements of the Seventh advanced through the Brenner Pass and on May 4 made contact with units of the U.S. Fifth Army moving northward from Italy. Meanwhile, the French First Army of Devers' army group swept south to the Swiss border.

The Russians, in the east, took Vienna April 13 and forced Berlin,

which they had completely surrounded, to capitulate on May 2.

To the British in the north now fell Lübeck and Wismar, as well as Hamburg (May 3). Two days later, all the German troops in northwest Germany, Denmark and the Netherlands surrendered to Montgomery. This was followed on May 7, 1945, by Nazi Germany surrendering unconditionally to General Eisenhower at Rheims.

With the end of hostilities, the Allies began to take over their respective occupation zones in Germany and Austria, which had been agreed upon by Roosevelt, Churchill and Stalin at Yalta in February 1945 (see inset map above).

U.S. and Russian troops celebrate after meeting at Torgau on the Elbe, April 25, 1945. Amid much backslapping and vodka drinking, a Soviet Major toasted the occasion: "Today we have the most happy day of our lives. . . . Long live our great countries."

433

VICTORY MESSAGE TO THE TROOPS

The route you have traveled through hundreds of miles is marked by the graves of former comrades. Each of the fallen died as a member of the team to which you belong, bound together by a common love of liberty and a refusal to submit to enslavement. Our common problems of the immediate and distant future can be best solved in the same conceptions of cooperation and devotion to the cause of human freedom as have made this Expeditionary Force such a mighty engine of righteous destruction.

Let us have no part in the profitless quarrels in which other men will inevitably engage as to what country, what service, won the European war. Every man, every woman, of every nation here represented has served according to his or her ability, and the efforts of each have contributed to the outcome. This we shall remember—and in doing so we shall be revering each honored grave and be sending comfort to the loved ones of comrades who could not live to see this day.

— DWIGHT D. EISENHOWER

The giant British liner Queen Elizabeth, loaded with GI's returning from Europe, steams toward New York in 1945. For the majority of those aboard, discharge and civilian life lay ahead. But in the Pacific the fighting continued.

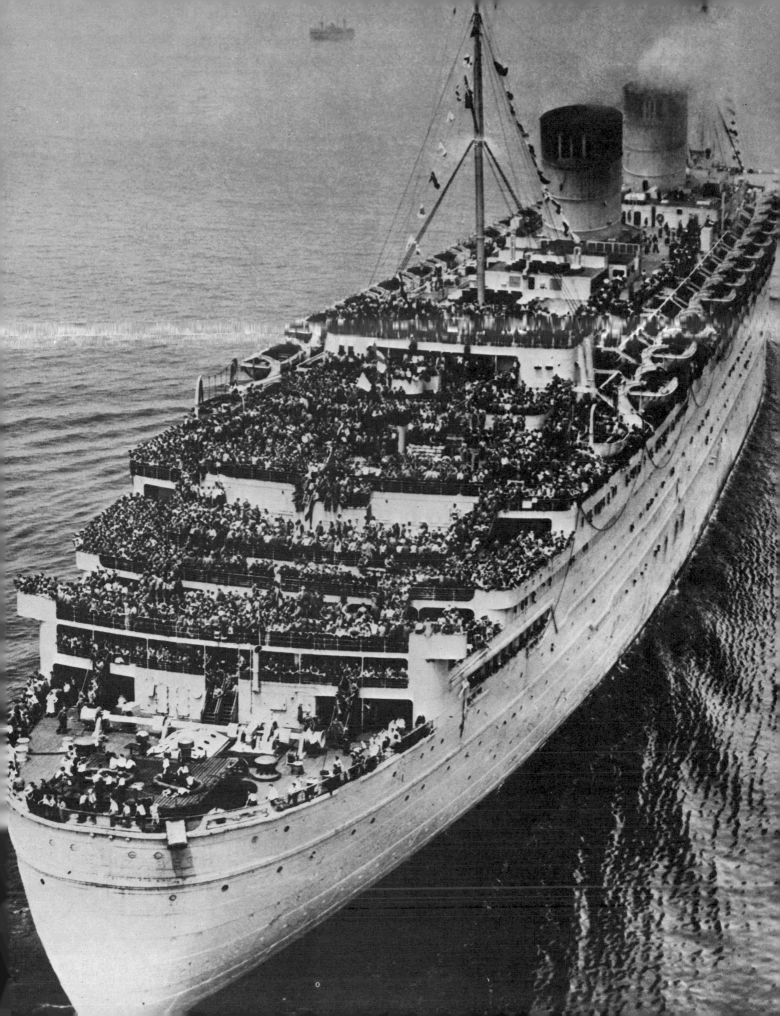

As the Allies drew closer to Japan, the enemy's resistance intensified. Whether running in a shrieking banzai charge or screaming down in a suicidal kamikaze dive, the Japanese made the Allies pay for every inch of their advance. Here U.S. marines move over the cinder beach of Iwo Jima, wary of enemy fire from Mount Suribachi.

BLOOD AND SAND:

DOOMSDAY COMES TO JAPAN

ISLAND-HOPPING: Phase II December 1943 to December 1944

The two branches of the Allied counteroffensive in the Pacific gained great momentum in 1944. American and Australian troops under command of Gen. Douglas MacArthur continued to press along the 1500-mile northern coast of New Guinea.

The string of their victories made up a timetable of progress: Saidor (January 2, 1944); Hollandia and Aitape (April 22); Madang and Alexishafen (April 24–26); Arare (May 17); Wakde Island (May 18); Biak Island (May 27); Noemfoor Island (July 2); and Sansapor (July 30), followed by the capture of Morotai in the Moluccas (September 15).

A second drive by MacArthur was aimed at isolating the key Japanese base at Rabaul on New Britain. Allied troops had gained control of the western end of that island in December 1943. On March 6 of the following year, Talasea on the Willaumez Peninsula was taken, causing the Japanese to begin a withdrawal, until by November 1944 they had been herded into the Gazelle Peninsula with no chance of escape.

Still more gains were won by MacArthur's men, notably the seizure of Los Negros in the Admiralty Islands (February 29) and the capture of the island of Manus in March. The possession of the Admiralties sealed off Rabaul from all contact with Truk, the major Japanese Naval and Air Force base some 800 miles to the north.

While the forces of MacArthur were making telling strikes, those of Adm. William F. Halsey's South Pacific Command (under the overall supervision of Adm. Chester W. Nimitz) were engaged in breaking the Japanese grip on the Solomon Islands. New Zealand troops under Admiral Halsey took the Green Islands to the north on February 15, followed by Emirau Island in the St. Matthias (Mussau) group on March 20. Here new airfields reinforced the network of air bases that ringed Rabaul and Kavieng on New Ireland, rendering both enemy garrisons helpless.

With the Solomon action concluded and the Bismarck Barrier broken, Halsey's forces were assigned to MacArthur while the Admiral himself was transferred to the Central Pacific. In this vast area the other spearhead of the Allied offensive under Admiral Nimitz had been vigorously carrying the fight to the enemy.

Nimitz' task forces captured the islands of Kwajalein and Roi-Namur in the Marshalls, January 31–February 7. The assault on Eniwetok Atoll, begun February 17, was completed five days later. Attacked by land- and carrier-based planes and bombarded by the fleet, Truk was rendered useless to the Japanese.

Nimitz now sent an armada of more than 500 ships, under the command of Adm. Raymond A. Spruance, against the Marianas. American landings were made on the island of Saipan on June 15 in the face of blazing opposition. To help repel the American attack, a Japanese fleet of 9 carriers, 18 battleships and cruisers, and 28 destroyers was dispatched from the Philippines. The ensuing aerial battle with planes from Vice Adm. Marc A. Mitscher's U.S. force of 15 carriers, 7 battleships, 21 cruisers and 69 destroyers, which took place in the vicinity of Guam on June 19, proved to be a staggering blow to Japanese air power from which it never recovered. (See "The Battle of the Philippine Sea," pages 451–457.)

On Saipan, meanwhile, the vicious battle raged until July 9, and mopping-up operations continued for another three weeks. More than 23,000 Japanese were killed; the American dead numbered close to 3500.

The next target was Guam, where landings began July 21 and the fighting lasted until August 10. Some 150 miles to the northeast, American troops were attacking the island of Tinian (July 23–August 1).

The loss of the Pacific islands, particularly Saipan, brought about the downfall of the Tojo Government in July 1944. The American counteroffensive was now close enough to the enemy's homeland to send B-29 Superfortress bombers to blast Japan itself.

Nimitz advanced his forces to the Palau Islands in the western Carolines, and on September 15 the island of Peleliu was assaulted by U.S. marines. Holed up in hundreds of fortified caves and tunnels, the Japanese resisted savagely for ten weeks.

The American forces were now close to their objective, the Philippines. The next phase would be General MacArthur's strike at the island of Leyte.

KOREA

SEA OF JAPAN

JAPAN

●Tokyo

●Osaka

CHINA

PACIFIC OCEAN

OKINAWA

RYUKYU ISLANDS

IWO JIMA

FORMOSA
(TAIWAN)

WAKE ISLAND

LUZON

PHILIPPINE
ISLANDS

●Manila

PHILIPPINE SEA

MARIANAS
ISLANDS

SAIPAN

TINIAN

GUAM

ENIWETOK

MARSHALL
ISLANDS

ROI-NAMUR

KWAJALEIN

LEYTE

PALAU
ISLANDS

PELELIU

CAROLINE ISLANDS

TRUK

MAKIN

MOROTAI

GILBERT
ISLANDS

TARAWA

Sansapor●

MOLUCCA ISLANDS

BIAK ISLAND

WAKDE ISLAND

Arare

ADMIRALTY
ISLANDS

ST. MATTHIAS
ISLANDS

EMIRAU ISLAND

Kavieng

CELEBES

NOEMFOOR ISLAND

Sarmi●

Aitape

MANUS ISLAND

LOS NEGROS

NEW IRELAND

GAZELLE PEN.

Hollandia●

Alexishafen●

Rabaul

GREEN ISLANDS

NETHERLANDS
NEW GUINEA

NORTH-EAST
NEW GUINEA

Talasea

SOLOMON ISLANDS

Saidor

WILLAUMEZ
PEN.

PAPUA

NEW
BRITAIN

BOUGAINVILLE

TIMOR

Buna●

GUADALCANAL

SANTA
CRUZ
ISLANDS

Darwin●

Port Moresby●

CORAL SEA

NEW
HEBRIDES

AUSTRALIA

(Above) *Paratroopers establish a stronghold on the Japanese-built Kamiri Airfield on Noemfoor Island as U.S. planes patrol overhead. Noemfoor was one of a series of small enemy-held islands captured by Allied forces in the course of the New Guinea campaign.*

(Left) *Under cover of naval and air bombardment, Southwest Pacific forces commanded by General MacArthur stream ashore from landing craft to seize a beachhead on the island of Morotai in the Moluccas on September 15, 1944. The small Japanese force that garrisoned the island was quickly overcome, and American casualties were exceptionally light. General MacArthur himself accompanied the invasion force aboard the light cruiser* Nashville.

441

BANZAI ON SAIPAN

BY CAPT. EDMUND G. LOVE, USA (RET.)

The biggest suicide operation of the war occurred on the island of Saipan during the night of July 7–8, 1944. Pushed into a tight pocket by the American invaders, the surviving Japanese forces erupted in a sudden maniacal death charge. Captain Love describes the grisly battle from the vantage point of the two battalions at the forward perimeter, suddenly overrun by the wild, disorganized avalanche of several thousand men bent on taking as many Americans as possible with them in a crazed orgy of self-destruction.

After the great banzai attack which ended the Battle of Attu in the Aleutians on May 30, 1943, in which more than 500 Japanese gave up their lives in rushing American lines, American soldiers in the Pacific war generally believed that every battle would end in such an all-out suicide raid. Evidence from other battlefields seemed to support this theory. Guadalcanal, Tarawa, Eniwetok all had their futile, crazed banzai attacks at one time or another. On Saipan soldiers and marines had been waiting for this, and it seemed ever more imminent.

According to the tradition of the Japanese Army, if the Emperor himself ordered such a raid, it was called *Gyokusai*—"Death with honor." It meant that every soldier facing the enemy must take up arms and give his life for his country. The battle cry on Saipan in the *Gyokusai* was characteristic: "Seven lives for the Emperor!" Each soldier, in dying, was to take seven Americans with him. The great charge on Attu was undoubtedly *Gyokusai;* the raids on the other islands probably were not.

Some Japanese later claimed that on the night of July 4, 1944, an airplane flew over northern Saipan and dropped a written message over the Japanese headquarters. It was purportedly from the Emperor, ordering the *Gyokusai*. But it is not generally believed by U.S. intelligence officers that any such direct order was delivered. More than likely this was a battlefield rumor that gained wide credence. There is also the possibility that Lt. Gen. Yoshitsugu Saito deliberately set this rumor in motion to justify his order for the attack. In any case, the charge of July 7 was a true *Gyokusai* because all those who took part *believed* that they were acting on the orders of the Emperor.

The Saipan *Gyokusai* was not a wild, blind rush without an objective. Saito, in his orders, instructed the Japanese that their attack was to push down the coast through Tanapag village and Garapan to Charan Kanoa, where they were to join forces with sizable portions of a Japanese division which was still holding out on Nafutan Point. The attacking force was to do as much damage as possible to all American installations on the way, particularly in the village of Garapan where, it was thought, the invasion headquarters had been established. The attack on the morning of July 7 was to be three-pronged. But the pattern laid out was never followed. Virtually all the enemy strength came down the coast. There are probably two reasons for this: One, a confusion in orders; and two, the absolute domination of the herd instinct in the component parts of the raiding party.

The general opinion, supported by testimony of all who saw the attack, and further substantiated by the number of known enemy on the island at the time, indicates that between 3000 and 4000 Japanese soldiers participated in the *Gyokusai*. The exact figure will never be known. After the raid was over, Japanese resistance on Saipan almost entirely collapsed, showing a complete draining off of available manpower.

The senior Japanese commanders on Saipan were Lieutenant General Saito and Vice Adm. Chuichi Nagumo. During the evening of July 5 the General feted his Naval counterpart at a ceremonial dinner that lasted all night. At 8 a.m. on July 6, he assembled his staff officers and read them his farewell message:

I am addressing the officers and men of the Imperial Army on Saipan. For more than twenty days since the American devils attacked, the officers, men and civilian employes of the Imperial

Army and Navy on this island have fought well and bravely. Everywhere they have demonstrated the honor and glory of the Imperial forces. I expected that every man would do his duty. Heaven has not given us the opportunity: we have not been able to utilize fully the terrain. We have fought in unison up to the present time, but now we have no material with which to fight, and our artillery for attack is completely destroyed. Our comrades have fallen one after another. Despite the bitterness of defeat we pledge seven lives to repay our country.

The barbarous attack of the enemy is being continued. Even though the enemy has occupied only a corner of Saipan, we are dying without avail under the violent shelling and bombing. Whether we attack or whether we stay where we are, there is only death. However, in death there is life. We must use this opportunity to exalt true Japanese manhood. I will advance with those who remain to deliver still another blow to the American devils and leave my bones on Saipan as a bulwark of the Pacific.

As it says in the *Senjinkun* ("Battle Ethics"): "I will never suffer the disgrace of being taken alive, and I will offer up the courage of my soul and calmly rejoice in living by the Eternal Principle." Here I pray with you for the eternal life of the Emperor and the welfare of our country. I advance to seek out the enemy. Follow me!

This remarkable document was found on the body of a Japanese officer killed in the *Gyokusai*. But Saito did not advance with his troops to die on the fields of Tanapag. Instead, after dispatching messengers with copies of his farewell address and instructions for the attack, Saito and Nagumo retired to their quarters. Both let blood in the traditional fashion and then were killed by their aides, by pistol shots in the head. This was at 10 a.m. on July 6, about eighteen hours before the attack was launched. Afterward, as they had ordered, the bodies of both officers were burned, although only partially. American authorities later disinterred the remains and carried them to Charan Kanoa, where they were buried with full military honors.

The Americans, of course, knew nothing about the preparations; the Japanese had not changed their pattern of defense one bit on July 6. At about 8 p.m. a Japanese soldier was captured. Under interrogation he said that his unit had been ordered to attack that night and that "all men alive at three a.m. on July seventh must commit suicide." This information was passed up through channels, and just before midnight a summary of the prisoner's statements was communicated to Corps Headquarters with the comment: "Though vague and contradictory in places, there seems to be something in the air. All units should be particularly alert."

The Japanese had begun to assemble at Makunsha —the place designated by Saito—soon after dark. Soldiers who were unable to walk or bear arms had been killed before the assembly started. Every man was armed with something. There were not enough rifles to go around, so officers gave away their pistols, keeping only their sabers. Daggers and hunting knives were parceled out; when these were used up, the men took long limbs of trees or bamboo poles—anything that would serve as a spear. Sometimes they sharpened the ends; sometimes they found a crude piece of iron or steel which they sharpened as best they could and tied onto the end of the stick.

Reports conflict as to the sobriety of the participants. After the attack subsided, the story went the rounds of the island that all the attackers had been drunk on sake. Prisoners interrogated later said that this was not entirely true. Naval and Army personnel participating in the attack had nothing more than a ceremonial toast before starting out. Admiral Nagumo had issued orders that the civilian construction workers on the island need not take part in the *Gyokusai* unless they wished to do so. Most of the 1000 laborers joined the final rush and were given bottles of sake to fortify themselves. By the time they reached Makunsha, they were almost all intoxicated.

On the American side, the key to the July 7 action lies in the 1st and 2d Battalions, 105th Infantry, which were in the advance positions and took the brunt of the assault. From the time the *Gyokusai* hit the perimeter, these units were the center of a whirlpool around which all other action passed.

The two battalions had dug in for the night 1200 yards south of Makunsha. Although enemy forces had been gathering nearby since 8 p.m., U.S. concentrated and sustained artillery fire dispersed and disorganized them to such an extent that they were not able to launch a full-scale effort until 4 a.m. At that time the entire Japanese force started south, following three general routes of advance. The main force went down the railroad track and on each side of it for about twenty-five yards. Another sizable column went along the base of the cliffs at the edge of the plain. The third, and much the smallest column, came down the beach, right at the water's edge.

It took approximately forty-five minutes for these columns to reach the perimeter of the two defending battalions. There they broke all at once. Major Edward A. McCarthy of the 2d Battalion later described the sight in a memorandum to his commanding officer:

It was like the movie stampede staged in the old Wild West movies. We were the cameramen. These Japs just kept coming and coming and didn't stop. It didn't make any difference if you shot one; five more would take his place. We would be in the foxholes looking up, just like those cameramen used to be. The Japs ran right over us.

This human avalanche literally swept over the two battalions. It was a raging, close-quarters fight. Grenades, bayonets, firearms of all descriptions, fists, spears and even feet were used by the participants.

At 5:10 a.m. a conservative estimate of casualties in both battalions was about 60 percent of all those suffered during the entire day. By that time the whole area of the perimeter was one boiling, fighting mass. There remained no semblance of unit organization.

Meanwhile, the two flanking columns of Japanese had surrounded the area. The east column, near the cliffs, had spread out over the entire field. Some of these attackers had branched off and joined the fighting at the perimeter. Large numbers of others had kept driving straight ahead. Some of these hit the Marine artillery battalion, others turned to the east and hit G Company of the 105th Infantry and then moved into the area between G Company and the 3d Battalion Command Post (CP), thus cutting communication between these two units. Those Japanese who overran the 3d Battalion, 10th Marines, kept on going to the south and eventually brought up against the 105th Infantry Command Post. The beach column also moved south, past the embattled battalions, and hit the 105th CP.

These flanking movements severed all communication lines to the rear and placed Japanese at every likely spot that might be used to interdict routes of retreat for the two frontline units. There was no possibility that supplies could get through to the men in front or that the wounded could be evacuated.

At the end of the first twenty-five minutes of fighting, the Americans began to run out of ammunition. Each man who fell removed one more rifle from the fighting. Furthermore, the Japanese, with their apparently inexhaustible manpower, were beginning to capture and man the American machine guns, which they used indiscriminately on the area. In addition, many key officers and noncommissioned officers had been killed, removing the vital element of leadership.

About this time Lt. Col. William J. O'Brien, commander of the 1st Battalion, got through his only message to his regimental headquarters, telling them of his situation. By the time the radio went out, the front lines of the perimeter had already disappeared, engulfed by the howling mob of Japanese. O'Brien jumped into a nearby foxhole, grabbed a rifle from a wounded man and fired away at the enemy until he was out of ammunition. He ran to one of the jeeps parked in the middle of the battalion perimeter, jumped aboard and manned the .50-caliber machine gun mounted on it. By this time he was surrounded by a large group of the enemy who were trying to get at him. These he mowed down with his machine gun until it, too, ran out of ammunition. Then he grabbed a saber from one of the Japanese and continued to stand on the vehicle, flailing away at his assailants, until he was literally cut to pieces. Around his body, lying beside the jeep, were thirty dead Japanese.

All along the line, men out of ammunition, most of them wounded, were starting to roam the area. Many of them stripped the equipment off the bodies of their dead or dying comrades and used it against the enemy. This was so widespread, and so many holes had developed in the line because of fallen soldiers, that there was no longer any organized resistance. Men who left to get ammunition could not return to their original foxholes. Others fought until only dead men remained around them, and then made their way back to a group of men behind them and fought from there. By 6 a.m. both battalions were moving south not as units but as individuals. The whole plain was filled with running men. Japanese hobbling along on crutches were trying to keep up with their comrades. Here and there an American could be seen moving down a path, sometimes alone, sometimes supporting or carrying a wounded comrade. In the withdrawal, the Americans were not driven in front of the oncoming Japanese, but ran *with* the enemy, or even behind them. Everyone was mixed together. This confused movement of forces would last until one man or another would notice an enemy and shoot him; then the whole group would stop and fight.

The American retreat was not entirely headlong. Here and there a leader would organize a holding party. The men would take up a position behind a tree or bush or in a ditch and try to hold off the enemy in order to give their wounded comrades a head start.

The rush stopped only as the vanguard of American troops was entering the outlying houses of Tanapag, where they ran into the vanguard of the left prong of the Japanese attack which had come down the plain next to the cliffs. This group had overrun three Marine batteries and then sped on into the 105th CP, where it stopped. In the process of getting this far, however, much of the Japanese force had become disorganized, and men were racing around in the fields aimlessly. Some of them had taken to the ditches, and others were hiding in the bushes. As the American wounded began to stream back toward them, the Japanese simply waited in ambush.

The Americans were now faced with the prospect of fighting their way through this new enemy force or of making a stand. Captain Earl White, who had been badly wounded in the early fighting and was now limping back to the rear, and Lieutenant King, commanding officer of B Company, took complete charge of the situation for the next few minutes. They directed the men to the houses in the village, exhorting them to dig in there and take up a stand. Together they managed to stem the pell-mell rush to the south. Most of the wounded were dragged into the houses or into ditches inside the village. Under the direction of Major McCarthy, who had come up meanwhile, and with the help of other officers and noncommissioned officers, a perimeter was organized that took up most of the village of Tanapag. By 8 a.m. this defensive establishment was completed.

For the next four hours this group of men put up one of the great defensive fights in the war. The whole area was surrounded by enemy soldiers, who made attempt after attempt to get inside the perimeter. Wounded men crawled about on the ground taking ammunition from fallen comrades and bringing it back to a central point where it was cleaned and put into clips. Then it was parceled out to the men on the firing line. The wounded men also had a weapons-cleaning line which operated all day. One of the factors that had contributed to the difficulties of the First Perimeter had been the fouling of weapons in a rainstorm the night before. The same trouble plagued the men within the Tanapag defense area, which was known as the Second Perimeter.

There was no adequate aid for the wounded. The first-aid men had nearly all been killed; only one or two were still left in the Second Perimeter. There were no medical supplies and no chance to get any. Most of the first aid was administered by one wounded man to another in the crudest fashion. One enlisted man performed an amputation without any previous experience or training. His patient lived.

Until 10 a.m. these men, all that were left of both battalions, fought on without any contact with the outside. Shortly before eight o'clock the 165th Infantry Command Post received a brief and baffling message over the radio: "There are only five hundred men left from the First and Second Battalions of the One Hundred and Fifth. For God's sake get us some ammunition and water and medical supplies right away." This message was viewed with such skepticism that it was not even recorded in the 165th Infantry journal.

Lieutenant Colonel Joseph Hart moved up to his observation post atop Hill 721 and looked down on the plain. The Japanese were "as thick as maggots." The regimental commander, whose best friend had been Colonel O'Brien, only needed one look at the burning vehicles and dead lying on the ground below to change his mind. He immediately dispatched a jeepload of ammunition which was just at the moment coming up the road to his own 1st Battalion. He then ordered three more jeeps to load as soon as possible and follow the first. All four vehicles tried to use the road that wound around the hillside, but none of them got any farther than the 3d Battalion, 105th Infantry. Hart's initial reaction was typical. Other units knew that a big counterattack was under way, but none of them realized how serious was the plight of Major McCarthy and his men.

Private, first class, J. C. Baird, radio operator of

On Saipan, U.S. aviation engineers struggle against flames and smoke in order to smother a blazing B-29 bomber with bulldozed earth, thus preventing the fire from spreading to other planes. The plane was hit and set afire during a Japanese bombing raid on the island.

(Left) Marines move away from an exploding charge of TNT which they have just tossed into an underground enemy bunker. On Saipan, as on other islands in the Pacific, many Japanese soldiers chose to die in battle rather than surrender to the invading Americans.

(Right) A U.S. bulldozer rumbles over the barren and rocky soil of Saipan as it carries out the grim task of digging a mass grave for hundreds of Japanese soldiers. These were among the more than 2000 enemy troops who were slaughtered in a great but futile banzai charge.

C Company, was asleep in the rear of the perimeter. He awoke to find Japanese rushing pell-mell at his foxhole. He lay down and played dead, and the enemy passed right on by. Then he jumped out of the hole, put his heavy radio on his back and carried it all the way back to the newly formed Second Perimeter in Tanapag. This in itself was a remarkable feat, but Baird sat down in the midst of the flying bullets and in between the times he was manning a position on the firing line, he fixed the damaged radio so that he was able to reach regimental headquarters. He reported his success to Major McCarthy at 10 a.m.

In the subsequent conversation between McCarthy and Lt. Col. Leslie Jensen at the regimental command post, McCarthy begged for tanks, ammunition and medical supplies. The regimental executive promised to do what he could, but the help did not get up to McCarthy until much later in the day.

The radio that Baird had repaired continued to work for about an hour, but reception was so poor after the first message that it was practically useless.

The next important phase of the defense of the Second Perimeter was to be its most tragic. With the disruption of communications and the movement of the battalions under the trees of the village, they were largely out of sight of the main division observation posts (OP's). But the men manning these OP's could see the plain quite easily and watch the Japanese moving around openly in the whole area. Artillery liaison planes had been flying overhead all morning, picking out targets. Cannon Company, 165th Infantry, led by Capt. Robert B. Marshall, had perched itself upon the shelf of ground under a hilltop, and the gunners threw shells into the swarms of Japanese below.

Shortly after 11 a.m. the men along the northeast side of the new perimeter were subjected to an extremely heavy mortar barrage which wounded several more of the dwindling number. Ammunition was getting scarcer and there seemed to be no help on the way. In view of the desperate situation, McCarthy decided that if he could muster a strong enough force, he might be able to fight his way back to the regimental command post and bring up help for the more seriously wounded. He asked for volunteers among those with minor wounds, and nearly 100 offered to go. McCarthy himself decided to stay with the men who were left to hold off the enemy.

It is evident that the activity which accompanied the organization of this flying wedge, as McCarthy called it, attracted the attention of both the Cannon Company and an artillery liaison plane. Although both units must have known that there were American troops somewhere in the area, they were unaware of the exact location and number. Major McCarthy's target maps had all been destroyed with the rest of his papers early in the raid, and he was unable to give accurate target squares of his location, but it is doubtful whether it would have had any effect if he could have done so. All units of the division had been firing all morning at anything that moved on the plain, assuming it was Japanese.

The flying wedge of volunteers drew the artillery fire of both Marshall's guns and elements of division artillery. The first rain of bullets drilled into the edge of the group and caused extremely severe casualties. The men immediately began to run at full speed southward along the edge of the road. Approximately 200 yards from Tanapag, almost on the edge of Bloody Run, as the creek was later called, a much more devastating concentration of fire landed directly in their midst. It not only blanketed the road, but covered the entire area between the highway and the beach.

Panic-stricken and without leadership, the men stampeded like cattle. Since there seemed to be no place else to go, most of them headed for the water. Observers on the high ground suddenly saw a large number of men splashing into the lagoon. Of the total of about 100 who had started out, seventy-one eventually managed to swim out to the reef, some 250 yards from the shore. Two or three of the more seriously wounded drowned. Others gave up and turned back to shore. Those who made the reef were later picked up by boats from a destroyer operating offshore.

The ill-fated attempt to break through to the American lines had resulted in a change in the situation of the survivors, about twenty-five in all. They now set themselves up in another perimeter, almost on the banks of Bloody Run. This came to be known as the Little Perimeter. During the afternoon it was augmented by men who managed to get through from the Second Perimeter. By the close of the day, it numbered close to seventy-five men.

The fury of the *Gyokusai* had now lessened to some extent. The Japanese were no longer massed as they had been in the morning. Casualties and the stone-wall defense put up by the CP group of the 105th Infantry had stopped and dispersed the enemy. But the situation remained menacing. Japanese lurked behind every tree and bush, in every ditch and under every obstruction, and continued to pour a deadly fire on anything that moved. They had set up machine guns that controlled virtually every foot of the road. They had men in every defiladed route to the rear, so that American soldiers who tried to escape back to our own lines invariably ran into one or more of them. There was no such thing as a front line. The two American perimeters were like islands in a sea of Japanese.

The first help to get through from the rear areas was a platoon of medium tanks which lumbered up the road from the 105th Infantry CP shortly after noon. Neither Major McCarthy nor anyone else had any means of communicating with these vehicles. They rolled to a stop just on the north side of the bridge that crossed Bloody Run and sat there for more than two hours. During that time they laid down a steady stream of fire and blasted anything in sight that looked as if it might be a Japanese hiding place. They did some damage, but because their visibility was poor and because they didn't know the real situation, they did not accomplish anything toward relieving the men in the two perimeters.

The men inside the tanks could hear an incessant drum of bullets on their armor and would neither unbutton nor come out. After two hours of helpless watching, McCarthy ran out to the vehicles and banged on the turrets with the butt of his pistol. While the bullets whizzed around his head, he coaxed the crew of one tank to open the turret hatch and he got inside with them. After some conversation with the tank commander, McCarthy used the radio to call the regimental command post. Again he pleaded for help, but he could get no intelligible answer. After this unsatisfactory exchange, he got out of the tank and returned to the opposite side of the road. But he still kept trying to get someone back to the command post with some sort of accurate information about his situation. All day long he sent party after party out in an attempt to find a way through. Invariably they ran into superior Japanese forces and had to turn back. Captain Louis Ackerman of Company A, who had been badly wounded in the neck earlier, started back with a patrol of twenty men. Shortly afterward he returned to report he had explored every possible route and found them all blocked. The battalion commander decided to try

it himself with the tanks, so he went over to one and told someone through the porthole that he was going to attempt to follow the vehicles back down the road.

McCarthy now organized a party of thirty-five men, all of them from among the walking wounded, and after the tank turned around, he led these men down the road after it. In this manner McCarthy and fifteen of his men finally reached the regimental command post at 3 p.m. He found that in the past hour some of the earlier parties had managed to push stragglers through with details of the two perimeters ahead, but he could sit down and give Lieutenant Colonel Jensen much more information as to where he had been and where the balance of the two battalions could be found.

A convoy of trucks loaded with medical supplies and ammunition was hastily organized, and at 4 p.m. the vehicles made a mad dash up the road toward the embattled men. Some of the trucks were knocked out on the way, but three managed to get through to the men who were still fighting. They were loaded with the most seriously wounded and turned around. In another dash down the highway to the south, all three trucks were able to get back to the command post.

McCarthy's information had convinced Maj. Gen. George W. Griner that the battalions could not continue fighting until they had been rested and reorganized. The 106th Infantry was already in line, so the problem now was to get the men back through the lines. General Griner sent Brig. Gen. Ogden J. Ross to the 105th CP to supervise this job. Acting upon McCarthy's information, Ross ordered elements of the 734th Amphibian Tractor Battalion to proceed up the lagoon and come ashore in the vicinity of the two perimeters to evacuate all the remaining men. They started out at once. At 5:30 p.m. the first amphibian tractors poked their noses into the beach opposite the point where the weary defenders were still killing Japanese. They brought with them elements of the 27th Reconnaissance Troop who now manned the perimeter, relieving the few remaining men who had not been wounded. The last man from the Reconnaissance Troop was evacuated at 10 p.m., just before a second counterattack hit the area.

This, in brief, is the story of the Saipan *Gyokusai*. Members of the two battalions refer to it, simply, as "the raid." These weary men had killed, by actual count, 2295 Japanese. This figure represents the number of dead enemy picked up in the area where the two battalions fought at the First, Second and Little Perimeters. Of the remaining 4311 enemy dead, 322 were found near the positions of the Marine artillery battalion, while 1694 were found in the areas defended by the 105th Infantry CP and its reinforcements—the 1st and 2d Battalions, 106th Infantry—which came up during the day.

In the 1st Battalion, 105th Infantry, only one officer, Lt. John F. Mulhem, survived unscathed. Major McCarthy of the 2d Battalion survived, but all of his company commanders were killed or wounded. The exact number of men on the line with the two battalions will never be known. This we do know: 406 men of both battalions were killed on July 7, and 512 wounded and evacuated. At least 25 percent of those

evacuated suffered amputations. At a muster of the two units on July 7, only 189 men answered from the companies which had been present on the night of July 6. This seems to indicate a total of 1107 men in the perimeter that night, but that is only an estimate, at best.

This is the simple story of the epic fight put up by the two battalions that bore the brunt of the Saipan *Gyokusai*. It lacks the smell of battle, and it lacks many of the tales of heroism that could be unfolded by going deeper. One Sergeant expressed himself later: "You can't pick out any heroes. Every man is a hero."

Every war claims civilian victims, and the war in the Pacific was no exception. An American marine takes time out from fighting the Japanese to help a terrified family escape from the wreckage of their once-peaceful Saipan village.

THE BATTLE OF THE PHILIPPINE SEA

BY PETER MAAS

With its fleet and naval air force rapidly melting away, the Japanese Imperial Navy chose to stake everything on one mighty blow against U.S. Task Force 58, in the Philippine Sea. The action, carried out by its First Mobile Force under Admiral Ozawa, was an overwhelming disaster for Japanese sea power. And American pilots bagged fifteen planes for every one they lost, giving the battle the unofficial name of the "Great Marianas Turkey Shoot."

On the afternoon of June 18, 1944, the First Mobile Force of Japan's Imperial Navy prowled warily through the Philippine Sea. Seven hundred miles to the east lay the besieged Japanese bastion of Saipan, now under attack by U.S. amphibian forces. Somewhere in between was a huge American fleet, covering the invasion.

Vice Admiral Jisaburo Ozawa had been searching for it all day. That afternoon, shortly after three o'clock, he finally found it. One of his scout planes sighted numerous enemy ships moving southwest toward him. Ozawa was on the bridge of his flagship, the carrier *Taiho,* when he received the report. His staff quickly gathered round. Some argued for a twilight torpedo attack. "Sir, why not hit them when they least expect it?" one officer blurted out.

Ozawa pursed his lips. He was a man of thoughtful habit and he was not prone to hasty action. His orders were to engage the enemy. Other than that, he was on his own. It was a terrible responsibility. He stood now, hands fiddling with his binoculars, as he deliberated. Then he decided against an immediate attack. Few of his pilots were trained in night landings. Besides, vastly superior U.S. carrier groups would soon be on top of him. The stakes were too high to risk it. He would wait until dawn, and gave orders accordingly.

His mission was an all-or-nothing bet. Japan teetered near total collapse. American naval might roamed the Pacific almost unchallenged. If Saipan, some 1200 miles from Tokyo, was taken, the home islands could be battered at will. Somehow the crunching American advance had to be stopped.

The problem had been thrashed out for months at Japan's Naval War College. A dozen different plans were tried out on the big game board and then discarded: the Japanese always lost. Only one idea seemed to stand any chance at all: Enter into decisive action; throw in everything in one mighty stroke; do it at an opportune moment with the support of land-based air power to help even the odds. The plan was given the code name "A-Go." Everyone agreed it was a gamble. But nobody came up with a better idea.

The opportune moment arrived the afternoon of June 15. While the First Mobile Force was refueling in the central Philippines, Adm. Soemu Toyoda, the new Commander of the Japanese Combined Fleet, radioed Ozawa: "Activate 'A-Go Operation' for decisive battle." The American landing on Saipan in the Marianas Islands, first thought to be a diversionary movement, had turned out to be a full-scale invasion. That same night Ozawa entered the Philippine Sea and headed northeast toward the Marianas.

By the 17th dispatches from Combined Fleet Headquarters had given Ozawa a pretty fair idea of what he was up against. He found the prospect joyless. The invasion was being protected by a "great force of carriers." Moreover, he had no precise idea where they were. The only message from the Japanese Marianas Air Command blithely advised: "Don't worry about us. Attack the carriers."

Then on the 18th, when they were sighted, Ozawa devised an ingenious maneuver. The Americans were proceeding southwest in his direction. Even so, he was confident that his position was unknown. Presumably U.S. picket submarines had seen the First Mobile Force from time to time, but no planes were tracking it. He swung his own ships around to the southwest. He wanted to maintain at least 400 miles between them and the enemy carriers. His planes, lightly armored, had greater range than U.S. aircraft. Thus he could strike in the morning without endangering himself.

451

That evening Ozawa ran a risk he ordinarily wouldn't take. But he counted heavily on help from the planes based in the Marianas. Since he had heard nothing more from the air command there, he broke radio silence and broadcast the enemy's position.

Now a last night of quiet settled over the darkened ships. Midnight passed. For the *Taiho*—the Imperial Navy's newest and biggest carrier—this was a significant day. She was going into combat for the first time. Across her huge hangar deck, plane crews finished up final battle preparations. They labored with none of the feverish excitement which preceded the strike against Pearl Harbor. There was, rather, an air of solemnity. Everyone was touched by Admiral Ozawa's terse call to arms: "This operation has immense bearing on the fate of the Empire."

Below, the *Taiho*'s pilots tossed restlessly in their bunks that night. Warrant Officer Sakio Komatsu was especially moved by Admiral Ozawa's words. He imagined bringing his "Judy" dive bomber in over an enemy carrier and scoring a direct hit amidships. He wondered what the antiaircraft fire would be like, and he wondered also if he would ever get back to the *Taiho*. In any event, Komatsu decided, he would attempt to crash into an American ship if he himself were hit.

Nothing had been spared for this effort. Every available ship the Japanese could muster, including nine carriers, was now assembled in the First Mobile Force. If it failed, there wouldn't be another chance. Then, a little after one o'clock in the morning, fate lent a momentary hand. A patrol bomber, at the limit of its range, discovered part of the American force. But its radio refused to work. By the time the patrol bomber could get back to its base, it would be too late.

At 3 a.m. Ozawa ordered his light-carrier division with its escorting cruisers and destroyers to turn northeast again. When he went into action, he intended to have this advance group about 100 miles ahead for better air defense. At 4:15 he brought the rest of his ships around and started his final thrust northeast. He was ready to throw 471 Japanese planes against an American fleet still not sure of his whereabouts.

Ozawa planned to launch his planes in a series of mighty waves, first from his front groups and then from his two heavy-carrier divisions. His chief concern was a critical lack of veteran pilots; some of his men had less than two months' training. His Zero fighters, once supreme, were now greatly outclassed by U.S. Hellcats.

On his side, the Japanese were sailing into the wind and could launch and recover planes without reversing course. If everything went well, his fighters and bombers could also land in the Marianas, gas up and hit what was left of the enemy. Ozawa was a realist. Like many of his fellow Naval officers, he had been against the whole idea of starting war in the first place. But maybe this would work. He began to let himself think so. At 4:45 a.m. his dawn search patrol took off.

An officer on the flag staff cheerfully noted, "Initiative was secured by us and so we will gain the victory. All staff members are heartily satisfied and Admiral Ozawa looks quite brilliant."

By now pilots on the *Taiho* and the other carriers were up and getting dressed. They breakfasted and then gathered around their little Shinto shrines to pray for success. Afterward they drank sake. Admiral Ozawa observed that the sea was so calm that none of the sake spilled from the shallow ceremonial cups.

Some 400 miles eastward, U.S. Task Force 58 had tacked back and forth all night off the Marianas. Dawn came shortly before six o'clock. The sky, that morning, blushed deep red against the gray, then paled to salmon pink and silver over an azure sea. It was warm and fair, with an easterly wind, and it was going to be beautifully clear. Farther east, the 2d and 4th Marine Divisions, joined by the Army's 27th Infantry Division, began their fifth consecutive day of smashing across the volcanic ridges and valleys of Saipan. In the first forty-eight hours of battle they had suffered 3500 casualties.

Task Force 58 was the most destructive armada in the history of naval warfare. It took up almost 900 square miles of ocean. Some 200 of its 956 planes had led the invasion assault, and they had caught the Japanese napping. Instead of the usual dawn strike for this sort of operation, they had flown in early in the afternoon of June 11, pounded the airfields and left the wreckage of 124 enemy planes strewed about on the ground. Desperate attempts to hit back had only brought additional woe to the Japanese. Of all the Marianas-based planes on which Admiral Ozawa placed such reliance, there were now no more than fifty still able to fly.

Soon after sunrise on the morning of June 19, Vice

Adm. Marc A. Mitscher, Task Force 58 commander, in a freshly laundered khaki uniform, his green cap with its huge visor pulled low over piercing blue eyes, appeared on the flag bridge of the carrier *Lexington* (she had replaced the first *Lexington,* sunk in the Coral Sea, May 8, 1942; see page 181). He went directly to his canvas swivel chair which always faced aft, crooked his arm over the bridge's edge and stared moodily down the flight deck. He was, this morning, an angry man. Throughout the fleet for the past four days, scuttlebutt had it that the Japanese were finally coming out to fight. Mitscher was sure that this was the day the Japanese would attack, and he loathed being on the defensive. He had been up most of the night arguing with Adm. Raymond A. Spruance, overall commander of the invasion forces, to let him go after the approaching Ozawa.

The peril was obvious enough to have postponed the landing on Guam, scheduled for June 18. Three days earlier the U.S. submarine *Flying Fish,* off the Philippine coast, had reported sighting a "large enemy task force heading east from the San Bernardino Strait. Speed twenty knots." On June 17 the submarine *Cavalla* had seen part of the fleet go by and noted in the log: "Got enemy contact report off. Chasing task force at four-engine speed. Hoping for a second chance." Then U.S. Pacific Fleet Headquarters at Pearl Harbor had flashed the news that a high-frequency fix—picked up when Ozawa broke radio silence—showed the enemy even nearer.

But from a report by a third submarine, the *Stingray,* Admiral Spruance had inferred that the Japanese fleet might be much farther south. Since his first aim was to protect the landings and he was fearful of a sweep around Task Force 58, he finally turned down Mitscher's urgent request.

The day's action started slowly. Around 6 a.m. a Hellcat from the *Monterey* downed one Japanese plane nosing about, and a destroyer bagged another. No one knew whether the planes were carrier-based or land-based. The lull continued until radar picked up a flight of bogeys (unidentified aircraft) winging into Guam from the southwest. They were reinforcements from the great Japanese Naval base at Truk. Hellcats from the *Belleau Wood* combat air patrol over Guam asked for help, and Mitscher sent it from the carriers *Cabot, Yorktown* (named for the *Yorktown* sunk off Midway, June 7, 1942; see pages 210–211) and *Hornet.*

The Japanese were taken by surprise and disappeared. Later in the morning, in a brief vicious duel, thirty-five Japanese planes were knocked down. Then it was quiet again.

When Ozawa's dawn search signaled the latest enemy position, he didn't waste time. At 8:30 a.m. his vanguard launched the first wave. The next would come from his own carrier division led by the *Taiho,* now racing through the sea at twenty-seven knots.

From the bridge Ozawa watched while engines sputtered and roared into life. A few minutes before nine, the signal flags went up and down. The dive bombers were the first to go, and plane crews waved and cheered as each one sped in swift succession down the flight deck. As Ozawa shifted his gaze for a moment, he suddenly saw three of his escorting destroyers heel sharply to the starboard. He instinctively knew what it meant: a sub had been sighted.

Some 9000 yards away, Comdr. J. W. Blanchard had the *Taiho* framed neatly in the periscope of the U.S.S. *Albacore.* His automatic computer had gone haywire. There was no time to start over again. He fired six torpedoes "by God and by guess," and the *Albacore* went into a crash-dive; she began to shudder as the first depth-charge blasts rolled in.

Warrant Officer Komatsu was barely aloft, when he saw the wake of a torpedo streaking directly toward the *Taiho.* He banked hard right and dove down at the torpedo. Incredibly, he hit it and blew it up, along with himself, before it reached the carrier. But Komatsu's sacrifice wasn't enough. A few seconds later, as the *Taiho*'s last plane took to the air, another of the *Albacore*'s hastily fired torpedoes struck the Japanese carrier's starboard side, near the forward gasoline tanks. Admiral Ozawa felt the great ship lurch beneath his feet, but she apparently was in little danger, and everyone breathed easier. Watertight compartments had sealed off the gaping hole at her waterline. Some forward gasoline-storage tanks were leaking but there was no fire, and speed was reduced by only one knot. Satisfied there was little to worry about, Ozawa prepared to launch the third wave.

Task Force 58's tense expectation of battle gradually subsided after the first alert had ended and no further sign of enemy activity had as yet cropped up. Breakfasts were eaten leisurely, and some officers even retired to their cabins for a nap. Ships' bullhorns

An enemy warship maneuvers to escape bombs from U.S. carrier planes as elements of Admiral Halsey's 3d Fleet close in on a Japanese Naval force off Luzon, October 1944. At top right is seen the wake of a Japanese destroyer which took evasive action to avoid being hit by an American aerial torpedo.

(Right) Antiaircraft fire from the U.S. carrier Yorktown turns a death-dealing Japanese torpedo plane into a mass of flaming wreckage. The encounter took place near the Japanese fortress of Kwajalein, in the Marshall Islands, in January 1944. That base was soon taken by American forces.

(Far right) The weaving wake behind this Japanese heavy cruiser indicates the warship's frantic attempt to evade bombs from American carrier-based planes. This photograph was taken during a U.S. raid on Manila Bay, November 5, 1944. Minutes later, the Japanese vessel was hit and destroyed.

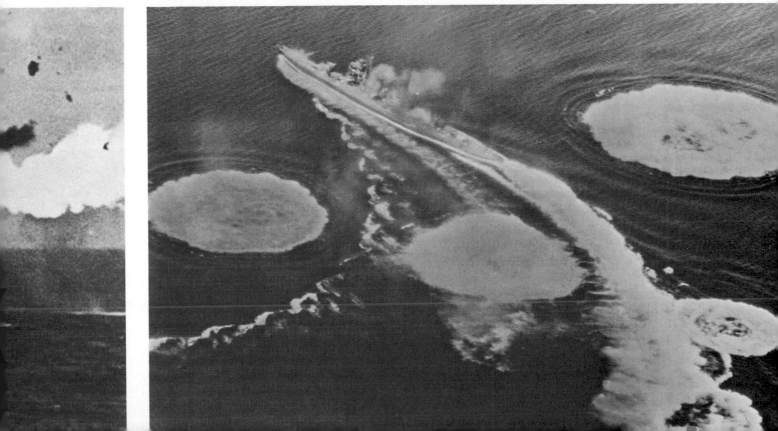

roared: "Sweepers, man your brooms." In the ready rooms pilots whiled away the time playing cribbage and acey-deucey. On the *Lexington* a work crew was assigned to repair the water-distillation system, which had gone out of order. In flag plot, operational brain of the fleet, staff officers bent over their charts trying to anticipate what would happen next. Radio traffic crackled steadily between the ships, and a stenographer stood by recording it. Admiral Mitscher remained on the flag bridge.

Then, at 9:59, radar picked up a flight in the first Japanese wave. A few minutes later a second flight was reported. General quarters sounded on all ships. Steel battle ports clanged shut. Helmets and lifejackets were donned and guns manned. Mitscher himself shouted the rallying cry, "Hey, Rube," over the radio, calling back his fighters on air patrol over the Marianas. At his command fifteen carriers, grouped out in a rough line some thirty miles long, swung into the wind. Plane directors in bright yellow caps and shirts spilled out on the flight decks. All torpedo and bomber pilots were ordered to take off and orbit east of Saipan, to get them out of the way. The bullhorns now chanted the bearing and distance of the oncoming Japanese: "Raid one now two-three-six, seventy-eight miles; raid two now two-three-eight, eighty-six miles."

At 10:17 fighter pilots were told: "Scramble all ready rooms!" And at 10:23 the Hellcats started to roar skyward.

Lieutenant Commander C. W. Brewer of the *Lexington*'s "Fighting 15" was first to tallyho the enemy planes, at 10:35. With eleven Hellcats stacked from 17,000 to 23,000 feet, he dived into a nest of twenty-four bombers and fighters at 18,000 feet, with sixteen others above and astern. Brewer singled out the lead Japanese plane as his target. He fired at 800 feet, and after two bursts it blew up. "My first was a 'Judy,'" Brewer observed over his radio as he whizzed through the burning debris. He pulled up and shot off the wing of another "Judy." It spiraled crazily into the sea. Brewer then overtook a Zero, fired at 400 feet and saw it explode moments later. Looking up, he found a second Zero diving at him. In the ensuing dogfight Brewer got on the Zero's tail. The enemy plane maneuvered violently, half-rolled, stayed briefly on its back, pulled up and went into a series of frantic barrel rolls. Brewer caught it at last on a wingover. A bright ribbon of flame darted along the fuselage of the Zero, and

it plunged downward in an ever-tightening spiral.

As the battle raged, the *Lexington*'s Hellcats were joined by more planes from the *Cowpens, Bunker Hill, Princeton* and *Enterprise*. Lieutenant Alexander Vraciu got his first of six this day, which would later make him the Navy's top ace, with nineteen confirmed kills. To the carriers, some fifteen miles away, the fighting was as silent as the sunlight. The sky was crisscrossed by twisting white vapor trails. Black puffs of smoke emerged as the protecting battle-line ships began to fire. The puffs mounted higher and higher until the horizon became a vast polka-dot pattern of exploding shrapnel. Great balls of fire burst forth brilliantly against the deep blue backdrop, and through the vapor trails long streamers of black smoke descended raggedly to the sea.

Watching the fight, Mitscher commented, "Jap planes still burn very well."

None of the first-wave planes reached the carriers. Four bombers managed to make runs in toward the battle line. One minor hit, on the *South Dakota*, was scored; but it was the only one that day for the Japanese. Lack of experience was hurting them. Back on the *Lexington*, Commander Brewer reported enemy bombers had considerable trouble keeping formation, while their fighter escorts rarely initiated combat.

A hundred and nineteen planes from Ozawa's second wave were picked up by radar when 115 miles away. *Essex* fighters scrambled, and Comdr. David McCampbell, leading his Hellcats, gave the tallyho, "Nine o'clock down, two miles." A few minutes later, augmented by other carrier squadrons, McCampbell noted, "They're falling like leaves." Some twenty Japanese planes finally got past the air defense, only to meet withering fire from the battleships, cruisers and destroyers. One lost both wings and fluttered down like a piece of paper. A second fell like a tired bird. A torpedo plane swung in toward the battleship *Indiana*. Every available gun trained on it. Somehow it staggered on through the bursting steel; no one knew what was keeping it up. Then, about fifty yards away, it was jolted badly. In a last desperate effort, the pilot kept on for a moment longer and crashed into the *Indiana*'s waterline. The ship held a collective breath. But nothing happened. The torpedo was a dud.

Six "Judy" dive bombers made for the *Wasp* and *Bunker Hill*. The *Wasp* received the brunt of the attack and escaped, though three men were killed by bomb fragments. On the *Bunker Hill* someone yelled, "Duck, it's a bomb!" The geyser from the near-miss splashed over a Hellcat ready to take off. "My cockpit," the pilot complained, "smelled like a fish market for a week." The *Princeton* had a spate of action. Her anti-aircraft fire brought down two planes, and she narrowly avoided a third trying to crash into her. A torpedo sped through the *Enterprise*'s wake. A dive bomber aiming at the *Lexington* was delicately held in tracer-bullet pincers by two of the ship's escorts. Then the plane flashed into flames.

One of Mitscher's task group commanders excitedly signaled for permission to call back the bombers orbiting east of Saipan for a try at the Japanese carriers. "Approved! Approved!" Mitscher responded. But combat radio traffic was so heavy that an attack could not be organized. Eventually the bombers were sent in to pound Saipan again and the main Guam airfield, Orote. Returning Hellcat pilots ducked into ready rooms to look at the latest scores chalked up on the big blackboards. Other pilots were being interviewed by intelligence officers. On the *Lexington* it was announced that the water-distillation system had been fixed. Up in flag plot, a mess attendant began serving ham sandwiches and iced lemonade.

Aboard the First Mobile Force nobody felt like relaxing. Admiral Ozawa, still sailing northeast into the wind, had launched two more waves of planes. Just as the last one roared off, the war came to an end for the 29,000-ton carrier *Shokaku,* a veteran of Pearl Harbor. The *Shokaku* ran into an old antagonist. For two days the submarine *Cavalla,* after reporting the presence of the Japanese in the Philippine Sea, had trailed far behind. But when Ozawa temporarily turned to the southwest the night of the 18th, the *Cavalla* continued northeast and now, near noon, they met once again. When the *Cavalla*'s skipper, Lt. Comdr. H. J. Kossler, raised his periscope, the *Shokaku* was only 1000 yards distant. "There was the Rising Sun," Kossler said, "big as hell." He promptly let go with six torpedoes. Three or four of them hit. Within minutes the carrier was rocked by explosions, and she fell apart in a couple of hours.

Gloom settled over the Japanese staff officers. No word, moreover, had been heard about the air strikes. Some entertained the faint hope that the planes had successfully attacked the enemy and gone on to Guam. While Ozawa debated his next step, a young damage-control officer decided to do something about the annoying gas seepage from the *Taiho*'s sprung storage tanks. Why not blow it away by opening all her ventilating ducts? Before anyone knew what was up, the huge ship was filled with fumes.

It took a few minutes for the gas to reach the fuel supply, and then it happened. An amazed officer aboard a nearby destroyer described the scene: "Suddenly a terrible explosion burst the flight deck of the *Taiho* into the shape of a mountain top." She sank quickly in 2500 fathoms. Less than a quarter of her crew was saved. As a dazed Ozawa was transferred to an escorting destroyer, he wondered vaguely how he could possibly land all his planes. It was the least of his worries.

Ozawa's fourth wave, launched just before the *Shokaku* was torpedoed, arrived in the afternoon. Unaware of the fate of its predecessors, the fourth wave flew into disaster. Of eighty-two planes, seventy-three failed to return or were too damaged for further use. Japanese pilots still in the air were hopelessly disorganized. Some of these, led astray by a green reconnaissance pilot, never did find a target. They wandered aimlessly for a while; then forty-nine of them finally headed for Guam. There they were spotted by Comdr. Gaylord B. Brown of the *Cowpens,* followed by more Hellcats from the *Essex* and *Hornet.* Thirty of the Japanese planes were shot down in short order, and the remaining nineteen were so badly torn up that they never fought again. Between Guam and Task Force 58, a patrolling pilot counted "seventeen fires or oil slicks within the radius of a mile."

Then, just at dusk, Lieutenant Commander Brewer led his fighters in a last sweep over Orote Field. Below, he spied a "Jill" dive bomber slipping in for a landing. With his wingman, Ens. Thomas Tarr, he went after it. Suddenly sixteen Zeros, hidden in the fading light, pounced. His remaining Hellcats got the attackers, but neither Brewer nor Tarr were seen again by their comrades. It was 6:45 p.m.

During the night the crippled Japanese First Mobile Force fled westward. Admiral Mitscher, however, having had to swing his carriers constantly around into the wind, was in about the same place that he had been at dawn. He now sailed in pursuit. The final tally showed twenty-nine U.S. planes lost, as compared with 426 Japanese losses. "Operation A-Go"—the decisive battle—was over.

THE GREATEST SEA FIGHT: LEYTE GULF

BY HANSON W. BALDWIN

The Battle for Leyte Gulf has been called the greatest naval engagement ever fought. In the number of ships involved and the magnitude of ocean surface covered, the battle is unparalleled in history. At its conclusion there was no doubt that the Japanese, no matter how long it might take them to admit it, had lost the war. Hanson W. Baldwin, former military editor of the New York Times, *depicts the many phases of this crucial battle.*

In October 1944 the greatest sea fight in history—perhaps the world's last great fleet action—broke the naval power of Japan and spelled the beginning of the end of the war in the Pacific. The Battle for Leyte Gulf, fought off the Philippine archipelago, sprawled across an area of almost 500,000 square miles, about twice the size of Texas. Unlike most of the actions of World War II, it included every element of naval power from submarines to planes. There was no dispute about the outcome. After Leyte Gulf, the Japanese Fleet was finished. Yet it was a battle of considerable controversy.

The Empire was dying, and there were some who faced the fact. The long retreat was over, the great spaces of the Pacific had been bridged by the countless ships of the American "barbarians," and the enemy was knocking upon the inner strongholds of the *samurai*. For Japan it was now the desperate gamble, the all-out stroke: to conquer or to die.

And so, the *Sho* ("Victory") plans were drawn: If the inner citadel—the Philippines, Formosa, the Ryukyus, the main islands—was penetrated by the U.S. Fleet, all the remaining Japanese Naval power

that could steam or fly would be mobilized for a desperate assault.

Four separate *Sho* plans were drawn up to deal with different contingencies, but, as Samuel Eliot Morison notes, Japanese intelligence was "betting on the Philippines.

"The Japanese High Command obtained very little advance intelligence from reconnaissance, but a good deal from other sources and by inference. One important bit came from Moscow on October 6."

The Soviet Foreign Office informed the Ambassador from Japan, representative of their "ally's enemy," that through diplomatic sources they had learned that the U.S. 14th and 20th Army Air Forces, then China-based, had been ordered to make attacks intended to isolate the Philippines. The U.S. assault on Leyte came sooner than the Japanese had expected but about where they expected it.

U.S. intelligence was far less perspicacious; indeed, it was grossly overoptimistic, as many of our estimates of Japanese island garrisons were throughout the Pacific War. Lieutenant General George C. Kenney, Commander, Allied Air Forces, Southwest Pacific, described the objective (Leyte) as "relatively undefended," and predicted that the Japanese would not offer strong resistance to an invasion and that a fleet action was unlikely.

From August 31 to September 24 the fast carriers, supported by the battleships, of Adm. William F. ("Bull") Halsey's 3d Fleet had raked over Japanese bases from Mindanao to Luzon, and on September 21, while Radio Manila was playing "Music for Your Morning Moods," Naval pilots combed Manila Bay. The bag throughout the islands was large, the enemy opposition was surprisingly feeble, and Admiral Halsey reported to Adm. Chester W. Nimitz, Commander in Chief, Pacific: "No damage to our surface forces and nothing on the screen but Hedy Lamarr."

The weak Japanese reaction led to a change in American strategy. The planned capture of Yap and step-by-step moves to Mindanao in the southern Philippines and then northward were eliminated; the amphibious assault upon the island of Leyte in the central Philippines was advanced by two months to October 20, 1944.

It started according to plan. A great armada of more than 700 U.S. ships steamed into Leyte Gulf at dawn on the 20th; a lone Japanese plane braved the skies. Initial Japanese opposition was weak; the vast American armada—the greatest of the Pacific war, with some 151 LST's (landing ships, tank), 58 transports, 221 LCT's (landing craft, tank), 79 LCI's (landing craft, infantry), and hundreds of other vessels—may have overawed the defenders. By the end of A plus 2—October 21—thousands of American troops had been landed on Leyte with few casualties, and only three warships had been damaged.

Light cruiser *Honolulu,* called Blue Goose by her men, was the first American casualty. On the afternoon of the landing, a Japanese torpedo plane put a "fish" into the cruiser's port side. The explosion tore a jagged hole in *Honolulu's* side, gave her a heavy list in a few minutes, killed sixty men and put the first of many ships out of action.

At 8:09 a.m. October 17, just nine minutes after the U.S.S. *Denver* fired the opening gun in the liberation of the Philippine Islands, Japanese forces had been alerted to carry out the *Sho* I plan. Admiral Soemu Toyoda, Commander in Chief of the Japanese Combined Fleet and leader of what he knew was a forlorn hope, had his last chance to "destroy the enemy who enjoys the luxury of material resources." From his headquarters at the Naval War College just outside Tokyo, he sent the word "Victory" to his widely scattered units.

For Toyoda, the Battle of the Philippine Sea and his futile gamble in defense of Formosa—when he had thrown his land-based planes and hastily trained carrier replacement pilots into the fight against Halsey's fleet—had left the Japanese Fleet naked to air attack. Toyoda had carriers, but with few planes and half-trained pilots. *Sho* I, therefore, must be dependent upon stealth and cunning, night operations and what air cover could be provided, chiefly by land-based planes operating from Philippine bases and working in close conjunction with the fleet.

Toyoda also confronted another handicap—a fleet widely separated by distance. He exercised command, from his land headquarters, over a theoretically "Combined Fleet," but Vice Adm. Jisaburo Ozawa, who flew his flag from carrier *Zuikaku* and who commanded the crippled carriers and some cruisers and destroyers, was still based in the Inland Sea in Japanese home waters. The bulk of the fleet's heavy units—Vice Adm. Takeo Kurita's First Attack Force of 7 battleships, 13 cruisers and 19 destroyers—was based

on Lingga Roads, near Singapore, close to its fuel sources. The Japanese Fleet was divided in the face of a superior naval force; it could not be concentrated prior to battle.

These deficiencies, plus the geography of the Philippines, dictated the enemy plan, which was hastily modified at the last minute, partially because of the Japanese weaknesses in carrier aviation. Two principal straits—San Bernardino, north of the island of Samar; and Surigao, between Mindanao and Leyte—give access from the South China Sea to Leyte Gulf, where the great armada of General MacArthur was committed to the invasion. The Japanese ships based near Singapore, the First Attack Force, were to steam north toward Leyte, with a stop at Brunei Bay, Borneo, to refuel. There the force would split: The Central Group, Vice Admiral Kurita, flying his flag in the heavy cruiser *Atago,* with a total of 5 battleships, 10 heavy cruisers, 2 light cruisers and 15 destroyers, would transit San Bernardino Strait at night; the Southern Group, Vice Adm. Shoji Nishimura, with 2 battleships, 1 heavy cruiser and 4 destroyers, was to be augmented at Surigao Strait by an auxiliary force of three more cruisers and four destroyers under Vice Adm. Kiyohide Shima, which was to steam through Formosa Strait, with a stop in the Pescadores, all the way from its bases in the home islands. These forces were to strike the great American armada in Leyte Gulf almost simultaneously at dawn on October 25 and wreak havoc among the thin-skinned amphibious ships like a hawk among chickens.

But the key to the operation was the emasculated Japanese carriers, operating under Vice Admiral Ozawa from their bases in the Inland Sea. These ships—one heavy carrier and three light carriers with about 116 planes aboard, "all that remained of the enemy's once-great carrier forces"—were to steam south toward Luzon and to act as deliberate decoys or sacrificial "lures" for Admiral Halsey's great 3d Fleet, which was "covering" the amphibious invasion of Leyte. The northern decoy force was to be accompanied by 2 battleship-carriers, the *Ise* and *Hyuga*—with the after turrets replaced by short flight decks, but with no planes—and by 3 cruisers and 8 destroyers. Ozawa was to lure Halsey's 3d Fleet to the north, away from Leyte, and open the way for Kurita and Nishimura to break into Leyte Gulf.

At the same time all three forces were to be aided,

not with direct air cover, but by intensive attacks by Japanese land-based planes upon American carriers and shipping. As a last-minute "spur-of-the-moment" decision, the Japanese "Special Attack Groups" were activated, and the kamikaze fliers commenced their suicidal attacks upon U.S. ships. As early as October 15, Rear Adm. Masabumi Arima, a subordinate Naval air commander, flying from a Philippine field, had made a suicide dive and had "lighted the fuse of the ardent wishes of his men." When Vice Adm. Takijiro Onishi took command of the First Air Fleet on October 17, there were only about 100 operational Japanese planes available in the entire Philippine archipelago. (They were subsequently reinforced.) There were at least—and Admiral Onishi knew this—twenty to thirty U.S. aircraft carriers nearby. To solve this equation the kamikaze was born. Admiral Onishi made the mission clear in an address to Japanese air group commanders in the Philippines on October 19.

The fate of the empire depends on this operation. . . . Our surface forces are already in motion. . . . The mission of our First Air Fleet is to provide land-based air cover for Admiral Kurita's advance. . . . To do this, we must hit the enemy's carriers and keep them neutralized for at least one week.

In my opinion, there is only one way of assuring that our meager strength will be effective to a maximum degree, and that is for our bomb-laden fighter planes to crash-dive into the decks of enemy carriers.

All these far-flung forces were under the common command of Admiral Toyoda far away in Tokyo. Such was the desperate *Sho* I—perhaps the greatest gamble, the most daring and unorthodox plan, in the history of naval war.

It committed to action virtually all that was left of the operational forces, afloat and in the air, of Japan's Navy: 4 carriers, 2 battleship-carriers, 7 battleships, 19 cruisers, 33 destroyers, and perhaps 500 to 700 Japanese aircraft—mostly land-based.

But the opposing American forces were far more powerful. Like the Japanese forces, which had no common commander closer than Tokyo, the U.S. Fleet operated under divided command. General MacArthur, as Supreme Allied Commander, Southwest

Pacific Area, was in overall charge of the Leyte invasion, and through Vice Adm. Thomas C. Kinkaid he commanded the 7th Fleet, which was in direct charge of the amphibious operation. But Admiral Halsey's powerful covering force of the 3d Fleet—the strongest fleet in the world—was not under MacArthur's command; it was a part of Admiral Nimitz' Pacific Command forces, and Nimitz had his headquarters in Hawaii. Above Nimitz and MacArthur the only unified command was in Washington.

The gun power of Kinkaid's 7th Fleet was provided by 6 old battleships, 5 of them raised from the mud of Pearl Harbor; but he had 16 escort carriers—small, slow-speed vessels, converted from merchant hulls—11 cruisers and scores of destroyers and destroyer escorts, frigates, motor-torpedo boats and other types. Kinkaid's job was to provide shore bombardment and close air support for the Army and antisubmarine and air defense for the amphibious forces.

Halsey, with 8 large attack carriers, 8 light carriers, 6 fast new battleships, 15 cruisers and 58 destroyers, was ordered to "cover and support" forces of the Southwest Pacific (MacArthur's command) "in order to assist in the seizure and occupation of objectives in the Central Philippines." He was to destroy enemy naval and air forces threatening the invasion. And, "in case opportunity for destruction of major portion of the enemy fleet is offered or can be created, such destruction becomes the primary task." He was to remain responsible to Admiral Nimitz, but "necessary measures for detailed coordination of operations between the [3d Fleet] . . . and . . . the [7th Fleet] will be arranged by their . . . commanders."

The combined 3d and 7th Fleets could muster 1000 to 1400 ship-based aircraft, 32 carriers, 12 battleships, 23 cruisers, more than 100 destroyers and destroyer escorts, numerous smaller types and hundreds of auxiliaries. The 7th Fleet also had a few tender-based patrol planes (flying boats). But not all of these forces participated in the far-flung air attacks and the three widely separated major engagements which later came to be called the Battle for Leyte Gulf. Such was the stage for the most dramatic naval battle in history.

It opens with first blood for the submarines. At dawn on October 23, the U.S. submarines *Darter* and *Dace,* patrolling Palawan Passage, intercept Admiral Kurita. The *Darter* puts five torpedoes into Kurita's flagship, the heavy cruiser *Atago,* at less than 1000 yards range, and damages the cruiser *Takao. Dace* hits the cruiser *Maya* with four torpedoes. The *Atago* sinks in about twenty minutes as Kurita shifts his flag to the destroyer *Kishinami* and later to the battleship *Yamato.* The *Maya* blows up and sinks in four minutes. *Takao,* burning and low in the water, is sent back to Brunei, escorted by two destroyers. Kurita steams on, implacable, toward San Bernardino Strait.

October 24

Aboard battleship *New Jersey,* flying "Bull" Halsey's flag, the plans are ready for this day as the sun quickly burns away the morning haze. In the carriers, bowing to the swell, the bullhorns sound on the flight decks: "Pilots, man your planes."

At 6 a.m. the 3d Fleet launches search planes to sweep a wide arc of sea covering the approaches to San Bernardino and Surigao straits. Submarine reports from *Darter, Dace* and *Guitarro* have alerted the Americans, but not in time to halt the detachment of 3d Fleet's Task Group 38.1, commanded by Vice Adm. John S. ("Slew") McCain, which had orders to retire to Ulithi for rest and supplies. The fleet's three other task groups are spread out over 300 miles of ocean to the east of the Philippines from central Luzon to southern Samar; one of them, to the north, has been tracked doggedly all night by enemy "snoopers." As the planes take off to search the reef-studded waters of the Sibuyan and Sulu seas and the approaches to San Bernardino and Surigao straits, Kinkaid's old battleships and little carriers off Leyte are supporting the GI's ashore.

At 8:12 a.m. Lt. (jg.) Max Adams, flying a Helldiver above the magnificent volcanic crags, the palm-grown islands and startling blue sea of the archipelago, reports a radar contact, and a few minutes later Admiral Kurita's First Attack Force lies spread out like toy ships upon a painted sea—the pagoda masts unmistakable in the sunlight.

The tension of action grips flag plot (tactical and navigational control center) in the *New Jersey* as the contact report comes in; the radio crackles "Urgent" and "Top Secret" messages—to Washington, to Nimitz, to Kinkaid, to all task group commanders. McCain, 300 miles to the eastward, en route to Ulithi and rest, is recalled, and 3d Fleet is ordered to concentrate off San Bernardino to launch strikes against the enemy.

But at 9:05, far to the south, the southern arm of the Japanese pincer is sighted for the first time: Vice Admiral Nishimura—with battleships *Fuso* and *Yamashiro,* heavy cruiser *Mogami* and four destroyers—steaming toward Surigao. *Enterprise* search planes attack through heavy antiaircraft fire; *Fuso*'s catapult is hit, her float planes are destroyed, and a fire rages; a gun mount in destroyer *Shigure* is knocked out, but Nishimura steams on to the east, his speed undiminished. And Halsey continues the concentration of his fleet near San Bernardino to strike the Japanese Central Force.

There has been no morning search to the north and northeast, and Ozawa's decoy carriers, steaming southward toward Luzon, are still undiscovered.

The *Sho* plan now moves toward its dramatic denouement. Japanese planes flying from Ozawa's carriers and Philippine bases commence the most furious assault since the landing upon the 7th and 3d Fleets. To the north off Luzon, carriers *Langley, Princeton, Essex* and *Lexington* face the brunt of the winged fury. Seven Hellcats from the *Essex,* led by Comdr. David McCampbell, intercept sixty Japanese planes—half of them fighters—and after a melee of an hour and thirty-five minutes of combat the Americans knock down at least twenty-five Japs with no losses. *Princeton* claims thirty-four enemy from another large raid; the *Lexington*'s and *Langley*'s "fly boys" are also busy; over the air come the pilots' exultant cries of "Tallyho" and "Splash one 'Betty'—splash two 'Zekes.' "

But the Japanese draw blood. At about 9:38 a.m., as 3d Fleet starts converging toward San Bernardino and the carriers prepare to launch deckloads to strike the enemy's center force, a Japanese "Judy" dives unseen and unrecorded on the radar screen out of a low cloud. She drops a 550-pound bomb square on *Princeton*'s flight deck; the bomb penetrates to the hangar deck, ignites gasoline in six torpedo planes, starts raging fires. The fight to save her starts, but at 10:02 a series of terrific explosions splits open the flight deck like the rind of a dropped melon, throws the after plane-elevator high into the air, and by 10:20 *Princeton*'s fire mains have failed and she is dead in the water, with a 1000-foot pall of smoke above her and hundreds of her crew in the water. The task group steams on southward to the San Bernardino rendezvous, while cruisers *Birmingham* and *Reno* and destroyers *Gatling, Irwin* and *Cassin Young* hover about the wounded

Ignoring heavy flak, an American B-25 bomber roars in to attack an 8000-ton Japanese transport off the coast of Leyte. The ship was part of a convoy carrying military supplies that the Japanese were rushing to the island to reinforce its defense. U.S. planes sank at least three ships.

An armada of U.S. troop transports moves toward landing beaches on Leyte at dawn on October 20, 1944, launching the invasion of the Philippines. Japan's Naval Command met this fleet with the bulk of its remaining strength and was beaten in the Battle for Leyte Gulf, which began three days later.

Princeton in a desperate daylong fight to save her.

But as *Princeton* flames and staggers, Kurita's Central Group of five battleships, accompanied by cruisers and destroyers, is running the gauntlet. Carrier strikes start coming in against Japan's First Attack Force about 10:25 a.m., and the exultant U.S. pilots concentrate against targets none of them had ever seen before—the largest battleships in the world. *Yamato* and *Musashi,* long the mysterious focus of intelligence reports, lie beneath the wings of Naval air power—their 68,000-ton bulks, 18.1-inch guns, twenty-seven-knot speeds dwarfing their sisters. *Musashi* is wounded early; oil smears trail on the blue water from her lacerated flank as a torpedo strikes home. But she is strong; her speed is undiminished. Not so *Myoko*'s. This heavy cruiser is badly hurt in the first attack; she drops to fifteen knots and is left astern to limp alone into port; Kurita has lost four out of the ten heavy cruisers that sortied so gallantly from Brunei.

But he has no respite. At three minutes past noon another strike comes out of the sun. The Japanese antiaircraft fire blossoms in pink and purple bursts; even the battleships' main batteries are firing. Several American planes are hit; one goes down flaming, but *Musashi* takes additional bombs and torpedoes; she loses speed and drops back slowly out of formation.

An hour and a half later *Yamato* takes two hits forward of her No. 1 turret, which start a fire, but her thick hide minimizes damages; the fire is extinguished. But *Musashi* is now sorely wounded; she takes four bomb hits in this attack and three more torpedoes; her upper works are a shambles, her bow almost under water, her speed down first to sixteen and then to twelve knots.

Kurita's slow agony drags on during this long and sunlit day. He hopes in vain for air cover. *Yamato* is hit again in the fourth attack and the older battleship *Nagato* damaged.

At 3 p.m. Kurita orders the limping *Musashi* to withdraw from the fight. But not in time. The final and largest attack of the day seeks her out as she turns heavily to find sanctuary. In fifteen minutes *Musashi* receives the *coup de grâce*—ten more torpedoes. She's down to six knots now, her bow is under water, and she lists steeply to port.

Kurita is shaken. He has had no air cover; he has been subjected to intense attack; his original strength of 5 battleships, 12 cruisers and 15 destroyers has

been reduced to 4 battleships, 8 cruisers and 11 destroyers; all his remaining battleships have been damaged. Fleet speed is limited to twenty-two knots. There is no sign that Ozawa's northern decoy force is succeeding in luring the 3d Fleet away from San Bernardino. At 3:30 p.m. Kurita reverses course and steams away toward the west. And American pilots report the "retreat" to Admiral Halsey aboard *New Jersey*.

To Admiral Halsey there is "one piece missing in the puzzle—the [Japanese] carriers."

The northern task group of 3d Fleet has been under attack by enemy carrier-type planes, which might have been land-based, but none of the sightings has reported enemy carriers. Where are they?

At 2:05 p.m., as Kurita's Central Group is pounded in the Sibuyan Sea, *Lexington*'s planes take off to find out. They are under orders to search to the north and northeast in the open seas untouched by the morning search.

The search planes fly through a cloud-speckled sky and intermittent rain squalls, leaving behind them a task group harassed by fierce, though intermittent, Japanese air attacks.

The flaming *Princeton,* billowing clouds of fire and smoke, is still afloat, with her covey of rescue ships around her. Despite intermittent explosions and singeing heat, cruisers *Birmingham* and *Reno* and destroyers *Morrison, Irwin* and *Cassin Young* have clustered alongside, pouring water from their pumps on the blazing carrier. Submarine contacts and enemy air attacks interrupt the fire fighting; the rescue ships pull off. At 2:45 p.m. cruiser *Birmingham* comes alongside *Princeton*'s blazing port side again. The cruiser's open decks are thick with men—fire fighters, line handlers, antiaircraft gunners, medical personnel, fire and rescue squads, watch standers. There are fifty feet of open water between blazing *Princeton* and her salvor, *Birmingham;* a spring line is out forward between carrier and cruiser.

Suddenly a "tremendous blast" rips off *Princeton*'s stern and after section of the flight deck; steel plates as big "as a house" fly through the air; jagged bits of steel, broken gun barrels, shrapnel, helmets, debris rake *Birmingham*'s bridge, upper works and crowded decks like grapeshot; in a fraction of a second the cruiser is a charnel house; her decks literally flowing blood—229 dead, 420 mangled and wounded—the ship's superstructure sieved.

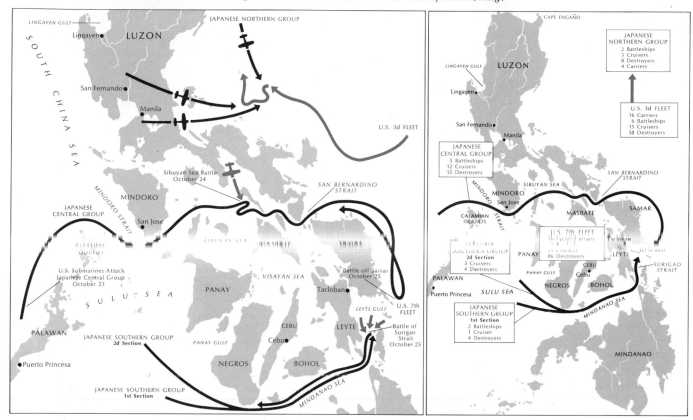

Aboard *Princeton* all the skeleton fire-fighting crew is wounded. Captain John M. Hoskins, who has been scheduled to take command of *Princeton* shortly and has remained aboard with the skipper he is relieving, puts a rope tourniquet around his leg, as his right foot hangs by a shred of flesh and tendon. The surviving medical officer cuts off the foot with a sheath knife, dusts the wound with sulfa powder, injects morphine. . . . Hoskins lives to become the Navy's first "peg-leg" admiral of modern times. But still *Princeton* floats on even keel, flaming like a volcano, manned by a crew of bloody specters.

At 4:40 p.m. the search to the north pays off. U.S. planes sight Ozawa's decoy force of carriers. The contact reports electrify 3d Fleet, but mislead it, too; Ozawa's Northern Group of ships, which were sighted about 130 miles east of the northern tip of Luzon, includes two battleship-carriers, but our fliers mistakenly report four. Nor do our fliers know Ozawa's carriers are virtually without planes.

The contact reports decide *Princeton*'s fate; her weary crew of fire fighters are removed, the daylong struggle is ended, and at 4:49 p.m. *Reno* puts two torpedoes into the flaming hulk and the carrier blows up. Mangled *Birmingham*, which has lost far more men than the ship she was trying to save, steams with her dead and dying to Ulithi—out of the fight.

Two hours later, near Sibuyan Island, the giant *Musashi*, pride of Kurita's Central Group, loses her long fight. Fatally wounded, she settles slowly deeper and deeper in the calm sea, and as the evening closes down, the greatest battleship in the world capsizes and takes with her to the depths almost half her crew. But no American sees her passing. . . . And no American has seen Kurita, earlier in the afternoon, alter his course once more and at 5:14 p.m. head once again with his battered but still powerful Central Group back toward San Bernardino Strait.

At 7:50 p.m., with the tropic dusk, "Bull" Halsey makes his decision and informs Kinkaid, commanding the 7th Fleet: "Central Force heavily damaged according to strike reports. Am proceeding north with three groups to attack carrier force at dawn."

Third Fleet concentrates and steams hard to the north in what irreverent historians of the future are to call Bull's Run. Snoopers from *Independence* shadow the Japanese Northern Group, and orders go to the carriers to launch planes at sunrise. San Bernardino

465

Strait is left uncovered—not even a submarine patrols its waters; Kinkaid and the 7th Fleet, protecting the Leyte invasion, believe it is barred by Halsey; Halsey, banking heavily on exaggerated claims from his pilots, thinks Kurita's Central Group has been stopped by the day's air attacks and the battered Japanese survivors can be left safely to Kinkaid. On such misunderstandings rest the course of history and the fate of nations.

Surigao Strait is dark under the loom of the land. Since the morning there have been no sightings of the Japanese Southern Group; even its exact composition is not known. But Kinkaid and the 7th Fleet have no doubts; the Japanese will try to break through this night. Kinkaid and Rear Adm. Jesse B. Oldendorf, his officer in tactical command (OTC), have made dispositions for a night surface battle. They have provided a suitable reception committee, including patrol-torpedo (PT) boats deep in the strait and covering its southern approaches, 3 destroyer squadrons near the center and, at the mouth, where the strait debouches into Leyte Gulf, 6 old battleships and 8 cruisers.

Into this trap the Japanese Southern Group blunders in two divisions, each independent of the other. Vice Admiral Nishimura, with battleships *Fuso* and *Yamashiro,* cruiser *Mogami* and 4 destroyers, leads the way. Cruising 20 miles behind Nishimura is Vice Admiral Shima with 3 cruisers and 4 destroyers from home bases. The two Japanese forces attack piecemeal and uncoordinated; neither knows much of the other's plans. Shima and Nishimura were classmates at the Japanese Naval Academy; their careers have bred rivalry; Nishimura, formerly the senior, has been passed in the processes of promotion by Shima, who commands the smaller force but is now six months senior in rank to Nishimura. But Nishimura, a seagoing admiral, has seen more war. Neither seems anxious to serve with the other; there is no common command.

Radars on the PT boats pick up the enemy about 10:36 p.m. as "sheet lightning dims the hazy blur of the setting moon and thunder echoes from the islands' hills."

Thirty-nine PT boats, motors muffled, head for Nishimura and attack in successive "waves" as the enemy advances. But the Japanese score first. Enemy destroyers illuminate the little boats with their searchlights long before the PT's reach good torpedo range;

a hit starts a fire in PT-152; a near-miss with its spout of water extinguishes it; PT-130 and PT-132 are also hit. But Nishimura is identified; course, speed and formation are radioed to Kinkaid's fleet and the harassing PT attacks continue.

Aboard destroyer *Remey,* flagship of Destroyer Squadron 54, Comdr. R. P. Fiala turns on the loudspeaker to talk to the crew: "This is the Captain speaking. Tonight our ship has been designated to make the first torpedo run on the Jap task force that is on its way to stop our landings in Leyte Gulf. It is our job to stop the Japs. May God be with us tonight."

The destroyers attack along both flanks of the narrow strait; their silhouettes merge with the land; the Japanese, in the middle, can scarcely distinguish dark shape of ship from dark loom of land; the radar fuzzes and the luminescent pips on the screen are lost in a vague blur.

It is deep in the midwatch—3:01 a.m. of October 25—when the first destroyer-launched torpedoes streak across the strait. In less than half an hour Nishimura is crippled. His slow and lumbering flagship, the battleship *Yamashiro,* is hit; destroyer *Yamagumo* is sunk; two other destroyers are out of the battle. Nishimura issues his last command: "We have received a torpedo attack. You are to proceed and attack all ships."

Battleship *Fuso,* cruiser *Mogami,* destroyer *Shigure* steam on toward Leyte Gulf. But before 4 a.m. a tremendous eruption of flames and pyrotechnics presages *Yamashiro*'s imminent passing; another American torpedo has found her magazine. At 4:19 the battleship capsizes and sinks, with Nishimura's flag still flying.

Fuso does not long outlive her sister. Up from the mud of Pearl Harbor, the avengers wait—the old battleships patrol back and forth across the mouth of the strait. This is an admiral's dream. Kinkaid and Oldendorf have capped the T; the remaining Japanese ships are blundering head on in single column against a column of American ships at right angles to the Japanese course. The concentrated broadsides of six battleships can be focused against the leading enemy ship, and only his forward turrets can be brought to bear against the Americans.

Climax of battle. As the last and heaviest destroyer attack goes home in answer to the command, "Get the big boys," the battle line and the cruisers open up; the night is streaked with flare of crimson.

466

Fuso and *Mogami* flame and shudder as the "rain of shells" strikes home; *Fuso* soon drifts helplessly, racked by great explosions, wreathed in a fiery pall. She breaks in two and dies before the dawn. *Mogami*, on fire, is finished later. Only destroyer *Shigure* escapes at thirty knots.

Into this mad melee, with the dying remnants of his classmate's fleet around him, steams Vice Admiral Shima—"fat, dumb and happy." He knows nothing of what has gone before; he has no cogent plan of battle. *Abukuma*, Shima's only light cruiser, is struck by a PT torpedo even before he is deep in the strait; she is left behind, speed dwindling, as the two heavy cruisers and four destroyers steam up the strait toward the gun flashes on the horizon. About 4 a.m. Shima encounters destroyer *Shigure*, sole survivor of Nishimura's fleet, retiring down the strait.

Shigure tells Shima nothing of the debacle. She simply signals: "I am the *Shigure;* I have rudder difficulties."

The rest is almost comic anticlimax. Shima pushes deeper into the strait, sees a group of dark shadows, fires torpedoes and manages an amazing collision between his flagship, the *Nachi,* and the burning stricken *Mogami,* which looms up flaming out of the dark waters of the strait like the Empire State Building. And that is all for futile Shima; discretion is the better part of valor; dying for the Emperor is forgotten, and Shima reverses course and heads back into the Mindanao Sea and the obscurity of history.

The Battle of Surigao Strait ends with the dawn—disaster for the Japanese. One PT boat destroyed, one destroyer damaged for the Americans. The southern pincer toward Leyte Gulf is broken.

October 25

By this day, more than 114,000 troops and almost 200,000 tons of supplies have been put ashore on Leyte, and most of the great amphibious fleet has cleared Leyte Gulf. But as the day of battle opens, there are still more than fifty thin-skinned Libertys, LST's and amphibious ships anchored in Leyte Gulf.

Dawn finds Admiral Ozawa with his decoy force eastward of Cape Engaño (fortuitous name: "Engaño" is Spanish for "lure," or "hoax"), prepared to die for the Emperor. At 7:12 a.m., when the first American planes appear from the southeast, Ozawa knows he has at last succeeded in his luring mission. The day be-

fore he despaired at times; more than 100 of his carrier planes—all he had, save for a small combat air patrol—joined Japanese land-based planes in attacks upon Halsey's northern task group. But his planes did not come back; many were lost, others flew on to Philippine bases. This day less than thirty aircraft—token remnants of Japan's once great flying fleets—are all that Ozawa commands. A few are in the air, to die quickly beneath American guns, as the first heavy attacks from Halsey's carriers come in.

The American carrier pilots have a field day; the air is full of the jabberwock of the fliers: "Pick one out, boys, and let 'em have it."

The Japanese formation throws up a convulsive carpet of antiaircraft fire; the colored bursts and tracers frame the sky-sea battle. The Japanese ships twist and turn, maneuver violently in eccentric patterns to avoid the bombs and torpedoes, but their time has come. The first strike reaches target at 8 a.m. With the day still young, some 150 U.S. carrier planes have wreaked havoc. Carrier *Chitose,* billowing clouds of smoke and fatally hurt, is stopped and listing heavily. Destroyer *Akitsuki* is blown up; light carrier *Zuiho* is hit; and Ozawa's flagship, the *Zuikaku,* takes a torpedo aft, which wrecks the steering engine so that she must be steered by hand.

A second strike at 9:45 cripples carrier *Chiyoda,* which dies a slow death, to be finished off later by U.S. surface ships. Light cruiser *Tama* is hit, to be sunk later. In early afternoon a third strike dooms *Zuikaku,* the last surviving carrier of the Japanese attack upon Pearl Harbor. She rolls over slowly and sinks, "flying a battle flag of tremendous size." At 3:27 p.m. *Zuiho* follows her down. The two Japanese battleships, with flight decks aft—*Hyuga* and *Ise,* "fattest of the remaining targets"—are bombed repeatedly, their bilges perforated, their decks inundated with tons of water from near-misses. *Ise*'s port catapult is hit, but the two ships bear charmed lives. Admiral Ozawa, his flag transferred to cruiser *Oyodo,* his work of luring done, struggles northward with his cripples from the battle off Cape Engaño. Throughout the day he is subject to incessant air attack, and in late afternoon and in the dark of the night of October 25, U.S. cruisers and destroyers detached from the 3d Fleet finish off the cripples.

The price of success for Admiral Ozawa's decoy force is high: all 4 carriers, 1 of his 3 cruisers and 2 of his 9 destroyers are gone. But he has accomplished

THE GREATEST SEA FIGHT: LEYTE GULF

his mission: Halsey has been lured, San Bernardino Strait is unguarded, and the hawk Kurita is down among the chickens.

Off Samar that morning of October 25, the sea is calm at sunup, the wind gentle, the sky overcast with spotted cumulus; occasional rain squalls dapple the surface. Aboard the sixteen escort carriers of 7th Fleet and their escorting "small boys" (destroyers and destroyer escorts), the dawn alert has ended. The early missions have taken off (though not the search planes for the northern sectors). Many of the carriers' planes are already over Leyte, supporting the ground troops; the combat air patrol and antisubmarine warfare (ASW) patrols are launched, and on the bridge of carrier *Fanshaw Bay,* Rear Adm. Clifton A. F. Sprague is having a second cup of coffee.

The coming day will be busy; the little escort carriers have support missions to fly for the troops ashore on Leyte, air defense and antisubmarine patrols, and a large strike scheduled to mop up the cripples and fleeing remnants of the Japanese force defeated in the night surface battle of Surigao Strait. The escort-carrier groups are spread out off the east coast of the Philippines from Mindanao to Samar; Sprague's northern group of 6 escort carriers, 3 destroyers and 4 destroyer escorts is steaming northward at fourteen knots, fifty miles off Samar and halfway up the island's coast.

The escort carriers, designated CVE's in naval abbreviation, are tinclads, unarmored, converted from merchant ships or tanker hulls, slow, carrying eighteen to thirty-six planes. They are known by many uncomplimentary descriptives—"baby flattops," "tomato cans," "jeep carriers"—and new recruits "coming aboard for the first time were told by the old hands that CVE stood for Combustible, Vulnerable, Expendable!" Their maximum of eighteen knots' speed (made all-out) is too slow to give them safety in flight; their thin skins and "popguns"—5-inchers and under—do not fit them for surface slugging; they are ships of limited utility, intended for air support of ground operations ashore, antisubmarine and air defense missions, never for fleet action. Yet they are to fight this

<hr>

Floating sailors and debris dot the waters surrounding a crippled and sinking Japanese warship, the victim of an attack by American planes in Leyte Gulf. The Battle for Leyte Gulf marked the virtual end of Japan as a great naval power.

morning a one-sided battle of jeeps against giants.

Admiral Sprague has scarcely finished his coffee when a contact report comes over the squawk box. An ASW pilot reports enemy battleships, cruisers and destroyers twenty miles away and closing fast.

"Check that identification," the Admiral says, thinking some green pilot has mistaken Halsey's fast battleships for the enemy. The answer is sharp and brief, the tension obvious. "Identification confirmed," the pilot's voice comes strained through the static. "Ships have pagoda masts."

Almost simultaneously radiomen hear Japanese chatter over the air; the northern CVE group sees antiaircraft bursts blossoming in the air to the northwest; blips of unidentified ships appear on the radar screens; and before 7 a.m. a signalman with a long glass has picked up the many-storied superstructures and the typical pagoda masts of Japanese ships.

Disbelief, amazement and consternation are felt; the escort carriers, Admiral Kinkaid himself, in fact most of the 7th Fleet, had been convinced the Japanese Central Group was still west of the Philippines and that, in any case, Halsey's fast battleships—now far away to the north with the carriers in the battle for Cape Engaño—were guarding San Bernardino Strait. But Kurita has arrived. And about all that stands between him and the transports, supply ships and amphibious craft in Leyte Gulf, and Army headquarters and supply dumps on the beach, are the "baby flattops" and their accompanying "small boys."

There's no time for planning; within five minutes of visual sighting, Japanese heavy stuff—18.1-inch shells from *Yamato,* sister ship of the foundered *Musashi*—is whistling overhead. Sprague, giving his orders over the voice radio, turns his ships to the east into the wind, steps up speed to maximum, orders all planes scrambled. By 7:05 escort carrier *White Plains,* launching aircraft as fast as she can get them off, is straddled several times, with red, yellow, green and blue spouts of water from the dye-marked shells foaming across her bridge, shaking the ship violently, damaging the starboard engine room, opening electrical circuit breakers and throwing a fighter plane out of its chocks on the flight deck.

White Plains makes smoke, and the Japanese shift fire to the *St. Lo,* which takes near-misses and casualties from fragments. The "small boys" make smoke, and the carriers, their boiler casings panting from maximum effort, pour out viscous clouds of oily black smoke from their stacks, which veil the sea. There is a moment of surcease; the planes are launched, most of them armed with small-size or antipersonnel or general-purpose bombs or depth charges—no good against armored ships. But there has been no time to rearm.

The air waves sound alarm. Sprague broadcasts danger in plain language at 7:01; at 7:04 Admiral Kinkaid, aboard his flagship *Wasatch* in Leyte Gulf, hears the worst has happened: the Japanese fleet is three hours' steaming from the beachhead; the little escort carriers may be wiped out. Just five minutes before, Kinkaid has learned that his assumption that a 3d Fleet cork was in the bottle of San Bernardino Strait was incorrect; in answer to a radioed query sent at 4:12, Halsey informs him that Task Force 34—modern, fast battleships—is with 3d Fleet's carriers off Cape Engaño far to the north.

Kinkaid in "urgent and priority" messages asks for the fast battleships, for carrier strikes, for immediate action. Even Admiral Nimitz in far-off Hawaii sends a message to Halsey: WHERE IS TASK FORCE 34—THE WORLD WONDERS?

But in Leyte Gulf and Surigao Strait the tocsin of alarm sounded via the radio waves puts 7th Fleet, red-eyed from days of shore bombardment and nights of battle, into frenetic action. Some of the old battleships and cruisers are recalled from Surigao Strait, formed into a task unit, and they prepare feverishly to ammunition and refuel. The 7th Fleet's heavy ships are in none too good shape for surface action; their ammunition is somewhat low from five days of constant shore bombardment, some of their armor-piercing projectiles having been used during the night battle; destroyers are low on torpedoes, many ships short of fuel.

And in the battle off Samar, Sprague is fighting for his life.

Within twenty minutes, as the baby carriers steam to the east, launching planes, the range to the enemy has been decreased to 25,000 yards—easy shooting for

U.S. troops and supplies pour out from LST's on a Leyte beach during an early stage of the American invasion of the Philippines. The landing vessels were manned by Navy and Coast Guard personnel. An antiaircraft gun points upward from the bow of each ship, on the alert for air attacks.

470

the big guns of the Japanese, far beyond the effective reach of the American 5-inchers.

Destroyer *Johnston,* Comdr. Ernest E. Evans commanding, sees her duty and does it. Anticipating orders (which are issued by Admiral Sprague at 7:16), she dashes in at almost thirty knots to launch a spread of ten torpedoes against an enemy heavy cruiser, *Kumano,* working up along a flank of the pounding carriers. She spouts smoke and fire as she charges, her 5-inchers firing continuously as she closes the range. She escapes damage until she turns to retire; then a salvo of three 14-inchers, followed by three 6-inch shells, hole her, wound her captain, wreck the steering engine, the after fire room and engine room, knock out her after guns and gyro compass, maim many of her crew and leave her limping sadly at seventeen knots.

Sprague and his carriers, veiled in part by smoke, find brief sanctuary in a heavy rain squall; the curtain of water saves temporarily the wounded *Johnston.* But well before 8 a.m. Kurita has sent some of his faster ships seaward to head off and flank the escort carriers; gradually Sprague turns southward, the enemy coming hard on both his flanks and astern.

"Small boys, launch torpedo attack," Sprague orders over the short-range radio (TBS) circuit. Destroyers *Heermann* and *Hoel* and wounded *Johnston,* her torpedoes already expended but her guns speaking in support, answer the command—3 destroyers in a daylight attack against the heaviest ships of the Japanese fleet—3 tinclads against 4 battleships, 8 cruisers and 11 destroyers.

Commander Amos T. Hathaway, skipper of the *Heermann,* remarks coolly to his officer of the deck, "Buck, what we need is a bugler to sound the charge."

Hoel and *Heermann,* followed by limping *Johnston,* sally forth to their naval immortality. In and out of rain squalls, wreathed in the black and oily smoke from the stacks and the white chemical smoke from the smoke generators on the fantails, the destroyers charge, backing violently to avoid collisions, closing the range. They hear that "express-train" roar of the 14-inchers going over; they fire spreads at a heavy cruiser, rake the superstructure of a battleship with their 5-inchers, launch their last torpedoes at 4400 yards range. Then Hathaway of the *Heermann* walks calmly into his pilothouse, calls Admiral Sprague on the TBS, and reports: "Exercise completed."

But the destroyers are finished. *Hoel* has lost her port engine; she is steered manually; her decks are a holocaust of blood and wreckage; fire control and power are off; No. 3 gun is wreathed in white-hot steam venting from the burst steam pipes and in flames from No. 3 handling room; No. 5 is frozen in train by a near-miss; half the barrel of No. 4 is blown off; but Nos. 1 and 2 guns continue to fire.

By 8:30 power is lost on the starboard engine; all engineering spaces are flooding; the ship slows to dead in the water and, burning furiously, is raked by enemy guns. At 8:40, with a 20° list, the order is given to "abandon ship." Fifteen minutes later she rolls on her port side and sinks stern first, holed repeatedly by scores of major-caliber shells.

In *Heermann* the crimson dye from enemy shell splashes mixes with the blood of men to daub bridge and superstructure reddish hues. A shell strikes a bean locker and spreads a brown paste across the decks. *Heermann* takes hits but, fishtailing and chasing salvos, she manages to live.

Not so, wounded *Johnston.* Spitting fire to the end, and virtually surrounded by the entire Japanese fleet, she is overwhelmed under an avalanche of shells and sinks about an hour after *Hoel.*

The four smaller and slower destroyer escorts join in the second torpedo attack. *Raymond* and *John C. Butler* live to tell about it; *Dennis* has her guns knocked out; but *Samuel B. Roberts,* deep in the smoke and framed by shell splashes, comes to her end in a mad melee. She is hit by many heavy-caliber projectiles, her speed is reduced, and by 9 a.m. a salvo of 14-inch shells rips open her port side like a can opener, wrecks an engine room, starts raging fires. The *Roberts,* abaft her stack, looks like "an inert mass of battered metal"; she has no power, she is dead in the water.

But the crew of No. 2 gun load, ram, aim and fire by hand. They know the chance they take; without compressed air to clear the bore of the burning bits of fragments from the previous charge, the silken powder bags may explode before the breach can be closed. But they fire six rounds, despite the risk. At the seventh, the gun explodes and instantly kills most of the gun crew; the breach is blown into a twisted inoperable mass of steel. Gunner's Mate, third class, Paul Henry Carr, the gun captain, his body ripped open from neck to groin, still cradles the last 54-pound shell in his arms, and his last gasping words before he dies are pleas for aid to load the gun.

But smoke screens, rain squalls and torpedo attacks have not saved the slow and lumbering baby flattops. Kurita has sent his cruisers curving seaward; slowly the fight swerves around from south to southwest; Sprague's carriers, strung out over miles of ocean, steam wounded toward Leyte Gulf, with the enemy destroyers coming hard on their landward flank, battleships astern and Japanese cruisers to seaward.

The flattops dodge in and out of the 150-foot waterspouts from the major-caliber Japanese shells; they chase salvos and fire their 5-inchers defiantly. *Fanshaw Bay* takes four hits and two near misses from 8-inch shells, which wreck the catapult, knock holes in the hull, start fires. *Kalinin Bay* takes fourteen hits; *White Plains* is racked from stem to stern by straddles. But their thin skins save them; most of the huge armor-piercing projectiles pass clean through the unarmored carriers without exploding.

Gambier Bay, trailing and on an exposed windward flank where the smoke screens do not shield her, takes a hit on the flight deck, a near-miss close alongside, loses an engine, drops to eleven knots, then loses all power—and is doomed. For an hour, far behind the chase, she dies in agony, hit about once a minute by enemy fire. She sinks about 9 a.m. flaming brightly, gasoline exploding, a Japanese cruiser still raddling her from only 2000 yards away.

Well before 9:30 the chase, which is drawing closer and closer to crowded Leyte Gulf, where frantic preparations are in progress, has enveloped the northern group of escort carriers; the central group is now under fire, and the sixteen jeep flattops have lost 105 planes.

Observers think it will be "only a matter of time" until the two groups are destroyed or crippled.

Two destroyers, a destroyer escort and a carrier are sunk or sinking; two carriers, a destroyer and a destroyer escort are badly hurt.

Aboard *Kitkun Bay* an officer quips, "It won't be long now, boys; we're sucking 'em into forty-millimeter range."

Suddenly at 9:11, Vice Admiral Kurita, with victory in his grasp, breaks off the action, turns his ships to the north and ends the surface phase of the battle off Samar. "Damn it, boys," a sailor says. "They're getting away."

Kurita's action, inexplicable at the time, has some,

though incomplete, justification. The charge of the American "small boys"—one of the most stirring episodes in the long history of naval war—and the desperate gallantry of the uncoordinated and improvised air strikes by the pilots of the escort carriers have had their effect. During the early action off Samar, U.S. carrier pilots from the little CVE's have harassed Kurita constantly, have shot down more than 100 enemy land-based planes and dropped 191 tons of bombs and 83 torpedoes. The enemy ships have turned and maneuvered violently to avoid torpedoes. Effective smoke screens have confused the Japanese. The air attacks have been mounting in intensity and effectiveness as planes have been launched from the center and southern groups of escort carriers and have been diverted from ground-support missions on Leyte to the new emergency. Pilots have strafed the Japanese ships recklessly, have dropped depth charges and antipersonnel bombs, have zoomed above Japanese mastheads with no ammunition and no weapons to win time and to divert and to distract.

The torpedo attacks by surface ship and aircraft have damaged enemy ships, and Kurita's fleet, composed of units now capable of widely differing speeds, is strung out over miles of ocean. Cruiser *Kumano,* torpedoed, is down to sixteen knots; cruisers *Chikuma* and *Chokai* are sunk; superstructures, charthouses and communication equipment in other ships are damaged by 5-inch shellfire and aircraft strafing. The Japanese are shaken. Kurita, who has lost close tactical control of his command, does not comprehend his closeness to victory; he thinks he has engaged some of the big, fast carriers of 3d Fleet instead of merely the escort carriers of 7th Fleet. Intercepted U.S. radio traffic convinces him—erroneously—that Leyte airstrips are operational. He believes the rest of Halsey's powerful forces are nearby; he knows that Nishimura's southern pincer has been defeated in Surigao Strait; he has never received messages from Ozawa, far to the north, reporting the success of his decoy mission. So Kurita recalls his ships and assembles his scattered forces—and his chance is gone.

Admiral Sprague notes (in his after-action report) his thankful bewilderment: "The failure of the enemy . . . to completely wipe out all vessels of this Task Unit can be attributed to our successful smoke screen, our torpedo counterattack—and the definite partiality of Almighty God."

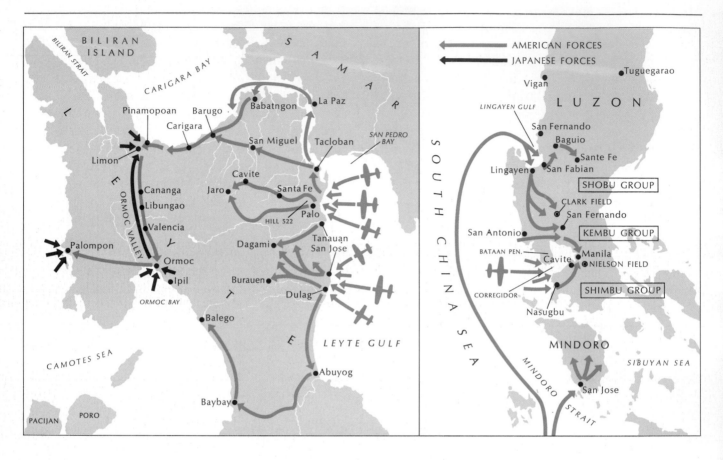

THE PHILIPPINE CAMPAIGN

The struggle to recapture the Philippines, vital to the Allied war plans, began on the morning of October 20, 1944, when four divisions of the U.S. Sixth Army under Lt. Gen. Walter Krueger landed on Leyte's east coast between Tacloban and Dulag. General Douglas MacArthur also went ashore, thus fulfilling his pledge to return.

The U.S. forces fanned out around and across the island. The embattled Japanese defenders fought back hard and, aided by torrential rains, blocked the U.S. advance for a time, but by December 26 only isolated enemy units still held out.

The next target was Luzon. Units of Krueger's Sixth Army were con-voyed to Lingayen Gulf on Luzon's western coast. Japanese kamikaze pilots took a deadly toll of the exposed convoys, although the actual landing met light resistance.

The Japanese commander, Gen. Tomoyuki Yamashita, had divided his force of some 250,000 men into three groups: *Shobu* to defend the north; *Kembu,* the center; *Shimbu,* the south. Despite his great numerical superiority (the U.S. troops numbered only 68,000), Yamashita was unable to hold back the U.S. advance. By January 20 U.S. forces had penetrated forty miles inland. Nine days later elements of the U.S. Eighth Army landed near San Antonio on the west coast, while a third landing was made at Nasugbu

on January 31. Manila was entered on February 3, Corregidor reclaimed on March 20 and Baguio on April 27. Although fighting continued in northern Luzon until the war's end, MacArthur declared the island liberated on June 28.

Meanwhile, in late February U.S. troops landed on Palawan Island, seized the islands of Panay, Cebu and Negros in March, and breached Mindanao in the middle of April.

The loss of the Philippines was a crippling blow to Japan. With her fleet decimated and her air strength shattered by the loss of some 9000 aircraft, Japan's cities now lay open to constant bludgeoning by Superfortress bombers based in the Philippines. The end was drawing near.

General Douglas MacArthur (center) and members of his staff stride ashore through the low surf on Leyte island in October 1944. The last rung of the "island-hopping" ladder was within the General's grasp.

A U.S. patrol carefully picks its way through the dense jungle of Leyte, in search of Japanese snipers. By early November 1944, the eastern half of the island was in American hands.

The quiet dignity of a Roman Catholic Mass provides a dramatic contrast to the unmistakable signs of war. This Philippine cathedral shelters wounded soldiers as well as worshiping villagers.

CLOSING IN ON JAPAN: IWO JIMA

BY ROBERT LECKIE

The story of the assault on the fantastically fortified volcanic island of Iwo Jima by U.S. marines, one of the most violent operations in the Pacific war, is summed up by Robert Leckie, who served as a scout and machine gunner with the 1st Marine Division in the Pacific until injured at Peleliu.

In early 1945, with Nazi Germany in its death throes, Adm. Chester W. Nimitz was reaching out for island bases in the Pacific for the final assault on Japan.

The two islands chosen were Iwo Jima in the Volcano Islands and Okinawa in the Ryukyus. Iwo Jima was to be taken first because it was believed to be easier, and because this tiny island's airfields posed both a threat and a potential advantage to B-29 Superforts returning from raids on Japan. Since November 24, 1944, the Superforts had been flying from Marianas bases to attack the Japanese home islands, and they had been suffering grievous losses. Radar based on Iwo alerted Japanese fighters to their approach, and many of these valuable U.S. bombers with their invaluable crews were either shot down or so crippled that they crashed into the sea during the 1500-mile flight back to base. Iwo, only 760 miles south of Tokyo, would be the ideal halfway haven for crippled B-29's. Moreover, if it was made a regular stopping point, the Superforts could carry less gas and more bombs and make more continuous attacks. Finally, possession of Iwo would knock out the enemy's warning system and allow the Superforts to have sorely needed fighter escort to the target and back.

It is not often that the value of an objective is so clearly understood beforehand, and in fact there was but one error in all the American estimates on Iwo Jima. This was that it would be easy to take. Just as,

three years previously, Gen. Douglas MacArthur had delayed the Japanese timetable of conquest, so the Japanese on Leyte and Luzon had held up MacArthur's advance. As a result, the target date for Iwo was delayed a month, and in that interval the Japanese put the finishing touches on what was probably the world's most formidable island bastion.

Iwo Jima, or Sulphur Island, is only 4½ miles long and 2½ miles wide. In shape it resembles a pork chop. To the south, at the tip of the pork chop's tail, the extinct volcano Mount Suribachi rises 550 feet above sea level. To either side of the tail are the island's only landing beaches, both lashed by high surf, terraced and covered with a mixture of brown volcanic ash and black cinders finer than sand. Widening to the meat of the chop, the island ends in a plateau with rocky, inaccessible bluffs. Difficult as it was to land at Iwo, the island might indeed have been easy to take in September 1944, when the Joint Chiefs of Staff were debating where to hit next. At that time Gen. Tadamichi Kuribayashi had only begun the task of transforming it into an all but invulnerable fortress.

Kuribayashi was a perfectionist martinet who had been impressed by the tactics of defense in depth worked out on the island of Peleliu in the Carolines. He began his Iwo assignment by convincing his 21,000-man garrison that each and every one of them must fight to the death. Before dying, each man was to kill ten Americans. Even if the island was lost, America would pay the kind of bloody butcher's bill which she would not readily incur again, and the U.S. timetable would be badly mangled.

At Mount Suribachi in the south, Kuribayashi constructed a labyrinth of positions for artillery, mortars and automatic weapons. From Suribachi observers could see most of the island and signal instructions to the positions in the north. Here a system of caves even more elaborate than Peleliu's housed the Japanese main body. Its characteristics were invisibility and flexibility. Positions were hidden by camouflage and usually so constructed that the guns could be fired in any direction. Finally, General Kuribayashi was wise

(Top right) *U.S. bombers, based in the newly liberated Marianas, pass beautiful Mount Fuji on their way to rain destruction on Japanese cities.* (Bottom) *This photograph, taken during the opening moments of an attack on the important Nipponese port of Osaka, shows a load of incendiary bombs plummeting on target toward the warehouse and dock areas.*

enough to instruct his men not to return fire and give away their positions when the Americans began their preinvasion bombardments.

As a result of this, the most prolonged preparatory bombardment of the war proved to be the most unrewarding. Some 6800 tons of bombs and 22,000 rounds of naval shells ranging from 5-inch to 16-inch were put on Iwo Jima. When two Marine divisions under Maj. Gen. Harry Schmidt went churning toward the landing beach on February 19, 1945, the target was obscured beneath a cloud of dust and smoke. Yet under the cloud was a virtually unscathed enemy crouching safely in his bombproof shelters, waiting only for the bombardment to lift before rushing back to his guns.

At first it seemed that bombardment had at last won an island on its own. There was only light opposition to the landing. Most of the difficulty seemed to be in Iwo's soil. Assault troops leaping out of their amtracs (amphibious tractor vehicles) sank calf-deep into that loose ash and cinder in which it was impossible to run or dig. They plodded forward, leaving elephant tracks behind them. The amtracs found no traction and could not move. Nor could they surmount the beach terraces ranging from five to eighteen feet in height. Vehicles began to pile up on each other. Confusion spread, and it was then that the guns of Iwo broke their silence and turned the beaches into bloody chaos.

Kuribayashi had deliberately allowed the Americans to come ashore lightly opposed. This would grant him surcease from naval gunfire and give the invaders just time enough to become bogged down. Then he could open up with everything he had, holding the Americans in front of his fixed positions while cutting them off from their supply craft, so that he could defeat them at leisure. Thus, only after the passage of almost an hour did Iwo Jima's black sands begin to clot red with blood. Artillery boomed from Suribachi and the northern heights, automatic weapons spat from innocent hummocks and antitank guns whammed from underground pillboxes. Until they could take cover among the wreckage of their own vehicles or behind their own dead, the marines on Iwo were naked to their

Marines of the 4th Division lunge from their landing craft onto the black volcanic sands of an Iwo Jima beach. In the background some men rush over the top of an embankment, and behind them others haul up equipment, while shells from U.S. Navy ships burst on the horizon. During the assault on Iwo Jima, twenty-six marines won the nation's top award, the Medal of Honor.

enemies. Yet they clung to their beachhead and expanded it. Gunfire from ships offshore covered their flanks and their front with rolling barrages, and after the assault signal companies came ashore to pinpoint targets, the naval fire became more accurate. Kuribayashi had given the marines one hour to build a beachhead and it had been too much. By nightfall it was clear that they had come to Iwo to stay.

Next day a Marine regiment turned south to strike at Suribachi. Blasting and burning pillboxes, sealing up interconnected caves with flamethrowers, grenades, rockets and demolition charges, the marines reached Suribachi in three days. On February 23 a patrol fought its way up to the volcano's summit and raised a flag there (see pages 482–486).

Meanwhile, the marines below had pivoted north and had begun their dreadful up-island advance into Kuribayashi's meat grinder. It was not possible to edge around the flanks, and to penetrate was to expose their own flanks to enemy fire. The Japanese entrenchments had to be pulverized piece by piece, sometimes with the aid of warships and aircraft, but most often with men on foot fighting among gullies, caverns, ledges and crevices, and using tanks or flamethrowers whenever they could. As Admiral Nimitz was to say later: "Among the Americans who served on Iwo Island, uncommon valor was a common virtue."

Eventually, elements of a third Marine division had to be fed into the battle. With this, and also by the impetus gained in a surprise night attack, the Japanese center was opened up and the defenses finally fragmented. Iwo was secured on March 26, but Kuribayashi had put a fearful price on the victory: ashore and in the fleet, 19,000 Americans were wounded and 7000 killed. Among the foot marines alone there were 5900 dead. But only 216 of the enemy's 21,000 survived to be taken prisoner.

"Let the world count our crosses!" Maj. Gen. Graves B. Erskine said in a moving speech saluting the fallen of his division. "Let them count them over and over. Then when they understand the significance of the fighting for Iwo Jima, let them wonder how few there are."

Even before the island fell, it had begun to pay enormous military dividends. On March 4 a B-29 running low on gasoline made a forced landing there, and before the war was over, 2251 Superforts with 24,761 crewmen were saved by emergency landings on Iwo.

TO THE SUMMIT OF SURIBACHI WITH THE FLAG

BY RICHARD WHEELER

Mount Suribachi is a name haloed with glory in the record of the Pacific war. The picture of weary bloodstained marines raising the American flag on its summit was destined to become an inspiring symbol of free men triumphant. Richard Wheeler, one of the survivors of the Iwo Jima invasion, writes about the famous episode of the struggle for Suribachi.

On February 21, 1945 (D plus 2), we began to breach the base defenses of Iwo Jima's Mount Suribachi. The assault was accompanied by a sustained din. Only our flamethrowers worked their slaughter quietly. They went into action with a metallic click and a long whoosh. But these were no doubt the most terrifying sounds the Japanese heard.

Hand-to-hand fighting sometimes resulted when enemy soldiers would suddenly dart from cover to attack or to make a break for the safety of more remote defenses. There were a number of bayonetings and knife killings. One marine, attacked by a saber-swinging Japanese officer, caught the blade with his bare hands, wrested it from the man and hacked him to death with it. I saw this marine later when he was brought aboard the hospital ship I occupied a mile or two offshore. He stopped by my bunk and told me his story. Both his hands were badly gashed and were swathed in bandages—but he still had the Japanese sword.

Several organized counterattacks were launched, but each was soon broken up. It isn't likely that the Japanese expected to accomplish much with these measures, but charging the advancing marines was a way of death that many doubtless preferred to being exterminated in their failing defenses.

Attacking on the extreme left, the 3d Platoon and the other units of Easy Company reached the volcano's base on the afternoon of the first day. Next they sliced around its left flank. Once they had reached the area where the defenses thinned, they were ordered by Lt. Col. Chandler W. Johnson to dig in and hold.

A similar attack was made by the 1st Battalion on the right. But in the center, where the 3d Battalion was operating, going was tougher. An extra day was required for these units to batter their way to the base.

By the end of D plus 3, the fight was largely won. There were still substantial numbers of the enemy in caves and other places of concealment, but hundreds had been slain and the pernicious power of the fortress had been broken.

It was time for our regiment to start climbing. But the craggy 550-foot dome was so steep that a cooperative move could not be made. It was discovered that the only route to the crater lay in the 2d Battalion zone, so the job of planning the climb fell to Colonel Johnson. And he soon decided to send one of his rifle platoons up as an assault patrol.

The twenty-five men of the 3d Platoon were by this time very dirty and very tired. They no longer looked or felt like crack combat troops. Although they had just spent a relatively free day, their rest had been marred by a chilling rain. They hardly yearned for the distinction of being the first marines to tackle the volcano. But the Colonel didn't bother to ask them how they felt about it.

About eight o'clock on the morning of D plus 4, 1st Lt. Harold Schrier, our company executive officer, assembled the platoon. After its thin ranks had been bolstered by replacements from other Easy Company units, he led it back around the volcano to 2d Battalion Headquarters near the northeast base.

The men found our dynamic battalion commander standing outside an improvised pup tent sipping from a cup of steaming coffee. He was wearing his fatigue cap with its visor bent upward, and this gave him a jaunty appearance that belied his stern nature. He was smiling this morning, however, so he must have been pleased with the way things were going.

While Johnson and Schrier consulted, the men were issued an abundant replenishment of cartridges, hand grenades, demolitions and flamethrower fuel. They

Four days after the Iwo Jima landing, weary marines of the 3d Platoon picked their way up Mount Suribachi. Their mission: to raise a flag on the summit of the squat, extinct volcano. Marine photographer Louis R. Lowery asked them to pause and show the flag, so that he could record their historic journey to the top.

Minutes later, the marines reached the dead volcano's rim with their precious flag. Then, while under attack by Japanese hand grenades, they crouch to mount the flag on a piece of pipe they had found within the shell-pocked crater.

were also provided with large water cans from which they filled their canteens. During these preparations they were joined by a radioman, two teams of stretcher bearers and a photographer, S. Sgt. Louis R. Lowery of *Leatherneck* magazine.

As the forty-man patrol loaded up to move out, the Colonel handed Schrier a folded American flag that had been brought ashore by our battalion adjutant, 1st Lt. George G. Wells. He had been carrying it in his map case. The flag had been obtained from the *Missoula,* the transport that had borne our battalion to Saipan, our staging area.

Johnson's orders were simple. The patrol was to climb to the summit, secure the crater and raise the flag. Though our men hoped fervently that their mission would prove as uncomplicated as the Colonel made it sound, most had serious misgivings.

Harold Keller said later: "When I looked at the two stretchers that were being sent along, I thought that we'd probably need a hell of a lot more than that."

However, Johnson had earlier sent two small patrols up the dome on reconnoitering missions, and both had reached the rim of the crater and had then withdrawn without running into any trouble.

Falling into an irregular column, our men headed directly for the volcano's base. They moved briskly at first, but when the route turned steep and going became difficult, the Lieutenant sent out flankers to guard the vulnerable column against surprise attack. Heavily laden with weapons and ammunition, the men climbed slowly and were forced to stop from time to time to catch their breath. Some areas were so steep they had to be negotiated on hands and knees. Though several cave entrances were sighted, no resistance developed.

Far below, the marines located about the northeast base watched the patrol's laborious ascent. Also observing, some through binoculars, were many men of the fleet.

Within a half hour after leaving battalion headquarters, the patrol reached the crater's rim. Schrier called a halt here while he took stock of the situation. He could see two or three battered gun emplacements

---

The flag is planted and flutters bravely above Iwo Jima as members of the 3d Platoon stand guard. From below, cheering marines had already spotted the high-flying banner. Seconds later, Japanese soldiers, hidden in surrounding caves, attacked the flag's defenders with rifle fire and a scattering of hand grenades.

and some cave entrances, but there were no Japanese in evidence. So he gave the signal for the men to start filing over.

My bold friend Howard Snyder went over first. Had I remained unwounded, I probably would have been second—whether I wanted to be or not. As it was, Harold Keller occupied this spot. Chick Robeson was third. Then came Harold Schrier, his radioman and Leo Rozek. Robert Leader was seventh, and fully expecting to be fired at, he hoped that number seven was really the lucky number it was supposed to be.

As the men entered the crater, they fanned out and took up positions just inside the rim. They were tensed for action, but the dim caves and the yawning trenches below them remained silent. Finally one of the men stood up and urinated down the crater's slope. But even this insulting gesture didn't bring the Japanese to life.

While half the patrol stayed at the rim, the other half now began to press into the crater to probe for resistance and to look for something that could be used as a flagpole.

Harold Keller, moving in the lead, made the first contact with the enemy. He says of this: "The Jap started to climb out of a deep hole, his back toward me. I fired three times from the hip, and he dropped out of sight."

Several caves now began to disgorge hand grenades. The marines in the hot spots took cover and replied with grenades of their own. Some of these came flying back out of the dark entrances before exploding.

Even while this action waxed, Robert Leader and Leo Rozek discovered a long piece of pipe, seemingly a remnant of a rain-catching system, and passed it to the summit. Waiting with the flag were Harold Schrier, Ernest Thomas, Hank Hansen and Chuck Lindberg. They promptly began fixing it to the pole.

It was about 10:30 a.m. when the pole was planted, and the Stars and Stripes, seized by the wind, began to whip proudly over the volcano. The date February 23, 1945, had suddenly become historically significant.

The marines watching from below raised the cry, "There goes the flag!" And the electrifying word quickly spread to all the units about the volcano's base and to the regiments fighting the main battle to the north. Our combat-weary troops felt a great swell of pride and exultation. They felt a certain relief, too. A part of the "impregnable" island had fallen. Victory seemed a little nearer now. Some men cheered, and some wiped at brimming eyes. The cry was also taken up by the fleet. Ship whistles tooted a spirited salute.

Though most of our men were aware of the significance of their accomplishment, no one at first did much thinking in terms of pride and glory. All were concerned about the effect the sight of the colors would have on the enemy. They were in danger of getting resistance not only from the Japanese close at hand but from artillery units in the north. The forty men had raised the flag, but they were by no means certain they would be able to defend it successfully.

Shells from the north wouldn't come until later, but the flag was promptly challenged by the Japanese on the summit. First a rifleman stepped out of a cave and fired at the photographer and Chick Robeson. The Japanese missed, but Robeson didn't. He swung his automatic rifle up for a long burst, and the man dropped heavily.

"You got him!" Harold Schrier said.

The body was quickly seized by the feet and dragged partway back into the cave. But now an officer stepped out. Grimacing bitterly, he charged toward the flag-raising group, brandishing a sword that had only half a blade. He had probably broken the weapon on purpose, so that it would have no value as a souvenir.

Howard Snyder advanced to meet this attack with a .45 pistol. He took deliberate aim as the frenzied man bore down. But when he pressed the trigger, there was only a metallic snap. The weapon misfired. Snyder had to scramble out of the way, but a dozen marines were now alerted to the cave threat. A volley of rifle fire, led off by Pfc. Clarence H. Garrett, turned the one-man charge into a headlong tumble.

Our men now moved against the resisting area, and they were met by a flurry of hand grenades. The cave turned out to be a large one with several entrances. Flanking the openings, the marines once more countered with grenades of their own. Then the entrances were hosed with flamethrowers and blown shut with demolitions.

Photographer Lowery, covering the action at considerable risk, soon had another close shave. A Japanese lobbed a grenade at him, and he was forced to leap down the side of the volcano. Tumbling for fifty feet before he was able to catch hold of a bush, he broke his camera.

This cave was a far greater threat to the flag raisers than was realized at the time. Howard Snyder and Chick Robeson would make the discovery a few days later, when they dug the cave open to look for souvenirs.

Robeson said of the venture: "The stench that met us was so foul that we had to put on gas masks. We went in with a small flashlight, and we found it to be a large cave in two parts. Dead Japs lay all about, so thick that we had to tread on some. I believe that there were at least one hundred and fifty."

Why these Japanese hadn't tried to bolt from the cave and overwhelm the flag-raising patrol is a mystery. They had our men outnumbered four to one. What made the situation even more unaccountable was that there were other occupied caves on the summit. While the number of Japanese who could have hurled themselves against the patrol can never be known, there were surely enough to have killed every man in it.

Other platoons soon joined the patrol at the summit and began to help with the crater mop-up. Similar operations were still going on at the volcano's base and had also been started on its outer slopes.

It was about three hours after the flag was planted that Colonel Johnson made the decision that it be replaced. The 3d Platoon's flag measured only 54 inches by 28 inches, and it was lost to distant view. Since the sight of the colors was important to the morale of our troops, who still had a lot of fighting to do before Iwo was secured, Johnson felt that a larger set was needed. So a flag that was 8 feet by 4 feet 8 inches was obtained from a ship beached near Suribachi's eastern base.

As the new flag was being carried up the volcano, Joe Rosenthal, a civilian photographer who was covering the Iwo operation for the Associated Press, learned of the move and decided to follow. And this decision resulted in the now-famous photograph, which pushed the 3d Platoon's heroic story into the background and rendered our flag raisers nameless. Although about half the platoon was present at the second raising, only one of our men, Corpsman John Bradley, is in the picture. It shows an authentic combat scene, though less impromptu and dangerous than the earlier one.

The raising of a larger flag atop Mount Suribachi was accomplished several hours after the first one had been hoisted. The decision to replace the small flag with a larger, more visible one was made to boost morale. This celebrated photograph was the model for the Marine Corps War Memorial in Arlington, Virginia.

HOLD THAT LINE... OR DIE

BY MITCHELL DANA

As the last great enemy bastion astride the ocean road for invasion of Japan—an invasion that would never take place—the island of Okinawa was of crucial strategic importance. Sixty miles long, from two to fifteen miles wide, it lay only 340 miles from the major Japanese island of Kyushu. On its ridges and cliffs, in its natural and man-made caves, a huge and well-equipped Japanese army had long been entrenched and ready. For the possession of this rugged outpost of empire, Americans from April 1, 1945, into late June fought one of the toughest and certainly the most costly of battles, for both sides, in the entire war. The United States paid for its victory with 12,500 killed or missing, 36,600 wounded; the Japanese, with 109,600 killed and 7800 taken prisoner.

In telling the story of Okinawa, journalists and historians most often concentrated on the furious ground fighting. But the soldiers and marines were mortally dependent on the continuing flow of troop reinforcements and supplies. To keep the sea-lanes open, the Navy deployed a picket line of destroyers and destroyer escorts. The ships and men of this force became the primary targets for the Japanese suicide squadrons—the kamikaze assault, a fanatic, half-mad and eventually futile enterprise born of Japanese desperation. It is the remarkable story of the picket line, a saga of incredible courage, that is told here.

Okinawa was the last insanely reckless struggle of the crashing Japanese Empire in World War II. It was the last battle, in truth, for many a man and many a ship and plane. But for the destroyer men of the United States it was a nightmare come true. What the destroyer men took, and what they dished out there, seems unbelievable now. In one final burst of teeth-grinding fury, Japan's suicide squadrons literally hurled themselves at the Americans.

It was men who wanted to live against men who wanted to die. Men in thin-skinned, skittering little "cans" against men in swift-hurtling planes, rockets and torpedoes. And, almost incredibly, it was the men in the little ships who won. Pure skill, bulldog tenacity and death-defying bravery won out. Men who were too proud to run defeated men who were determined on self-destruction.

There were many good little ships in the picket line that surrounded bloody Okinawa. Many good men in them, too. It would be hard to say, *"This* ship and crew was better than *that* one," in the stubborn line. But there was one destroyer, the U.S.S. *Hugh W. Hadley,* that somehow symbolized the spirit of all the gallant "small boys" of the American fleets.

Destroyer *Hadley* had been commissioned in November 1944. She was the latest thing in swift surface ships when she headed west with her new crew. "DD 774" was her battle number. Commander Baron J. Mullaney was her skipper when she underwent her ordeal by fire in April and May 1945. Her men were to win a Presidential Unit Citation in an unparalleled series of blazing life-or-death battles. But ninety-five of them were destined for death or serious injury from a howling hell of kamikazes. The *Hadley* herself was to emerge a shattered, staggering wreck.

The kamikazes were the reason for the bloody, fire-seared chaos off Okinawa. To Americans, to whom the individual and his life are sacred, the Japanese kamikaze seemed an insane horror produced by diseased minds. Not so to the fatalistic Nipponese.

Suicide weapons had been tried before, but never on the horrible scale of Okinawa. Japan's Imperial Navy had secretly launched a whole *kikusui* ("floating chrysanthemums") plan of mass kamikaze attacks, using a new Special Attack Corps of suicide volunteers. The kamikaze ("divine wind") operations were well under way as 1945 began. By March some

190 Japanese pilots, sworn to seek death, already had crashed about 130 planes into American ships and almost sixty more into the sea in near-misses.

Often dressed in ceremonial hara-kiri (ritual suicide) robes, insanely fanatic Japanese pilots flew the kamikaze planes or steered the one-way *okas* ("cherry blossoms")—jet-propelled, flying-bomb rockets. The torpedo-shaped, stub-winged rockets were called bakas by the Yanks. (*Baka* is the Japanese word for "idiot.") They were flying bombs, packed with 3000–4700 pounds of high explosives, carried under the belly of a medium or heavy bomber. Once near the target they were released, to be ridden into the target by a suicide pilot who served as a living aim and exploder device.

Besides the plane and rocket pilots, there were other death-dedicated suicide volunteers. Speedboats packed with high explosives were used, too; and midget submarines, operated by one or two suiciders, served as living torpedoes. Before it was stopped, the grisly "divine wind" took a terrible toll: more than 12,000 Americans killed and many times that number wounded. On Okinawa itself over 7000 GI's and marines died. At sea the U.S. Navy lost more men and ships than in any other comparable battle-time campaign: nearly 5000 seamen dead; another 4800 wounded; 13 destroyers and 1 destroyer escort sunk; 13 carriers, 10 battleships and 5 cruisers severely damaged; and 47 destroyers and destroyer escorts mauled and battered. How many Japanese died, no one will ever know.

The picket line at Okinawa was the worst ordeal ever faced by the American Navy. Most of the blows were taken by the swift "small boy" ships. Their eggshell hulls, built for speed, not for slugging, were ill-suited to such brutal, head-on smashes. Nevertheless, they choked the "divine wind" in the throats of their foes. No less than ninety-eight destroyers and fifty-two destroyer escorts fought in this last great struggle of the Japanese. Sixty-one of them were hit in the furious day and night battles.

"Operation Iceberg" was the code name of the American invasion plan for Okinawa. It aimed to seize the big island as the base for the final invasion of the Japanese home islands. As March 1945 ended, the 5th Fleet headed for the East China Sea—and Okinawa. April 1 was the opening day.

Well aware of the ferocity of defense to be expected, Adm. Chester W. Nimitz sent a huge force to tackle the formidable task—more than 1500 American ships,

manned by over half a million men. More than 1200 transport and supply ships, carrying 182,000 assault troops, aimed for Okinawa, with some 300 fighting ships to protect them.

In the great anchorage area off the west coast of the long, narrow island, the vast transport fleet would have to sit for days and weeks. Such a huge assemblage of juicy targets would tempt the Japanese to wild attacks. If they could destroy the transports, they would isolate the invasion army.

Protection of the transport area would depend on a distant screen of swift fighting ships—the destroyers (DD's) and destroyer escorts (DE's). In a ring encircling the island, the DD's and DE's would patrol in constant radar picket duty. They would guard the vital convoy lanes and flash warnings of aircraft or other enemies approaching the vulnerable transport area. More important, they were to stop the attackers with a wall of antiaircraft fire—and with their ships and bodies, if need be.

Seventy miles out from the island coast the first picket line took stations. Forty miles from shore the second line began its picket runs. Then, twenty miles out from the transport area, the last line was set up. The rings of picket groups were named Task Flotilla 5.

In each little picket group a fighter-director team kept in constant touch with some assigned fighter squadron. Two support landing craft (LCS) or other support went with each picket group. They were called the Pallbearers, with typically salty navy humor.

At first only one destroyer was assigned to each picket group. But as days of furious attacks followed one another, more were added. Toward the end, in May, there were two or three DD's in each station. Four to twelve planes were on call solely as cover for each group. Destroyer escorts, which were not heavily enough armed for the outer line, served in the inner lines.

As many as nineteen picket groups ringed the island until shore radar stations could be set up. In each, 2, 3 or 4 DD's and 2 to 4 LCS's cruised, each group usually in an Indian-fighting circle, for mutual help. Whenever enemy planes were spotted, timely warning enabled the transport area guards to blanket the helpless transports with protective smoke.

It was up to the "tin cans." The big carriers, much too clumsy for this job, stood far away beyond the horizon. Their fighter planes came on call. Bombardment

(Above) *Kamikazes, or suicide pilots, swore an oath to die in the defense of their homeland and Emperor. Six young pilots pose proudly in their flight uniforms before taking off on final, tragic missions.*

(Left) *Flight to death: As antiaircraft shells churn the sea, a kamikaze plane makes its last, suicidal run toward an American carrier off Truk in the Carolines, during the fierce air-sea fight in 1944.*

(Right) *This U.S. carrier has just been hit by a kamikaze plane, and her crew works feverishly to extinguish the lethal fires. As U.S. forces moved ever closer, island by island, to the home islands of Japan, these suicide attacks grew more ferocious.*

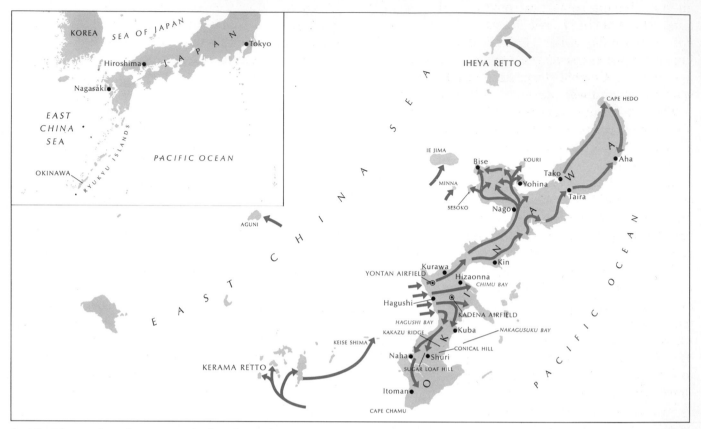

battleships and cruisers came in for short-time gun attacks on the island and as quickly drew back from the danger zone. Blockading submarines stood far out, to warn of approaching surface attack. But it was from the air that danger would come. For that, the destroyer men were sent out.

U.S.S. *Hadley* joined one of the picket lines (Station 15, north of the transport area) and settled down to alert patrolling. It was not a new job to many of her men, but it was to some. A fighter-director team was aboard to control the twelve fighter planes assigned to this group's control.

The *Hadley* was a good ship with a good crew. It was well for the men that they knew their business. Their lives were to depend on their skill and fortitude.

The ship worked in a team with another crack DD, the *Evans*. Between them they were to blast some fifty suicide planes and rockets out of the air in one terrific day, incredible as it sounds. One day of furious action —May 11—was typical of how the iron men in the "tin ships" could fight.

Early in the morning of the 11th the kamikazes came like flies. Out of a misty haze to the north the first one came, straight for the *Hadley*.

Lookouts shrilled the alarm, and tense men at the guns crouched ready. The tiny spot in the sky grew rapidly bigger. It was a float plane, the first of the scores of mad death seekers that were to attack the two destroyers that day.

As the racing kamikaze came into range, the guns of the *Hadley* opened up with a snarling roar. Tracers and bursting shells began to spot the sky around the Japanese plane. Suddenly there was a terrific explosion about 1500 yards from the destroyer. The plane disappeared in a blasting flash of yellow flame and gray smoke. Direct hit—right on the nose! One kamikaze had gone to join his ancestors: first score for the *Hadley*.

Another plane came hurtling out of the mist, higher up this time. The gun muzzles on the destroyer rose swiftly, like insect feelers, pointing toward the new enemy. Behind the guns tight-lipped crewmen braced for the next attack. Mount captains and gun captains spoke tersely to their crews. Ammunition and powder men swung to their jobs. Pointers peered through their sights.

While the guns lifted their muzzles, the fighter-director chief studied his radar screen and spoke to his air unit. "Bandits coming in from the north. We've got a snowstorm of bogeys, one-five-zero. Big raid coming up." Back on the carriers, far over the horizon, waiting fighter planes roared along flight decks and leaped into the air. Combat Air Patrol (CAP) would be wanted—the mist was swarming with kamikazes.

The approaching plane was a "Val." Snapping gunfire on the *Hadley* mounted to a roar, as the ship heeled around to bring all guns to bear. Fire control men sweated suddenly as the careening plane swerved and maneuvered, swinging around in an arc to hit from the rear. How could they figure the deflection rate? The plane swerved from side to side, skidding, slipping and barrel rolling, speeding up and slowing down, in a great circle.

At 5000 yards the air around the careening "Val" was plastered with 5-inch bursts, while streaming 40-mm. tracers seemed to frame the darting, dancing plane. Still it came on, closer and closer. At 2000 yards it turned sharply and bored in toward the ship. The 20-mm. guns opened up, adding their shrill racket to the uproar. A thin wisp of black smoke began to stream from the onrushing plane.

As it came on, right over the ship's wake, the after 5-inchers crashed savagely. Each blast almost knocked down the crew of the nearby aft 20-mm. gun. Cold sweat beaded the gunners' brows.

The "Val" was smoking badly now, but it still came on like a rocket. Yammering guns ripped desperately at the plunging kamikaze, tearing at the wings and fuselage. Suddenly a wing seemed to detach itself from the onrushing plane. It floated like a leaf, swaying to and fro as it dropped. Then the plane turned lazily up into a long graceful arch and flipped over on one side. Its dead pilot, riddled by flying steel, no longer controlled the explosive-packed machine. It dropped suddenly, nose first, and plunged into the sea in a splashing column of foam—less than 100 yards from the *Hadley.*

As the guns suddenly fell silent, the men of the *Hadley* stared at each other, ashen-faced. How much of this sort of thing could they take? How long can men who want to live fight off men who want to die? This wasn't battle: it was insanity—lunatic idiocy!

That was the reaction of all the men, in all the racing DD's and DE's of the great picket line. Each ship in the whole long scattered line was to go through this soul-searing experience, not just once, but many times.

Off Okinawa the seamen of America fought not only men, but grim, brain-addled death itself. That they stayed on and fought this nightmare enemy to the end, almost passes belief.

But they stayed.

Here and there on the crowded little ships a man's nerves broke. Some men became hysterical; but the ones who cracked were very few. Sick with horror and disgust, almost every man stayed put and beat off the swarming lunatics and patched their ships.

More than 150 suicide planes hurled themselves at the *Hadley* and the *Evans* on that awful day in May. Wave after wave came hurtling out of the sky. How many more were shot down, high above, in wild aerial dogfights, no one will ever know.

Each time, after the first solo attacks, 4, 5 or 6 Japanese would plunge at the *Hadley* together. One would dive straight from above. One would come screaming down at a 45° angle. Another would come gliding in at 30°. And another would skim the waves, low and level. From every quarter of the compass, they bored in on the racing destroyer—some bow-on, some from astern and some from the sides.

Like a porcupine, the *Hadley's* guns bristled in all directions, fighting off attackers. A canopy of streaming steel, flame and smoke hung over her, like a wall to hold off the swarms above. Her men labored and sweated, feeding and firing their guns like lost souls who were doomed to everlasting labor in the fiery pits of hell.

By 9 a.m. the *Evans* was three miles away, desperately fighting for her own life. Then the *Evans* was hit and out of action and the *Hadley* was alone.

From 8:30 to 9 the keen-eyed gunners on the *Hadley* speared one plane after another—twelve in all. At 9:05 the weird attackers pierced her defenses. A high-flying Japanese bomber released a baka. Like a jet-propelled stone the huge rocket fell straight onto the *Hadley.* With a terrific explosion it tore through her deck, shattering power and control connections. A spout of flame boiled up from the stricken destroyer. Torn fragments of dead men littered her seared decks, as repair crews ran to stop her wounds. Burning and racked with pain, the little ship fought on. Then a hurtling bomb smashed into her, tearing at her vitals. Then a "Nate" plummeted down, crashing aft on the deck. Shattering explosion tore through the ship,

blowing her after gunners to shreds. But the other guns kept right on firing.

Another "Val" was driving for the hull of the stricken destroyer. Oblivious to the storm of flying steel, the fanatic Japanese pilot held his plane straight in line to crash. It struck square amidships.

A dull, jarring boom signaled the smash. Terrific concussion drove in the side of the staggering ship. Water rushed in. Drunkenly the *Hadley* began to heel over. Tons of green water pressed her down. She began to list and settle. But the men on the *Hadley* were still fighting. Every gun that had not been blasted continued to lash out its defiance.

The last of the howling kamikazes came on, to finish the job. Clawing, spitting gunfire ripped it out of the sky, plunging it to its death in a foaming geyser in the sea. It was as though the furious men of the *Hadley* were reaching up with long talon-tipped claws, tearing their tormentors down. Then suddenly they were gone. There were no more left.

Wallowing heavily, the *Hadley* seemed to be mortally wounded. Damage-repair crews appeared to be losing the grim struggle with fire and water. At any moment she might roll over and sink.

Calm and restrained, Commander Mullaney's voice sounded the order to prepare to abandon ship, but

494

grief and pain racked him even when he gave the necessary order. The Captain himself and some forty officers and men stayed aboard.

In quick, orderly fashion, life rafts were pushed over the side. The wounded were carried gently to safety on the rafts, and most of the crew went over the side, too. Their LCS's (the "Pallbearers") were coming up fast to lend a hand.

On board the few remaining men labored in frantic haste, lightening the laboring ship and stopping her wounds. In a frenzied half hour of heroic effort the damage was brought under control. A miracle had happened; the *Hadley* would live, after all!

Battered, torn and fiercely triumphant, the *Hadley* did survive after her unbelievable ordeal. Laboring heavily, she was towed to safety at Ie Shima, just west of Okinawa. She would ride the seas again. Her mission was accomplished. She had given the Japanese a bitter bellyful of suicide. And the transports she had protected were safe.

The U.S.S. *Hugh W. Hadley* paid the price, as did so many other destroyers of the immortal picket line. Twenty-eight of her men were dead. Sixty-seven of them were badly wounded. The ship was a battered mess. But she was still there, and her indomitable men were triumphant. The *kikusui* had blown itself out.

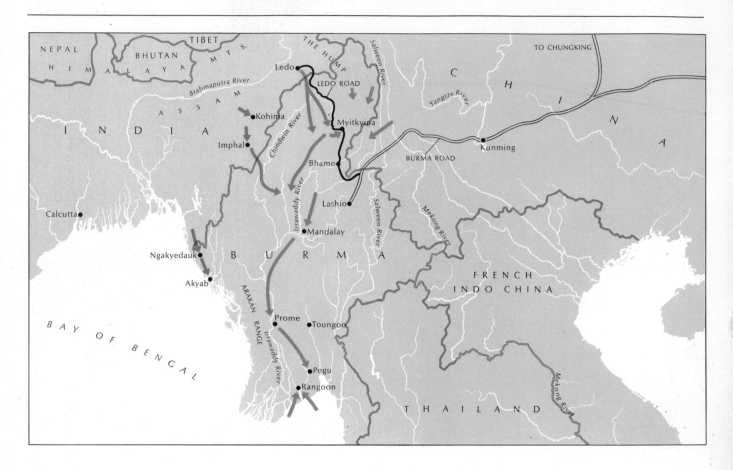

THE CHINA-BURMA THEATER

The conquest of Burma by the Japanese in mid-1942 slammed shut the door to the Burma Road, the Allies' only land route to embattled China. Allied pilots began flying large amounts of war goods across the Himalayas (the Hump) from India to Generalissimo Chiang Kai-shek, but the supply was never enough to meet the needs of the Chinese armies.

In December 1943, U.S. Lt. Gen. Joseph W. Stilwell, who had been forced to retreat to India with his two divisions of Chinese troops, struck back into Burma from Ledo, with Myitkyina as his target. Accompanying him were engineers to build a new highway (the Ledo Road) linking up with the Burma Road. They met vigorous opposition.

A short time later, a British Army corps, pushing down the coast of the Bay of Bengal toward Akyab, also encountered strong resistance. The Japanese were defeated at the Battle of Ngakyedauk.

As part of their plan to invade India, Japanese forces now launched a massive drive against the British in the north. Sixty thousand British and Indian troops were isolated at Imphal and Kohima. The siege lasted for almost three months before it was broken.

Meanwhile, guerrilla warfare was being waged by British Maj. Gen. Orde C. Wingate's Raiders and U.S. Brig. Gen. Frank D. Merrill's Marauders. Another unusual fighting force in the China-Burma theater was Maj. Gen. Claire L. Chennault's Flying Tigers, later a part of the U.S. 14th Air Force (see pages 110–111).

The campaign in Burma began to draw to a close when Allied troops under the overall command of British Lord Louis Mountbatten captured Myitkyina in August 1944, resulting in the opening of the Ledo-Burma Road. Mandalay fell to Mountbatten's men on March 20, 1945, followed by Prome, on the lower Irrawaddy, and Pegu on May 1. Two days later, British troops captured Rangoon.

The Japanese, now thoroughly beaten, left Burma, their dream of empire gone.

The reopened Burma Road, twisted like a crazed snake in its "twenty-one curves" section, was used to carry supplies from India to China in 1945.

(Left) *Chinese troops, laden with equipment for their drive against the Japanese, cross the swift Salween River on a temporary bridge. All supplies in this Yunnan Province campaign of the summer of 1944 had to be carried or air-dropped.*

(Right) *Bicycles were the perfect vehicles for traveling swiftly and silently along the narrow jungle paths of embattled Burma. Here a Japanese unit pedals toward Rangoon shortly before the city fell.*

(Below) *Hundreds of Chinese refugees with their household belongings cling to every available space on a train headed away from the rapidly advancing Japanese armies during fierce fighting on the Chinese mainland in November 1944.*

THE ULTIMATE WEAPON

BY FLETCHER KNEBEL AND
CHARLES W. BAILEY II

August 6, 1945 — the day a single bomb dropped on Hiroshima, wiped out the city and killed about 70,000 persons. It led to the unconditional surrender of Japan and ushered in the Nuclear Age. Here is the gripping story of the technological miracle that produced the apocalyptic weapon; the diplomatic impasse that led to the soul-searing Allied decision to annihilate Japanese cities; the vast Air Force planning behind the successful delivery of the bomb; and the nightmare of death and destruction visited on the ill-fated population of Hiroshima and, later, Nagasaki.

The U.S.S. *Augusta* hurried westward across the Atlantic. It was wartime—the date was August 5, 1945—but with Germany defeated the war was half a world away, and the heavy cruiser sparkled with lights.

In the wardroom the officers entertained President Harry S Truman, who was traveling home from the conference with his British and Russian allies at Potsdam, Germany. Over dessert and coffee the ship's doctor raised a question they had all been wondering about. Had there been any commitments at Potsdam to bring Russia into the Pacific war?

The President responded with a statement that his listeners would never forget. No, he said, there had been no such deal made. And if the Russians had been difficult at Potsdam it did not matter; the United States now had a new weapon of such force that we did not need the Russians. "It is so powerful," he said, "that one weapon is equal to twenty thousand tons of TNT."

Truman told them that the new weapon had been developed in total secrecy, that it already had been tested and that it could end the war. "It is the biggest gamble in history," he said. "Two billion dollars have been spent on it. We will have the final answer on its effectiveness within a very short time."

While President Truman ate Sunday dinner in the *Augusta*'s wardroom on the Atlantic, it was already the next day in the Marianas Islands in the western Pacific. There U.S. Navy Seabees had been working since 3 a.m., as they had every morning, seven days a week, for over a month. They were the last link in a chain that was working frantically to supply the U.S. 20th Air Force with high-explosive and incendiary bombs. Major General Curtis E. LeMay's B-29 bombers had unloaded 40,000 tons of bombs on Japanese cities in July; on the preceding Thursday, August 2, his pilots had dropped a single-day record total of 6632 tons.

The 13th U.S. Marines, one of the regiments of the 5th Marine Division, was now restaging in Hawaii. Pulled out of Iwo Jima in March, the division had been getting ready for the next job: the assault landing on Kyushu, southernmost of the Japanese home islands. Overall initial casualties of 100,000 seemed to the planners a conservative estimate.

Similarly, men in Pearl Harbor, Guam and Manila were putting the final touches on a plan called Olympic. This was to be the first assault on Japan and was intended to capture the southern portion of Kyushu, so that its airfields and harbors could be used for a final thrust at Tokyo a few months later. "Olympic" was on its way, approved by President Truman and the Joint Chiefs of Staff. The details were set down in more than 400 single-spaced pages of "top-secret operations." In all, three quarters of a million men would be involved.

In a radish field outside Tokyo, a crew of expert radiomen kept a round-the-clock watch over a room jammed with 181 powerful radio receivers. They were assigned to detect and record all radio signals emanating from U.S. transmitters. Now, early on August 6, they picked up a call sign they had first heard almost three weeks earlier. The monitors had located it on the island of Tinian, and as it was heard daily during late July they had tagged it New Task Company.

Now the signal came out of the air again—merely one more item to be logged and reported. The Japanese did not know that the "New Task Company" was the highly secret 509th Composite Group, whose ultimate mission would be to end the war by dropping the first atomic bomb.

Three hundred miles to the east, one of the most powerful striking forces ever assembled steamed into the morning sun. Twenty-four hours earlier, the U.S. Navy's 3d Fleet had been lunging toward prearranged targets in southern Japan. Now it had been ordered to turn around and run out to sea—and its admirals were baffled and angry.

The order, from Pacific Fleet Headquarters, read:

It is imperative that there be noninterference with the operations of the 509th Bomb [Composite] Group. It is accordingly directed that you send no planes over Kyushu or western Honshu until specifically authorized.

The Japanese Cabinet hoped to persuade the U.S.S.R., still neutral in the Pacific war, to act as intermediary in arranging a peace agreement. Foreign Minister Shigenori Togo had already ordered his Ambassador in Moscow, Naotake Sato, to raise the subject and to seek permission for a special Imperial convoy to come to the Russian capital.

Sato was a seasoned career diplomat. From the embassy in Moscow he could clearly see the hopelessness of his country's position. On July 1 he had advised his Government to end the war in any way possible, even unconditional surrender. Bluntly he pointed out that Japan, now alone and friendless, could look to no one for help or sympathy.

Sato's advice was sound, as both Togo and Prime Minister Kantaro Suzuki knew very well. But they also knew what Sato, long absent from home, could not know: while Japan was being torn apart by American bombs and naval gunfire, a desperate private struggle was also taking place.

From the day he took office in April 1945, Suzuki had been trying to arrange an end to the war. In this effort he had the backing of two other members of the Supreme War Council—Togo and Navy Minister Mitsumasa Yonai. But War Minister Korechika Anami and the chiefs of the Army and Navy General Staffs wanted to fight on. There was thus a three-to-three deadlock in the Council.

Emperor Hirohito wanted to end the war and had in fact been quietly sounding out the nation's senior statesmen. But, though deified by his subjects, he had no solid political power. He could influence individual leaders, but he could not dictate policy.

On June 18 a small break occurred in this stalemate: the Council agreed to propose, through neutral nations, that an effort be made to negotiate a peace. This could hardly be called a decision to surrender, but it was a beginning.

On the same day, in Washington, President Truman's inner council of war advisers also held a meeting, but with quite a different aim. At the end, the President put his stamp of approval on "Olympic." The invasion of Japan was scheduled for November.

In the United States, as in Japan, the search for peace was under way even as both sides braced for final combat. That same day Joseph C. Grew, Under Secretary of State, privately urged Truman to give Japan a chance to keep its Emperor if it capitulated, arguing that such an offer would greatly facilitate the surrender.

He suggested that the President issue a statement calling for Japanese surrender, but holding out the possibility that the Emperor might be allowed to remain in power. The proposal also had the support of Secretary of War Henry L. Stimson. Truman liked the idea, but wanted to hold it up until he could talk to the Allies at Potsdam.

Meanwhile, in Japan things were moving at last. The day after the Supreme Council's reversal, Togo asked ex-Prime Minister Koki Hirota to see Soviet Ambassador Jacob A. Malik in an effort to persuade Russia to act as broker in peace talks. He got no encouragement from the taciturn Russian.

The Suzuki Government did not know how little time was left. In Potsdam on July 24 Stimson conferred with Truman for fifteen minutes. He had heard from James F. Byrnes, Secretary of State, that it had been decided not to mention the Emperor specifically in the ultimatum approved by Truman and Churchill. The declaration would merely state that the final form of government in Japan was to be left up to the people.

One day later, in the most momentous decision he had to make as President, Truman approved an order to use the atomic bomb if the Japanese should refuse the Potsdam ultimatum. That order was put into writing in Washington, then flown across the Pacific to Tinian.

On July 26 the United States and Great Britain,

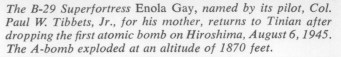

Albert Einstein, whose theories contributed greatly to the creation of the bomb, is seen here with J. Robert Oppenheimer, director of the nuclear research project at Los Alamos, New Mexico, where the first atomic bomb was built.

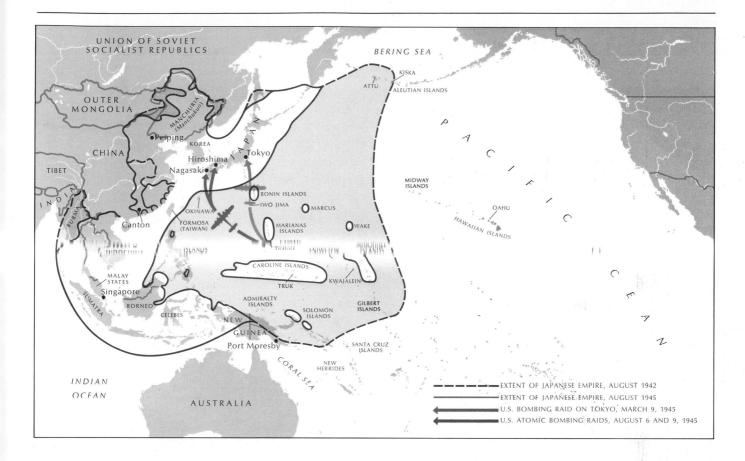

UNION OF SOVIET SOCIALIST REPUBLICS

BERING SEA

OUTER MONGOLIA

MANCHURIA (Manchukuo)

Peiping

KOREA

CHINA

TIBET

Hiroshima
Nagasaki
Tokyo
JAPAN

INDIA

BURMA

Canton

OKINAWA

FORMOSA (TAIWAN)

KISKA
ATTU
ALEUTIAN ISLANDS

PACIFIC

MIDWAY ISLANDS

OAHU
HAWAIIAN ISLANDS

BONIN ISLANDS
IWO JIMA
MARCUS

MARIANAS ISLANDS
WAKE

MALAY STATES

Singapore

SUMATRA

BORNEO

CELEBES

CAROLINE ISLANDS
TRUK

KWAJALEIN

ENIWETOK

OCEAN

ADMIRALTY ISLANDS

SOLOMON ISLANDS

GILBERT ISLANDS

NEW GUINEA
Port Moresby

CORAL SEA

NEW HEBRIDES

SANTA CRUZ ISLANDS

INDIAN OCEAN

AUSTRALIA

———— EXTENT OF JAPANESE EMPIRE, AUGUST 1942
———— EXTENT OF JAPANESE EMPIRE, AUGUST 1945
⟵ U.S. BOMBING RAID ON TOKYO, MARCH 9, 1945
⟵ U.S. ATOMIC BOMBING RAIDS, AUGUST 6 AND 9, 1945

END OF THE JAPANESE EMPIRE

By the end of 1944, the Allies had seized most of the island groups that shielded Japan from attack: New Guinea, the Admiralties and the Solomons, parts of the Marshalls, the Marianas, the Carolines and the Philippines.

Before invading Japan itself, the Allies hoped to smash her war machine and destroy her will to resist by massive bombing. Beginning on November 24, 1944, wave after wave of giant B-29 bombers roared westward from Saipan in the Marianas to make daylight raids on Japanese cities. The B-29 was capable of carrying upward of four tons of bombs and of flying at 38,000 feet at a speed of 350 miles per hour. It seemed the ideal aircraft for the six-

teen-hour, 3000-mile mission to Japan and back. Yet in the beginning the superbombers did little damage. High winds and cloud cover scattered bombs and hid targets. Engines were overstrained; planes ran out of gas.

In January 1945 Maj. Gen. Curtis E. LeMay took over the 21st Bomber Command in the Marianas. A tough veteran of bombing missions over Germany, he quickly saw what needed to be done. He ordered that the B-29's be stripped of their heavy armaments in order to make room for more bombs, that they set out at night and come in low over their targets to avoid enemy interception, and that they drop only fire bombs. On March 9, 325 B-29's took off for

Tokyo to test LeMay's theory, with the result that sixteen square miles of crowded slum dwellings were flattened.

From then until the war's end the Japanese night sky was filled with planes as U.S. bombers struck sixty-six cities. The conquest of Iwo Jima and Okinawa (February–July 1945) laid Japan open to the invasion that both she and the Allies dreaded.

But events elsewhere, outside the field of battle, made the costly invasion unnecessary. The first atomic bomb was tested at Alamogordo, New Mexico, on July 16, 1945. After two such bombs destroyed Hiroshima (August 6) and Nagasaki (August 9), Japan surrendered.

with China as a co-signer and Soviet Russia approving, issued the Potsdam Declaration. There was instant concern in Japan, as Stimson and Grew had warned there would be. The ultimatum made no mention of the future status of the Emperor. The Cabinet, after long discussion, decided not to answer, but to disregard, the ultimatum.

Truman received this advice shortly after he had been told by Stalin that the Japanese proposals for mediation were still thought by the Soviets to be "too vague" for consideration. Stalin's attitude, combined with the report that Japan had decided to ignore the Potsdam ultimatum, left the President convinced that he now had no choice but to let the order he had started toward Tinian on July 25 stand as written. And on that tiny island events were already in motion that would sweep away all subtleties of diplomacy and politics in a single overwhelming blow.

The steps which led to these events had their beginning six years earlier. In January 1939 American newspapers reported that German scientists had succeeded in splitting the atom. To the initiated it was obvious that Hitler might one day have a weapon of terrible proportions. Leo Szilard, a brilliant Hungarian who had fled to America, went with a fellow Hungarian physicist to see Albert Einstein in his summer home on Long Island. Representing a group of scientists, the two hoped to persuade Einstein to warn President Franklin D. Roosevelt of atomic progress in Germany. Einstein was not abreast of the latest atomic developments, but agreed to sign a letter to Roosevelt. The two Hungarians then enlisted the New York economist Alexander Sachs, who was an unofficial adviser to the President, to deliver the letter in person.

Sachs took the letter to the White House in October 1939. Roosevelt was obviously impressed, but seemed reluctant to add a major undertaking to the score of new defense projects just started. Having wangled an invitation to breakfast at the White House the next morning, Sachs spent a sleepless night at his hotel. How could he capture the President's imagination?

FDR was alone at breakfast in the second-floor study of the White House when Sachs called.

"What bright idea do you have this morning?" Roosevelt asked cheerily.

"Just a story," Sachs replied.

He told the President about one of Napoleon Bona-

parte's missed opportunities. Hungering to conquer England, Napoleon was frustrated by the erratic Channel tides, which blocked an invasion by French sailing vessels. The young American inventor Robert Fulton proposed that France construct a fleet of steamboats which could negotiate the Channel with ease. But Napoleon rudely brushed aside the idea as being visionary. How, asked Sachs, might the history of Europe have been changed if Napoleon had heeded Robert Fulton? And in the world of 1939, who would first sponsor the atomic scientists as they sought to pioneer a weapon of untold force?

Roosevelt summoned Brig. Gen. Edwin M. ("Pa") Watson, who served as a secretary, and handed him the relevant data. "Pa," he said, "this requires action." The United States Government had begun to take an interest in the atomic bomb.

Not until the summer of 1941, however, was a uranium section formed in the National Research Committee in Washington, and it was the end of 1941 before real Government muscle was put into it. Vannevar Bush, head of the Office of Scientific Research and Development, reported to the President on progress at that time and got a pledge of more men and money for the effort. On December 6 Bush announced the new all-out drive to his colleagues. It was none too soon. The next day Japanese carrier planes bombed Pearl Harbor.

What followed was an only-in-America miracle. A nation that had performed many industrial feats now undertook, in rigorous secrecy, the most prodigious scientific-industrial-military enterprise ever conceived by man. Years later many of those who had played leading roles in it still could not quite believe that it had really happened.

By the end of the summer of 1942, the Manhattan District Engineers, as the bomb's builders were originally designated, had been assigned AAA priority. Brigadier General Leslie R. Groves, a forty-six-year-old West Point engineer, took command of the operation that September and set out—without known tools, blueprints or materials—to transform an invisible compound of equations, theory and scientific faith into a practical military weapon. To do it, Groves drafted industrial magnates like so many privates, upstaged Congress, trusted no one and coaxed incredible sums of money from the U.S. Treasury.

The scale of Manhattan's operations was staggering.

Since nobody knew which of three different methods of separating U-235 was best, all three were initiated. All were costly, and all developed two new problems for every solution. Although less than 100 pounds of fissionable material was produced for the three bombs ready by the summer of 1945, at its peak the project and its allied payrolls reached 539,000 persons.

The Manhattan Project (as it was now known) became the melting pot of American science. Such homegrown zealots of the new physics as J. Robert Oppenheimer mingled with physicists from England's atomic program and with refugee scientists from Italy, Germany and Hungary. Doctors of Philosophy outnumbered the clerical help in some facilities, and Nobel Prize winners marched as privates in the ranks.

Within months of its establishment, Manhattan achieved a historic triumph. On the afternoon of December 2, 1942, in a squash court under the football stands at the University of Chicago, its scientists produced man's first controlled chain reaction. Their apparatus was crude, but before evening the physicists knew that the fission process they had created would someday make a weapon of untold power.

Still, there were stubborn practical problems. The scientists calculated that one pound of U-235 (about the size of a golf ball) would release energy equivalent to about 9000 tons of TNT. But a single pound of this bomb material by itself was too small to sustain a chain reaction. There had to be a certain amount, the so-called critical mass—its quantity was as yet unknown—before an explosion could develop. And the scientists had to keep the components of this mass separated enough so that it would be noncritical until the exact moment for firing. To solve these problems, the Manhattan Project built a bomb laboratory on an isolated mesa near Los Alamos, New Mexico, and Oppenheimer was appointed scientific director.

Security regulations at this plant, where the weapon itself was being designed and fabricated, were rigid. Mail was censored, telephone calls monitored, scientists shadowed from city to city when they left the laboratory. Precautions at other installations were only slightly less rigorous. No German or Japanese agent ever acquired significant atomic intelligence. Few Americans had any inkling of the revolutionary weapon being developed in their midst.

Meanwhile, to ensure that the as yet nonexistent A-bomb could actually be delivered to enemy targets,

1500 officers and men were gathered into the singular 509th Composite Group, the only complete do-it-yourself unit in the Air Force. Its men were all carefully hand-picked.

For the top job, Gen. Henry H. ("Hap") Arnold, chief of the Army Air Force, selected Col. Paul W. Tibbets, Jr., a handsome twenty-nine-year-old flier who appeared to be quietly dependable. He had been a crack bomber pilot in European combat.

Within an hour of receiving his assignment, Tibbets felt as though he had been set down on another planet. He was instructed in the mysteries of the split atom, told what we hoped from it militarily and learned that if an A-bomb was ever produced, he himself might pilot the plane that dropped the first one.

When Tibbets set out in a B-29 to pick a training field, his first stop was at Wendover, Utah. He looked no farther. Wendover was a barren expanse of desert 115 miles from Salt Lake City. Its broad, treeless flats and bright skies made it ideal for the unorthodox operations the new group would be practicing.

The 509th was different from the outset. Tibbets enjoined the top officers to secrecy without informing them what it was they weren't supposed to reveal. Flight operations were unlike anything ever seen by airmen. Bombing practice was constant from 30,000 feet, and each plane always dropped only one 10,000-pound bomb. Relentless emphasis was placed on visual bombing.

The reasons were plain to those initiated into Manhattan's secrets. When only one precious bomb, worth hundreds of millions of dollars, would be in the bomb bay, they simply could not afford to miss the target.

In the Manhattan Project the frantic effort to create an A-bomb never once flagged. By December 30, 1944, Major General Groves felt able to announce his timetable. "The first bomb should be ready about August 1, 1945," he wrote in a memorandum to the Chief of Staff, Gen. George C. Marshall. Since this would be too late to use the bomb against Germany, where the Nazi regime was already tottering toward collapse, Groves suggested that the Pacific Naval Command be alerted; the 509th would need a base from which it could reach Japan.

The island of Tinian in the American-held Marianas was selected for basing the 509th. A level limestone platform, about five miles wide in the middle and eleven miles long, the island made an ideal anchored aircraft carrier, and its very smallness adapted it to secrecy. Moreover, it had a network of good roads built by the Japanese, and its four-runway North Field had already been planned as the biggest bomber base in the world.

Late in April, Tibbets' men, who now had fifteen stripped-down B-29's, began moving overseas. Almost at once the 509th became the local curiosity. Tokyo Rose greeted its arrival by radio from Japan, but that was the last "official" news the other B-29 crews had of this strange outfit.

It was chiefly the 509th's flying that raised eyebrows among other B-29 crews. Never did Tibbets and his men participate in the mass raids or share the sight of empty bunks afterward. Instead, they flew solo missions, occasionally bombing a Japanese-held island, or making the round trip of almost 3000 miles to Japanese cities just to drop one bomb each—or so the rumor ran in Air Wing headquarters.

General Groves' timetable for the completed A-bomb—August 1—proved to be nearly correct. The place chosen for testing it was an arid expanse of land in New Mexico, fifty miles from Alamogordo; the time, 5:30 a.m. July 16.

On that date the Atomic Age opened with a flash that lighted the skies 250 miles away and brightened ground zero with the dazzle of many suns. Men who looked directly at it against orders were temporarily blinded. A giant sphere of fire laced with hues of deep purple and orange spread out for a mile. The earth shook. A blast of hot air rolled out in a wave. The 100-foot tower on which the bomb rested was vaporized. A column of white smoke shot straight up, then flowered into a mushroom that finally climbed to 40,000 feet. Miles away a blind woman cried out that she had seen a light.

A press release, prepared in advance, with a fake explanation for the unearthly eruption, was handed to newspapermen in Albuquerque:

An ammunition magazine exploded early today in a remote area of the Alamogordo Air Base reservation, producing a brilliant flash and blast which were reported to have been observed as far away as Gallup, 235 miles northwest.

The scientists were awestruck at their triumph. "The test was successful beyond our most optimistic hopes,"

Groves wrote in a confidential memorandum delivered by air courier to Secretary Stimson at Potsdam. The bomb had generated energy estimated as equaling 20,000 tons of TNT.

The decision to drop atomic bombs on Japan had been made with great reluctance after months of soul-searching. From the start some scientists had hoped that Manhattan's research would prove futile, and when the A-bomb was nevertheless produced many of them wrote impassioned memorandums and got up petitions asking that it not be used.

Even some war leaders made no effort to mask their repugnance toward the bomb. But most military chieftains believed the new bomb presented no ethical questions not found in TNT or the fire bomb.

Soon after Roosevelt's death in April 1945, Secretary Stimson urged the new President, Harry S Truman, to appoint a committee on certain phases of atomic policy. The Interim Committee, as it was called, consisted of eight men, and it had a four-man panel of scientific advisers.

The Committee's report to the White House recommended that the bomb be dropped on Japan as soon as possible, without specific warning. Truman had already come to the same conclusion independently, and it was now settled that we would use the bomb against the Japanese unless they surrendered first.

To make the maximum imprint, it was decided to explode the atomic weapon over a city hitherto relatively untouched by bombing. There were few such cities left in Japan by now, and the list submitted for consideration contained only four names: Kyoto, Kokura, Niigata and Hiroshima—Nagasaki was added at the last moment. Eventually the list of primary target cities was narrowed to one. On August 2 a top-secret field order was issued at Guam, stating that the bomb was to be dropped on August 6. Primary target: *Hiroshima urban industrial area.*

Hiroshima was known throughout Japan as a place where exceptionally beautiful willow trees grew. This big port and manufacturing city, now marked for death, had in 3½ years of war felt the concussion of only twelve enemy bombs. In spite of this, the city's

A mushroom cloud looms 40,000 feet over Nagasaki, August 9, 1945. More than 70,000 Japanese perished in this second atomic-bomb drop. The primary target, Kokura, was obscured by clouds, and an alternate city, Nagasaki, was chosen in its place.

After the holocaust: This photograph was taken a few hours after the first atomic bomb exploded over the center of Hiroshima. Dazed and disfigured victims are waiting to receive first aid. Many who managed to survive the blast died three or four weeks later.

people knew very well that the war was going badly.

Down by the docks, from which almost every Nipponese soldier who went to the southwestern Pacific fighting area had sailed, a deathlike quiet hung over the big embarkation facilities. Where the city in earlier years had bulged with as many as 100,000 troops en route to the front, it now held only one division, and that was preparing for defense, not attack. Including support troops, there were about 24,000 soldiers in Hiroshima. The once-busy harbor was almost dead.

Under military orders, the citizens of Hiroshima themselves did what the Americans had not done, and destroyed great chunks of their city. Almost 70,000

dwellings were demolished to make three broad firebreaks. Over 90,000 of the city's peak wartime population of 380,000 had been ordered to leave in five mass evacuations. The factories, warehouses and railway yards of Hiroshima were running hard, trying to turn out supplies and equipment for an army that would soon have to meet a terrible American onslaught on the home islands.

The average citizen in Hiroshima might know only that his rice ration was smaller, but the Japanese Cabinet knew more. An official study in June had predicted that minimum requirements for rice to support the people on a subsistence basis would outrun supplies by

14 million tons in 1945. The Cabinet knew, too, that the Armed Forces had been desperately short of fuel for almost a year.

The Japanese Army was making shell cases out of dull-gray substitute metals, for there was no more brass. Some regular military units were being issued bamboo spears. Every foot of shoreline was being prepared for defense; but in most cases this meant only barbed wire (there was little cement for fortifications), machine guns (there were almost no artillery pieces available) and caves in the hills (it was obvious the Americans could not be kept off the beaches). The Navy, not only short of fuel but also decimated by U.S. guns and bombs, had adopted the kamikaze tactics of the Air Force. In July 700 small craft, loaded with explosives and intended for one-way voyages only, were being prepared in southern Japanese harbors against the inevitable day when America's invasion fleet would appear over the horizon.

August 6, 1945, was little different in Hiroshima from previous Mondays. Busy with morning routines of one kind or another, most people paid little attention to the air-raid alert that sounded at 7:09 a.m. Those who looked up at the faint drone of engines found, if their eyes were sharp, a single B-29, flying very high. Probably it was a weather plane of the kind that often flew over in the morning. It crossed the city twice and then, at 7:25, flew out to sea. The warning system sounded the all clear at 7:31.

The single B-29 *was* a weather plane. Its name was *Straight Flush*. The order which sent it over Hiroshima was designated as Special Bombing Mission No. 13. Seven of Tibbets' fifteen B-29's had been assigned to this mission.

On August 4 the seven crews were summoned to the briefing hut, and U.S. Navy Capt. William S. Parsons, who was to arm the A-bomb, showed movies of the atomic test at Alamogordo. After viewing its chilling and awful majesty, every man there knew why the pilots had practiced steep breakaway turns at high altitudes. Parsons also warned pilots not to fly through the mushroom cloud because of the danger of radioactivity. He stated frankly that no one could be sure what would happen; even exploding at the planned altitude of 1850 feet, the bomb might crack the crust of the earth.

The next day, August 5, was a Sunday, hot with a glaring sun. At the 509th's bomb-assembly hut on Tinian, physicists, ordnance men, military police, security agents and Air Corps brass gathered to peer respectfully at the A-bomb as it swung from its chain hoist.

About fourteen feet long and five feet in diameter, the bomb weighed just under 10,000 pounds. The fissionable core was far less than .5 percent of this weight and was tucked away in the interior. A proximity fuse would be set for 1850 feet. When the falling projectile reached this altitude, the fuse would detonate an explosive charge which would shoot a small chunk of U-235 forward at a speed of 5000 feet per second until it collided with a larger chunk of U-235, a cup-shaped piece in the nose. At that instant the atomic explosion would occur.

Two special couriers had brought that vital, cup-shaped target to Tinian in a lead cylinder. Their orders had been explicit: if the ship sank—it was the heavy cruiser *Indianapolis*—the U-235 was to have the first motor launch or life raft. From San Francisco the cruiser had raced for Tinian, pausing only a few hours at Pearl Harbor to refuel, and had delivered the U-235 to the island on July 26. (Three days later the ill-starred *Indianapolis* was torpedoed and sank.) Three smaller chunks of U-235 had also been shipped to Tinian by air, each on a separate plane.

Around midnight the chaplain of the 509th said a brief prayer for the mission. Then the seven crews had breakfast, and at 1:37 a.m. the three weather planes took off for Hiroshima, Kokura and Nagasaki, respectively. (If Hiroshima was fogged over, the other two cities would be alternate targets.)

A little over an hour later—the time was 2:45 a.m. August 6—Tibbets' heavily loaded plane, the *Enola Gay* (named for his mother), rolled down the coral runway. It was followed at two-minute intervals by two other B-29's—one to measure blast and radiation, one to take photographs. Another B-29, which would stand by to transfer the bomb at Iwo Jima and carry on in case the *Gay* developed trouble, had left earlier. Special Bombing Mission No. 13 was now on the way.

As it climbed above the Pacific with a sharp upward thrust, the *Enola Gay* shuddered with the strain of the lift. The crew breathed easier when Tibbets had gained sufficient altitude to swing left and seek his compass heading for Iwo, 622 miles to the north. At 4000 feet Tibbets throttled back to cruising speed. Parsons knocked out a cold pipe, lowered himself into

the forward bomb bay and began completing the final assembly. It took only about twenty-five minutes.

Aside from its revolutionary nuclear character, the weapon, now fully armed and ready to go, was a maze of electronic ingenuity. When it was dropped, a series of intricate timers would shut off for the first fifteen seconds, so that the device could not possibly detonate during that interval. Another cluster of instruments prevented the bomb from exploding above 10,000 feet. After fifteen seconds of fall, barometric gauges would alert the radio proximity fuses, set to trigger the explosion at 1850 feet. All these devices had to operate within the estimated forty-three seconds from the moment of bomb release to the instant of explosion.

At 4:55, well after daylight, the *Enola Gay* rendezvoused over Iwo Jima with the two following B-29's that were to accompany her. Then in a wide V formation, maintaining strict radio silence, the three B-29's headed northwest toward the Japanese island of Shikoku.

Presently Tibbets called all hands over the intercom. From here on in, he said, every man must be at his station. And when they reached the coast of Japan, all intercom conversation would be recorded.

"This is for history," said Tibbets, "so watch your language. We're carrying the first atomic bomb." It was the first time most of the crew had heard the phrase.

At 7:09, far ahead of them, the weather plane *Straight Flush* approached the outskirts of Hiroshima. A solid undercast covered Japan as far as the eye could see. Minutes later, however, a view of the entire city opened up. At the point where the *Enola Gay* was scheduled to release its cargo, the city was so clear below that the crew could see patches of green grass. A ten-mile hole in an otherwise solid cloud bank marked Hiroshima as though fate had driven a spike into the city's heart.

At 7:25 the *Straight Flush* radioed its report, which ended, "Advice: bomb primary." At 7:50 the *Enola Gay* passed over the edge of Shikoku Island. Crew members pulled on their flak suits. The monitoring console showed all the bomb's electrical circuits in

perfect order, with no evidence of Japanese jamming. By 8:09 the outlines of Hiroshima were in view through an opening in the clouds. Tibbets announced, "When you hear the signal, pull on your goggles until after the flash." All hands had specially manufactured goggles in which quinine crystals would admit only one color, purple, through the lenses.

As the *Enola Gay* flew west at 31,600 feet, Hiroshima lay open and bare beneath the plane. Through the bombsight it unrolled in a pattern familiar to bombardier Maj. Thomas W. Ferebee. It could have been the target photograph he had studied a dozen times. The aiming point, the center of a main bridge over the Ota River's main stream, lay immediately in the crosshairs.

"I've got it," Ferebee said and started the automatic synchronization for the final minute of the bomb run. Forty-five seconds later he turned on the radio tone signal which meant that in fifteen seconds the bomb would drop.

At 8:15 plus 17 seconds the bomb-bay doors sprang open and the aircraft lurched up, suddenly 10,000 pounds lighter. Tibbets nosed the plane over to the right in a 60° bank and tight turn of 158°. The fuselage screamed with the violence of the maneuver.

Hastily instructing Bob Caron, the tail gunner, to tell everyone what he saw, Tibbets began measuring the forty-three seconds mentally. Each moment now seemed endless.

First Lieutenant Morris R. Jeppson, in charge of the console which had been monitoring the bomb's circuits, had started his own count and was now nearing the end: 40 . . . 41 . . . 42 . . . Jeppson stopped the count. The thought flashed through his brain, "It's a dud."

At that instant the world went purple in a flash before Caron's eyes. His eyelids shut involuntarily behind his goggles. "I must be blinded," he thought. He was too stunned at first to report on the intercom.

Caron had been looking at an explosion which, in a slice of time too small for any stopwatch to measure, had become a ball of fire 1800 feet across, with a temperature at its center of 100 million degrees.

Hiroshima was already a missing city.

The sounding of the all-clear signal in Hiroshima at 7:31 a.m. on August 6 made little change in the tempo of the city. Most people had been too busy or too lazy to pay much attention to the alert. At 8:15 the few people in Hiroshima who caught sight of a new small

Ruins of Hiroshima, after the atomic bomb had been dropped on the city. Such devastation—and that suffered by Nagasaki three days later—left Emperor Hirohito no choice but to surrender. "I cannot bear," he said, "to see my innocent people suffer any longer."

formation of planes noticed that three parachutes blossomed from one of them. These had been dropped from the blast- and radiation-measuring plane; they supported instruments to broadcast such measurements. Seeing the parachutes, some people cheered, thinking the enemy planes were in trouble.

For three quarters of a minute there was nothing but the parachutes in the sky over the city. Then suddenly, without a sound, there was no sky left over Hiroshima.

For those who survived to recall it, the first instant of the atomic explosion was pure light, blinding, intense, but of awesome beauty and variety. One witness described a flash that turned from white to pink and then to blue as it rose and blossomed. Others seemed to see five or six bright colors. Some saw merely flashes of gold in a white light that reminded them—this was perhaps the most common description—of a huge photographic flashbulb exploding over the city. The sole impression was visual. If there was sound, no one heard it.

Thousands did not see anything at all. They were simply incinerated where they stood by the radiant heat that turned central Hiroshima into a gigantic oven. Thousands of others survived for perhaps a second or two, only to be shredded by the scattered window glass that flew before the blast waves, or crushed underneath walls, beams, bricks or other solid objects.

Several factors combined to produce more devastation than the nuclear experts had predicted. First, the precision of the drop. For Major Ferebee's aim was nearly perfect. The bomb was detonated only a little more than 200 yards from the designated aiming point.

Then, the time of the explosion. All over Hiroshima, thousands of charcoal braziers were full of hot coals for the breakfast cooking. Almost every stove, knocked over by the massive blast waves, became a torch to fire the wood-and-paper houses. Oppenheimer had assumed that most people would be in air-raid shelters and had estimated 20,000 casualties. But there had been no specific alert, and most people were on their way to work. Thus there were more than 70,000 casualties.

The initial flash spawned a succession of calamities. First came heat. It lasted only an instant but was so intense that it melted roof tiles, fused the quartz crystals in granite blocks, charred the exposed sides of telephone poles for almost two miles, and destroyed nearby humans so thoroughly that nothing remained except the outline of their shadows, burned into asphalt pavements or stone walls.

At 2½ miles from ground zero, the heat still burned skin. At 1½ miles a printed page exposed to the heat rays had the black letters burned completely out of the white paper. Hundreds of women had the darker parts of their clothing burned out while lighter shades remained unscorched, leaving the skin underneath etched with the flower patterns of their kimonos.

After the heat came the blast, sweeping outward from the fireball with the force of a 500-mile-an-hour wind. Only objects which offered a minimum of surface resistance—handrails on bridges, pipes, utility poles—withstood its force. The walls of a few office buildings, which had been especially constructed to resist earthquakes, remained standing. But they enclosed only wreckage. Between them, blast and fire destroyed every single building within an area of almost five square miles.

A few minutes after the explosion, a strange rain began to fall. The raindrops were as big as marbles—and they were black. This frightening phenomenon resulted from the vaporization of moisture in the fireball and condensation in the cloud that spouted up from it. There was not enough of this black rain to put out the fires, but enough to heighten the panic.

After the rain came a wind, the great fire wind which blew back in toward the center of the catastrophe, increasing in force as the air over Hiroshima grew hotter because of the great fires. The wind blew so hard that it uprooted huge trees in the parks where survivors were collecting. It whipped up high waves on the rivers and drowned many who had gone into the water to escape from the heat and flames.

Tibbets had been warned that a shock wave would probably hit the plane about a minute after the bomb exploded. Anticipating this, he pointed the nose upward to gain altitude and lose speed—a tactic which aerodynamics experts calculated would lessen the impact.

From the rear turret Caron presently saw a shimmering line rushing toward the plane. It resembled a heat wave as seen far down an asphalt highway, but it extended in a long curve like a ripple from a rock tossed in a pond. It was visible because the heavy compression of air was followed by a vacuum in which vapor condensed instantaneously, forming a belt of speeding mist. The shock wave raced at the plane at a speed of twelve miles a minute. It felt as though a large antiaircraft shell had burst twenty feet from the plane.

"Here comes another one," Caron warned on the intercom from his rear vantage point.

A reflection of the blast from the ground, this second shock wave hit them; and then the peril was over. In formation with the two accompanying planes, the *Enola Gay* now flew south along the outskirts of Hiroshima, and for the first time the crew observed what they had done.

Dust boiled up from the entire city and long swirling gray shafts rushed toward the center. A column of white smoke, incredibly tidy in form, stood straight up. At the base it was flecked with red and orange and at the top it spilled into an almost perfect mushroom. Within minutes the cloud mushroom pushed upward almost four miles.

Conflicting emotions jostled the minds of the airmen over the ruined city. Some were elated that the bomb had worked and hoped it would end the war. Some were torn between pride and dismay. Some simply could not relate what they saw to reality.

Captain Robert A. Lewis, Tibbets' copilot, was one of the first to speak. "My God," he said, "what have we done?"

Tibbets ordered a radio message sent in the clear, notifying Tinian that the *Enola Gay* had bombed its primary target visually with good results; no fighters, no flak. Then, as they settled down to the long flight back to Tinian, the report was elaborated in code: "Clear-cut, successful in all respects. Visible effect greater than Trinity [the New Mexico test]."

When the *Enola Gay* returned, she had barely taxied to her stand, before 200 officers and enlisted men crowded under her wings. The greeting delegation included Gen. Carl ("Tooey") Spaatz, new Strategic Bombing Force boss, Lt. Gen. Nathan F. Twining, new chief of the Marianas Air Force, Brig. Gen. John Davies, 313th Wing Commander—more generals and admirals than the plane's crew had ever seen.

"Attention to orders!" barked General Davies.

Spaatz stepped forward and pinned the Distinguished Service Cross on the breast of Tibbets' dirty flight overalls. Tibbets, his eyes red-rimmed from lack of sleep, was caught off guard. Spaatz shook his hand and the crowd milled around again. Later, every air-

man participating in the mission was also decorated.

A moment after 8:16 a.m., the Tokyo control operator of the Japanese Broadcasting Corporation noticed that his telephone line to the radio station in Hiroshima had gone dead. He tried to reestablish his connection but found he could not get a call through to the city.

Twenty minutes later the men in the railroad-signal center in Tokyo realized that the main-line telegraph had stopped working. The break seemed to be just north of Hiroshima. Reports began to come in from stations near Hiroshima that there had been some kind of an explosion in the city. It was nearly ten o'clock when the Tokyo newspaper *Asahi* learned that Hiroshima had almost completely collapsed as the result of bombing by enemy planes.

At about the same time, Maj. Tosaku Hirano, a staff officer of II Army Corps, was in General Headquarters (GHQ) in Tokyo. He had come up from Hiroshima a week earlier and had been scheduled to fly back on Sunday. Now his telephone rang. It was a call from Central Headquarters in Osaka, an installation under the control of II Army Corps in Hiroshima, reporting that its communications to Hiroshima had failed.

Tokyo GHQ tried several times to raise the Hiroshima communications center but could not get through. Then, shortly after 1 p.m., GHQ finally heard from II Army Corps. The message was short but stunning: "Hiroshima has been annihilated by one bomb, and fires are spreading." This flash came from the Army shipping depot on the Hiroshima waterfront, which was outside the blast area.

Reports continued to trickle in. By the middle of the afternoon, the Army knew that only three enemy planes had been over Hiroshima when the bomb exploded. It had been told that two of these did not drop any bombs. In midafternoon the managing editors of the five big Tokyo newspapers were called to the office of the Government Information and Intelligence Agency. An Army press officer addressed the group: "We believe that the bomb dropped on Hiroshima is different from an ordinary one. We intend to make some announcement when proper information has been obtained. Until then, run the story in an obscure place in your papers and as one no different from the report of an ordinary air raid."

In other words, the lid was on. The Army already had a strong suspicion that the Hiroshima bomb might be an atomic weapon. But, anxious to keep the war going so that it could fight a showdown, hand-to-hand battle with the Americans on Japanese soil, it was determined to withhold the news from the Japanese people as long as it could.

The truth about Hiroshima was soon to be revealed, however. In Saitama prefecture north of Tokyo, Domei, the quasi-Governmental news agency, operated a big monitoring station where nearly fifty workers, many of them nisei girls born in the United States, listened to American broadcasts. About 1 a.m. on August 7 (noon on the 6th in Washington, D.C.), Hideo Kinoshita, chief of the monitoring room, was informed that U.S. stations were all broadcasting a statement by President Truman describing the weapon dropped on Hiroshima as an atomic bomb.

The news was quickly transmitted to Prime Minister Suzuki. He knew immediately, he said later, ". . . that if the announcement were true, no country could carry on a war. . . . The chance had come to end the war. It was not necessary to blame the military side, the manufacturing people or anyone else—just the atomic bomb. It was a good excuse."

The Army, however, was unwilling to accept this attitude. The generals, sitting in an emergency Cabinet meeting on August 7, argued that the bomb was not atomic but merely a huge conventional projectile. They flatly refused Foreign Minister Togo's proposal to take up for immediate consideration the possibility of surrender on the terms of the Potsdam ultimatum, and insisted on keeping the Truman atomic statement from the Japanese people until the Army could conduct an investigation on the ground at Hiroshima.

The military had already started such a check. Major Hirano, whose desire to spend a couple of extra nights in Tokyo had saved his life, called Yoshio Nishina, the nation's ranking nuclear scientist. He told Nishina of the Truman claims and asked him to fly to Hiroshima to investigate the matter.

It was almost seven in the evening when Hirano's little plane came down over Hiroshima. It was still light, however, so he got the full picture with shocking suddenness. Long before they began their formal investigation the next morning, the men from Tokyo knew the truth. Hirano, in fact, had known it the moment he caught sight of what was left of Hiroshima.

In Washington it was agreed that news of the atomic strike should be released to the general public at once.

Correspondents immediately went to work on what they recognized as one of the greatest stories of all time. As official bulletins about the bomb were released, the news startled the entire world. The first official communiqué came from the White House. After briefly describing the nature and power of the weapon, the dispatch continued:

> It was to spare the Japanese people from utter destruction that the ultimatum of July 26 was issued at Potsdam. Their leaders promptly rejected that ultimatum. If they do not now accept our terms, they may expect a rain of ruin from the air the like of which has never been seen.

To speed the Empire's surrender, Washington decided to launch an intensive propaganda campaign, dropping 16 million leaflets on forty-seven Japanese cities. They also moved up a scheduled second atomic strike from August 11 to August 9, reasoning that a swift one-two sequence would convince Japanese leaders that Hiroshima was not some freak of nature.

The second atomic-bomb flight was jinxed from the start and, in the end, almost nothing about it went right. The bomb was plutonium, the type that had been exploded in New Mexico. (The Hiroshima bomb had been uranium, a type hitherto untested.) The weapon was flown by Maj. Charles W. Sweeney in a plane not his own. The primary target, Kokura, was so closed in that three passes over the city failed to disclose the smallest hole. When Sweeney flew on to Nagasaki, the alternate target, it, too, was hidden by clouds. Commander Fred Ashworth, the weaponeer aboard the plane, ordered a radar drop if necessary. The entire bomb run was made by radar, and although the bombardier found a hole at the last minute, he missed the aiming point by three miles. Even so, the devastation was enormous.

On the following day the Japanese Cabinet agreed to send a message through Switzerland accepting the terms of the Potsdam ultimatum, with the "understanding" that the Emperor would remain in power. Except for the formalities, the war was over.

In the shadow of Tokyo, the Pacific war ends. As Allied soldiers and sailors look on, Japanese Foreign Minister Mamoru Shigemitsu signs the formal surrender documents on board the U.S. battleship Missouri, *anchored in Tokyo Bay. World War II officially came to an end at 9:04 a.m. on September 2, 1945.*

Chronology: Important Dates of World War II

1939

Sept. 1—Germans invade Poland in first Nazi blitzkrieg ("lightning war").

Sept. 3—Britain and France declare war on Germany.

Sept. 17—Soviet Russia, under a secret understanding with Germany, invades Poland from the east.

Sept. 27—Poland surrenders unconditionally to the Germans.

Nov. 30—Soviet Armed Forces invade Finland and bomb the capital, Helsinki.

1940

March 12—Peace treaty is signed in Moscow between Soviet Russia and Finland, ceding territory to Russia.

April 9—Germans invade Denmark and Norway. Denmark offers no resistance, but Norway fights.

May 10—Germans smash into the Netherlands, Belgium and Luxembourg.

Winston Churchill becomes British Prime Minister after the resignation of Neville Chamberlain.

May 14—Germans cross the French frontier. The Armed Forces of the Netherlands capitulate.

May 28—Belgian Army surrenders, by order of King Leopold III.

May 26–June 4—Some 340,000 British, French and other Allied troops are dramatically evacuated across the English Channel, through the Dunkirk beachhead.

June 10—Italy declares war on Britain and France.

June 14—Hitler's forces enter undefended Paris.

June 16—Marshal Henri Philippe Pétain becomes Premier of France when Paul Reynaud resigns.

June 22—France and Germany sign an armistice at Compiègne, on terms dictated by the Nazi conquerors.

July 10—First large-scale German attack on the United Kingdom marks the beginning of the Battle of Britain.

Sept. 7—London suffers its first air blitz.

Sept. 27—Japan joins the Rome-Berlin Axis in the Tripartite Pact for mutual defense.

Dec. 15—British drive the Italian Army out of Egypt.

1941

Jan. 10—Lend-Lease bill introduced in U.S. Congress, touching off a great debate between isolationists and interventionists.

March 11—U.S. Congress passes Lend-Lease Act, giving President power to provide all-out aid to Britain and other enemies of Axis powers.

March 27—Military leaders in Yugoslavia overthrow the government of Prince Regent Paul and put Peter II in power, to prevent their country from joining the Axis.

March 28—British fleet wins a decisive battle with the Italian Navy at Cape Matapan, gaining supremacy in the Mediterranean.

March 30—Hitler's *Afrika Korps* launches a counteroffensive in North Africa.

April 6—Nazi forces invade Greece and Yugoslavia.

April 18—Yugoslav Army surrenders to the Germans, but guerrilla resistance continues.

May 10—Rudolf Hess, Deputy Fuehrer, parachutes into Scotland on his own peace mission to Britain.

May 20—Germans invade British-held island of Crete in eastern Mediterranean.

May 27—German battleship *Bismarck* is sunk in North Atlantic by British.

June 1—British surrender Crete.

June 14—President Franklin D. Roosevelt freezes Axis assets in United States; State Department orders closing of all German consular and propaganda offices.

June 22—Germany declares war on the Soviet Union; launches invasion on a 1000-mile front from the Baltic to the Black Sea.

July 26—Roosevelt orders freezing of all Japanese assets in the United States and discontinuing trade with Japan.

Aug. 9–14—Churchill and Roosevelt meet in secret conference at sea off Newfoundland and issue statement of common war aims known as the Atlantic Charter.

Sept. 8—Germans complete land encirclement of Leningrad, starting a 900-day siege of the city.

Sept. 19—Nazis occupy Kiev, capital of Soviet Ukraine.

Oct. 17—General Hideki Tojo, war minister and leader of military extremists, becomes Prime Minister of Japan.

Oct. 31—U.S. destroyer *Reuben James,* on convoy duty with arms shipments, sunk by a German submarine, with loss of 115 lives.

Nov. 14—Saburo Kurusu, special envoy from Tokyo, arrives in the United States to discuss the Japanese-American crisis.

Nov. 18—British Eighth Army in North Africa begins desert offensive in Libya.

Dec. 7—At 7:55 a.m. (Hawaiian time), Japan unleashes surprise air attack on Pearl Harbor, imposing immense damage on U.S. naval and military forces. Tokyo declares war on the United States and Britain.

Dec. 8—U.S. Congress adopts declaration of war against Japan; Churchill informs Parliament that Britain is at war with Japan.

Japanese forces invade Thailand and Malaya.

Japan makes first landings and massive air attacks on Philippines. Defending forces are under command of Gen. Douglas MacArthur.

Dec. 10—British warships *Prince of Wales* and *Repulse* are sunk by Japanese air attacks off Malayan coast.

Dec. 11—Germany and Italy declare war on the United States. Congress recognizes existence of state of war with both countries.

Dec. 13—Hungary and Bulgaria declare war on the United States.

Dec. 22—Churchill arrives in Washington for conference with Roosevelt.

Dec. 25—British colony of Hong Kong surrenders to Japan.

1942

Jan. 1—Twenty-six countries sign the Declaration of the United Nations, forming a great coalition against the Axis.

Jan. 2—Japanese take over Manila, as MacArthur's forces retire to Bataan Peninsula.

Jan. 11—Japanese invade Netherlands East Indies.

Feb. 15—General Tomoyuki Yamashita receives the surrender of Singapore from British Gen. Arthur E. Percival.

Feb. 27–March 1—Small Allied fleet under Dutch command destroyed in Battle of the Java Sea.

March 7—British evacuate Rangoon, capital and main port of Burma.

March 9—Java is unconditionally surrendered to Japanese by Dutch, British and American defenders.

April 9—U.S. forces on Bataan surrender to Japanese. General Jonathan M. Wainwright retreats to Corregidor with small group.

April 18—U.S. Army planes, commanded by Col. James H. Doolittle, carry out bombing raid on Tokyo.

May 4–8—Both Americans and Japanese claim victory in the Battle of the Coral Sea; aircraft carrier U.S.S. *Lexington* is sunk.

May 6—General Wainwright surrenders Corregidor to the Japanese.

June 3–6—Japanese planes attack Midway Islands, lose heavily in the great air and sea Battle of Midway.

June 21—German Gen. Erwin Rommel captures Tobruk in North Africa.

June 25—Lieutenant General Dwight D. Eisenhower is appointed commander of U.S. forces in European theater.

July 1—Sevastopol, main Russian stronghold on Black Sea, falls to German-Rumanian forces after twenty-five-day siege.

Aug. 7—U.S. marines land on Guadalcanal in Solomon Islands.

Aug. 19—British and Canadian Commandos raid Dieppe, on French coast of English Channel, suffering heavy losses.

Aug. 31—British, led by Lt. Gen. Bernard L. Montgomery, defeat Rommel's *Afrika Korps* in the Battle of Alam Halfa in Egypt.

Nov. 5—Rommel's forces, beaten at the Battle of Alamein, begin retreat to Tunisia.

Nov. 8—Troops of Allied Army, Navy and Air Force, with Eisenhower in overall command, land in North Africa.

Nov. 11—Nazis invade the unoccupied part of France.

Nov. 13—British retake Tobruk from the Germans.

Nov. 19–22—In the Battle of Stalingrad, Soviet forces, commanded by Gen. Georgi K. Zhukov, begin a counteroffensive.

1943

Jan. 14–24—Roosevelt, Churchill and military leaders hold Casablanca Conference.

Jan. 30—British Air Force makes first daylight bombing raid on Berlin.

Feb. 2—Battle of Stalingrad ends when exhausted German troops surrender; Gen. Friedrich von Paulus had been taken prisoner two days earlier.

Feb. 7—Japanese evacuate Guadalcanal, ending six months' resistance.

March 2–4—Battle of the Bismarck Sea is fought off the New Guinea coast; large portion of the Japanese fleet is destroyed.

May 11—U.S. forces land on Attu in Aleutian Islands.

May 12—Organized Axis resistance ends in Tunisia, marking Allied victory in all of North Africa. Rommel flees to Germany.

July 9–10—Allied forces, under the overall command of Eisenhower, invade Sicily.

July 25—Mussolini resigns as Italian Premier and is replaced by Marshal Pietro Badoglio.

Aug. 1—Rumanian oil fields in Ploesti are bombed by U.S. Liberator planes.

Aug. 17—Conquest of Sicily is completed by the Allies.

Sept. 3—Allies invade southern Italy across Strait of Messina.

Sept. 8—Italy announces its surrender to the Allies.

Sept. 10—Germans shell and seize Rome. Italian Navy is turned over to the Allies.

Oct. 1—U.S. Fifth Army captures Naples.

Oct. 13—Italy declares war on Germany.

Oct. 19–Nov. 1—Foreign Ministers of leading members of United Nations hold a conference in Moscow; Secretary of State Cordell Hull represents the United States.

Nov. 1—American troops land on Bougainville in the Solomon Islands.

Nov. 6—Russians recapture Kiev from the Germans.

Nov. 20—American forces land on Tarawa and Makin in the Gilbert Islands.

Nov. 23–26—First Cairo Conference is held in Egyptian capital by Roosevelt, Churchill and Chiang Kai-shek.

Nov. 28–Dec. 1—Conference at Teheran, Iran, of "Big Three": Roosevelt, Churchill and Stalin.

Dec. 24—Eisenhower appointed Supreme Commander of Allied Expeditionary Forces, to plan and direct the invasion of Europe.

Dec. 26—German battleship *Scharnhorst* sunk by British off North Cape.

1944

Jan. 22—American and British troops land behind German lines at Anzio, Italy.

Feb. 2—Soviet Army enters Estonia and launches offensive against Latvia.

U.S. marines capture Roi-Namur in the Marshalls; take Kwajalein Island five days later.

Feb. 21—Hideki Tojo, named chief of Japanese Army General Staff, becomes military dictator.

March 20—Nazi forces invade Hungary to meet threat to Balkans.

April 5—General Charles de Gaulle becomes head of the French Provisional Government in London.

April 22—MacArthur leads American landings at Hollandia, Netherlands New Guinea.

May 9—Soviet forces recapture naval base of Sevastopol.

May 18—Nazis evacuate Cassino monastery, ending three-month siege.

May 23—Allies unleash offensive from Anzio, Italy, beachhead.

May 25—Germans yield entire coastline from Anzio to Terracina.

June 4—Anglo-American troops take Rome, left undamaged by the Germans.

June 6—D day. Allies, in vast strength, with Eisenhower in supreme command, invade Normandy for long-planned offensive against Hitler's Fortress Europe.

June 13—First German V-1 rockets attack England.

June 14—General de Gaulle, visiting liberated Normandy coast, returns to France for the first time in four years.

June 15—U.S. Superfortresses (B-29's) make first raids on Japan.

June 19—Carrier-borne U.S. aircraft attack the Japanese fleet between Luzon in Philippines and the Marianas, in the Battle of the Philippine Sea.

June 21—Okinawa falls to Americans, as organized Japanese resistance ends.

July 9—American forces take Saipan, in Marianas, after twenty-five-day struggle.

July 11—Red Army penetrates borders of Latvia and Lithuania.

July 18—British Second Army breaks through German lines at Caen, France.

July 20—Hitler is slightly wounded in bomb attempt on his life at Rastenburg, his headquarters in East Prussia; plot is a failure.

July 21—U.S. marines and infantry establish beachheads on Guam.

July 26—American forces make breakthrough west of St.-Lô in France.

Aug. 10—Americans complete conquest of Guam after three-week battle.

Aug. 11—Nazis abandon Florence, undamaged, as Allies close in on the historic city.

Aug. 15—Allied troops invade southern France between Cannes and Toulon.

Aug. 21—U.S. armored columns reach the Seine River to the north and south of Paris.

Aug. 23—Rumania surrenders to Russians and joins the Allies.

Aug. 25—Paris liberated; German commandant surrenders to Gen. Jacques LeClerc.

Aug. 27—General Eisenhower enters Paris with Lt. Gen. Omar N. Bradley.

Sept. 3—British Second Army, under Lt. Gen. Sir Miles C. Dempsey, liberates Brussels, Belgian capital.

Sept. 4—Armistice declared between Finland and Soviet Russia.

Sept. 5—Soviet Russia declares war on Bulgaria.

Sept. 8—First German V-2 rockets land on London.

Sept. 9—Bulgaria signs armistice with the Soviet Union.

Sept. 10—Roosevelt and Churchill meet in Quebec, their second conference in that city, ninth conference during war.

Sept. 17—Allied airborne troops land deep in the Netherlands.

Sept. 24—Russian Army advances twenty miles into Czechoslovakia from Poland.

Oct. 3—Warsaw Resistance Army under Gen. Tadeusz Bor-Komorowski surrenders to Germans after two months' struggle.

Oct. 20—U.S. forces land on Leyte, in central Philippines.

Oct. 23–26—Battle of Leyte Gulf; Japanese fleet suffers heavy losses; U.S. carrier *Princeton* sunk.

Nov. 6—Stalin renounces neutrality pact with Japan.

Nov. 7—Roosevelt elected to fourth term as President.

Nov. 12—German battleship *Tirpitz* sunk by Royal Air Force off Tromso, Norway.

Nov. 24—U.S. B-29's, based on Saipan, bomb Tokyo.

Dec. 16—Germans launch massive counteroffensive in Ardennes, known as the Battle of the Bulge.

Dec. 26—U.S. forces at Bastogne, a key point in the Battle of Bulge, commanded by Brig. Gen. Anthony C. McAuliffe, are relieved by Allied spearhead from the south.

1945

Jan. 9—MacArthur's forces land on Luzon at Lingayen Gulf, 100 miles north of Manila.

Jan. 17—Soviet Army captures Warsaw, capital of Poland.

Jan. 20—Provisional Government of Hungary signs armistice with Allies.

Jan. 27—Memel, Lithuania, liberated; country entirely under control of Soviet Army.

Jan. 31—Churchill and Roosevelt meet at British island of Malta, in prelude to Yalta Conference.

Feb. 3—U.S. troops enter Manila.

Feb. 4–11—Roosevelt, Churchill and Stalin hold Yalta Conference, plan occupation of Germany and other liberated countries in eastern Europe.

Feb. 19—U.S. marines land on Iwo Jima, island 750 miles from Tokyo.

Feb. 23—Marines capture Mount Suribachi on Iwo Jima.

March 4—Finland declares war on Germany, postdating it to September 15, 1944.

March 7—U.S. First Army crosses Ludendorff Bridge at Remagen on the Rhine. Cologne falls to Allies.

March 9—Biggest B-29 bombing of Tokyo flattens sixteen square miles of city and kills 100,000.

March 26—Iwo Jima secured.

April 1—American forces invade Okinawa, 340 miles south of Japan.

April 7—Baron Kantaro Suzuki becomes Japan's Prime Minister in shake-up.

April 12—President Roosevelt dies; is succeeded by Harry S Truman.

April 13—Vienna falls to the Russians.

April 16—Soviet Army begins its final push toward Berlin on forty-five-mile front.

April 25—American and Soviet forces meet in ceremonial juncture near Torgau on the Elbe River.

April 28—Mussolini, his mistress and sixteen Fascist henchmen are assassinated in the village of Giulino di Messegra on Lake Como.

April 30—Adolf Hitler commits suicide in bunker underneath Reich Chancellery in Berlin; Soviet Russian flag is raised on Berlin Reichstag; Americans free 33,000 inmates of Dachau concentration camp.

May 2—Berlin falls to Russia; German troops in northern Italy surrender.

May 3—Rangoon, Burma port, recaptured by British.

May 7—Germany surrenders unconditionally to Allies and Russia in ceremony at Rheims, France.

May 8—V-E (Victory in Europe) Day celebrated by U.S. and Allied nations.

May 9—Ratification of surrender signed in Berlin by Marshal Zhukov for the Soviet Union and Field Marshal Wilhelm Keitel for Germany.

June 5—Four Powers (United States, Britain, Soviet Union, France) sign declaration of German defeat; they assume supreme power in Germany.

June 21—Battle of Okinawa ends with complete victory for the United States.

June 26—Representatives of fifty nations in San Francisco sign World Security Charter establishing United Nations.

July 4—General MacArthur announces liberation of all the Philippines.

July 5—Churchill is defeated in general election; Labour Party, led by Clement Attlee, gains power.

July 16—First atom bomb tested successfully at Alamogordo, New Mexico.

July 17—Potsdam Conference begins in Germany, attended by Truman, Churchill (later replaced by Attlee) and Stalin.

Aug. 2—Potsdam Declaration, imposing a hard peace on Germany, is made public.

Aug. 6—U.S. atom bomb is dropped on Hiroshima, virtually wiping out the Japanese city.

Aug. 8—Soviet Russia declares war on Japan; invades Manchuria.

Aug. 9—Atom bomb is dropped on Nagasaki, Japan.

Aug. 14—Japan surrenders unconditionally; Emperor Hirohito announces defeat to his people.

Sept. 2—Japanese Foreign Minister Mamoru Shigemitsu and military leaders sign surrender terms on U.S.S. *Missouri* in Tokyo Bay.

Acknowledgments

I LED THE ATTACK ON PEARL HARBOR, by Capt. Mitsuo Fuchida, from United States Naval Institute Proceedings, September 1952, © 1952, U.S. Naval Institute, Annapolis, Md. REMEMBER PEARL HARBOR! by Blake Clark, from the book, © 1942, Blake Clark; pub. by Modern Age Books, Inc. WHY THE SNEAK ATTACK SUCCEEDED, by Louis L. Snyder, from *The War: A Concise History 1939–1945*, © 1960, Louis L. Snyder; reprinted by permission of Simon & Schuster, Inc. THE FALL OF SINGAPORE, by Noel Barber, from *A Sinister Twilight: The Fall of Singapore 1942*, © 1968, Noel Barber; pub. by Houghton Mifflin Co. HITLER'S SEIZURE OF EUROPE, by William L. Shirer, from *The Rise and Fall of the Third Reich*, © 1959, 1960, William L. Shirer; pub. by Simon & Schuster, Inc. MEIN KAMPF, by Adolf Hitler, excerpts from the book (translated by Ralph Manheim), © 1943 and pub. by Houghton Mifflin Co. HOW AND WHY JAPAN PREPARED FOR WORLD WAR, by Rear Adm. Samuel Eliot Morison, USNR (Ret.), from *History of United States Naval Operations in World War II*, © 1947, Samuel Eliot Morison; pub. by Little, Brown and Co. THE FLYING TIGERS, by Russell Whelan, cond. from the book, © 1942, Russell Whelan; pub. by The Viking Press, Inc. THE MIRACLE OF DUNKIRK and THE BATTLE OF BRITAIN, by Winston S. Churchill, excerpts from *Their Finest Hour*, © 1949 and pub. by Houghton Mifflin Co. THE VOICE FROM LONDON, by Edward R. Murrow, from *In Search of Light*, © 1940, 1941, Edward R. Murrow, © 1967 by the Estate of Edward R. Murrow; reprinted by permission of Alfred A. Knopf, Inc. THE SINKING OF THE "BISMARCK," by Capt. Russell Grenfell, R.N., from *The "Bismarck" Episode*, © 1948, Russell Grenfell; pub. by The Macmillan Company. ON BOARD THE "BISMARCK," by Edwin Muller,

from *Harper's Magazine*, © 1942, Harper & Brothers. DISASTER—AND GLORY—IN THE PHILIPPINES, by General of the Army Douglas MacArthur, USA, excerpts from *Reminiscences*, © 1964, Time Inc.; pub. by McGraw-Hill. DEATH MARCH FROM BATAAN, by Lt. Col. William Dyess, USA, from *The Dyess Story*, © 1944, Marajen Stevick Dyess; reprinted by permission of G. P. Putnam's Sons. THE BATTLE OF THE CORAL SEA, by Rear Adm. Samuel Eliot Morison, USNR (Ret.), from *The Two-Ocean War*, © 1963, Samuel Eliot Morison; pub. by Little, Brown and Co. DRESS REHEARSAL: THE STORY OF DIEPPE, by Quentin Reynolds, cond. from the book, © 1943, Random House, Inc.; reprinted by permission of the publisher. MIDWAY: TURNING POINT IN THE PACIFIC, by J. Bryan III, as "Never a Battle Like Midway" in *The Saturday Evening Post*, © 1949, The Curtis Pub. Co.; used by permission of Brandt & Brandt. ACTION AT GUADALCANAL, "ISLAND OF DEATH," by Maj. Frank O. Hough, USMC, from *The Island War*, © 1947, Frank O. Hough; reprinted by special arrangement with the publisher J. B. Lippincott Co. FIGHTING BACK IN NEW GUINEA, by George H. Johnston, from *The Toughest Fighting in the World*, © 1943, George H. Johnston; pub. by Duell, Sloan and Pearce, Inc. TARAWA: CONQUEST OF THE UNCONQUERABLE, by Robert Leckie, from *Strong Men Armed*, © 1962, Robert Leckie; reprinted by permission of Random House, Inc. THE GERMANS INVADE RUSSIA, by William L. Shirer, from *The Rise and Fall of the Third Reich*, © 1959, 1960, William L. Shirer; pub. by Simon & Schuster, Inc. TWO BATTLES THAT STOPPED ROMMEL: THE BATTLE OF ALAM HALFA AND THE BATTLE OF ALAMEIN, excerpts from *The Memoirs of Field Marshal Montgomery*, © 1958, Bernard Law, Viscount Montgomery of Alamein; cond. by permission of The World Pub. Co. "OPERATION TORCH," by Col. Karl Detzer, from *The Mightiest Army,* © 1945, Karl Detzer, Col. G.S.C. THE AMERICAN SOLDIER IN NORTH AFRICA, by Ernie Pyle, from *Here Is Your War,* © 1943, Lester Cowan; reprinted by permission of Holt, Rinehart and Winston, Inc. RAID ON REGENSBURG, by Lt. Col. Beirne Lay, Jr., USAF, as "I Saw Regensburg Destroyed," in *The Saturday Evening Post,* © 1943, Beirne Lay, Jr.; reprinted by permission of Harold Ober Associates, Inc. THE INVASION OF ITALY, by Maj. Gen. J. F. C. Fuller, from *The Second World War;* pub. by Eyre and Spottiswoode, London. OVERLORD: THE ALLIES' TRIUMPH IN NORMANDY, by Kenneth S. Davis, from *Experience of War,* © 1965, Kenneth S. Davis; used by permission of Doubleday & Co., Inc. AIRDROP: BEGINNING OF THE LONGEST DAY, by Cornelius Ryan, from *The Longest Day,* © 1959, Cornelius Ryan; reprinted by permission of Simon & Schuster, Inc. FIRST WAVE AT OMAHA BEACH, by Brig. Gen. S. L. A. Marshall, USAR (Ret.), from *Battle at Best,* © 1964, S. L. A. Marshall; pub. by William Morrow and Co., Inc. THE PLOT TO KILL HITLER, by Georges Blond, from *The Death of Hitler's Germany,* © 1954 and pub. by The Macmillan Company. THE CAPTURE OF REMAGEN BRIDGE, by Lt. Col. Ken Hechler, USAR, from *The Bridge at Remagen,* © 1957, Ken Hechler, pub. by Ballantine Books, Inc. ROOSEVELT'S DEATH, by John Toland, from *The Last 100 Days,* © 1965, 1966, John Toland; reprinted by permission of Random House, Inc. THE BATTLE FOR BERLIN, by Cornelius Ryan, from *The Last Battle,* © 1966, Cornelius Ryan; reprinted by permission of Simon & Schuster, Inc. THE END OF A TYRANT, by H. R. Trevor-Roper, cond. from Chapter 7 of *The Last Days of Hitler,* © 1947, H. R. Trevor-Roper; printed by permission of The Macmillan Company. NAZI DEATH FACTORY AT BUCHENWALD, by Edward R. Murrow, from *Masterpieces of War Reporting,* © 1962 and pub. by Julian Messner, Inc. VICTORY MESSAGE TO THE TROOPS, by Dwight D. Eisenhower, excerpt from *Crusade in Europe,* © 1948, Doubleday & Co., Inc.; reprinted by permission. BANZAI ON SAIPAN, by Capt. Edmund G. Love, USA (Ret.), from *The 27th Infantry Division in World War II,* © 1949, *Infantry Journal Press.* THE GREATEST SEA FIGHT: LEYTE GULF, by Hanson W. Baldwin, from *Battles Lost and Won, Great Campaigns of World War II,* © 1966, Hanson W. Baldwin; reprinted by permission of Harper & Row, Publishers. CLOSING IN ON JAPAN: IWO JIMA, by Robert Leckie, from *The Wars of America,* © 1968, Robert Leckie; reprinted by permission of Harper & Row, Publishers. TO THE SUMMIT OF SURIBACHI WITH THE FLAG, by Richard Wheeler, from *The Bloody Battle for Suribachi,* © 1965, Richard Wheeler; reprinted by permission of Thomas Y. Crowell Co. HOLD THAT LINE . . . OR DIE, by Mitchell Dana, from *Heroic Battles of World War II,* compiled by Maj. Howard Oleck, © 1962, Belmont Productions, Inc. THE ULTIMATE WEAPON, by Fletcher Knebel and Charles W. Bailey II, from *No High Ground,* © 1960, Fletcher Knebel and Charles W. Bailey II; reprinted by permission of Harper & Row, Publishers.

Illustration Credits

Pages *14–15, 18:* Navy Department. *21:* (top left) Wide World; (top right) from Tora, Tora, Tora; (bottom) Navy Department. *22, 23, 24:* Navy Department. *27:* (top) Navy Department; (bottom) Wide World. *29:* Navy Department. *31:* from Tora, Tora, Tora. *33:* Wide World. *36:* (top, left and right) Culver; (bottom) Wide World. *37:* (top left) Wide World; (top right) U.S. Army; (bottom) Photo World. *39:* U.P.I. *41:* (top) Wide World; (bottom) U.P.I. *45:* (top) Imperial War Museum; (bottom) U.P.I. *46–47:* Photo World. *51:* Ullstein. *54:* (top) D.P.A./Pictorial Parade; (bottom) Wide World. *55:* (top) Wide World; (bottom) Photo World. *58:* Wide World. *61:* (top) Radio Times Hulton Picture Library; (bottom left) Photo Goldner; (bottom right) Wide World. *64:* Wide World. *69:* (top) U.S. Army; (bottom) U.P.I. *70:* Ullstein. *75:* Ullstein/Photo Reporters. *76:* (top) Wide World; (bottom) Imperial War Museum. *78:* (top) Ullstein/Photo Reporters; (bottom) Suddeutscher Verlag. *79:* U.P.I. *81:* Suddeutscher Verlag. *83:* Roger Schall. *85:* (top) U.P.I.; (bottom) Imperial War Museum. *87:* Pictorial Parade. *90–91:* Keystone. *95:* Mainichi Graphic/Photo Reporters. *96:* Wide World. *97:* (top) Pix; (bottom) Photo World. *99:* Wide World. *100–101:* U.P.I. *102, 107:* Wide World. *108–109:* Imperial War Museum. *111:* (top) R. T. Smith/Flying Tiger Line; (bottom) Wide World. *113:* Fox Photos. *114:* Etablissement Cinématographique des Armées. *115:* U.P.I. *117:* (top) Wide World; (bottom) Radio Times Hulton Picture Library. *119:* Pix. *121:* Sport and General Press Agency Ltd. *122:* (top) Rene Dazy; (bottom) Ullstein. *124:* (top) Odhams Press; (bottom) Keystone. *125:* Ullstein. *127:* Imperial War Museum. *132:* (top) Imperial War Museum; (bottom) Brown Bros. *133:* (top left) Ullstein/Photo Reporters; (top right) Imperial War Museum; (bottom) Keystone. *134, 141, 146:* Imperial War Museum. *147:* Camera Press/Pix. *150:* (top) Keystone; (bottom) Wide World. *154:* U.P.I. *155:* (top) Keystone; (bottom) U.P.I. *159:* U.S. Coast Guard. *162, 163, 166, 167:* U.P.I. *174:* U.S. Air Force. *175:* Wide World. *180:* Brown Bros. *184:* Suddeutscher Verlag. *185:* Bibliothèque Nationale, Paris. *190–191:* U.S. Army. *195:* U.S.I.S. *197:* (top) Office of War Information/National Archives; (bottom) Pictorial Parade. *204:* (top) Paris Match/Pictorial Parade; (bottom) Wide World. *207:* (top) Wide World; (bottom) Pictorial Parade. *210–211:* U.P.I. *213:* Wide World. *214:* U.S. Marine Corps. *220:* U.P.I. *221:* (top) Pictorial Parade; (bottom) Navy Department. *224–225:* Camera Press/Pix. *228:* U.S. Air Force. *232:* U.P.I. *233:* U.S. Marine Corps. *238–239:* Wide World. *242:* U.S. Marine Corps. *243:* (top) Navy Department; (bottom) U.S. Marine Corps. *250:* U.S. Marine Corps. *251:* (top) U.P.I.; (bottom) U.S. Marine Corps. *256:* U.S. Marine Corps. *260–261:* Imperial War Museum. *266:* (top) Imperial War Museum; (bottom) Ullstein/Photo Reporters. *267:* Photo X. *269:* Bibliothek Zeitgeschichte. *270:* Pictorial Parade. *273:* Imperial War Museum. *276:* Camera Press/Pix. *277:* (top) Soviet Life/Sovfoto; (bottom left) Sovfoto; (bottom right) Wide World. *279:* Ullstein/Photo Reporters. *280–281:* Camera Press/Pix. *283:* (top) Imperial War Museum; (bottom) Wide World. *285:* Agence Mella. *290:* Photo Reporters. *291:* Pictorial Parade. *299:* (top) Wide World; (bottom) Imperial War Museum. *304:* U.S. Army. *308:* U.P.I. *311:* Brown Bros. *313:* U.P.I. *318:* Brown Bros. *319:* Robert Capa/Magnum. *323:* U.P.I. *325:* Wide World. *328–329:* U.S. Air Force. *333:* U.S. Army. *336:* (top) U.S. Coast Guard; (bottom) U.P.I. *337:* U.S. Air Force. *341, 342, 343, 344–345:* U.S. Army. *348–349, 351, 355:* U.S. Coast Guard. *356:* Paris Match/Pictorial Parade. *360:* (top) Paris Match/Pictorial Parade; (bottom) Camera Press/Pix. *364–365:* (top) U.S. Coast Guard; (bottom) Wide World. *368:* (top) Photo X; (bottom) Wide World. *369:* (top) Imperial War Museum; (bottom) U.S.I.S. *371:* U.S. Coast Guard. *372:* U.S. Army. *374:* (top) Presse Liberation; (bottom) U.S. Army. *375:* (left) Paris Match/Pictorial Parade; (right) U.S. Army. *378:* Photo Reporters. *379:* (top) Photo World; (bottom) Keystone. *387:* U.S. Air Force. *388, 389, 390, 396, 397, 398, 400:* U.S. Army. *405:* (top) D.P.A./Pictorial Parade; (bottom) Photo Reporters. *411:* Paris Match/Pictorial Parade. *413:* Pictorial Parade. *419:* Wide World. *423:* (top) Copress Munich; (bottom) Wide World. *425:* (top) U.S. Army; (bottom) Ullstein. *427:* Imperial War Museum. *429:* Ullstein. *431:* Archives Documentation Francaise. *433:* Paris Match/Pictorial Parade. *435:* Office of War Information/National Archives. *436–437:* U.S. Marine Corps. *440:* Navy Department. *441:* U.S. Air Force. *446:* (top) U.S. Air Force; (bottom) U.S. Marine Corps. *447:* U.P.I. *450:* U.S. Coast Guard. *454:* Navy Department. *455:* Photo World. *462–463:* (top) U.S. Air Force; (bottom) U.S. Coast Guard. *468:* Pictorial Parade. *470–471:* U.S. Coast Guard. *475:* Wide World. *476:* U.S. Coast Guard. *477:* W. Eugene Smith. *479:* (top) U.S. Air Force; (bottom) U.P.I. *480:* Wide World. *483, 484:* Louis R. Lowery/Leatherneck Magazine. *487:* Office of War Information/National Archives. *490:* (top) Paris Match/Pictorial Parade; (bottom) Keystone. *491:* Paris Match/Pictorial Parade. *494, 495:* U.S. Marine Corps. *497:* U.S. Army. *498:* (top) U.S. Army; (bottom) U.P.I. *499:* Photo World. *502:* (top) Photo X; (bottom) Keystone. *507:* Office of War Information/National Archives. *508:* Wide World. *510:* Pictorial Parade. *515:* Navy Department.

MAPS DESIGNED BY: JOSEPH W. WAGNER.

SPECIAL CONSULTANT ON MAPS: THOMAS S. COLAHAN, Vice Dean of Columbia College, Columbia University.

The Story of World War II in Maps

*The maps listed below provide
an account of major campaigns
and battles of the war.*

Index

Page numbers in italics indicate illustrations.

Page numbers in italics indicate illustrations.

Page numbers in italics indicate illustrations.

Page numbers in italics indicate illustrations.

Page numbers in italics indicate illustrations.

Page numbers in italics indicate illustrations.